D0128576

Exploring
Macroeconomics

Second Canadian Edition

Robert L. Sexton
Pepperdine University

Peter N. Fortura
Algonquin College

Colin C. Kovacs
Algonquin College

NELSON / EDUCATION

NELSON / EDUCATION

Exploring Macroeconomics, Second Canadian Edition

by Robert L. Sexton, Peter N. Fortura, and Collin C. Kovacs

**Associate Vice President,
Editorial Director:**
Evelyn Veitch

**Editor-in-Chief,
Higher Education:**
Anne Williams

Senior Acquisitions Editor:
Craig Dyer

Marketing Manager:
David Ward

Developmental Editor
My Editor Inc.

**Photo Researcher and Permissions
Coordinator:**
Nicola Winstanley

Content Production Manager:
Susan Wong

Production Service:
S4Carlisle Publishing Services

Copy Editor:
Liba Berry

Proofreader:
S4Carlisle Publishing Services

Indexer:
S4Carlisle Publishing Services

Production Coordinator:
Ferial Suleman

Design Director:
Ken Phipps

Managing Designer:
Franca Amore

Interior Design Modifications:
Nelson Gonzalez

Cover Design:
Dianna Little

Cover Image:
© Brad Wrobleski/Masterfile

Compositor:
S4Carlisle Publishing Services

Printer:
Courier-Kendallville

COPYRIGHT © 2010, 2007 by Nelson Education Ltd.

Printed and bound in the United States
1 2 3 4 12 11 10 09

For more information contact Nelson Education Ltd., 1120-Birchmount Road, Toronto, Ontario, M1K 5G4. Or you can visit our Internet site at http://www.nelson.com

Statistics Canada information is used with the permission of Statistics Canada. Users are forbidden to copy this material and/or redisseminate the data, in an original or modified form, for commercial purposes, without the expressed permissions of Statistics Canada. Information on the availability of the wide range of data from Statistics Canada can be obtained from Statistics Canada's Regional Offices, its World Wide Web site at <http://www.statcan.ca>, and its toll-free access number 1-800-263-1136.

ALL RIGHTS RESERVED. No part of this work covered by the copyright herein may be reproduced, transcribed, or used in any form or by any means—graphic, electronic, or mechanical, including photocopying, recording, taping, Web distribution, or information storage and retrieval systems—without the written permission of the publisher.

For permission to use material from this text or product, submit all requests online at www.cengage.com/permissions. Further questions about permissions can be emailed to permissionrequest@cengage.com

Every effort has been made to trace ownership of all copyrighted material and to secure permission from copyright holders. In the event of any question arising as to the use of any material, we will be pleased to make the necessary corrections in future printings.

**Library and Archives Canada
Cataloguing in Publication Data**

Sexton, Robert L.
Exploring macroeconomics / Robert L. Sexton, Peter Fortura, Colin Kovacs.—
2nd Canadian ed. Previously published as part of: Exploring Economics. 1st Canadian ed.

Includes bibliographical references and index.
ISBN 978-0-17-650141-9

1. Macroeconomics—Textbooks. I. Fortura, Peter II. Kovacs, Colin III. Title.

HB172.5.S49 2009 339
C2008-907355-X

ISBN-13: 978-0-17-650141-9
ISBN-10: 0-17-650141-X

Additional Photo Credits
Page 15: Alan Crosthwarte/Acclaim Stock Photography; Page 7: Wilfried Krecichwost/ Photographer's Choice RF
Active Learning Exercise boxes; In the News boxes

To Cynthia, Laura, and Nicholas

P.N.F.

To Lindsay, Rowan, and Seth

C.C.K.

To Julie, Elizabeth, Katherine, and Tommy

R.L.S.

Brief Contents

Detailed Contents

About the Authors

Robert L. Sexton is Distinguished Professor of Economics at Pepperdine University. Professor Sexton has also been a Visiting Professor at the University of California at Los Angeles in the Anderson Graduate School of Management and the Department of Economics.

Professor Sexton's research ranges across many fields of economics: economics education, labour economics, environmental economics, law and economics, and economic history. He has written several books and has published more than 40 research papers, many in top economic journals such as the *American Economic Review, Southern Economic Journal, Economics Letters, Journal of Urban Economics,* and the *Journal of Economic Education.* Professor Sexton has also written more than 100 other articles that have appeared in books, magazines, and newspapers.

He received the Pepperdine Professor of the Year Award in 1991 and 1997, and the Howard A. White Memorial Teaching Award in 1994; he was named a Harriet and Charles Luckman Teaching Fellow in 1994.

Professor Sexton resides in Agoura Hills, California, with his wife, Julie, and their three children, Elizabeth, Katherine, and Tommy.

Peter N. Fortura earned his undergraduate degree from Brock University, where he was awarded the Vice-Chancellor's Medal for academic achievement, and his graduate degree (Master of Arts) from the University of Western Ontario. He has taught economics at Algonquin College, in Ottawa, for 20 years. Prior to that, he was an economist in the International Department of the Bank of Canada, in Ottawa.

He has published articles on Canadian housing prices, Canada's automotive industry, and Canada's international competitiveness. As well, he is the author of the *Study Guide to Accompany Principles of Macroeconomics,* by Mankiw, Kneebone, McKenzie, and Rowe (Nelson Education, 4th edition), and the co-author of the statistics textbook *Contemporary Business Statistics with Canadian Applications* (Pearson, 3rd edition).

He lives in Ottawa with his wife, Cynthia, and their children, Laura and Nicholas.

Colin C. Kovacs received his Master of Arts degree from Queen's University after completing his Bachelor of Arts at the University of Western Ontario. He has taught economics, statistics, and finance for over 15 years at both the DeVry College of Technology, in Toronto, and Algonquin College, in Ottawa. His research papers have included *Determinants of Labour Force Participation Among Older Males in Canada,* and *Minimum Wage—The Past and Future for Ontario.*

He lives in Ottawa with his wife, Lindsay, and their children, Rowan and Seth.

Preface

Exploring Macroeconomics, Second Canadian Edition, offers students a lively, back-to-the-basics approach designed to take the intimidation out of economics. With its short, self-contained active learning units and its carefully chosen pedagogy, graphs, and photos, this text helps students master and retain the principles of economics. In addition, the current-events focus and modular format of presenting information makes *Exploring Macroeconomics* a very student-accessible and user-friendly text. Driven by a combined 60 years of experience teaching the economic principles course, Bob Sexton, Peter Fortura, and Colin Kovacs' dedication and enthusiasm shine through in *Exploring Macroeconomics*.

NEW TO THE SECOND CANADIAN EDITION
Overall Highlights

The Second Canadian Edition of *Exploring Macroeconomics* is now a separate split edition, as compared to the combined Micro/Macro first-edition text. With this edition, "In the News" features have been reviewed and replaced where needed for greater Canadian content and continued relevance. As well, all statistical information has been updated.

CHAPTER HIGHLIGHTS
Chapter 1: The Role and Method of Economics

This chapter combines the first two chapters of the first edition, thereby producing one complete introductory chapter. Topics have been carefully reviewed to eliminate any unnecessary repetition.

Chapter 2: Scarcity, Trade-Offs, and Economic Growth

Greater detail has been added to the development of both the circular flow and production possibility curve models.

Chapter 3: Supply and Demand

This newly created chapter is solely dedicated to explaining the demand and supply curves as well as those factors responsible for shifting them.

Chapter 4: Bringing Supply and Demand Together

This newly created chapter focuses on the concepts of market equilibrium and price floors and price ceilings.

Chapter 6: Measuring Economic Performance

The section "Problems in Calculating an Accurate GDP" has been reworked. The new discussion of the Consumer Price Index and the GDP Deflator provides improved clarity to these important components of macroeconomic measurement.

Chapter 7: Economic Growth in the Global Economy

A new section describing the impact that population has on economic growth has been added to this edition, providing added depth and application to the chapter material.

Chapter 9: Aggregate Supply and Macroeconomic Equilibrium

To accompany the aggregate demand/aggregate supply model developed in Chapters 8 and 9, an abbreviated discussion of the Keynesian Expenditure Model (Aggregate Expenditure Model) has been included as an appendix to this chapter.

Chapter 12: The Bank of Canada

Individual attention to paid is the Bank of Canada, the role it plays in macroeconomic management, as well as the equation of exchange in this revised chapter.

Chapter 13: Monetary Policy

This newly created chapter discusses the operation of monetary policy in the economy. The connection between the money market, interest rates, and aggregate demand is provided, as well as a simplified and improved discussion of both expansionary and contractionary monetary policy. In addition, a new section details the development of the Phillips curve model for Canada.

Chapter 14: International Trade

The impact of exports and imports on the Canadian economy is the focus of this newly formed chapter. Specific improvements include a separate section detailing Canada's international trade agreements, as well as an improved and expanded discussion of absolute and comparative advantage.

Chapter 15: International Finance

This newly created chapter focuses its attention on the impact of international finance on the Canadian economy. In addition to discussing Canada's balance of payments and the determination of exchange rates, a new section on flexible exchange rates has been added.

FEATURES OF THE BOOK

The Section-by-Section Approach

Exploring Macroeconomics uses a section-by-section approach in which economic ideas and concepts are presented in short, self-contained units rather than in large blocks of text. Each chapter comprises approximately six to eight bite-sized sections, typically presented in two to eight pages, that include all of the relevant graphs, tables, applications, boxes, photos, and definitions, for the topic at hand. Our enthusiasm for and dedication to this approach stems from studying research on *learning theory*, which indicates that students retain information much better when it is broken down into short, intense, and exciting bursts of "digestible" information. Students prefer information divided into smaller, self-contained sections that are less overwhelming, more manageable, and easier to review before going on to new material. In short, students will be more successful in mastering and retaining economic principles using this approach, which is distinctly more compatible with modern communication styles.

But students aren't the only ones to benefit from this approach. The self-contained sections allow instructors greater flexibility in planning their courses. They can simply select or delete sections of the text as it fits their syllabus.

Learning Tools

Key Questions   Each section begins with key questions designed to preview ideas and to pique students' interest in the material to come. These questions also serve as landmarks for students: If they can answer these questions after reading the material, they may go forward with confidence.

Section Checks   Section Checks appear at the end of each section and are designed to reinforce the key questions presented in the section. Key points that summarize major ideas give students an opportunity to confirm their mastery before proceeding to the next topic.

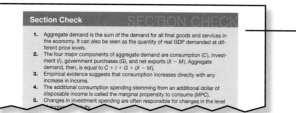

Exhibits   Graphs, tables, and charts are used throughout *Exploring Macroeconomics* to illustrate, clarify, and reinforce economic principles. Text exhibits are designed to be as clear and simple as possible and are carefully coordinated with the text material.

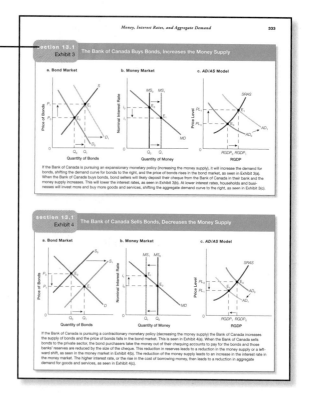

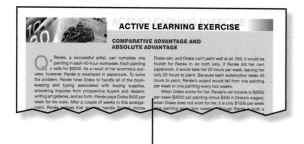

Active Learning Exercises   Active learning exercises are scattered throughout the text as a way of reinforcing and checking student comprehension of important or more difficult concepts. Students can check their work against the answer given at the bottom of the box, providing them with immediate feedback and encouragement in the learning process.

In 1993, the North American Free Trade Agreement (NAFTA) was passed. This lowered the trade barriers between Mexico, Canada, and the United States. Proponents of free trade, especially economists, viewed the agreement as a way to gain greater wealth through specialization and trade for all three countries—one of our ten powerful ideas. Opponents thought the agreement would take away Canadian and U.S. jobs and lower living standards.

net gain of area b + d. However, part of the domestic producers' gain comes at domestic consumers' expense. Specifically, consumers had a consumer surplus equal to area a + b before the trade (at P_{BT}), but they now only have area a (at P_{AT})—a loss of area b.

Area b reflects a redistribution of income because producers are gaining exactly what consumers are losing. Is that good or bad? We can't say objectively whether consumers or producers are more deserving. However, the net benefits from allowing free trade and exports are clearly visible in area d. Without free trade, no one gets area d. That is, on net, members of the domestic society gain when domestic wheat producers are able to sell their wheat at the higher world price. Although domestic wheat consumers lose from the free trade, those negative effects are more than offset by the positive gains captured by producers. Area d is the net increase in domestic welfare (the welfare gain) from free trade and exports.

FREE TRADE AND IMPORTS—DOMESTIC CONSUMERS GAIN MORE THAN DOMESTIC PRODUCERS LOSE

Now suppose that our economy does not produce shirts as well as other countries of the world. In other words, other countries have a comparative advantage in producing shirts. This means that the domestic price for shirts is above the world price. This scenario is illustrated in Exhibit 3. At the new, lower world price, the domestic producer will supply quantity Q_{AT}^D. However, at the lower world price, the domestic producers will not produce the entire amount demanded by domestic consumers, Q_{AT}^D. At the world price, reflecting the world supply and demand for shirts, the difference between what is domestically supplied and what is domestically demanded is supplied by imports.

Photos *Exploring Macroeconomics* contains a large number of colourful pictures. They are not, however, mere decoration; rather, these photos are an integral part of the book, for both learning and motivational purposes. The photos are carefully placed where they reinforce important concepts, and they are accompanied by captions designed to encourage students to extend their understanding of particular ideas.

In the News Boxes In the News boxes focus primarily on current events in Canada and abroad that are relevant and thought-provoking. These articles are placed strategically throughout the text to solidify particular concepts and to help students find the connection between economics and their lives.

In The NEWS

CANADIAN FIRMS SURVIVE THE DROP IN TARIFFS UNDER THE CANADA-U.S. FREE TRADE AGREEMENT

BY ERIC BEAUCHESNE

The reduction in tariffs between Canada and the United States under free trade boosted the odds of survival for more than two-thirds of Canadian manufacturing firms, according to a ... Statistics Canada study released [in 2004].

And those most likely to survive the drop in tariffs were firms that had relatively low levels of debt and were relatively more productive, concluded the study, which bolsters claims that, on balance, free trade has been good for Canadian businesses.

"Somewhat surprisingly, firm size does not affect the sensitivity of firms to changes in tariffs," stated the study, titled Changing Trade Barriers and Canadian Firms: Survival and Exit After the Canada-U.S. Free Trade Agreement.

"On one hand, tariff reductions effectively increase competition by exposing firms to foreign competitors in the domestic market," it noted. "This decline in protection threatens to reduce the market share of domestic firms less efficient than their foreign rivals.

"However, declining tariffs also provide domestic firms with access to foreign markets without the cost disadvantages imposed by high tariffs," it said. "Access to this larger market may be advantageous for domestic firms able to compete with foreign producers."

The report noted there was a dramatic drop in tariffs under free trade.

protected by tariffs of 10% or more, but by 1995, there were no industries in this position.

On balance, the combined Canadian and American tariff reductions were associated with an improved probability of survival for 69% of Canadian firms.

It appears higher productivity and low debt levels shelter firms from the impact of falling tariff protection, it concluded. "However, this general conclusion was not true for all firms," it noted.

The chances of survival increased significantly in industries where the reduction in U.S. tariffs was much greater than the drop in Canadian tariffs, and that was the case even for Canadian firms with lower levels of productivity and higher debt loads, it said.

SOURCE: Adapted from Eric Beauchesne, "Free Trade Benefits Canada, StatsCan Finds," *National Post*, April 29, 2004, p. FP8. Reprinted with permission by Canwest News Service.

CONSIDER THIS:
In 1988, prior to the Canada-U.S. Free Trade Agreement, 21 percent of Canadian manufacturing industries were protected by tariffs of 10 percent or more. By 1995, no Canadian industries had that level of tariff protection. The Canadian firms that were most likely to survive the drop in tariffs were firms that had relatively low levels of debt

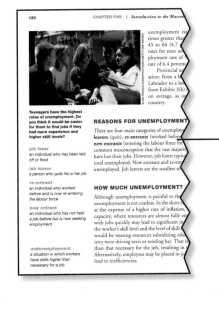

unemployment ra... times greater tha... 45 to 64 (4.7... rates for men an... ployment rate of... rate of 6.4 percen...

Provincial un... ation: from a h... Labrador to a lo... from Exhibit 3(b)... on average, as ou... country.

Teenagers have the highest rates of unemployment. Do you think it would be easier for them to find jobs if they had more experience and higher skill levels?

job loser
an individual who has been laid off or fired

job leaver
a person who quits his or her job

re-entrant
an individual who worked before and is now re-entering the labour force

new entrant
an individual who has not held a job before but is now seeking employment

underemployment
a situation in which workers have skills higher than necessary for a job

REASONS FOR UNEMPLOYMENT

There are four main categories of unemploye... **leavers** (quit), **re-entrants** (worked befor... **new entrants** (entering the labour force fo... common misconception that the vast majori... have lost their jobs. However, job losers typic... total unemployed. New entrants and re-ent... unemployed. Job leavers are the smallest so...

HOW MUCH UNEMPLOYMENT?

Although unemployment is painful to th... unemployment is not costless. In the short r... at the expense of a higher rate of inflation,... capacity, where resources are almost fully em... with jobs quickly may lead to significant in... the worker's skill level and the level of skill... would be wasting resources subsidizing edu... istry were driving taxis or tending bar. That i... than that necessary for the job, resulting in... Alternatively, employees may be placed in jo... lead to inefficiencies.

Marginal Key Terms When key terms and concepts are first introduced within the text, they are highlighted in boldface and the definitions appear in the margin for ease of student learning.

Summary

Section 9.1
- The short-run aggregate supply curve measures how much RGDP suppliers will be willing to produce at different price levels given fixed input prices.
- In the short run, profitability induces producers to supply more as the price level increases because wages and other input prices tend to be slower to change than output prices.
- Producers also may be fooled into thinking that the relative price of the item they are producing is rising, so they increase production.
- In the long run, the aggregate supply curve is vertical as input prices change proportionally with output prices.
- The position of the *LRAS* curve is determined by the level of capital, land, labour, and technology at the natural rate of output, $RGDP_{NR}$.

Section 9.2
- Any increase... the quantity... y of the fac... of...

- A short-run equilibrium is also a long-run equilibrium only if it is at potential output on the long-run aggregate supply curve.
- If short-run equilibrium occurs at less than the potential output of the economy, $RGDP_{NR}$, there is a contractionary gap.
- If short-run equilibrium temporarily occurs beyond $RGDP_{NR}$, there is an expansionary gap.
- Demand-pull inflation occurs when the price level rises as a result of an increase in aggregate demand.
- A contractionary gap can be caused by cost-push inflation, which is caused by a leftward shift in the short-run aggregate supply curve, or insufficient aggregate demand.
- Most recoveries from contractions occur because of increases in aggregate demand; however, it is possible that the economy could self-correct through declining wages and other input prices.

End-of-Chapter Summaries Each chapter ends with a point-form summary that highlights the most important concepts of the chapter. Summary points are grouped by section for quick and easy review.

End-of-Chapter Key Terms and Concepts

There is a list of key terms and concepts at the end of each chapter that allows students to test their mastery of new concepts. Page references are included so students can easily find key terms within the chapter.

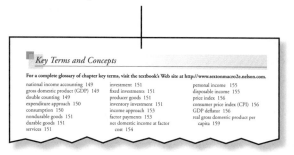

Key Terms and Concepts

For a complete glossary of chapter key terms, visit the textbook's Web site at http://www.sextonmacro2e.nelson.com.

national income accounting 149	investment 151	personal income 155
gross domestic product (GDP) 149	fixed investments 151	disposable income 155
double counting 149	producer goods 151	price index 156
expenditure approach 150	inventory investment 151	consumer price index (CPI) 156
consumption 150	income approach 153	GDP deflator 156
nondurable goods 151	factor payments 153	real gross domestic product per
durable goods 151	net domestic income at factor	capita 159
services 151	cost 154	

End-of-Chapter Review Questions   Questions at the end of the chapter allow students to test their understanding of chapter concepts. Some of the questions are designed for review whereas others are designed to help students extend their thinking about core concepts.

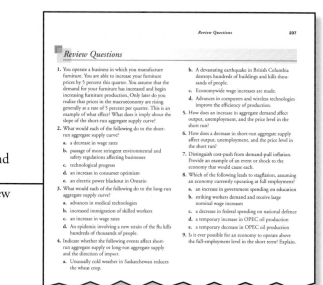

Review Questions   237

Review Questions

1. You operate a business in which you manufacture furniture. You are able to increase your furniture prices by 5 percent this quarter. You assume that the demand for your furniture has increased and begin increasing furniture production. Only later do you realize that prices in the macroeconomy are rising generally at a rate of 5 percent per quarter. This is an example of what effect? What does it imply about the slope of the short-run aggregate supply curve?

2. What would each of the following do to the short-run aggregate supply curve?
   a. a decrease in wage rates
   b. passage of more stringent environmental and safety regulations affecting businesses
   c. technological progress
   d. an increase in consumer optimism
   e. an electric power blackout in Ontario

3. What would each of the following do to the long-run aggregate supply curve?
   a. advances in medical technologies
   b. increased immigration of skilled workers
   c. an increase in wage rates
   d. An epidemic involving a new strain of the flu kills hundreds of thousands of people.

4. Indicate whether the following events affect short-run aggregate supply or long-run aggregate supply and the direction of impact.
   a. Unusually cold weather in Saskatchewan reduces the wheat crop.

   b. A devastating earthquake in British Columbia destroys hundreds of buildings and kills thousands of people.
   c. Economywide wage increases are made.
   d. Advances in computers and wireless technologies improve the efficiency of production.

5. How does an increase in aggregate demand affect output, unemployment, and the price level in the short run?

6. How does a decrease in short-run aggregate supply affect output, unemployment, and the price level in the short run?

7. Distinguish cost-push from demand-pull inflation. Provide an example of an event or shock to the economy that would cause each.

8. Which of the following leads to stagflation, assuming an economy currently operating at full employment?
   a. an increase in government spending on education
   b. striking workers demand and receive large nominal wage increases
   c. a decrease in federal spending on national defence
   d. a temporary increase in OPEC oil production
   e. a temporary decrease in OPEC oil production

9. Is it ever possible for an economy to operate above the full-employment level in the short term? Explain.

Study Guide   chapter 6

Fill in the Blanks

Section 6.1

1. _____ accounting was created to provide a reliable, uniform method of measuring economic performance.

2. _____ is defined as the value of all final goods and services produced in a country in a period of time, almost always one year.

3. A _____ good or service is one that is ready for its designated ultimate use, in contrast to _____ goods or services that are used in the production of other goods.

4. There are two primary ways of calculating economic output: the _____ approach and the _____ approach.

Section 6.2

5. With the _____ approach, GDP is calculated by adding up the expenditures of market participants on final goods and services over a period of time.

6. For analytical purposes, economists usually categorize expenditures into four categories: _____, _____, _____, and _____.

7. Consumption spending is usually broken down into three subcategories: _____ goods, _____ goods, and _____.

8. Consumption refers to the purchase of consumer goods and services by _____.

9. The most important single category of consumer durable goods is consumer _____.

10. Sales of nondurable consumer goods tend to be _____ stable over time than sales of durable goods.

11. Investment, as used by economists, refers to the creation of _____ goods whose purpose is to _____.

12. The two categories of investment purchases measured in the expenditures approach are _____ investment and _____ investment.

13. When the economy is booming, investment purchases tend to _____ dramatically.

14. _____ payments are not included in government purchases because that spending does not go to purchase newly produced goods or services.

15. Imports must be _____ from GDP in order to obtain an accurate measure of domestic production.

Section 6.3

16. The _____ approach to measuring GDP involves summing the incomes received by producers of goods and services.

17. Output creates _____ of equal value.

18. Factor payments include _____ for the use of labour services; _____ for land; _____ payments for the use of capital goods; and _____ for entrepreneurs who put labour, land, and capital together.

Self-Contained Study Guide   Providing added value for the student, each chapter concludes with a 6 to 12-page study guide that includes Fill in the Blanks, True or False, and Multiple Choice questions as well as Problems. The Study Guide questions for each chapter have been organized into sections that correspond to the relevant section in the chapter.

SUPPLEMENTARY MATERIALS

Student Web Site

The Student Web Site at **http://www.sextonmacro2e.nelson.com** provides access to many learning tools. It allows students to access PowerPoint presentations, online quizzes, and other resources they can use to test their understanding of key economic concepts.

Supplements for the Instructor

Computerized Test Bank   ExamView allows for quick test creation. All items in the test bank are available in computerized test bank software format. Questions and answers may be added, edited, or deleted. Instructors can easily vary the sequence of questions in order to create multiple versions of the same test. Answer keys are generated quickly with each version of the test. The program is available for both Mac and Windows.

A Word version of the test bank is available for those instructors who wish to take advantage of this option. Both the Computerized Test Bank and the Word version are available on the Instructor's Resource CD-ROM.

Instructor's Manual and Test Bank   The Instructor's Manual follows the textbook's concept-by-concept approach in two parts: chapter outlines and teaching tips. The Teaching Tips section provides analogies, illustrations, and examples to help instructors reinforce each section of the text. The answers to the end-of-chapter text questions can be found in the Instructor's Manual. The Test Bank, prepared by Michael Leonard, Kwantlen University, includes approximately 150 test questions per chapter, consisting of multiple choice, true/false, and short-answer questions.

Lecture Presentation in PowerPoint   This PowerPoint presentation covers all the essential sections presented in each chapter of the book. Graphs, tables, lists, and concepts are animated sequentially, much as one might develop them on the blackboard. Additional examples and applications are used to reinforce major lessons, and instructors may adapt or add slides to customize their lectures. These are available on the Instructor's Resource CD-ROM and from the Instructor's Web site.

Instructor's Web Site   The Instructor's portion of the Web site to accompany *Exploring Macroeconomics* contains electronic versions of valuable instructor resources described. Adopters of the textbook may obtain a password from their local sales representative for access to the Instructor's Manual and Powerpoint presentation slides.

Instructor's Resource CD-ROM   Included on the CD-ROM are the key supplements designed to aid instructors:

- Instructor's Manual
- PowerPoint presentation slides
- Computerized Test Bank
- A printable Test Bank for ease of use.

Acknowledgments

Producing the Second Canadian Edition of *Exploring Macroeconomics* has truly been a team effort. We would like to thank the editorial, production, and marketing teams at Nelson Education for their hard work and effort. First, our appreciation goes to Anne Williams, editorial director, who has provided the vision and leadership for both editions of the text.

We would like to extend special thanks to Katherine Goodes, senior developmental editor at My Editor Inc., for her helpful advice and constant encouragement. This book reflects her hard work and effort. Thanks also to Susan Wong, content production editor, and all the marketing and sales representatives at Nelson Education Ltd.

Finally, we would like to acknowledge the reviewers listed below for their comments and feedback:

Bruno Fullone, *George Brown College*
Russell Turmer, *Fleming College*
Aurelia Best, *Centennial College*
Jim Butko, *Niagara College*
Geoffrey Prince, *Centennial College*
Carl Weston, *Mohawk College*

Their thoughtful suggestions were very important to us in providing input and useful examples for the Second Canadian Edition of this book.

P.N.F.
C.C.K.

chapter

1

The Role and Method of Economics

1.1 ECONOMICS: A BRIEF INTRODUCTION
What is economics?

1.2 ECONOMIC THEORY
Why do we need a theory?

1.3 SCARCITY
Can all of our wants be satisfied in a world of limited resources?

1.4 OPPORTUNITY COST
Can we have our cake and eat it too?

1.5 MARGINAL THINKING
What is the rule of rational choice?

1.6 INCENTIVES MATTER
Do people respond to incentives?

1.7 SPECIALIZATION AND TRADE
How can specialization and trade lead to greater wealth?

1.8 MARKET PRICES COORDINATE ECONOMIC ACTIVITY
How do the market economy and the price system coordinate economic activity?

---

section

1.1

Economics: A Brief Introduction

- Why study economics?
- What is economics?
- What is scarcity?
- What distinguishes macroeconomics from microeconomics?

WHY STUDY ECONOMICS?

As you begin your first course in economics, you may be asking yourself why you're here. What does economics have to do with your life? Although there are many good reasons to study economics, perhaps the best reason is that many issues in our lives are at least partly economic in character. For example, a good understanding of economics would allow you to answer such questions as: Why do 10 A.M. classes fill up quicker than 8 A.M. classes during registration? Why is teenage unemployment always higher than adult unemployment? Why are the prices of prescription drugs so high? Will higher taxes on cigarettes reduce the number of people smoking? Why do professional athletes make so much money? Why do North American auto producers like tariffs (taxes) on imported

© Monkey Business/Shutterstock

The front pages of our daily newspapers are filled with articles related to economics—either directly or indirectly. News headlines might read: "Gasoline Prices Soar; Stocks Rise; Stocks Fall; Prime Minister Vows to Increase National Defence Spending; Health-Care Costs Continue to Rise."

cars? The study of economics improves your understanding of these and many other concerns.

Another reason to study economics is that it may teach you how to "think better"—economics helps develop a disciplined method of thinking about problems. Although economics may not always give you clear-cut answers, it will give you something even more powerful: the economic way of thinking. The problem-solving tools you will develop by studying economics will prove valuable to you both in your personal and professional life, regardless of your career choice. A student of economics becomes aware that, at a basic level, much of economic life involves choosing among alternative courses of action—making choices between our conflicting wants and desires in a world of limited resources. Economics provides some clues as to how to intelligently evaluate these options and determine the most appropriate choices in given situations.

ECONOMICS—A WORD WITH MANY DIFFERENT MEANINGS

Some individuals think economics involves the study of the stock market and corporate finance, and it does—in part. Others think that economics is concerned with the wise use of money and other matters of personal finance, and it is—in part. Still others think that economics involves forecasting or predicting what business conditions will be like in the future, and again, it does—in part.

A Unique Way of Looking at Human Behaviour

Economics is a unique way of analyzing many areas of human behaviour. Indeed, the range of topics to which economic analysis is applied is quite broad. Many researchers have discovered that the economic approach to human behaviour sheds light on social problems that have been with us for a long time: discrimination, education, crime, divorce, political favouritism, and many more. In fact, economics is front-page news almost every day, whether it involves politicians talking about tax cuts, inflation, interest rates, or unemployment; business executives talking about restructuring their companies to cut costs; or the average citizen trying to figure out how to make ends meet each month. Economics is all of this and more.

Growing Wants and Scarce Resources

economics
the study of the allocation of our limited resources to satisfy our unlimited wants

resources
inputs used to produce goods and services

the economic problem
scarcity forces us to choose, and choices are costly because we must give up other opportunities that we value

Precisely defined, **economics** is the study of the allocation of our limited resources to satisfy our unlimited wants. **Resources** are inputs—such as land, human effort and skills, and machines and factories—used to produce goods and services. The problem is that our wants exceed our limited resources, a fact that we call scarcity. Scarcity forces us to make choices on how to best use our limited resources. This is **the economic problem:** Scarcity forces us to choose, and choices are costly because we must give up other opportunities that we value. This economizing problem is evident in every aspect of our lives. Choosing between a trip to the grocery store or the mall, or between finishing an assignment or going to a movie, can be understood more easily when one has a good handle on the "economic way of thinking."

ECONOMICS IS ALL AROUND US

Although many things that we desire in life are considered to be "noneconomic," economics concerns anything that is considered worthwhile to some human being. For instance, love, sexual activity, and religion have value for most people. Even these have an economic dimension. Consider religion, for example. Concern for spiritual matters has led to the development of institutions such as churches, mosques, and temples that provide religious and spiritual services. These services are goods that many people desire. Love and sex likewise have received economists' scrutiny. One product of love, the institution of the family, is an important economic decision-making unit. Also, sexual activity results in the birth of children, one of the most important "goods" that humans desire.

Even time has an economic dimension. In fact, perhaps the most precious single resource is time. We all have the same limited amount of time per day, and how we divide our time between work and leisure (including perhaps study, sleep, exercise, etc.) is a distinctly economic matter. If we choose more work, we must sacrifice leisure. If we choose to study, we must sacrifice time with friends, or time spent sleeping or watching TV. Virtually everything we decide to do, then, has an economic dimension.

Living in a world of scarcity means trade-offs. And it is important that we know what these trade-offs are so we can make better choices about the options available to us.

ECONOMICS IS A SOCIAL SCIENCE

Like psychology, sociology, anthropology, and political science, economics is considered a social science. Economics, like the other social sciences, is concerned with reaching generalizations about human behaviour. Economics is the study of people. It is the social science that studies the choices people make in a world of limited resources.

Economics and the other social sciences often complement one another. For example, a political scientist might examine the process that led to the adoption of a certain tax policy, whereas an economist might analyze the impact of that tax policy. Or, whereas psychologist may try to figure out what makes the criminal mind work, an economist might study the factors causing a change in the crime rate. Social scientists, then, may be studying the same issue but from different perspectives.

MACROECONOMICS AND MICROECONOMICS

Conventionally, we distinguish two main branches of economics: macroeconomics and microeconomics. **Macroeconomics** deals with the **aggregate,** or total economy; it looks at economic problems as they influence the whole of society. Topics covered in macroeconomics include discussions of inflation, unemployment, business cycles, and economic growth. **Microeconomics,** by contrast, deals with the smaller units within the economy, attempting to understand the decision-making behaviour of firms and households and their interaction in markets for particular goods or services. Microeconomic topics include discussions of health care, agricultural subsidies, the price of everyday items such as running shoes, the distribution of income, and the impact of labour unions on wages. To put it simply, microeconomics looks at the trees whereas macroeconomics looks at the forest.

macroeconomics
the study of the whole economy including the topics of inflation, unemployment, and economic growth

aggregate
the total amount—such as the aggregate level of output

microeconomics
the study of household and firm behaviour and how they interact in the marketplace

Section Check

1. Economics is a problem-solving science.
2. Economics is the study of the allocation of our limited resources to satisfy our unlimited wants.
3. Our unlimited wants exceed our resources, so we must make choices.
4. Economics is concerned with reaching generalizations about human behaviour.
5. Macroeconomics deals with the aggregate, or total, economy.
6. Microeconomics focuses on smaller units within the economy—firms and households, and how they interact in the marketplace.

section
1.2

Economic Theory

- What are economic theories?
- Why do we need to abstract?
- What is a hypothesis?
- What is the *ceteris paribus* assumption?
- What is the fallacy of composition?
- What is positive and normative analysis?
- Why do economists disagree?

ECONOMIC THEORIES

theory
statement or proposition used to explain and predict behaviour in the real world

A **theory** is an established explanation that accounts for known facts or phenomena. Specifically, economic theories are statements or propositions about patterns of human behaviour that are expected to take place under certain circumstances. These theories help us to sort out and understand the complexities of economic behaviour. We expect a good theory to explain and predict well. A good economic theory, then, should help us to better understand and, ideally, predict human economic behaviour.

ABSTRACTION IS IMPORTANT

Economic theories cannot realistically include every event that has ever occurred. This is true for the same reason that a newspaper or history book does not include every world event that has ever happened. We must abstract. A road map of Canada may not include every creek, ridge, and valley between Calgary and Halifax—indeed, such an all-inclusive map would be too large to be of value. However, a small road map with major details will provide enough information to travel by car from Calgary to Halifax. Likewise, an economic theory provides a broad view, not a detailed examination, of human economic behaviour.

© RYAN MCVAY/PHOTODISC/GETTY ONE IMAGES

How is economic theory like a map? Because of the complexity of human behaviour, economists must abstract to focus on the most important components of a particular problem. This is similar to maps that highlight the important information (and assume away many minor details) to help people get from here to there.

DEVELOPING A TESTABLE PROPOSITION

hypothesis
a testable proposition

The beginning of any theory is a **hypothesis,** a testable proposition that makes some type of prediction about behaviour in response to certain changes in conditions. In economic theory, a hypothesis is a testable prediction about how people will behave or react to a change in economic circumstances. For example, if the price of compact discs (CDs) increased, we might hypothesize that fewer CDs would be sold, or if the price of CDs fell, we might hypothesize that more CDs would be sold. Once a hypothesis is stated, it is tested by comparing what it predicts will happen to what actually happens.

Using Empirical Analysis

empirical analysis
the use of data to test a hypothesis

To see if a hypothesis is valid, we must engage in an **empirical analysis.** That is, we must examine the data to see if the hypothesis fits well with the facts. If the hypothesis is consistent with real-world observations, it is accepted; if it does not fit well with the facts, it is "back to the drawing board."

Determining whether a hypothesis is acceptable is more difficult in economics than it is in the natural or physical sciences. Chemists, for example, can observe chemical reactions under laboratory conditions. They can alter the environment to meet the assumptions of the hypothesis and can readily manipulate the variables (chemicals, temperatures, and so on) crucial to the proposed relationship. Such controlled experimentation is seldom possible in economics. The laboratory of economists is usually the real world. Unlike a chemistry lab, economists cannot easily control all the other variables that might influence human behaviour.

FROM HYPOTHESIS TO THEORY

After gathering their data, economic researchers must then evaluate the results to determine whether the hypothesis is supported or refuted. If supported, the hypothesis can then be tentatively accepted as an economic theory.

Economic theories are always on probation. A hypothesis is constantly being tested against empirical findings. Do the observed findings support the prediction? When a hypothesis survives a number of tests, it is accepted until it no longer predicts well.

VIOLATION OF THE *CETERIS PARIBUS* ASSUMPTION

One condition common to virtually all theories in economics is usually expressed by use of the Latin expression **ceteris paribus.** This roughly means "let everything else be equal" or "holding everything else constant." In trying to assess the effect of one variable on another, we must isolate their relationship from other events that might also influence the situation that the theory tries to explain or predict. To make this clearer, we will illustrate this concept with a couple of examples.

ceteris paribus
holding all other things constant

Suppose you develop your own theory describing the relationship between studying and exam performance: If I study harder, I will perform better on the test. That sounds logical, right? Holding other things constant *(ceteris paribus)*, this is likely to be true. However, what if you studied harder but inadvertently overslept the day of the exam? What if you were so sleepy during the test that you could not think clearly? Or what if you studied the wrong material? Although it may look as if additional studying did not improve your performance, the real problem may lie in the impact of other variables, such as sleep deficiency or how you studied.

Researchers must be careful to hold other things constant *(ceteris paribus)*. For example, in 1936, cars were inexpensive by modern standards, yet few were purchased; in 1949, cars were much more expensive, but more were bought. This statement appears to imply that people prefer to buy more when prices are higher. However, we know from ample empirical observations that this is not the case—buyers are only willing to buy more at lower prices, *ceteris paribus.* The reason people bought more cars at the higher prices was that several other important variables were not held constant over this period (the *ceteris paribus* assumption): the purchasing power of dollars, the income of potential car buyers, and the quality of cars to mention just a few.

CONFUSING CORRELATION AND CAUSATION

Without a theory of causation, no scientist could sort out and understand the enormous complexity of the real world. But one must always be careful not to confuse correlation with causation. In other words, the fact that two events usually occur together (**correlation**) does not necessarily mean that one caused the other to occur (**causation**). For example, say a groundhog awakes after a long winter of hibernation, climbs out of his hole, sees his shadow,

correlation
two events that usually occur together

causation
when one event brings on another event

© Steve Estvanik/Shutterstock

People tend to drive slower when the roads are covered with ice. In addition, more traffic accidents occur when the roads are icy. So, does driving slower cause the number of accidents to rise? No, it is the icy roads that lead to both lower speeds and increased accidents.

and then six weeks of bad weather ensue. Did the groundhog cause the bad weather? It is highly unlikely.

Perhaps the causality may run in the opposite direction. Although a rooster may always crow before the sun rises, it does not cause the sunrise; rather, the early light from the sunrise causes the rooster to crow.

Why Is There a Positive Correlation Between Ice Cream Sales and Crime?

Did you know that when ice cream sales rise, so do crime rates? What do you think causes the two events to occur together? Some might think that the sugar "high" in the ice cream causes the higher crime rate. Excess sugar in a snack was actually used in court testimony in a murder case—the so-called "Twinkie defence." However, it is more likely that crime peaks in the summer because of weather, more people on vacation (leaving their homes vacant), teenagers out of school, and so on. It just happens that ice cream sales also peak in those months because of weather. The lesson: One must always be careful not to confuse correlation with causation and to be clear on the direction of the causation.

THE FALLACY OF COMPOSITION

fallacy of composition
the incorrect view that what is true for the individual is always true for the group

One must also be careful with problems associated with aggregation (summing up all the parts), particularly the **fallacy of composition.** This fallacy states that even if something is true for an individual, it is not necessarily true for many individuals as a group. For example, say you are at a concert and you decide to stand up to get a better view of the stage. This works as long as no one else stands up. But what would happen if everyone stood up at the same time? Then, standing up would not let you see better. Hence, what may be true for an individual does not always hold true in the aggregate. The same can be said of arriving to class early to get a better parking place—what if everyone arrived early? Or studying harder to get a better grade in a class that is graded on a curve—what if everyone studied harder? All of these are examples of the fallacy of composition.

POSITIVE ANALYSIS

positive analysis
an objective testable statement—how the economy is

Most economists view themselves as scientists seeking the truth about the way people behave. They make speculations about economic behaviour, and then (ideally) they try to assess the validity of those predictions based on human experience. Their work emphasizes how people *do* behave, rather than how people *should* behave. In the role of scientist, an economist tries to observe, objectively, patterns of behaviour without reference to the appropriateness or inappropriateness of that behaviour. This objective, value-free approach, utilizing the scientific method, is called **positive analysis.** In positive analysis, we want to know the impact of variable A on variable B. We want to be able to test a hypothesis. For example, the following is a positive statement: If rent controls are imposed, vacancy rates will fall. This statement is testable. A positive statement does not have to be a true statement, but it does have to be a testable statement.

However, keep in mind that it is doubtful that even the most objective scientist can be totally value-free in his or her analysis. An economist may well emphasize data or evidence that supports his hypothesis, putting less weight on other evidence that might be contradictory. This, alas, is human nature. But a good economist/scientist strives to be as fair and objective as possible in evaluating evidence and in stating conclusions based on the evidence.

NORMATIVE ANALYSIS

Like everyone, economists have opinions and make value judgments. When economists, or anyone else for that matter, express opinions about some economic policy or statement, they are indicating in part how they believe things should be, not just facts as to the way things are. **Normative analysis** expresses opinions about the desirability of various actions. Normative statements involve judgments about what should be or what ought to happen. For example, one could judge that incomes should be more equally distributed. If there is a change in tax policy that makes incomes more equal, there will be positive economic questions that can be investigated, such as how work behaviour will change. But we cannot say, as scientists, that such a policy is good or bad; rather, we can point to what will likely happen if the policy is adopted.

normative analysis
a subjective, non-testable statement—how the economy should be

POSITIVE VERSUS NORMATIVE STATEMENTS

The distinction between positive and normative analysis is important. It is one thing to say that everyone should have universal health care, a normative statement, and quite another to say that universal health care would lead to greater worker productivity, a

In The **NEWS**

FEDERAL GOVERNMENT URGED TO KEEP FOCUSED ON DEBT CUTS

BY ERIC BEAUCHESNE

Despite years of federal budget surpluses, the interest charges on the nation's $501-billion debt still run at about $35 billion a year, or $95 million a day, say Canada's chartered accountants.

The Canadian Institute of Chartered Accountants, amid a flurry of last-minute, pre-budget appeals . . . , urged Finance Minister Ralph Goodale to limit spending and keep cutting the debt in [the 2005] budget.

"With a minority government facing increased spending pressures and an annual debt service cost approximating $35 billion, the federal government should not forget that the interest meter is still running at a pace of $95 million each day," David Hope, chair of the institute, said . . . .

Almost 20 cents of every dollar in federal revenue still goes toward interest payments on the debt, noted the group.

"This is similar to an individual earning $50,000 a year being obligated to pay a $9,600 interest bill at the start of each year," it said.

The accountants calculated that Ottawa will save $50 million a year in reduced charges for each $1-billion reduction in interest-bearing debt.

"We have seen good progress on paying down the debt, but the total debt still accounts for almost 40 per cent of annual GDP," Hope said. "There remains a long way to go to reach the government's 25 per cent of GDP target."

The accountants, in calling for increased debt reduction, urged the government to do more than just restrain spending. It also wants Ottawa to improve its accountability of expenditures.

"Even if the government were to keep future spending essentially constant in per-capita terms there would be very little latitude for new initiatives in the next two years," it said.

Meanwhile, a report by a right-wing economic think-tank urged Goodale to focus on improving productivity and economic performance, as well as controlling spending.

The Fraser Institute recommended stringent controls on new spending, prioritizing existing expenditures, a multi-year tax relief program—including elimination of the federal capital tax—reductions in corporate and personal income taxes and reforms in the way services are delivered.

"Since 1997, the year Canada finally balanced its books, there have been continued excessive spending increases, a lack of meaningful tax relief, and avoidance of competitiveness and productivity-related issues," said institute economist Jason Clemens. "The depth of new spending has been truly startling."

It calculated that since the government balanced its books in 1997, program spending has increased by $42.1 billion or 39.8 per cent, outstripping by a wide margin the 6.8 per cent increase in population and 15.8 per cent rise in inflation.

SOURCE: Eric Beauchesne. "Feds urged to keep focus on debt cuts." *The Windsor Star.* February 19, 2005. p. A19. Material reprinted with the express permission of: "CANWEST NEWS SERVICE", a CanWest Partnership.

CONSIDER THIS:
When the Canadian Institute of Chartered Accountants urged the finance minister to cut the debt and to limit spending in the upcoming budget, it was expressing its opinion about economic policy. This is an example of normative analysis.

testable positive statement. It is important to distinguish between positive and normative analysis because many controversies in economics revolve around policy considerations that contain both. When economists start talking about how the economy should work rather than how it does work, they have entered the normative world of the policymaker.

DISAGREEMENT IS COMMON IN MOST DISCIPLINES

Although economists differ frequently on economic policy questions, there is probably less disagreement than the media would have you believe. Disagreement is common in most disciplines: Seismologists differ over predictions of earthquakes or volcanic eruption; historians can be at odds over the interpretation of historical events; psychologists disagree on proper ways to rear children; and nutritionists debate the merits of large doses of vitamin C.

The majority of disagreements in economics stem from normative issues, as differences in values or policy beliefs result in conflict. As we discussed earlier in this chapter, economists may emphasize specific facts over other facts when trying to develop support for their own hypothesis. As a result, disagreements can result when one economist gives weight to facts that have been minimized by another, and vice versa.

Freedom Versus Fairness

Some economists are concerned about individual freedom and liberty, thinking that any encroachment on individual decision making is, other things equal, bad. People with this philosophic bent are inclined to be skeptical of any increased government involvement in the economy.

On the other hand, some economists are concerned with what they consider an unequal, "unfair," or unfortunate distribution of income, wealth, or power, and view governmental intervention as desirable in righting injustices that they believe exist in a market economy. To these persons, the threat to individual liberty alone is not sufficiently great to reject governmental intervention in the face of perceived economic injustice.

The Validity of an Economic Theory

Aside from philosophic differences, there is a second reason why economists may differ on any given policy question. Specifically, they may disagree as to the validity of a given economic theory for the policy in question. Suppose two economists have identical philosophical views that have led them to the same conclusion: To end injustice and hardship, unemployment should be reduced. To reach the objective, the first economist believes the government should lower taxes and increase spending, whereas the second economist believes increasing the amount of money in public hands by various banking policies will achieve the same results with fewer undesirable consequences. The two economists differ because the empirical evidence for economic theories about the cause of unemployment appears to conflict. Some evidence suggests government taxation and spending policies are effective in reducing unemployment, whereas other evidence suggests that the prime cause of unnecessary unemployment lies with faulty monetary policy. Still other evidence is consistent with the view that, over long periods, neither approach mentioned here is of much value in reducing unemployment, and that unemployment will be part of our existence no matter what macroeconomic policies we follow.

ECONOMISTS DO AGREE

Although you may not believe it after reading the previous discussion, economists don't always disagree. In fact, according to a survey among members of the American Economic Association, most economists agree on a wide range of issues, including rent control, import tariffs, export restrictions, the use of wage and price controls to curb inflation, and the minimum wage.

Section Check

SECTION CHECK

1. Economic theories are statements used to explain and predict patterns of human behaviour.
2. A hypothesis makes a prediction about human behaviour and is then tested.
3. In order to isolate the effects of one variable on another, we use the *ceteris paribus* assumption.
4. The fact that two events are related does not mean that one caused the other to occur.
5. What is true for the individual is not necessarily true for the group.
6. Positive analysis is objective and value-free.
7. Normative analysis involves value judgments and opinions about the desirability of various actions.
8. Most disagreement among economists stems from normative issues.

Scarcity

- What is scarcity?
- What are goods and services?

KNOW A FEW PRINCIPLES WELL

Most of economics is really knowing certain principles well and knowing when and how to apply them. In the following sections, some important tools are presented that will help you understand the economic way of thinking. These few basic ideas will repeatedly occur throughout the text. If you develop a good understanding of these principles and master the problem-solving skills inherent in them, they will serve you well for the rest of your life.

SCARCITY

As we have already mentioned, economics is concerned primarily with **scarcity**—how we satisfy our unlimited wants in a world of limited resources. We may want more "essential" items like food, clothing, schooling, and health care. We may want many other items, like vacations, cars, computers, and concert tickets. We may want more friendship, love, knowledge, and so on. We also may have many goals—perhaps an A in this class, a university education, and a great job. Unfortunately, people are not able to fulfill all of their wants—material desires and nonmaterial desires. And as long as human wants exceed available resources, scarcity will exist.

scarcity
exists when human wants (material and nonmaterial) exceed available resources

SCARCITY AND RESOURCES

The scarce resources used in the production of goods and services can be grouped into four categories: labour, land, capital, and entrepreneurship.

   Labour is the total of both physical and mental effort expended by people in the production of goods and services.

labour
the physical and human effort used in the production of goods and services

land
the natural resources used in the production of goods and services

capital
the equipment and structures used to produce goods and services

human capital
the productive knowledge and skill people receive from education and on-the-job training

entrepreneurship
the process of combining labour, land, and capital together to produce goods and services

Land includes the "gifts of nature" or the natural resources used in the production of goods and services. Trees, animals, water, minerals, and so on are all considered to be "land" for our purposes, along with the physical space normally thought of as land.

Capital is the equipment and structures used to produce goods and services. Office buildings, tools, machines, and factories are all considered capital goods. When we invest in factories, machines, research and development, or education, we increase the potential to create more goods and services in the future. Capital also includes **human capital**, the productive knowledge and skills people receive from education and on-the-job training.

Entrepreneurship is the process of combining labour, land, and capital together to produce goods and services. Entrepreneurs make the tough and risky decisions about what and how to produce goods and services. Entrepreneurs are always looking for new ways to improve production techniques or to create new products. They are lured by the chance to make a profit. It is this opportunity to make a profit that leads entrepreneurs to take risks.

However, entrepreneurs are not necessarily a Bill Gates (Microsoft), a Ted Rogers (Rogers Communications), or a Paul Desmarais (Power Corporation). In some sense, we are all entrepreneurs when we try new products or when we find better ways to manage our households or our study time. Rather than money, then, our profits might take the form of greater enjoyment, additional time for recreation, or better grades.

GOODS AND SERVICES

goods
items we value or desire

service
an intangible act that people want, like treatment from a doctor or a dentist

Goods are those items that we value or desire. Goods tend to be tangible—objects that can be seen, held, heard, tasted, or smelled. **Services** are intangible acts for which people are willing to pay, such as legal services, medical services, and dental care. Services are intangible because they are less overtly visible, but they are certainly no less valuable than goods. All goods and services, whether tangible or intangible, are produced from scarce resources and can be subjected to economic analysis. If there are not enough goods and services for all of us, we will have to compete for those scarce goods and services. That is, scarcity ultimately leads to competition for the available goods and services, a subject we will return to often in the text.

EVERYONE FACES SCARCITY

We all face scarcity because we cannot have all of the goods and services that we desire. However, because we all have different wants and desires, scarcity affects everyone differently. For example, a child in a developing country may face a scarcity of food and clean drinking water, whereas a rich person may face a scarcity of garage space for his growing antique car collection. Likewise, a harried middle-class working mother may find time for exercise particularly scarce, whereas a pharmaceutical company may be concerned with the scarcity of the natural resources it uses in its production process. Although its effects vary, no one can escape scarcity.

Section Check

1. We all have many wants and goals.
2. Scarcity exists when our wants exceed the available resources.
3. Scarce resources can be categorized as: land (all of our natural resources), labour (the physical and mental efforts expended in the production of goods and services), capital (the equipment and structures used to produce goods and services, the productive knowledge and skills people receive from education and on-the-job traning), and entrepreneurship (the process of combining land, labour, and capital into production of goods and services).
4. Goods and services are things that we value.

Opportunity Cost

- Why do we have to make choices?
- What do we give up when we have to choose?
- Why are "free" lunches not free?

SCARCITY AND CHOICES

We may want nice homes, two luxury cars in every garage, wholesome and good-tasting food, a personal trainer, and a therapist, all enjoyed in a pristine environment with zero pollution. If we had unlimited resources, and thus an ability to produce all of the goods and services anyone wanted, we would not have to choose among those desires. If we did not have to make meaningful economic choices, the study of economics would not be necessary. The essence of economics is to understand fully the implications that scarcity has for wise decision making. This suggests another way to define economics: *Economics is the study of the choices we make among our many wants and desires.*

TO CHOOSE IS TO LOSE

We are all faced with scarcity and, as a consequence, we must make choices. Because none of us can "afford" to buy everything we want, each time we do decide to buy one good or service, we reduce our ability to buy other things we would also like to have. If you buy a new car this year, you may not be able to afford your next best choice—the vacation you've been planning. You must choose. The cost of the car to you is the value of the vacation that must be forgone. The highest or best forgone opportunity resulting from a decision is called the **opportunity cost.** For example, time spent running costs time that could have been spent doing something else that is valuable—perhaps spending time with friends or studying for an upcoming exam. Another way to put this is that "to choose is to lose" or "an opportunity cost is an opportunity lost." To get more of anything that is desirable, you must accept less of something else that you also value.

opportunity cost
the value of the best forgone alternative that was not chosen

THE OPPORTUNITY COST OF GOING TO UNIVERSITY OR HAVING A CHILD

The average person often does not correctly consider opportunity costs when thinking about costs. For example, the cost of going to university is not just the direct costs of tuition and books. It also includes the opportunity cost of your time, which for many people is the greatest part of their costs. Specifically, the time spent going to school is time that could have been spent on a job earning, say, $25 000 a year. And how often do people consider the cost of raising a child to the age of 18? There are the obvious costs: food, visits to the dentist, clothes, piano lessons, time spent at soccer practices, and so on. But there are also other substantial opportunity costs incurred in rearing a child. Consider the opportunity cost if one parent chooses to give up his or her job to stay at home. Then, the time spent in child-rearing is time that could have been used making money and pursuing a career.

IS THAT REALLY A FREE LUNCH, OR A FREE LIBRARY?

The expression *"there's no such thing as a free lunch"* clarifies the relationship between scarcity and opportunity cost. Suppose the school cafeteria is offering "free" lunches today. Although the lunch is free to you, is it really free from society's perspective? The answer is no, because some of society's scarce resources will have been used in the preparation of the lunch. The issue is whether the resources that went into creating that lunch could have been used to produce something else of value. Clearly, the scarce resources that went into the production of the lunch like the labour and materials (food-service workers, lettuce, meat, ploughs, tractors, fertilizer, and so forth) could have been used in other ways. They had an opportunity cost, and thus were not free. Whenever you hear the word "free"— free libraries, free admission, and so on—an alarm should go off in your head. Very few things are free in the sense that they use none of society's scarce resources. So what does a free lunch really mean? It is, technically speaking, a "subsidized" lunch—a lunch using society's scarce resources, but one for which you personally do not have to pay.

In The **NEWS**

THE COST OF ELECTRICITY

BY WILLIAM WATSON

What's a thing worth? It's a question philosophers have worried about at least since Plato. We economists have a partial and in many ways unsatisfactory answer, but at least it's an answer: One measure of a thing's worth is what people are willing to pay for it.

Take electricity. In Quebec, we produce lots of electricity and don't actually charge ourselves very much for it: a little over six cents per kilowatt/hour for residential customers (as of April 2004) and even less for big industrial users. Nearby U.S. cities pay a lot more: over 15 cents in Boston, over 18 cents in New York.

So what's Quebec's electricity worth: six cents, which is what we charge ourselves for it, or almost three times that, which is what Americans would pay for it?

Why, people say, should we charge ourselves much more than our cost of producing a valuable natural resource that supports energy-intensive industry that hires lots of local people and pays them good wages?

"For the money," is the answer to that one. Suppose Hydro-Quebec did charge American rates for energy that costs less than six cents to produce. Its profits would soar—by more than $5 billion, according to its own estimates. That money could be used to reduce taxes or public debts or to finance spending on health or education or anything the gov-

ernment fancied. If [Quebecers] had lower taxes, better roads, a health-care system people could depend on, better universities and so on, wouldn't that create jobs?

Would hikes in electricity prices hit poor people disproportionately? Maybe they would, but to prevent that we could provide rebates to poor people that cover the higher costs they'd face. Would that defeat a key purpose of higher prices, namely getting people to economize on their use of a valuable scarce resource, which is what energy is? It might, a bit. But think about it. If I gave you $500 to compensate for the increase in your energy bill, would it be rational for you to take the $500 and spend it all on now much higher-priced energy? Probably not. What's more likely is that you would substitute away from energy and buy other things.

SOURCE: Adapted from William Watson, "Higher Electicity Prices Make Cents," *Ottawa Citizen*, March 22, 2005, p. A13. Reprinted with permission from the author.

CONSIDER THIS:
The real cost of electricity is its opportunity cost, which is the benefit Quebecers give up by consuming it themselves rather than selling it to Americans, who would pay up to three times the price.

Section Check

1.   Scarcity means we all have to make choices.
2.   When we are forced to choose, we give up the next highest-valued alternative.
3.   Opportunity cost is what you give up when you make a choice.

Marginal Thinking

■ What do we mean by marginal thinking?
■ What is the rule of rational choice?
■ Why do we use the word "expected" with marginal benefits and costs?

CHOICES ARE PRIMARILY MARGINAL—NOT ALL OR NOTHING

Most choices involve how *much* of something to do, rather than whether or not to do something. It is not *whether* you eat, but *how much* you eat. Hopefully, the question is not *whether* to study this semester but instead *how much* to study this semester. For example, "If I studied a little more, I might be able to improve my grade," or "If I had a little better concentration when I was studying, I could improve my grade." This is what economists call **marginal thinking** because the focus is on the additional, or marginal, choices. Marginal choices involve the effects of adding to or subtracting from the current situation. In short, it is the small (or large) incremental changes to a plan of action.

Always watch out for the difference between average and marginal costs. Suppose the cost to an airline of flying 250 passengers from Edmonton to Montreal was $100 000. The average cost per seat would be $400 (the total cost divided by the number of seats— $100 000/250). If ten people are on standby and willing to pay $300 for a seat on the flight, should the airline sell them a ticket? Yes! The unoccupied seats earn nothing for the airline. The airline pays the $400 average cost per seat regardless of whether or not someone is sitting in the seat or not. What the airline needs to focus on are the additional (marginal) costs of a few extra passengers. The marginal costs are minimal—slight wear and tear on the airplane, handling some extra baggage, and ten extra inflight meals. In this case, thinking at the margin can increase total profits, even it if means selling at less-than-average cost of production.

Another good example of marginal thinking is auctions. Prices are bid up marginally as the auctioneer calls out one price after another. When a bidder views the new price (the marginal cost) to be greater than the value she places on the good (the marginal benefit), she withdraws from further bidding.

In trying to make themselves better off, people alter their behaviour if the expected marginal benefits from doing so outweigh the expected marginal costs—this is the **rule of rational choice.** The term *expected* is used with marginal benefits and costs because the world is uncertain in many important respects, so the actual result of changing behaviour may not always make people better off—but on average it will. However, as a matter of rationality, people are assumed to engage only in behaviour that they think ahead of time will make them better off. That is, individuals will only pursue an activity if expected marginal benefits are greater than the expected marginal costs, or *E(MB) > E(MC)*. This fairly unrestrictive and realistic view of individuals seeking self-betterment can be used to analyze a variety of social phenomena.

marginal thinking
focusing on the additional, or marginal, choices; marginal choices involve the effects of adding to or subtracting from the current situation, the small (or large) incremental changes to a plan of action

rule of rational choice
individuals will pursue an activity if the expected marginal benefits are greater than the expected marginal costs

Zero Pollution Would Be Too Costly

Let's use the concept of marginal thinking to evaluate pollution levels. We all know the benefits of a cleaner environment, but what would we have to give up—that is, what marginal costs would we have to incur—in order to achieve zero pollution? A lot! You could not drive a car, fly in a plane, or even ride a bike, especially if everybody else was riding bikes too (because congestion is a form of pollution). How would you get to school or

© PHOTODISC/GETTY ONE IMAGES

What would you be willing to give up to eliminate the rush-hour congestion you face? Think of the number of hours drivers waste each year sitting in traffic in Canada's largest cities. It costs the Canadian economy hundreds of millions of dollars a year in lost wages and wasted fuel.

work, or go to the movies or the grocery store? Everyone would have to grow their own food because transporting, storing, and producing food uses machinery and equipment that pollutes. And even growing your own food would be a problem because many plants emit natural pollutants. We could go on and on. The point is *not* that we shouldn't be concerned about the environment; rather, we have to weigh the expected marginal benefits of a cleaner environment against the expected marginal costs of a cleaner environment. This is not to say the environment should not be cleaner, only that zero pollution levels would be far too costly in terms of what we would have to give up.

Optimal (Best) Levels of Safety

Just as we can have optimal (or best) levels of pollution that are greater than zero, it is also true for crime and safety. Take crime. What would it cost society to have zero crime? It would be prohibitively costly to divert a tremendous amount of our valuable resources towards the total elimination of crime. In fact, it would be impossible to eliminate crime totally. But it would also be costly to reduce crime significantly. Since lower crime rates are costly, society must decide how much it is willing to give up: The additional resources for crime prevention can only come from limited resources, which could be used to produce something else possibly valued even more.

The same is true for safer products. Nobody wants defective tires on their cars, or cars that are unsafe and roll over at low speeds. However, there are optimal amounts of safety that are greater than zero too. The issue is not safe versus unsafe products but rather *how much* safety consumers want. It is not risk versus no-risk but rather *how much* risk are we willing to take? Additional safety can only come at higher costs. To make all products perfectly safe would be impossible, so we must weigh the benefits and costs of safer products. In fact, according to one U.S. study by Sam Peltzman, a University of Chicago economist, additional safety regulations in cars (mandatory safety belts, padded dashboards) in the late 1960s may have had little impact on highway fatalities. Peltzman found that making cars safer led to more reckless driving and more accidents. Although the safety regulations did result in fewer deaths per automobile accident, the total number of deaths remained unchanged because there were more accidents.

Reckless driving has benefits—getting somewhere more quickly—but it also has costs—possibly causing an accident or even a fatality. Rational people will compare the marginal benefits and marginal costs of safer driving and make the choices that they believe will get them to their destination safely. We would expect that even thrill-seekers would slow down if there were higher fines and/or increased law enforcement. It would change the benefit–cost equation for reckless driving (as would bad brakes, bald tires, and poor visibility). On the other hand, compulsory seat belts and air bags might cause motorists to drive more recklessly.

Section Check

SECTION CHECK

1. Economists are usually interested in the effects of additional, or marginal, changes in a given situation.
2. People try to make themselves better off.
3. People make decisions based on what they expect to happen.
4. The rule of rational choice states that individuals will pursue an activity if they expect the marginal benefits to be greater than the marginal costs, or $E(MB) > E(MC)$.
5. The optimal (best) levels of pollution, crime, and safety are greater than zero.

Incentives Matter

- Can we predict how people will respond to changes in incentives?
- What are positive incentives?
- What are negative incentives?

PEOPLE RESPOND TO INCENTIVES

In acting rationally, people are responding to incentives. That is, they are reacting to the changes in expected marginal benefits and expected marginal costs. In fact, much of human behaviour can be explained and predicted as a response to incentives. Consider the economic view of crime. Why do criminals engage in their "occupation"? Presumably because the "job," even with its risks, is preferred to alternative forms of employment. For criminals, the benefits of their actions are higher and/or the opportunity costs of them are lower than is the case for noncriminals. In some cases, criminals cannot get a legitimate job at a wage they would find acceptable, so the cost of crime in terms of other income forgone may be quite low. At other times, the likelihood of being caught is small, so the expected cost is negligible. Also, for some, the moral cost of a crime is low, whereas for others it is high. The benefits, in terms of wealth gained, are clear. If the expected gains or benefits from committing a crime outweigh the expected costs, the activity is pursued. For most policy purposes, the primary concern is not what causes the level of crime to be what it is but, rather, what causes the level of crime to change. Changes in the crime rate can be largely explained in terms of such a benefit–cost framework. If the benefits of crime rise, say, in the form of larger real "hauls," and/or if the costs fall due to a reduced likelihood of being caught or of being imprisoned if caught, then economists would expect the amount of crime to rise. Likewise, economists would expect the crime rate to fall in response to increased police enforcement, stiffer punishments, or an increase in the employment rate. Whether or not this analysis tells the complete story is debatable, but the use of the economic framework in thinking about the problem provides valuable insight.

POSITIVE AND NEGATIVE INCENTIVES

Almost all of economics can be reduced to incentive [$E(MB)$ versus $E(MC)$] stories, where consumers and producers are driven by incentives that affect expected costs or benefits. Prices, wages, profits, taxes, and subsidies are all examples of economic incentives.

ACTIVE LEARNING EXERCISE

DO INCENTIVES MATTER?

Q: The penalty for drug trafficking in Singapore is death. Do you think there would be more drug traffickers in Singapore if the mandatory sentence were five years with parole for good behaviour?

A: Singapore's tough drug-trafficking penalty would clearly impact the cost–benefit ratios of would-be smugglers. Lighter sentences would probably result in more drug smuggling because the overall cost of breaking the law would be reduced.

positive incentives
incentives that either reduce costs or increase benefits resulting in an increase in the activity or behaviour

negative incentives
incentives that either increase costs or reduce benefits resulting in a decrease in the activity or behaviour

Incentives can be classified into two types: positive and negative. **Positive incentives** are those that either increase benefits or reduce costs and thus result in an increased level of the related activity or behaviour. **Negative incentives,** on the other hand, either reduce benefits or increase costs, resulting in a decreased level of the related activity or behaviour. For example, a tax on cars that emit lots of pollution (an increase in costs) would be a negative incentive that would lead to a reduction in emitted pollution. On the other hand, a subsidy (the opposite of a tax) to hybrid cars—part electric, part internal combustion—would be a positive incentive that would encourage greater production and consumption of hybrid cars. Human behaviour is influenced in predictable ways by such changes in economic incentives, and economists use this information to predict what will happen when the benefits and costs of any choice are changed. In short, economists study the incentives and consequences of particular actions.

A subsidy on hybrid electric vehicles (HEVs) would be a positive incentive that would encourage greater production and consumption of these vehicles. Honda's Insight is expected to go 1100 kilometres on a single tank of gas; the Toyota Prius is expected to go about 700 kilometres.

© Jose Gil/Shutterstock

In The **NEWS**

MORE MONEY FOR HEALTH CARE WON'T HELP

BY ANDREW COYNE

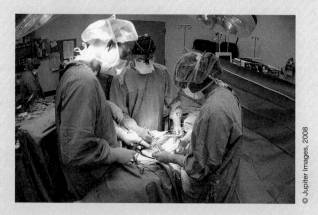

© Jupiter Images, 2008

In . . . 2003–04, provincial and territorial governments across Canada spent roughly $80 billion on health care, according to figures compiled by the Canadian Institute for Health Information. Per capita, that works out to just under $2,500—the highest it has ever been.

In 1978–79, by way of comparison, government spending on health care totalled just $12.6 billion. Adjusting for differences in population and prices, that's about $1,450 per capita, in today's dollars. In other words, governments today are spending nearly twice as much real dollars on each citizen as they did a generation ago, just to provide basic health care.

That's not counting the growing cost of things for which Canadians are required to pay out of pocket, including the lengthening list of services that are no longer covered by medicare. These add another $40 billion or so to the national

tab, or roughly two and a half times as much as in 1979—again, that's per capita, after inflation.

And yet the one thing on which everyone agrees—and I mean everyone: doctors, nurses, Ottawa, the provinces, conservatives, liberals—is that the system is in desperate need of more money. Left-wingers want more public funds to be ploughed into it. Right-wingers want to open it up to user fees, parallel private systems, and the like. But both are united in the belief that there's nothing wrong with medicare that a little more cash (well, a lot more) couldn't solve.

We spend 10% of GDP on health care today, in return for which we wait six months or more for many surgeries. Thirty years ago, we spent just 7% of GDP on health, and waiting lists were unknown. Possibly the issue is not how much is spent, but how well. Perhaps, if resources were used more efficiently, we might find it possible to provide more services with shorter wait times—out of existing funds. Yet many analysts continue to insist there is very little in savings to be squeezed out of the system.

Just one question: How do they know? A few years ago, a Canadian Policy Research Networks study estimated it was possible to save as much as $7 billion, merely by getting the provinces to adopt existing "best practices" across the country: that is, without requiring any innovation or discovery, but simply on the basis of known methodologies, already in place in one part of the system or another. But that's a little like treating a patient with the help of the best medical minds, circa 1350: What is unknown vastly exceeds what is known.

The system is often and aptly described as a "black box," in which resources are allocated without the most elementary data on the costs and benefits of different procedures. The Kirby committee was startled to find, in interviews with hospital administrators across the country—people with three and four degrees, and years of managerial experience—that, in the blunt language of its report, "no one knows what anything costs."

How can this be? Quite simply, it had never occurred to anyone to ask. The system of funding is positively Soviet: Hospitals typically get so much for scalpels, so much for rubber gloves, and so forth. There's often no connection with how many patients they treat, or what procedures they perform. In the absence of such information, there is no real basis for competition among hospitals, and in the absence of competition, there is no incentive to collect it. But put a price on the services hospitals provide, and fund them

accordingly, as Kirby recommends, and suddenly a functioning market becomes possible: an "internal market," wholly within the publicly funded universe.

Doctors, on the other hand, are paid on a fee for service basis, and so could be said to operate under a rudimentary price system. But since they can always just pass the tab on to the government, they too have little incentive to economize: In fact, as countless studies have concluded, they have every incentive to load a patient up with services they don't need. That's why many reform models include shifting doctors to a "capitation" system of payment, allotting them a fixed annual budget depending on the number of patients they see. This has much the same practical effect as user fees—i.e., imposing budget discipline at a "micro" level—without raising the same issues of accessibility.

In an odd sense, medicare's weakness is its strength. Had we any reason to believe the system was operating at maximum efficiency, and still found waiting lists and other signs of strain, then it would indeed be time to think about injecting more cash, whether public or private. But since in fact there is every reason to think the system is massively inefficient, it should be possible to make quite significant improvements, without spending more money and without departing from the ideal of public funding.

SOURCE: Adapted from Andrew Coyne, "Tossing Money at Medicare Won't Help," *National Post*, September 8, 2004, p. A1. Material reprinted with the express permission of: "The National Post Company", a CanWest Partnership.

CONSIDER THIS:
If the health-care system is inefficient in its use of resources, then it could be possible to make improvements in the health-care system without spending more money. One way to improve efficiency is to change the incentives in the system. For example, by putting a price on the services, hospitals would have an incentive to economize on their use of resources. Similarly, by shifting doctors to a capitation system of payment, they would not have the incentive to load a patient up with services the patient does not need.

Section Check

1. People respond to incentives in predictable ways.
2. A negative incentive increases costs or reduces benefits, thus discouraging consumption or production.
3. A positive incentive decreases costs or increases benefits, thus encouraging consumption or production.

Specialization and Trade

- What is the relationship between opportunity cost and specialization?
- What are the advantages of specialization in production?

WHY DO PEOPLE SPECIALIZE?

As you look around, you can see that people specialize in what they produce. They tend to dedicate their resources to one primary activity, whether it be child-rearing, driving a bus, or making bagels. Why is this? The answer, short and simple, is opportunity costs. By concentrating their energies on only one, or a few, activities, individuals are **specializing.** This allows them to make the best use of (and thus gain the most benefit from) their limited resources. A person, a region, or a country can gain by specializing in the production of the good in which they have a comparative advantage. That is, if they can produce a good or service at a lower opportunity cost than others, we say that they have a **comparative advantage** in the production of that good or service.

specializing
concentrating in the production of one, or a few, goods

comparative advantage
producing a good or service at a lower opportunity cost than other producers

WE ALL SPECIALIZE

We all specialize to some extent and rely on others to produce most of the goods and services we want. The work that we choose to do reflects our specialization. For example, we may specialize in selling or fixing automobiles. The wages from that work can then be used to buy goods from a farmer who has chosen to specialize in the production of food. Likewise, the farmer can use the money earned from selling his produce to get his tractor fixed by someone who specializes in that activity.

Specialization is evident not only among individuals but among regions and countries as well. In fact, the story of the economic development of Canada involves specialization. Within Canada, the prairies with their wheat, the Maritime provinces of Eastern Canada with their fishing fleets, and British Columbia with its lumber are all examples of regional specialization.

ACTIVE LEARNING EXERCISE

COMPARATIVE ADVANTAGE

Q: Should a lawyer who types 100 words per minute hire an administrative assistant to type her legal documents, even though he can only type 50 words per minute? If the lawyer does the job, she can do it in five hours; if the administrative assistant does the job, it takes him ten hours. The lawyer makes $100 an hour, and the administrative assistant earns $10 an hour. Which one has the comparative advantage (the lowest opportunity cost) in typing documents?

A: If the lawyer types her own documents, it will cost $500 ($100 per hour × 5 hours). If she has the administrative assistant type her documents, it will cost $100 ($10 per hour × 10 hours). Clearly, then, the lawyer should hire the administrative assistant to type her documents because the administrative assistant has the comparative advantage (lowest opportunity cost) in this case, despite being half as good in absolute terms.

THE ADVANTAGES OF SPECIALIZATION

In a small business, employees may perform a wide variety of tasks—from hiring to word processing to marketing. As the size of the company increases, each employee can perform a more specialized job, with a consequent increase in output per worker. The primary advantages of specialization are that employees acquire greater skill from repetition, they avoid wasted time in shifting from one task to another, and they do the types of work for which they are best suited, and it promotes the use of specialized equipment for specialized tasks.

The advantages of specialization are seen throughout the workplace. For example, in larger firms, specialists conduct personnel relations and accounting is in the hands of full-time accountants instead of someone with half a dozen other tasks to perform. The owner of a small retail store selects the location for the store primarily through guesswork, placing it where she believes sales would be high or where an empty, low-rent building is available. In contrast, larger chains have store sites selected by experts who have experience in analyzing the factors that make different locations relatively more desirable, like traffic patterns, income levels, demographics, and so on.

SPECIALIZATION AND TRADE LEAD TO GREATER WEALTH AND PROSPERITY

Trade, or voluntary exchange, directly increases wealth by making both parties better off (or they wouldn't trade). It is the prospect of wealth-increasing exchange that leads to productive specialization. That is, trade increases wealth by allowing a person, a region, or a nation to specialize in those products that it produces at a lower opportunity cost and to trade for those products that others produce at a lower opportunity cost. For example, say Canada is better at producing wheat than Brazil, and Brazil is better at producing coffee than Canada. Canada and Brazil would each benefit if Canada produces wheat and trades some of it to Brazil for coffee. Coffee growers in Canada could grow coffee in expensive greenhouses, but it would result in higher coffee costs and prices, while leaving fewer resources available for employment in more productive jobs, such as wheat production. This is true for individuals, too. Imagine Tom had 10 kilograms of tea and Katherine had 10 kilograms of coffee. However, Tom preferred coffee to tea and Katherine preferred tea to coffee. So if Tom traded his tea to Katherine for her coffee, both parties would be better off. Trade simply reallocates existing goods, and voluntary exchange increases wealth by making both parties better off, or they would not agree to trade.

Section Check

1. We all specialize.
2. Specialization is important for individuals, businesses, regions, and nations.
3. Specialization and trade increase wealth.
4. The person, region, or country that can produce a good or service at a lower opportunity cost than other producers has a comparative advantage in the production of that good or service.

Market Prices Coordinate Economic Activity

■ How does a market system allocate scarce resources?
■ What are the important signals that market prices communicate?
■ What are the effects of price controls and price supports?
■ What are unintended consequences?
■ What is a market failure?

HOW DOES THE MARKET SYSTEM WORK TO ALLOCATE RESOURCES?

In a world of scarcity, competition is inescapable, and one method of allocating resources among competing uses is the market system. The market system provides a way for millions of producers and consumers to allocate scarce resources. Buyers and sellers indicate their wants through their actions and inaction in the marketplace, and it is this collective "voice" that determines how resources are allocated. But how is this information communicated? Market prices serve as the language of the market system. By understanding what these market prices mean, you can get a better understanding of the vital function that the market system performs.

MARKET PRICES PROVIDE IMPORTANT INFORMATION

Market prices communicate important information to both buyers and sellers. These prices communicate information about the relative availability of products to buyers, and they provide sellers with critical information about the relative value that consumers place on those products. In effect, market prices provide a way for both buyers and sellers to communicate about the relative value of resources. This communication results in a shifting of resources from those uses that are less valued to those that are more valued. We will see how this works beginning in Chapter 3.

The basis of market economy is the voluntary exchange and the price system that guide people's choices and produces solutions to the questions of what goods to produce and how to produce those goods and distribute them.

Take something as simple as the production of a pencil. Where did the wood come from? Perhaps British Columbia or Quebec. The graphite may have come from the mines in Northern Ontario, and the rubber maybe from Malaysia. The paint, the glue, the metal piece that holds the eraser—who knows? The point is that market forces coordinated this activity among literally thousands of people, some of whom live in different countries and speak different languages. The market system brought these people together to make a pencil that sells for 25 cents at your bookstore. It all happened because the market system provided the incentive for people to pursue activities that benefit others. This same process produces millions of goods and services around the world from automobiles and computers to pencils and paper clips.

In countries that do not rely on the market system, there is no clear communication between buyers and sellers. In the former Soviet Union, where quality was virtually nonexistent, there were shortages of quality goods and surpluses of low-quality goods. For example, there were thousands of tractors without spare parts and millions of pairs of shoes that were left on shelves because the sizes did not match those of the population.

In The **NEWS**

RISING FOOD PRICES CAUSING CONSUMERS TO CHANGE HABITS

BY ERIC BEAUCHESNE

OTTAWA—Canadians are not only cutting back on the use of their cars in the wake of surging gasoline prices but are also starting to change their food-buying habits in anticipation of higher food prices, according to new poll results. "Buffeted by continuing increases in gas and energy prices, Canadians are also preparing to change their eating habits and how they shop for food," stated the analysis of the Investors Group poll, released Tuesday. Many of those polled say they are buying more local produce, giving up exotic or out-of-season fruits and vegetables, eating less meat and having more meals at home rather than going to a restaurant.

The results of the survey earlier this month also suggest consumers' inflation fears are dovetailing with their concerns about the viability of non-renewable energy resources. "While concern about rising prices appears to be prompting lifestyle changes, a number of Canadians are also worried about the sustainability of non-renewable resource supplies," the analysis said, noting that 46 per cent fear the world's supply of such resources will be depleted within the next generation.

However, it appears that it took price increases, or in the case of food, the fear of higher prices, to prompt consumers to start acting on those environmental concerns, said Myron Knodel, tax and estate planning specialist with Investors Group, Canada's biggest mutual fund company. "The two, it

appears, are linked to a certain extent but I think the change in behaviour when it comes to spending habits currently . . . was the result of the increase in prices," he said in an interview.

"When prices went up that was an initial shock and people thought we've got to adjust our budgets . . . be more prudent in our spending, and along with that there is a greater awareness of the sustainability of our natural resources, and the two went hand in hand," he said. "But had the price pressures not occurred I do not know that their reaction or behaviour would have changed as much as it has did."

The survey indicated that the "most significant change in behaviour" is where prices have increased the most, at the pumps. For example, 83 per cent plan to buy a more fuel-efficient vehicle when they make their next car purchase.

SOURCE: Eric Beauchesne, "Rising food prices causing consumers to change habits; Higher fuel costs altering spending decisions," *Edmonton Journal*, June 18, 2008, p. E3. Material reprinted with the express permisson of: "CANWEST NEWS SERVICE," a CanWest Partnership.

CONSIDER THIS:

Rising gas prices have communicated important information to consumers about the relative availability of non-renewable resources such as oil. The resulting changes to consumer behaviour—in terms of new-car purchases, what type of food to buy, and where to buy it—are of interest to producers.

WHAT EFFECT DO PRICE CONTROLS HAVE ON THE MARKET SYSTEM?

Government policies called **price controls** sometimes force prices above or below what they would be in a market economy. Unfortunately, these controls often impose harm on the same people they are trying to help, in large part by short-circuiting the market's information transmission function. That is, price controls effectively strip the market price of its meaning for both buyers and sellers (which we will see in Chapters 3 and 4). A sales tax will also distort price signals, leading to a misallocation of resources (which we will see in Chapter 5).

price controls
government-mandated minimum or maximum prices

MARKET FAILURE

The market mechanism is a simple but effective and efficient general means of allocating resources among alternative uses. When the economy fails to allocate resources efficiently on its own, however, it is known as **market failure.** For example, a steel mill might put soot and other forms of "crud" into the air as a by-product of making steel. When it does this, it imposes costs on others not connected with using or producing steel from the steel mill. The soot may require homeowners to paint their homes more often, entailing a cost. And studies show that respiratory diseases are greater in areas with more severe air pollution, imposing costs and often shortening life itself. In addition,

market failure
when the economy fails to allocate resources efficiently on its own

the steel mill might discharge chemicals into a stream, thus killing wildlife and spoiling recreational activities for the local population. In this case, the steel factory does not bear the cost of its polluting actions and emits too much pollution. In other words, by transferring the pollution costs onto society, the firm has lowered its costs of production and is now producing more than the ideal output—this is inefficient because it is an overallocation of resources.

Markets can also produce too little of a good—research, for example. The government might decide to subsidize promising scientific research that may benefit many people—like cancer research.

Whether the market economy has produced too little (underallocation) or too much (overallocation), the government can improve society's well-being by intervening. The case of market failure will be taken up in more detail in Chapter 6.

In addition, we cannot depend on the market economy to always communicate accurately. Some firms may have market power to distort prices in their favour. For example, the only regional cement company in the area has the ability to charge a higher price and provide a lower-quality product than if the company was in a highly competitive market. In this case, the lack of competition can lead to higher prices and reduced product quality. And without adequate information, unscrupulous producers may be able to misrepresent their products to the disadvantage of unwary consumers.

Does the Market Distribute Income Fairly?

Sometimes a painful trade-off exists between how much an economy can produce efficiently and how that output is distributed—the degree of equality. There is no guarantee that the market economy will provide everyone with adequate amounts of food, shelter, and transportation. That is, not only does the market determine what goods are going to be produced, and in what quantities, but it also determines the distribution of output among members of society. For example, in 2006, the richest 20 percent of Canadian households received 47 percent of the total national income, whereas the poorest 20 percent of Canadian households received only 4 percent of the total national income. Although one person may find it terribly unfair for some individuals to earn many times the amount that other individuals who work equally hard earn, another person may find it highly unfair to ask one group, the relatively rich, to pay a much higher proportion of their income in taxes than another group.

Section Check

1. Scarcity forces us to allocate our limited resources.
2. Market prices provide important information to buyers and sellers.
3. Price controls distort market signals.
4. A market failure is said to occur when the economy fails to allocate resources efficiently.

Summary

Section 1.1

- Economics is the study of the allocation of our limited resources to satisfy our unlimited wants.
- Scarcity refers to "the economic problem" we all face—our wants exceed our limited resources.

- Scarcity forces us to choose, and choices are costly because we must give up other opportunities that we value.
- Economics provides the tools to intelligently evaluate and decide on choices.

- The two branches of economics are microeconomics and macroeconomics: microeconomics focuses on smaller units within the economy—firms and households; macroeconomics deals with the aggregate, or total, economy.

Section 1.2

- Economic theories are statements about patterns of human behaviour.
- Economic theories are tested by using empirical analysis to examine the data and see if our hypothesis fits well with the facts.
- Common pitfalls to avoid when studying economics are: violating the *ceteris paribus* assumption, confusing causation and correlation, and the fallacy of composition.
- Positive analysis is testable and objective ("what is").
- Normative analysis is subjective ("what should or ought to be").

Section 1.3

- Scarcity refers to how we satisfy our unlimited wants with limited resources.
- Resources are defined as inputs—land, labour, capital, and entrepreneurship.
- Goods and services are those items (both tangible and intangible) that we value or desire.

Section 1.4

- Economics is the study of the choices we make among our many wants and desires.
- The opportunity cost of a decision refers to the value of the next-best foregone alternative.

Section 1.5

- Economists are usually interested in the effects of additional, or marginal, changes in a given situation.

- A rational person will generally pursue an activity if he or she perceives the marginal benefits to be greater than the marginal costs, or $E(MB) > E(MC)$—this is sometimes called the rule of rational choice.

Section 1.6

- Economists predict that people will change their behaviour in predictable ways when responding to changes in incentives.
- Positive incentives decrease costs or increase benefits, thus encouraging a particular activity or behaviour.
- Negative incentives increase costs or reduce benefits, thus discouraging a particular activity or behaviour.

Section 1.7

- Trade is generally mutually beneficial, whether it is between two individuals or two countries.
- A person, region, or country that can produce a good or service at a lower opportunity cost than other producers is said to have a comparative advantage in the production of that good or service.
- Trade allows individuals or countries to do what they do best—specialize.
- Specialization and trade increase wealth.

Section 1.8

- Through voluntary exchange and the price system, the market system provides a way for producers and consumers to allocate scarce resources.
- Price controls sometimes force prices above or below what they would be in a market economy.
- A market failure occurs when an economy fails to allocate resources efficiently on its own.

Key Terms and Concepts

For a complete glossary of chapter key terms, visit the textbook's Web site at http://www.sextonmacro2e.nelson.com.

economics 2
resources 2
the economic problem 2
macroeconomics 3
aggregate 3
microeconomics 3
theory 4
hypothesis 4
empirical analysis 4
ceteris paribus 5
correlation 5

causation 5
fallacy of composition 6
positive analysis 6
normative analysis 7
scarcity 9
labour 9
land 10
capital 10
human capital 10
entrepreneurship 10
goods 10

service 10
opportunity cost 11
marginal thinking 13
rule of rational choice 13
positive incentives 16
negative incentives 16
specializing 18
comparative advantage 18
price controls 21
market failure 21

Review Questions

1. Why should we use the *ceteris paribus* assumption in these statements?

   a. Car prices increased and people bought more cars as their incomes rose.

   b. The price of generic shampoo fell and people bought less of it as their income rose.

2. After reading this chapter, see if you can come up with a list of ten topics where you think the economic way of thinking would be helpful in your life.

3. Identify which of the following economic statements are positive and which are normative:

   a. A tax increase will increase unemployment.

   b. The government should reduce funding for social assistance programs.

   c. Tariffs on imported wine will lead to higher prices for domestic wine.

   d. A decrease in the capital gains tax rate will increase investment.

   e. Goods purchased on the Internet should be subject to provincial sales taxes.

   f. A reduction in interest rates will cause inflation.

4. The following statement represents which fallacy in thinking, and why: "I earn $12 per hour. If I am able to earn $12 per hour, everyone should be able to find work for at least that wage rate."

5. Which of the following goods are scarce?

   a. garbage

   b. salt water in the ocean

   c. clothes

   d. clean air in a big city

   e. dirty air in a big city

   f. a public library

6. List the opportunity costs of the following:

   a. going to university

   b. missing a lecture

   c. withdrawing and spending $100 from your savings account, which earns 5 percent interest annually

   d. going snowboarding on the weekend before final examinations

7. Which of the following are positive incentives? negative incentives? Why?

   a. a fine for not cleaning up after your dog defecates in the park

   b. a trip to Quebec City paid for by your parents or significant other for earning an A in your economics course

   c. a higher tax on cigarettes and alcohol

   d. a subsidy for installing solar panels on your house

8. Which region has a comparative advantage in the following goods?

   a. Wheat: Colombia or Canada

   b. Coffee: Colombia or Canada

   c. Lumber: Alberta or British Columbia

   d. Oil: Alberta or British Columbia

9. Why is it important that the country or region with the lower opportunity cost produce the good? How would you use the concept of comparative advantage to argue for reducing restrictions on trade between countries?

10. Imagine that you are trying to decide whether or not to cross a street without using the designated crosswalk at the traffic signal. What are the expected marginal benefits of crossing? the expected marginal costs? How would the following conditions change your benefit–cost equation?

    a. The street was busy.

    b. The street was empty and it was 3 A.M.

    c. You were in a huge hurry.

    d. There was a police officer 10 metres away.

    e. The closest crosswalk was 1 kilometre away.

    f. The closest crosswalk was 5 metres away.

Appendix

GRAPHS ARE AN IMPORTANT ECONOMIC TOOL

Sometimes the use of visual aids, such as graphs, greatly enhances our understanding of a theory. It is much the same as finding your way to a friend's house with the aid of a map rather than with detailed verbal or written instructions. Graphs are important tools for economists. They allow us to understand better the workings of the economy. To economists, a graph can be worth a thousand words. This text will use graphs throughout to enhance the understanding of important economic relationships. This appendix provides a guide on how to read and create your own graphs.

The most useful graph for our purposes is one that merely connects a vertical line (the **Y-axis**) with a horizontal line (the **X-axis**), as seen in Exhibit 1. The intersection of the two lines occurs at the origin, which is where the value of both variables is equal to zero. In Exhibit 1, the graph has four quadrants or "boxes." In this textbook we will be primarily concerned with the shaded box in the upper right-hand corner. This portion of the graph deals exclusively with positive numbers. Always keep in mind that moving to the right on the horizontal axis and up along the vertical axis each lead to higher values.

USING GRAPHS AND CHARTS

Exhibit 2 presents three common types of graphs. The **pie chart** in Exhibit 2(a) shows what college students earn. That is, each slice in the pie chart represents the percent of college students in a particular earnings category. Therefore, pie charts are used to show the relative size of various quantities that add up to a total of 100 percent.

Exhibit 2(b) is a **bar graph** that shows the sales of wireless phone service by province for a new company that has just entered the Canadian market. The height of the line represents sales in millions of dollars. Bar graphs are used to show a comparison of the sizes of quantities of similar items.

Exhibit 2(c) is a **time-series graph.** This type of graph shows changes in the value of a variable over time. This is a visual tool that allows us to observe important trends over a certain time period. In Exhibit 2(c) we see a graph that shows trends in the stock price of Fly-by-Chance Airlines for the period January to December 2008. The horizontal axis shows us the passage of time, and the vertical axis shows us the stock price in dollars per share.

USING GRAPHS TO SHOW THE RELATIONSHIP BETWEEN TWO VARIABLES

Although the graphs and chart in Exhibit 2 are important, they do not allow us to show the relationship between two vari-

Y-axis
the vertical axis on a graph

X-axis
the horizontal axis on a graph

pie chart
a circle subdivided into proportionate slices that represent various quantities that add up to 100 percent

bar graph
represents data using vertical bars rising from the horizontal axis

time-series graph
a type of line chart that plots data trends over time

appendix
Exhibit 1 — Plotting a Graph

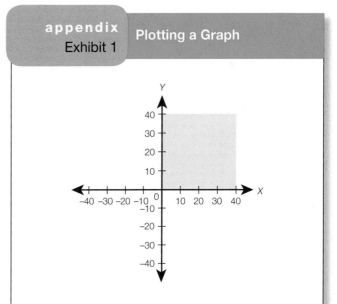

In the upper right-hand corner, we see that the graph includes a positive figure for the Y-axis and the X-axis. As we move to the right along the horizontal axis, the numerical values increase. As we move up along the vertical axis, the numerical values increase.

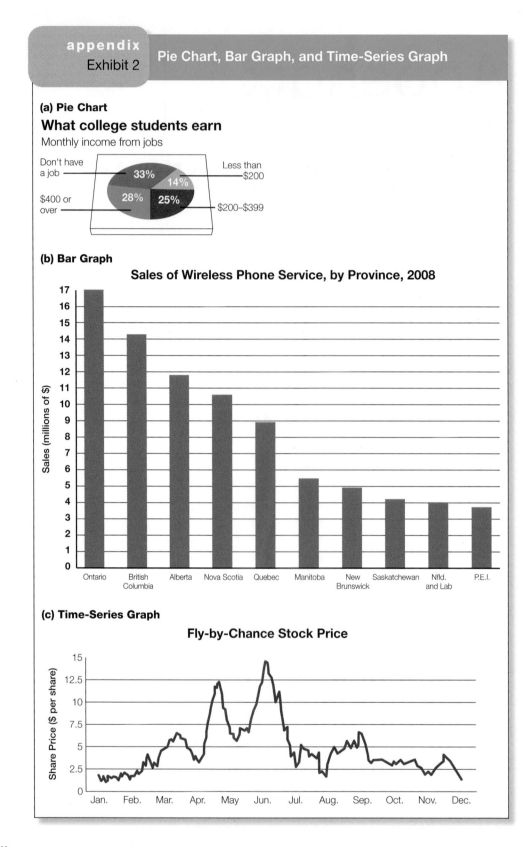

appendix
Exhibit 2   Pie Chart, Bar Graph, and Time-Series Graph

(a) Pie Chart
What college students earn
Monthly income from jobs

Don't have a job — 33%
Less than —$200 — 14%
$400 or over — 28%
$200–$399 — 25%

(b) Bar Graph
Sales of Wireless Phone Service, by Province, 2008

Sales (millions of $)

Ontario British Columbia Alberta Nova Scotia Quebec Manitoba New Brunswick Saskatchewan Nfld. and Lab P.E.I.

(c) Time-Series Graph
Fly-by-Chance Stock Price

Share Price ($ per share)

Jan. Feb. Mar. Apr. May Jun. Jul. Aug. Sep. Oct. Nov. Dec.

variable
something that is measured by a number, such as your height

positive relationship
when two variables change in the same direction

ables (a **variable** is something that is measured by a number, such as your height). To more closely examine the structure of and functions of graphs, let us consider the story of Katherine, an avid inline skater who has aspirations of winning the Z Games next year. To get there, however, she will have to put in many hours of practice. But how many hours? In search of information about the practice habits of other skaters, she logged onto the Internet, where she pulled up the results of a study conducted by ESPM 3 that indicated the score of each Z Games competitor and the amount of practice time per week spent by each skater. The results of this study (see Exhibit 3) indicated that skaters had to practise 10 hours per week to receive a score of 4.0, 20 hours per week to receive a score of 6.0, 30 hours per week to get a score of 8.0, and 40 hours per week to get a perfect score of 10. What does this information tell Katherine? By using a graph, she can more clearly understand the relationship between practice time and overall score.

A Positive Relationship

The study on scores and practice times revealed what is called a direct relationship, also called a positive relationship. A **positive relationship** means that the variables change in the same direction. That is, an increase in one variable (practice time) is accompanied by an increase in the other variable (overall score), or a decrease in one variable (practice time) is accompanied by a decrease in the other variable (overall score). In short, the variables change in the same direction.

A Negative Relationship

When two variables change in opposite directions, we say they are inversely related, or have a **negative relationship.** That is, when one variable rises, the other variable falls, or when one variable decreases, the other variable increases.

THE GRAPH OF A DEMAND CURVE

Let us now examine one of the most important graphs in all of economics—the demand curve. In Exhibit 4, we see Emily's individual demand curve for compact discs. It shows the price of CDs on the vertical axis and the quantity of CDs purchased per month on the horizontal axis. Every point in the space shown represents a price and quantity combination. The downward-sloping line, labelled demand curve, shows the different combinations of price and quantity purchased. Note that the higher you go up on the vertical (price) axis, the smaller the quantity purchased on the horizontal (quantity) axis, and the lower the price on the vertical axis, the greater the quantity purchased.

In Exhibit 4, we see that moving up the vertical price axis from the origin, the price of CDs increases from $5 to $25 in increments of $5. Moving out along the horizontal quantity axis, the quantity purchased increases from zero to five CDs per month. Point A represents a price of $25 and a quantity of one CD, point B represents a price of $20 and a quantity of two CDs, point C, $15 and a quantity of three CDs, and

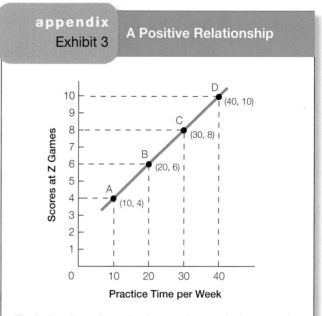

appendix Exhibit 3 **A Positive Relationship**

The in-line skaters' practice times and scores in the competition are plotted on the graph. Each participant is represented by a point. The graph shows that those skaters who practised the most scored the highest. This is called a positive, or direct, relationship.

negative relationship
when two variables change in opposite directions

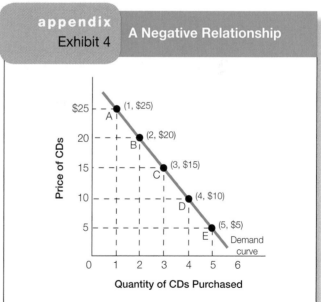

appendix Exhibit 4 **A Negative Relationship**

The downward slope of the curve means that price and quantity purchased are inversely, or negatively, related: when one increases, the other decreases. That is, moving down along the demand curve from point A to point E, we see that as price falls, the quantity purchased increases. Moving up along the demand curve from point E to point A, we see that as the price increases, the quantity purchased falls.

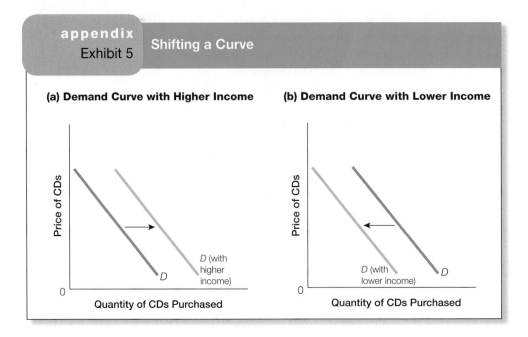

appendix
Exhibit 5   Shifting a Curve

(a) Demand Curve with Higher Income   **(b) Demand Curve with Lower Income**

so on. When we connect all the points, we have what economists call a curve. As you can see, curves are sometimes drawn as straight lines for ease of illustration. Moving down along the curve, we see that as the price falls, a greater quantity is demanded; moving up the curve to higher prices, a smaller quantity is demanded. That is, when CDs become less expensive, Emily buys more CDs. When CDs become more expensive, Emily buys fewer CDs, perhaps choosing to go to the movies or buy a pizza instead.

USING GRAPHS TO SHOW THE RELATIONSHIP BETWEEN THREE VARIABLES

Although only two variables are shown on the axes, graphs can be used to show the relationship between three variables. For example, say we add a third variable—income—to our earlier example. Our three variables are now income, price, and quantity purchased. If Emily's income rises, say she gets a raise at work, she is now able and willing to buy more CDs than before at each possible price. As a result, the whole demand curve shifts outward (rightward) compared to the old curve. That is, with the new income, she uses some of it to buy more CDs. This is seen in the graph in Exhibit 5(a). On the other hand, if her income falls, say she quits her job to go back to school, she now has less income to buy CDs. This causes the whole demand curve to shift inward (leftward) compared to the old curve. This is seen in the graph in Exhibit 5(b).

The Difference Between a Movement Along and a Shift in the Curve

It is important to remember the difference between a movement between one point and another along a curve and a shift in the whole curve. A change in one of the variables on the graph, like price or quantity purchased, will cause a movement along the curve, say from point A to point B, as shown in Exhibit 6. A change in one of the

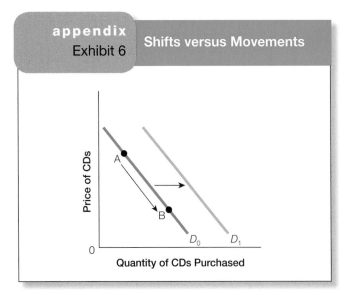

appendix
Exhibit 6   Shifts versus Movements

variables not shown (held constant in order to show only the relationship between price and quantity), like income in our example, will cause the whole curve to shift. The change from D_0 to D_1 in Exhibit 6 shows such a shift.

SLOPE

In economics, we sometimes refer to the steepness of the lines or curves on graphs as the **slope.** A slope can be either positive (upward sloping) or negative (downward sloping). A curve that is downward sloping represents an inverse, or negative, relationship between the two variables and slants downward from left to right, as seen in Exhibit 7(a). A curve that is upward sloping represents a direct, or positive, relationship between the two variables and slants upward from left to right, as seen in Exhibit 7(b). The numeric value of the slope shows the number of units of change of the Y-axis variable for each unit of change in the X-axis variable. Slope provides the direction (positive or negative) as well as the magnitude of the relationship between the two variables.

slope
the ratio of rise (change in the Y variable) over the run (change in the X variable)

Measuring the Slope of a Linear Curve

A straight-line curve is called a linear curve. The slope of a linear curve between two points measures the relative rates of change of two variables. Specifically, the slope of a linear curve can be defined as the ratio of the change in the Y value to the change in the X value. The slope can also be expressed as the ratio of the rise to the run, where the rise is the change in the Y variable (along the vertical axis) and the run is the change in the X variable (along the horizontal axis).

In Exhibit 8, we show two linear curves, one with a positive slope and one with a negative slope. In Exhibit 8(a), the slope of the positively sloped linear curve from point A to B is 1/2, because the rise is 1 (from 2 to 3) and the run is 2 (from 1 to 3). In Exhibit 8(b), the negatively sloped linear curve has a slope of -4, a rise of -8 (a fall of 8 from 10 to 2) and a run of 2 (from 2 to 4), which gives us a slope of -4 $(-8/2)$. Note the appropriate signs on the slopes: The negatively sloped line carries a minus sign and the positively sloped line, a plus sign.

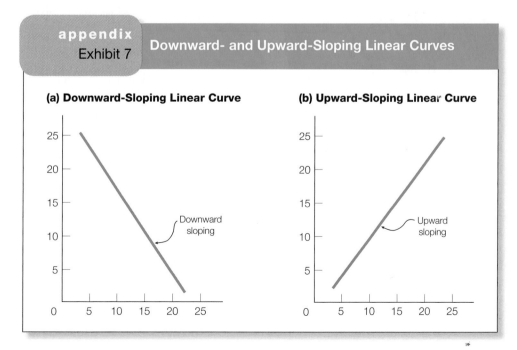

appendix Exhibit 7 — Downward- and Upward-Sloping Linear Curves

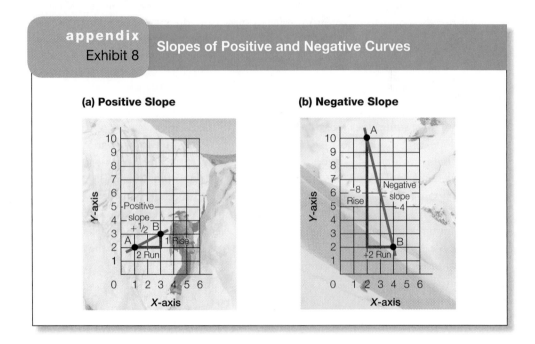

appendix Exhibit 8 — Slopes of Positive and Negative Curves

(a) Positive Slope

(b) Negative Slope

Finding the Slope of a Nonlinear Curve

In Exhibit 9, we show the slope of a nonlinear curve. A nonlinear curve is a line that actually curves. Here the slope varies from point to point along the curve. However, we can find the slope of this curve at any given point by drawing a straight line tangent to that point on the curve. A tangency is when a straight line just touches the curve without actually crossing it. At point A, we see that the positively sloped line that is tangent to the curve has a slope of 1—the line rises one unit and runs one unit. At point B, the line is horizontal, so it has zero slope. At point C, we see a slope of −2 because the negatively sloped line has a rise of −2 units (a fall of two units) for every one unit run.

Remember, many students have problems with economics simply because they fail to understand graphs, so make sure that you understand this material before going on to Chapter 2.

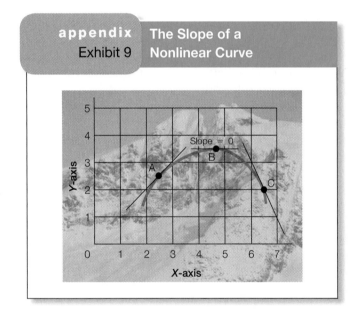

appendix Exhibit 9 — The Slope of a Nonlinear Curve

Key Terms and Concepts

For a complete glossary of chapter key terms, visit the textbook's Web site at http://www.sextonmacro2e.nelson.com.

Y-axis 25	bar graph 25	positive relationship 26
X-axis 25	time-series graph 25	negative relationship 27
pie chart 25	variable 26	slope 29

Fill in the Blanks

Section 1.1

1. Economics is the study of the allocation of _____ resources to satisfy _____ wants for goods and services.

2. _____ is the problem that our wants exceed our limited resources.

3. Resources are _____ used to produce goods and services.

4. The economic problem is that _____ forces us to choose, and choices are costly because we must give up other opportunities that we _____.

5. Living in a world of scarcity means _____.

6. _____ deals with the aggregate (the forest), or total economy, whereas _____ deals with the smaller units (the trees) within the economy.

Section 1.2

7. Economic _____ are statements or propositions used to _____ and _____ patterns of human economic behaviour.

8. A _____ in economic theory is a testable prediction about how people will behave or react to a change in economic circumstances.

9. In order to isolate the effects of one variable on another, we use the _____ assumption.

10. When two events usually occur together, it is called _____.

11. The _____ is the incorrect view that what is true for an individual is always true for the group.

12. "A tax increase will lead to a lower rate of inflation" is a _____ economic statement.

Section 1.3

13. As long as human _____ exceed available _____, scarcity will exist.

14. The scarce resources that are used in the production of goods and services can be grouped into four categories: _____, _____, _____, and _____.

15. Capital includes human capital, the _____ people receive from _____.

16. Entrepreneurs are always looking for new ways to improve _____ or _____, driven by the lure of a positive incentive—_____.

17. Scarcity ultimately leads to _____ for the available goods and services.

18. Because we all have different _____, scarcity affects everyone differently.

Section 1.4

19. Economics is the study of the _____ we make among our many _____.

20. The highest or best forgone alternative resulting from a decision is called the _____.

Section 1.5

21. Most choices involve _____ of something to do rather than whether or not to do something.

22. Economists emphasize _____ thinking because the focus is on additional, or _____, choices, which involve the effects of _____ or _____ the current situation.

23. The rule of rational choice is that in trying to make themselves better off, people alter their behaviour if the _____ to them from doing so outweigh the _____ they will bear.

Section 1.6

24. If the benefits of some activity _____ and/or if the costs _____, economists expect the amount of that activity to rise. Likewise, if the benefits of some activity _____ and/or if the costs _____, economists expect the amount of that activity to fall.

25. _____ incentives either reduce costs or increase benefits, resulting in an increase in the activity or behaviour.

Section 1.7

26. People _____ by concentrating their energies on the activity to which they are best suited because individuals incur _____ opportunity costs as a result.

27. If a person, a region, or a country can produce a good or service at a lower opportunity cost than others can, we say that they have a _____ in the production of that good or service.

28. The primary advantages of specialization are that employees acquire greater _____ from repetition, they avoid _____ time in shifting from one task to another, and they do the types of work for which they are _____ suited.

Section 1.8

29. Market prices serve as the _____ of the market system. They communicate information about the _____ to buyers, and they provide sellers with critical information about the _____ that buyers place on those products. This communication results in a shifting of resources from those uses that are _____ valued to those that are _____ valued.

30. The basis of a market economy is _____ exchange and the _____ system that guides people's choices about questions of what goods to produce and how to produce those goods and distribute them.

31. _____ can lead the economy to fail to allocate resources efficiently, as in the cases of pollution and scientific research.

True or False

Section 1.1

1. Choices are costly because we must give up other opportunities that we value.

2. When our limited wants exceed our unlimited resources, we face scarcity.

3. If we valued leisure more highly, the opportunity cost of working would be lower.

4. Economics is a social science because it is concerned with reaching generalizations about human behaviour.

5. Microeconomics would deal with the analysis of a small individual firm, whereas macroeconomics would deal with very large global firms.

Section 1.2

6. Economic theories do not abstract from very many particular details of situations so they can better focus on every aspect of the behaviour to be explained.

7. Determining whether or not an economic hypothesis is acceptable is more difficult than in the natural or physical sciences in that, unlike a chemist in a chemistry lab, economists cannot control all the other variables that might infiuence human behaviour.

8. A positive statement must be both testable and true.

9. Normative analysis involves subjective, nontestable statements.

10. The majority of disagreements in economics stem from normative issues.

11. A hypothesis is a normative statement.

Section 1.3

12. In economics, labour includes more than physical effort, and land includes more than what people usually think of as land.

13. Entrepreneurship is the process of combining labour, land, and capital together to produce goods and services.

14. All goods and services can be subjected to economic analysis.

15. Even the wealthy individual who decides to donate all of her money to charity faces the constraints of scarcity.

16. Increases in production could enable us to eliminate scarcity.

17. If we had unlimited resources, we would not have to choose among our desires.

Section 1.4

18. Opportunity cost is the value of the best forgone alternative that was not chosen.

19. Scarcity implies that "there's no such thing as a free lunch."

Section 1.5

20. The actual result of changing behaviour following the rule of rational choice will always make people better off.

21. In terms of the rule of rational choice, zero levels of pollution, crime, and safety would be far too costly in terms of what we would have to give up to achieve them.

22. Most choices in economics are all or nothing.

23. Good economic thinking requires thinking about average amounts rather than marginal amounts.

24. The safety issue is generally not whether a product is safe, but rather how much safety consumers want.

Section 1.6

25. Positive incentives are those that either increase benefits or reduce costs, resulting in an increase in the level of the related activity or behaviour.

26. Negative incentives are those that either increase costs or reduce benefits, resulting in an increase in the level of the related activity or behaviour.

Section 1.7

27. People can gain by specializing in the production of the good in which they have a comparative advantage.

28. Without the ability to trade, people would not tend to specialize in those areas where they have a comparative advantage.

29. Voluntary trade directly increases wealth by making both parties better off, and it is the prospect of wealth-increasing exchange that leads to productive specialization.

Section 1.8

30. Government price controls can short-circuit the market's information transmission function.

31. When the economy produces too little or too much of something, the government can potentially improve society's well-being by intervening.

32. Not only does the market determine what goods are going to be produced and in what quantities, it also determines the distribution of output among members of society.

Multiple Choice

Section 1.1

1. Which of the following is true of resources?
   a. Their availability is unlimited.
   b. They are the inputs used to produce goods and services.
   c. Increasing the amount of resources available could eliminate scarcity.
   d. Both b and c.

2. What do economists mean when they state that a good is scarce?
   a. There is a shortage of the good at the current price.
   b. It is impossible to expand the availability of the good.
   c. People will want to buy more of the good regardless of price.
   d. Our wants exceed our limited resources.

3. Economics is concerned with
   a. the choices people must make because resources are scarce.
   b. human decision makers and the factors that influence their choices.
   c. the allocation of limited resources to satisfy virtually unlimited desires.
   d. all of the above.

4. Scarcity would cease to exist as an economic problem if
   a. we learned to cooperate and not compete with each other.
   b. there were new discoveries of an abundance of natural resources.
   c. output per worker increased.
   d. none of the above.

5. When we look at a particular segment of the economy, such as a given industry, we are studying
   a. macroeconomics.
   b. microeconomics.
   c. normative economics.
   d. positive economics.

6. Which of the following is most likely a topic of discussion in macroeconomics?
   a. an increase in the price of a pizza
   b. a decrease in the production of DVD players by a consumer electronics company
   c. an increase in the wage rate paid to automobile workers
   d. a decrease in the unemployment rate
   e. the entry of new firms into the software industry

Section 1.2

7. Economists use theories to
   a. abstract from the complexities of the world.
   b. understand economic behaviour.
   c. explain and help predict human behaviour.
   d. do all of the above.
   e. do none of the above.

8. The importance of the *ceteris paribus* assumption is that it
   a. allows one to separate normative economic issues from positive economic ones.
   b. allows one to generalize from the whole to the individual.
   c. allows one to analyze the relationship between two variables apart from the infiuence of other variables.
   d. allows one to hold all variables constant so the economy can be carefully observed in a suspended state.

9. Ten-year-old Tommy observes that people who play hockey are larger than average and tells his mom that he's going to play hockey because it will make him big and strong. Tommy is
   a. committing the fallacy of composition.
   b. violating the *ceteris paribus* assumption.
   c. mistaking correlation for causation.
   d. committing the fallacy of decomposition.

10. Which of the following correlations is likely to involve primarily one variable causing the other, rather than a third variable causing them both?
   a. The amount of time a team's third string plays in the game tends to be greater, the larger the team's margin of victory.
   b. Higher ice cream sales and higher crime rates both tend to increase at the same time.
   c. A lower price of a particular good and a higher quantity purchased tend to occur at the same time.
   d. The likelihood of rain tends to be greater after you have washed your car.

11. Which of the following is a statement of positive analysis?
   a. New tax laws are needed to help the poor.
   b. Teenage unemployment should be reduced.
   c. We should increase pension payments to the elderly.
   d. An increase in tax rates will reduce unemployment.
   e. It is only fair that firms protected from competition by government-granted monopolies pay higher corporate taxes.

12. "Mandating longer sentences for any criminal's third arrest will lead to a reduction in crime. That is the way it ought to be, as such people are a menace to society." This quotation
   a. contains positive statements only.
   b. contains normative statements only.
   c. contains both normative and positive statements.
   d. contains neither normative nor positive statements.

Section 1.3

13. Which of the following is part of the economic way of thinking?
   a. When an option becomes less costly, individuals will become more likely to choose it.
   b. Costs are incurred whenever scarce resources are used to produce goods or services.
   c. The value of a good is determined by its cost of production.
   d. Both a and b are part of the economic way of thinking.

14. An example of a capital resource is
   a. stock in a computer software company.
   b. the funds in a savings account at a bank.
   c. a bond issued by a company selling electric generators.
   d. a dump truck.

Section 1.4

15. Who would be most likely to drop out of university before graduation?
   a. an economics major who wishes to go to graduate school
   b. a math major with a B+ average
   c. a chemistry major who has just been reading about the terrific jobs available for those with chemistry degrees
   d. a star hockey player who has just received a multimillion-dollar contract offer

16. "If I hadn't been set up on this blind date tonight, I would have saved $50 and spent the evening watching TV." The opportunity cost of the date is
   a. $50.
   b. $50, plus the cost to you of giving up a night of TV.
   c. smaller, the more you enjoy the date.
   d. higher, the more you like that night's TV shows.
   e. described by both b and d.

17. Say you had an 8 A.M. economics class, but you would still come to campus at the same time even if you skipped your economics class. The cost of coming to the economics class would include:
   a. the value of the time it took to drive to campus.
   b. the cost of the gasoline it took to get to campus.
   c. the cost of insuring the car for that day.
   d. both a and b.
   e. none of the above.

18. Which of the following would be likely to raise your opportunity cost of attending a big hockey game this Saturday night?
   a. A friend calls you up and offers you free tickets to a concert by one of your favourite bands on Saturday night.
   b. Your employer offers you double your usual wage to work this Saturday night.
   c. Late Friday afternoon, your statistics professor makes a surprise announcement that there will be a major exam on Monday morning.
   d. All of the above.

19. Which of the following statements is true?
   a. The opportunity cost of a decision is always expressed in monetary terms.
   b. The opportunity cost of a decision is the value of the best forgone alternative.
   c. Some economic decisions have zero opportunity cost.
   d. The opportunity cost of postsecondary education is the same for all students at the same university but may differ among students at different universities.
   e. None of the above statements is true.

20. The opportunity cost of attending university is likely to include all except which of the following?
   a. the cost of required textbooks
   b. tuition fees
   c. the income you forgo in order to attend classes
   d. the cost of haircuts received during the school term
   e. the cost of paper, pencils, and laptop needed to take notes

Section 1.5

21. Ted has decided to buy a burger and fries at a restaurant but is considering whether or not to buy a drink as well. If the price of a burger is $2, fries are $1, drinks are $1, and a value meal with all three costs $3.40, the marginal cost to Ted of the drink is
   a. $1.
   b. $0.40.
   c. $1.40.
   d. $3.40.
   e. impossible to determine from the above information.

22. Which of the following demonstrates marginal thinking?
   a. deciding never to eat meat
   b. deciding to spend one more hour studying economics tonight because you think the improvement on your next test will be large enough to make it worthwhile to you
   c. deciding to go to a marketing class you usually skip because there is a guest lecturer you are really interested in hearing that day
   d. both b and c

23. If a driver who had no change and whose cellphone battery was dead got stranded near a pay phone and chose to buy a quarter from a passerby for a $5 bill,
   a. the passerby was made better off and the driver was made worse off by the transaction.
   b. both the passerby and the driver were made better off by the transaction.
   c. the transaction made the driver worse off by $4.75.
   d. both a and c are true.

24. The expected marginal benefit to you from purchasing a new sport-utility vehicle is $30 000. The price of the new sport-utility vehicle is $32 000.
   a. If you are acting rationally, you will borrow $2000 and purchase a new sport-utility vehicle.
   b. You will not purchase the new sport-utility vehicle at this time if you are acting rationally.
   c. If you do not purchase the new sport-utility vehicle, your net loss will be $2000.
   d. If you are acting rationally, you will not purchase a sport-utility vehicle until the marginal cost of doing so falls to $30 000.

25. Litres of milk at a local grocery store are priced at one for $2 or two for $3. The marginal cost of buying a second litre of milk equals
    a. $3.
    b. $2.
    c. $1.
    d. $0.

26. Which of the following statements is most consistent with the rule of rational choice?
    a. Environment Canada should strive to eliminate virtually all air and water pollution.
    b. When evaluating new prescription drugs, Health Canada should weigh each drug's potential health benefits against the potential health risks posed by known side effects.
    c. Police forces should be enlarged until virtually all crime is eliminated.
    d. Manufacturers of automobiles should seek to make cars safer, no matter the costs involved.

Section 1.6
27. Government subsidies designed to encourage automobile manufacturers to produce more "environmentally friendly" cars is an example of _____.
    a. a negative incentive
    b. a positive incentive
    c. inverse legislation
    d. a waste of time

28. The fines and penalties associated with breaking the law in Canada are an example of _____.
    a. a negative incentive
    b. a positive incentive
    c. inverse legislation
    d. a waste of time

Section 1.7
29. If a country wanted to maximize the value of its output, each job should be carried out by the person who
    a. has the highest opportunity cost.
    b. has a comparative advantage in that activity.
    c. can complete the particular job most rapidly.
    d. enjoys that job the least.

30. If resources and goods are free to move across provinces, and if Quebec producers choose to specialize in growing apples and Ontario producers choose to specialize in growing peaches, then we could reasonably conclude that
    a. Ontario has a comparative advantage in producing peaches.
    b. Quebec has a comparative advantage in producing peaches.
    c. the opportunity cost of growing peaches is lower in Ontario than in Quebec.
    d. the opportunity cost of growing apples is lower in Quebec than in Ontario.
    e. all of the above except b are true.

31. Which of the following is not true?
    a. Voluntary exchange is expected to be advantageous to both parties to the exchange.
    b. What one trader gains from a trade, the other must lose.
    c. If one party to a potential voluntary trade decides it does not advance his interests, he can veto the potential trade.
    d. The expectation of gain motivates people to engage in trade.

32. Kelly is a lawyer and also an excellent typist. She can type 120 words per minute, but she is pressed for time because she has all the legal work she can handle at $75 per hour. Kelly's friend Todd works as a waiter and would like some typing work (provided that he can make at least his wage as a waiter, which is $25 per hour). Todd can type only 60 words per minute.
   a. Kelly should do all the typing because she is faster.
   b. Todd should do the typing as long as his earnings are more than $25 and less than $37.50 per hour.
   c. Unless Todd can match Kelly's typing speed, he should remain a waiter.
   d. Todd should do the typing, and Kelly should pay him $20 per hour.
   e. Both a and c are correct.

Section 1.8

33. When the market mechanism fails to allocate resources efficiently, which of the following has happened?
   a. the natural functioning of the market
   b. positive incentive
   c. market failure
   d. all of the above

34. Who is primarily responsible for imposing price controls in a market economy?
   a. producers
   b. consumers
   c. the government
   d. all of the above

Problems

1. [Section 1.1]
Are the following topics ones that would be covered in microeconomics or macroeconomics?
   a. the effects of an increase in the supply of lumber on the home-building industry
   b. changes in the national unemployment rate
   c. the effect of interest rates on the machine-tool industry
   d. the effect of interest rates on the demand for investment goods in society
   e. the way a firm maximizes profits

2. [Section 1.2]
Are the following statements normative or positive, or do they contain both normative and positive statements?
   a. A higher income-tax rate would generate increased tax revenues. Those extra revenues should be used to give more government aid to the poor.
   b. The study of physics is more valuable than the study of sociology, but both should be studied by all college students.
   c. An increase in the price of wheat will decrease the amount of wheat purchased. However, it will increase the amount of wheat supplied to the market.
   d. A decrease in the price of butter will increase the amount of butter purchased, but that would be bad because it would increase Canadians' cholesterol levels.
   e. The birth rate is reduced as economies urbanize, but that also leads to an increased average age of developing countries' populations.

3. [Section 1.5]

Assume the total benefits to Mark from trips to a local amusement park during the year are given by the following schedule: 1 trip, $60; 2 trips, $115; 3 trips, $165; 4 trips, $200; 5 trips, $225; 6 or more trips, $240.

a. What is Mark's marginal benefit of the third trip? the fifth trip?

b. If the admission price to the amusement park were $45 per day, how many times would Mark be willing and able to go in a year? What if the price were $20 per day? Explain.

c. If the amusement park offered a year-long pass for $200 rather than a per-day admission, would Mark be willing to buy one? If so, how many times would he go? Explain.

4. [Section 1.5]

Assume the total cost of producing widgets was $4200 for 42 units; $4257 for 43 units; $4332 for 44 units; and $4420 for 45 units.

a. What is the marginal cost of producing the forty-third unit? the forty-fifth unit?

b. If the widget producer could sell however many he could produce at $60 per unit, how many would he choose to produce? If he could sell however many he could produce at $80 per unit? Explain.

Scarcity, Trade-Offs, and Economic Growth

section
2.1

The Three Economic Questions Every Society Faces

- What is to be produced?
- How are the goods to be produced?
- For whom are the goods produced?

SCARCITY AND THE ALLOCATION OF RESOURCES

Collectively, our wants far outstrip what can be produced from nature's scarce resources. So how should we allocate those scarce resources? Some methods of resource allocation might seem bad and counterproductive, like the "survival of the fittest" competition that exists on the floor of the jungle. Physical violence has been used since the beginning of time, as people, regions, and countries attacked one another to gain control over resources. One might argue that government should allocate scarce resources on the basis of equal shares or according to need. However, this approach poses problems because of diverse individual preferences, the problem of ascertaining needs, and the negative work and investment incentives involved. In reality, society is made up of many approaches to resource allocation. For now, we will focus on one form of allocating goods and services found in most countries—the market system.

Because of scarcity, certain economic questions must be answered, regardless of the level of affluence of the society or its political structure. We will consider three fundamental questions that inevitably must be faced: (1) What is to be produced? (2) How are the goods to be produced? (3) For whom are the goods produced? These questions are unavoidable in a world of scarcity.

WHAT IS TO BE PRODUCED?

How do individuals control production decisions in market-oriented economies? Questions arise such as "should we produce lots of cars and just a few school buildings, or relatively few cars and more school buildings?" The answer to these and other such questions is that people "vote" in economic affairs with their dollars (or pounds or yen). This concept is called **consumer sovereignty.** Consumer sovereignty explains how individual consumers in market economies determine what is to be produced.

Televisions, DVD players, cellular telephones, pagers, camcorders, and computers, for example, became part of our lives because consumers "voted" hundreds of dollars apiece on these goods. As they bought more colour TVs, consumers "voted" fewer dollars on black-and-white TVs. Similarly, record albums gave way to tapes and CDs as consumers voted for these items with their dollars.

consumer sovereignty
consumers vote with their dollars in a market economy; this explains what is produced

How Different Types of Economic Systems Answer the Question "What Is to Be Produced?"

Economies are organized in different ways to answer the question of what is to be produced. The dispute over the best way to answer this question has inflamed passions for centuries. Should central planning boards make the decisions, as in North Korea and Cuba? Sometimes these highly centralized economic systems are referred to as **command economies.** Under this type of regime, decisions about how many tractors or automobiles to produce are largely determined by a government official or committee associated with the central planning organization. That same group decides on the number and size of school buildings, refrigerators, shoes, and so on. Other countries—including Canada, the United States, much of Europe, and, increasingly, Asia and elsewhere—have largely adopted a decentralized decision-making process where literally millions of individual producers and

command economies
economies where the government uses central planning to coordinate most economic activities

In The **NEWS**

THE RISE OF THE CUV?

BY ERIC BEAUCHESNE

OTTAWA—Canada should benefit from the shift from gas-guzzling SUVs to more fuel-efficient CUVs, a trend that will continue to rob the Big Three North American automakers of market share, a new analysis of the troubled industry says.

Automakers are now scrambling to introduce new more fuel-efficient vehicles, including so-called crossover utility vehicles (CUVs), which make up the fastest-growing segment in the North American auto market, Scotiabank said in a report on the slump in market share by North American automakers.

That slump to about 50 per cent or less of the Canadian market last month, and just over 50 per cent of the U.S. market, is in part due to the growing share of the market being taken by CUVs from SUVs, it said. CUVs, such as Honda's CR-V, and Toyota's RAV4/EV, are smaller than SUVs, and look more like cars, but have more cargo space than cars.

The bad news for the Big Three North American automakers is that offshore producers, led by Honda,

dominate the CUV market, with a near 60 per cent market share, it said. Honda alone has 19 per cent of the CUV market, compared with General Motors' 15 per cent, it said.

The report noted the slide in market share held by North American automakers has accelerated over the past three months as soaring gasoline prices intensified the shift from SUVs to CUVs.

SOURCE: Adapted from Eric Beauchesne, "Vehicle shift may benefit Canada," *Windsor Star,* Final Edition, November 29, 2005, p. D8. Materials reprinted with the express permission of: "CANWEST NEWS SERVICE", a CanWest Partnership.

CONSIDER THIS:
Consumers have voted and it looks like the gas-guzzling SUVs' days may be numbered. Crossover utility vehicles (CUVs) make up the fastest-growing segment of the North American auto market, a segment dominated by offshore producers. Will we eventually look at SUVs the same way we look at black-and-white TVs and record albums? Only time will tell.

consumers of goods and services determine what goods, and how many of them, will be produced. A country that uses such a decentralized decision-making process is often referred to as a **market economy.** Actually, no nation has a pure market economy. Most countries, including Canada, are said to have a **mixed economy.** In such economies, the government and the private sector together determine the allocation of resources.

market economy
an economy that allocates goods and services through the private decisions of consumers, input suppliers, and firms

mixed economy
an economy where government and the private sector determine the allocation of resources

HOW ARE THE GOODS TO BE PRODUCED?

All economies, regardless of their political structure, must decide how to produce the goods and services that they want—because of scarcity. Goods and services can generally be produced in several ways. For example, a ditch can be dug by many workers using their hands, by a few workers with shovels, or by one person with a backhoe. Someone must decide which method is most appropriate. The larger the quantity of the good and the more elaborate the form of capital, the more labour that is saved and is thus made available for other uses. (Remember, goods like shovels or large earthmoving machines used to produce goods and services are called capital.) From this example, you might be tempted to conclude that it is desirable to use the biggest, most elaborate form of capital. But would you really want to plant your spring flowers with huge earthmoving machinery? That is, the most capital-intensive method of production may not always be the best. The best method is the least-cost method.

What Is the Best Form of Production?

The best or "optimal" form of production will usually vary from one economy to the next. For example, earthmoving machinery is used in digging large ditches in Canada, the United States, and Europe, whereas in developing countries, such as India, China, or Pakistan, shovels are often used. Similarly, when a person in Canada cuts the grass, he or she may use a power lawn mower, whereas in a developing country, a hand mower might be used or grass might not be cut at all. Why do these "optimal" forms of production vary so drastically? Compared to capital, labour is relatively cheap and plentiful in developing

ACTIVE LEARNING EXERCISE

MARKET SIGNALS

Q: Adam was a university graduate with a double major in economics and art. A few years ago, Adam decided that he wanted to pursue a vocation that utilized both of his talents. In response, he shut himself up in his studio and created a watercolour collection, "Graphs of Famous Recessions." With high hopes, Adam put his collection on display for buyers. After several years of displaying his econ art, however, the only one interested in the collection was his eight-year-old sister, who wanted the picture frames for her room. Recognizing that Adam was having trouble pursuing his chosen occupation, Adam's friend Karl told him that the market had failed. What do you think? Is Karl right?

A: No. Markets provide important signals, and the signal being sent in this situation is that Adam should look for some other means of support—something that society values. Remember the function of

consumer sovereignty in the marketplace. Clearly, consumers were not voting for Adam's art.

"We feel he's either going to be an artist or an economist."

© STAYSKAL/CHICAGO TRIBUNE

labour intensive
production that uses a large amount of labour

capital intensive
production that uses a large amount of capital

countries but relatively scarce and expensive in Canada. In contrast, capital (machines and tools, mainly) is comparatively plentiful and cheap in Canada but scarcer and more costly in developing countries. That is, in developing countries, production would tend to be more **labour intensive,** or labour driven. In Canada, production would tend to be more **capital intensive,** or capital driven. Each nation tends to use the production processes that conserve its relatively scarce (and thus relatively more expensive) resources and use more of its relatively abundant resources.

FOR WHOM ARE THE GOODS PRODUCED?

In every society, some mechanism must exist to determine how goods and services are to be distributed among the population. Who gets what? Why do some people get to consume or use far more goods and services than others? This question of distribution is so important that wars and revolutions have been fought over it. Both the French and Russian Revolutions were concerned fundamentally with the distribution of goods and services. Even in societies where political questions are usually settled peacefully, the question of the distribution of income is an issue that always arouses strong emotional responses. As we shall see, in a market economy with private ownership and control of the means of production, the amount of goods and services one is able to obtain depends on one's income, which depends on the quantity and quality of the scarce resources the individual controls. For example, Tiger Woods makes a lot of money because he has unique and marketable skills as a golfer. This may or may not be viewed as "fair," an issue we shall look at in detail later in this book.

Avril Lavigne gets paid a lot of money because she controls a scarce resource: her talent and name recognition. As we will see in the next chapter, people's talents and other goods and services in limited supply relative to demand will command high prices.

Section Check

1. Every economy has to decide what to produce.
2. In a decentralized market economy, millions of buyers and sellers determine what and how much to produce.
3. In a mixed economy, the government and the private sector determine the allocation of resources.
4. The best form of production is the one that conserves the relatively scarce (more costly) resources and uses more of the abundant (less costly) resources.
5. When capital is relatively scarce and labour plentiful, production tends to be labour intensive.
6. When capital is relatively abundant and labour relatively scarce, production tends to be capital intensive.
7. In a market economy, the amount of goods and services one is able to obtain depends on one's income.
8. The amount of one's income depends on the quantity and the quality of the scarce resources that the individual controls.

section 2.2

The Circular Flow Model

- What are product markets?
- What are factor markets?
- What is the goods and services flow?
- What is the income flow?
- What is the circular flow model?

How do we explain how millions of people in an economy interact when it comes to buying, selling, producing, working, hiring, and so on? In a simple economy, there are two decision makers, the producers of goods and services, which we call firms, and households, the buyers of goods and services. Exchanges between these two decision makers take place in product markets and factor markets and involve flows of goods, services, and money.

PRODUCT MARKETS

Product markets are the markets for consumer goods and services. In the product market, households are buyers and firms are sellers. Households buy the goods and services that firms produce and sell.

product markets
the market where households are buyers and firms are sellers of goods and services

FACTOR MARKETS

Factor, or, **input markets** are the markets where households sell the use of their inputs (capital, land, labour, and entrepreneurship) to firms. In the factor markets, households are the sellers and the firms are the buyers.

factor (input) markets
the market where households sell the use of their inputs (capital, land, labour, and entrepreneurship) to firms

THE GOODS AND SERVICES FLOW

The **goods and services flow** represents the continuous flow of inputs and outputs in an economy. Households make inputs available to producers through the factor markets. These inputs are then turned into outputs which are then bought by households.

goods and services flow
the continuous flow of inputs and outputs in an economy

THE INCOME FLOW

The **income flow** represents the continuous flow of income and expenditure in an economy. Households receive money payments from firms as compensation for the labour, land, capital, and entrepreneurship needed to produce goods and services. These payments take the form of wages (salaries), rent, interest payments, and profits, respectively. The payments from households to firms are for the purchase of goods and services.

income flow
the continuous flow of income and expenditure in an economy

THE SIMPLE CIRCULAR FLOW MODEL

The simple **circular flow model of income and output** is illustrated in Exhibit 1. In the top half of the exhibit, the product market, households purchase goods and services that firms have produced. In the lower half of the exhibit, the factor (or input) market, households sell the inputs that firms use to produce goods and services. The income flow (going clockwise in Exhibit 1) describes how households receive income—money income—and use that income to buy goods and services—consumption spending. The goods and services flow (going counter-clockwise in Exhibit 1) details how households supply inputs—capital, land, labour, and entrepreneurship—to firms who use them in the production of outputs—goods and services.

circular flow model of income and output
an illustration of the continuous flow of goods, services, inputs, and payments between firms and households

Let's take a simple example to see how the circular flow model works. Suppose a teacher's supply of labour generates personal income in the form of wages (the factor market), which she can use to buy automobiles, vacations, food, and other goods (the product market). Suppose she buys an automobile (product market); the automobile dealer now has revenue to pay for his inputs (factor market)—wages to workers, purchase of new cars to replenish his inventory, rent for his building, and so on. So we see that in the simple circular flow model that income flows from firms to households (factor markets) and spending flows from households to firms (product markets). The simple circular

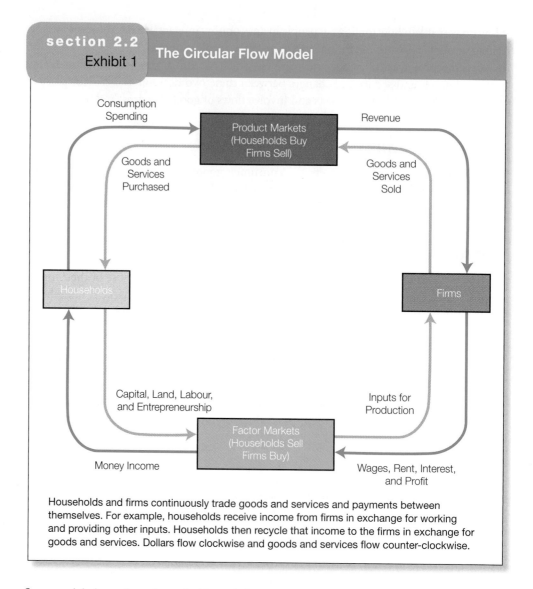

section 2.2
Exhibit 1   **The Circular Flow Model**

Consumption Spending

Product Markets
(Households Buy Firms Sell)

Revenue

Goods and Services Purchased

Goods and Services Sold

Households

Firms

Capital, Land, Labour, and Entrepreneurship

Inputs for Production

Factor Markets
(Households Sell Firms Buy)

Money Income

Wages, Rent, Interest, and Profit

Households and firms continuously trade goods and services and payments between themselves. For example, households receive income from firms in exchange for working and providing other inputs. Households then recycle that income to the firms in exchange for goods and services. Dollars flow clockwise and goods and services flow counter-clockwise.

flow model shows how households and firms interact in product markets and in factor markets and how product markets and factor markets are interrelated.

The circular flow model can become much more complex but here it is presented merely to introduce the major markets and players in the economy. For example, the model can be extended to show the role of government, financial, and foreign markets. Our simple model also does not show how firms and households send some of their income to the government for taxes or how households save some of their income for savings. Households are not the only buyers in the economy—firms, government, and foreigners buy some of the goods and services.

Section Check

1. In the product market, households are buyers and firms are sellers.
2. In the factor markets, households are the sellers and firms are the buyers.
3. Wages, rent, interest, and profits are the payments for the labour, land, capital, and entrepreneurship needed to produce goods and services. These transactions are carried out in factor, or input, markets.
4. The circular flow model illustrates the flow of goods, services, and payments among firms and households.

The Production Possibilities Curve

- What is a production possibilities curve?
- What is the law of increasing opportunity costs?
- What are unemployed resources?
- What are underemployed resources?
- What is efficiency?

THE PRODUCTION POSSIBILITIES CURVE

The economic concepts of scarcity, choice, and trade-offs can be shown with a simple graph called a production possibilities curve. The **production possibilities curve** represents the potential total output combinations of any two goods for an economy, given the inputs and technology available to the economy. That is, it illustrates an economy's potential for allocating its limited resources in producing various combinations of goods, in a given time period.

production possibilities curve
the potential total output combinations of any two goods for an economy

A Straight-Line Production Possibilities Curve— Grades in Economics and Accounting

What would the production possibilities curve look like if you were "producing" grades in two of your classes—say, economics and accounting? In Exhibit 1, we draw a hypothetical production possibilities curve for your expected grade in economics on the vertical axis and your expected grade in accounting on the horizontal axis. Assume, because of a part-time restaurant job, you choose to study ten hours a week and that you like both courses and are equally adept at studying for both courses.

We see in Exhibit 1 that the production possibilities curve is a straight line. For example, if all ten hours are spent studying economics, the expected grade in economics is 85 percent (an A) and the expected grade in accounting is 45 percent (an F). Moving down the production possibilities curve, we see that as you spend more of your time studying accounting, and less on economics, you can raise your expected grade in accounting but only at the expense of lowering your expected grade in economics. Specifically, moving down along the straight-line production possibilities curve, the trade-off is one letter-grade lower in economics for one higher letter-grade in accounting.

Of course, if you increased your study time it would be possible to expect higher grades in both courses. But that would be on a new production possibilities curve; along this production possibilities curve we are assuming that technology and the number of study hours are given. In the next section, the coverage is expanded to cover the more realistic case of a bowed production possibilities curve.

Production Possibilities Curve: "Producing" Grades in Economics and Accounting

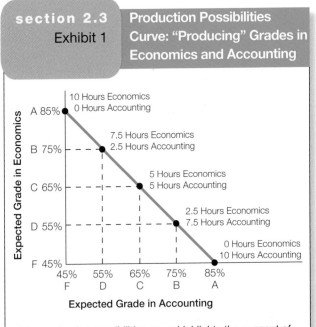

The production possibilities curve highlights the concept of trade-offs. Assuming you choose to study a total of ten hours a week, moving down the production possibilities curve shows that if you use your time to study accounting instead of economics you can raise your expected grade in accounting but only at the expense of lowering your expected grade in economics. With a straight-line production possibilities curve, the opportunity costs are constant.

The Bowed Production Possibilities Curve

To more clearly illustrate the production possibilities curve, imagine an economy that produces just two goods: food and shelter. The fact that we have many goods in the real world makes actual decision making more complicated, but it does not alter the basic principles being illustrated. Each point on the production possibilities curve shown in Exhibit 2 represents the potential amounts of food and shelter that can be produced in a given time period, given the quantity and quality of resources available in the economy for production.

Note in Exhibit 2 that if we devoted all of our resources to making shelters, we could produce 10 units of shelter, but no food (point A). If, on the other hand, we chose to devote all of our resources to food, we could produce 80 units of food, but no shelter (point E).

In reality, nations would rarely opt for production possibility A or E, preferring instead to produce a mixture of goods. For example, the economy in question might produce 9 units of shelter and 20 units of food (point B), or perhaps 7 units of shelter and 40 units of food (point C). Still other combinations along the curve, such as point D, are possible.

Off the Production Possibilities Curve

The economy cannot operate at point N (not attainable) during the given time period because there are presently not enough resources to produce that level of output. However, it is possible the economy can operate inside the production possibilities curve, at point I (inefficient). If the economy is operating at point I, or any other point inside the production possibilities curve, it is not at full capacity, and is operating inefficiently. In short, the economy is not using all of its scarce resources efficiently; as a result, actual output is less than potential output.

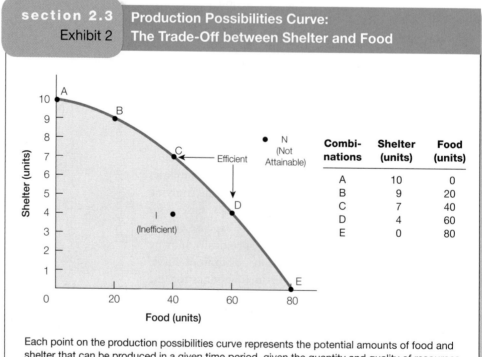

section 2.3 Exhibit 2   Production Possibilities Curve: The Trade-Off between Shelter and Food

Combi-nations	Shelter (units)	Food (units)
A	10	0
B	9	20
C	7	40
D	4	60
E	0	80

Each point on the production possibilities curve represents the potential amounts of food and shelter that can be produced in a given time period, given the quantity and quality of resources available in the economy to use for production. All the points on the production possibility curve are efficient. Any points in the shaded area, like point I, are inefficient. Any point outside the production possibilites curve, like point N, is not attainable at the present time.

USING RESOURCES EFFICIENTLY

Most modern economies have resources that are idle, at least for some period of time—like during periods of high unemployment. If those resources were not idle, people would have more scarce goods and services available for their use. Unemployed resources create a serious problem. For example, consider an unemployed fisherman who is unable to find work at a "reasonable" wage, or those unemployed in depressed times when factories are already operating below capacity. Clearly, the resources of these individuals are not being used efficiently.

The fact that factories can operate below capacity suggests that it is not just labour resources that should be most effectively used. Rather, all resources entering into production must be used effectively. However, for several reasons, social concern focuses on labour. First, labour costs are the largest share of production costs. Also, unemployed or underemployed labourers (whose resources are not being used to their full potential) may have mouths to feed at home, whereas an unemployed machine does not (although the owner of the unemployed machine may).

INEFFICIENCY AND EFFICIENCY

Suppose for some reason there is widespread unemployment or resources are not being put to their best use. The economy would then be operating at a point, such as I, inside the production possibilities curve where the economy is operating inefficiently. At point I, 4 units of shelter and 40 units of food are being produced. By putting unemployed resources to work or by putting already employed resources to better use, we could expand the output of shelter by 3 units (moving to point C) without giving up any units of food. Alternatively, we could boost food output by 20 units (moving to point D) without reducing shelter output. We could even get more of both food and shelter moving to a point on the curve between C and D. Increasing or improving the utilization of resources, then, can lead to greater output of all goods. An efficient use of our resources means more of everything we want can be available for our use. Thus, **efficiency** requires society to use its resources to the fullest extent—getting the most from our scarce resources; that is, there are no wasted resources. If resources are being used efficiently, that is, at some point along a production possibilities curve, then more of one good or service requires the sacrifice of another good or service. Efficiency does not tell us which point along the production possibilites curve is *best,* but it does tell us that points inside the curve cannot be best because some resources are wasted.

efficiency
getting the most from society's scarce resources

THE MEASUREMENT OF OPPORTUNITY COST

When an economy is operating efficiently, the decision to increase the production of one good or service will carry with it a related opportunity cost. Within the framework of the production possibility model, the determination of opportunity cost is greatly simplified since the next best alternative is the only alternative—therefore, in our example, the opportunity cost of increasing the production of shelter would be measured in corresponding forgone units of food, and the opportunity cost of expanding food production would be measured in units of forgone shelter.

Note in Exhibit 2 if the economy is currently operating at point D (producing 4 units of shelter and 60 units of food) the decision to increase the amount of shelter it produces to 7 units will have an opportunity cost of 20 units of food—as this is the amount of food that the economy must give up to gain the additional units of shelter. In the diagram, this gain of shelter and related opportunity cost would involve the movement along the production possibilities curve from point D to point C.

THE LAW OF INCREASING OPPORTUNITY COSTS

Note that in Exhibits 2 and 3, the production possibilities curve is not a straight line like that in Exhibit 1. It is concave from below (that is, bowed outward from the origin). Looking at the figures, you can see that at very low food output, an increase in the amount of food produced will lead to only a small reduction in the units of shelter produced. For example, increasing food output from 0 to 20 (moving from point A to point B on the curve) requires the use of resources capable of producing 1 unit of shelter. This means that for the first 20 units of food, 1 unit of shelter must be given up. When food output is higher, however, more units of shelter must be given up when switching additional resources from the production of shelter to food. Moving from point D to point E, for example, an increase in food output of 20 (from 60 to 80) reduces the production of shelter from 4 to 0. At this point, then, the cost of those 20 additional units of food is 4 units of shelter, considerably more than the 1 unit of shelter required in the earlier scenario. This difference shows us that opportunity costs have not remained constant, but have risen, as more units of food and fewer units of shelter are produced. It is this increasing opportunity cost, then, that is represented by the bowed production possibilities curve.

What Is the Reason for the Law of Increasing Opportunity Cost?

increasing opportunity cost
the opportunity cost of producing additional units of a good rises as society produces more of that good

The basic reason for the **increasing opportunity cost** is that some resources and skills cannot be easily adapted from their current uses to alternative uses. For example, at low levels of food output, additional increases in food output can be obtained easily by switching relatively low-skilled carpenters from making shelter to producing food. However, to get even more food output, workers that are less well suited or appropriate for producing food (i.e., they are better adapted to making shelter) must be released from shelter making in order to increase food output. For example, a skilled carpenter may be an expert at making shelter but a very bad farmer, because he lacks the training and skills necessary in that occupation. So, using the skilled carpenter to farm results in a relatively greater opportunity cost than using the poor carpenter to farm. Hence, the production of additional units of food becomes increasingly costly as progressively even lower-skilled farmers (but good carpenters) convert to farming.

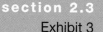

section 2.3
Exhibit 3   Increasing Opportunity Cost and the Production Possibilities Curve

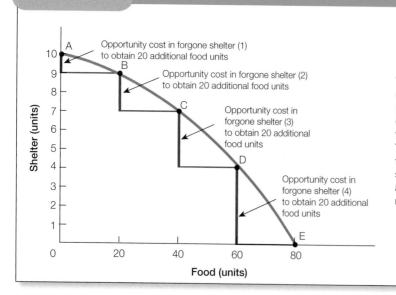

The production possibilities curve also illustrates the opportunity cost of producing more of a given product. For example, if we were to increase food output from 40 units to 60 units (moving from point C to point D), we must produce 3 fewer units of shelter. The opportunity cost of those 20 additional units of food is the 3 units of shelter we must forgo. We can see that moving down the curve from A to E, each additional 20 units of food costs society more and more shelter—the law of increasing opportunity cost.

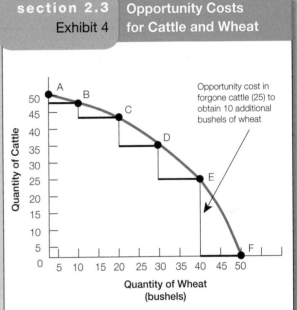

ACTIVE LEARNING EXERCISE

THE PRODUCTION POSSIBILITIES CURVE

Q: Imagine that you are the overseer on a small island that only produces two goods: cattle and wheat. About a quarter of the land is not fertile enough for growing wheat, so cattle graze on it. What would happen if you tried to produce more and more wheat, extending your planting even to the less fertile soil?

A: This is the law of increasing opportunity costs in action. As you planted more and more of your land in wheat, we would move into some of the rocky, less fertile land and, consequently, wheat yields on the additional land would fall. If we tried to plant the entire island with wheat, we would find that some of the rocky, less fertile land would yield virtually no extra wheat. It would, however, have been great for cattle grazing—a large loss. Thus, the opportunity cost of using that marginal land for wheat rather than cattle grazing would be very high. The law of increasing opportunity cost occurs because resources are not homogeneous (identical) and are not equally adaptable for producing cattle and wheat; some land is more suitable for cattle grazing, whereas some land is more suitable for wheat

growing. This is seen in Exhibit 4, where the vertical lines represent the opportunity cost of growing ten more bushels of wheat in terms of cattle production sacrificed. You can see that as wheat production increases, the opportunity costs in terms of lost cattle production rise.

section 2.3	Opportunity Costs
Exhibit 4	for Cattle and Wheat

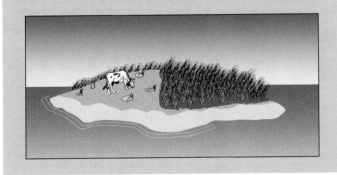

The opportunity cost of each ten bushels of wheat in terms of forgone cattle is measured by the vertical distances. As we move from A to F, the opportunity cost of wheat in terms of forgone cattle rises.

Section Check

1. The production possibilities curve represents the potential total output combinations of two goods available to a society given its resources and existing technology.
2. If the economy is operating within the production possibilities curve, the economy is operating inefficiently; this means that actual output is less than potential output.
3. Efficiency requires society to use its resources to the fullest extent—no wasted resources.
4. A bowed production possibilities curve means that the opportunity costs of producing additional units of a good rise as society produces more of that good (the law of increasing opportunity costs).

Economic Growth and the Production Possibilities Curve

- How much should we sacrifice today to get more in the future?
- How do we show economic growth on the production possibilities curve?

GENERATING ECONOMIC GROWTH

How have some nations been able to rapidly expand their output of goods and services over time, whereas others have been unable to increase their standards of living at all?

The economy can only grow with qualitative or quantitative changes in the factors of production—land, labour, capital, and entrepreneurship. Advancement in technology, improvements in labour productivity, or new sources of natural resources (such as previously undiscovered oil) could all lead to outward shifts of the production possibilities curve.

This idea can be clearly illustrated by using the production possibilities curve (Exhibit 1). In terms of the production possibilities curve, economic growth means an outward shift in the possible combinations of goods and services produced. With growth comes the possibility to have more of both goods than were previously available. Suppose we were producing at point C (7 units of shelter, 40 units of food) on our original production possibilities curve. Additional resources and/or new methods of using them (technological progress) can lead to new production possibilities creating the potential for more of all goods (or more of some with no less of others). These increases would push the production possibilities curve outward. For example, if you invest in human capital, such as training the workers making the shelter, it will increase the productivity of those workers. As a result, they will produce more units of shelter. This means, ultimately, that fewer resources will be used to make shelter, freeing them to be used for farming—resulting in more units of food. Notice that at point F (future) on the new curve, it is possible to produce 9 units of shelter and 70 units of food, more of both goods than was previously produced, at point C.

GROWTH DOESN'T ELIMINATE SCARCITY

With all of this discussion of growth, it is important to remember that growth, or increases in a society's output, does not make scarcity disappear. Even when output has grown more rapidly than the population so that people are made better off, they still face trade-offs: At any point

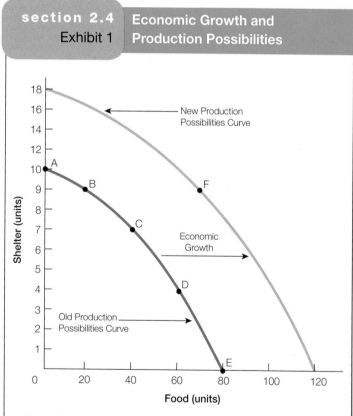

section 2.4

Exhibit 1

Economic Growth and Production Possibilities

Economic growth shifts the production possibilities curve outward, allowing increased output of both food and shelter (compare point F with point C).

along the production possibilities curve, in order to get more of one thing, you must give up something else. There are no free lunches on the production possibilities curve.

Capital Goods versus Consumption Goods

Economies that choose to invest more of their resources for the future will grow faster than those that don't. To generate economic growth, a society must produce fewer consumer goods—like pizza, DVD players, cellphones, cars, and so on—in the present and produce more capital goods. The society that devotes a larger share of its productive capacity to capital goods (machines, factories, tools, and education), rather than consumption goods (video games, pizza, and vacations), will experience greater economic growth. It must sacrifice some present consumption of consumer goods and services in order to experience growth in the future. Why? Investing in capital goods, like computers and other new technological equipment, as well as upgrading skills and knowledge, expands the ability to produce in the future. It shifts the economy's production possibilities outward, increasing the future production capacity of the economy. That is, the economy that invests more now (consumes less now) will be able to produce, and therefore consume, more in the future. In Exhibit 2, we see that Economy A invests more in capital goods than Economy B. Consequently, Economy A's production possibilities curve shifts out further than Economy B's over time.

SUMMING UP THE PRODUCTION POSSIBILITIES CURVE

The production possibilities curve shown in Exhibit 3 illustrates the choices faced by an economy that makes military goods and consumer goods. How are the economic concepts of scarcity, choice, opportunity costs, efficiency, and economic growth illustrated in this production possibilities curve framework? In Exhibit 3, we can show scarcity because resource combinations outside the initial production possibilities curve, like point D, are

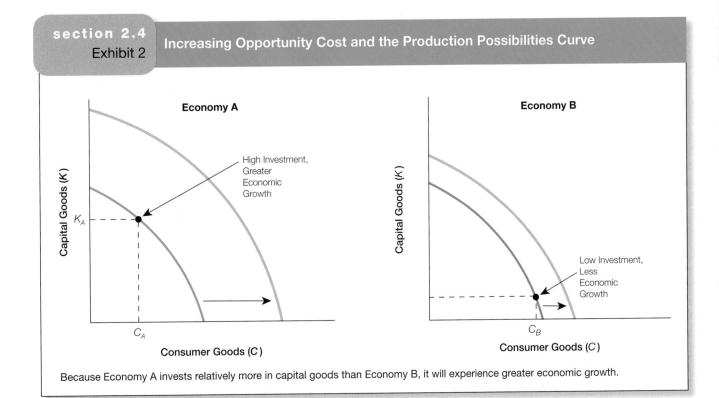

section 2.4
Exhibit 2   **Increasing Opportunity Cost and the Production Possibilities Curve**

Because Economy A invests relatively more in capital goods than Economy B, it will experience greater economic growth.

unattainable without economic growth. If the economy is operating efficiently, we are somewhere on that production possibilities curve, like point B or point C. However, if the economy is operating inefficiently, we are operating inside that production possibilities curve, like point A. We can also see in this graph that to get more military goods you must give up consumer goods—that is, there is an opportunity cost. Finally, we see that over time, with economic growth, the whole production possibilities curve can shift outward, making point D now attainable.

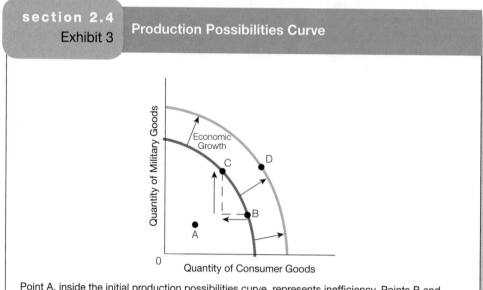

section 2.4
Exhibit 3   **Production Possibilities Curve**

Point A, inside the initial production possibilities curve, represents inefficiency. Points B and C, on the curve, are efficient points and represent two possible output combinations. Point D can only be attained with economic growth, illustrated by the outward shift in the production possibilities curve.

In The **NEWS**

TOURISM VERSUS ECOSYSTEMS

BY JON KRAKAUER

Canada's main transcontinental railway and transcontinental highway roll side-by-side down the length of Banff's main valley. On the busiest weekends, the road is clotted with cars, RVs, and tour buses, and a brown haze of exhaust fumes veils the celebrated vistas. Within the park lie three ski resorts and the town of Banff— home to 7000 permanent residents. On the typical summer day, the townies may see 25 000 tourists streaming through their streets.

One local businessman and town council member remarked, "Environmentalists love to talk gloom and doom— but all you have to do is drive five miles out of town and you're in the middle of miles and miles of nothing but nature. You get tired of looking at all these big bare mountains; what's wrong with putting a restaurant or a little chalet up there to make it nicer for the people who come here?"

One thing that is wrong with it, according to a biologist who has studied wildlife throughout the Rocky Mountains, is that the human presence in Banff is wreaking havoc on the area's fragile makeup. "I'd say the park is in very, very poor condition compared with what it was 10 years ago, 20 years ago, 30 years ago," declared the biologist. "There's been a major decline in most of our large predators—black bears, grizzlies, wolverines, lynx, cougars. Such species are one of our best indicators of overall ecological health, and the way things are going, most of these animals will not survive here."

IN THE NEWS *(continued)*

© MARK DOWNEY/PHOTODISC/GETTY ONE IMAGES

Can Banff currently have more tourism and a better environment? Society can choose high environmental quality but only at the cost of lower tourism or more tourism and commercialization at the expense of the ecosystem, but society must choose. It involves a trade-off, and in this case Canada must presently choose between tourism and ecosystems.

SOURCE: Adapted from Jon Krakauer, "Rocky Times in Banff," *National Geographic,* July 1995, pp. 46–69. By permission of John Ware Literary Agency.

CONSIDER THIS:
The principal point of this article is that there are trade-offs that require choice and those choices have costs. In order to totally preserve the ecosystem of Banff, it would mean far fewer tourists and commercial ventures. In this case, society must make a value judgment. If Banff is developed further, what will be the cost to future generations who will not be able to appreciate the visual splendours of this special "hamlet" nestled in the Canadian Rockies? On the other hand, how can you possibly accommodate the growing numbers of daily visitors without building additional restaurants, motels, and so on? Society must choose.

Section Check

1. Economies must decide how much current consumption they are willing to sacrifice for greater growth in the future.
2. Economic growth is represented by an outward shift of the production possibilities curve.
3. Economic growth increases the possibility of producing more of all goods.
4. Despite economic growth, scarcity inevitably remains a fact of life.

Summary

Section 2.1
- Every economy has to decide what goods to produce, how to produce the goods, and how to distribute the goods.
- In command economies, central planning (the government) is solely responsible for coordinating economic activities.
- In a mixed economy, the government and the private sector determine the allocation of resources.
- In a market economy, the amount of output one is able to obtain depends on one's income. The amount of one's income depends on the quantity and the quality of the scarce resources that the individual controls.
- The best form of production is the one that conserves the relatively scarce (more costly) resources and uses more of the abundant (less costly) resources.

- When capital is relatively scarce and labour plentiful, production tends to be labour intensive.
- When capital is relatively abundant and labour relatively scarce, production tends to be capital intensive.

Section 2.2
- The circular flow model illustrates the flow of goods, services, and payments among businesses and households.
- In the product market, households purchase goods and services that firms have produced.
- In the factor (or input) market, households sell the inputs that firms use to produce goods and services.
- The flow of money illustrates how households receive income (wages, rent, interest, and profit) from firms for

their inputs (labour, land, capital, and entrepreneurship) and use it to purchase goods and services.

■ The flow of goods and services illustrates the transition of inputs into outputs.

Section 2.3

■ The production possibilities curve represents the potential total output combinations of two goods available to a society.

■ Efficiency requires society to use its resources to the fullest extent—no wasted resources.

■ If the economy is operating within the production possibilities curve, the economy is operating inefficiently.

■ A bowed (or concave from the origin) production possibilities curve means that the opportunity costs of producing additional units of a good rise as society produces more of that good (the law of increasing opportunity costs).

Section 2.4

■ Economic growth is represented by an outward shift of the production possibilities curve.

Key Terms and Concepts

For a complete glossary of chapter key terms, visit the textbook's Web site at http://www.sextonmacro2e.nelson.com.

consumer sovereignty 42
command economies 42
market economy 43
mixed economy 43
labour intensive 44

capital intensive 44
product markets 45
factor (input) markets 45
goods and services flow 45
income flow 45

circular flow model of income and output 45
production possibilities curve 47
efficiency 49
increasing opportunity cost 50

Review Questions

1. What is the significance of the three basic economic questions?

2. How would the following events be shown using a production possibilities curve for shelter and food?

   a. The economy is experiencing double-digit unemployment.

   b. Economic growth is increasing at over 5 percent per year.

   c. Society decides it wants less shelter and more food.

   d. Society decides it wants more shelter and less food.

3. Using the table below, answer the following questions:

Combinations

	A	B	C	D	E
Guns	1	2	3	4	5
Butter	20	18	14	8	0

   a. What are the assumptions for a given production possibilities curve?

   b. What is the opportunity cost of one gun when moving from point B to point C? When moving from point D to point E?

   c. Do these combinations demonstrate constant or increasing opportunity costs?

4. Economy A produces more capital goods and fewer consumer goods than Economy B. Which economy will grow more rapidly? Draw two production possibilities curves, one for Economy A and one for Economy B. Demonstrate graphically how one economy can grow more rapidly than the other.

5. How does education add to a nation's capital stock?

6. How does a technological advance that increases the efficiency of shoe production affect the production possibilities curve between shoes and pizza? Is it possible to produce more shoes and pizza or just more shoes? Explain.

7. The leader of a political party running in an upcoming provincial government election promises to build new schools and new hospitals during the next four years without sacrificing any other goods and services. Explain using a production possibilities curve between schools and hospitals under what conditions the politician would be able to keep her promise.

8. In 2003, the United States waged war on Iraq. Illustrate a production possibilities curve showing Iraq's ability to produce tanks and consumer goods both pre-war and post-war.

Fill in the Blanks

Section 2.1

1. Because of scarcity, certain economic questions must be answered regardless of the level of affluence of the society or its political structure. Three fundamental questions that inevitably must be faced in a world of scarcity are (1) _____ is to be produced? (2) _____ are these goods to be produced? (3) _____ are the goods produced?

2. Market economies largely rely on a _____ decision-making process, where literally millions of individual producers and consumers of goods and services determine what will be produced.

3. Most countries, including Canada, have _____ economies, in which the government and private sector determine the allocation of resources.

4. The _____-cost method is the most appropriate method for producing a given product.

5. Methods of production used where capital is relatively scarce will be _____, and methods of production used where labour is relatively scarce will be _____.

Section 2.2

6. The markets where households are buyers and firms are sellers of goods and services are called _____ markets.

7. The markets where households sell the use of their _____ (capital, land, labour, and entrepreneurship) to _____ are called _____ or _____ markets.

8. The simple _____ model shows the continuous flow of goods, services, inputs, and payments through the _____ and _____ markets among households and _____.

Section 2.3

9. A _____ curve represents the potential total output combinations of any two goods for an economy.

10. On a production possibilities curve, we assume that the economy has a given quantity and quality of _____ and _____ available to use for production.

11. If an economy is operating inside its production possibilities curve, it is not at full capacity and is operating _____. Such an economy's actual output is less than _____ output.

12. By putting _____ resources to work or by putting already employed resources to _____ uses, we could expand output.

13. _____ requires society to use its resources to the fullest extent—getting the _____ we can out of our scarce resources.

14. If the production possibilities curve is _____ from below (that is, bowed outward from the origin), it reflects _____ opportunity costs of producing additional amounts of a good.

15. When easily adaptable resources are exhausted and resources and workers that are less well suited or appropriate must then be employed to increase output further, the _____ of production _____.

Section 2.4

16. To generate economic growth, a society must produce _____ consumer goods and _____ capital goods in the present.

17. Advancements in _____, improvements in _____, or new _____ could all lead to outward shifts of the production possibilities curve.

18. Increases in a society's output do not make _____ disappear. Even when output has grown more rapidly than the population so that people are made better off, they still face _____.

19. The production possibilities curve can be used to illustrate the economic concepts of _____ (resource combinations outside the production possibilities curve are unattainable), _____ (selecting among the alternative bundles available along the production possibilities curve), _____ (how much of one good you give up to get another unit of the second good as you move along the production possibilities curve), _____ (being on the production possibilities curve rather than inside it), and _____ (shifting the production possibilities curve outward).

True or False

Section 2.1

1. Consumer sovereignty describes how individual consumers in market economies determine what is to be produced.

2. Command economies rely on central planning, where decisions about what and how many are largely determined by a government official associated with the central planning organization.

3. All economies, regardless of political structure, must decide how, from several possible ways, to produce the goods and services that they want.

4. In any economy, it would always be less efficient to dig ditches by having many workers use their hands than to use workers with shovels or a backhoe.

5. Each nation tends to use the production processes that conserve its relatively scarce (and thus relatively more expensive) resources and use more of its relatively abundant resources.

6. In a market economy, with private ownership and control of the means of production, the amount of output one is able to obtain depends on the quantity and quality of the scarce resources that the individual controls.

Section 2.2

7. The market where households sell the use of their inputs to firms is called the product market.

8. The circular flow model illustrates the continuous flow of goods, services, inputs, and payments between firms and households.

Section 2.3

9. With a straight-line production possibilities curve, the opportunity cost of producing another unit of a good increases with its output.

10. The economy cannot produce beyond the levels indicated by the production possibilities curve during a given time period, but it is possible to operate inside the production possibilities curve.

11. Underutilized resources or those not being put to their best uses are illustrated by output combinations along the production possibilities curve.

12. We all have an interest in the efficient use of all of society's resources because there can be more of everything we care about available for our use as a result.

13. If resources are being used efficiently, at a point along a production possibilities curve, more of one good or service requires the sacrifice of another good or service as a cost.

14. The basic reason for increasing opportunity cost is that some resources and skills cannot be easily adapted from their current uses to alternative uses.

Section 2.4

15. Investing in capital goods will increase the future production capacity of an economy, so an economy that invests more now (consumes less now) will be able to produce, and therefore consume, more in the future.

16. An economy can grow despite a lack of qualitative and quantitative improvements in the factors of production.

17. Economic growth means a movement along an economy's production possibilities curve in the direction of producing more consumer goods.

18. From a point inside the production possibilities curve, in order to get more of one thing, an economy must give up something else.

Multiple Choice

Section 2.1

1. Which of the following is not a question that all societies must answer?
   a. How can scarcity be eliminated?
   b. What goods and services will be produced?
   c. Who will get the goods and services?
   d. How will the goods and services be produced?
   e. All of the above are questions that all societies must answer.

2. Economic disputes over the distribution of income are generally associated with which economic question?
   a. Who should produce the goods?
   b. What goods and services will be produced?
   c. Who will get the goods and services?
   d. How will the goods and services be produced?

3. Three economic questions must be determined in all societies. What are they?
   a. How much will be produced? When will it be produced? How much will it cost?
   b. What will the price of each good be? Who will produce each good? Who will consume each good?
   c. What is the opportunity cost of production? Does the society have a comparative advantage in production? Will consumers desire the goods being produced?
   d. What goods will be produced? How will goods be produced? For whom will the goods be produced?

4. The private ownership of property and the use of the market system to direct and coordinate economic activity are most characteristic of
   a. a command economy.
   b. a mixed economy.
   c. a market economy.
   d. a traditional economy.

5. The degree of government involvement in the economy is greatest in
   a. a command economy.
   b. a mixed economy.
   c. a market economy.
   d. a traditional economy.

6. When a command economy is utilized to resolve economic questions regarding the allocation of resources, then
   a. everyone will receive an equal share of the output produced.
   b. the preferences of individuals are of no importance.
   c. economic efficiency will be assured.
   d. the role of markets will be replaced by political decision making.

7. Which of the following is true?
   a. An advanced market economy would tend to use labour-intensive production methods.
   b. An economy in which labour is relatively scarce would tend to use capital-intensive production methods.
   c. An increase in the availability of labour relative to capital in an economy would tend to increase how labour intensive the production processes in that economy would be.
   d. All of the above are true.
   e. Both b and c are true.

Section 2.2

8. In a circular flow diagram,
   a. goods and services flow in a clockwise direction.
   b. goods and services flow in a counter-clockwise direction.
   c. product markets appear at the top of the diagram.
   d. factor markets appear at the left of the diagram.
   e. both b and c are true.

9. Which of the following is true?
   a. In the product markets, firms are buyers and households are sellers.
   b. In the factor markets, firms are sellers and households are buyers.
   c. Firms receive money payments from households for capital, land, labour, and entrepreneurship.
   d. All of the above are true.
   e. None of the above is true.

10. In the circular flow model,
    a. firms supply both products and resources.
    b. firms demand both products and resources.
    c. firms demand resources and supply products.
    d. firms supply resources and demand products.

Section 2.3

11. A point beyond the boundary of an economy's production possibilities curve is
  a. efficient.
  b. inefficient
  c. attainable.
  d. unattainable.
  e. both attainable and efficient.

Use the diagram below to answer questions 12 through 15.

12. Currently, it is not possible to produce at
  a. point A.
  b. point B.
  c. point E.
  d. point G.
  e. either point E or point G.

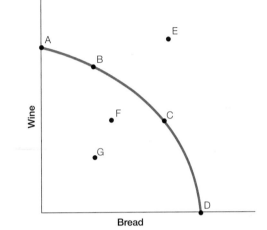

13. An economy is operating at full employment, and then workers in the bread industry are laid off. This change is portrayed in the movement from
  a. A to B.
  b. B to E.
  c. C to F.
  d. G to F.
  e. None of the above is correct.

14. Along the production possibilities curve, the most efficient point of production depicted is
  a. point B.
  b. point C.
  c. point D.
  d. point G.
  e. All points on the production possibilities curve are equally efficient.

15. The opportunity cost of one more unit of bread is greater at point _____ than at point _____.
  a. G; B
  b. C; A
  c. A; C
  d. None of the above. The opportunity cost of a good is constant everywhere along the production possibilities curve.

16. Which of the following is consistent with the implications of the production possibilities curve?
  a. If the resources in an economy are being used efficiently, scarcity will not be a problem.
  b. If the resources in an economy are being used efficiently, more of one good can be produced only if less of another good is produced.
  c. Producing more of any one good will require smaller and smaller sacrifices of other goods as more of that good is being produced in an economy.
  d. An economy will automatically attain that level of output at which all of its resources are fully employed.
  e. Both b and c are consistent with the implications of the production possibilities curve.

17. Which of the following is the most accurate statement about a production possibilities curve?
   a. An economy can produce at any point inside or outside its production possibilities curve.
   b. An economy can produce only on its production possibilities curve.
   c. An economy can produce at any point on or inside its production possibilities curve, but not outside the curve.
   d. An economy can produce at any point inside its production possibilities curve, but not on or outside the curve.

Section 2.4

18. Which of the following is most likely to shift the production possibilities curve outward?
   a. an increase in unemployment
   b. a decrease in the stock of physical or human capital
   c. a decrease in the labour force
   d. a technological advance

19. Which of the following is least likely to shift the production possibilities curve outward?
   a. a change in preferences away from one of the goods and toward the other
   b. an invention that reduces the amount of natural resources necessary for producing a good
   c. the discovery of new natural resources
   d. a reduction in people's preferences for leisure

20. Inefficiency is best illustrated by which of the following?
   a. forgoing civilian goods in order to produce more military goods
   b. limiting economic growth by reducing capital spending
   c. having high levels of unemployment of labour and other resources that could be productively employed
   d. producing outside the production possibilities frontier
   e. all of the above

21. Suppose Country A produces few consumption goods and many investment goods whereas Country B produces few investment goods and many consumption goods. Other things being equal, you would expect
   a. per-capita income to grow more rapidly in Country B.
   b. population to grow faster in Country B.
   c. the production possibilities curve for Country A to shift out more rapidly than that of Country B.
   d. that if both countries started with identical production possibilities curves, in 20 years, people in Country B would be able to produce more consumer goods than people in Country A.
   e. that both c and d are true.

22. A virulent disease spreads throughout the population of an economy, causing death and disability. This can be portrayed as
   a. a movement from a point on the production possibilities curve to a point inside the curve.
   b. a movement from a point on the production possibilities curve to the northeast.
   c. a movement along the production possibilities curve to the southeast.
   d. an outward shift of the production possibilities curve.
   e. an inward shift of the production possibilities curve.

23. Say that a technological change doubles an economy's ability to produce good X and triples the economy's ability to produce Y. As a result,

   a. the economy will tend to produce less X and more Y than before.

   b. the opportunity cost of producing units of Y in terms of X forgone will tend to fall.

   c. the production possibilities curve will shift out further along the *X*-axis than along the *Y*-axis.

   d. both b and c would be true.

Problems

1. [Section 2.2]

Identify where the appropriate entries go in the circular flow diagram below.

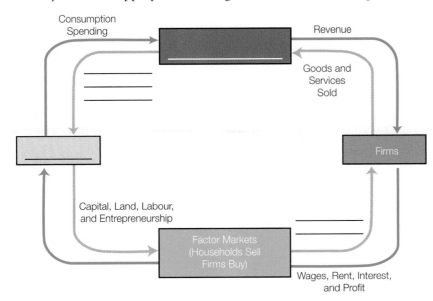

2. [Section 2.3]

Assume that the production possibilities for Alberta are the following combinations of kegs of beer and sides of beef.

Beer	Beef
55	0
54	1
52	2
49	3
45	4
40	5
34	6
27	7
19	8
10	9
0	10

a. Construct the production possibilities frontier for beer and beef on the grid below.

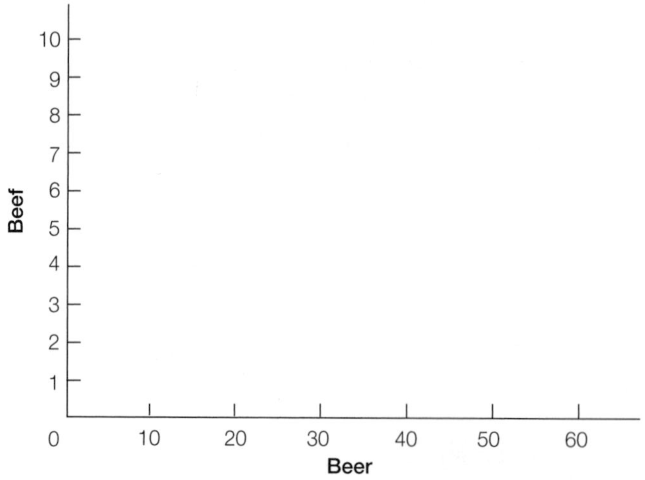

(Graph with vertical axis labeled "Beef" ranging from 1 to 10, and horizontal axis labeled "Beer" ranging from 0 to 60 in increments of 10.)

b. Given the information above, what is the opportunity cost of the fifty-fifth keg of beer in Alberta? of the sixth side of beef? of the ninth side of beef?

c. Suppose Alberta is currently producing 4 sides of beef and 45 kegs of beer. What is the opportunity cost of 5 more sides of beef in Alberta?

d. Would the combination of 40 kegs of beer and 4 sides of beef be efficient? Why or why not?

e. Is the combination of 9 kegs of beer and 10 sides of beef possible for Alberta? Why or why not?

3. [Section 2.4]

Given the following production possibilities curve:

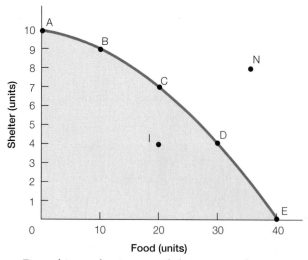

a. Does this production possibilities curve show increasing opportunity costs? Explain.

b. What is the opportunity cost of moving from point I to point D? Explain.

c. What is the opportunity cost of moving from point C to point B?

d. Which of points A–E is the most efficient? Explain.

e. Which of the identified production alternatives is currently impossible for this economy to achieve? What must happen in order for this production alternative to become attainable?

f. Which of the identified production alternatives is currently attainable but inefficient? What must happen in order for this production alternative to become efficient?

chapter

3

Supply and Demand

Markets

section
3.1

- What is a market?
- Why is it so difficult to define a market?

DEFINING A MARKET

Although we usually think of a market as a place where some sort of exchange occurs, a market is not really a place at all. A **market** is the process of buyers and sellers exchanging goods and services. This means that supermarkets, the Toronto Stock Exchange, drugstores, roadside stands, garage sales, Internet stores, and restaurants are all markets.

Every market is different. That is, the conditions under which the exchange between buyers and sellers takes place can vary. These differences make it difficult to precisely define a market. After all, an incredible variety of exchange arrangements exists in the real world—organized securities markets, wholesale auction markets, foreign exchange markets, real estate markets, labour markets, and so forth.

Goods being priced and traded in various ways at various locations by various kinds of buyers and sellers further compound the problem of defining a market. For some goods, such as housing, markets are numerous but limited to a geographic area. Homes in Niagara Falls, Ontario, for example (about 130 kilometres from downtown Toronto), do not compete directly with homes in Toronto. Why? Because people who work in Toronto will generally look for homes within commuting distance. Even within cities, there are separate markets for homes, differentiated by amenities such as bigger houses, newer houses, larger lots, and better schools.

In a similar manner, markets are numerous but geographically limited for a good such as cement. Because transportation costs are so high relative to the selling price, the

market
the process of buyers and sellers exchanging goods and services

good is not shipped any substantial distance, and buyers are usually in contact only with local producers. Price and output are thus determined in a number of small markets. In other markets, like those for gold or automobiles, markets are global. The important point is not what a market looks like, but what it does—it facilitates trade.

BUYERS AND SELLERS

The roles of buyers and sellers in markets are important. The buyers, as a group, determine the demand side of the market. Buyers include the consumers who purchase the goods and services and the firms that buy inputs—labour, capital, and raw materials. Sellers, as a group, determine the supply side of the market. Sellers include the firms that produce and sell goods and services, and the resource owners who sell their inputs to firms—workers who "sell" their labour and resource owners who sell raw materials and capital. It is the interaction of buyers and sellers that determines market prices and output—through the forces of supply and demand.

In this chapter, we focus on how supply and demand work in a **competitive market.** A competitive market is one in which there are a number of buyers and sellers offering similar products and no single buyer or seller can influence the market price; that is, buyers and sellers have very little market power. Because most markets contain a large degree of competitiveness, the lessons of supply and demand can be applied to many different types of problems.

competitive market
a market where the many buyers and sellers have very little market power—each buyer's and seller's effect on market price is negligible

---

Section Check

1. Markets consist of buyers and sellers exchanging goods and services with one another.
2. Markets can be regional, national, or global.
3. Buyers determine the demand side of the market and sellers determine the supply side of the market.

Demand

- What is the law of demand?
- What is an individual demand curve?
- What is a market demand curve?
- What is a money price?
- What is a relative price?

THE LAW OF DEMAND

law of demand
the quantity of a good or service demanded varies inversely (negatively) with its price, ceteris paribus

Some laws are made to protect us, such as "no speeding" or "no drinking and driving." Other times observed behaviour is so pervasive it is called a law—like the law of demand. According to the **law of demand,** the quantity of a good or service demanded varies inversely (negatively) with its price, *ceteris paribus*. More directly, the law of demand says that, other things being equal, when the price (P) of a good or service falls, the quantity demanded (Q_D) increases, and conversely, if the price of a good or service rises, the quantity demanded decreases.

$$P \uparrow \Rightarrow Q_D \downarrow \text{ and } P \downarrow \Rightarrow Q_D \uparrow$$

The law of demand puts the concept of basic human "needs," at least as an analytical tool, to rest. Needs are those things that you must have at any price. That is, there are no substitutes. There are usually plenty of substitutes available for any good, some better than others. The law of demand, with its inverse relationship between price and quantity demanded, implies that even so-called needs are more or less urgent depending on the circumstances (opportunity costs). Whenever you hear somebody say, "I need a new car," "I need a new CD player," or "I need new clothes," always be sure to ask: What does the person really mean? At what price does that person "need" the good?

WHY IS THERE A NEGATIVE RELATIONSHIP BETWEEN PRICE AND THE QUANTITY DEMANDED?

The law of demand describes a negative (inverse) relationship between price and quantity demanded. When price goes up, the quantity demanded goes down, and vice versa. But why is this so? The primary reason for this inverse relationship is the **substitution effect.** At higher prices, buyers increasingly substitute other goods for the good that now has a higher relative price. For example, if the price of orange juice increases, some consumers may substitute out of orange juice into other juices, such as apple or tomato juice, or perhaps water, milk, or coffee. This is what economists call the substitution effect of a price change. Of course, if the relative price of orange juice fell, then consumers would substitute out of other products and increase their quantity of orange juice demanded, because the lower relative price now makes it a more attractive purchase.

Another reason for the inverse relationship between price and quantity demanded is referred to as the **income effect.** In this explanation, higher prices make the buyer feel poorer, since they cannot buy the same quantity of goods as they did when prices were lower. As a result, quantity demanded decreases. When prices decline, this makes buyers feel richer, therefore causing quantity demanded to increase.

AN INDIVIDUAL DEMAND SCHEDULE

The **individual demand schedule** shows the relationship between the price of the good and the quantity demanded. For example, suppose Elizabeth enjoys eating apples. How many kilograms of apples would Elizabeth be willing and able to buy at various prices during the year? At a price of $3 a kilogram, Elizabeth buys 15 kilograms of apples over the course of a year. If the price is higher, at $4 per kilogram, she might buy only 10 kilograms; if it is lower, say $1 per kilogram, she might buy 25 kilograms of apples during the year. Elizabeth's demand for apples for the year is summarized in the demand schedule in Exhibit 1. Elizabeth might not be consciously aware of the amounts that she would purchase at prices other than the prevailing one, but that does not alter the fact that she has a schedule in the sense that she would have bought various other amounts had other prices prevailed. It must be emphasized that the schedule is a list of alternative possibilities. At any one time, only one of the prices will prevail, and thus a certain quantity will be purchased.

COURTESY OF ROBERT SEXTON

Need water? What if the price of water increases significantly? At the new higher price, consumers will still use almost as much water for essentials like drinking and cooking. However, they may no longer "need" to wash their cars as often, water their lawns daily, hose off their sidewalks, run the dishwasher so frequently, take long showers, or flush the toilet as often.

substitution effect
at higher prices, buyers increasingly substitute other goods for the good that now has a higher relative price

income effect
at higher prices, buyers feel poorer, causing a lowering of quantity demanded

individual demand schedule
a schedule that shows the relationship between price and quantity demanded

section 3.2 Exhibit 1	Elizabeth's Demand Schedule for Apples

Price (per kilogram)	Quantity Demanded (kilograms per year)
$5	5
4	10
3	15
2	20
1	25

AN INDIVIDUAL DEMAND CURVE

individual demand curve
a graphical representation that shows the inverse relationship between price and quantity demanded

By plotting the different prices and corresponding quantities demanded in Elizabeth's demand schedule in Exhibit 1 and then connecting them, we can create an **individual demand curve** for Elizabeth (Exhibit 2). From the curve, we can see that when the price is higher, the quantity demanded is lower, and when the price is lower, the quantity demanded is higher. The demand curve shows how the quantity demanded of the good changes as its price varies.

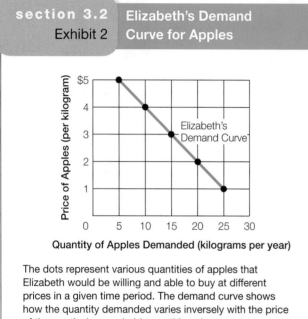

section 3.2
Exhibit 2
Elizabeth's Demand Curve for Apples

The dots represent various quantities of apples that Elizabeth would be willing and able to buy at different prices in a given time period. The demand curve shows how the quantity demanded varies inversely with the price of the good when we hold everything else constant—*ceteris paribus*. Because of this inverse relationship between price and quantity demanded, the demand curve is downward sloping.

market demand curve
the horizontal summation of individual demand curves

WHAT IS A MARKET DEMAND CURVE?

Although we introduced this concept in terms of the individual, economists usually speak of the demand curve in terms of large groups of people—a whole nation, a community, or a trading area. As you know, every single individual has his or her demand curve for every product. The horizontal summation of the demand curves of many individuals is called the **market demand curve.**

Suppose the consumer group comprises Homer, Marge, and the rest of their small community, Springfield, and that the product is still apples. The effect of price on the quantity of apples demanded by Marge, Homer, and the rest of Springfield is given in the demand schedule and demand curves shown in Exhibit 3. At $4 per kilogram, Homer would be willing and able to buy 20 kilograms of apples per year, Marge would be willing and able to buy 10 kilograms, and the rest of Springfield would be willing and able to buy 2970 kilograms. At $3 per kilogram, Homer would be willing and able to buy 25 kilograms of apples per year, Marge would be willing and able to buy 15 kilograms, and the rest of Springfield would be willing and able to buy 4960 kilograms. The market demand curve is simply the (horizontal) sum of the quantities Homer, Marge, and the rest of Springfield demand at each price. That is, at $4, the quantity demanded in the market would be 3000 kilograms

What if this house had been on the market for a year at the same price and not sold? Although no one may want this house at the current asking price, a number of people may want it at a lower price—the law of demand.

© KRISTIINA PAUL

of apples (20 + 10 + 2970 = 3000), and at $3, the quantity demanded in the market would be 5000 kilograms of apples (25 + 15 + 4960 = 5000).

In Exhibit 4, we offer a more complete set of prices and quantities from the market demand for apples during the year. Remember, the market demand curve shows the amounts that all the buyers in the market would be willing and able to buy at various prices. For example, if the price of apples is $2 per kilogram, consumers in the market

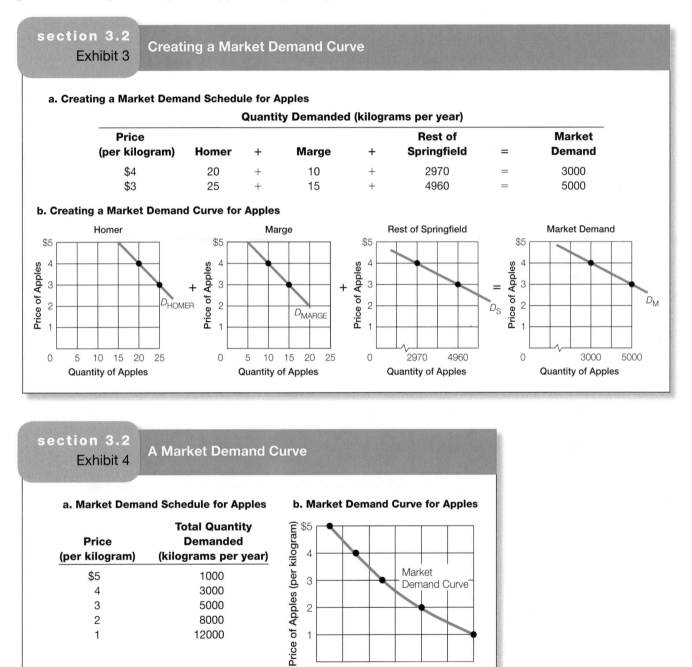

section 3.2 **Exhibit 3** — **Creating a Market Demand Curve**

a. Creating a Market Demand Schedule for Apples

Price (per kilogram)	Homer	+	Marge	+	Rest of Springfield	=	Market Demand
			Quantity Demanded (kilograms per year)				
$4	20	+	10	+	2970	=	3000
$3	25	+	15	+	4960	=	5000

b. Creating a Market Demand Curve for Apples

section 3.2 **Exhibit 4** — **A Market Demand Curve**

a. Market Demand Schedule for Apples

Price (per kilogram)	Total Quantity Demanded (kilograms per year)
$5	1000
4	3000
3	5000
2	8000
1	12000

b. Market Demand Curve for Apples

The market demand curve shows the amounts that all buyers in the market would be willing to buy at various prices. If the price of apples is $2 per kilogram, consumers in the market would collectively be willing to buy 8000 kilograms per year. At $1 per kilogram, the amount demanded would be 12 000 kilograms per year.

would collectively be willing and able to buy 8000 kilograms per year. At $1 per kilogram, the amount demanded would be 12 000 kilograms per year.

A MONEY PRICE

money price
the price that one pays in dollars and cents, sometimes called an absolute or nominal price

Over the past 50 years, few goods have fallen in **money price**—that is, the price that you would pay in dollars and cents. The money price is sometimes called the *absolute* or *nominal price,* expressed in dollars of current purchasing power. Some well-known examples of falling money prices include cellular telephones, DVD players, digital cameras, and home computers, but the evidence indicates that most prices have risen in money terms.

MONEY PRICES VERSUS RELATIVE PRICES

relative price
the price of one good relative to other goods

Money prices themselves are of little importance to most economic decisions in a world where virtually all prices are changing. It is **relative price,** the price of one good relative to other goods, that is crucial.

Suppose you were exploring the Canadian inflation rate of the 1980s and 1990s. You found that from 1980 to 2000, the price of new cars rose, but the quantities of cars demanded did not fall. Is this a flaw in the law of demand? No. Although car prices in dollars rose significantly over this period, so did just about everything else—including wages. The relative price of cars, the price of cars as compared to that of other goods, did not change much over this period. Thus, we would not expect this to cause a fall in the quantity demanded (holding other things constant, especially income). That is, because the relative price did not rise, we would not expect a fall in car sales.

Section Check

1. The law of demand states that when the price of a good falls (rises), the quantity demanded rises (falls), *ceteris paribus.*
2. An individual demand curve is a graphical representation of the relationship between the price and the quantity demanded.
3. The market demand curve shows the amount of a good that all the buyers in the market would be willing and able to buy at various prices.
4. The money price is what one pays in terms of dollars and cents.
5. The relative price is the price of one good relative to another.

---

section

3.3

Shifts in the Demand Curve

- What is the difference between a change in demand and a change in quantity demanded?
- What are the determinants of demand?
- What are substitutes and complements?
- What are normal and inferior goods?
- How does the number of buyers affect the demand curve?
- How do changes in taste affect the demand curve?
- How do changing expectations affect the demand curve?

A CHANGE IN DEMAND VERSUS A CHANGE IN QUANTITY DEMANDED

Economists think consumers are influenced by the prices of goods when they make their purchasing decisions. At lower prices, people prefer to buy more of a good than at higher prices, holding other factors constant. Why? Primarily, it is because many goods are substitutes for one another. For example, an increase in the price of apples might tempt some buyers to switch from buying apples to buying oranges or peaches.

Understanding this relationship between price and quantity demanded is so important that economists make a clear distinction between it and the various other factors that can influence consumer behaviour. A change in a good's price is said to lead to a **change in quantity demanded.** That is, it "moves you along" a given demand curve. The demand curve is drawn under the assumption that all other things are held constant, except the price of the good. However, economists know that price is not the only thing that affects the quantity of a good that people buy. The other factors that influence the demand curve are called *determinants of demand* and a change in these other factors *shifts the entire demand curve.* These determinants of demand are called demand shifters and they lead to a **change in demand.**

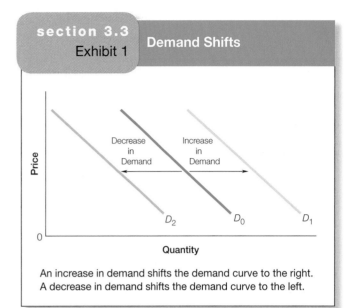

section 3.3
Exhibit 1

Demand Shifts

An increase in demand shifts the demand curve to the right. A decrease in demand shifts the demand curve to the left.

change in quantity demanded
a change in a good's price leads to a change in quantity demanded, a move along a given demand curve

change in demand
the prices of related goods, income, number of buyers, tastes, and expectations can change the demand for a good. That is, a change in one of these factors shifts the entire demand curve

SHIFTS IN DEMAND

An increase in demand shifts the demand curve to the right; a decrease in demand shifts the demand curve to the left, as seen in Exhibit 1. Some of the possible demand shifters are the prices of related goods, income, number of buyers, tastes, and expectations. We will now look more closely at each of these variables.

THE PRICES OF RELATED GOODS

In deciding how much of a good or service to buy, consumers are influenced by the price of that good or service, a relationship summarized in the law of demand. However, consumers are also influenced by the prices of *related* goods and services—substitutes and complements.

Substitutes

Suppose you go into a store to buy a couple of six packs of Coca-Cola and you see that Pepsi is on sale for half its usual price. Is it possible that you might decide to buy Pepsi instead of Coca-Cola? Economists argue that this is the case, and empirical tests have confirmed that people are responsive to both the price of the good in question and the prices of related goods. In this example, Pepsi and Coca-Cola are said to be substitutes. Two goods are **substitutes** if an increase (a decrease) in the price of one good causes an increase (a decrease) in the demand for another good, a direct (or positive) relationship. Because personal tastes differ, what are substitutes for one person may not be so for another person. Furthermore, some substitutes are better than others. For most people, good substitutes include butter and margarine, movie tickets and video rentals, jackets and sweaters, and peas and carrots.

substitute
an increase (a decrease) in the price of one good causes the demand curve for another good to shift to the right (left)

Complements

complement

an increase (a decrease) in the price of one good shifts the demand curve for another good to the left (right)

If an increase (a decrease) in the price of one good causes a decrease (an increase) in the demand of another good (an inverse or negative relationship), the two goods are called **complements.** Complements are goods that "go together," often consumed and used simultaneously, such as skis and bindings, hot dogs and buns, DVDs and DVD players, or printers and ink cartridges. For example, if the price of motorcycles rises and it causes the demand for motorcycle helmets to fall (shift to the left), the two goods are complements. Or if a decrease in the price of DVD players leads to an increase in the demand (a rightward shift) for DVDs, then DVD players and DVDs are complements.

Substitutes	**Complements**
$P_{\text{GOOD A}} \uparrow \Rightarrow \uparrow D_{\text{GOOD B}}$	$P_{\text{GOOD A}} \uparrow \Rightarrow \downarrow D_{\text{GOOD B}}$
$P_{\text{GOOD A}} \downarrow \Rightarrow \downarrow D_{\text{GOOD B}}$	$P_{\text{GOOD A}} \downarrow \Rightarrow \uparrow D_{\text{GOOD B}}$

INCOME

Economists have observed that generally the consumption of goods and services is positively related to the income available to consumers. Empirical studies support the notion that as individuals receive more income they tend to increase their purchases of

ACTIVE LEARNING EXERCISE

SUBSTITUTE GOODS

Q: Can you describe the change we would expect to see in the demand curve for Pepsi if the relative price for Coca-Cola increased significantly?

A: If the price of one good increases and, as a result, an individual buys more of another good, the two related goods are substitutes. That is, buying more of one reduces purchases of the other. In Exhibit 2(a),

we see that as the price of Coca-Cola increased—a movement up along your demand curve for it—you increased your demand for Pepsi, resulting in a shift in the demand for Pepsi (Exhibit 2(b)). If you hated a particular brand of soft drink, however, it might not matter if someone was giving it away, but that is highly unlikely. The substitution effect varies among individuals, but in the aggregate we can recognize substitutes fairly well.

section 3.3
Exhibit 2

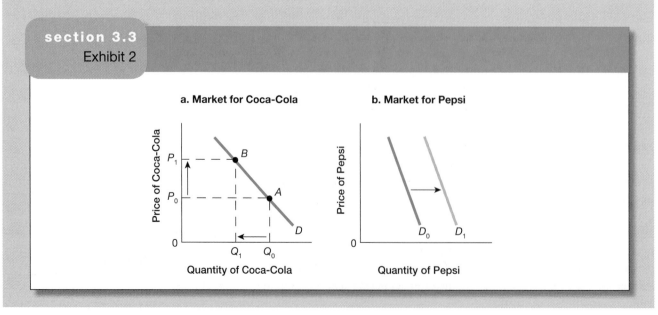

a. Market for Coca-Cola

b. Market for Pepsi

ACTIVE LEARNING EXERCISE

COMPLEMENTARY GOODS

Q: As he looked over the racquets hanging on the wall of the local sports shop, an aspiring young tennis player, Clay Kort, noticed that the price of the racquets was much higher (due to cost increases) than last month. Clay predicted that this increase in the relative price of tennis racquets would probably lead to a reduced demand for tennis balls. Do you agree with Clay?

A: Yes, Clay has correctly indentified tennis racquets and tennis balls as possessing a strong complementary relationship. That is, tennis racquets and tennis balls "go together." In Exhibit 3(a), we see that as the price of tennis racquets increases, the quantity demanded of tennis racquets falls (a movement in demand). And with fewer tennis racquets being purchased, we would expect people to decrease their demand (a leftward shift) for tennis balls (Exhibit 3(b)). There are many other examples of complements in athletic equipment: skis and bindings, golf clubs and golf balls, hockey sticks and hockey pucks, and so on.

section 3.3
Exhibit 3

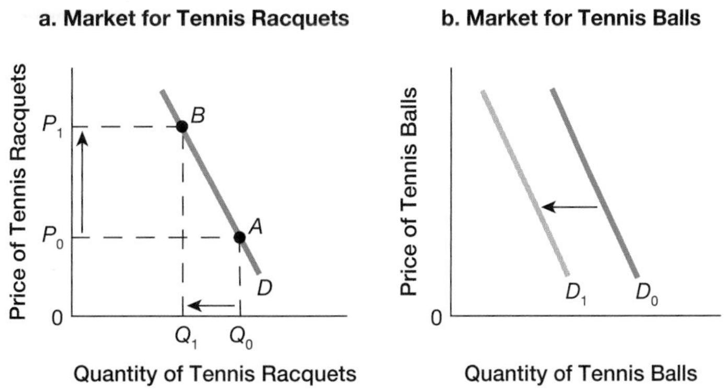

a. Market for Tennis Racquets

b. Market for Tennis Balls

most goods and services. Other things held equal, rising income usually leads to an increase in the demand for goods (a rightward shift of the demand curve), and decreasing income usually leads to a decrease in the demand for goods (a leftward shift of the demand curve).

Normal and Inferior Goods

If demand for a good increases when incomes rise and decreases when incomes fall, the good is called a **normal good.** Most goods are normal goods. Consumers will typically buy more CDs, clothes, pizzas, and trips to the movies as their incomes rise. However, if demand for a good decreases when incomes rise and increases when incomes fall, the good is called an **inferior good.** For example, for most people inferior goods might include do-it-yourself haircuts, used cars, thrift-shop clothing, macaroni and cheese, and so on. The term *inferior* in this sense does not refer to the quality of the good in question but shows that when income changes, demand changes in the opposite direction (inversely).

normal good
if income increases, the demand for a good increases; if income decreases, the demand for a good decreases

inferior good
if income increases, the demand for a good decreases; if income decreases, the demand for a good increases

ACTIVE LEARNING EXERCISE

NORMAL AND INFERIOR GOODS

Q: Chester owns a furniture shop. If there was a recent boom in the economy (higher average income per person and fewer people unemployed), can Chester expect to sell more furniture?

A: Yes, furniture is generally considered a normal good, so a rise in income will increase the demand for furniture (Exhibit 4(a)). However, if Chester sells unfin-

ished, used, or lower-quality furniture, the demand for his products may fall, as higher incomes allow customers to buy furniture that is finished, new, or of higher quality. Chester's furniture would then be an inferior good (Exhibit 4(b)).

section 3.3
Exhibit 4

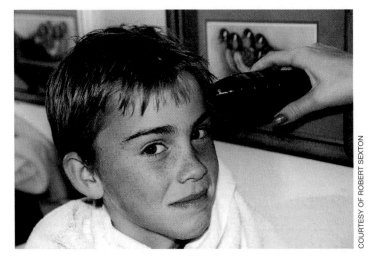

For example, if people's incomes rise and they increase their demand for movie tickets, we say that movie tickets are a normal good. But if people's incomes fall and they increase their demand for bus rides, we say bus rides are an inferior good. Whether goods are normal or inferior, the point here is that income influences demand—usually positively, but sometimes negatively.

Normal Good	**Inferior Good**
Income ↑ ⇒ Demand ↑	Income ↑ ⇒ Demand ↓
Income ↓ ⇒ Demand ↓	Income ↓ ⇒ Demand ↑

COURTESY OF ROBERT SEXTON

For most people, do-it-yourself haircuts are an inferior good. That is, an increase in income will lead to a reduction in do-it-yourself haircuts.

NUMBER OF BUYERS

The demand for a good or service will vary with the size of the potential consumer population. The demand for wheat, for example, rises as population increases because the added population wants to consume wheat products, like bread or cereal. Marketing experts, who closely follow the patterns of consumer behaviour with regards to a particular good or service, are usually vitally concerned with the "demographics" of the product—the vital statistics of the potential consumer population, including size, income, and age characteristics. For example, market researchers for baby-food companies keep a close watch on the birth rate.

TASTES

The demand for a good or service may increase or decrease suddenly with changes in fashions or fads. Taste changes may be triggered by advertising or promotion, by a news story, by the behaviour of some popular public figure, and so on. Taste changes are particularly noticeable in apparel. Skirt lengths, coat lapels, shoe styles, and tie sizes change frequently.

Changes in preferences naturally lead to shifts in demand. Much of the predictive power of economic theory, however, stems from the assumption that tastes are relatively stable, at least over a substantial period of time. Tastes *do* change, though. A person may grow tired of one type of recreation or food and try another type. Changes in occupation, number of dependants, state of health, and age also tend to alter preferences. The birth of a baby may cause a family to spend less on recreation and more on food and clothing. Illness increases the demand for medicine and lessens purchases of other goods. A cold winter increases the demand for natural gas. Changes in customs and traditions also affect preferences, and the development of new products draws consumer preferences away from other goods. Compact discs have replaced record albums, just as in-line skates have replaced traditional roller skates.

EXPECTATIONS

Sometimes the demand for a good or service in a given time period will dramatically increase or decrease because consumers expect the good to change in price or availability at some future date. For example, in the summer of 1997, many buyers expected coffee harvests to be lower because of El Niño. As a result of their expectations of higher future coffee prices, buyers increased their current demand for coffee. That is, the current demand for coffee shifted to the right. Other examples, such as waiting to buy a home computer because price reductions may be even greater in the future, are also common. Or, if you expect to earn additional income next month, you may be more willing to dip into your current savings to buy something this month.

CHANGES IN DEMAND VERSUS CHANGES IN QUANTITY DEMANDED REVISITED

Economists put particular emphasis on the impact on consumer behaviour of a change in the price of a good. We are interested in distinguishing between consumer behaviour related to the price of a good itself (movement *along* a demand curve) from behaviour related to other factors changing (shifts of the demand curve).

As indicated earlier, if the price of a good changes, we say that this leads to a *"change in quantity demanded."* If one of the other factors (determinants) influencing consumer behaviour changes, we say there is a *"change in demand."* The effects of some of the determinants that cause a change in demand (shifters) are reviewed in Exhibit 5.

section 3.3
Exhibit 5   Possible Demand Shifters

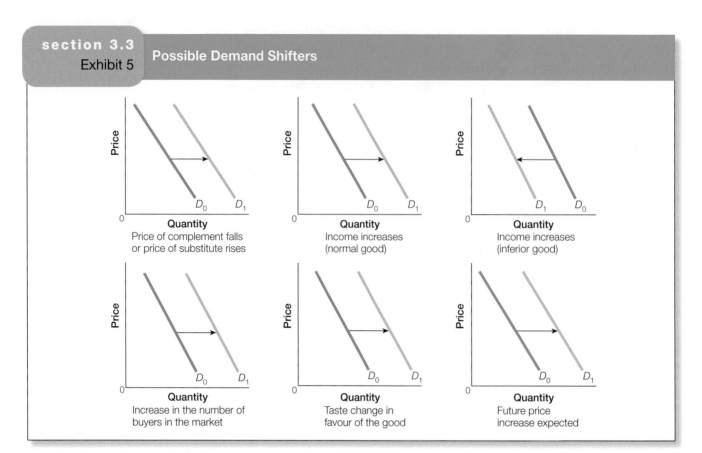

Price of complement falls
or price of substitute rises

Income increases
(normal good)

Income increases
(inferior good)

Increase in the number of
buyers in the market

Taste change in
favour of the good

Future price
increase expected

In The NEWS

CHINA AND INDIA ARE GROWTH DRIVERS FOR GLOBAL AUTO INDUSTRY

BY ERIC BEAUCHESNE

Developing countries will provide the growth markets for global auto sales, a Canadian financial institution says.

Global auto sales, which hit a record [in 2004], will edge ahead [in 2005] as sales growth in developing markets, especially China and India, offset stagnant sales in industrial markets such as North America, Europe and Japan, Scotiabank predicted in a year-end auto report.

Sales worldwide rose three per cent to an estimated all-time high 45.5 million vehicles [in 2004], thanks to a synchronized global economic recovery and despite record oil prices, it said. And sales will rise a more moderate two per cent in 2005 to nearly 46.2 million.

Vehicle sales in China rose by an estimated 15 per cent [in 2004] to about 2.3 million, surpassing both Italy and France to become the fourth-largest car market in the world.

While sales growth slowed from a 71 per cent explosion in 2003, it was still a strong increase, noted Scotiabank economist and auto industry analyst Carl Gomes. Higher incomes and falling car prices are more than offsetting rising interest rates aimed at dampening inflation there.

By the end of the decade China is expected to be the world's second-largest car market—surpassing both Germany

and Japan—with sales only behind the United States, he said. India's market is only half that of China, but [in 2004] surpassed China as the fastest growing market in the world.

"These two nations are now the major growth drivers for the global auto industry," Gomes said. "India has the world's second-largest population with 1.05 billion people—and its population growth is outpacing China's."

Just to keep pace with the growth in the population, sales in India must rise by 20 per cent a year, he noted. That doesn't include the sales growth that will come from an expected increase in vehicle ownership rates in India from only 10 per 1000 population, which compares with 19 per 1000 in China and 600 in Canada.

SOURCE: Adapted from Eric Beauchesne, "Developing countries will power auto sales: study: china is driving force," *Calgary Herald*, December 31, 2004, p. E3. Material reprinted with the express permission of: "CANWEST NEWS SERVICE", a CanWest Partnership.

CONSIDER THIS:

The global demand for automobiles will increase because of rising demand in two important markets: China and India. Rising incomes and rising populations are the major factors increasing demand in the two markets.

ACTIVE LEARNING EXERCISE

CHANGES IN DEMAND VERSUS CHANGES IN QUANTITY DEMANDED

Q: How would you use a graph to demonstrate the two following scenarios? (1) Someone buys more CDs because the price of CDs has fallen; and (2) a student buys more CDs because she just got a 20 percent raise at work, giving her additional income.

A: In Exhibit 6, the movement from A to B is called *an increase in quantity demanded,* and the movement from B to A is called a *decrease in quantity demanded*. Economists use the phrase "increase or decrease in quantity demanded" to describe movements along a given demand curve. However, the change from A to C is called an *increase in demand,* and the change from C to A is called a *decrease in demand*. The phrase "increase or decrease in demand" is reserved for a shift in the whole curve. So if an individual buys more CDs because the price fell, we say there was an increase in quantity demanded. However, if she buys more CDs even at the current price, say $10, we say there is an increase in demand. In this case, the increase in income was responsible for the increase in demand, as she chose to spend some of her new income on CDs.

section 3.3
Exhibit 6

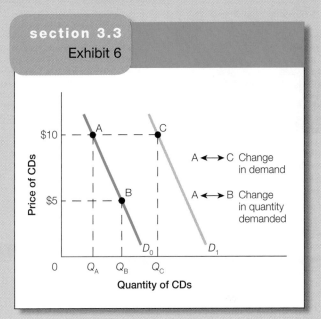

Section Check

SECTION CHECK

1. A change in the quantity demanded describes a movement along a given demand curve in response to a change in the price of the good.
2. A change in demand shifts the entire demand curve. An increase in demand shifts the demand curve to the right; a decrease shifts it to the left.
3. A change in the price of a substitute shifts the demand curve for the good in question. The relationship is direct.
4. A change in the price of a complement shifts the demand curve for the good in question. The relationship is inverse.
5. Changes in income cause demand curve shifts. For normal goods the relationship is direct; for inferior goods it is inverse.
6. The position of the demand curve will vary according to the number of consumers in the market.
7. Taste changes will shift the demand curve.
8. Changes in expected future prices and income can shift the current demand curve.

Supply

■ What is the law of supply?
■ What is an individual supply curve?
■ What is a market supply curve?

law of supply
the higher (lower) the price of the good, the greater (smaller) the quantity supplied

© SIMON PEDERSEN/SHUTTERSTOCK

In order to get more oil, drillers must sometimes drill deeper or go into unexplored areas, and they still may come up with a dry hole. If it costs more to increase oil production, then oil prices would have to rise in order for producers to increase their output.

individual supply curve
a graphical representation that shows the positive relationship between the price and the quantity supplied

THE LAW OF SUPPLY

In a market, the answer to the fundamental question "What do we produce, and in what quantities?" depends on the interaction of both buyers and sellers. Demand is only half the story. The willingness and ability of suppliers to provide goods are equally important factors that must be weighed by decision makers in all societies. As in the case of demand, factors other than the price of the good are also important to suppliers, such as the cost of inputs or advances in technology. As with demand, the price of the good is an important factor. Although behaviour will vary among individual suppliers, economists expect, other things being equal, that the quantity supplied will vary directly with the price of the good, a relationship called the **law of supply.** According to the law of supply, the higher the price of the good (P), the greater the quantity supplied (Q_S), and the lower the price of the good, the smaller the quantity supplied.

$$P\uparrow \Rightarrow Q_S\uparrow \text{ and } P\downarrow \Rightarrow Q_S\downarrow$$

The relationship described by the law of supply is a direct, or positive, relationship, because the variables move in the same direction.

A POSITIVE RELATIONSHIP BETWEEN PRICE AND QUANTITY SUPPLIED

Firms supplying goods and services want to increase their profits, and the higher the price per unit, the greater the profitability generated by supplying more of that good. For example, if you were an apple grower, wouldn't you much rather be paid $5 a kilogram than $1 a kilogram?

There is another reason that supply curves are upward sloping. The law of increasing opportunity costs demonstrated that when we hold technology and input prices constant, producing additional units of a good will require increased opportunity costs. That is, when we produce more of anything, we use the most efficient resources first (those with the lowest opportunity cost) and then draw on less efficient resources (those with higher opportunity cost) as more of the good is produced. So if costs are rising for producers as they produce more units, they must receive a higher price to compensate them for their higher costs. In short, increasing production costs mean that suppliers will require higher prices to induce them to increase their output.

AN INDIVIDUAL SUPPLY CURVE

To illustrate the concept of an **individual supply curve,** consider the amount of apples that an individual supplier, John Macintosh, is willing and able to supply in one year. The law of supply can be illustrated, like the law of demand, by a table or graph. John's supply schedule for apples is shown in Exhibit 1(a). The price–quantity supplied combinations were then plotted and joined to create the individual supply curve shown in Exhibit 1(b). Note that the individual supply curve is upward sloping as you move from left to right. At higher prices, it will be more attractive to increase production. Existing firms, or growers, will produce more at higher prices than at lower prices.

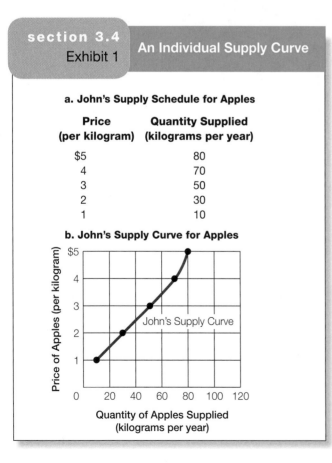

section 3.4
Exhibit 1   **An Individual Supply Curve**

a. John's Supply Schedule for Apples

Price (per kilogram)	Quantity Supplied (kilograms per year)
$5	80
4	70
3	50
2	30
1	10

b. John's Supply Curve for Apples

John's Supply Curve

Quantity of Apples Supplied (kilograms per year)

section 3.4
Exhibit 2

A Market Supply Curve

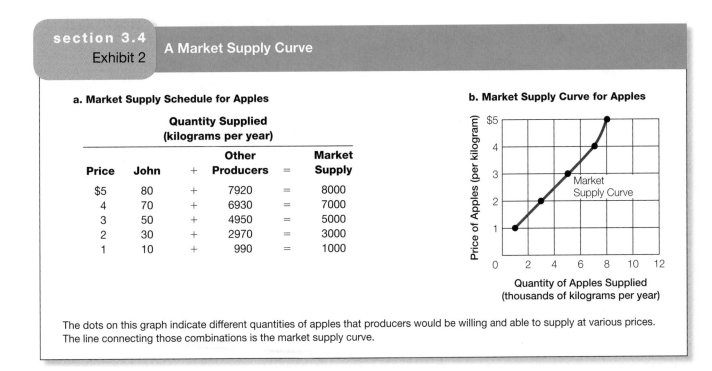

a. Market Supply Schedule for Apples

Price	John	+	Other Producers	=	Market Supply
$5	80	+	7920	=	8000
4	70	+	6930	=	7000
3	50	+	4950	=	5000
2	30	+	2970	=	3000
1	10	+	990	=	1000

Quantity Supplied (kilograms per year)

b. Market Supply Curve for Apples

The dots on this graph indicate different quantities of apples that producers would be willing and able to supply at various prices. The line connecting those combinations is the market supply curve.

THE MARKET SUPPLY CURVE

The **market supply curve** may be thought of as the horizontal summation of the supply curves for individual firms. The market supply schedule, which reflects the total quantity supplied at each price by all of the apple producers, is shown in Exhibit 2(a). Exhibit 2(b) illustrates the resulting market supply curve for this group of apple producers.

market supply curve
a graphical representation of the amount of goods and services that suppliers are willing and able to supply at various prices

Section Check

1. The law of supply states that the higher (lower) the price of the good, the greater (smaller) the quantity supplied.
2. There is a positive relationship between price and quantity supplied because profit opportunities are greater at higher prices and because the higher production costs of increased output mean that suppliers will require higher prices.
3. The market supply curve is a graphical representation of the amount of goods and services that suppliers are willing and able to supply at various prices.

section
3.5

Shifts in the Supply Curve

- What is the difference between a change in supply and a change in quantity supplied?
- How does the number of suppliers affect the supply curve?
- How does technology affect the supply curve?
- How do taxes affect the supply curve?

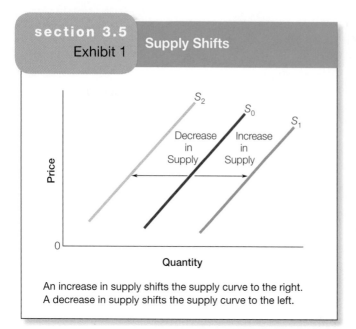

section 3.5
Exhibit 1
Supply Shifts

An increase in supply shifts the supply curve to the right.
A decrease in supply shifts the supply curve to the left.

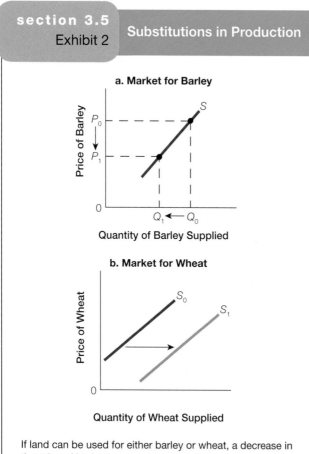

section 3.5
Exhibit 2
Substitutions in Production

If land can be used for either barley or wheat, a decrease in the price of barley (a movement along the supply curve) may cause some farmers to shift out of the production of barley and into wheat—shifting the wheat supply curve to the right.

A CHANGE IN QUANTITY SUPPLIED VERSUS A CHANGE IN SUPPLY

Changes in the price of a good lead to changes in quantity supplied by suppliers, just as changes in the price of a good lead to changes in quantity demanded by buyers. Similarly, a change in supply, whether an increase or a decrease, will occur for reasons other than changes in the price of the product itself, just as changes in demand are due to factors (determinants) other than the price of the good. In other words, a change in the price of the good in question is shown as a movement along a given supply curve, leading to a change in quantity supplied. A change in any other factor that can affect supplier behaviour (input prices, the prices of related products, expectations, number of suppliers, technology, regulation, taxes and subsidies, and weather) results in *a shift in the entire supply curve,* leading to a change in supply.

SHIFTS IN SUPPLY

An increase in supply shifts the supply curve to the right; a decrease in supply shifts the supply curve to the left, as seen in Exhibit 1. We will now look at some of the possible determinants of supply—factors that determine the position of the supply curve—in greater depth.

INPUT PRICES

Suppliers are strongly influenced by the costs of inputs used in the production process, such as steel used for automobiles or microchips used in computers. For example, higher labour, materials, energy, or other input costs increase the costs of production, causing the supply curve to shift to the left at each and every price. If input prices fall, this will lower the costs of production, causing the supply curve to shift to the right—more will be supplied at each and every price.

THE PRICES OF RELATED PRODUCTS

Suppose you own your own farm, on which you plant wheat and barley. Then, the price of barley falls and farmers reduce the quantity supplied of barley, as seen in Exhibit 2(a). What effect would the lower price of barley have on your wheat production? Easy—it would increase the supply of wheat. You would want to produce relatively less of the crop that had fallen in price (barley) and relatively more of the now more attractive other crop (wheat). Wheat and barley are *substitutes in production* because both goods can be produced using the same resources. This example demonstrates why the price of related products is important as a supply shifter as well as a demand shifter. Producers tend to substitute the production of more profitable products for that of less profitable products. This is desirable from society's perspective as well because more profitable products tend to be those considered more valuable by society, whereas less profitable products are usually considered less valuable. Hence, the lower price in the barley market has caused an increase in supply (a rightward shift) in the wheat market, as seen in Exhibit 2(b).

EXPECTATIONS

Another factor shifting supply is suppliers' expectations. If producers expect a higher price in the future, they will supply less now than they otherwise would have, preferring to wait and sell when their goods will be more valuable. For example, if an oil producer expected the future price of oil to be higher next year, he might decide to store some of his current production of oil for next year when the price would be higher. Similarly, if producers expect now that the price will be lower later, they will supply more now.

NUMBER OF SUPPLIERS

We are normally interested in market demands and supplies (because together they determine prices and quantities) rather than in the behaviour of individual consumers and firms. As we discussed earlier, the supply curves of individual suppliers can be summed horizontally to create a market supply curve. An increase in the number of suppliers leads to an increase in supply, denoted by a rightward shift in the supply curve. An exodus of suppliers has the opposite impact, a decrease in supply, which is indicated by a leftward shift in the supply curve.

TECHNOLOGY

Most of us think of prices as constantly rising, given the existence of inflation, but, in fact, decreases in costs often occur because of technological progress, and such advances can lower prices. Human creativity works to find new ways to produce goods and services using fewer or less costly inputs of labour, natural resources, or capital. In recent years, despite generally rising prices, the prices of electronic equipment such as computers, cellular telephones, and DVD players have fallen dramatically. At any given price this year, suppliers are willing to provide many more (of a given quality of) computers than in the 1970s, simply because technology has dramatically reduced the cost of providing them. Graphically, the increase in supply is indicated by a shift to the right in the supply curve.

REGULATION

Supply may also change because of changes in the legal and regulatory environment in which firms operate. Government regulations can influence the costs of production to the firm, leading to cost-induced supply changes similar to those just discussed. For example, if new safety or anti-pollution requirements increase labour and capital costs, the increased cost will result, other things equal, in a decrease in supply, shifting the supply curve to the left, or up. An increase in a government-imposed minimum wage may have a similar effect by raising labour costs and decreasing supply in markets that employ many low-wage workers. However, deregulation—the process by which governments reduce or outright eliminate restrictions on individuals or businesses—can shift the supply curve to the right.

TAXES AND SUBSIDIES

Certain types of taxes can also increase the costs of production borne by the supplier, causing the supply curve to shift to the left at each price. The opposite of a tax (a subsidy) can lower the firm's costs and shift the supply curve to the right. For example, the government sometimes provides farmers with subsidies to encourage the production of certain agricultural products.

WEATHER

In addition, weather can certainly affect the supply of certain commodities, particularly agricultural products and transportation services. A drought or freezing temperatures will almost certainly cause the supply curves for many crops to shift to the left, whereas exceptionally good weather can shift a supply curve to the right.

CHANGE IN SUPPLY VERSUS CHANGE IN QUANTITY SUPPLIED—REVISITED

If the price of a good changes, we say this leads to a change in the quantity supplied. If one of the other factors influences sellers' behaviour, we say this leads to a change in supply. For example, if production costs rise because of a wage increase or higher fuel costs, other things remaining constant, we would expect a decrease in supply—that is, a leftward shift in the supply curve. Alternatively, if some variable, like lower input prices, causes the costs of production to fall, the supply curve will shift to the right. Exhibit 3 illustrates the effect of some of the determinants that cause shifts in the supply curve.

section 3.5
Exhibit 3   Possible Supply Shifts

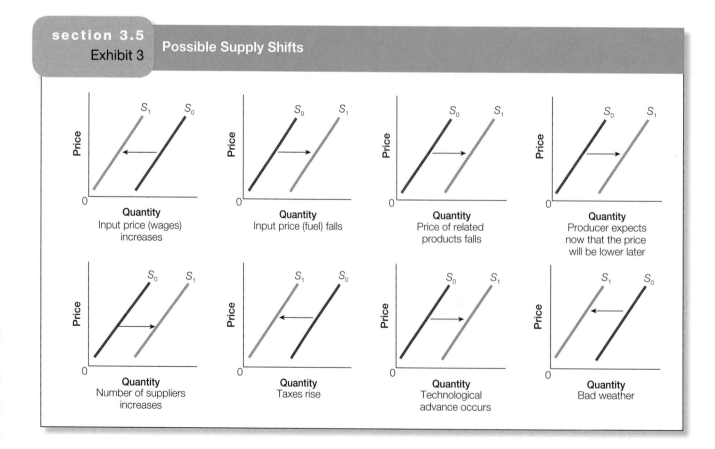

In The **NEWS**

ALBERTA FARMERS PLANT RECORD CANOLA; AGRICULTURE BOOM CREATES BUOYANT MOOD

BY GINA TEEL

Fat prices for canola motivated Alberta farmers to plant a record number of hectares of the cash crop this year, seeing the province notch the biggest percentage increase on the canola-loving Prairies, in terms of new acreage devoted to the popular oilseed.

Provincially, the area seeded to canola is expected to reach 2.1 million hectares, or 263,000 more hectares than in 2007, and well above the five-year average of 1.7 million hectares, Statistics Canada said Tuesday in its latest principal field crop report.

Prairie-wide, it's estimated a whopping 405,000 more hectares were seeded to canola this year, to 6.3 million hectares.

David Burroughs, an analyst with Statistics Canada, said the seeding estimates suggest a similar story is afoot across the board.

"If you're asking about canola, the prices there were pretty darn good, and it just seems there isn't anything you can plant this year that you can't make money on," he said.

The 405,000-hectare increase in canola is equal to 650,000 tonnes of production—assuming normal weather from here to harvest, he said.

Prairie farmers have made room for the canola by ripping up fallow hectares, he said—land most industry observers thought would be going into barley and oats. Seeded hectares of both those crops are down in Alberta this year.

SOURCE: Adapted from Gina Teel, "Alberta farmers plant record canola; Agriculture boom creates buoyant mood," *Calgary Herald*, June 25, 2008, p. D1. Material reprinted with the express permission of: "Calgary Herald Group Inc.", a CanWest Partnership.

CONSIDER THIS:

Why did Alberta farmers choose to plant more canola in 2008 as compared to previous years? The answer is simple: price. Since Alberta farmers can use their land to plant any number of crops (canola, wheat, barley, oats), the increase in the price of canola (a movement along the supply curve) has caused some farmers to shift out of the production of these other crops and into canola—shifting the supply curves for the other crops to the left.

ACTIVE LEARNING EXERCISE

CHANGE IN SUPPLY VERSUS CHANGE IN QUANTITY SUPPLIED

Q: How would you graph the following two scenarios: (1) the price of wheat has risen; and (2) good weather has caused an unusually abundant wheat harvest?

A: In the first scenario, there is an increase in the price of wheat, so there is a change in quantity supplied (i.e., a movement along the supply curve). In the second scenario, the good weather causes the supply curve for wheat to shift to the right. This is called a change in supply (not quantity supplied). A shift in the whole supply curve is caused by one of the other variables, not by a change in the price of the good in question.

As shown in Exhibit 4, the movement from A to B is called an increase in quantity supplied, and the movement from B to A is called a decrease in quantity supplied. However, the change from B to C is called an increase in supply and the movement from C to B is called a decrease in supply.

section 3.5

Exhibit 4

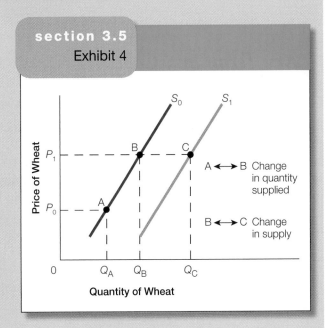

Section Check

1. A movement along a given supply curve is caused by a change in the price of the good in question. As we move along the supply curve, we say there is a change in the quantity supplied.
2. A shift of the entire supply curve is called a change in supply.
3. An increase in supply shifts the supply curve to the right; a decrease shifts it to the left.
4. Input prices, the prices of related products, expectations, the number of suppliers, technology, regulation, taxes and subsidies, and weather can all lead to changes in supply.
5. The supply of a good increases (decreases) if the price of one of its substitutes in production falls (rises).

Summary

Section 3.1
- A market is the process of buyers and sellers exchanging goods and services.

Section 3.2
- The law of demand states that when the price of a good falls (rises), the quantity demanded rises (falls), *ceteris paribus*.

Section 3.3
- A change in the price of the good leads to a change in quantity demanded (this is referred to as a *movement* along a demand curve).
- A change in the price of related goods (substitutes and complements), income, number of buyers, tastes, and expectations can lead to a change in demand (this is referred to as a *shift* of the demand curve).

Section 3.4
- The law of supply states that the higher (lower) the price of the good, the greater (smaller) the quantity supplied, *ceteris paribus*.

Section 3.5
- A change in the price of the good leads to a change in the quantity supplied (this is referred to as a *movement* along a supply curve).
- Input prices, the prices of related products, expectations, the number of suppliers, technology, regulation, taxes and subsidies, and weather can all lead to a change in supply (this is referred to as a *shift* of the supply curve).

Key Terms and Concepts

For a complete glossary of chapter key terms, visit the textbook's Web site at http://www.sextonmacro2e.nelson.com.

market 65
competitive market 66
law of demand 66
substitution effect 67
income effect 67
individual demand schedule 67
individual demand curve 68

market demand curve 68
money price 70
relative price 70
change in quantity demanded 71
change in demand 71
substitute 71

complements 72
normal good 73
inferior good 73
law of supply 78
individual supply curve 78
market supply curve 79

Review Questions

1. Using the demand curve, show the effect of the following events on the market for beef:
   a. Consumer income increases.
   b. The price of beef increases.
   c. There is an outbreak of mad cow disease.
   d. The price of chicken (a substitute) increases.
   e. The price of barbecue grills (a complement) increases.

2. Draw demand curves for the following goods. If the price of the first good listed rises, what will happen to the demand for the second good and why?
   a. hamburger and ketchup
   b. Coca-Cola and Pepsi
   c. camera and film
   d. golf clubs and golf balls

3. Show the impact of each of the following events on the demand for or the supply of oil.
   a. OPEC becomes more effective in limiting the supply of oil.
   b. OPEC becomes less effective in limiting the supply of oil.
   c. The price for natural gas (a substitute for heating oil) rises.
   d. New oil discoveries occur in Alberta.
   e. Electric and hybrid cars become subsidized and their prices fall.

4. Which of the following will cause an increase in the quantity of cell phones demanded? in the demand for cellphones?
   a. The price of cellphones falls.
   b. Your income increases.
   c. The price of cellphone service (a complement) increases.
   d. The price of pagers (a substitute) falls.

5. Which curve (supply or demand) would shift and in which direction in the following cases?
   a. an increase in income and a decreasing price of a complement, for a normal good
   b. a technological advance and lower input prices
   c. a decrease in the price of a substitute and a decrease in income, for an inferior good
   d. producers' expectations that prices will soon fall, and increasingly costly government regulations

6. If the price of ice cream increased,
   a. what would be the effect on the demand for ice cream?
   b. what would be the effect on the demand for frozen yogurt?

7. If the price of corn rose,
   a. what would be the effect on the supply of corn?
   b. what would be the effect on the supply of wheat?

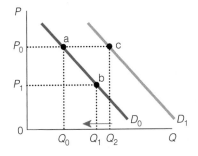

8. Using the graph above, answer the following questions:
   a. What is the shift from D_0 to D_1 called?
   b. What is the movement from *b* to *a* called?

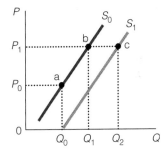

9. Using the graph above, answer the following questions:
   a. What is the shift from S_0 to S_1 called?
   b. What is the movement from *a* to *b* called?
   c. What is the movement from *b* to *a* called?
   d. What is the shift from S_1 to S_0 called?

Fill in the Blanks

Section 3.1

1. A _____ is the process of buyers and sellers _____ goods and services.

2. The important point about a market is what it does—it facilitates _____.

3. _____, as a group, determine the demand side of the market. _____, as a group, determine the supply side of the market.

4. A _____ market consists of many buyers and sellers where no single buyer or seller can influence the market price.

Section 3.2

5. According to the law of demand, other things being equal, when the price of a good or service falls, the _____ increases.

6. The primary reason for the inverse relationship between price and quantity demanded in the law of demand is the _____ effect.

7. An _____ reveals the different amounts of a particular good a person would be willing and able to buy at various possible prices in a particular time interval, other things being equal.

8. The _____ for a product is the horizontal summation of the demand curves of the individuals in the market.

9. The _____ price of a good is the price you would pay for it in dollars and cents, expressed in dollars of current purchasing power. The _____ price of a good is its price in terms of other goods.

Section 3.3

10. A change in _____ leads to a change in quantity demanded, illustrated by _____ a demand curve.

11. A change in demand is caused by changes in any of the other factors (besides the good's price) that would affect how much of the good is purchased: the _____, _____, the _____ of buyers, _____, and _____.

12. An increase in demand is represented by a _____ shift in the demand curve; a decrease in demand is represented by a _____ shift in the demand curve.

13. Two goods are called _____ if an increase in the price of one causes an increase in the demand for the other.

14. For normal goods an increase in income leads to a(n) _____ in demand, and a decrease in income leads to a(n) _____ in demand, other things being equal.

15. An increase in the expected future price of a good or an expected future income increase may _____ current demand.

Section 3.4

16. According to the law of supply, the higher the price of the good, the greater the _____, and the lower the price of the good, the smaller the _____.

17. The quantity supplied is positively related to the price because firms supplying goods and services want to increase their _____, and because increasing _____ costs mean that the suppliers will require prices to induce them to increase their output.

18. An individual supply curve is a graphical representation that shows the _____ relationship between the price and the quantity supplied.

19. The market supply curve is a graphical representation of the amount of goods and services that suppliers are _____ and _____ to supply at various prices.

Section 3.5

20. Possible supply determinants (factors that determine the position of the supply curve) are _____ prices; _____; _____ of suppliers; and _____, _____, _____, and _____.

21. If input prices fall, this will _____ the costs of production, causing the supply curve to shift to the _____.

22. The supply of a good _____ if the price of one of its substitutes in production falls.

23. The supply of a good _____ if the price of one of its substitutes in production increases.

True or False

Section 3.1

1. The differences in the conditions under which the exchange between buyers and sellers occurs make it difficult to precisely define a market.

2. All markets are effectively global in scope.

Section 3.2

3. The law of demand puts the concept of basic human "needs" to rest as an analytical tool because there are usually plenty of substitutes available for any good.

4. There is an inverse or negative relationship between price and quantity demanded.

5. The market demand curve is the vertical summation of individual demand curves.

6. A relative price is the price of one good relative to the price of other goods.

Section 3.3

7. A change in a good's price does not change its demand.

8. A change in demand is illustrated by a shift in the entire demand curve.

9. Because personal tastes differ, what are substitutes for one person may not be substitutes for another person.

10. Two goods are complements if an increase in the price of one causes an increase in the demand for the other.

11. Those goods for which falling income leads to decreased demand are called inferior goods.

12. Either an increase in the number of buyers or an increase in tastes or preferences for a good or service will increase the market demand for a good or service.

13. A decrease in the price of ice cream would cause an increase in the demand for frozen yogurt, a substitute.

Section 3.4

14. The law of supply states that, other things being equal, the quantity supplied will vary directly (a positive relationship) with the price of the good.

15. The market supply curve for a product is the vertical summation of the supply curves for individual firms.

Section 3.5

16. A change in the price of a good leads to a change in the quantity supplied, but not a change in its supply.

17. An increase in supply leads to a movement up along the supply curve.

18. A decrease in supply shifts the supply curve to the left.

19. Just as demanders will demand more now if the price of a good is expected to rise in the near future, sellers will supply more now if the price of a good is expected to rise in the near future.

20. Both technological progress and cost-increasing regulations will increase supply.

Multiple Choice

Section 3.1

1. Which of the following is a market?
   a. a garage sale
   b. a restaurant
   c. the Toronto Stock Exchange
   d. an eBay auction
   e. all of the above

2. In a competitive market,
   a. there are a number of buyers and sellers.
   b. sellers, but not buyers, have significant control over the market price.
   c. no single buyer or seller can appreciably affect the market price.
   d. both a and c are true.

Section 3.2

3. If the demand for milk is downward sloping, then an increase in the price of milk will result in a(n)
   a. increase in the demand for milk.
   b. decrease in the demand for milk.
   c. increase in the quantity of milk demanded.
   d. decrease in the quantity of milk demanded.
   e. decrease in the supply of milk.

4. If the dollar price of Good A rises by 15 percent while the prices of other goods rise an average of 25 percent, then Good A's nominal price has _____ and its relative price has _____.
   a. risen, risen
   b. risen, fallen
   c. fallen, risen
   d. fallen, fallen

Section 3.3

5. Which of the following would not cause a change in the demand for cheese?
   a. an increase in the price of crackers, which are consumed with cheese
   b. an increase in the income of cheese consumers
   c. an increase in the population of cheese lovers
   d. an increase in the price of cheese
   e. none of the above

6. *Ceteris paribus,* an increase in the price of DVD players would tend to
   a. decrease the demand for DVD players.
   b. increase the price of televisions, a complement to DVD players.
   c. increase the demand for DVD players.
   d. increase the demand for VCRs, a substitute for DVD players.
   e. decrease the quantity of DVD players supplied.

7. CBC Newsworld announces that bad weather in Central America has greatly reduced the number of cocoa-bean plants and as a result, the price of chocolate is expected to rise soon. As a result,
   a. the current market demand for chocolate will decrease.
   b. the current market demand for chocolate will increase.
   c. the current quantity demanded for chocolate will decrease.
   d. there is no change in the current market for chocolate, but there will be after the current crop of cocoa-bean plants is processed into chocolate.

8. Whenever the price of Good A increases, the demand for Good B increases as well. Goods A and B appear to be
   a. complements.
   b. substitutes.
   c. inferior goods.
   d. normal goods.
   e. inverse goods.

Section 3.4

9. An upward-sloping supply curve shows that
   a. buyers are willing to pay more for particularly scarce products.
   b. suppliers expand production as the product price falls.
   c. suppliers are willing to increase production of their goods if they receive higher prices for them.
   d. buyers are willing to buy more as the product price falls.
   e. buyers are not affected either directly or indirectly by the sellers' costs of production.

10. Along a supply curve,
    a. supply changes as price changes.
    b. quantity supplied changes as price changes.
    c. supply changes as technology changes.
    d. quantity supplied changes as technology changes.

Section 3.5

11. All of the following factors will affect the supply of shoes except one. Which will not affect the supply of shoes?
    a. higher wages for shoe-factory workers
    b. higher prices for leather

c. a technological improvement that reduces waste of leather and other raw materials in shoe production

d. an increase in consumer income

12. Which of the following is not a determinant of supply?
  a. input prices
  b. technology
  c. tastes
  d. expectations
  e. the prices of related products

13. If a farmer were choosing between growing wheat on his own land and growing soybeans on his own land,
  a. an increase in the price of soybeans would increase his supply of soybeans.
  b. an increase in the price of soybeans would increase his supply of wheat.
  c. an increase in the price of soybeans would decrease his supply of soybeans.
  d. an increase in the price of soybeans would decrease his supply of wheat.
  e. an increase in the price of soybeans would not change his supply of either wheat or soybeans.

14. Antonio's makes the greatest pizza and delivers it hot to all the dorms around the campus. Last week Antonio's supplier of pepperoni informed him of a 25 percent increase in price. Which variable determining the position on the supply curve has changed, and what effect does it have on supply?
  a. future expectations; supply decreases
  b. future expectations; supply increases
  c. input prices; supply decreases
  d. input prices; supply increases
  e. technology; supply increases

Problems

1. [Section 3.2]
   Assume the following demand schedule information:

Ben		Bill		Bob	
P	Q_D	P	Q_D	P	Q_D
$5	1	$5	2	$5	3
4	2	4	4	4	6
3	3	3	6	3	9
2	4	2	8	2	12
1	5	1	10	1	15

  a. Show the market demand schedule if Ben and Bob are the only demanders.

P	Q_D
$5	
4	
3	
2	
1	

b. Show the market demand schedule if Bill joins Ben and Bob in the market.

P	Q_D
$5	
4	
3	
2	
1	

c. Show the market demand schedule if Ben now leaves the market, and only Bill and Bob remain.

P	Q_D
$5	
4	
3	
2	
1	

2. [Section 3.3]

Graph and explain the effect of an increase in the price of ice cream in the frozen yogurt market.

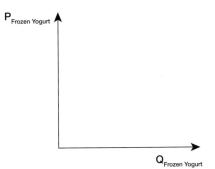

3. [Section 3.3]

Show and describe what would happen to the market demand curve for a good in each of the following cases:

a. An increase in the price of a substitute and a decrease in the price of a complement.

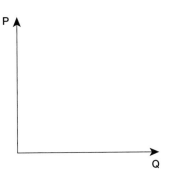

b. A decrease in the price of a substitute and an increase in the price of a complement.

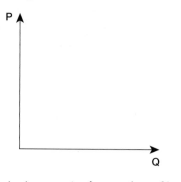

c. An increase in the number of buyers and an increase in income, for a normal good.

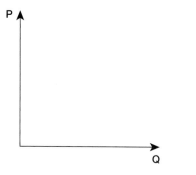

d. A decrease in the number of buyers and an increase in income, for an inferior good.

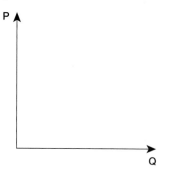

e. A decrease in expected future prices and a shift in tastes away from the good.

4. [Section 3.4]

Assume the following supply schedule information:

Stan		Steve		Stu	
P	Q_S	P	Q_S	P	Q_S
$5	10	$5	15	$5	5
4	8	4	12	4	4
3	6	3	9	3	3
2	4	2	6	2	2
1	2	1	3	1	1

a. Show the market supply schedule if Stan and Steve are the only suppliers.

P	Q_S
$5	
4	
3	
2	
1	

b. Show the market supply schedule if Stu joins Stan and Steve in the market.

P	Q_S
$5	
4	
3	
2	
1	

c. Show the market supply schedule if Stan now leaves the market, and only Steve and Stu remain.

P	Q_S
$5	
4	
3	
2	
1	

5. [Section 3.5]

Graph and explain the effect of a decrease in the price of corn on the soybean market, assuming corn and soybeans can be grown on the same land.

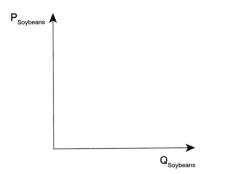

6. [Section 3.5]

Show and describe what would happen to the market supply curve for a good in each of the following cases:

a. An increase in the number of suppliers and an increase in subsidies.

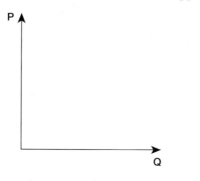

b. An decrease in the number of suppliers and an increase in taxes.

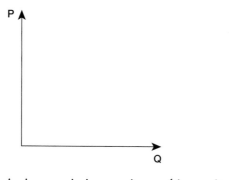

c. An increase in input prices and increasing costs of regulation.

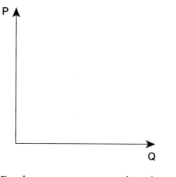

d. Producers expect now that the price will be lower later.

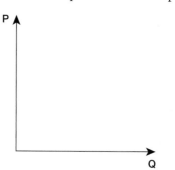

Bringing Supply and Demand Together

4.1 MARKET EQUILIBRIUM PRICE AND QUANTITY

Why is the concept of market equilibrium such a valuable tool?

4.2 CHANGES IN EQUILIBRIUM PRICE AND QUANTITY

What happens to equilibrium price and quantity when we shift the supply or demand curve?

4.3 PRICE CONTROLS

What are price ceilings and price floors?

Market Equilibrium Price and Quantity

- What is the equilibrium price?
- What is the equilibrium quantity?
- What is a shortage?
- What is a surplus?

In the last chapter, we learned about demand and supply separately. Bearing in mind our discussion of the "fuzzy" nature of many real-world markets, we now bring the market supply and market demand together.

EQUILIBRIUM PRICE AND QUANTITY

The price at the intersection of the market demand curve and the market supply curve is called the **equilibrium price** and the quantity is called the **equilibrium quantity.** At the equilibrium price, the amount that buyers are willing and able to buy is exactly equal to the amount that sellers are willing and able to produce. If the market price is above or below the equilibrium price, there will be shortages or surpluses. However, the actions of many buyers and sellers will move the price back to the equilibrium level. Let us see how this happens.

equilibrium price
the price at the intersection of the market supply and demand curves; at this price the quantity demanded equals the quantity supplied

equilibrium quantity
the quantity at the intersection of the market supply and demand curves; at the equilibrium quantity, the quantity demanded equals the quantity supplied

SHORTAGES AND SURPLUSES

surplus
a situation where quantity supplied exceeds quantity demanded

shortage
a situation where quantity demanded exceeds quantity supplied

The equilibrium market solution is best understood with the help of a simple graph. Let's return to the apple example we used in our earlier discussions of supply and demand in Chapter 3. Exhibit 1 combines the market demand curve for apples with the market supply curve. At $3 per kilogram, buyers are willing to buy 5000 kilograms of apples and sellers are willing to supply 5000 kilograms of apples. Neither may be "happy" about the price, because the buyers would like a lower price and the sellers would like a higher price. But both buyers and sellers are able to carry out their purchase and sales plans at that $3 price. However, at any other price, either suppliers or demanders would be unable to trade as much as they would like.

As you can see in Exhibit 1, at $4 per kilogram, the quantity of apples demanded would be 3000 kilograms, but the quantity supplied would be 7000 kilograms. At that price, a **surplus,** or excess quantity supplied, would exist. That is, at this price, growers would be willing to sell more apples than demanders would be willing to buy. To cut growing inventories, frustrated suppliers would cut their price and cut back on production. And as price falls, consumers would buy more, ultimately eliminating the unsold surplus and returning the market to the equilibrium.

What would happen if the price of apples were cut to $1 per kilogram? The yearly quantity demanded of 12 000 kilograms would be greater than the 1000 kilograms that producers would be willing to supply at that low price. So, at $1 per kilogram, a **shortage,** or excess quantity demanded, would exist. Because of the apple shortage, frustrated buyers would be forced to compete for the existing supply, bidding up the price. The rising price would have two effects: (1) producers would be willing to increase the quantity supplied; and (2) the higher price would decrease the quantity demanded. Together, these two effects would ultimately eliminate the shortage, returning the market to the equilibrium.

LEARNING THE FIRST LESSON OF SUPPLY *and* DEMAND...

© 1999 Wiley Miller / dist. by The Washington Post Writers Group
E-mail: wiley@wileytoons.com   Web Site: www.wileytoons.com   2-24

NON SEQUITUR © 1999 Wiley Miller. Distributed by UNIVERSAL PRESS SYNDICATE. Reprinted with permission. All rights reserved.

---

section 4.1
Exhibit 1 — A Hypothetical Market Supply and Demand Schedule for Apples

Price	Quantity Supplied	Quantity Demanded	Difference	State of Market
$5	8 000	1 000	7 000	Surplus
4	7 000	3 000	4 000	Surplus
3	5 000	5 000	0	Equilibrium
2	3 000	8 000	−5 000	Shortage
1	1 000	12 000	−11 000	Shortage

The equilibrium is $3 per kilogram and 5000 kilograms of apples, where quantity demanded and quantity supplied are equal. At higher prices, quantity supplied exceeds quantity demanded, resulting in a surplus. Below $3, quantity demanded exceeds quantity supplied, leading to a shortage.

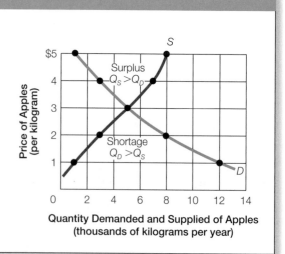

Quantity Demanded and Supplied of Apples
(thousands of kilograms per year)

ACTIVE LEARNING EXERCISE

SHORTAGES

Q: Imagine that you own a butcher shop. Recently, you have noticed that at about noon, you run out of your daily supply of chicken. Puzzling over your predicament, you hypothesize that you are charging less than the equilibrium price for your chicken. Should you raise the price of your chicken? Explain using a simple graph.

A: If the price you are charging is below the equilibrium price (P_E), you can draw a horizontal line from that price straight across Exhibit 2 and see where it intersects the supply and demand curves. The point where this horizontal line intersects the demand curve indicates how much chicken consumers are willing to buy at that below-equilibrium price (P_{BE}). Likewise, the intersection of this horizontal line with the supply curve indicates how much chicken producers are willing to supply at P_{BE}. From this, it is clear that a shortage (or excess quantity demanded) exists, because consumers want more chicken (Q_D) than producers are willing to supply (Q_S) at this relatively low price. This excess quantity demanded results in competition among buyers, which will push prices up and reduce or eliminate the shortage. That is, it would make sense to raise your price on the chicken. As price moves upward toward the equilibrium price, consumers are willing to purchase less (some will

substitute fish, steak, and ground round), and producers will have an incentive to supply more chicken.

section 4.1
Exhibit 2

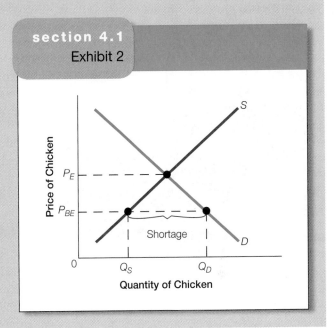

Section Check

1. The intersection of the supply and demand curve shows the equilibrium price and equilibrium quantity in a market.
2. A surplus is a situation where quantity supplied exceeds quantity demanded.
3. A shortage is a situation where quantity demanded exceeds quantity supplied.
4. Shortages and surpluses set in motion actions by many buyers and sellers that will move the market toward the equilibrium price and quantity unless otherwise prevented.

Changes in Equilibrium Price and Quantity

section
4.2

- What happens to equilibrium price and quantity when the demand curve shifts?
- What happens to equilibrium price and quantity when the supply curve shifts?
- What happens when both supply and demand shift in the same time period?
- What is an indeterminate solution?

© CP Photo (Jacques Boissinot)

When one of the many determinants of demand or supply changes, the demand and supply curves will shift, leading to changes in the equilibrium price and equilibrium quantity. When analyzing a change in demand or supply, it is important to answer three key questions to help ensure that the analysis is complete:

1. Which side of the market is being affected by the event in question, demand or supply?
2. Is the event in question a "shift" or a "movement"?
3. Is the event in question having an expansionary or contractionary impact on the market?

We first consider a change in demand.

A CHANGE IN DEMAND

A shift in the demand curve—caused by a change in the price of a related good (substitutes or complements), income, the number of buyers, tastes, or expectations—results in a change in both equilibrium price and equilibrium quantity. But how and why does this happen? This result can be most clearly explained through the use of an example. What happens in the gasoline market during the summer months when people typically do more travelling?

1. This event has a demand side effect, since we are looking at the impact of consumer behaviour.
2. The event is a shift, since it does not directly involve a change in the price of gasoline.
3. The event is expansionary, since we are looking at how consumers buy more gasoline in the summer months than in the winter months.

Therefore, the demand for gasoline increases during the summer. The greater demand for gasoline during the summer sends prices upward, *ceteris paribus*. As shown in Exhibit 1, the rightward shift of the demand curve results in an increase in both equilibrium price and quantity.

A CHANGE IN SUPPLY

Like a shift in demand, a shift in the supply curve will also influence both equilibrium price and equilibrium quantity, assuming that demand for the product has not changed. Let's look at another example: Why are strawberries less expensive in summer than in winter (assuming that consumers' tastes and preferences are fairly constant throughout the year)?

1. This event has a supply side effect, since the behaviour of consumers is assumed to be constant.
2. The event is a shift, since it does not directly involve a change in the price of strawberries.
3. The event is expansionary, since producers can make more fresh strawberries available in the summer, when they are in season, than in the winter.

Therefore, as shown in Exhibit 2, this increase in supply shifts the supply curve to the right, resulting in a lower equilibrium price (from P_{WINTER} to P_{SUMMER}) and a greater equilibrium quantity (from Q_{WINTER} to Q_{SUMMER}).

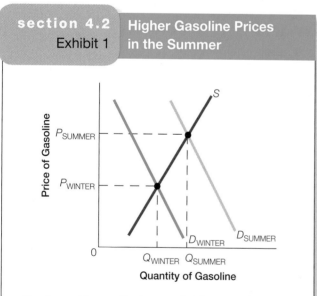

section 4.2
Exhibit 1
Higher Gasoline Prices in the Summer

The demand for gasoline is generally higher in the summer than in the winter. The increase in demand during the summer, coupled with a fixed supply, means a higher price and a greater quantity.

ACTIVE LEARNING EXERCISE

section 4.2
Exhibit 2   **Lower Strawberry Prices in the Summer**

In the summer the supply of fresh strawberries is greater and this leads to a lower equilibrium price and a greater equilibrium quantity, *ceteris paribus.* In the winter, the supply of fresh strawberries is lower and this leads to a higher equilibrium price and a lower equilibrium quantity, *ceteris paribus.*

ACTIVE LEARNING EXERCISE

CHANGE IN DEMAND

Q: In ski resorts like Whistler, BC, hotel prices are higher in January and February (in-season when there are more skiers) than in November (off-season when there are fewer skiers). Why is this the case?

A: In the (likely) event that supply is not altered significantly, demand is chiefly responsible for the higher prices in the prime skiing months. In Exhibit 3, we see that the demand is higher in-season (February) than off-season (November).

section 4.2
Exhibit 3

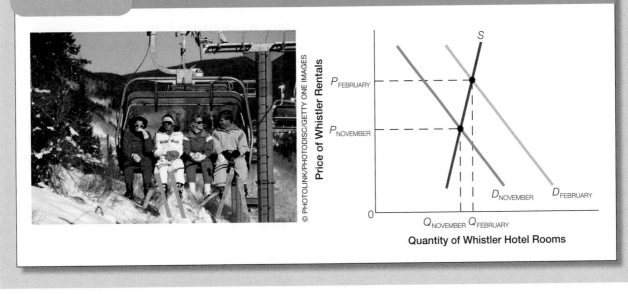

In The **NEWS**

MAD COW CRISIS HITS CANADIAN CATTLE INDUSTRY

BY JUDY MONCHUK

Nicki Murray's world turned upside down [in May 2003] when mad cow disease was detected in an Alberta animal. Suddenly, the cattle that had provided a livelihood and a history to her family weren't wanted anywhere in the world.

Adversity may be part of farm life, but nothing prepared rural families for the unprecedented economic crisis, which has no end in sight.

For almost 10 months, Murray has ridden an emotional roller coaster trying to keep life as normal as possible for her five young sons.

"It's like we're waiting in limbo, you can't dream of anything," said Murray of Picture Butte, Alta. She can look out her front door and see the feedlot operation her husband Shawn has struggled to keep going—and knows her neighbours are facing the same thing.

"There's no vision as to where you're going to be in a month or a year," said Murray, whose husband's grandfather began raising cattle in 1905. "And that's emotionally draining."

It's here in an area known as Feedlot Alley that the mad cow crisis has hit particularly hard. In this southern Alberta expanse of rolling valley, 650,000 cattle are fattened for slaughter, most in family-run operations that hold anywhere from 3,000 to upwards of 15,000 head of cattle.

Cattle prices collapsed in the wake of the detection of bovine spongiform encephalopathy (BSE) in a northern Alberta breeder cow. For months there were no international markets for Canadian beef: a huge blow to an industry which exports up to 60 per cent of its product, much of it to the United States.

The feedlot industry has taken the hardest hit. Many producers have seen equity built up over a lifetime of work evaporate by 75 per cent. As bills pile up, the bankers have begun knocking.

Businesses that rely on the beef industry have also been hurt. Farm machinery sales are down. Restaurants sit empty. Truckers who used to haul live cattle to the U.S. have found other ways to survive.

The Murrays have tried to shelter their boys from much of the stress, but that doesn't always work. Their eldest son sees the toll. "Dad's more depressed, he's not smiling as much," said 14-year-old Taner. "He's usually talking to Mom because Mom helps him get through it."

Taner expects his family will get through the crisis, although that seems a long way off. But when Taner looks at his future, he sees it away from cattle farming.

That's not a surprise to his mother.

"My youngest boys seem to have more love for the land and love for animals," said Murray. "Taner has always said he wouldn't farm, but I'm sure this wouldn't convince him of anything different."

SOURCE: Adapted from Judy Monchuk, "Farm Life in Limbo," *Star-Phoenix* (Saskatoon), March 30, 2004, p. B8. © The Canadian Press. Reprinted with permission from *The Canadian Press*.

CONSIDER THIS:
Alberta and Saskatchewan produce 80 percent of Canada's finished cattle, animals used for prime cuts and export. The mad cow crisis in 2003 caused a massive decrease in the demand for Canadian cattle, resulting in a collapse in cattle prices.

CHANGES IN BOTH SUPPLY AND DEMAND

We have discussed that as part of the continual adjustment process that occurs in the marketplace, supply and demand can each shift in response to many different factors, with the market then adjusting toward the new equilibrium. We have, so far, only considered what happens when just one such change occurs at a time. In these cases, we learned that the results of these adjustments in supply and demand on the equilibrium price and quantity are predictable. However, very often supply and demand will both shift in the same time period. Can we predict what will happen to equilibrium prices and equilibrium quantities in these situations?

As you will see, when supply and demand move at the same time, we can predict the change in one variable (price or quantity), but we are unable to predict the direction of the effect on the other variable with any certainty. This change in the second variable, then, is said to be indeterminate because it cannot be determined without additional information about the size of the relative shifts in supply and demand. This concept will become clearer to you as we work through the following example.

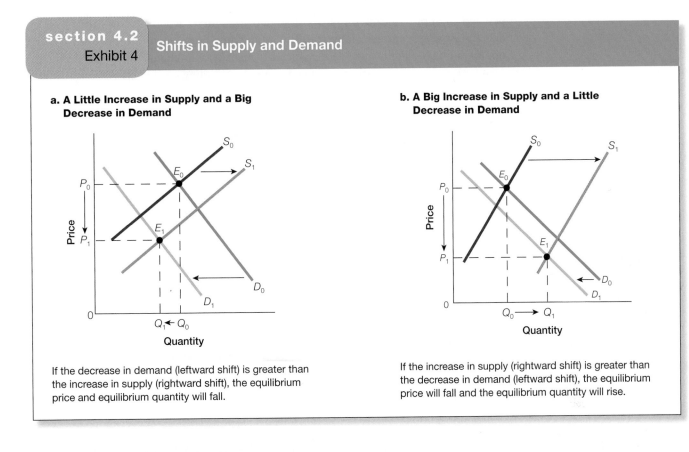

section 4.2
Exhibit 4   **Shifts in Supply and Demand**

a. A Little Increase in Supply and a Big Decrease in Demand

If the decrease in demand (leftward shift) is greater than the increase in supply (rightward shift), the equilibrium price and equilibrium quantity will fall.

b. A Big Increase in Supply and a Little Decrease in Demand

If the increase in supply (rightward shift) is greater than the decrease in demand (leftward shift), the equilibrium price will fall and the equilibrium quantity will rise.

An Increase in Supply and a Decrease in Demand

When considering this scenario, it might help you to break it down into its individual parts. As you learned in the last section, an increase in supply (a rightward shift in the supply curve) results in a decrease in the equilibrium price and an increase in the equilibrium quantity. A decrease in demand (a leftward movement of the demand curve), on the other hand, results in a decrease in both the equilibrium price and the equilibrium quantity. These shifts are shown in Exhibit 4(a). Taken together, then, these changes will clearly result in a decrease in the equilibrium price because both the increase in supply and the decrease in demand work to push this price down. This drop in equilibrium price (from P_0 to P_1) is shown in the movement from E_0 to E_1.

The effect of these changes on equilibrium price is clear, but how does the equilibrium quantity change? The impact on equilibrium quantity is indeterminate because the increase in supply increases the equilibrium quantity and the decrease in demand decreases it. In this scenario, the change in the equilibrium quantity will vary depending on the relative changes in supply and demand. If, as shown in Exhibit 4(a), the decrease in demand is greater than the increase in supply, the equilibrium quantity will decrease. If, however, as shown in Exhibit 4(b), the increase in supply is greater than the decrease in demand, the equilibrium quantity will increase.

THE COMBINATIONS OF SUPPLY AND DEMAND SHIFTS

The eight possible changes in demand and/or supply are presented in Exhibit 5, along with the resulting changes in equilibrium quantity and equilibrium price. Although you could memorize the impact of the various possible changes in demand and supply, it would be more profitable to draw a graph, such as shown in Exhibit 6, whenever a situation of changing demand and/or supply arises. Remember that an increase in either demand or supply means a rightward shift in the curve, whereas a decrease in either demand or supply means a leftward shift. Also, when both demand and supply change, one of the two equilibrium values, price or quantity, will change in an indeterminate manner (can increase, decrease, or stay the same) depending on the relative magnitude of the changes in supply and demand.

section 4.2
Exhibit 5
The Effect of Changing Demand and/or Supply

If Demand	and Supply	then Equilibrium Quantity	and Equilibrium Price
1. Increases	Stays unchanged	Increases	Increases
2. Decreases	Stays unchanged	Decreases	Decreases
3. Stays unchanged	Increases	Increases	Decreases
4. Stays unchanged	Decreases	Decreases	Increases
5. Increases	Increases	Increases	Indeterminate*
6. Decreases	Decreases	Decreases	Indeterminate*
7. Increases	Decreases	Indeterminate*	Increases
8. Decreases	Increases	Indeterminate*	Decreases

*May increase, decrease, or remain the same, depending on the size of the change in demand relative to the change in supply.

section 4.2
Exhibit 6
The Combinations of Supply and Demand Shifts

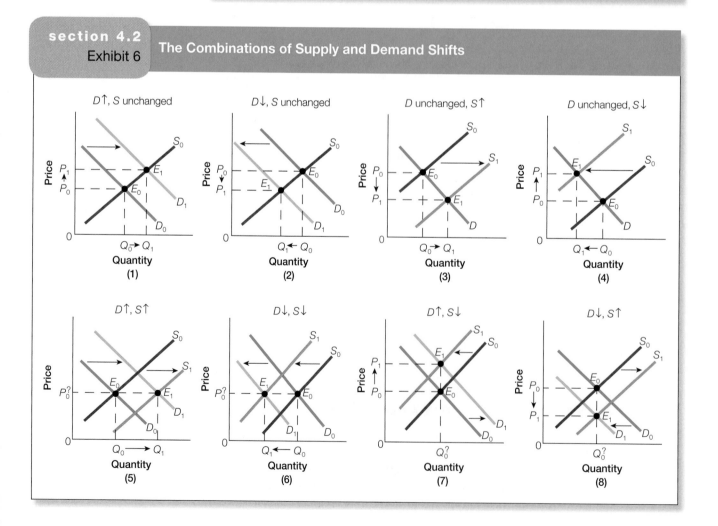

SECTION CHECK

Section Check

1. Changes in demand will cause a change in the equilibrium price and quantity, *ceteris paribus.*
2. Changes in supply will cause a change in the equilibrium price and quantity, *ceteris paribus.*
3. Supply and demand curves can shift simultaneously in response to changes in both supply and demand determinants.
4. When there are simultaneous shifts in both supply and demand curves, we will be able to determine one, but not both, of the variables. Either the equilibrium price or the equilibrium quantity will be indeterminate without more information.

Price Controls

■ What are price controls?
■ What are price ceilings?
■ What are price floors?

PRICE CONTROLS

Although nonequilibrium prices can occur naturally, reflecting uncertainty, they seldom last for long. Governments, however, may impose nonequilibrium prices for significant time periods. Price controls involve the use of the power of the government to establish prices different from the equilibrium prices that would otherwise prevail. The motivations for price controls vary with the market under consideration. For example, a **price ceiling,** a legal maximum price, is often set for goods deemed important to low-income households, like housing. Or a **price floor,** a legal minimum price, may be set on wages because wages are the primary source of income for most people.

Price controls are not always implemented by the federal government. Provincial governments can and do impose local price controls. One fairly well-known example is rent controls, which limit how much landlords can charge for rental housing.

price ceiling
a legally established maximum price

price floor
a legally established minimum price

PRICE CEILINGS: RENT CONTROL

Rent controls have been imposed in some provinces. Although the rules may vary, generally the price (or rent) of an apartment remains fixed over the tenure of an occupant, except for allowable annual increases tied to the cost of living or some other price index. When an occupant moves out, the owners can usually, but not always, raise the rent to a near-market level for the next occupant. The controlled rents for existing occupants, however, are generally well below market rental rates.

Results of Rent Controls

Rent controls distort market signals and lead to shortages. In addition, they often do not even help the intended recipients—low-income households. Most people living in rent-controlled apartments have a good deal, one that they would lose by moving as their family circumstances or income changes. Tenants thus are reluctant to give up their governmentally granted right to a below-market-rent apartment. In addition, because the rents received by landlords are constrained and below market levels, the rate of return (roughly, the profit) on housing investments falls compared to that on other forms of real estate not subject to rent controls, like office rents or mortgage payments on condominiums. Hence, the incentive to construct new housing is reduced. Where rent controls are truly effective, there is generally little new construction going on and a shortage of apartments that persists and grows over time.

Also, when landlords are limited in what rent they can charge, there is little incentive to improve or upgrade apartments, such as by putting in new kitchen appliances or new carpeting, in order to get more rent. In fact, there is some incentive to avoid routine maintenance, thereby lowering the cost of apartment ownership to a figure approximating the controlled rental price, although the quality of the housing stock will deteriorate over time.

Another impact of rent control is that it promotes housing discrimination. Where rent controls do not exist, a prejudiced landlord might willingly rent to someone he believes is undesirable simply because the undesirable family is the only one willing to pay the requested rent (and the landlord is not willing to lower the rent substantially to get a desirable family, since this could translate into the loss of thousands of dollars in income). With rent controls, many families are likely to want to rent the controlled apartment, some desirable and some undesirable as seen by the landlord, simply because the rent is at a below-equilibrium price. The landlord can indulge in his "taste" for discrimination without any additional financial loss beyond that required by the controls.

Consequently, he will be more likely to choose to rent to a desirable family, perhaps a family without children or pets, rather than an undesirable one, perhaps one with lower income and so a greater risk of nonpayment.

Exhibit 1 shows the impact of rent control. If the price ceiling is set below the market price, the quantity demanded will increase to Q_D from Q^* and the quantity supplied will fall to Q_S from Q^*. The rent control policy will therefore create a shortage, the difference between Q_S and Q_D.

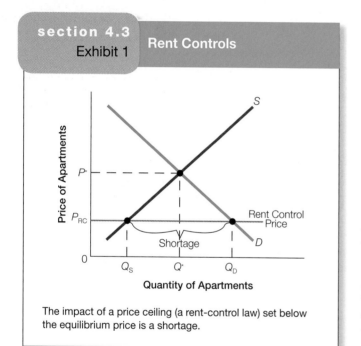

section 4.3
Exhibit 1   Rent Controls

The impact of a price ceiling (a rent-control law) set below the equilibrium price is a shortage.

PRICE FLOORS: THE MINIMUM WAGE

The argument for a minimum wage is simple: Existing wages for workers in some types of labour markets do not allow for a very high standard of living, and a minimum wage allows those workers to live better than before. Provincial government legislation makes it illegal to pay most workers an amount below the current legislated minimum wage.

Let us examine graphically the impact of a minimum wage on low-skilled workers. In Exhibit 2, suppose the government sets the minimum wage, W_{MIN}, above the market equilibrium wage, W_E. In Exhibit 2, we see that the price floor is binding; that is, there is a surplus of low-skilled workers at W_{MIN} because the quantity of labour supplied is greater than the quantity of labour demanded. The reason for the surplus of low-skilled workers (unemployment) at W_{MIN} is that more people are willing to work than employers are willing and able to hire.

Notice that not everyone loses from a minimum wage. Those workers who continue to hold jobs now have higher incomes (those workers between 0 and Q_D in Exhibit 2). However, many low-skilled workers suffer from a minimum wage—they either lose their jobs or are unable to get them in the first place (those between Q_D and Q_S in Exhibit 2). Although studies disagree somewhat on the precise magnitudes, they largely agree that minimum-wage laws do create some unemployment, and that the unemployment is concentrated among teenagers—the least-experienced and least-skilled members of the labour force.

Most Canadian workers are not affected by the minimum wage because in the market for their skills, they earn wages that exceed the minimum wage. For example, a minimum wage will not affect the unemployment rate for accountants. In Exhibit 3, we see the labour market for skilled and experienced workers. In this market the minimum wage (the price floor) is not binding because these workers are earning wages that far exceed the minimum wage—W_E is much higher than W_{MIN}.

The above analysis does not "prove" minimum-wage laws are "bad" and should be abolished. To begin with, there is the empirical question of how much unemployment is caused by minimum wages. Secondly, some might believe that the cost of unemployment resulting from a minimum wage is a reasonable price to pay for assuring that those with jobs get a "decent" wage. The analysis does point out, however, that there is a cost to having a minimum wage, and the burden of the minimum wage falls not only on low-skilled workers and employers but also on consumers of products made more costly by the minimum wage.

What do you think would happen to the number of low-skilled workers getting jobs if we raised the minimum wage to $20 an hour?

UNINTENDED CONSEQUENCES

When markets are altered for policy reasons it is wise to remember that the actual results of actions are not always as initially intended or result in **unintended consequences.** As economists, we must always look for the secondary effects of an action that may occur along with the initial effects. For example, the government is often well intentioned when

unintended consequences
the secondary effects of an action that may occur after the initial effects

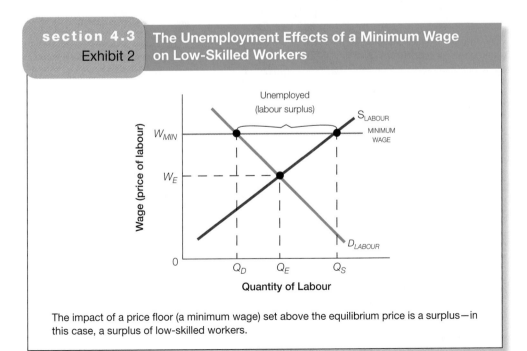

section 4.3
Exhibit 2
The Unemployment Effects of a Minimum Wage on Low-Skilled Workers

The impact of a price floor (a minimum wage) set above the equilibrium price is a surplus—in this case, a surplus of low-skilled workers.

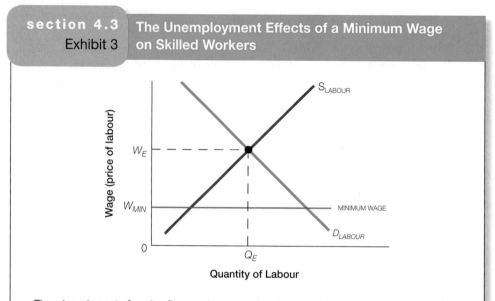

section 4.3
Exhibit 3   **The Unemployment Effects of a Minimum Wage on Skilled Workers**

There is no impact of a price floor on the market for skilled and experienced workers. In this market, the price floor (the minimum wage) is not binding.

In The **NEWS**

MINIMUM-WAGE WORKERS TEND TO BE TEENS OR YOUNG ADULTS

Minimum-wage workers in 2003 tended to be teens or young adults with lower levels of education in service-sector jobs, employed part time with short job tenure, says Statistics Canada.

They represented about four per cent of paid workers, down from 5.7 per cent in 1997, and across the country they totalled 547,000 people.

"Some were working to finance their education or support their families, while others were older workers looking to supplement their pension," the agency said....

Women accounted for almost two-thirds of minimum-wage workers in 2003. One in 20 women was a minimum-wage worker, compared with one in 35 men.

Individuals aged 24 and under were eight times as likely to be minimum-wage workers as those over 24.

And "nearly half of minimum-wage workers were aged 15 to 19, with more than three-quarters of these attending school either full or part time. Another 15 per cent were between 20 and 24, four out of 10 of whom were students."

About 41 per cent of all minimum-wage workers did not have a high-school diploma, compared with 15 per cent of all employees.

"This would explain the high rates of minimum-wage work among young people, many of whom have not yet completed their studies."

Most of them worked in accommodation and food services or retail trade.

However, some 27,000 heads of family with no spouse worked for minimum wage or less.

SOURCE: "Minimum-Wage Earners Tend to Be Young, Says Statistics Canada Study," *The Province* (Vancouver), March 28, 2004, p. A61. © The Canadian Press. Reprinted with permission from *The Canadian Press.*

CONSIDER THIS:
Nearly half of minimum-wage workers were aged 15 to 19, with the majority of these attending school either full- or part-time. However, some 27 000 heads of family with no spouse worked for minimum wage.

it adopts price controls to help low-skilled workers, or tenants in search of affordable housing; however, such policies can also cause unintended consequences, which may completely undermine the intended effects. For example, rent controls may have an immediate effect of lowering rents, but secondary effects may well include very low vacancy rates, discrimination against low-income and large families, and deterioration of the quality of rental units. Similarly, a sizeable increase in the minimum-wage rate may help many low-skilled workers or apprentices, but will result in higher unemployment and/or a reduction in fringe benefits, such as vacations and discounts to employees. Society has to make tough decisions, and if the government subsidizes some program or groups of people in one area, then something must always be given up somewhere else. The "law of scarcity" cannot be repealed!

Section Check

1. Price controls involve government mandates to keep prices above or below the market-determined equilibrium price.
2. Price ceilings are government-imposed maximum prices.
3. If price ceilings are set below the equilibrium price, shortages will result.
4. Price floors are government-imposed minimum prices.
5. If price floors are set above the equilibrium price, surpluses will result.
6. The law of unintended consequences states that the results of certain actions may not always be as clear as they initially appear.

Summary

Section 4.1

- The intersection of the supply and demand curves determines the equilibrium price and equilibrium quantity in a market.
- At the equilibrium price, quantity supplied equals quantity demanded.
- When the market price is above the equilibrium price, there will be a surplus, which causes the market price to fall.
- When the market price is below the equilibrium price, there will be a shortage, which causes the market price to rise.

Section 4.2

- Changes in demand and supply will cause a change in the equilibrium price and/or quantity.

Section 4.3

- A price ceiling, like rent control, is a legal maximum price.
- If a price ceiling is set below the equilibrium price (therefore binding), it will lead to a shortage.
- A price floor, like a minimum wage, is a legal minimum price.
- If a price floor is set above the equilibrium price (therefore binding), it will lead to a surplus.

Key Terms and Concepts

For a complete glossary of chapter key terms, visit the textbook's Web site at http://www.sextonmacro2e.nelson.com.

equilibrium price 95
equilibrium quantity 95
surplus 96
shortage 96

price ceiling 103
price floor 103
unintended consequences 105

Review Questions

1. Using supply and demand curves, show the effect of each of the following events on the market for wheat.

   a. Saskatchewan suffers a drought.

   b. The price of corn decreases (assume that many farmers can grow either corn or wheat).

   c. The prairie provinces have great weather.

   d. The price of fertilizer declines.

   e. More farmers start growing wheat.

2. If a price is above the equilibrium price, explain the forces that bring the market back to the equilibrium price and quantity. If a price is below the equilibrium price, explain the forces that bring the market back to the equilibrium price and quantity.

3. The market for hockey tickets at your university arena, which seats 2000, is the following:

Price	Q_D	Q_S
$2	4000	2000
$4	2000	2000
$6	1000	2000
$8	500	2000

   a. What is the equilibrium price?

   b. What is unusual about the supply curve?

   c. At what price would there be a shortage?

   d. At what price is there a surplus?

   e. Suppose that the addition of new students (all big hockey fans) next year will add 1000 to the quantity demanded at each price. What will this do to next year's demand curve? What is the new equilibrium price?

4. What would be the impact of a rental price ceiling set above the equilibrium rental price for apartments? below the equilibrium rental price?

5. What would be the impact of a price floor set above the equilibrium price for dairy products? Below the equilibrium price?

6. Why do both price floors and price ceilings reduce the quantity of goods traded in those markets?

7. Why do 10 a.m. classes fill up before 8 a.m. classes during class registration? Use the supply and demand curves to help explain your answers.

8. What would happen to the equilibrium price and equilibrium quantity in the following cases?

   a. an increase in income for a normal good and a decrease in the price of an input

   b. a technological advance and a decrease in the number of buyers

   c. an increase in the price of a substitute and an increase in the number of suppliers

   d. producers' expectations that prices will soon fall and a reduction in consumer tastes for the good

Fill in the Blanks

Section 4.1

1. The price at the intersection of the market demand curve and the market supply curve is called the _____ price, and the quantity is called the _____ quantity.

2. A situation where quantity supplied is greater than quantity demanded is called a _____.

3. A situation where quantity demanded is greater than quantity supplied is called a _____.

4. At a price greater than the equilibrium price, a _____, or excess quantity supplied, would exist. Sellers would be willing to sell _____ than demanders would be willing to buy. Frustrated suppliers would _____ their price and consumers would buy _____, returning the market to equilibrium.

Section 4.2

5. An increase in demand results in a _____ equilibrium price and a _____ equilibrium quantity.

6. A decrease in supply results in a _____ equilibrium price and a _____ equilibrium quantity.

7. If demand decreases and supply increases, but the decrease in demand is greater than the increase in supply, the equilibrium quantity will _____.

8. If supply decreases and demand increases, the equilibrium price will _____ and the equilibrium quantity will _____.

Section 4.3

9. A price _____ is a legally established maximum price; a price _____ is a legally established minimum price.

10. Rent controls distort market signals and lead to _____ of rent-controlled apartments.

11. The quality of rent-controlled apartments would tend to _____ over time.

12. An increase in the minimum wage would tend to create _____ unemployment for low-skilled workers.

13. The secondary effects of an action that may occur after the initial effects are called _____.

True or False

Section 4.1

1. If the quantity demanded does not equal quantity supplied, a shortage will always occur.

2. At the equilibrium price the quantity demanded equals the quantity supplied.

Section 4.2

3. A decrease in demand results in a lower equilibrium price and a higher equilibrium quantity.

4. An increase in supply results in a lower equilibrium price and a higher equilibrium quantity.

5. An increase in supply, combined with a decrease in demand, will decrease the equilibrium price but result in an indeterminate change in the equilibrium quantity.

6. If supply increases and demand decreases, but the increase in supply is greater than the decrease in demand, the equilibrium quantity will decrease.

7. An increase in both demand and supply increases the equilibrium quantity.

Section 4.3

8. Neither a price ceiling at the equilibrium price nor a price floor at the equilibrium price would have any effect on the market price or quantity exchanged.

9. A price ceiling decreases the quantity of a good exchanged, but a price floor increases the quantity of a good exchanged.

10. A minimum wage (price floor) is likely to be binding in the market for experienced and skilled workers.

Multiple Choice

Section 4.1

1. Which of the following is true at market equilibrium?
   a. quantity supplied exceeds quantity demanded
   b. quantity supplied is less than quantity demanded
   c. quantity supplied is equal to quantity demanded
   d. all of the above

2. A market will experience a _____ in a situation where quantity supplied exceeds quantity demanded, and a _____ in a situation where quantity demanded exceeds quantity supplied.
   a. shortage; shortage
   b. surplus; surplus
   c. shortage; surplus
   d. surplus; shortage

3. The price of a good will tend to rise when
   a. a temporary shortage at the current price occurs (assuming no price controls are imposed).
   b. a temporary surplus at the current price occurs (assuming no price controls are imposed).
   c. demand decreases.
   d. supply increases.

Section 4.2

4. If incomes are rising, in the market for an inferior good,
   a. its price will rise, and the quantity exchanged will rise.
   b. its price will rise, and the quantity exchanged will fall.
   c. its price will fall, and the quantity exchanged will rise.
   d. its price will fall, and the quantity exchanged will fall.

5. If many cooks view butter and margarine to be substitutes, and the price of butter rises, then in the market for margarine
    a. the equilibrium price will rise, whereas the change to equilibrium quantity is indeterminate.
    b. the equilibrium price will rise, and the equilibrium quantity will decrease.
    c. both the equilibrium price and quantity will rise.
    d. the equilibrium price will fall, and the equilibrium quantity will fall.
    e. the equilibrium price will fall, and the equilibrium quantity will increase.

6. If you observed that the market price of a good rose while the quantity exchanged fell, which of the following could have caused the change?
    a. an increase in supply
    b. a decrease in supply
    c. an increase in demand
    d. a decrease in demand
    e. none of the above

7. If both supply and demand decreased, but supply decreased more than demand, the result would be
    a. a higher price and a lower equilibrium quantity.
    b. a lower price and a lower equilibrium quantity.
    c. no change in the price and a lower equilibrium quantity.
    d. a higher price and a greater equilibrium quantity.
    e. a lower price and a greater equilibrium quantity.

8. If you observed the price of a good decreasing and the quantity exchanged increasing, it would be most likely caused by
    a. an increase in demand.
    b. a decrease in demand.
    c. an increase in supply.
    d. a decrease in supply.

9. If you observed the price of a good decreasing and the quantity exchanged decreasing, it would be most likely caused by
    a. an increase in demand.
    b. a decrease in demand.
    c. an increase in supply.
    d. a decrease in supply.

10. If, in a given market, the price of inputs increases and income increases (assuming it is a normal good), then
    a. price would increase but the change in quantity exchanged would be indeterminate.
    b. price would decrease but the change in quantity exchanged would be indeterminate.
    c. quantity exchanged would increase but the change in price would be indeterminate.
    d. quantity exchanged would decrease but the change in price would be indeterminate.

Section 4.3

11. If the equilibrium price of widgets is $22, and then a price floor of $20 is imposed by the government, as a result,
  a. there will be no effect on the widget market.
  b. there will be a shortage of widgets.
  c. there will be a surplus of widgets.
  d. the price of widgets will decrease.

12. Which of the following is true?
  a. A price ceiling reduces the quantity exchanged in the market, but a price floor increases the quantity exchanged in the market.
  b. A price ceiling increases the quantity exchanged in the market, but a price floor decreases the quantity exchanged in the market.
  c. Both price floors and price ceilings reduce the quantity exchanged in the market.
  d. Both price floors and price ceilings increase the quantity exchanged in the market.

13. Which of the following will most likely occur with a 20 percent increase in the minimum wage?
  a. higher unemployment rates among the experienced and skilled workers
  b. higher unemployment rates among the young and low-skilled workers
  c. lower unemployment rates for the young and low-skilled workers
  d. the price floor (minimum wage) will be binding in the young and low-skilled labour market but not in the experienced and skilled labour market
  e. both b and d

14. If a price floor was set at the current equilibrium price, which of the following would cause a surplus as a result?
  a. an increase in demand
  b. a decrease in demand
  c. an increase in supply
  d. a decrease in supply
  e. either b or c

15. A current shortage is due to a price ceiling. If the price ceiling is removed,
  a. price would increase, quantity supplied would increase, and quantity demanded would decrease.
  b. price would increase, quantity supplied would decrease, and quantity demanded would increase.
  c. price would decrease, quantity supplied would increase, and quantity demanded would decrease.
  d. price would decrease, quantity supplied would decrease, and quantity demanded would increase.

16. A current surplus is due to a price floor. If the floor is removed,
  a. price would increase, quantity demanded would increase, and quantity supplied would decrease.
  b. price would increase, quantity demanded would decrease, and quantity supplied would increase.
  c. price would decrease, quantity demanded would increase, and quantity supplied would decrease.
  d. price would decrease, quantity demanded would decrease, and quantity supplied would increase.

Problems

1. [Sections 4.1 and 4.2]

Assume the following information for the demand and supply schedules for Good Z.

Demand		Supply	
Price	Quantity Demanded	Price	Quantity Supplied
$10	10	$1	10
9	20	2	15
8	30	3	20
7	40	4	25
6	50	5	30
5	60	6	35
4	70	7	40
3	80	8	45
2	90	9	50
1	100	10	55

a. Draw the corresponding supply and demand curves.
b. What is the equilibrium price and quantity traded?
c. If the price were $9, would there be a shortage or a surplus? How large?
d. If the price were $3, would there be a shortage or a surplus? How large?
e. If the demand for Z increased by 15 units at every price, what would the new equilibrium price and quantity traded be?
f. Given the original demand for Z, if the supply of Z were increased by 15 units at every price, what would the new equilibrium price and quantity traded be?

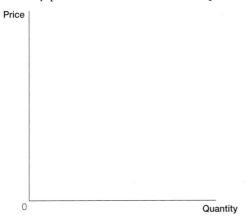

2. [Sections 4.2 and 4.3]

Refer to the following supply and demand curve diagram.

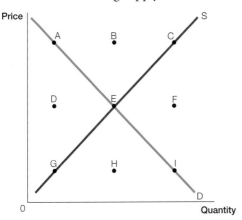

a. Starting from an initial equilibrium at E, what shift or shifts in supply and/or demand could move the equilibrium price and quantity to each of points A through I?

b. Starting from an initial equilibrium at E, what would happen if there were both an increase in the price of an input and an increase in income, if it is a normal good?

c. Starting from an initial equilibrium at E, what would happen if there were both an increase in the price of an input and an advance in technology?

d. If a price floor is imposed above the equilibrium price, which of A through I would tend to be the quantity supplied, and which would tend to be the quantity demanded? Which would be the new quantity exchanged?

e. If a price ceiling is imposed below the equilibrium price, which of A through I would tend to be the quantity supplied, and which would tend to be the quantity demanded? Which would be the new quantity exchanged?

3. [Section 4.3]

Draw a supply and demand curve diagram with a price floor above the equilibrium price, and indicate the quantity supplied and quantity demanded at that price and the resulting surplus.

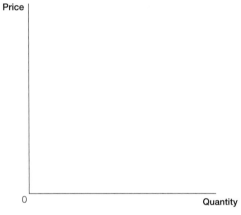

a. What happens to the quantity supplied, the quantity demanded, and the surplus if the price floor is raised? if it is lowered?

b. What happens to the quantity supplied, the quantity demanded, and the surplus if, for a given price floor, the demand curve shifts to the right?

c. What happens to the quantity supplied, the quantity demanded, and the surplus if, for a given price floor, the supply curve shifts to the right?

4. [Section 4.3]

Draw a supply and demand curve diagram with a price ceiling below the equilibrium price, and indicate the quantity supplied and quantity demanded at that price, and the resulting shortage.

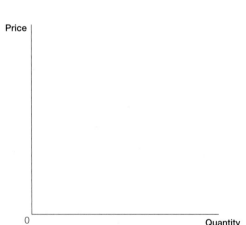

a. What happens to the quantity supplied, the quantity demanded, and the shortage if the price ceiling is raised? if it is lowered?

b. What happens to the quantity supplied, the quantity demanded, and the shortage if, for a given price ceiling, the demand curve shifts to the right?

c. What happens to the quantity supplied, the quantity demanded, and the shortage if, for a given price ceiling, the supply curve shifts to the right?

Introduction to the Macroeconomy

Macroeconomic Goals

- What are the most important macroeconomic goals in Canada?
- Are these goals universal?

THREE MAJOR MACROECONOMIC GOALS

Recall from Chapter 1 that macroeconomics is the study of the whole economy—the study of the forest, not the trees. A macroeconomist may study the changes in the inflation rate or the unemployment rate, the impact of changing monetary policy or fiscal policy on output and inflation, or alternative policies that may contribute to long-term economic growth.

Nearly every society has been interested in three major macroeconomic goals: (1) maintaining employment of human resources at relatively high levels, meaning that jobs are relatively plentiful and financial suffering from lack of work and income is relatively uncommon; (2) maintaining prices at a relatively stable level so that consumers and producers can make better decisions; and (3) achieving a high rate of economic growth, meaning a growth in real output over time. We use the term **real gross domestic product (RGDP)** to measure output or production. The word "real" is used to indicate that the output is adjusted for the general increase in prices over time. Technically, gross domestic product (GDP) is defined as the total value of all final goods and services produced in a given time period such as a year or a quarter. Exhibit 1 provides data on Canada's macroeconomic performance since 1990. Economic growth increased sharply after 1994, which helped to lower Canada's unemployment rate from relatively high levels in the early 1990s. Over the 1990–2007 period, the inflation rate remained below 3 percent per year.

real gross domestic product (RGDP)
the total value of all final goods and services produced in a given time period such as a year or a quarter, adjusted for inflation

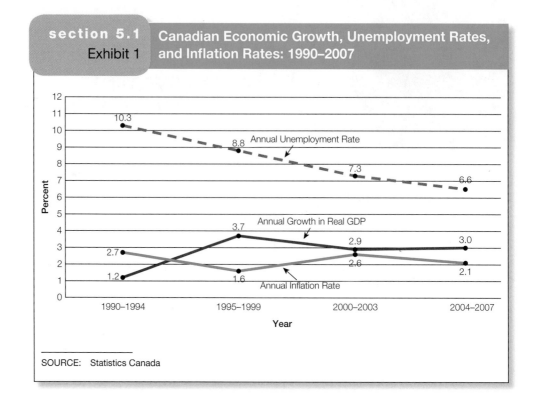

section 5.1
Exhibit 1   Canadian Economic Growth, Unemployment Rates, and Inflation Rates: 1990–2007

SOURCE: Statistics Canada

WHAT OTHER GOALS ARE IMPORTANT?

In addition to these primary goals, concern has been expressed at various times and places about other economic issues, some of which are essentially microeconomic in character. For example, concern about the "quality of life" has prompted some societies to try to reduce "bads" such as pollution and crime, and increase goods and services such as education and health services. Another goal has been "fairness" in the distribution of income or wealth. Still another goal pursued in many nations at one time or another has been self-sufficiency in the production of certain goods or services, such as food and energy.

HOW DO VALUE JUDGMENTS AFFECT ECONOMIC GOALS?

In stating that nations have economic goals, we must acknowledge that nations are made up of individuals. Individuals within a society may differ considerably in their evaluation of the relative importance of certain issues, or even whether certain "problems" are really problems after all. For example, economic growth, viewed positively by most persons, is not considered so favourably by others. Although some citizens may think the income distribution is just about right, others might think it provides insufficient incomes to the poorer members of society; still others think it involves taking too much income from the relatively well-to-do and thereby reduces incentives to carry out productive, income-producing activities.

Section Check

1.   The most important Canadian macroeconomic goals are full employment, price stability, and economic growth.
2.   Individuals each have their own reasons for valuing certain goals more than others.

Employment and Unemployment

- What are the consequences of high unemployment?
- What is the unemployment rate?
- Does unemployment affect everyone equally?
- What causes unemployment?
- How long are people typically unemployed?

THE CONSEQUENCES OF HIGH UNEMPLOYMENT

Nearly everyone agrees that it is unfortunate when a person who wants a job cannot find one. A loss of a job can mean financial insecurity and a great deal of anxiety. High rates of unemployment in a society can increase tensions and despair. A family without income from work undergoes great suffering; as its savings fade, it wonders where it is going to obtain the means to survive. Society loses some potential output of goods when some of its productive resources—human or nonhuman—remain idle, and potential consumption is also reduced. Clearly, then, there is a loss in efficiency when people willing to work and productive equipment remain idle. That is, other things equal, relatively high rates of unemployment are viewed almost universally as undesirable.

WHAT IS THE UNEMPLOYMENT RATE?

When discussing unemployment, economists and politicians refer to the unemployment rate. In order to calculate the unemployment rate, you must first understand another important concept—the **labour force.** Exhibit 1 shows the population categories used by Statistics Canada in its analysis of the labour market. First, it calculates the population 15 years of age and over, which was 26.554 million people in 2007. This population is

labour force
persons 15 years of age and over who are employed or are unemployed and seeking work

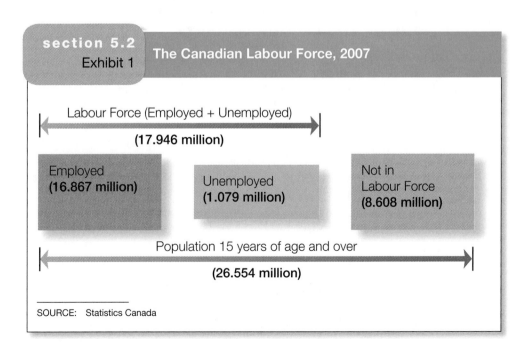

section 5.2
Exhibit 1
The Canadian Labour Force, 2007

Labour Force (Employed + Unemployed)
(17.946 million)

Employed
(16.867 million)

Unemployed
(1.079 million)

Not in
Labour Force
(8.608 million)

Population 15 years of age and over
(26.554 million)

SOURCE: Statistics Canada

broken down into two categories: those in the labour force and those not in the labour force. Those not in the labour force, 8.608 million people, are people who are not working and are not seeking work. For example, they may be retired persons, full-time homemakers, or full-time students. Those in the labour force, 17.946 million people, are people who are employed or are unemployed and seeking work.

unemployment rate
*the percentage of the people in
the labour force who are
unemployed*

The **unemployment rate** is defined as the percentage of the people in the labour force who are unemployed. To calculate the unemployment rate, we divide the number of unemployed people by the number of people in the labour force.

$$\text{Unemployment rate} = (\text{Number of unemployed} / \text{Labour force}) \times 100$$

For 2007, 1.079 million people were unemployed from a labour force of 17.946 million people.

$$\text{Unemployment rate} = (1.079 \text{ million} / 17.946 \text{ million}) \times 100$$
$$= 0.060 \times 100$$
$$= 6.0 \text{ percent}$$

THE WORST CASE OF CANADIAN UNEMPLOYMENT

By far the worst employment downturn in Canadian history was the Great Depression, which began in late 1929 and continued until 1939. Unemployment rose from only 2.9 percent of the labour force in 1929 to more than 19 percent in the early 1930s, and double-digit unemployment persisted through 1939. Some economists would argue that modern macroeconomics, with its emphasis on the determinants of unemployment and its elimination, truly began in the 1930s.

VARIATIONS IN THE UNEMPLOYMENT RATE

Exhibit 2 shows the unemployment rate since 1976. Unemployment has ranged from a high of 11.9 percent in 1983 to a low of 6.0 percent in 2007.

ARE UNEMPLOYMENT STATISTICS ACCURATE REFLECTIONS OF THE LABOUR MARKET?

In periods of prolonged economic recession and high unemployment, some individuals think that the chances of landing a job are so bleak that they quit looking. These people are called **discouraged workers.** Individuals who have not actively sought work are not counted as unemployed; instead, they fall out of the labour force. Also, people looking for full-time work who grudgingly settle for a part-time job are counted as "fully" employed, yet they are only "partly" employed. However, at least partially balancing these two biases in official employment statistics are a number of jobs in the underground economy (drugs, prostitution, gambling, and so on) that are not reported at all. In addition, many people may claim they are actually seeking work when, in fact, they may just be going through the motions so that they can continue to collect employment insurance or receive other government benefits.

discouraged worker
*an individual who has left the
labour force because he or she
could not find a job*

WHO ARE THE UNEMPLOYED?

Unemployment varies between different segments of the population and by region of the country. Unemployment tends to be much greater among teenagers, and female unemployment tends to be slightly lower than male unemployment. As Exhibit 3 indicates, the

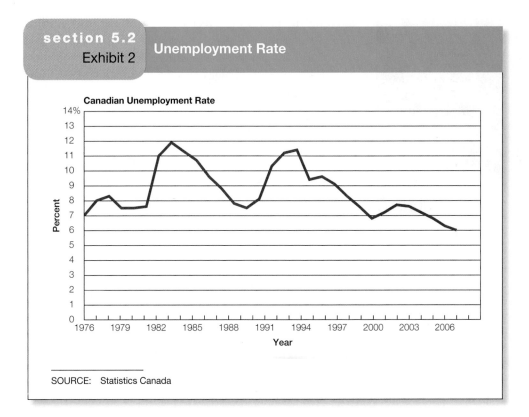

section 5.2
Exhibit 2 **Unemployment Rate**

Canadian Unemployment Rate

SOURCE: Statistics Canada

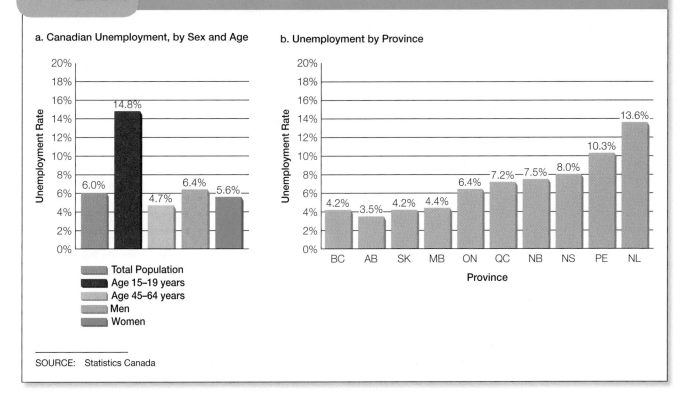

section 5.2
Exhibit 3 **Unemployment in Canada by Age, Sex, and Region, 2007**

a. Canadian Unemployment, by Sex and Age

- Total Population
- Age 15–19 years
- Age 45–64 years
- Men
- Women

6.0% 14.8% 4.7% 6.4% 5.6%

b. Unemployment by Province

BC 4.2% | AB 3.5% | SK 4.2% | MB 4.4% | ON 6.4% | QC 7.2% | NB 7.5% | NS 8.0% | PE 10.3% | NL 13.6%

SOURCE: Statistics Canada

Teenagers have the highest rates of unemployment. Do you think it would be easier for them to find jobs if they had more experience and higher skill levels?

job loser
an individual who has been laid off or fired

job leaver
a person who quits his or her job

re-entrant
an individual who worked before and is now re-entering the labour force

new entrant
an individual who has not held a job before but is now seeking employment

underemployment
a situation in which workers have skills higher than necessary for a job

unemployment rate for teenagers (14.8 percent) is three times greater than the unemployment rate for workers aged 45 to 64 (4.7 percent). The difference in unemployment rates for men and women is slighter, with a female unemployment rate of 5.6 percent versus a male unemployment rate of 6.4 percent.

Provincial unemployment rates show considerable variation: from a high of 13.6 percent in Newfoundland and Labrador to a low of 3.5 percent in Alberta. It is also clear from Exhibit 3(b) that the unemployment rate tends to rise, on average, as one moves from west to east, across the country.

REASONS FOR UNEMPLOYMENT

There are four main categories of unemployed workers: **job losers** (laid off or fired), **job leavers** (quit), **re-entrants** (worked before and now re-entering the labour force), and **new entrants** (entering the labour force for the first time—primarily teenagers). It is a common misconception that the vast majority of workers are unemployed because they have lost their jobs. However, job losers typically account for only 50 to 60 percent of the total unemployed. New entrants and re-entrants also make up a large component of the unemployed. Job leavers are the smallest source of unemployment.

HOW MUCH UNEMPLOYMENT?

Although unemployment is painful to those who have no source of income, reducing unemployment is not costless. In the short run, a reduction in unemployment may come at the expense of a higher rate of inflation, especially if the economy is close to full capacity, where resources are almost fully employed. Also, trying to match employees with jobs quickly may lead to significant inefficiencies because of mismatches between the worker's skill level and the level of skill required for a job. For example, the economy would be wasting resources subsidizing education if people with a Ph.D. in biochemistry were driving taxis or tending bar. That is, the skills of the employee may be higher than that necessary for the job, resulting in what economists call **underemployment.** Alternatively, employees may be placed in jobs beyond their abilities, which would also lead to inefficiencies.

THE AVERAGE DURATION OF UNEMPLOYMENT

The *duration* of unemployment is equally as important as the amount of unemployment. The financial consequences of a head of household being unemployed four or five weeks are usually not extremely serious, particularly if the individual is covered by employment insurance. The impact becomes much more serious if a person is unemployed for many months. Therefore, it is useful to look at the average duration of unemployment to discover what percent of the labour force is unemployed for more than a certain time period, say, 13 weeks. Canadian data indicates that long-term unemployment (greater than 13 weeks) accounts for approximately 40 to 50 percent of total unemployment. The duration of unemployment tends to be greater when the amount of unemployment is high, and smaller when the amount of unemployment is low. Unemployment of any duration, of course, means a potential loss of output. This loss of current output is permanent; it is not made up when unemployment starts falling again.

In The **NEWS**

LABOUR MARKET IN GOOD SHAPE

BY ERIC BEAUCHESNE

Canada's labour market is in better shape than those in most industrial nations, especially in the youth job market, due in part to the fact young Canadians commonly gain work experience while still in school, says the report by the Organization for Economic Cooperation and Development.

But it's not a workers' paradise . . .

"Labour market discrimination is still a big obstacle," said OECD Secretary General Angel Gurria. "Many workplaces not only have a glass ceiling but also a glass door, which keeps out women and ethnic minorities."

The report, meanwhile, noted the proportion of Canadian adults who are working is at an all-time high of 74 per cent, three percentage points higher than at the start of the decade, seven percentage points higher than the average for the world's industrial countries and two percentage points higher than in the U.S.

Canada's jobless rate, at 6.1 per cent, is currently higher than the 5.5 per cent U.S. rate. However, if adjusted for measurement differences in the two countries, Statistics Canada said Canada's unemployment rate already slipped below the U.S. rate in May [2008] for the first time in more than a quarter century and to what in U.S. terms would be 5.3 per cent.

"The strong export earnings of extractive industries are unlikely to be sufficient to totally delink the Canadian economy from the U.S. slowdown, but the labour market should be less adversely affected north of the border," the OECD report said.

Canada also has a relatively healthy youth-labour market, it said.

"One factor accounting for the high youth employment rate in Canada is that it is quite common for students to hold part-time jobs," it said. "This pattern may also ease the transition from study to full-time work in Canada, since youth typically gain some familiarity with the world of work while still in school."

The recent relative strong performance of the youth labour market in Canada is also due to sustained economic growth and a very flexible labour market, which have contributed to rising employment rates and falling overall unemployment for all, it said.

"Canada combines a high youth employment rate with the second-highest rate of higher education completion in the OECD," it also noted.

However, as in other industrial countries, some groups in Canadian society are not doing as well as others, it said. "Employment opportunities continue to lag for women and some ethnic minorities."

The employment rate for prime-age women in Canada is eight percentage points lower than for men, the report said, adding, however, that's less than one-half of the average 20 per cent gender employment gap in industrial countries. Also, average hourly wages for prime-age Canadian women were nearly 20 per cent lower than for men, a slightly larger gap than the average 17 per cent in industrial countries.

"Similarly, the employment rates and wages of non-white Canadians lag [behind] those of whites," it said.

In Canada, the employment gap between native-born "non-white" and "white" groups with identical levels of education is about 12 per cent, and their wage gap about 14 per cent. In comparison, the U.S. employment gap was only six per cent but the wage gap was about 16 per cent.

"While many factors explain why employment rates and earnings are lower for women and some ethnic minorities, new evidence . . . suggests that discrimination in the labour market continues to play a role."

And in Canada, that's despite "federal anti-discrimination legislation [that] is among the most advanced in the OECD."

"Experience in a number of OECD countries indicates that repressive legislation alone cannot guarantee a level playing field for all workers," it said. "Informational and educational campaigns may also need to be reinforced in order to induce the needed cultural change.

"Discriminatory practices appear to be pervasive in the labour markets of all OECD countries," it said, noting ethnic minorities typically have to search up to 50 per cent longer than members of the majority group with identical resumes before receiving a job offer.

"Similarly, a job applicant from a minority group needs to be substantially better qualified in order to have the same probability of receiving a call back for an interview after submitting a written job application," it said.

SOURCE: Eric Beauchesne, "Labour market in good shape; But women, ethnic minorities continue to face discrimination," *Star-Phoenix*, Saskatoon, Saskatchewan, July 3, 2008, p. C1. Eric Beauchesne; Material reprinted with the express permission of: *The National Post Company*, a CanWest Partnership.

CONSIDER THIS:

The pace of economic growth, the high degree of flexibility found within the Canadian labour market, and the fact that the majority of Canadian students work part-time while in school gave a labour market advantage to Canadian youth compared to other industrialized countries. There was also notable improvement for the overall labour market, as the Canadian unemployment rate—corrected for measurement differences—slipped below the U.S. rate for the first time in 25 years. Unfortunately, all the news from the labour front was not positive, as women and visible minorities continue to encounter discrimination—this despite some of the most advanced anti-discrimination legislation amongst industrialized nations.

Labour Force Participation Rates for Men and Women

	1976	1986	1996	2007
Total	61.5%	66.0%	64.7%	67.6%
Men	77.6	76.8	72.2	72.7
Women	45.7	55.5	57.5	62.7

SOURCE: Statistics Canada

LABOUR FORCE PARTICIPATION RATE

labour force participation rate

the percentage of the population (aged 15 years and over) in the labour force

The percentage of the population (aged 15 years and over) that is in the labour force is what economists call the **labour force participation rate.** Since 1976, there has been an increase in the labour force participation rate from 61.5 percent to 67.6 percent. The increase in the labour force participation rate can be attributed in large part to the entry of the baby boomers into the labour force and a 17.0 percentage point increase in the women's labour force participation rate.

Over the last 30 years, the number of women working has shifted dramatically, reflecting the changing role of women in the workforce. In Exhibit 4, we see that in 1976 only 46 percent of women were working or looking for work. Today that figure is roughly 63 percent. In 1976, over 77 percent of men were working or looking for work. Today the labour force participation rate for men has fallen to roughly 73 percent, as many men stay in school longer or opt to retire earlier.

Section Check

1. The consequences of unemployment to society include a reduction in potential output and consumption—a decrease in efficiency.
2. The unemployment rate is found by taking the number of people officially unemployed and dividing by the number in the labour force.
3. Unemployment rates are higher for teenagers, men, and those living in eastern Canada.
4. There are four main categories of unemployed workers: job losers, job leavers, re-entrants, and new entrants.
5. The duration of unemployment tends to be greater (smaller) when the amount of unemployment is high (low).

section 5.3

Different Types of Unemployment

- What are the three types of unemployment?
- What is frictional unemployment?
- What is structural unemployment?
- What is cyclical unemployment?
- What is the natural rate of unemployment?

In examining the status of and changes in the unemployment rate, it is important to recognize that there are numerous types of unemployment. In this section, we will examine these different types of unemployment and evaluate the relative impact of each on the overall unemployment rate.

FRICTIONAL UNEMPLOYMENT

Some unemployment results from people being temporarily between jobs. For example, consider an advertising executive who was laid off in Montreal on March 1 and is now actively looking for similar work in Calgary. This is an example of **frictional unemployment.** Of course, not all unemployed workers were laid off from their jobs; some may voluntarily quit their jobs. In either case, frictional unemployment is short term and results from the normal turnover in the labour market, such as when people change from one job to another.

frictional unemployment
unemployment from normal turnovers in the economy, such as when individuals change from one job to another

SHOULD WE WORRY ABOUT FRICTIONAL UNEMPLOYMENT?

Geographic and occupational mobility are considered good for the economy because they generally lead human resources to go from activities of relatively low productivity or value to areas of higher productivity, increasing output in society as well as the wage income of the mover. Hence, frictional unemployment, although not good in itself, is a by-product of a healthy phenomenon, and because it is often short-lived, it is generally not viewed as a serious problem. The amount of frictional unemployment varies somewhat over time; it tends to be greater in periods of low unemployment, when job opportunities are plentiful. This high level of job opportunities stimulates mobility, which, in turn, creates some frictional unemployment.

structural unemployment
unemployment persisting due to lack of skills necessary for available jobs

STRUCTURAL UNEMPLOYMENT

A second type of unemployment is structural unemployment. Like frictional unemployment, **structural unemployment** is related to occupational movement or mobility, or in this case, to a lack of mobility. Structural unemployment occurs when workers lack the necessary skills for jobs that are available or have particular skills that are no longer in demand. For example, if a machine operator in a manufacturing plant loses his job, he could still remain unemployed despite the openings for computer programmers in his community. The quantity of unemployed workers conceivably could equal the number of job vacancies, but the unemployment persists because the unemployed lack the appropriate skills. Given the existence of structural unemployment, it is wise to look at both unemployment and job vacancy statistics in assessing labour market conditions. Structural unemployment, like frictional unemployment, reflects the dynamic dimension of a changing economy. Over time, new jobs open up that require new skills, whereas old jobs that required different skills disappear. It is not surprising, then, that many people advocate government-subsidized retraining programs as a means of reducing structural unemployment.

The dimensions of structural unemployment are debatable, in part because of the difficulty in precisely defining the term in an operational sense. Structural unemployment

© JULES FRAZIER/PHOTODISC/GETTY ONE IMAGES

What type of unemployment would occur if these miners lost their jobs as a result of a reduction in demand for their output and needed retraining to find other employment? Usually structural unemployment occurs because of poor skills or long-term changes in demand. Consequently, it generally lasts for a longer period of time than frictional unemployment. In this situation, both might come into play.

varies considerably—sometimes it is low and at other times, like the 1970s and 1980s, it is high. To some extent, in this latter period, jobs in the traditional sectors like manufacturing and mining gave way to jobs in the computer and financial services sectors. Consequently, structural unemployment was higher.

IMPERFECTIONS AND UNEMPLOYMENT

Some unemployment is actually normal and important to the economy. Frictional and structural unemployment is simply unavoidable in a vibrant economy. To a considerable extent, one can view both frictional and structural unemployment as phenomena resulting from imperfections in the labour market. For example, if individuals seeking jobs and employers seeking workers had better information about each other, the amount of frictional unemployment would be considerably lower. It takes time for suppliers of labour to find the demanders of labour services, and it takes time and money for labour resources to acquire the necessary skills. But because information is not costless, and because job search also is costly, the bringing of demanders and suppliers of labour services together does not occur instantaneously.

CYCLICAL UNEMPLOYMENT

cyclical unemployment
unemployment due to short-term cyclical fluctuations in the economy

Often, unemployment is composed of more than just frictional and structural unemployment. In years of relatively high unemployment, some joblessness may result from short-term cyclical fluctuations in the economy. We call this **cyclical unemployment.** Whenever the unemployment rate is greater than the natural rate, or during a recession, there is cyclical unemployment.

REDUCING CYCLICAL UNEMPLOYMENT

Most economists believe cyclical unemployment is the most volatile form of unemployment. Given its volatility and dimensions, governments, rightly or wrongly, have viewed unemployment resulting from inadequate demand to be especially correctable through government policies. Most of the attempts to solve the unemployment problem have placed an emphasis on increasing aggregate demand to counter recessions. Attempts to reduce frictional unemployment by providing better labour market information and to reduce structural unemployment through job retraining have also been made, but these efforts have received fewer resources and much less attention from policymakers.

THE NATURAL RATE OF UNEMPLOYMENT

natural rate of unemployment
the "average" unemployment rate, equal to the sum of frictional and structural unemployment

Looking back at Exhibit 2 in Section 5.2, we see that the unemployment rate averaged around 6.9 percent during the 2000–2007 period. Some economists call this "average" unemployment rate the **natural rate of unemployment.** When unemployment rises well above 6.9 percent, we have abnormally high unemployment; when it falls below 6.9 percent, we have abnormally low unemployment. The natural rate of unemployment of approximately 6.9 percent equals the sum of frictional and structural unemployment. When unemployment rises above the natural rate, it reflects the existence of cyclical unemployment. In short, the natural rate of unemployment is the unemployment rate when there is neither a recession nor a boom.

The natural rate of unemployment can change over time as technological, demographic, institutional, and other conditions vary. For example, as baby boomers have

ACTIVE LEARNING EXERCISE

ACTIVE LEARNING EXERCISE

CYCLICAL UNEMPLOYMENT

Q: Are layoffs more prevalent during a recession than a recovery? Do most resignations occur during a recovery?

A: Layoffs are more likely to occur during a recession. When times are bad, employers are often forced to let workers go. Resignations are relatively more prevalent during good economic times because there are more job opportunities for those seeking new jobs.

aged, the natural rate has fallen because middle-aged workers generally have lower unemployment rates than younger workers. Thus, the natural rate is not fixed because it can change with demographic changes over time. In fact, it is estimated that the natural rate of unemployment was as low as about 5 percent in the 1960s, and then rose to about 8 percent in the 1980s. Today, most economists estimate the natural rate of unemployment to lie in a range between 6.0 and 7.0 percent.

Full Employment and Potential Output

When all of the economy's labour resources and other resources like capital are fully employed, the economy is said to be producing its potential level of output: that is, the amount these resources could produce if they were fully employed. Literal full employment of labour means that the economy is providing employment for all who are willing and able to work, with no cyclical unemployment. It also means that capital and land are fully employed. That is, at the natural rate of unemployment, all resources are fully employed and the economy is producing its **potential output** and there is no cyclical unemployment. This does not mean the economy will always be producing at its potential output of resources. For example, when the economy is experiencing cyclical unemployment, the unemployment rate is greater than the natural rate. It is also possible that the economy's output can temporarily exceed the potential output as workers take on overtime or moonlight by taking on extra employment.

potential output
the amount of real output the economy would produce if its labour and other resources were fully employed—that is, at the natural rate of unemployment

EMPLOYMENT INSURANCE

Losing a job can lead to considerable hardships, and employment insurance is designed to partially offset the severity of the unemployment problem. The program does not cover those who quit their jobs. To qualify, recipients must have worked a certain length of time. Although the program is intended to ease the pain of unemployment, it also leads to more frictional unemployment, as job seekers stay unemployed for longer periods of time searching for new jobs.

For example, some unemployed people may show little drive in seeking new employment, because employment insurance lowers the opportunity cost of being unemployed. Say a worker making $400 a week when employed receives $220 in compensation when unemployed; as a result, the cost of losing his job is not $400 a week in forgone income, but only $180.

Without employment insurance, job seekers would more likely take the first job offered even if did not match their preferences or skill levels. A longer job search might mean a better match but at the expense of lost production and greater amounts of tax dollars.

Will new technology in one industry displace workers in the whole economy? No. There may be some job loss of specific jobs or within certain industries. But the overall effect of technological improvements is the release of scarce resources for the expansion of output and employment in other areas and ultimately more economic growth and a higher standard of living.

DOES NEW TECHNOLOGY LEAD TO GREATER UNEMPLOYMENT?

Although many believe that technological advances inevitably result in the displacement of workers, this is not necessarily the case. New inventions are generally cost saving, and these cost savings will generally generate higher incomes for producers, and lower prices and better products for consumers, benefits that will ultimately result in the growth of other industries. If the new equipment is a substitute for labour, then it might displace workers. For example, many fast-food restaurants have substituted self-service beverage bars for workers. However, new capital equipment requires new workers to manufacture and repair the new equipment. The most famous example of this is the computer, which was supposed to displace thousands of workers. Although it did displace workers, the total job growth it generated exceeded the number of lost jobs. The problem is that it is easy to see just the initial effect of technological advances (displaced workers), without recognizing the implications of that invention for the whole economy over time.

Section Check

1. The three types of unemployment are frictional unemployment, structural unemployment, and cyclical unemployment.
2. Frictional unemployment results when a person moves from one job to another as a result of normal turnovers in the economy.
3. Structural unemployment results when people who are looking for jobs lack the required skills for the jobs that are available or a long-term change in demand occurs.
4. Cyclical unemployment is caused by a recession.
5. When cyclical unemployment is eliminated, our economy is said to be operating at full employment, or at a natural rate of unemployment.
6. Some unemployed persons may show little drive in seeking new employment, given the existence of employment insurance, which lowers the opportunity cost of being unemployed.

section 5.4 Inflation

- Why is the overall price level important?
- Who are the winners and losers during inflation?
- Can wage earners avoid the consequences of inflation?

price level
the average level of prices in the economy

inflation
a rise in the overall price level, which decreases the purchasing power of money

STABLE PRICE LEVEL AS A DESIRABLE GOAL

Just as full employment brings about economic security of one kind, an overall stable **price level** increases another form of security. Most prices in the Canadian economy tend to rise over time. The continuing rise in the *overall* price level is called **inflation.** Even when the level of prices is stable, some prices will be rising while others are falling.

However, when inflation is present, the goods and services with rising prices will outweigh the goods and services with falling prices. Without stability in the price level, consumers and producers will experience more difficulty in coordinating their plans and decisions. When the *overall* price level is falling, there is **deflation.**

In general, the only thing that can cause a *sustained* increase in the price level is a high rate of growth in money, a topic we will discuss thoroughly in the coming chapters.

deflation
a decrease in the overall price level, resulting in an increase of the purchasing power of money

THE PRICE LEVEL OVER THE YEARS

Unanticipated and sharp changes in the price level are almost universally considered to be "bad" and to require a policy remedy. What is the historical record of changes in the overall Canadian price level? Exhibit 1 shows changes in the consumer price index (CPI), the standard measure of inflation, from 1915 to 2007. As you can see from the chart, the Canadian economy experienced deflation in the early 1920s and the early 1930s. High rates of inflation, on the other hand, were experienced in the mid-1970s and early 1980s. Notice that since 1992, the annual inflation rate has remained below 3 percent, implying a substantial period of relatively low and stable inflation. Remember, however, that even when the inflation rate is only 3 percent per year, prices on average are rising, and the price level will double in 24 years.

WHO LOSES WITH INFLATION?

Inflation brings about changes in real incomes of persons, and these changes may be either desirable or undesirable. Suppose you retire on a fixed pension of $3000 per month. Over time, the $3000 will buy less and less if prices generally rise. Your real income—your income adjusted to reflect changes in purchasing power—falls. Inflation lowers income in real terms for people on fixed-dollar incomes. Likewise, inflation can hurt creditors. Suppose you loaned someone $1000 in 1997 and were paid back $1000 plus interest in 2007. The $1000 in principal you were paid back actually is worth less in 2007 than it was in 1997 because inflation has eroded the purchasing power of the dollar. Thus, inflation erodes the real wealth of the creditor. Another group that sometimes loses from inflation, at least temporarily, is people whose incomes are tied to long-term contracts. If inflation begins shortly after a labour union signs a three-year wage

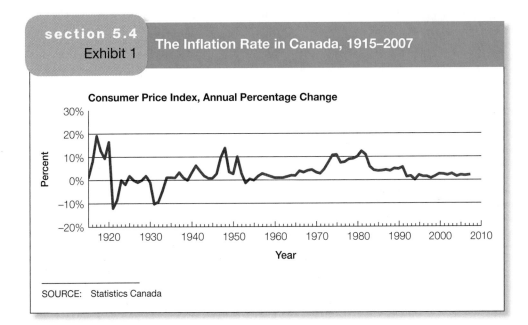

section 5.4
Exhibit 1   **The Inflation Rate in Canada, 1915–2007**

Consumer Price Index, Annual Percentage Change

SOURCE: Statistics Canada

agreement, it may completely eat up the wage gains provided by the contract. The same applies to businesses that agree to sell a quantity of something, say, phone service, for a fixed price for a given number of years.

If some people lose because of changing prices, others must gain. The debtor pays back dollars worth less in purchasing power than those she borrowed. Corporations that can quickly raise the prices on their goods may have revenue gains greater than their increases in costs, providing additional profits. The redistributional impact of inflation is not the result of conscious public policy; it just happens.

The uncertainty that inflation creates can also discourage investment and economic growth. Moreover, inflation can raise one nation's price level relative to that in other countries. In turn, this can make that nation's goods and services less competitive in international markets, or can decrease the value of the national currency relative to that of other countries. In its extreme form, inflation can lead to a complete erosion in faith in the value of the pieces of paper we commonly call money. In Germany after both world wars, prices rose so fast that people in some cases finally refused to take paper money, insisting instead on payment in goods or metals whose prices tend to move predictably with inflation. Unchecked inflation can feed on itself and ultimately lead to hyperinflation of 300 percent or more per year. We saw these rapid rates of inflation in Argentina in the 1980s and Brazil in the 1990s.

UNANTICIPATED INFLATION DISTORTS PRICE SIGNALS

In periods of high and variable inflation, households and firms have a difficult time distinguishing between changes in the relative prices of individual goods and services and changes in the general price level of all goods and services. Inflation distorts the information that flows from price signals. Does the good have a higher price because it has become relatively more scarce, and therefore more valuable relative to other goods, or did the price rise along with all other prices because of inflation? This muddying of price information undermines good decision making.

MENU AND SHOE-LEATHER COSTS

Another cost of inflation is that incurred by firms as a result of being forced to change prices more frequently. For example, a restaurant may have to print new menus, or a department or mail-order store may have to print new catalogues to reflect changing prices. These costs are called **menu costs,** and they are the costs of changing posted prices. In some South American economies in the 1980s, inflation increased at over 300 percent

menu costs
the costs imposed on a firm from changing listed prices

ACTIVE LEARNING EXERCISE

INFLATION

Q. Evaluate the following three statements: Inflation means: (1) that people have less money to spend; (2) that there are fewer goods available; and (3) that one must pay more money for goods purchased.

A. Of the three statements, only one is correct: With inflation, we must, on average, pay more money for the goods we purchase. Inflation does not necessarily mean we have fewer goods but rather that, on net, these goods have higher price tags. Inflation does not necessarily mean that people have less money to spend. Employees and unions will bargain for higher wages when there is inflation.

per year, with prices changing on a daily, or even hourly, basis in some cases. Imagine how large the menu costs could be in an economy such as that!

There is also the **shoe-leather cost** of inflation: the cost of going to and from the bank (and thus wearing out the leather on your shoes) to check on your assets. Specifically, high rates of inflation erode the value of a currency; this means that people will want to hold less currency—perhaps going to the ATM once a week rather than twice a month. That is, the higher inflation rates lead to higher nominal interest rates and this may induce more individuals to put money in a savings account at the bank rather than allowing it to depreciate in their pockets. The effects of shoe-leather costs of inflation, like menu costs, are very modest in countries with low inflation rates but can be quite large in countries where inflation is substantial.

shoe-leather cost
the cost incurred when individuals reduce their money holdings because of inflation

INFLATION AND INTEREST RATES

The interest rate is usually reported as the **nominal interest rate.** We determine the actual **real interest rate** by taking the nominal rate of interest and subtracting the inflation rate.

nominal interest rate
the reported interest rate that is not adjusted for inflation

real interest rate
the nominal interest rate minus the inflation rate; also called the inflation-adjusted interest rate

$$\text{Real interest rate} = \text{Nominal interest rate} - \text{Inflation rate}$$

For example, if the nominal interest rate was 5 percent and the inflation rate was 3 percent, then the real interest rate would be 2 percent.

If people can correctly anticipate inflation, they will behave in a manner that will largely protect them against loss. Consider the creditor who believes that the overall price level will rise 6 percent a year, based on the immediate past experience. Would that creditor lend money to someone at a 5 percent rate of interest? No. A 5 percent rate of interest means that a person borrowing $1000 now will pay back $1050 ($1000 plus 5 percent of $1000) one year from now. But if prices go up 6 percent, it will take $1060 to buy what $1000 does today. (That is, $1060 is 6 percent more than $1000.) Thus, the person who lends at 5 percent will get paid back an amount ($1050) that is less than the purchasing power of the original loan ($1060) at the time it was paid back. The real interest rate, then, would actually be negative. Hence, to protect themselves, lenders will demand a rate of interest large enough to compensate for the deteriorating value of the dollar.

ANTICIPATED INFLATION AND THE NOMINAL INTEREST RATE

The economic theory behind the behavioural responses of creditors and debtors to anticipated inflation is straightforward and can be expressed in a simple diagram (Exhibit 2). An interest rate is, in effect, the price that one pays for the use of funds. Like other prices, interest rates are determined by the interaction of demand and supply forces. The lower the interest rate (price), the greater the quantity of loanable funds demanded, *ceteris paribus;* the higher the interest rate (price), the greater the quantity of loanable funds supplied by individuals and institutions like banks, *ceteris paribus.* Suppose that in an environment where prices in general are expected to remain stable in the near future, the demand for loanable funds is depicted by D_0 and the supply of such funds is indicated by S_0. In this scenario, the equilibrium price, or interest rate, will be r_0, where the quantity demanded equals the quantity supplied.

When people start expecting future inflation, creditors such as banks will become less willing to lend funds at any given interest rate because they fear they will be repaid in dollars of lesser value than those they loaned. This is depicted by a leftward shift in the supply curve of loanable funds (a decrease in supply) to S_1. Likewise, demanders of funds (borrowers) are more anxious to borrow because they think they will pay their loans back in

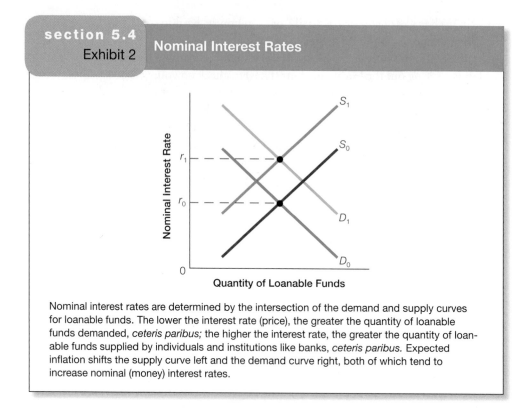

section 5.4
Exhibit 2

Nominal Interest Rates

Nominal interest rates are determined by the intersection of the demand and supply curves for loanable funds. The lower the interest rate (price), the greater the quantity of loanable funds demanded, *ceteris paribus;* the higher the interest rate, the greater the quantity of loanable funds supplied by individuals and institutions like banks, *ceteris paribus.* Expected inflation shifts the supply curve left and the demand curve right, both of which tend to increase nominal (money) interest rates.

dollars of lesser purchasing power than the dollars they borrowed. Thus, the demand for funds increases from D_0 to D_1. Both the decrease in supply and the increase in demand push up the interest rate to a new equilibrium, r_1. Whether the equilibrium quantity of loanable funds will increase or decrease depends on the relative sizes of the shifts in the respective curves.

DO CREDITORS ALWAYS LOSE DURING INFLATION?

Usually lenders are able to anticipate inflation with reasonable accuracy. For example, in the early 1980s, when the inflation rate was over 10 percent a year, nominal interest rates on a three-month Treasury bill were relatively high. Since 2000, with low inflation rates, the nominal interest rate has been relatively low. If the inflation rate is anticipated accurately, new creditors will not lose nor will debtors gain from a change in the inflation rate. However, nominal interest rates and real interest rates do not always run together. For example, in periods of high *unexpected* inflation, the nominal interest rates can be very high whereas the real interest rates may be very low or even negative.

PROTECTING OURSELVES FROM INFLATION

Some groups try to protect themselves from inflation by using cost-of-living clauses in contracts. In labour union contracts with these clauses, workers automatically get wage increases that reflect rising prices. The same is true of some private pension plans that are adjusted for inflation, as well as the government-run Canada Pension Plan. Personal income taxes also are now indexed (adjusted) for inflation. However, some of the tax code is still not indexed for inflation. This can affect the incentives to work, save, and invest.

Some economists have argued that we should go one step further and index everything, meaning that all contractual arrangements would be adjusted frequently to take account of changing prices. Such an arrangement might reduce the impact of inflation,

ACTIVE LEARNING EXERCISE

ACTIVE LEARNING EXERCISE

ANTICIPATED INFLATION AND INTEREST RATES

Q: Suppose you had a five-year, fixed-interest mortgage on a home, which you purchased three years ago. In the meantime, the inflation rate has fallen considerably and probably will not reach that higher level again. Did you get a good interest rate on your loan?

A: No. You will be paying a higher interest rate to borrow money than others who have borrowed money more recently. In other words, the real interest rate you paid in the first years of your loan was less than the real interest you will pay on the final years of your loan.

but it would also entail additional contracting costs. An alternative approach has been to try to stop inflation through various policies relating to the amount of government spending, tax rates, or the amount of money created.

Section Check

SECTION CHECK

1. Unanticipated inflation causes unpredictable transfers of wealth and reduces the efficiency of the market system by distorting price signals.
2. Inflation generally hurts creditors and those on fixed incomes and pensions; debtors generally benefit from inflation.
3. The nominal interest rate is the actual amount of interest you pay. The real interest rate is the nominal rate minus the inflation rate.
4. Wage earners attempt to keep pace with inflation by demanding higher wages each year or by indexing their annual wage to inflation.

Economic Fluctuations

- What are short-term economic fluctuations?
- What are the four stages of a business cycle?
- Is there a difference between a recession and a depression?

SHORT-TERM FLUCTUATIONS IN ECONOMIC GROWTH

The aggregate amount of economic activity in Canada and most other nations has increased markedly over time, even on a per capita basis, indicating long-term economic growth. Short-term fluctuations in the level of economic activity also occur. We sometimes call these short-term fluctuations **business cycles.** Exhibit 1 illustrates the distinction between long-term economic growth and short-term economic fluctuations. Over a long period of time, the line representing economic activity slopes upward, indicating increasing real output. Over short time periods, however, there are downward, as well as upward, output changes. Business cycles refer to the short-term ups and downs in economic activity, not to the long-term trend in output, which in modern times has been upward.

business cycles
short-term fluctuations in the economy relative to the long-term trend in output

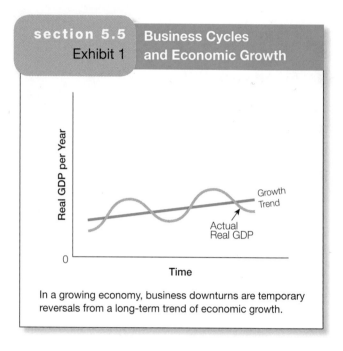

section 5.5
Exhibit 1
Business Cycles and Economic Growth

In a growing economy, business downturns are temporary reversals from a long-term trend of economic growth.

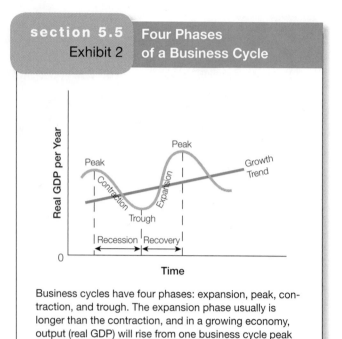

section 5.5
Exhibit 2
Four Phases of a Business Cycle

Business cycles have four phases: expansion, peak, contraction, and trough. The expansion phase usually is longer than the contraction, and in a growing economy, output (real GDP) will rise from one business cycle peak to the next.

THE PHASES OF A BUSINESS CYCLE

expansion

when output (real GDP) is rising significantly—the period between the trough of a recession and the next peak

peak

the point in time when the expansion comes to an end, when output is at the highest point in the cycle

contraction

when the economy's output is falling—measured from the peak to the trough

recession

a period of significant decline in output and employment

trough

the point in time when output stops declining; it is the moment when business activity is at its lowest point in the cycle

A business cycle has four phases—expansion, peak, contraction, and trough—as illustrated in Exhibit 2. The period of **expansion** occurs when output (real GDP) is rising significantly. Usually during the expansion phase, unemployment is falling and both consumer and business confidence is high. Thus, investment spending by firms is rising, as well as expenditures for expensive durable consumer goods, such as automobiles and household appliances. The **peak** is the point in time when the expansion comes to an end, when output is at the highest point in the cycle. The **contraction** is a period of falling real output, and is usually accompanied by rising unemployment and declining business and consumer confidence. The contraction phase is measured from the peak to the trough. Investment spending by firms and expenditures on consumer durable goods fall sharply in a typical contraction. This contraction phase is also called **recession,** a period of significant decline in output and employment (lasting at least six months). The **trough** is the point in time when output stops declining; it is the moment when business activity is at its lowest point in the cycle. Unemployment is relatively high at the trough, although the actual maximum amount of unemployment may not occur exactly at the trough. Often, unemployment remains fairly high well into the expansion phase. The expansion phase is measured from the trough to the peak.

Exhibit 3 shows the growth in Canadian real GDP over the 1962–2007 period. On an annual basis, you can see that there were two major recessions during this period; in 1982, the economy declined by 2.9 percent, whereas in 1991, the economy contracted by 2.1 percent. The sharp drop in output in 1982 was the deepest recession the economy had experienced since the Great Depression of the 1930s. The 1982 recession was accompanied by a sharp rise in unemployment, with the unemployment rate rising to 11.0 percent, from 7.6 percent in 1981.

You will notice from Exhibit 3 that the 1991 recession was different from the 1982 recession in that it was much more prolonged. The economy actually stagnated in 1990,

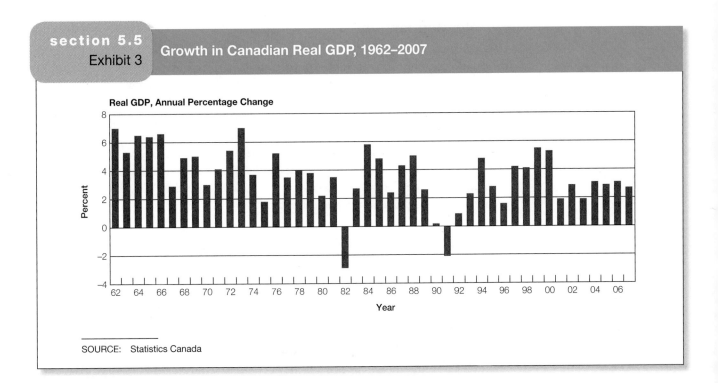

Growth in Canadian Real GDP, 1962–2007

Real GDP, Annual Percentage Change

SOURCE: Statistics Canada

contracted in 1991, and stayed in a state of decline for most of 1992. Again, this recession was accompanied by a sharp rise in unemployment, with the unemployment rate rising to 11.2 percent in 1992, from 7.5 percent in 1989. In fact, the unemployment rate remained above 10 percent through 1994, even as the economy entered the expansion phase, which is a characteristic of unemployment that we discussed previously.

You will also notice that the expansion phase of the business cycle is characterized by varying rates of economic growth. In 1962 and 1973, for example, the economy grew at a very rapid pace of 7.0 percent per year. In other years, economic growth can be much more sluggish, as in 1975 and 2003, when the economy grew by less than 2 percent each year.

HOW LONG DOES A BUSINESS CYCLE LAST?

As you can see from Exhibit 3, there is no uniformity to a business cycle's length. This is why economists often call them economic fluctuations rather than business cycles, since there is not the regularity that a cycle implies. Severe recessions are called **depressions.** Likewise, a prolonged expansion in economic activity is sometimes called a **boom.** For example, during the Great Depression, real GDP contracted for four consecutive years, from 1930 to 1933. An economic boom occurred during the 1960s when real GDP grew by about 6 percent a year on average over that decade.

depressions
severe recessions, or contraction in output

boom
period of prolonged economic expansion

FORECASTING CYCLICAL CHANGES

The farmer and the aviator rely heavily on weather forecasters for information on climatic conditions in planning their activities. Similarly, businesses, government agencies, and, to a lesser extent, consumers rely on economic forecasts to learn of forthcoming developments in the business cycle. If it looks like the economy will continue in an expansionary phase, businesses might expand production to meet a perceived forthcoming need; if it looks like contraction is coming, perhaps they will be more cautious.

Forecasting Models

Using theoretical models, which will be discussed in later chapters, economists gather statistics on economic activity in the immediate past, including, for example, consumer expenditures, business inventories, the supply of money, governmental expenditures, tax revenues, and so on. Using past historical relationships between these factors and the overall level of economic activity (which form the basis of the economic theories), they formulate *econometric models*. Statistics from the immediate past are plugged into the model and forecasts are made. Because human behaviour changes and we cannot correctly make assumptions about certain future developments, our numbers are imperfect and our econometric models are not always accurate. Like the weather forecasts, although the econometric models are not perfect, they are helpful.

Leading Economic Indicators

leading economic indicators
factors that typically change before changes in economic activity

One less sophisticated but very useful forecasting tool is watching trends in **leading economic indicators.** Some types of economic activity change before the economy as a whole changes. Statistics Canada has identified ten such leading indicators: furniture and applicance sales, other durable goods sales, length of average workweek, new orders in manufacturing, shipments-to-inventory ratio, housing starts, business and personal services employment, index of stock prices, money supply, and the U.S. leading indicator. Statistics Canada combines all of these into a composite index of leading indicators. If the index rises sharply for two or three months, it is likely (but not certain) that increases in the overall level of activity will follow.

Although the leading economic indicators do provide a warning of a likely downturn, they do not provide accurate information on the depth or the duration of the downturn.

In The **NEWS**

RECESSION? WE'LL KNOW SOON

BY WILLIAM WATSON

It would be nice if we had a rule that said, for instance, housing falls more than x%, Recession happens. Or: cut interest rates y-hundred basis points, Recession averted. But of course economics isn't like that. Too many things happen at once. Every economic event is different. Every event in physics is different, too, but somehow all the physics events seem to follow the rules. In economics, we write "law" only with quotation marks.

So will there be a recession? Ed Leamer, who teaches at UCLA and is one of the leading academic economists in the United States, just wrote a paper whose title suggests something very close to an economic law: "Housing is the Business Cycle." In fact, he concludes that the "business cycle" is actually a "consumer cycle" and that housing largely runs it. A serious downturn in housing has preceded eight of the 10 post-war U.S. recessions. The two exceptions were 1953, when peace in Korea killed defence spending, and 2000–01, when the Internet got its "comeuppance."

Only twice has the United States experienced a housing downturn without a recession following, in 1951 and 1967. Both times, Leamer writes, "the Department of Defense came to the rescue, because of the Korean War and the Vietnam War. We don't want that kind of rescue this time, do we?"

What do the Fates have in store for Canada for 2008? I'm with Sam Goldwyn: "Never forecast, especially about the future." But *evidence suggests* that if a Recession is coming, we'll know soon enough. Between August, 1981, and August, 1982, the unemployment rate rose five full points. Between March, 1990, and March, 1991, it jumped more than three points. If it happens, it will happen fast.

SOURCE: William Watson, *National Post,* Don Mills, Ontario, December 21, 2007, p. FP15. Material reprinted with the express permission of: *The National Post Company,* a CanWest Partnership.

CONSIDER THIS:

Unfortunately, the "laws of economics" do not have the same predictability as the "laws of nature." The housing downturn in the Unites States, the soaring price of oil, the value of the Canadian dollar, and the list goes on. . . The one thing we can predict about the economy is that the future is largely unpredictable.

Section Check

1. Business cycles (or economic fluctuations) are short-term fluctuations in the amount of economic activity, relative to the long-term growth trend in output.
2. The four phases of a business cycle are expansion, peak, contraction, and trough.
3. Recessions occur during the contraction phase of a business cycle. Severe, long-term recessions are called depressions.
4. The economy often goes through short-term contractions even during a long-term growth trend.

Summary

Section 5.1
- The most important macroeconomic goals are full employment, price stability, and economic growth.

Section 5.2
- The consequences of unemployment to society include a reduction in potential output and consumption—a decrease in efficiency.
- The unemployment rate is found by taking the number of people officially unemployed and dividing by the number in the labour force.
- There are four main categories of unemployed workers: job losers, job leavers, re-entrants, and new entrants.
- The duration of unemployment tends to be greater (smaller) when the amount of unemployment is high (low).

Section 5.3
- The three types of unemployment are frictional unemployment, structural unemployment, and cyclical unemployment.
- Frictional unemployment results from people moving from one job to another.
- Structural unemployment results when people who are looking for jobs lack the required skills for the available jobs.
- Cyclical unemployment is caused by a recession.

- The natural rate of unemployment is attributable to structural and frictional unemployment only; no cyclical unemployment is thought to be present.

Section 5.4
- Price stability provides security in the marketplace by ensuring constant purchasing power of a nation's currency.
- Inflation generally hurts creditors and those on fixed incomes and pensions; debtors generally benefit from unexpected inflation whereas creditors generally are hurt.
- Inflation distorts price signals, leads to shoe-leather costs and menu costs, arbitrarily redistributes wealth, and discourages long-term planning and investment.
- The nominal interest rate is the actual amount of interest you pay.
- The real interest rate is the nominal rate minus the inflation rate.

Section 5.5
- Business cycles are short-term fluctuations in economic activity, relative to the long-term trend in output.
- The four phases of a business cycle are expansion, peak, contraction, and trough.
- Recessions occur during the contraction phase of a business cycle.
- Severe, long-term recessions are called depressions.

Key Terms and Concepts

For a complete glossary of chapter key terms, visit the textbook's Web site at http://www.sextonmacro2e.nelson.com.

real gross domestic product (RGDP) 115
labour force 117
unemployment rate 118

discouraged worker 118
job loser 120
job leaver 120
re-entrant 120

new entrant 120
underemployment 120
labour force participation rate 122
frictional unemployment 123

structural unemployment 123
cyclical unemployment 124
natural rate of unemployment 124
potential output 125
price level 126
inflation 126
deflation 127

menu costs 128
shoe-leather cost 129
nominal interest rate 129
real interest rate 129
business cycles 131
expansion 132
peak 132

contraction 132
recession 132
trough 132
depressions 133
boom 133
leading economic indicators 134

Review Questions

1. Which of the following individuals would economists consider unemployed?

   a. Sam looked for work for several weeks, but has now given up his search and is going back to university.

   b. A 12-year-old wants to mow lawns for extra cash but is unable to find neighbours willing to hire him.

   c. A factory worker is temporarily laid off but expects to be called back to work soon.

   d. A receptionist, who works only 20 hours per week, would like to work 40 hours per week.

   e. A high-school graduate spends his days backpacking across the country rather than seeking work.

2. Identify whether each of the following reflects structural, frictional, or cyclical unemployment.

   a. A real estate agent is laid off due to slow business after housing sales fall.

   b. An automotive worker is replaced by robotic equipment on the assembly line.

   c. A salesperson quits a job in Ontario and seeks a new career after moving to Alberta.

   d. An employee is fired due to poor job performance and searches the want ads each day for work.

3. Calculate the unemployment rate for an economy using the following data:

Number of employed:	8 million
Number of unemployed:	1.5 million
Number of discouraged workers:	0.5 million
Total adult population:	16 million

4. Employment insurance benefits in the United States tend to be both less generous and available for shorter periods of time than in Canada. What impact do you think this is likely to have on the unemployment rate in the United States? Why?

5. How can unions result in higher unemployment rates? How would the results differ for someone who wants to be employed in the union sector than for someone who currently has a job in the union sector?

6. You borrow $10 000 at a nominal interest rate of 6 percent. What is the real rate of interest when the inflation rate is

   a. 2 percent?

   b. 6 percent?

   c. 8 percent?

7. You borrow money at a fixed rate of interest to finance your university education. If the rate of inflation unexpectedly slows down between the time you take out the loan and the time you begin paying it back, is there a redistribution of income? What if you already expected the inflation rate to slow at the time you took out the loan? Explain.

8. How does a variable rate mortgage agreement protect lenders against inflation? Who bears the inflation risk?

Fill in the Blanks

Section 5.1

1. There are three major macroeconomic goals: maintaining employment at _____ levels; maintaining prices at a _____ level; and achieving a _____ rate of economic growth.

2. We use _____ to measure output or production.

Section 5.2

3. With high rates of unemployment, society loses some potential _____ of goods and services.

4. The unemployment rate is the number of people officially _____ divided by _____.

5. The labour force is the number of people aged 15 and over who are either _____ or _____.

6. _____ workers who have not actively sought work are not counted as unemployed; instead, they fall out of the _____.

7. Some people working fewer hours than they desire might be considered to be _____ employed.

8. There are four main categories of unemployed workers: job _____ (laid off or fired), job _____ (quit), _____ (worked before and now re-entering the labour force), and _____ entrants (entering the labour force for first time).

9. _____ typically account for the largest fraction of those unemployed.

10. In the short run, a reduction in unemployment may come at the expense of a higher rate of _____, especially if the economy is close to full capacity.

11. Trying to match employees with jobs quickly may lead to significant inefficiencies because of _____ between a worker's skill level and the level of skill required for a job.

12. The duration of unemployment tends to be greater when the amount of unemployment is _____ and smaller when the amount of unemployment is _____.

13. The percentage of the adult population that is in the labour force is called the _____ rate.

Section 5.3

14. Frictional unemployment is _____ term and results from the _____ turnover in the labour market.

15. Frictional unemployment tends to be somewhat _____ in periods of low unemployment, when job opportunities are plentiful.

16. If individuals seeking jobs and employers seeking workers had better information about each other, the amount of frictional unemployment would be considerably _____.

17. _____ unemployment reflects the existence of persons who lack the necessary skills for jobs that are available.

18. _____ unemployment is the most volatile form of unemployment.

19. Most of the attempts to solve the unemployment problem have placed an emphasis on increasing _____.

20. Job-retraining programs have the potential to reduce _____ unemployment.

21. The natural rate of unemployment equals the sum of _____ and _____ unemployment.

22. One can view unemployment rates below the _____ rate as reflecting the existence of a below-average level of frictional and structural unemployment.

23. The natural rate of unemployment is the "average" unemployment rate, equal to the sum of _____ and _____ unemployment.

24. The natural rate of unemployment may change over time as _____, _____, _____, and other conditions vary.

25. When all of the economy's labour resources and other resources, like capital, are fully employed, the economy is said to be producing its _____ level of output.

26. When the economy is experiencing cyclical unemployment, the unemployment rate is _____ than the natural rate.

27. The economy can _____ exceed potential output as workers take on overtime or moonlight by taking on extra employment.

Section 5.4

28. Without price stability, consumers and producers will experience more difficulty in _____ their plans and decisions.

29. In general, the only thing that can cause a sustained increase in the price level is a _____ rate of growth in money.

30. The _____ is the standard measure of the price level.

31. Retirees on fixed pensions, creditors, and those whose incomes are tied to long-term contracts can be hurt by inflation because inflation _____ the purchasing power of the money they receive.

32. The _____ that inflation creates can discourage investment and economic growth.

33. Inflation can _____ one nation's price level relative to price levels in other countries, which can lead to a loss in competitiveness or to a decline in the value of the national currency relative to that of other countries.

34. In periods of high and variable inflation, households and firms have a difficult time distinguishing changes in _____ prices from changes in the general price level, distorting the information that flows from price signals.

35. _____ costs are the costs of changing posted prices.

36. _____ costs are the costs of checking on your assets.

37. The real interest rate equals the _____ interest rate minus the _____ rate.

38. The _____ the interest rate, the greater the quantity of funds people will demand, *ceteris paribus;* the _____ the interest rate, the greater the quantity of loanable funds supplied, *ceteris paribus.*

39. When creditors start expecting future inflation, there will be a _____ shift in the supply curve of loanable funds. Likewise, demanders of funds (borrowers) are more willing to borrow because they think they will pay their loans back in dollars of lesser purchasing power than the dollars they borrowed. Thus, the demand for funds increases.

40. If the inflation rate is _____ anticipated, new creditors do not lose, nor do debtors gain, from inflation.

41. Groups try to protect themselves from inflation by using _____ clauses in contracts.

Section 5.5

42. Business cycles refer to the _____-_____ fluctuations in economic activity, not to the _____-_____ trend in output.

43. A business cycle has four phases: _____, _____, _____, and _____.

44. Expansion occurs when output is _____ significantly, unemployment is _____, and both consumer and business confidence is _____.

45. The _____ occurs when an expansion comes to an end, when output is at the highest point in the business cycle; whereas the _____ is the point in time when output stops declining, when business activity is at its lowest point in the business cycle.

46. Businesses, government agencies, and, to a lesser extent, consumers rely on economic _____ to learn of forthcoming developments in the business cycles.

47. If the index of _____ increases sharply for two or three months, it is likely (but not certain) that increases in the overall level of activity will follow.

48. Although the leading economic indicators do provide a warning of a likely downturn, they do not provide accurate information on the _____ or _____ of the downturn.

True or False

Section 5.1

1. Economic growth means a growth in real output over time.

2. Individuals, because they may differ considerably in their evaluation of the relative importance of certain issues, may disagree about whether certain "problems" are really problems after all.

3. Economic growth is considered positively by all persons.

Section 5.2

4. Other things being equal, relatively high rates of unemployment are almost universally viewed as bad.

5. The unemployment rate is the number of people officially unemployed divided by a country's population aged 15 or over.

6. The labour force figure excludes homemakers, retirees, and full-time students because they are not considered to be currently looking for employment.

7. By far the worst employment downturn in Canadian history was the Great Depression.

8. During the Great Depression the unemployment rate reached almost 20 percent.

9. Discouraged workers, who have not actively sought work, are counted as unemployed.

10. People looking for full-time work who grudgingly settle for a part-time job are counted as employed, even though they are only "partly" employed.

11. Some people working in the underground economy may be counted in labour statistics as unemployed, whereas others may be counted as not in the labour force.

12. Unemployment rates are usually very similar across different provinces in Canada.

13. In the short run, a reduction in unemployment may come at the expense of a higher rate of inflation.

14. The duration of unemployment tends to be greater when the amount of unemployment is low, and smaller when the amount of unemployment is high.

15. Unemployment means a loss of potential output.

16. When the baby boom generation began entering the labour force, it raised the labour force participation rate.

Section 5.3

17. Frictional unemployment results from persons being temporarily between jobs.

18. Frictional unemployment, although not good in itself, is a by-product of a healthy phenomenon, and because it is short-lived, it is not generally viewed as a serious problem.

19. Structural employment can arise because jobs that require particular skills disappear.

20. Structural unemployment is easily measured and stable over time.

21. Cyclical unemployment may result from an insufficient level of demand for goods and services.

22. Given its volatility and dimensions, governments have viewed unemployment resulting from inadequate demand to be especially correctable through government policies.

23. The natural rate of unemployment equals the sum of frictional and cyclical unemployment.

24. When unemployment rises above the natural rate, it reflects the existence of cyclical unemployment.

25. The natural rate of unemployment does not change over time.

26. At the natural rate of unemployment, the economy is producing its potential output.

27. When the economy is experiencing cyclical unemployment, the unemployment rate is less than the natural rate.

Section 5.4

28. In both inflation and deflation, a country's currency unit changes in purchasing power.

29. Unanticipated and sharp price changes are almost universally considered to be a "bad" thing that needs to be remedied by some policy.

30. Debtors lose from inflation.

31. Wage earners will lose from inflation if wages rise at a slower rate than the price level.

32. Inflation brings about changes in real incomes of persons.

33. Menu costs and shoe-leather costs are modest, regardless of the rate of inflation.

34. The real interest rate equals the nominal interest rate plus the inflation rate.

35. If people correctly anticipate inflation, they will behave in a manner that will largely protect them against loss.

36. When people start expecting future inflation, creditors become less willing to lend funds at any given interest rate because they fear they will be repaid in dollars of lesser value than those they loaned.

37. When borrowers of funds start expecting future inflation, the demand for funds decreases.

38. When both suppliers and demanders of funds begin to expect inflation, it will push up the interest rate to a new higher equilibrium level.

39. In periods of high unexpected inflation, the nominal interest rate can be very high whereas the real interest rate is low or even negative.

Section 5.5

40. In a growing economy, real GDP will tend to rise from one business cycle peak to the next.

41. In an expansion, investment spending is rising, but expenditures for expensive durable consumer goods are falling.

42. A contraction is a period of falling real output and is usually accompanied by rising unemployment and declining business and consumer confidence.

43. Unemployment falls substantially as soon as the economy enters the expansion phase of the business cycle.

44. There is no uniformity to a business cycle's length.

Multiple Choice

Section 5.1

1. Which is *not* one of society's major economic goals?
   a. maintaining employment at high levels
   b. maintaining prices at a stable level
   c. maintaining a high rate of economic growth
   d. All of the above are major economic goals of society.

2. The three major macroeconomic goals of nearly every society are
   a. maintaining stable prices, reducing interest rates, and achieving a high rate of economic growth.
   b. maintaining high levels of employment, increasing the supply of money, and achieving a high rate of economic growth.
   c. maintaining stable prices, maintaining high levels of employment, and achieving high rates of economic growth.
   d. achieving high rates of economic growth, reducing unemployment, and reducing interest rates.

3. With regard to macroeconomic goals, which is *not* true?
   a. Individuals differ considerably in their evaluation of the relative importance of certain issues.
   b. Individuals disagree on whether certain "problems" are really problems.
   c. Everyone views economic growth positively.
   d. Some individuals disagree about the appropriate distribution of income.
   e. All of the above *are* true.

4. Economic growth is measured by changes in
   a. nominal GDP.
   b. the money supply.
   c. real GDP.
   d. the rate of unemployment.
   e. none of the above.

Section 5.2

5. High rates of unemployment
   a. can lead to increased tensions and despair.
   b. result in the loss of some potential output in society.
   c. reduce the possible level of consumption in society.
   d. represent a loss of efficiency in society.
   e. All of the above are true.

6. The unemployment rate is the number of people officially unemployed divided by
   a. the labour force.
   b. the adult population.
   c. the total population.
   d. the number of people employed.
   e. none of the above.

7. The labour force consists of
   a. discouraged workers, employed workers, and those actively seeking work.
   b. all persons aged 15 and over who are working or actively seeking work.
   c. all persons aged 15 and over who are able to work.
   d. all persons aged 15 and over who are working, plus those not working.
   e. discouraged workers, part-time workers, and full-time workers.

8. The labour force includes which of the following groups?
   a. discouraged workers
   b. those who are currently working part-time
   c. homemakers
   d. retirees
   e. all of the above

9. Discouraged workers
   a. are considered unemployed.
   b. are considered as not in the labour force.
   c. are considered as in the labour force.
   d. are considered as both unemployed and in the labour force.
   e. are considered as unemployed but not in the labour force.

10. Which of these provinces tends to have the lowest unemployment rate?
    a. Quebec
    b. Ontario
    c. Alberta
    d. Newfoundland and Labrador

11. The largest fraction of those counted as unemployed is due to
    a. job losers.
    b. job leavers.
    c. new entrants.
    d. re-entrants.

12. In Littletown, there are 1000 people aged 15 and over; 800 are in the labour force, and 600 are employed. The unemployment rate is
    a. 33 percent.
    b. 25 percent.
    c. 20 percent.
    d. 75 percent.
    e. none of the above.

13. The official unemployment rate may overstate the extent of unemployment because
    a. it excludes discouraged workers.
    b. it counts part-time workers as fully employed.
    c. it does not count those with jobs in the underground economy as employed.
    d. it includes those who claim to be looking for work as unemployed, even if they are just going through the motions in order to get government benefits.
    e. of both c and d.

14. The unemployment rate may underestimate the true extent of unemployment if
    a. employees increase the number of hours they work overtime.
    b. many people become discouraged and cease looking for work.
    c. there are a large number of people working in the underground economy.
    d. any of the above occur.

15. If employment insurance benefits increase and that leads more people to claim to be seeking work when they are not really seeking work, the measured unemployment rate would
    a. rise.
    b. fall.
    c. be unaffected.
    d. change in an indeterminate direction.

16. After looking for a job for more than eight months, Kyle has become frustrated and stopped looking. Economists view Kyle as
    a. unemployed.
    b. part of the labour force, but neither employed nor unemployed.
    c. a discouraged worker.
    d. cyclically unemployed.
    e. both b and c.

17. Persons who do not have jobs and who do not look for work are considered
    a. unemployed.
    b. out of the labour force.
    c. underemployed.
    d. overemployed.
    e. part of the underground economy.

18. If the unemployment rate is 6 percent and the number of persons unemployed is 6 million, the number of people employed is equal to
    a. 100 million.
    b. 94 million.
    c. 106 million.
    d. 6 million.
    e. none of the above.

19. The four main categories of unemployed workers are
    a. discouraged workers, part-time workers, the cyclically unemployed, and the frictionally unemployed.
    b. discouraged workers, job losers, new entrants, and the underemployed.
    c. new entrants, job losers, job leavers, and re-entrants.
    d. job losers, job leavers, the structurally unemployed, and the frictionally unemployed.

Section 5.3

20. Frictional unemployment is
    a. unemployment that is due to normal turnover in the labour market.
    b. unemployment caused by automation in the workplace.
    c. unemployment caused by lack of training and education.
    d. unemployment that is due to the friction of competing ideological systems.
    e. all of the above.

21. Unemployment caused by a contraction in the economy is called
    a. frictional unemployment.
    b. cyclical unemployment.
    c. structural unemployment.
    d. seasonal unemployment.

22. A federal government program aimed at retraining the unemployed workers of the declining fishing industry is designed to reduce which type of unemployment?
    a. seasonal
    b. cyclical
    c. structural
    d. frictional

23. When unemployment rises above the natural rate, it reflects the existence of _____ unemployment.
    a. frictional
    b. structural
    c. seasonal
    d. cyclical

24. When an economy is operating at full employment,
    a. the unemployment rate will equal zero.
    b. frictional unemployment will equal zero.
    c. cyclical unemployment will equal zero.
    d. structural unemployment will equal zero.
    e. both b and d are correct.

25. The natural rate of unemployment would increase when which of the following increases?
    a. frictional unemployment
    b. structural unemployment
    c. cyclical unemployment
    d. any of the above
    e. either frictional or structural unemployment

26. If a nation's labour force receives a significant influx of young workers,
    a. the natural rate of unemployment is likely to increase.
    b. the natural rate of unemployment is likely to decrease.
    c. the natural rate of unemployment is unlikely to change.
    d. frictional unemployment will likely decrease to zero.

27. Which of the following is false?
    a. At the natural rate of unemployment, the economy is considered to be at full employment.
    b. At full employment, the economy is producing at its potential output.
    c. If unemployment is greater than its natural rate, the economy is producing at greater than its potential output.
    d. If we are at less than full employment, some cyclical unemployment exists.

Section 5.4

28. When would consumers and producers experience increased difficulty in coordinating their plans and decisions?
    a. in a period of inflation
    b. in a period of deflation
    c. in either a period of inflation or deflation
    d. none of the above

29. Inflation can harm
    a. retirees on fixed pensions.
    b. borrowers who have long-term fixed interest rate loans.
    c. wage earners whose incomes grow slower than inflation.
    d. either a or c.
    e. all of the above.

30. Inflation will be least harmful if
    a. interest rates are not adjusted accordingly when inflation occurs.
    b. worker wages are set by long-term contracts.
    c. it is correctly anticipated and interest rates adjust accordingly.
    d. it is not fully anticipated.

31. Unexpected inflation generally benefits
    a. lenders.
    b. borrowers.
    c. the poor.
    d. people on fixed incomes.

32. The costs of inflation include
   a. menu costs.
   b. shoe-leather costs.
   c. a distortion of price signals.
   d. all of the above.

33. If the nominal interest rate is 9 percent and the inflation rate is 3 percent, the real interest rate is
   a. 3 percent.
   b. 6 percent.
   c. 9 percent.
   d. 12 percent.
   e. 27 percent.

34. What is the real interest rate paid on a loan bearing 7 percent nominal interest per year if the inflation rate is 6 percent?
   a. 13 percent
   b. 7 percent
   c. 6 percent
   d. 1 percent

35. If people correctly anticipate inflation, it will
   a. benefit borrowers.
   b. benefit lenders.
   c. benefit neither borrowers nor lenders.
   d. harm both borrowers and lenders.

36. If there is an increase in the expected future rate of inflation, it will
   a. increase the supply of funds.
   b. decrease the supply of funds.
   c. increase the demand for funds.
   d. decrease the demand for funds.
   e. do both b and c.

Section 5.5

37. A business cycle reflects changes in economic activity, particularly real GDP. The stages of a business cycle in order are
   a. expansion, peak, contraction, and trough.
   b. expansion, trough, contraction, and peak.
   c. contraction, recession, expansion, and boom.
   d. trough, expansion, contraction, and peak.

38. In the contraction phase of the business cycle,
   a. output is rising.
   b. unemployment is falling.
   c. consumer and business confidence is high.
   d. investment is rising.
   e. none of the above are true.

39. The contractionary phase of the business cycle is characterized by
   a. reduced output and increased unemployment.
   b. reduced output and reduced unemployment.
   c. increased output and increased unemployment.
   d. increased output and reduced unemployment.

Problems

1. **[Section 5.2]**

   Answer the following questions about unemployment.

   a. If a country had an adult population (those 15 years of age and over) of 200 million and a labour force of 160 million, and 140 million people were employed, what is its labour force participation rate and its unemployment rate?

   b. If 10 million new jobs were created in the country, and it attracted 20 million of the people previously not in the labour force into the labour force, what would its new labour force participation rate and its unemployment rate be?

   c. Beginning from the situation in a, if 10 million unemployed people became discouraged and stopped looking for work, what would its new labour force participation rate and its unemployment rate be?

   d. Beginning from the situation in a, if 10 million current workers retired, but their jobs were filled by others still in the labour force, what would its new labour force participation rate and its unemployment rate be?

2. **[Section 5.2]**

   Answer the following questions about reasons for unemployment.

   a. In a severe recession, explain what would tend to happen to the number of people in each of the following categories:

   job losers
   job leavers
   re-entrants
   new entrants

   b. In very good economic times, why might job leavers, re-entrants, and new entrants all increase?

3. **[Section 5.4]**

   Answer the following questions about inflation.

   a. What would be the effect of unexpected inflation on each of the following?

   retirees on fixed incomes
   workers
   debtors
   creditors
   shoe-leather costs
   menu costs

   b. How would your answers change if the inflation was expected?

4. **[Section 5.4]**

   Answer the following questions about the nominal and real interest rate.

   a. What would be the real interest rate if the nominal interest rate were 14 percent and the inflation rate were 10 percent? if the nominal interest rate were 8 percent and the inflation rate were 1 percent?

   b. What would happen to the real interest rate if the nominal interest rate went from 9 percent to 15 percent when the inflation rate went from 4 percent to 10 percent? if the nominal interest rate went from 11 percent to 7 percent when the inflation rate went from 8 percent to 4 percent?

Measuring Economic Performance

section

6.1 National Income Accounting: Measuring Economic Performance

- What reasons are there for measuring our economy's performance?
- What is gross domestic product?
- What are the different methods of measuring GDP?

WHY DO WE MEASURE OUR ECONOMY'S PERFORMANCE?

There is a great desire to measure the success, or performance, of our economy. Are we getting "bigger" (and hopefully better) or "smaller" (and worse) over time? Aside from intellectual curiosity, the need to evaluate the magnitude of our economic performance is important to macroeconomic policymakers who want to know how well the economy is performing so that they can set goals and develop policy recommendations.

Measurement of the economy's performance is also important to private businesses because inaccurate measurement can lead to bad decision making. Traders in stocks and bonds are continually checking economic statistics—buying and selling in response to the latest economic data.

WHAT IS NATIONAL INCOME ACCOUNTING?

To fulfill the desire for a reliable method of measuring economic performance, **national income accounting** was born early in the twentieth century. The establishment of a uniform means of accounting for economic performance was such an important accomplishment that one of the first Nobel Prizes in economics was given to the late Simon Kuznets, a pioneer of national income accounting in the United States.

Several measures of aggregate national income and output have been developed, the most important of which is gross domestic product (GDP). We will examine GDP and other indicators of national economic performance in detail later in this chapter.

national income accounting
a uniform means of measuring economic performance

WHAT IS GROSS DOMESTIC PRODUCT?

The measure of aggregate economic performance that gets the most attention in the popular media is **gross domestic product (GDP),** which is defined as the value of all final goods and services produced within a country during a given period of time. By convention, that period of time is almost always one year. But let's examine the rest of this definition. What is meant by "final good or service" and "value"?

gross domestic product (GDP)
the measure of economic performance based on the value of all final goods and services produced in a given period

double counting
adding the value of a good or service twice by mistakenly counting intermediate goods and services in GDP

Measuring the Value of Goods and Services

Value is determined by the market prices at which goods and services sell. Underlying the calculations, then, are the various equilibrium prices and quantities for the multitude of goods and services produced.

What Is a Final Good or Service?

The word "final" means that the good is ready for its designated ultimate use. Many goods and services are intermediate goods or services; that is, used in the production of other goods. For example, suppose Stelco produces some steel that it sells to General Motors for use in making an automobile. If we counted the value of steel used in making the car as well as the full value of the finished auto in the GDP, we would be engaging in **double counting**—adding the value of the steel in twice, first in its raw form and second its final form, the automobile.

© JANIS CHRISTIE/PHOTODISC/GETTY ONE IMAGES

The paper used in this book is an intermediate good; it is the book, the final good, that is included in the GDP.

MEASURING GROSS DOMESTIC PRODUCT

Economic output can be calculated primarily two ways: the expenditure approach and the income approach. Although these methods differ, their result, GDP, is the same, apart from minor "statistical discrepancies." In the following two sections, we will examine each of these approaches in turn.

Section Check

1. We measure our economy's status in order to see how its performance has changed over time. These economic measurements are important to government officials, private businesses, and investors.
2. National income accounting, pioneered by Simon Kuznets, is a uniform means of measuring national economic performance.
3. Gross domestic product (GDP) is the value of all final goods and services produced within a country during a given time period.
4. Two different ways to measure GDP are the expenditure approach and the income approach.

The Expenditure Approach to Measuring GDP

- What are the four categories of purchases included in the expenditure approach?
- What types of government purchases are included in the expenditure approach?
- How are net exports calculated?

THE EXPENDITURE APPROACH TO MEASURING GDP

expenditure approach
calculation of GDP by adding the expenditures of market participants on final goods and services over a given period

One approach to measuring GDP is the **expenditure approach.** With this method, GDP is calculated by adding up how much market participants spend on final goods and services over a period of time. For convenience and for analytical purposes, economists usually categorize spending into four categories: consumption, identified symbolically by the letter C; investment, I; government purchases, G; and net exports, which equals exports (X) minus imports (M), or $(X - M)$. Following the expenditure method, then

$$GDP = C + I + G + (X - M)$$

CONSUMPTION (*C*)

consumption
purchases of consumer goods and services by households

Consumption refers to the purchase of consumer goods and services by households. For most of us, a large percentage of our income in a given year goes for consumer goods and services. The consumption category does not include purchases by business or government. As Exhibit 1 indicates, in 2007 consumption expenditures totalled $853 billion. This figure was 56 percent of GDP.

Consumption spending, in turn, is usually broken down into three subcategories: nondurable goods, durable goods, and services.

section 6.2 Exhibit 1	2007 Canadian GDP by Type of Spending	
Category	**Amount (billions of current dollars)**	**Percent of GDP**
Gross domestic product	$1536	
Consumption (*C*)	853	55.5%
Investment (*I*)	311	20.2
Government purchases (*G*)	342	22.3
Net exports of goods and services (*X − M*)	30	2.0

SOURCE: Statistics Canada

What Are Nondurable and Durable Goods?

Nondurable goods include tangible consumer items that are typically consumed or used up in a relatively short period of time. Food and pencils are examples, as are such quickly consumable items as drugs, toys, magazines, soap, razor blades, light bulbs, and so on. Nearly everything purchased in a supermarket or drugstore is a nondurable good.

Durable goods include longer-lived consumer goods, the most important single category of which is automobiles. Appliances, consumer electronics like DVD players, and furniture are also included in the durable goods category. On occasion, it is difficult to decide whether a good is durable or nondurable, and the definitions are, therefore, somewhat arbitrary.

The distinction between durables and nondurables is important because consumer buying behaviour is somewhat different for each of these categories of goods. In boom periods, when GDP is rising rapidly, expenditures on durables often increase dramatically, whereas in years of stagnant or falling GDP, sales of durable goods often plummet. By contrast, sales of nondurables like food tend to be more stable over time because purchases of such goods are more difficult to shift from one time period to another. You can "make do" with your car for another year, but not your lettuce.

nondurable goods
tangible items that are consumed in a short period of time, such as food

durable goods
longer-lived consumer goods, such as automobiles

What Are Services?

Services are intangible items of value, as opposed to physical goods. Legal services, dental services, recreational services, automobile repair, haircuts, airplane transportation—all of these are services. In recent years, service expenditures have been growing faster than spending on goods; the share of total consumption going for services is now over 50 percent. As incomes have risen, service industries such as health, education, financial, and recreation have grown dramatically.

services
intangible items of value provided to consumers, such as haircuts

INVESTMENT (*I*)

Investment, as used by economists, refers to the creation of capital goods—inputs like machines and tools whose purpose is to produce other goods. This definition of investment deviates from the popular use of that term. It is common for people to say that they invested in stocks, meaning that they have traded money for a piece of paper, called a stock certificate, that says they own a share in some company. Such transactions are not investment as defined by economists (i.e., an increase in capital goods), even though they might provide the enterprises selling the stock the resources for new capital goods, which *would* be counted as investment by economists.

There are two categories of investment purchases measured in the expenditures approach: fixed investment and inventory investment.

investment
the creation of capital goods to augment future production

Fixed Investments

Fixed investments include all spending on capital goods—sometimes called **producer goods**—such as machinery, tools, and factory buildings. All of these goods increase future production capabilities. Residential construction is also included as an investment expenditure in GDP calculations. The construction of a house allows for a valuable consumer service—shelter—to be provided, and is thus considered an investment. Residential construction is the only part of investment that is tied directly to household expenditure decisions.

fixed investments
all new spending on capital goods by producers

producer goods
capital goods that increase future production capabilities

Inventory Investment

Inventory investment includes all purchases by businesses that add to their inventories—stocks of goods kept on hand by businesses to meet customer demands. Every business needs

inventory investment
purchases that add to the stocks of goods kept by the firm to meet consumer demand

inventory and, other things equal, the greater the inventory, the greater the amount of goods and services that can be sold to a consumer in the future. Thus, inventories are considered a form of investment. Consider a grocery store. If the store expands and increases the quantity and variety of goods on its shelves, future sales can rise. An increase in inventories, then, is presumed to increase the firm's future sales, and this is why we say it is an investment.

How Stable Are Investment Expenditures?

In recent years, investment expenditures have generally been around 20 percent of gross domestic product. Investment spending is the most volatile category of GDP, however, and tends to fluctuate considerably with changing business conditions. When the economy is booming, investment purchases tend to increase dramatically. In downturns, the reverse happens.

GOVERNMENT PURCHASES (*G*)

The part of government purchases that is included in GDP is expenditures on goods and services. For example, the government (which includes all four levels of government: federal, provincial, regional, and municipal) must pay the salaries of its employees, and it must also make payments to the private firms with which it contracts to provide various goods and services, such as highway construction companies and computer companies. All of these payments would be included in GDP. However, transfer payments (such as employment insurance benefits and Canada Pension Plan payments) are not included in government purchases because that spending does not go to purchase newly produced goods or services, but is merely a transfer of income among that country's citizens (which is why such expenditures are called transfer payments). The government purchase proportion of GDP, at 22 percent, has grown over the last 50 years, in part because of rising spending on publicly funded health care.

NET EXPORTS (*X* − *M*)

Some of the goods and services that are produced in Canada are exported for use in other countries. The fact that these goods and services were made in Canada means that they should be included in a measure of Canadian production. Thus, we include the value of exports when calculating GDP. At the same time, however, some of our expenditures in other categories (consumption and investment in particular) were for foreign-produced goods and services. These imports must be excluded from GDP in order to obtain an accurate measure of Canadian production. Thus, GDP calculations measure net exports, which equals total exports (*X*) minus total imports (*M*).

In 2007, Canada's net exports were $30 billion, or 2 percent of GDP. However, exports of goods and services themselves were $532 billion, or 35 percent of GDP. Likewise, imports of goods and services were $502 billion, or 33 percent of GDP. These numbers mean that about 35 percent of all Canadian production of goods and services is sold to foreigners, whereas about 33 percent of all Canadian expenditure is on foreign-produced goods and services. These high proportions reflect the fact that Canada is very much an "open" economy; that is, the Canadian economy is highly dependent on foreign markets in terms of both buying and selling goods and services. Because the value of Canada's exports is greater than the value of its imports, net exports are a positive number, and Canada runs a trade surplus. For some countries, the value of imports exceeds the value of exports, resulting in a trade deficit.

SECTION CHECK

Section Check

1. The expenditure approach to measuring GDP involves adding up the purchases of final goods and services by market participants.
2. Four categories of spending are used in the GDP calculation: consumption (*C*), investment (*I*), government purchases (*G*), and net exports (*X* − *M*).
3. Consumption includes spending on nondurable consumer goods, tangible items that are usually consumed in a short period of time; durable consumer goods, longer-lived consumer goods; and services, intangible items of value.
4. Fixed investment includes all spending on capital goods, such as machinery, tools, and buildings. Inventory investment includes the net expenditures by businesses to increase their inventories.
5. Purchases of goods and services are the only part of government spending included in GDP. Transfer payments are not included in these calculations because that spending is not a payment for a newly produced good or service.
6. Net exports are calculated by subtracting total imports from total exports.

The Income Approach to Measuring GDP

section

6.3

- What are factor payments?
- What does personal income measure?

THE INCOME APPROACH TO MEASURING GDP

In the last section, we outlined the expenditure approach to GDP calculation. There is, however, also an alternative method called the **income approach.** This approach involves summing the incomes received by producers of goods and services.

When someone makes an expenditure for a good or service, that spending creates income for someone else. For example, if you buy $10 in groceries at the local supermarket, your $10 in spending creates $10 in income for the grocery store owner. The owner, then, must buy more goods to stock her shelves as a consequence of your consumer purchases; in addition, she must pay her employees, her electricity bill, and so on. Consequently, much of the $10 spent by you will eventually end up in the hands of someone other than the grocer. The basic point, however, is that someone (one person or many) receives the $10 you spent, and that receipt of funds is called income. Therefore, by adding up all of the incomes received by producers of goods and services, we can also calculate the gross domestic product, because output creates income of equal value.

income approach
calculation of GDP based on the summation of incomes received by the owners of resources used in the production of goods and services

FACTOR PAYMENTS

Incomes received by people providing goods and services are actually payments to the owners of productive resources. These payments are sometimes called **factor payments.** Factor payments include wages for the use of labour services; rent for land; payments for

factor payments
wages (salaries), rent, interest payments, and profits paid to the owners of productive resources

net domestic income at factor cost

a measure of income earned by the owners of factors of production

the use of capital goods in the form of interest; and profits for entrepreneurs who put labour, land, and capital together. Exhibit 1 presents the income approach to measuring GDP. Wages and salaries are the payment for labour services. They total $788 billion, or 51 percent of GDP. Corporate profits are the profits of corporations before tax. Interest income is the interest that households earn on loans they make minus the interest that households pay on their borrowing. Net income of farm and unincorporated businesses is the earnings of farmers and proprietors from their own businesses. The sum of these four categories of income is called **net domestic income at factor cost,** which totalled $1,169 billion in 2007.

We have to make two adjustments to net domestic income at factor cost to arrive at GDP. Net domestic income is the cost of the factor payments, but GDP is the value of the output at market prices. Therefore, the first adjustment we have to make to net domestic income is to add indirect taxes and subtract subsidies. An indirect tax is a tax paid by consumers when they buy goods and services (such as sales taxes, the GST, and excise taxes). Because of indirect taxes, the market price of a product bought by consumers (for example, $1 plus 7 percent tax = $1.07) is greater than the factor payments to the owners of the resources who produced the good ($1). A subsidy is a payment by the government to producers (such as payments to airplane manufacturers or grain farmers). Because of subsidies, the market price of a product bought by consumers is less than the cost of the factor payments.

The second adjustment to net domestic income is to add depreciation (or capital consumption allowances). When firms purchase capital equipment, the cost of such goods must be allocated over the time that the capital equipment will be used, possibly 10 to 20 years for some types of equipment. The cost allocated, which is called depreciation, is an estimate of the amount of the equipment being used up each year in production. Depreciation is a cost of production and is included in the market value of output, but it is not part of any factor's income and is not included in net domestic income.

Adding indirect taxes less subsidies, $167 billion, and depreciation, $200 billion, to net domestic income at factor cost gives us GDP.

In Exhibit 2, we see the circular flow of income and expenditures. People earn income from producing goods and services (aggregate income) and then spend on goods and services (aggregate expenditures), $C + I + G + (X - M)$. The main point is that buyers have sellers—that is, aggregate expenditures are equal to aggregate income.

section 6.3 Exhibit 1	2007 Canadian GDP by Type of Income	

Category	Amount (billions of current dollars)	Percent of GDP
Gross Domestic Product	$1536	
Wages and salaries	788	51.3%
Corporate profits	219	14.2
Interest income	72	4.7
Net income of farm and unincorporated businesses	90	5.9
Indirect taxes less subsidies	167	10.9
Depreciation	200	13.0

SOURCE: Statistics Canada

section 6.3
Exhibit 2

section 6.3 Exhibit 2   Circular Flow of Income and Expenditures

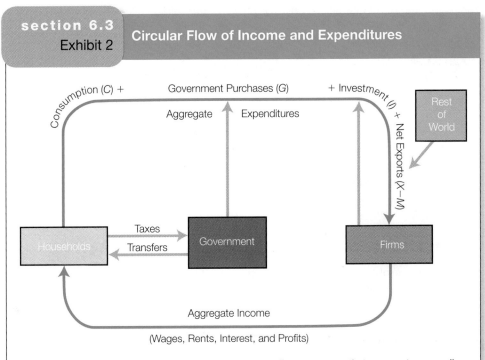

In the simple circular flow model of income and expenditures, we see that aggregate expenditures equal aggregate income. On the top of the figure, aggregate expenditures are added ($C + I + G + (X − M)$). Firms receive this aggregate spending for producing the goods and services. The firms pay households for their wages, rents, interest, and profits. The government receives taxes and makes transfer payments and government purchases.

PERSONAL INCOME AND DISPOSABLE INCOME

Often, we are interested in the income people *receive* rather than the income they *earn*, because the income received reflects the total amount available for spending before taxes. **Personal income** measures the amount of income received by households (including transfer payments) before income taxes. **Disposable income** is the personal income available to individuals after taxes. Disposable income can be used by households in two ways: consumption or saving.

personal income
the amount of income received by households before taxes

disposable income
the personal income available after taxes

Section Check

1. The income approach to measuring GDP involves summing the incomes received by the producers of goods and services. These payments to the owners of productive resources are also known as factor payments.
2. The income approach to GDP adds together wages and salaries, corporate profits, interest income, and net income of farm and unincorporated businesses to get net domestic income at factor cost. Adding indirect taxes less subsidies and depreciation to net domestic income gives us GDP.
3. Personal income measures the amount of income received by households (including transfer payments) before taxes.
4. Disposable income is the personal income available after taxes.

Problems in Calculating an Accurate GDP

- ■ What are the problems with GDP in measuring output?
- ■ What is the purpose of a price level index?
- ■ What inherent problems exist with a price level index?
- ■ What is per capita real GDP?

PROBLEMS IN CALCULATING AN ACCURATE GDP

The primary problem in calculating accurate GDP statistics becomes evident when attempts are made to compare the GDP over time. Between 1971 and 1976, a period of relatively high inflation, GDP in Canada rose over 100 percent. What great progress! Unfortunately, however, the measure used in adding together the values of different products, the Canadian dollar, also changed in value over this time period. A dollar in 1976, for example, would certainly not buy as much as a dollar in 1971, because the *overall* price level for goods and services increased.

One solution to this problem would be to use physical units of output—which, unlike the Canadian dollar, don't change in value from year to year—as our measure of total economic activity. The major problem with this approach is that different products have different units of measurement. How do you add together tonnes of steel, bushels of wheat, kilowatts of electricity, litres of paint, cubic metres of natural gas, kilometres of air passenger travel, number of games of bowling, and number of magazines sold? In order to compare GDP values over time, a common or standardized unit of measure, which only money can provide, must be used in the calculations.

The dollar, then, is the measure of value that we can use to correct the inflation-induced distortion of the GDP. We must adjust for the changing purchasing power of the dollar by constructing a **price index.** Essentially, a price index attempts to provide a measure of the trend in prices paid for a certain bundle of goods and services over time. The price index can be used to deflate the nominal or current dollar GDP values to a real GDP expressed in dollars of constant purchasing power.

There are many different types of price indices. The best-known price index, the **consumer price index (CPI),** measures the trend in the prices of certain goods and services purchased for consumption purposes. The CPI may be the most relevant price index to households trying to evaluate their changing financial position over time. Another price index, the **GDP deflator,** corrects GDP statistics for changing prices. The GDP deflator measures the average level of prices of all final goods and services produced in the economy.

Constructing the consumer price index is complicated. There are literally thousands of consumer goods and services. Attempting to include all of them in the index would be cumbersome, make the index expensive to compute, and take a long period of time to gather necessary price data. Therefore, a "bundle" or "basket" of representative goods and services is selected by Statistics Canada. The CPI is based on over 600 consumer goods and services that are purchased by a typical Canadian household. Each month the prices of these goods and services are recorded all across Canada.

price index
a measurement that attempts to provide a measure of the trend in prices paid for a certain bundle of goods and services over a given period

consumer price index (CPI)
a measure of the prices of a basket of consumable goods and services that serves to gauge inflation

GDP deflator
a price index that helps to measure the average price level of all final goods and services produced in the economy

CALCULATING THE CPI

Suppose a consumer typically buys 24 loaves of bread and 12 kilograms of oranges in a year. The following table indicates the prices of bread and oranges and the cost of the consumer's typical market basket in the years 2006 to 2008.

Year	Price of Bread	Price of Oranges	Cost of Market Basket
2006	$1.00	$2.00	(24 × $1.00) + (12 × $2.00) = $48.00
2007	1.15	2.10	(24 × 1.15) + (12 × 2.10) = 52.80
2008	1.40	2.20	(24 × 1.40) + (12 × 2.20) = 60.00

We calculate the CPI by comparing the cost of the market basket in the current year to the cost of the market basket in the base year. The base year is arbitrarily chosen; in our example we will designate 2006 as the base year. The CPI for each year is calculated using the following formula:

$$\text{CPI} = \frac{\text{Cost of market basket in current year}}{\text{Cost of market basket in base year}} \times 100$$

The following table shows the CPI from 2006 to 2008. In 2006, the base year, the CPI equals 100. In 2007 and 2008, the CPI is 110 and 125, respectively, meaning that the average price level has risen in each of these two years.

Year	Consumer Price Index
2006	$48/$48 × 100 = 100.0
2007	$52.80/$48 × 100 = 110.0
2008	$60/$48 × 100 = 125.0

A comparison of the CPI shows that between 2006 and 2007, prices increased an average of 10 percent. Between 2006 and 2008, 25 percent inflation occurred. And between 2007 and 2008 the inflation rate was 13.6 percent, $(125 - 110)/110 \times 100$.

The CPI is not a completely accurate measure of the cost of living. Three factors cause the CPI to overestimate changes in the cost of living. First, goods and services change in quality over time, so the observed price change may, in reality, reflect a quality change in the product rather than a change in the purchasing power of the dollar. A $300 television set today is dramatically better than a television set in 1950. The CPI is not able to adjust for all the quality increases that take place in goods and services, but does adjust for quality changes for some products. Second, new products come on the market and occasionally old products disappear. For example, colour-TV sets did not exist in 1950 but are a major consumer item now. How do you calculate changes in prices over time when some products did not even exist in the earlier period? Third, the CPI measures the price changes of a fixed basket of goods and services. Thus, the CPI does not capture the fact that consumers are able to keep their cost of living down by substituting towards those goods whose prices have risen by relatively less and away from those goods whose prices have risen by relatively more.

CALCULATING REAL GDP

To correct the nominal or current dollar GDP values for inflation, the appropriate price index to use is the GDP deflator. Once the GDP deflator has been calculated, the actual procedure for adjusting nominal, or current dollar, GDP to get real GDP is not complicated. Remember, real GDP gives us a measure of GDP in constant dollars that have been corrected for inflation.

The formula for converting any year's nominal GDP into real GDP (in constant dollars) is as follows:

$$\text{Real GDP} = \frac{\text{Nominal GDP}}{\text{GDP deflator}} \times 100$$

Say, for example, the GDP deflator was expressed in terms of 2002 dollars (2002 = 100), and the GDP deflator for 2008 was 115. This means that prices were 15 percent higher in 2008 than they were in 2002. Now, in order to correct the 2008 nominal GDP, we take the nominal GDP figure for 2008, suppose it is $1000 billion, and divide it by the GDP deflator, 115, which results in a quotient of $8.695 billion. We then multiply this number by 100, giving us $869.5 billion, which is the 2008 GDP in 2002 dollars (that is, 2008 real GDP, in terms of a 2002 base year).

Exhibit 1 presents data on nominal GDP, real GDP, and the GDP deflator for the Canadian economy for the 2002–2007 period. The base year for the GDP deflator is 2002, so real GDP is expressed in billions of 2002 dollars. (You may want to calculate real GDP yourself, in order to confirm your understanding of the adjustment process.) Notice that nominal GDP (in current dollars) increased from $1152.9 billion in 2002 to $1535.6 billion in 2007, an increase of 33.2 percent. However, over the same time period, the GDP deflator rose from 100.0 to 116.4, an increase of 16.4 percent. Thus, the average price level of all the final goods and services produced in the economy increased by 16 percent, meaning the economy experienced 16 percent inflation over this five-year period. This inflation was one of the factors that led to the growth in nominal (current dollar) GDP. The other factor was growth in real GDP, or the economy's actual physical production of final goods and services. As we can see, real GDP (measured in 2002 dollars) increased from $1152.9 billion in 2002 to $1319.7 billion in 2007, an increase of 14.5 percent. This is the economy's "real" economic growth.

When there is inflation, the adjustment of nominal (current dollar) GDP to real GDP (measured in constant dollars) will reduce the growth in GDP suggested by the nominal GDP figures. Thus, it is important when comparing GDP over time that we use real GDP as our measure of the economy's production of final goods and services, as this measure corrects nominal GDP for the distortions caused by inflation.

section 6.4
Exhibit 1 — Nominal GDP, Real GDP, and the GDP Deflator

Year	Nominal GDP (billions of current dollars)	GDP Deflator (2002 = 100)	Real GDP (billions of 2002 dollars)
2002	$ 1152.9	100.00	$ 1152.9
2003	1213.2	103.29	1174.6
2004	1290.9	106.58	1211.2
2005	1372.6	110.15	1246.1
2006	1450.5	112.90	1284.8
2007	1535.6	116.36	1319.7

SOURCE: Statistics Canada

REAL GDP PER CAPITA

The measure of economic well-being, or standard of living, most often used is **real gross domestic product per capita.** We use a measure of real GDP for reasons already cited. To calculate real GDP per capita, we divide the real GDP by the total population to get the value of real output of final goods and services per person. *Ceteris paribus,* people prefer more goods to fewer, so a higher GDP per capita would seemingly make people better off, improving their standard of living. Economic growth, then, is usually considered to have occurred anytime the real GDP per capita has risen. In Exhibit 2, we see that in Canada, the real gross domestic product per capita has exactly doubled between 1971 and 2007. However, the growth in real GDP per capita was not steady, as seen by the shaded areas that represent recessions in Exhibit 2. Falling real GDP per capita can bring on many human hardships like rising unemployment, lower profits, stock market losses, and bankruptcies. Note, in particular, the prolonged stagnation in standard of living during the early 1990s, when real GDP per capita was the same level in 1994 as it was in 1989.

Because one purpose of using GDP is to relate output to human desires, we need to adjust for population change. If we do not take population growth into account, we can

real gross domestic product per capita
real output of goods and services per person

section 6.4
Exhibit 2   Canadian Real Gross Domestic Product per Capita

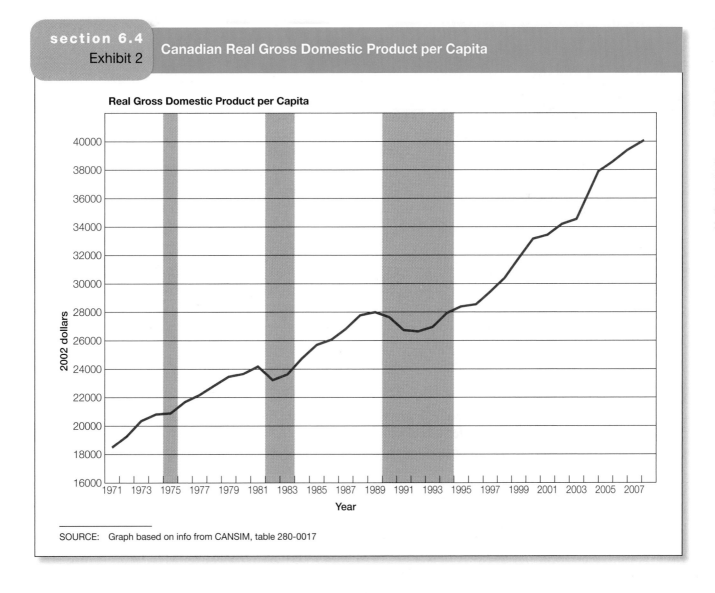

Real Gross Domestic Product per Capita

SOURCE: Graph based on info from CANSIM, table 280-0017

be misled by changes in real GDP values. For example, in some less-developed countries in some time periods, real GDP has risen by perhaps 2 percent a year but the population has grown just as fast. In these cases, the real output of goods and services per person has remained virtually unchanged, but this would not be apparent in an examination of real GDP trends alone.

Section Check

1. It is difficult to compare nominal GDP over time because of the changing value of money over time.
2. A price index allows us to compare prices paid for goods and services over time. The consumer price index (CPI) is the best-known price index.
3. The GDP deflator is a price index that measures the average level of prices of all final goods and services produced in the economy.
4. Per capita real GDP is real output of goods and services per person. In some cases, real GDP may increase, but per capita real GDP may actually drop as a result of population growth.

section 6.5

Problems with GDP as a Measure of Economic Welfare

- What are some of the deficiencies of GDP as a measure of economic welfare?
- What are nonmarket transactions?
- What is the underground economy?

As we have noted earlier, real GDP is often used as a measure of the economic welfare of a nation. The accuracy of this measure for that purpose is, however, questionable because several important factors are excluded from its calculations. These factors include nonmarket transactions, the underground economy, leisure, externalities, and the quality of the goods purchased.

NONMARKET TRANSACTIONS

Nonmarket transactions include the provision of goods and services outside of traditional markets for which no money is exchanged. We simply do not have reliable enough information on this output to include it in the GDP. The most important single nonmarket transaction omitted from the GDP is the services of housewives (or househusbands). These services are not sold in any market, so they are not entered into the GDP, but they are nonetheless performed. For example, if a single woman hires a tax accountant, those payments enter into the calculation of GDP. Suppose, though, that the woman marries her tax accountant. Now the woman no longer pays her husband for his accounting services. Reported GDP falls after the marriage, although output does not change.

In less-developed countries, where a significant amount of food and clothing output is produced in the home, the failure to include nonmarket economic activity in GDP is a serious deficiency. Even in Canada, homemade meals, housework, and the vegetables and flowers produced in home gardens are excluded, even though they clearly represent an output of goods and services.

THE UNDERGROUND ECONOMY

It is impossible to know for sure the magnitude of the underground economy, which includes unreported income from both legal and illegal sources. For example, illegal drug dealing and prostitution are not included in the GDP, leading to underreporting of an unknown dimension. The reason these activities are excluded, however, has nothing to do with the morality of the services performed, but rather results from the fact that the payments made for these services are not reported to governmental authorities. Likewise, cash payments made to employees "under the table" slip through the GDP net. The estimates of the size of the underground economy vary from 5 percent to 15 percent of GDP. It also appears that a good portion of this unreported income comes from legal sources, such as self-employment.

COURTESY OF ROBERT SEXTON

Are her household production efforts included in GDP? If a family hires someone to clean the house, provide child care, mow the lawn, or cook, this is included in GDP; when members of the household provide these services, it is not. Neglecting household production in GDP distorts measurements of economic growth and leads to potential policy problems. Is it time to include household activities in GDP? An estimate of the value of these services could be obtained by calculating the cost to buy these services in the marketplace.

MEASURING THE VALUE OF LEISURE

The value that individuals place on leisure is omitted in calculating GDP. Most of us could probably get a part-time job if we wanted to, earning some additional money by working in the evening or on weekends. Yet we choose not to do so. Why? The opportunity cost is too high—we would have to forgo some leisure. If you work on Saturday nights, you cannot visit your friends, go to parties, see concerts, watch television, or go to the movies. The opportunity cost of the leisure is the income forgone by not working. For example, if people start taking more three-day weekends, GDP will surely fall, but can we necessarily say that the standard of living will fall? GDP will fall but economic well-being may rise.

Leisure, then, has a positive value that does not show up in the GDP accounts. To put leisure in the proper perspective, ask yourself if you would rather live in Country A, which has a per capita GDP of $25 000 a year and a 30-hour work week, or Country B, with a $25 000 per capita GDP and a 50-hour work week. Most would choose Country A. The problem that this omission in GDP poses can be fairly significant in international comparisons, or when one looks at one nation over time.

GDP AND EXTERNALITIES

Economists have observed that side effects can accompany the production of some goods and services. These additional impacts (in the form of either benefits or costs) are referred to as externalities. As a result of these positive and negative externalities, the equilibrium prices of goods and services—the figures used in GDP calculations—do not reflect their true value to society (unless the externality has been internalized).

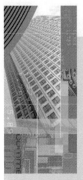

In The **NEWS**

GROWING UNDERGROUND

Underground economies are large and growing rapidly in most countries. High taxes and labour market regulations are the reasons why 17 percent of economic activity goes unreported in OECD countries, while corruption explains the large black market in some developing ones.

By definition, national income statistics capture economic activity reported by individuals and corporations. A large and growing portion of economic activity, however, goes unrecorded in most countries. This "underground" economy consists of legal activities that are concealed, mainly for reasons of tax evasion. Underground activity grew during the 1970s, when government became pervasive in national economies. As tax rates were raised to finance public spending programs, an increasing number of individuals risked dodging taxes. It is only since the 1980s that economists have attempted to estimate the size of underground economies. This is an inherently difficult task.

Nevertheless, it is important to estimate the size and growth of all economic activity, not only the reported kind. For one thing, cross-country comparisons of per capita income depend on it. By one account, Italy would be one of the richest European countries if its large black market were included alongside reported income. More importantly, GDP growth figures and unemployment rates may be severely distorted if a sudden increase in taxes pushes more people underground. Accurate statistics about overall economic activity and true unemployment are essential for effective economic policy decisions.

An article in the *Journal of Economic Literature* takes a closer look at the size, causes, and consequences of underground economies. Its authors, Friedrich Schneider of the University of Linz and Dominick Enste of the University of Cologne, claim that no cross-country comparison of underground economies has yet been undertaken. In their research, the authors compare the relative size of underground economies for 76 countries, and track their growth over time. They point out that even though estimates of underground economies are naturally inexact, economists generally agree that they are growing in most countries. Moreover, underground economies vary significantly in size, from a small fraction of "official" GDP (Switzerland), to nearly three-quarters of economic output (Nigeria, Egypt, and Thailand).

But first, what drives people underground? The authors argue that underground activity grows when tax rates rise. This is most noticeable in Scandinavian countries where governments have created some of the most generous public programs over the past few decades, and have consequently witnessed a substantial rise in their underground economies. This unsurprising claim is substantiated by the data. Norway, for example, has seen its underground economy grow from a negligible 1.5 percent of GNP in 1960 to a staggering 18 percent in 1995 (based on the currency demand approach). The high fiscal burden in other Scandinavian countries has led to a similar growth in their underground economies. In contrast, countries with relatively small public sectors—such as Switzerland and the United States—have developed much smaller underground markets.

The study shows that underground economies have grown in all OECD countries over the past few decades, representing an alarming 17 percent of reported GDP by 1997. In countries like Spain, Portugal, Italy, Belgium, and Greece, the estimated size of unreported economic activity stood at 22 to 30 percent. "In the European Union at least 20 million workers and in OECD countries about 35 million work in the unofficial economy. Moreover, the amount doubled within 20 years."

The authors find evidence that fewer regulations (that are properly enforced), lower tax rates, and a better rule of law lead to smaller underground economies, and consequently generate higher tax revenues. These factors are absent in many countries of Latin America, where underground economies amount to one-quarter to one-third of official GNP, and in the former Soviet Union, where underground economies stand at more than one-third of reported income.

SOURCE: Friedrich Schneider and Dominick H. Enste, "Shadow Economies: Size, Causes and Consequences," *Journal of Economic Literature*, March 2000, and *Economic Intuition*, Summer 2000.

CONSIDER THIS:
As the federal government and most provincial governments in Canada have lowered taxes since the late 1990s, it is possible that the size of the underground economy may have become smaller. With lower tax rates, there is less incentive to try to hide income from the government.

QUALITY OF GOODS

GDP can also miss important changes in the improvements in the *quality* of goods and services. For example, there is a huge difference between the quality of a computer bought today and one that was bought ten years ago, but it will not lead to an increase in measured GDP. The same is true of many goods from cellular phones to automobiles to medical care.

In The **NEWS**

AN INVALUABLE ENVIRONMENT

Environmentalists have long felt cross with the way governments measure national incomes and wealth. These figures for GDP, they point out, fail to value a country's environmental assets, such as fine public parks. They treat the use of natural capital differently from that of man-made capital: a country that depletes its stock of production equipment grows poorer, while one that chops down its forests appears to grow richer. And they treat the costs of cleaning up environmental damage as an addition to national income without subtracting the environmental loss caused by the damage in the first place.

The answer might seem obvious: adjust national accounts to take account of changes in the environment. Statisticians have laboured for more than a decade to find ways to do this. The difficulties of creating environmental statistics that are comparable to national income and wealth statistics are serious. GDP is measured in money, but putting monetary values on environmental assets is a black art. Some assets, such as timber, may have a market value, but that value does not encompass the trees' role in harboring rare beetles, say, or their sheer beauty. Methods for valuing such benefits are controversial. To get round these problems, the U.N. guidelines suggest measuring the cost of repairing environmental damage. But some kinds of damage, such as extinction, are beyond costing, and others are hard to estimate.

For economists, the average value of a good or service is usually less important than the marginal value—the cost or benefit of one more unit. Marginal value, however, is a tricky concept to bring into environmental analysis. It may be clear that the cost of wiping out an entire species of beetle would be high, but what value should be attached to the extermination of a few hundred bugs?

Putting environmental concepts into economic terms raises other difficulties as well. Geography weighs differently: a ton of sulphur dioxide emitted in a big city may cause more harm than the same ton emitted in a rural area, while a dollar's worth of output counts the same wherever it is produced. And the exploitation of natural resources may not always have a cost. Is a country depleting resources if it mines a ton of coal? All other things equal, the mining of that ton might raise the value of the coal that remains in the ground, leaving the value of coal assets unchanged.

SOURCE: "An Invaluable Environment," *The Economist*, April 18, 1998, p. 75. http://www.economist.com/displaystory.cfm?story_ID=160621. © 1998 The Economist Newspaper Group, Inc. Reprinted with permission. Further reproduction prohibited. www.economist.com.

© DOUG MENUEZ/PHOTODISC/GETTY ONE IMAGES

CONSIDER THIS:

GDP doesn't measure everything that contributes to or detracts from our well-being; it is very difficult to measure the value of those effects. Environmentalists believe that national income accounts should adjust for changes in the environment. But this leads to many conceptual problems, such as measuring the marginal values of goods and services not sold in markets, and adjusting for geographical differences in environmental damage. The critical issue is whether there are important trends in "uncounted" goods and services that result in questionable conclusions about whether we are getting better or worse off.

Section Check

1. There are several factors that make it difficult to use GDP as a welfare indicator, including nonmarket transactions, the underground economy, leisure, and externalities.
2. Nonmarket transactions are the exchange of goods and services that do not occur in traditional markets, and so no money is exchanged.
3. The underground economy is the unreported production and income that come from legal and illegal activities.
4. The presence of positive and negative externalities makes it difficult to measure GDP accurately.

Summary

Section 6.1

- Gross domestic product (GDP) is the value of all final goods and services produced within a country during a given time period.
- Two different ways to measure GDP are the expenditure approach and the income approach.

Section 6.2

- The expenditure approach to measuring GDP involves adding up the purchases of final goods and services by market participants.
- The four categories of spending used in the GDP calculation are consumption (*C*), investment (*I*), government purchases (*G*), and net exports (*X* − *M*).

Section 6.3

- The income approach to measuring GDP involves summing the incomes received by the producers of goods and services.
- Payments received by owners of productive resources are known as factor payments.
- Net domestic income adds together wages and salaries, corporate profits, interest income, and net income of farm and unincorporated businesses.
- Adding indirect taxes less subsidies and depreciation to net domestic income gives GDP.

Section 6.4

- It is difficult to compare nominal GDP over time because of the changing value of money over time.
- A price index allows us to compare prices paid for goods and services over time
- The consumer price index (CPI) is the best-known price index.
- The GDP deflator is a price index that measures the average level of prices of all final goods and services produced in the economy.
- The consumer price index fails to fully account for increased quality in goods, introduction of new goods, or changes in the relative quantities of goods purchased.

Section 6.5

- Several factors make it difficult to use GDP as a welfare indicator, including nonmarket transactions, the underground economy, leisure, and externalities.
- Nonmarket transactions are the exchange of goods and services that do not occur in traditional markets, and so no money is exchanged.
- The underground economy is the unreported production and income that come from legal and illegal activities.
- The presence of positive and negative externalities makes it difficult to measure GDP accurately.

Key Terms and Concepts

For a complete glossary of chapter key terms, visit the textbook's Web site at http://www.sextonmacro2e.nelson.com.

national income accounting 149
gross domestic product (GDP) 149
double counting 149
expenditure approach 150
consumption 150
nondurable goods 151
durable goods 151
services 151

investment 151
fixed investments 151
producer goods 151
inventory investment 151
income approach 153
factor payments 153
net domestic income at factor cost 154

personal income 155
disposable income 155
price index 156
consumer price index (CPI) 156
GDP deflator 156
real gross domestic product per capita 159

Review Questions

1. Which of the following are included in Canadian GDP calculations?

a. cleaning services performed by Molly Maid corporation

b. washing your own car

c. drugs sold illegally on a local street corner

d. prescription drugs manufactured in Canada and sold at a local pharmacy

e. a rug woven by hand in Turkey

f. air pollution that diminishes the quality of the air you breathe

g. toxic waste cleanup performed by a local company

h. car parts manufactured in Canada for assembly of a car in Mexico

i. a purchase of 1000 shares of RIM stock

j. monthly Canada Pension Plan payment received by a retiree

2. To which Canadian GDP expenditure category does each of the following correspond?

a. Ministry of Transportation snow-clearing services

b. automobiles exported to Europe

c. a refrigerator

d. a newly constructed four-bedroom house

e. a restaurant meal

f. additions to inventory at a furniture store

g. purchases of new computers by Statistics Canada

h. a new steel mill

3. The expenditures on tires by the Ford Motor Company of Canada are not included directly in GDP statistics whereas consumer expenditures on replacement tires are included. Why?

4. Using any relevant information below, calculate GDP via the expenditure approach.

Inventory investment	$ 50 billion
Fixed investment	120 billion
Consumer durables	420 billion
Consumer nondurables	275 billion
Interest	140 billion
Indirect business taxes	45 billion
Government wages and salaries	300 billion
Government purchases of goods and services	110 billion
Imports	80 billion
Exports	40 billion
Profits	320 billion
Consumer services	600 billion

5. Nominal GDP in Nowhereland in 2008 and 2009 is as follows:

NGDP 2008	NGDP 2009
$400 billion	$440 billion

Can you say that the production of goods and services in Nowhereland has increased between 2008 and 2009? Why or why not?

6. Calculate a consumer price index for 2006, 2007, and 2008, using the following information about prices. Let the market basket consist of one pizza, two soft drinks, and three video rentals. Let the year 2006 be the base year (with an index value of 100).

Year	Price of a Pizza	Price of a Soft Drink	Price of a Video Rental
2006	$ 9.00	$0.50	$2.00
2007	9.50	0.53	2.24
2008	10.00	0.65	2.90

How much inflation occurred between 2006 and 2007? between 2007 and 2008?

7. Calculate real GDP for the years 2004 to 2008 using the following information:

Year	Nominal GDP	GDP Deflator	Real GDP
2004	$720 billion	100	
2005	750 billion	102	
2006	800 billion	110	
2007	900 billion	114	
2008	960 billion	120	

What was the real economic growth rate in 2008?

8. Evaluate the following statement: "Real GDP in the United States is higher than real GDP in Canada. Therefore, the standard of living in the U.S. must be higher than in Canada."

9. Population and real GDP in Country A are as follows:

Year	Population	Real GDP
1980	1.25 million	$4000 million
1990	1.6 million	6750 million
2000	1.8 million	9000 million

Calculate real GDP per capita in 1980, 1990, and 2000. Does real output per person increase or decrease over time?

Fill in the Blanks

Section 6.1

1. _____ accounting was created to provide a reliable, uniform method of measuring economic performance.

2. _____ is defined as the value of all final goods and services produced in a country in a period of time, almost always one year.

3. A _____ good or service is one that is ready for its designated ultimate use, in contrast to _____ goods or services that are used in the production of other goods.

4. There are two primary ways of calculating economic output: the _____ approach and the _____ approach.

Section 6.2

5. With the _____ approach, GDP is calculated by adding up the expenditures of market participants on final goods and services over a period of time.

6. For analytical purposes, economists usually categorize expenditures into four categories: _____, _____, _____, and _____.

7. Consumption spending is usually broken down into three subcategories: _____ goods, _____ goods, and _____.

8. Consumption refers to the purchase of consumer goods and services by _____.

9. The most important single category of consumer durable goods is consumer _____.

10. Sales of nondurable consumer goods tend to be _____ stable over time than sales of durable goods.

11. Investment, as used by economists, refers to the creation of _____ goods whose purpose is to _____.

12. The two categories of investment purchases measured in the expenditures approach are _____ investment and _____ investment.

13. When the economy is booming, investment purchases tend to _____ dramatically.

14. _____ payments are not included in government purchases because that spending does not go to purchase newly produced goods or services.

15. Imports must be _____ from GDP in order to obtain an accurate measure of domestic production.

Section 6.3

16. The _____ approach to measuring GDP involves summing the incomes received by producers of goods and services.

17. Output creates _____ of equal value.

18. Factor payments include _____ for the use of labour services; _____ for land; _____ payments for the use of capital goods; and _____ for entrepreneurs who put labour, land, and capital together.

19. The incomes received by persons providing goods and services are actually payments to the owners of _____ resources and are sometimes called _____ payments.

20. _____ and indirect taxes less subsidies must be added to net domestic income to get GDP.

21. _____ income is the personal income available to individuals after taxes.

Section 6.4

22. We must adjust for the changing purchasing power of the dollar by constructing a price _____.

23. The best-known price index is the _____, which provides a measure of the trend in the prices of goods and services purchased for consumption purposes.

24. The GDP deflator measures the average level of prices of all _____ goods and services produced in the economy.

25. The CPI is the price index that is most relevant to _____ trying to evaluate their changing financial position over time.

26. A consumer price index is equal to the cost of the chosen market basket in the _____ year, divided by the cost of the same market basket in the _____ year, times 100.

27. The formula for converting any year's nominal GDP into real GDP (in base-year dollars) is real GDP equals _____ divided by the _____, times 100.

28. To calculate real per capita GDP, we divide _____ GDP by the _____ to get the value of real output of final goods and services per person.

Section 6.5

29. We do not have _____ enough information on the output of nonmarket transactions to include it in the GDP.

30. The most important nonmarket transactions omitted from GDP are services provided directly _____.

31. The value that individuals place on leisure is _____ in calculating GDP.

True or False

Section 6.1

1. Measuring the performance of our economy is important to private businesses and to macroeconomic policymakers in setting goals and developing policy recommendations.

2. All goods and services exchanged in the current period are included in this year's GDP.

3. The value of a good or service is determined by the market prices at which goods and services sell.

4. If we counted the value of intermediate goods as well as the full value of the final products in GDP, we would be double counting.

5. Although the expenditure approach and the income approach differ, their result, GDP, is the same, apart from minor "statistical discrepancies."

Section 6.2

6. According to the expenditure method, $GDP = C + I + G + X$.

7. The distinction between whether a good is durable or nondurable is clear and easy to apply.

8. In boom periods, expenditures on consumer durables often increase more than expenditures on nondurables.

9. As incomes have risen, consumer expenditures on services have been growing slower than expenditures on goods.

10. The share of total consumption going for services now exceeds 50 percent.

11. Purchases of stock are included as part of investment in the national income accounts.

12. Fixed investments include all spending on capital goods, as well as on residential construction.

13. Investment spending is the most volatile category of GDP.

14. Government expenditures on goods and services as a proportion of GDP have fallen over the last 30 years.

15. Because exports are consumed in other countries, they are omitted from measures of domestic GDP.

16. Net exports are a small proportion of GDP.

Section 6.3

17. When someone makes an expenditure for a good or service, that spending creates income for someone else.

18. Depreciation is the amount of equipment being used up each year.

19. Net domestic income is a measure of the income earned by owners of resources and available for spending after taxes.

Section 6.4

20. The primary problem in calculating accurate Canadian GDP statistics is that the measure used in adding together the values of different products, the Canadian dollar, changes in value over time.

21. The GDP deflator can be used to deflate current dollar GDP to real GDP expressed in dollars of constant purchasing power.

22. The consumer price index measures the average level of prices of all final goods and services produced in the economy.

23. Our ability to accurately calculate inflation is complicated by changing qualities of goods and services over time and the creation of new products.

24. There are many factors that could potentially distort the CPI.

25. Nominal GDP equals real GDP divided by the GDP deflator, times 100.

26. In periods of inflation, real GDP growth will tend to be greater than nominal GDP growth.

27. The measure of economic welfare most often cited is real per capita gross domestic product.

28. In a country with a growing population, real GDP per capita could be falling at the same time that real GDP was rising.

Section 6.5

29. Nonmarket transactions, the underground economy, and the value of leisure are all omitted from official measures of GDP.

30. Real GDP is a highly accurate measure of the economic welfare of a nation.

31. Marrying one's housekeeper would leave reported GDP unchanged.

32. In less-developed countries, where a significant amount of food and clothing output is produced in the home, the failure to include nonmarket economic activity in GDP is a serious deficiency.

33. Almost all of the underground economy represents income from illegal sources, such as drug dealing.

34. GDP is decreased to reflect pollution resulting from production.

35. There are severe defects with real GDP as a welfare measure. Nonetheless, at the present time, there is no alternative measure that is generally accepted as better.

Multiple Choice

Section 6.1

1. GDP is defined as the
   a. value of all final goods and services produced in a country in a period of time.
   b. value of all final goods produced in a country in a period of time.
   c. value of all goods and services produced in a country in a period of time.
   d. value of all final services produced in a country in a period of time.

2. GDP measures
   a. the value of all intermediate goods produced domestically within a given period.
   b. the value of all goods and services sold in an economy within a given period.
   c. the value of all final goods and services produced domestically within a given period.
   d. the government's domestic product.

3. An example of an intermediate product is
   a. the purchase of tires by Ford Motor Company to put on its Ford Explorers.
   b. the purchase of wood by a home construction firm.
   c. the purchase of leather by a shoe manufacturer.
   d. All of the above are examples of intermediate products.

4. Which of the following is *not* included in the calculated gross domestic product?
   a. the purchase of Canadian wine
   b. dinner at Burger King
   c. a construction firm's purchase of lumber to build a four-bedroom home
   d. the purchase of a newly constructed home

5. GDP is calculated including
   a. intermediate products but not final products.
   b. manufactured goods but not services.
   c. final products but not intermediate products.
   d. only goods purchased by consumers in a given year.

Section 6.2

6. The expenditure measure of GDP accounting adds together
   a. consumption, interest, government purchases, and net exports.
   b. consumption, government purchases, wages and salaries, and net exports.
   c. consumption, investment, government purchases, and net exports.
   d. wages and salaries, rent, interest, and profit.
   e. wages and salaries, rent, investment, and profit.

7. Which category of consumption spending tends to be the most unstable over the business cycle?
   a. nondurable consumer goods
   b. durable consumer goods
   c. services
   d. All of these categories of consumer spending are highly unstable over the business cycle.

8. Which of the following are most likely classified by economists as consumer durable goods?
   a. stocks, bonds
   b. automobiles, furniture, CD players
   c. drugs, toys, magazines, books
   d. food, clothing

9. Investment includes
   a. fixed investment.
   b. fixed investment plus government purchases.
   c. fixed investment plus additions to business inventories.
   d. fixed investment plus subtractions from business inventories.
   e. fixed investment plus government purchases plus additions to business inventories.

10. Included in the investment category under the expenditure approach to GDP accounting is (are)
    a. additions to inventory.
    b. machines and tools.
    c. newly constructed residential housing.
    d. all of the above.

11. Which of the following is *not* included in government purchases?
    a. government purchases of goods
    b. transfer payments
    c. government spending on services
    d. None of the above is included in government purchases.
    e. Neither b nor c is included in government purchases.

12. A negative amount of net exports in the GDP expenditures accounting means
    a. exports are less than imports.
    b. imports are less than exports.
    c. the sum of this period's exports and imports has declined from the previous period.
    d. net exports have declined from the previous period.
    e. none of the above.

13. We can be certain that net exports fall if
    a. both exports and imports rise.
    b. both exports and imports fall.
    c. exports rise and imports fall.
    d. exports fall and imports rise.
    e. either b or d occurs.

14. French perfume that is purchased in Canada is accounted for in which expenditure category of Canadian GDP?
    a. consumption
    b. investment
    c. government purchases
    d. net exports
    e. consumption and net exports

15. If Canada imported $1.5 billion worth of goods and services and sold $2.9 billion worth of goods and services outside its borders, net exports would equal
    a. −$4.4 billion.
    b. $4.4 billion.
    c. $1.4 billion.
    d. −$1.4 billion.
    e. none of the above.

16. The largest category of GDP is _____, and the most unstable category of GDP is _____.
    a. consumption, consumption
    b. government, investment
    c. consumption, investment
    d. consumption, government purchases
    e. investment, consumption

17. Which of the following will be counted as part of this year's Canadian GDP?
    a. goods produced last year but not sold until this year
    b. goods produced this year by a Canadian working in Paris
    c. purchases of Bank of Montreal stock
    d. sales of used lawn mowers that take place this year
    e. none of the above

Section 6.3

18. In the income approach to measuring GDP, factor payments do *not* include
    a. wages and salaries for the use of labour services.
    b. rent for land.
    c. interest payments for the use of capital goods.
    d. profits for entrepreneurs.
    e. All of the above are included as factor payments.

19. Which of the following is *not* considered a factor payment?
    a. wages
    b. interest
    c. rent
    d. profit
    e. transfer payments

20. What is added to net domestic income to get GDP?
    a. depreciation
    b. indirect taxes less subsidies
    c. personal income taxes
    d. both a and b.

21. Disposable income is
    a. a measure of the market value of total output.
    b. a measure of the income households have to spend before paying taxes.
    c. a measure of the income households have to spend after paying taxes.
    d. a measure of household income from investment income, such as dividends and capital gains.

22. Disposable income will increase when
    a. taxes rise and transfer payments rise.
    b. taxes rise and transfer payments fall.
    c. taxes fall and transfer payments rise.
    d. taxes fall and transfer payments fall.

Section 6.4

23. The CPI is a measure of
    a. the overall price of goods and services produced in the economy.
    b. the overall price of inputs purchased by a typical producer.
    c. the overall price of goods and services bought by a typical consumer.
    d. the overall price of stocks on the Toronto Stock Exchange.

24. If the consumer price index was 100 in the base year and 110 in the following year, the inflation rate was
    a. 110 percent.
    b. 100 percent.
    c. 11 percent.
    d. 10 percent.

25. The current cost of a market basket of goods is $6000. The cost of the same basket of goods in the base year was $4000. The current price index is
    a. 600.
    b. 160.
    c. 150.
    d. 133.
    e. 66.7.

26. The CPI overestimates changes in the cost of living because
    a. new products enter the marketplace, which increases economic welfare, but the CPI does not pick up the increase in welfare.
    b. the CPI does not adequately deal with changes in the quality of products over time.
    c. the CPI deals with a fixed market basket and doesn't capture the savings households enjoy when they substitute cheaper alternatives in response to a price change.
    d. of all of the above.

27. Nominal GDP is
    a. the base year market value of all final goods and services produced domestically during a given period.
    b. the current year market value of all final goods and services produced domestically during a given period.
    c. usually less than real GDP.
    d. the current year market value of domestic production of intermediate goods.
    e. none of the above.

28. Nominal GDP differs from real GDP in that
    a. nominal GDP tends to increase when total production of output in the economy increases, whereas real GDP does not.
    b. nominal GDP is measured in base year prices, whereas real GDP is measured in current year prices.
    c. nominal GDP is measured in current year prices, whereas real GDP is measured in base year prices.
    d. real GDP excludes taxes paid to the government, whereas nominal GDP does not.

29. The consumer price index
    a. takes government purchases into account, unlike the GDP deflator.
    b. takes business investment purchases into account, unlike the GDP deflator.
    c. equals 100 in the base year, unlike the GDP deflator.
    d. is generally used to adjust nominal GDP to calculate real GDP.
    e. None of the above is true.

30. Real GDP in base year dollars equals
    a. nominal GDP divided by the GDP deflator, times 100.
    b. nominal GDP divided by the GDP deflator.
    c. nominal GDP times the GDP deflator.
    d. nominal GDP times the GDP deflator, divided by 100.
    e. none of the above.

31. Suppose that nominal GDP in 2000 equals $800 billion, and in 2001, nominal GDP equals $850 billion. It can be concluded that
    a. total production of output decreased from 2000 to 2001.
    b. total production of output increased from 2000 to 2001.
    c. the economy experienced inflation from 2000 to 2001.
    d. the economy experienced deflation from 2000 to 2001.
    e. None of the above is necessarily true.

32. If real GDP increases and population increases, then real GDP per capita
    a. will rise.
    b. will fall.
    c. will remain unchanged.
    d. could either rise, fall, or remain unchanged.

33. If nominal GDP rises from $5 billion to $6 billion, when the GDP deflator goes from 100 to 120, real GDP
    a. rises.
    b. falls.
    c. stays the same.
    d. could either be rising or falling.

Section 6.5

34. Important factors that are excluded from GDP measurements include
    a. leisure.
    b. the underground economy.
    c. nonmarket transactions.
    d. the value of changes in the environment.
    e. all of the above.

35. Which of the following is measured in GDP?
  a. leisure
  b. underground economic transactions
  c. the services of homemakers
  d. external benefits and costs
  e. none of the above

36. If Country A had a bigger underground economy than Country B, and Country A's citizens worked fewer hours per week than the citizens of Country B, other things being equal, then
  a. GDP comparisons between the countries would overstate the economic welfare of Country A compared to B.
  b. GDP comparisons between the countries would understate the economic welfare of Country A compared to B.
  c. it is impossible to know which direction GDP comparisons between the countries would be biased as measures of the economic welfare of the two countries.
  d. it would not introduce any bias in using GDP to compare economic welfare between the countries.
  e. none of the above would be true.

Problems

1. [Section 6.1]
Answer the following questions about GDP.
  a. What is the definition of GDP?
  b. Why does GDP measure only the final value of goods and services?
  c. Why does GDP measure only the value of goods and services produced within a country?
  d. How does GDP treat the sales of used goods?
  e. How does GDP treat sales of corporate stock from one shareholder to another?

2. [Section 6.2]
Fill in the missing data for the following table (in millions).

Consumption:	_____
Consumption of durable goods:	$1200
Consumption of nondurable goods:	$1800
Consumption of services:	$2400
Investment:	_____
Fixed investment:	$800
Inventory investment:	$600
Government expenditures on goods and services:	$1600
Government transfer payments:	$500
Exports:	$500
Imports:	$650
Net exports:	_____
GDP:	_____

3. [Section 6.4]

Fill in the missing data for the following table.

Year	GDP Deflator	Nominal GDP (in billions)	Real GDP (in billions)
2004	90.9	$700	
2005	100		$800
2006		$1000	$800
2007	140	$1400	
2008	150		$1200

4. [Section 6.4]

Say that the bundle of goods purchased by a typical consumer in the base year consisted of 20 kilograms of apples, at a price of $1 per kilogram, and 15 loaves of bread, at a price of $2 per loaf. What would the consumer price index be in a year in which

a. apples cost $2 per kilogram and bread cost $1 per loaf?

b. apples cost $3 per kilogram and bread cost $2 per loaf?

c. apples cost $2 per kilogram and bread cost $4 per loaf?

Economic Growth in the Global Economy

Economic Growth

- What is economic growth?
- What is the Rule of 70?
- What is productivity?

SHORT RUN VERSUS LONG RUN

John Maynard Keynes, one of the most influential economic thinkers of all time, once said that "in the long run, we are all dead." The reason Keynes said this is that he was primarily concerned with explaining and reducing short-term fluctuations in the level of business activity. He wanted to smooth out the business cycle, largely because of the implications that cyclical fluctuations had for buyers and sellers in terms of unemployment and price instability. No one would deny that Keynes's concerns were important and legitimate.

At the same time, however, Keynes's flippant remark about the long run ignores the fact that human welfare is greatly influenced by long-term changes in a nation's capacity to produce goods and services. Emphasis on short-run economic fluctuations ignores the longer-term dynamic changes that affect output, leisure, real incomes, and lifestyles.

What are the determinants of long-run economic growth? What are some of the consequences of rapid economic change? Why are some nations rich whereas others are poor? Does growth in output improve our economic welfare? These are a few questions that we need to explore.

DEFINING ECONOMIC GROWTH

Economic growth is usually measured by the annual percent change in real output of goods and services per capita (real GDP per capita). In Chapter 2, we introduced the production possibilities curve. Along the production possibilities curve, the economy is producing at its potential output. How much the economy will produce at its potential output, sometimes called its *natural rate of output,* depends on the quantity and quality of an economy's resources, including labour, capital (like factories, machinery, and tools), land (fish, lumber, and so on), and entreprenurial activity. In addition, technology can increase the economy's production capabilities. As shown in Exhibit 1, improvements in and greater stocks of land, labour, capital, and entrepreneurial activity will shift the production possibilities curve out. Another way of saying that economic growth has shifted the production possibilities curve out is to say that it has increased potential output.

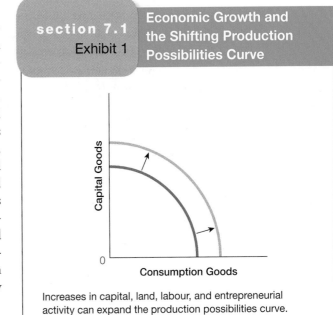

section 7.1
Exhibit 1

Economic Growth and the Shifting Production Possibilities Curve

Increases in capital, land, labour, and entrepreneurial activity can expand the production possibilities curve.

THE RULE OF 70

If Nation A and Nation B start off with the same size population and the same level of real GDP but grow at only slightly different rates over a long period of time, will it make much of a difference? Yes. In the first year or two the differences will be small but even over a decade the differences will be large, and huge after 50 to 100 years. And the final impact will be a much higher standard of living in the nation with the greater economic growth, *ceteris paribus.*

economic growth
an upward trend in the real per capita output of goods and services

A simple formula, called the Rule of 70, shows how long it will take a nation to double its output at various growth rates. If you take a nation's growth rate and divide it into 70, you will have the approximate time it will take to double the income level. For example, if a nation grows at 3.5 percent per year, then the economy will double every 20 years (70/3.5). However, if an economy only grows at 2 percent per year, then the economy will double every 35 years (70/2). And at a 1 percent annual growth rate, it will take 70 years to double income (70/1). So even a small change in the growth rate of a nation will have a large impact over a lengthy period.

In Exhibit 2, we see the growth rates in real per capita GDP for selected industrial countries. Because of differences in growth rates, some countries will become richer than others over time. With relatively slower economic growth, today's richest countries will not be the richest for very long. And with even slight improvements in economic growth, today's poorest countries will not remain poor for very long. We see, in Canada's case, that our growth rate in the 1989–1998 period was the worst of the seven countries listed; however, our growth rate rebounded in the 1999–2008 period, surpassing that of the United States. In order to close the gap in standard of living with the United States, Canada's growth in real GDP per capita must exceed that of the United States.

Because of past economic growth, the "richest" or "most-developed" countries today have many times the

section 7.1
Exhibit 2

Growth in Real per Capita GDP, Selected Industrial Countries

	Ten-Year Averages	
	1989–1998	**1999–2008**
Canada	0.9%	2.1%
United States	1.8	1.8
Japan	1.7	1.4
Germany	1.8	1.4
France	1.4	1.5
Italy	1.5	1.1
United Kingdom	1.7	2.3

SOURCE: World Economic Outlook, April 2007. International Monetary Fund. Printed by permission from the International Monetary Fund.

market output per person of the "poorest" or "least-developed" countries. Put differently, the most-developed countries produce and market per person more output in a day than the least-developed countries do in a year. The international differences in income, output, and wealth are indeed striking and have caused a great deal of friction between developed and less-developed countries. Canada, the United States, Japan, and the nations of the European Union have had sizeable increases in real output over the past two centuries, but even in 1900 most of these nations were better off in terms of real GDP per capita than impoverished countries such as Ethiopia, India, or Nepal are today.

PRODUCTIVITY: THE KEY TO A HIGHER STANDARD OF LIVING

productivity
the amount of goods and services a worker can produce per hour

Will the standard of living in Canada rise, level off, or even decline over time? The answer depends on productivity growth. **Productivity** is the amount of goods and services a worker can produce per hour. Productivity is especially important because it determines a country's standard of living. For example, slow growth of capital investment can lead to lower labour productivity and, consequently, lower wages. On the other hand, increases in productivity and higher wages can occur as a result of carefully crafted economic policies, such as tax policies that stimulate investment or programs that encourage research and development.

The link between productivity and the standard of living can most easily be understood by recalling our circular flow model in Section 6.3. The circular flow model showed that aggregate expenditures are equal to aggregate income. In other words, the aggregate values

In The **NEWS**

PEOPLE WORK MORE HOURS, BUT GROWTH IN OUTPUT LAGS

CBC NEWS

Canadian business productivity grew at the slowest rate in three years in 2007—increasing by just 0.5 per cent—and actually shrank in the fourth quarter, Statistics Canada reported.

By comparison, U.S. productivity increased by 1.9 per cent in 2007, the federal agency said. In the previous two years, Canadian businesses had bigger productivity gains than their U.S. counterparts.

Productivity, measured as real gross domestic product per hour worked, shows the trend in economic output, adjusted for inflation, of workers' efforts and the capital and equipment they use.

In the fourth quarter, when Canadian output was hit by a 2.2 per cent fall in exports, productivity fell 0.8 per cent, Statistics Canada said.

The good news in the latest report is that Canadians worked more hours last year [although not in the troubled manufacturing sector] and saw their hourly earnings rise.

The bad news is that growth in output slowed. By definition, productivity declines when hours worked increase faster than GDP.

A tightening Canadian labour market in Canada, especially in the West, continued to push up hourly wages in 2007.

The gain for the year was 3.7 per cent, down from 4.2 per cent in 2006 and 5.2 per cent in 2005 but well above the 2001–2004 average of 2.6 per cent.

The modest 0.5 per cent rise in productivity, combined with this growth in pay, resulted in a 3.2 per cent increase in labour costs per unit of production.

In manufacturing, productivity fell by 0.4 per cent in the fourth quarter after gains earlier in the year. This brought the growth in manufacturing productivity for 2007 to 1.9 per cent, compared with a bare 0.1 per cent in 2006.

Hours worked in manufacturing fell 1.2 per cent in the quarter, the seventh straight quarterly decline, reflecting continued restructuring in this sector, the agency said.

SOURCE: CBC News, http://www.cbc.ca/money/story/2008/03/14/labour-productivity.html Last Updated: Friday, March 14, 2008 11:18 A.M. ET. Reprinted with permission from *The Globe and Mail*.

CONSIDER THIS:

Due to productivity, modern economies are able to produce significantly more goods and services for less work effort. The result is rising standards of living. In Canada's case, the results are mixed; a productivity gain of just 0.5 percent in 2007 is the slowest growth rate in the last three years.

of all final goods and services produced in the economy must equal the payments made to the factors of production—the wages and salaries paid to workers, the interest payment to capital, the profits, and so on. That is, the only way an economy can increase its rate of consumption in the long run is if it increases the amount it produces. But why are some countries so much better than others at producing goods and services? We will see the answer in the next section, as we examine the determinants of productivity—quantity and quality of labour resources, land, physical capital, and techonological advances.

Section Check

1. Economic growth is usually measured by the annual percent change in real output of goods and services per capita. Improvements in and greater stocks of land, labour, capital, and entrepreneurial activity will lead to greater economic growth and shift the production possibilities curve outward.
2. According to the Rule of 70, if you take a nation's growth rate and divide it into 70, you have the approximate time it will take to double the income level.

Determinants of Economic Growth

■ What factors contribute to economic growth?
■ What is human capital?

FACTORS THAT CONTRIBUTE TO ECONOMIC GROWTH

Many separate explanations of the process of economic growth have been proposed. Which is correct? None of them, by themselves, can completely explain economic growth. However, each of the explanations may be part of a more complicated reality. Economic growth is a complex process involving many important factors, not one of which completely dominates. We can list at least several factors that nearly everyone would agree have contributed to economic growth in some or all countries:

1. The quantity and quality of labour resources (labour and human capital)
2. Increase in the use of inputs provided by the land (natural resources)
3. Physical capital inputs (machines, tools, buildings, inventories)
4. Technological knowledge (new ways of combining given quantities of labour, natural resources, and capital inputs), allowing greater output than previously possible

Labour

We know that labour is needed in all forms of productive activity. But other things being equal, an increase in the quantity of labour inputs does not necessarily increase output per capita. For example, if the increase in the quantity of labour input is due to an increase in population, per capita growth might not occur because the increase in output could be offset by the increase in population. However, if a greater proportion of the population works (that is, the labour force participation rate rises) or if workers put in longer hours, output per capita will increase—assuming that the additional work activity adds something to output.

human capital
the productive knowledge and skill people receive from education and on-the-job training

Qualitative improvements in workers (learning new skills, for example) can also enhance output. Indeed, it has become popular to view labour skills as **"human capital"** that can be augmented or improved by education and on-the-job training. Human capital has to be produced like physical capital with teachers, schoolrooms, libraries, computer labs, and time devoted to studying.

Natural Resources

The abundance of natural resources, like fertile soils, and other raw materials, like lumber and oil, can enhance output. Many scholars have cited the abundance of natural resources in Canada as one reason for its historical economic success. Resources are, however, not the whole story, as is clear with reference to Japan or especially Hong Kong, both of which have had tremendous success with relatively few natural resources. Similarly, Brazil has a large and varied natural resource base yet its income per capita is relatively low compared to many developed countries. It appears that a natural resource base can affect the initial development process but sustained growth is influenced by other factors. However, most economists would agree that a limited resource base does pose an important obstacle to economic growth.

innovation
applications of new knowledge that create new products or improve existing products

Physical Capital

Even in primitive economies, workers usually have some rudimentary tools to further their productive activity. Take the farmer who needs to dig a ditch to improve drainage in his fields. If he used just his bare hands, it might take years to complete the job. If he used a shovel, he could dig the ditch in hours or days. But with a big earthmoving machine, he could do it in minutes. There is nearly universal agreement that capital formation has played a significant role in the economic development of nations.

Countries that do not keep up with technology will generally be unable to keep up their economic growth and standard of living. If a country is technologically backward, it will lose global competitiveness and often rely on a narrow range of exports that will eventually lose their profitability in the global economy. For example, a country that relied on exporting copper may lose its market as other countries around the world convert their phone and cable lines to fibre optics.

Technological Advances

Technological advances stem from human ingenuity and creativity in developing new ways of combining the factors of production to enhance the amount of output from a given quantity of resources. The process of technological advance involves invention and innovation. **Innovation** is the adoption of the product or process. For example, the invention and innovation of the combine machine in agriculture, the assembly line in manufacturing, and the railroad were important stimuli to economic growth. New technology, however, must be introduced into productive use by managers or entrepreneurs who must weigh the perceived estimates of benefits of the new technology against estimates of costs. Thus, the entrepreneur is an important economic factor in the growth process.

Technological advance permits us to economize on one or more inputs used in the production process. It can permit savings of labour, such as when a new machine does the work of many workers. When this happens, technology is said to be embodied in capital and to be labour saving. Technology, however, can also be land (natural resource) saving or even capital saving. For example, nuclear fission has permitted us to build power plants that economize on the use of coal, a natural resource. The reduction in transportation time that accompanied the invention of the railroad allowed businesses to reduce the capital they needed in the form of inventories. Because goods could be obtained more quickly, businesses could reduce the stock kept on their shelves.

© LAWRENCE LOWERY/PHOTODISC/GETTY ONE IMAGES

In The **NEWS**

THE NEW ECONOMY?

BY JOHN BROWNING AND SPENCER REISS

Working with information is very different from working with the steel and glass from which our grandparents built their wealth. Information is easier to produce and harder to control than stuff you can drop on your foot. For a start, computers can copy it and ship it anywhere, almost instantly and almost for free. Production and distribution, the basis of industrial power, can increasingly be taken for granted. Innovation and marketing are all.

So an information economy is more open—it doesn't take a production line to compete, just a good idea. But it's also more competitive. Information is easy not just to duplicate, but to replicate. Successful firms have to keep innovating to keep ahead of copycats nipping at their heels. The average size of companies shrinks. New products and knockoffs alike emerge in months rather than years, and market power is increasingly based on making sense of an overabundance of ideas rather than rationing scarce material goods. Each added connection to a network's pool of knowledge multiplies the value of the whole. . . . The result:

new rules of competition, new sorts of organization, new challenges for management.

SOURCE: John Browning and Spencer Reiss, "Encyclopedia of the New Economy," *Wired*. http://www.hotwired.com/special/ene/index .html?word=intro_two. © *Wired*. By permission of John Browning and Spencer Reiss.

CONSIDER THIS:
The move to the information economy is shaping the way we think about the future. However, it is difficult to accurately measure the gains computers and telecommunications equipment are generating. Almost 75 percent of all computers are used in the service sector, in areas like finance, banking, education, and government administration. In these areas, productivity gains have been difficult to measure. In addition, many of the benefits come in the form of quality or convenience, like 24-hour-a-day automated bank tellers. Some of these quality-of-life improvements are not accurately measured in macroeconomic data.

Section Check

1. The factors that contribute to economic growth are increased quantity and quality of labour, natural resources, physical capital, and technological advances.
2. Labour can be improved through investment in human capital—that is, education, on-the-job training, and experience can improve the quality of labour.

section
7.3

Raising the Level of Economic Growth

- Why is the saving rate so important to increasing economic growth?
- Why is research and development so important to economic growth?
- Why are property rights so important to increasing economic growth?
- What impact will free trade have on economic growth?
- Why is education so important to economic growth?

THE IMPACT OF ECONOMIC GROWTH

Economic growth means more than an increase in the real income (output) of the population. A number of other important changes accompany changes in output. Some have even claimed that economic growth stimulates political freedom or democracy, but the correlation here is far from conclusive. Although there are rich democratic societies and poor authoritarian ones, the opposite also holds. That is, some features of democracy, such as majority voting and special interest groups, may actually be growth retarding. For example, if the majority decides to vote in large land reforms and wealth transfers, this will lead to higher taxes and market distortions that will reduce incentives for work, investment, and ultimately economic growth. However, there are a number of policies that a nation can pursue to increase economic growth.

SAVING RATES, INVESTMENT, CAPITAL STOCK, AND ECONOMIC GROWTH

One of the most important determinants of economic growth is the saving rate. In order to consume more in the future, we must save more now. Generally speaking, higher levels of saving will lead to higher rates of investment and capital formation and, therefore, to greater economic growth. Individuals can either consume or save their disposable income. If individuals choose to consume all of their disposable income, there will be nothing left for saving, which businesses could use for investment purposes to build new plants or replace worn-out or obsolete equipment. With little investment in capital stock, there will be little economic growth. Capital can also increase as a result of capital injections from abroad (foreign direct investments), but the role of national saving rates in economic growth is of particular importance.

Exhibit 1 clearly shows that sustained rapid economic growth is associated with high rates of saving and investment around the world. However, investment alone does not

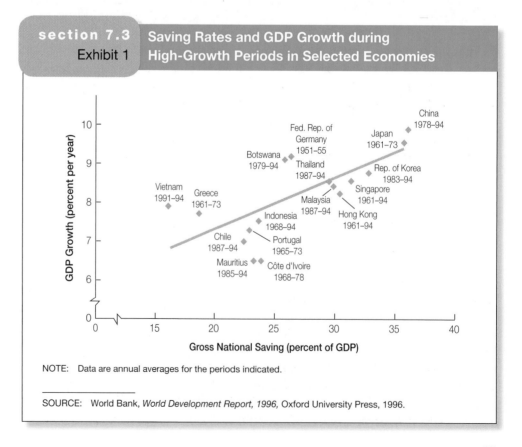

**section 7.3
Exhibit 1**   Saving Rates and GDP Growth during High-Growth Periods in Selected Economies

NOTE: Data are annual averages for the periods indicated.

SOURCE: World Bank, *World Development Report, 1996,* Oxford University Press, 1996.

guarantee economic growth. Economic growth hinges on the quality and the type of investment as well as on investments in human capital and improvements in technology.

RESEARCH AND DEVELOPMENT

Some scholars believe that the importance of **research and development (R&D)** is understated. The concept of R&D is broad indeed—it can include new products, management improvements, production innovations, or simply learning-by-doing. However, it is clear that investing in R&D and rewarding innovators with patents have paid big dividends in the past 50 to 60 years. Some would argue that even larger rewards for research and development would spur even more rapid economic growth. In addition, an important link exists between research and development and capital investment. As already noted, when capital depreciates over time, it is replaced with new equipment that embodies the latest technology. Consequently, R&D may work hand in hand with investment to improve growth and productivity.

research and development (R&D)
activities undertaken to create new products and processes that will lead to technological progress

THE PROTECTION OF PROPERTY RIGHTS IMPACTS ECONOMIC GROWTH

Economic growth rates tend to be higher in countries where the government enforces property rights. Property rights give owners the legal right to keep or sell their property—land, labour, or capital. Without property rights, life would be a huge free-for-all, where people could take whatever they wanted; in this scenario, protection for property, such as alarm systems and private security services, would have to be purchased.

In most developed countries, property rights are effectively protected by the government. However, in developing countries, this is not usually the case. And if the government is not enforcing these rights, the private sector must respond in costly ways that stifle economic growth. For example, an unreliable judiciary system means that entrepreneurs are often forced to rely on informal agreements that are difficult to enforce. As a result, they may have to pay bribes to get things done, and even then, they may not get the promised services. Individuals will have to buy private security or pay organized crime for protection against crime and corruption. In addition, landowners and business owners might be fearful of coups or takeovers from a new government, which might confiscate their property altogether. In short, if government is not adequately protecting property rights, the incentive to invest will be hindered, and political instability, corruption, and lower rates of economic growth will be likely.

Free trade and a stable monetary environment are important to economic growth, but governance is important too. The government has to protect private property and individual rights and enforce contracts, otherwise globalization can lead to corruption and violence. Russians have high levels of education, but the failure of the legal system has led to a dismal economic performance.

FREE TRADE AND ECONOMIC GROWTH

Allowing free trade can also lead to greater output because of the principle of comparative advantage. Essentially, the principle of comparative advantage suggests that if two nations or individuals with different resource endowments and production capabilities specialize in producing a smaller number of goods and services and engage in trade, both parties will benefit. Total output and consumption will rise. This will be discussed in greater detail in Chapter 14.

© ISTOCKPHOTO.COM/CAYUWE KULZER.

BIRUTE VIJEIKIENE, SHUTTERSTOK

Better education in poor countries is a relatively inexpensive method to enrich the lives of those in poorer countries. Education allows these countries to produce more advanced goods and services and enjoy the wealth created from trading in the global economy. Taiwan, India, and Korea are now all part of the high-tech global economy, but most of Africa, with the lowest levels of education, has been left behind.

However, it is important to note that for a country like Canada, which is a significantly open economy that trades considerably with the rest of the world, international trade has played a central role in it's economic growth over the last half century.

EDUCATION

Education, investment in human capital, may be just as important as improvements in physical capital. At any given time, an individual has a choice between current work and investment activities like education that can increase future earning power. People accept reductions in current income to devote current effort to education and training. In turn, a certain return on the investment is expected, for in later years they will earn a higher wage rate (the amount of the increase depending on the nature of the education and training as well as individual natural ability). For example, in Canada, a person with a college or university degree can be expected to earn almost twice as much per year as a high-school graduate.

One argument for government subsidizing education is that this investment can increase the skill level of the population and raise the standard of living. However, even if the individual does not benefit financially from increased education, society may benefit socially and in other respects from having its members highly educated. For example, more education may lead to lower crime rates, new ideas that may benefit the society at large, and more informed voters.

With economic growth, illiteracy rates fall and formal education grows. Exhibit 2 shows the adult literacy rates for selected countries. The correlation between per capita output and the proportion of the population that is able to read or write is striking. Improvements in literacy stimulate economic growth by reducing barriers to the flow of information; when information costs are high, out of ignorance many resources flow to

---

section 7.3
Exhibit 2   **Literacy and Economic Development**

Country	Output Per Capita (U.S. $)	Adult Literacy Rates
United States	$41 890	99.0%
Canada	33 375	99.0
Japan	31 267	99.0
Brazil	8 402	88.6
India	3 452	61.0
Haiti	1 663	54.8
Ethiopia	1 055	35.9

NOTE: The literacy rates are based on the ability to read and write at an elementary school level.

SOURCE: United Nations Human Development Report, 2007/2008.

or remain in uses that are rather unproductive. Moreover, education imparts skills that are directly useful in raising labour productivity, whether it is mathematics taught to a sales clerk, engineering techniques taught to a college or university graduate, or just good ideas that facilitate production and design.

However, in developing poor countries, the higher opportunity costs of education present an obstacle. Children in developing countries are an important part of the labour force starting at a young age. But children who are attending school cannot help in the field—planting, harvesting, fence building, and many other tasks that are so important in the rural areas of developing countries. A child's labour contribution to the family is far less important in a developed country. Thus the higher opportunity cost of an education in developing countries is one of the reasons that school enrolments are lower.

Education may also be a consequence of economic growth, because as incomes rise, people's tendency to consume education increases. People increasingly look to education for more than the acquisition of immediately applicable skills. Education becomes a consumption good as well as a means of investing in human capital.

Section Check

1. Generally speaking, higher levels of saving will lead to higher rates of investment and capital formation and, therefore, to greater economic growth.
2. Larger rewards for research and development would spur even more rapid economic growth.
3. Economic growth rates tend to be higher in countries where the government enforces property rights more vigorously.
4. Allowing free trade can also lead to greater output because of the principle of comparative advantage.
5. Education, investment in human capital, is important to improving standards of living and economic growth.

Population and Economic Growth

- When is population growth beneficial to per capita economic growth?
- When is population growth detrimental to per capita economic growth?

POPULATION GROWTH AND ECONOMIC GROWTH

At the beginning of the English Industrial Revolution (c. 1750), the world's population was perhaps 700 million. It took 150 years (to 1900) for that population to slightly more than double to 1.6 billion. Just 64 years later (in 1964), it had doubled again to 3.2 billion.

After another 41 years (in 2005), the population doubled yet again to more than 6.4 billion. Economic development occurred amidst all this growth in population, but what role does population play in economic growth?

The effect of population growth on per capita economic growth is far from obvious. If population were to expand faster than output, per capita output would fall; population growth would inhibit growth. With a larger population, however, comes a larger labour force. Also, economies of large-scale production may exist in some forms of production, so larger markets associated with greater populations lead to more efficient-sized production units.

The general feeling, however, is that in many of the developing countries today, rapid population growth threatens the possibility of attaining sustained economic growth. These countries are predominantly agricultural with modest natural resources, especially land. The land-labour ratio is low. Why is population growth a threat in these countries? One answer was provided nearly two centuries ago by an English economist, the Reverend Thomas Malthus.

THE MALTHUSIAN PREDICTION

Malthus formulated a theoretical model that predicted that per capita economic growth would eventually become negative and that wages would ultimately reach equilibrium at a subsistence level, or just large enough to provide enough income to stay alive. To create this model, Malthus made three assumptions: (1) the economy was agricultural, with goods produced by two inputs, land and labour; (2) the supply of land was fixed; and (3) human sexual desires worked to increase population.

THE LAW OF DIMINISHING MARGINAL RETURNS

As population increases, the number of workers increases, and with greater labour inputs available, output also goes up. At some point, however, output will increase by diminishing amounts because of the law of diminishing returns, which states that if you add variable amounts of one input (in this case, labour) to fixed quantities of another input (in this case, land), output will rise but by diminishing amounts (because as the land-labour ratio falls, less land is available per worker). For example, a rapid growth in the labour force might make it more difficult to equip each worker with sufficient capital, and lower amounts of capital per worker lead to lower productivity and a lower real GDP per capita. In short, the increase in the one factor of production, labour, might cause the other factors of production to be spread too thinly.

AVOIDING MALTHUS'S PREDICTION

Fortunately, Malthus's theory proved spectacularly wrong for much of the world. Although the law of diminishing returns is a valid concept, Malthus's other assumptions were unrealistic. The quantity or quality of tillable land is not completely fixed. Irrigation, fertilizer, and conservation techniques effectively increase arable land. More important, Malthus implicitly neglected the potential for technological advances and ignored the real possibility that improved technology, often embodied in capital, could overcome the impact of the law of diminishing returns. Further, the Malthusian assumption that sexual desire would necessarily lead to population increase is not accurate. True, sexual desire will always be with us, but the number of births can be reduced by birth control techniques.

As we discussed earlier, some economists believe that population growth can lead to greater economic growth. In some countries, a larger population may lead to more entrepreneurs, engineers, and scientists who will contribute to even greater economic growth through technological progress. These factors turn Malthus's theory on its head; instead of population being the villain, it could actually turn out to be the hero.

DO SOME DEVELOPING COUNTRIES STILL FIT MALTHUS'S PREDICTION TODAY?

Unfortunately, the Malthusian assumptions don't vary widely from reality for several developing countries today. Some developing nations of the world are having substantial population increases, with a virtually fixed supply of land, slow capital growth, and few technological advances. For example, in some African nations, the population growth rate is 3 percent per year, whereas food output is growing at only 2 percent per year. In these cases, population growth causes a negative effect on per capita output because the added output derived from having more workers on the land is small.

In fact, some developing countries have tried to reduce the rate of population growth to achieve greater economic growth per capita and higher standards of living. For example, China tried to reduce its population growth rate through laws regulating the number of children a family may have. It is true that in many poor countries, the population growth rate is much higher, nearly 3 percent per year, than in richer countries, about 1 percent per year. High population growth rates may be one explanation for lower standards of living, but many non-Malthusian explanations help explain the recurring poverty that exists in developing countries today, such as political instability, the lack of defined and enforceable property rights, and inadequate investment in human capital.

Section Check

1. Population growth may increase per capita output in resource-rich countries such as Canada, the United States, Australia, and Saudi Arabia, because they have more resources for each labourer to produce with. They are more likely to be able to exploit economies of large-scale production, and they are more likely to have rapidly expanding technology.
2. In some countries, the Malthusian dilemma posed by population growth and diminishing returns is a problem, and they may suffer as a result of population growth.

Summary

Section 7.1
- Economic growth is usually measured by the annual percent change in real output of goods and services per capita—real GDP per capita.

Section 7.2
- The factors that contribute to economic growth are increased quantity and quality of labour, natural resources, physical capital, and technological advances.

Section 7.3
- Higher savings rates generally lead to greater investment and capital formation, which lead to economic growth.
- Research and development can spur more rapid economic growth.

- Economic growth rates tend to be higher in countries where the government enforces property rights vigorously.
- Freer trade can also lead to greater output because of specialization and trade.
- Education—investment in human capital—is important in improving standards of living and economic growth.

Section 7.4
- Population growth has the potential to both improve and diminish a country's growth.
- Malthusian population theory predicted that per capita economic growth would eventually become negative for all economies. It proved wrong for much of the world.

Key Terms and Concepts

For a complete glossary of chapter key terms, visit the textbook's Web site at http://www.sextonmacro2e.nelson.com.

economic growth 177
productivity 178

human capital 180
innovation 180

research and development
(R&D) 183

Review Questions

1. Which of the following best measures economic growth?
   a. the change in nominal GDP
   b. the change in real GDP
   c. the annual percentage change in real GDP
   d. the annual percentage change in nominal GDP per capita
   e. the annual percentage change in real GDP per capita
   f. the inflation rate

2. Which of the following will shift the Canadian production possibilities curve out?
   a. the discovery of new oil reserves
   b. increased immigration of scientists and engineers to Canada
   c. a nuclear war that destroys both people and structures
   d. producing fewer pizzas in order to produce more tractors
   e. producing fewer strawberries in order to produce more corn

3. Explain why choosing between consumer goods and capital goods in the current period is really an intertemporal choice between present and future consumption.

4. Suppose that two poor countries experience different growth rates over time. Country A's real GDP per capita grows at a rate of 7 percent per year on average whereas Country B's real GDP per capita grows at a rate of only 3 percent per annum. Predict how the standard of living will vary between these two countries over time as a result of divergent growth rates.

5. Estimate the number of years needed for an economy's real GDP per capita to double if the annual growth rate in real GDP per capita is
   a. 10 percent.
   b. 5 percent.
   c. 2 percent.
   d. 0.5 percent.

6. What is the difference between "labour" and "human capital"? How does one increase human capital?

7. What is the implication for an economic system with weak enforcement of patent and copyright laws? Why does weak property right enforcement create an incentive problem?

8. Which of the following are likely to improve the productivity of labour and thereby lead to economic growth?
   a. on-the-job experience
   b. college education
   c. a decrease in the amount of capital per worker
   d. improvements in management of resources

Fill in the Blanks

Section 7.1

1. John Maynard Keynes was primarily concerned with explaining and reducing _____ fluctuations in the level of business activity.

2. Many would argue that in the long run, economic growth is a _____ determinant of people's well-being.

3. Economic growth is usually measured by the annual percent change in _____.

4. How much the economy will produce at its potential output depends on the _____ and _____ of an economy's resources.

5. _____ in technology can increase the economy's production capabilities.

6. A nation with _____ economic growth will end up with a much higher standard of living, *ceteris paribus.*

7. The Rule of 70 says that the number of years necessary for a nation to double its output is approximately equal to the nation's _____ rate divided into 70.

8. The international differences in income, output, and wealth are striking and have caused a great deal of friction between _____ and _____ countries.

Section 7.2

9. There are several factors that nearly everyone agrees have contributed to economic growth in some or all countries: (1) growth in the quantity and quality of _____ resources used (human capital); (2) increase in the use of inputs provided by the _____ (natural resources); (3) growth in physical _____ inputs (machines, tools, buildings, inventories); (4) _____ advances (new ways of combining given quantities of labour, natural resources, and capital inputs) allowing greater output than previously possible.

10. If the labour force participation rate in a country _____ or if workers put in _____ hours, output per capita will tend to increase.

11. It has become popular to view labour as _____ capital that can be augmented or improved by education and on-the-job training.

12. There is nearly universal agreement that _____ formation has played a significant role in the economic development of nations.

13. _____ is the adoption of a new product or process.

14. Technological advance permits us to economize on _____, _____, or even _____.

Section 7.3

15. Generally speaking, higher levels of saving will lead to _____ levels of investment and capital formation and, therefore, to _____ economic growth.

16. Investment alone does not guarantee economic growth, which hinges on the _____ and the _____ of investment as well.

17. Research and development can result in _____ products, management _____, production _____, or learning by _____.

18. Economic growth rates tend to be higher in countries where the government enforces _____.

19. _____ can lead to greater output because of the principle of comparative advantage.

20. With economic growth, illiteracy rates _____ and formal education _____.

21. Improvements in literacy stimulate economic growth by _____ barriers to the flow of information and _____ labour productivity.

22. One problem of providing enough education in poorer countries is that because children in developing countries are an important part of the labour force at a young age, there is a _____ opportunity cost of education in terms of forgone contribution to family income.

Section 7.4

23. If population were to expand faster than output, per capita output would _____.

24. According to Malthusian population theory, per capita economic growth would eventually become _____ and wages would ultimately reach equilibrium at a _____ level.

25. Malthusian explanations help explain the recurring poverty that exists in _____ countries today.

True or False

Section 7.1

1. Human welfare is greatly influenced by long-term changes in a nation's capacity to produce goods and services.

2. Emphasis on the short run of the business cycle can ignore the longer-term dynamic changes that affect output and real incomes.

3. Economic growth is usually measured by the annual percent change in the nominal output of goods and services per capita.

4. Along the production possibilities curve, the economy is producing at its potential output, sometimes called its natural level of output.

5. Another way of saying that economic growth has shifted the production possibilities curve out is that it has increased potential output.

6. Greater stocks of land, labour, or capital can shift out the production possibilities curve.

7. The Rule of 70 says that the number of years necessary for a nation to double its output is approximately equal to the nation's growth rate divided by 70.

8. The "richest" or "most-developed" countries today have many times the per capita output of the "poorest" or "least-developed" countries.

Section 7.2

9. Economic growth is a complex process involving many important factors, no one of which completely dominates.

10. If there were an increase in the quantity of physical capital in a country at the same time that the quantity or quality of labour resources used fell, that country would experience economic growth as a result.

11. Technological advances, even if there is no change in the quantity or quality of the labour resources used, tend to lead to economic growth.

12. An increase in labour input does not necessarily increase output per capita.

13. A limited resource base is no obstacle to economic growth.

14. Both the initial development process and the sustained growth of an economy are dependent on a large natural resource base.

15. Technological advances involve both invention and innovation.

16. Because new technology must be introduced into productive use by someone who must weigh estimates of the benefits of the new technology against estimates of the costs, the entrepreneur is an important economic factor in the growth process.

Section 7.3

17. One of the most important determinants of economic growth is the saving rate.

18. Investment alone does not guarantee economic growth.

19. There is an important link between research and development and capital investment, in that when capital depreciates over time, it is replaced with new equipment that embodies the latest technology.

20. In most developed countries, property rights are effectively protected by the government, but in developing countries, this is not normally the case.

21. Free-trade policies will tend to increase the value of total output in an economy.

22. The correlation between per capita output and the proportion of the population that is unable to read or write is very small.

23. Education is both a consequence of economic growth and a cause of economic growth.

Section 7.4

24. The time it takes the world's population to double has been increasing.

25. Malthusian population theory has proved remarkably accurate for most of the world.

26. Some developing countries have tried to reduce population growth to achieve greater economic growth.

Section 7.1

1. Economists typically measure economic growth by tracking
   a. the employment rate.
   b. the unemployment rate.
   c. the expansion index.
   d. real GDP per capita.
   e. nominal GDP.

2. Economic growth refers to a(n) _____ in the output of goods and services in an economy. The greater the economic growth, the _____ goods citizens and their descendants will have to consume.
   a. decrease; less
   b. decrease; more
   c. increase; more
   d. increase; less

3. Economic growth is usually measured by the annual percent change in
   a. nominal GDP.
   b. nominal GDP per capita.
   c. real GDP.
   d. real GDP per capita.

4. The standard of living will decline if
   a. nominal GDP grows at a faster rate than real GDP.
   b. nominal GDP grows at a slower rate than real GDP.
   c. the rate of population growth exceeds the rate of growth of real GDP.
   d. the rate of population growth is less than the rate of growth of real GDP.

5. According to the Rule of 70, if a nation's economy grows at a rate of 5 percent per year, it will take roughly _____ for national income to double.
   a. 10 years
   b. 20 years
   c. 70 years
   d. 14 years
   e. none of the above

6. A country will roughly double its GDP in 10 years if its annual growth rate is
   a. 5 percent.
   b. 7 percent.
   c. 10 percent.
   d. 12 percent.
   e. 20 percent.

7. According to the Rule of 70,
   a. if a country is growing at 7 percent per year, its output will double in approximately 10 years.
   b. if a country is growing at 3.5 percent per year, its output will double in approximately 20 years.
   c. if a country is growing at 1 percent per year, its output will double in approximately 70 years.
   d. all of the above are true.
   e. none of the above is true.

8. According to the Rule of 70, if a country's growth rate doubled, the amount of time before its output doubled would be
   a. quartered.
   b. halved.
   c. doubled.
   d. quadrupled.

Section 7.2

9. How much the economy can produce at its natural rate of output depends on
   a. technology.
   b. the quantity of available natural resources.
   c. the productivity of labour.
   d. the stock of available capital.
   e. all of the above.

10. The natural level of real output in a country will tend to fall if
   a. technology advances.
   b. an increasing fraction of the population retires.
   c. increased investment adds to the capital stock.
   d. existing supplies of natural resources are depleted.
   e. either b or d occurs.

11. An economy's production possibilities curve will shift outward over time if
   a. technological progress occurs.
   b. the stock of available capital decreases.
   c. emigration results in a decrease in the supply of available labour.
   d. the productivity of labour increases.
   e. either a or d occurs.

12. In the long run, the most important determinant of a nation's standard of living is
   a. its rate of productivity growth.
   b. its ability to export cheap labour.
   c. its ability to control the nation's money supply.
   d. its endowment of natural resources.

13. Per capita real output would tend to rise, other things being equal,
   a. if the labour force participation rate in the country rose.
   b. if the population rose.
   c. if the population fell and the labour force participation rate in the country fell.
   d. in all of the above cases.
   e. in none of the above cases.

14. If there were both an increase in the capital stock and an increase in technology in a country, other things being equal, the country's potential output would
   a. rise.
   b. fall.
   c. remain unchanged.
   d. change in an indeterminate direction.

15. Technological advances can be
   a. labour saving.
   b. capital saving.
   c. land (natural resource) saving.
   d. any of the above.

16. If Goodland's population grows faster than Badland's population, but Badland's labour force participation rate is growing faster than that in Goodland, other things being equal,
    a. real GDP will be growing faster in Badland.
    b. real GDP per capita will be growing faster in Badland.
    c. real GDP will be growing faster in Goodland.
    d. real GDP per capita will be growing faster in Goodland.

Section 7.3

17. Which of the following statements is incorrect?
    a. One of the most important determinants of economic growth is a nation's saving rate.
    b. Injections of foreign capital from abroad may contribute to a nation's economic growth.
    c. Economic growth depends on the quality and type of investments made.
    d. Economic growth rates tend to be lower in countries where property rights are better enforced by government.

18. Which of the following is considered a factor that contributes to economic growth?
    a. government protection of property rights
    b. increased specialization of labour
    c. research and development
    d. improved efficiencies through economies of scale
    e. all of the above

19. Economic growth tends to be greater in countries where
    a. the government effectively protects property rights.
    b. more resources are devoted to research and development.
    c. there is greater freedom to trade freely.
    d. any of the above is true.

20. During the Klondike gold rush, the first prospectors in the region arrived before any government authority was established. They followed a long goldfield tradition and created "miners' laws," which described how gold claims could be staked and how these claims would be enforced. The creation of "miners' laws" showed that these prospectors recognized the importance of which of the following factors that affect economic growth?
    a. increasing physical capital
    b. economies of scale
    c. well-defined and enforced property rights
    d. technological advance

21. In a country that has an unstable government or judiciary, would you expect to see more entrepreneurial activity, or less?
    a. Less, because in an unstable economy there are fewer entrepreneurs.
    b. Less, because there would be an unreliable infrastructure for protecting property rights.
    c. More, because there would be fewer governmental restrictions.
    d. More, because in general there would be less taxation of commercial and research activities.

22. Investment in human capital
    a. is of minor importance to economic growth.
    b. can be acquired through on-the-job training.
    c. is an important source of economic growth.
    d. does not affect economic growth; only physical capital does.
    e. is characterized by both b and c.

23. Other things being equal, the higher the rate of savings across countries,
    a. the higher the rate of change of real GDP per capita.
    b. the lower the rate of change of real GDP per capita.
    c. the lower the productivity of labour.
    d. the lower the rate of investment.

24. Reduced levels of illiteracy
    a. are, in part, a cause of economic growth.
    b. are, in part, caused by economic growth.
    c. are, in part, both a cause of economic growth and caused by economic growth.
    d. are largely unrelated to economic growth.

Section 7.4

25. Which of the following statements regarding population change and economic growth is true?
    a. If population expands faster than output, per capita ouput increases.
    b. If population expands slower than output, per capita output decreases.
    c. If population expands faster than output, per capita output decreases.
    d. There is no connection between population expansion and per capita output.

26. Malthusian population theory describes the reality in which region of the globe?
    a. developing economies.
    b. industrialized economies.
    c. European economies.
    d. North American economies.

Problems

1. **[Section 7.1]**

   Answer the following questions.

   a. According to the Rule of 70, how many years will it take a country to double its output at each of the following annual growth rates?

0.5 percent:	_____ years
1 percent:	_____ years
1.4 percent:	_____ years
2 percent:	_____ years
2.8 percent:	_____ years
3.5 percent:	_____ years
7 percent:	_____ years

   b. If a country had $100 billion of real GDP today, what would its real GDP be in 50 years if it grows at an annual growth rate of

1.4 percent?	_____
2.8 percent?	_____
7 percent?	_____

2. [Sections 7.2 and 7.3]

Which direction would the following changes alter GDP growth and per capita GDP growth in a country (increase, decrease, or indeterminate), other things being equal?

	Real GDP Growth	Real GDP Growth per Capita
An increase in population	_____	_____
An increase in labour force participation	_____	_____
An increase in population and labour force participation	_____	_____
An increase in current consumption	_____	_____
An increase in technology	_____	_____
An increase in illiteracy	_____	_____
An increase in tax rates	_____	_____
An increase in productivity	_____	_____
An increase in tariffs on imported goods	_____	_____
An earlier retirement age in the country	_____	_____
An increase in technology and a decrease in labour force participation	_____	_____
An earlier retirement age and an increase in the capital stock	_____	_____

chapter

8

Aggregate Demand

section
8.1

The Determinants of Aggregate Demand

- What is aggregate demand?
- What is consumption?
- What is investment?
- What are government purchases?
- What are net exports?

WHAT IS AGGREGATE DEMAND?

Aggregate demand (*AD*) is the sum of the demand for all final goods and services in the economy. It can also be seen as the quantity of real GDP demanded at different price levels. The four major components of aggregate demand are consumption (C), investment (I), government purchases (G), and net exports ($X - M$). Aggregate demand, then, is equal to $C + I + G + (X - M)$.

aggregate demand (*AD*)
the total demand for all the final goods and services in the economy

CONSUMPTION (*C*)

Consumption is by far the largest component in aggregate demand. Expenditures for consumer goods and services typically absorb almost 60 percent of total economic activity, as measured by GDP. Understanding the determinants of consumption, then, is critical to an understanding of the forces leading to changes in aggregate demand, which in turn, change total output and income.

Does Higher Income Mean Greater Consumption?

The notion that the higher a nation's income, the more it spends on consumer items, has been validated empirically. At the level of individuals, most of us spend more money when we have higher incomes. But what matters most to us is not our total income but our after-tax or *disposable income*. Moreover, other factors might explain consumption. Some consumer goods are "lumpy"; that is, the expenditures for these goods must come in big amounts rather than in small dribbles. Thus, in years in which a consumer buys a new car, takes the family on a European trip, or goes to college or university, consumption may be much greater in relation to income than in years in which the consumer does not buy such high-cost consumer goods or services. Interest rates also affect consumption because they affect savings. At higher real interest rates, people save more and consume less. At lower real interest rates, people save less and consume more.

The Average and Marginal Propensity to Consume

average propensity to consume (APC)
the fraction of total disposable income that households spend on consumption

marginal propensity to consume (MPC)
the additional consumption resulting from an additional dollar of disposable income

Households typically spend a large portion of their disposable income and save the rest. The fraction of their total disposable income that households spend on consumption is called the **average propensity to consume (APC).** For example, a household that consumes $450 out of $500 disposable income has an *APC* of 0.9 ($450/$500). However, households tend to behave differently with additional income than with their income as a whole. How much increased consumption results from an increase in income? That depends upon the **marginal propensity to consume (MPC),** which is the additional consumption that results from an additional dollar of disposable income. If consumption goes from $450 to $600 when disposable income goes from $500 to $700, what is the marginal propensity to consume out of disposable income? First, we calculate the change in consumption: $600 − $450 = $150. Next, we calculate the change in income: $700 − $500 = $200. The marginal propensity to consume, then, equals change in consumption divided by change in disposable income. In this example,

$$MPC = \frac{\text{Change in consumption}}{\text{Change in disposable income}} = \frac{\$150}{\$200} = \frac{3}{4} = 0.75$$

For each additional dollar in after-tax income over this range, this household consumes three-fourths of the addition, or 75 cents.

INVESTMENT (*I*)

Because investment spending (purchases of investment goods) is an important component of aggregate demand, which in turn is a determinant of the level of GDP, changes in investment spending are often responsible for changes in the level of economic activity. If consumption is determined largely by the level of disposable income, what determines the level of investment expenditures? As you may recall, investment expenditures is the most unstable category of GDP; it is sensitive to changes in economic, social, and political variables. In 2007, investment was roughly 20 percent of GDP.

If firms expect higher sales and profits, they will increase investment spending on capital goods, such as factories, machinery, and equipment.

Many factors are important in determining the level of investment. Good business conditions "induce" firms to invest because a healthy growth in demand for products in the future is likely based on current experience. We will consider the key variables that influence investment spending in the next section.

© STEVE COLE/PHOTODISC/GETTY ONE IMAGES

GOVERNMENT PURCHASES (G)

Government purchases, another component of aggregate demand, are spending by the federal, provincial, and local governments on the purchases of new goods and services produced. Government purchases include health, education, highways, and police protection.

NET EXPORTS (X − M)

The interaction of the Canadian economy with the rest of the world is becoming increasingly important. Models that include international trade effects are called **open economy** models.

    Remember, exports are Canadian-made goods and services that we sell to foreign customers, like lumber, wheat, or telecommunications equipment; imports are goods and services that we buy from foreign companies, like BMWs, French wine, or Sony TVs. Exports and imports can alter aggregate demand. It makes no difference to Canadian sellers if buyers are in this country or in some other country. A buyer is a buyer, foreign or domestic, so exports (X) must be added to the demand side of our equation. But what about goods and services that are consumed here but not produced by the domestic economy? When Canadian consumers, firms, or the government buy foreign goods and services, there is no direct impact on the total demand for Canadian goods and services, so imports (M) must be subtracted from our equation.

    Exports minus imports is what we call **net exports.** If exports are greater than imports, we have positive net exports ($X > M$). If imports are greater than exports, net exports are negative ($X < M$).

    The impact that net exports ($X − M$) have on aggregate demand is similar to the impact that government purchases have on aggregate demand. Suppose that Canada has no trade surplus and no trade deficit—zero net exports. Now say that foreign consumers start buying more Canadian goods and services whereas Canadian consumers continue to buy imports at roughly the same rate. This will lead to *positive net exports* ($X > M$) and result in greater demand for Canadian goods and services, a higher level of aggregate demand. From a policy standpoint, this might explain why countries that are currently in a recession might like to run a trade surplus by increasing exports.

    Of course, it is also possible that a country could run a trade deficit. Again let us assume that the economy was initially in a position with zero net exports. A trade deficit, or *negative net exports* ($X < M$), *ceteris paribus,* would lower Canadian aggregate demand.

open economy
a type of model that includes international trade effects

net exports
the difference between the value of exports and the value of imports

---

Section Check

1. Aggregate demand is the sum of the demand for all final goods and services in the economy. It can also be seen as the quantity of real GDP demanded at different price levels.
2. The four major components of aggregate demand are consumption (C), investment (I), government purchases (G), and net exports (X − M). Aggregate demand, then, is equal to C + I + G + (X − M).
3. Empirical evidence suggests that consumption increases directly with any increase in income.
4. The additional consumption spending stemming from an additional dollar of disposable income is called the marginal propensity to consume (MPC).
5. Changes in investment spending are often responsible for changes in the level of economic activity.
6. Government purchases are made up of federal, provincial, and local purchases of goods and services.
7. Trade deficits lower aggregate demand, other things equal; trade surpluses increase aggregate demand, other things equal.

The Investment and Saving Market

- What is the investment demand curve?
- What is the saving supply curve?
- How is the real interest rate determined?

section 8.2 **The Investment**
Exhibit 1 **Demand Curve**

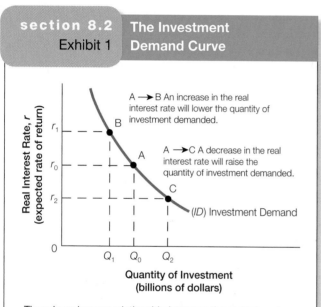

A ➝ B An increase in the real interest rate will lower the quantity of investment demanded.

A ➝ C A decrease in the real interest rate will raise the quantity of investment demanded.

(*ID*) Investment Demand

Quantity of Investment
(billions of dollars)

There is an inverse relationship between the real interest rate and the quantity of investment demanded. At higher real interest rates, firms will only pursue those investment activities with the highest expected return and the quantity of investment demanded will fall—a movement from point A to point B. As the real interest rate falls, projects with lower expected returns become potentially profitable for firms and the quantity of investment demanded rises—a movement from point A to point C.

If we put the investment demand for the whole economy and national savings together, we can establish the real interest rate in the saving and investment market. We begin by revisiting investment, and then follow with the introduction of the saving supply curve and equilibrium.

Exhibit 1 shows the investment demand curve for all the firms in the whole economy. The investment demand (*ID*) curve is downward sloping, reflecting the fact that investment spending varies inversely with the real interest rate—the amount borrowers pay for their loans. At high real interest rates, firms will only pursue those few investment activities with even higher expected rates of return. As the real interest rate falls, additional projects with lower expected rates of return become profitable for firms, and the quantity of investment demanded rises. In other words, the investment demand curve shows the dollar amount of investment forthcoming at different real interest rates. Because lower interest rates stimulate the quantity of investment demanded, governments often try to combat recessions by lowering interest rates.

SHIFTING THE INVESTMENT DEMAND CURVE

Several other determinants will shift the investment demand curve. If firms expect higher rates of return on their investments, for a given interest rate, the *ID* curve will shift to the right, as seen in Exhibit 2. If firms expect lower rates of return on their investments, for a given interest rate, the *ID* curve will shift to the left, also seen in Exhibit 2. Possible investment demand curve shifters include changes in technology, inventories, expectations, and business taxes.

Technology

Product and process innovation can cause the *ID* curve to shift out. For example, the development of new machines that can improve the quality and the quantity of products or lower the costs of production will increase the rate of return on investment, independent of the interest rate. The same is true for new products like handheld computers, the Internet, genetic applications in medicine, or HDTV. Imagine how many different firms increased their investment demand during the computer revolution.

Inventories

When inventories are high and goods are stockpiled in warehouses all over the country, there is a lower expected rate of return on new investment—*ID* shifts to the left. Firms with excess inventories of finished goods have very little incentive to invest in new capital. Alternatively, if inventories are depleted below the levels desired by firms, the expected rate of return on new investment increases, as firms look to replenish their shelves to meet the growing demand—*ID* shifts to the right.

Expectations

If sales and profit rates are expected to be higher in the future, firms will invest more in plant and equipment now, causing the *ID* curve to shift to the right—more investment will be desired at a given interest rate. If lower sales and profits are forecast, the *ID* curve shifts to the left—fewer investments will be desired at a given interest rate.

Business Taxes

If business taxes are lowered—such as with an investment tax credit—potential after-tax profits on investment projects will increase and shift the *ID* curve to the right. Higher business taxes will lead to lower potential after-tax profits on investment projects and shift the *ID* curve to the left.

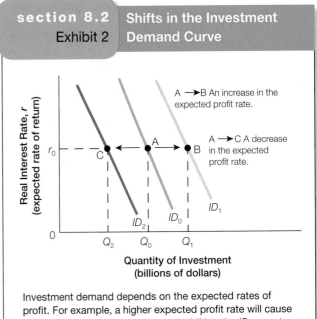

section 8.2
Exhibit 2
Shifts in the Investment Demand Curve

Investment demand depends on the expected rates of profit. For example, a higher expected profit rate will cause an increase in investment demand, shifting the *ID* curve to the right from point A to point B. A lower expected profit rate will cause a decrease in investment demand, shifting the *ID* curve to the left from point A to point C. Any change in technology, inventories, expectations, and business taxes can cause the investment demand curve to shift.

THE SUPPLY OF NATIONAL SAVING

The supply of **national saving** is composed of both private saving and public saving. Households, firms, and the government can supply savings. The supply curve of savings is upward sloping, as seen in Exhibit 3. At a higher real interest rate, there is a greater quantity of savings supplied. Think of the interest rate as the reward for saving and supplying funds to financial markets. At a lower real interest rate, a lower quantity of savings is supplied.

As with the investment demand curve, there are non-interest determinants of the saving supply curve. Two such saving supply curve shifters are disposable (after-tax) income and future expected earnings.

national savings
the sum of private saving and public saving

Disposable Income

If taxes are lowered—allowing disposable income to increase—the supply of saving would shift to the right—more saving would occur at any given interest rate. If taxes increased, causing disposable income to decline, there would be less saving at any given interest rate.

Earnings Expectation

If you expected lower future earnings, you would tend to save more now at any given interest rate—shifting the saving supply curve to the right. If you expected higher future earnings, you would tend to consume more and save less now, knowing that more income is right around the corner—shifting the saving supply curve to the left.

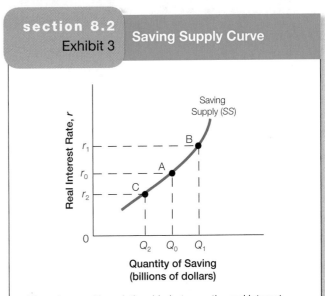

section 8.2
Exhibit 3
Saving Supply Curve

There is a positive relationship between the real interest rate and the quantity of saving supplied. At a higher real interest rate, there is a greater quantity of saving supplied—the movement from point A to point B. At a lower real interest rate, there is a lower quantity of saving supplied—the movement from point A to point C.

In Exhibit 4, we see that an increase in disposable income or lower expected future earnings shifts the saving supply curve to the right. A decrease in disposable income or higher expected future earnings will shift the saving supply curve to the left.

EQUILIBRIUM IN THE SAVING AND INVESTMENT MARKET

In equilibrium, desired investment equals desired national saving at the intersection of the investment demand curve and the saving supply curve. The real equilibrium interest rate is shown by the intersection of these two curves, as seen in Exhibit 5. If the real interest rate, r_1, is above the equilibrium real interest rate, r_E, forces within the economy would tend to restore the equilibrium. At a higher-than-real equilibrium interest rate, the quantity of savings supplied would be greater than the quantity of investment demanded—there would be a surplus of savings at this real interest rate. As savers (lenders) compete against each other to attract investment demanders (borrowers), the real interest rate falls. Alternatively if the real interest rate, r_2, is below the equilibrium real interest rate, r_E, the quantity of investment demanded is greater than the quantity of saving supplied at that interest rate—a shortage of saving occurs. As investment demanders (borrowers) compete against each other for the available saving, the real interest rate is bid up to r_E.

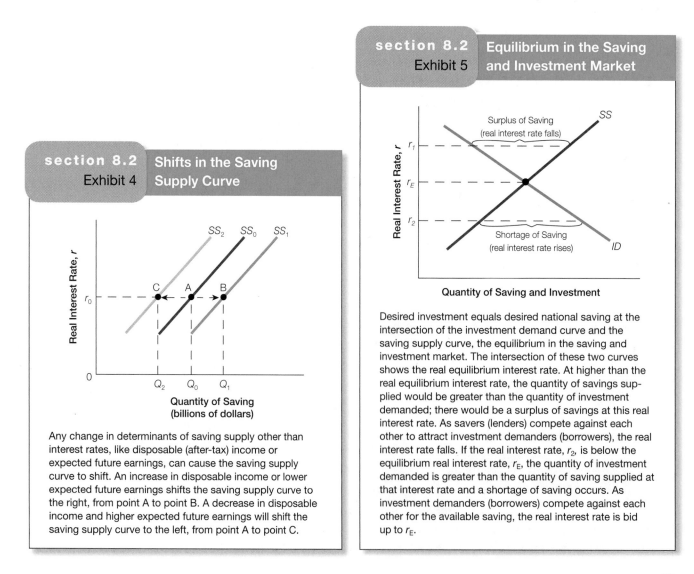

section 8.2
Exhibit 4
Shifts in the Saving Supply Curve

section 8.2
Exhibit 5
Equilibrium in the Saving and Investment Market

Any change in determinants of saving supply other than interest rates, like disposable (after-tax) income or expected future earnings, can cause the saving supply curve to shift. An increase in disposable income or lower expected future earnings shifts the saving supply curve to the right, from point A to point B. A decrease in disposable income and higher expected future earnings will shift the saving supply curve to the left, from point A to point C.

Desired investment equals desired national saving at the intersection of the investment demand curve and the saving supply curve, the equilibrium in the saving and investment market. The intersection of these two curves shows the real equilibrium interest rate. At higher than the real equilibrium interest rate, the quantity of savings supplied would be greater than the quantity of investment demanded; there would be a surplus of savings at this real interest rate. As savers (lenders) compete against each other to attract investment demanders (borrowers), the real interest rate falls. If the real interest rate, r_2, is below the equilibrium real interest rate, r_E, the quantity of investment demanded is greater than the quantity of saving supplied at that interest rate and a shortage of saving occurs. As investment demanders (borrowers) compete against each other for the available saving, the real interest rate is bid up to r_E.

GOVERNMENT AND FINANCIAL MARKETS

We know from our earlier circular flow discussion that the total output of firms equals the total income of households—that is, in a simple economy with just households and firms, where households spend all their incomes, total spending must equal total output. Recall from our discussion of national income accounts that GDP (or Y) = $C + I + G$ + $(X - M)$. That is, aggregate expenditures (Y) must equal the sum of its four components, $C + I + G + (X - M)$. For simplicity, we begin working in a **closed economy,** without the complications introduced by the international, or net export $(X - M)$, component. In a closed economy, net exports are zero because there is no international trade—that is, exports are zero and imports are zero. So we can now write

$$(1)\ Y = C + I + G$$

That is, GDP (Y) is the sum of consumption plus investment plus government purchases. You might ask, what does this have to do with financial markets? If we subtract C and G from both sides of the equation, we have

$$(2)\ Y - C - G = I$$

The left side of the equation ($Y - C - G$) is what remains of total income (Y) when you subtract consumption and government purchases. This is called national saving or saving (S) for short. If we substitute S for $Y - C - G$, we can write

$$(3)\ S = I$$

That is, saving equals investment.

However, to truly understand what happens to saving, we must add net taxes (T). Net taxes are total tax revenues minus transfer payments (like Canada Pension Plan benefits, welfare payments, and Employment Insurance). Transfer payments are that part of tax revenues the government takes from one part of the household sector to give to another part of the household sector. Combining equations (2) and (3), we can write the saving equation as

$$(4)\ S = Y - C - G$$

This can be rewritten as

$$(5)\ S = (Y - T - C) + (T - G)$$

Because the two Ts cancel each other out in equation (5), it is easy to see that these two equations are the same. However, equation (5) does give us some useful information. It divides saving into private saving and public saving. **Private saving** is the amount of income households have left over after consumption and net taxes. **Public saving** is the amount of income the government has left over after paying for its spending.

Most people are familiar with the idea that households and firms can save but are less familiar with the idea that the government can also save. If the government collects more in taxes than it spends ($T > G$), it runs a surplus and public saving is positive. If the government spends more than it collects in taxes ($G > T$), it runs a deficit and public saving is negative. In the next section, we use the tools of supply and demand to examine how budget surpluses and budget deficits affect the real interest rate, national saving, and investment.

Budget Surpluses and Budget Deficits. First, let's see how a budget surplus affects the real interest rate and the amount of saving and investment. In Exhibit 6, suppose that the

closed economy
an economy with no international trade—net exports are zero because exports and imports are zero

private savings
the amount of income households have left over after consumption and net taxes

public savings
the amount of income the government has left over after paying for its spending

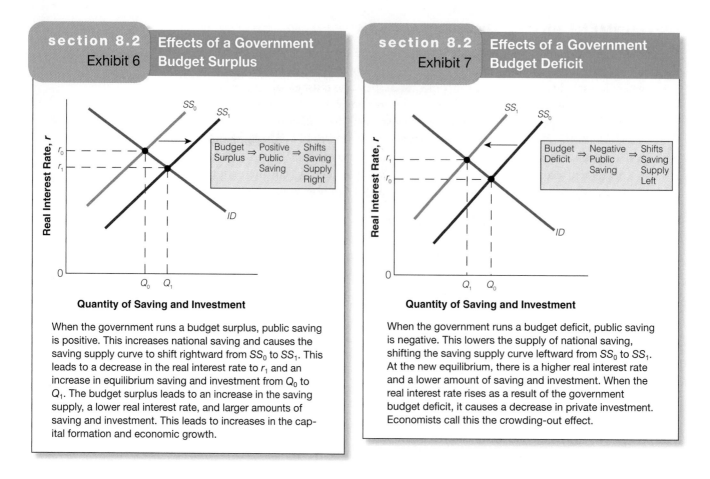

section 8.2   Effects of a Government
   Exhibit 6   Budget Surplus

Quantity of Saving and Investment

When the government runs a budget surplus, public saving is positive. This increases national saving and causes the saving supply curve to shift rightward from SS_0 to SS_1. This leads to a decrease in the real interest rate to r_1 and an increase in equilibrium saving and investment from Q_0 to Q_1. The budget surplus leads to an increase in the saving supply, a lower real interest rate, and larger amounts of saving and investment. This leads to increases in the capital formation and economic growth.

section 8.2   Effects of a Government
   Exhibit 7   Budget Deficit

Quantity of Saving and Investment

When the government runs a budget deficit, public saving is negative. This lowers the supply of national saving, shifting the saving supply curve leftward from SS_0 to SS_1. At the new equilibrium, there is a higher real interest rate and a lower amount of saving and investment. When the real interest rate rises as a result of the government budget deficit, it causes a decrease in private investment. Economists call this the crowding-out effect.

dissaving

consuming more than total available income

government has a balanced budget, the saving supply curve is SS_0, and the investment demand curve is ID_0, resulting in an equilibrium real interest rate equal to r_0 and an equilibrium quantity of saving and investment equal to Q_0. If the government now runs a budget surplus—the government receives more in tax revenues than it spends—there is an increase in public saving, assuming that private saving is unchanged. Because national saving is the sum of private saving and public saving, national saving increases, shifting the saving supply curve from SS_0 to SS_1. What impact does this budget surplus (government saving) have on the real interest rate, saving, and investment? The increase in the saving supply from SS_0 to SS_1 leads to a decrease in the real interest rate to r_1 and an increase in equilibrium saving and investment from Q_0 to Q_1, as shown in Exhibit 6. The budget surplus leads to an increase in the saving supply, a lower real interest rate, and larger amount of saving and investment. This increase in capital formation will tend to increase long-term economic growth.

When the government spends more than it receives in tax revenues, it experiences a budget deficit; the government is actually **dissaving** (saving negatively or borrowing), which decreases national saving. That is, the budget deficit reduces the national supply of saving, shifting the saving supply curve leftward from SS_0 to SS_1 in Exhibit 7. At the new equilibrium, there is a higher real interest rate and a lower amount of saving and investment. When the real interest rate rises because of the government budget deficit, private investment decreases. Economists call this the crowding-out effect, a topic we will expand on in the chapter entitled Fiscal Policy. In sum, when the government runs a budget deficit, it reduces national saving, which leads to a higher real interest rate and lower investment. Because investment is critical for capital formation, long-term economic growth is reduced by budget deficits.

Section Check

1. The investment demand curve is downward sloping, reflecting the fact that the quantity of investment demanded varies inversely with the real interest rate.
2. At high real interest rates, firms will only pursue those few investment activities with still higher expected rates of return. At lower real interest rates, projects with lower expected rates of return become profitable for firms, and the quantity of investment demanded rises.
3. Technology, inventories, expectations, and business taxes can shift the investment demand curve at a given real interest rate.
4. The supply of national saving is composed of both private saving and public saving.
5. The supply curve of saving is upward sloping. At a higher real interest rate, there is an increase in the quantity of saving supplied. At a lower real interest rate, there is a decrease in the quantity of saving supplied.
6. Two noninterest determinants of the saving supply curve are disposable (after-tax) income and expected future earnings.
7. In equilibrium, desired investment equals desired national saving at the intersection of the investment demand curve and the saving supply curve. If the real interest rate is above the equilibrium real interest rate, the quantity of saving supplied is greater than the quantity of investment demanded at that interest rate; lenders will compete against each other to attract borrowers and the real interest rate falls. If the real interest rate is below the equilibrium real interest rate, the quantity of investment demanded is greater than the quantity of saving supplied at that interest rate; borrowers compete with each other for the available saving and drive the real interest rate up.
8. Private saving is the amount of income households have left over after consumption and net taxes.
9. Public saving is the amount of income the government has left over after paying for its spending.
10. National saving is the sum of private saving and public saving.

The Aggregate Demand Curve

- How is the aggregate demand curve different from the demand curve for a particular good?
- Why is the aggregate demand curve downward sloping?

The **aggregate demand curve** reflects the total amount of real goods and services that all groups together want to purchase in a given time period. In other words, it indicates the quantities of real gross domestic product (RGDP) demanded at different price levels. Note that this is different from the demand curve for a particular good presented in Chapter 3, which looked at the relationship between the relative price of a good and the quantity demanded.

aggregate demand curve
graph that shows the inverse relationship between the price level and RGDP demanded

HOW IS THE QUANTITY OF REAL GDP DEMANDED AFFECTED BY THE PRICE LEVEL?

The aggregate demand curve slopes downward, which means that there is an inverse (or opposite) relationship between the price level and real gross domestic product demanded. Exhibit 1 illustrates this relationship, where the quantity of RGDP demanded is measured

section 8.3
Exhibit 1

The Aggregate Demand Curve

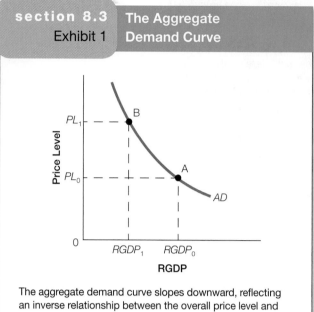

The aggregate demand curve slopes downward, reflecting an inverse relationship between the overall price level and the quantity of real GDP demanded. When the price level increases, the quantity of RGDP demanded decreases; when the price level decreases, the quantity of RGDP demanded increases.

on the horizontal axis and the overall price level is measured on the vertical axis. As we move from point A to point B on the aggregate demand curve, we see that an increase in the price level causes RGDP demanded to fall. Conversely, if there is a reduction in the price level, a movement from B to A, quantity demanded of RGDP increases. Why do purchasers in the economy demand less real output when the price level rises, and more real output when the price level falls?

WHY IS THE AGGREGATE DEMAND CURVE NEGATIVELY SLOPED?

Three complementary explanations exist for the negative slope of the aggregate demand curve: the real wealth effect, the interest rate effect, and the open economy effect.

The Real Wealth Effect

Imagine that you are living in a period of high inflation on a fixed pension that is not indexed for the changing price level. As the cost of goods and services rises, your monthly pension cheque remains the same. Therefore, the purchasing power of your pension will continue to decline as long as inflation is occurring. The same would be true of any asset of fixed dollar value, like cash. If you had $1000 in cash stashed under your bed while the economy suffered a serious bout of inflation, the purchasing power of your cash would be eroded by the extent of the inflation. That is, an increase in the price level reduces real wealth and would consequently decrease your planned purchases of goods and services, lowering the quantity of RGDP demanded.

In the event that the price level falls, the reverse would hold true. A falling price level would increase the real value of your cash assets, increasing your purchasing power and increasing RGDP. The connection can be summarized as follows:

$$\uparrow \text{Price level} \Rightarrow \downarrow \text{Real wealth} \Rightarrow \downarrow \text{Purchasing power} \Rightarrow \downarrow \text{RGDP demanded}$$

and

$$\downarrow \text{Price level} \Rightarrow \uparrow \text{Real wealth} \Rightarrow \uparrow \text{Purchasing power} \Rightarrow \uparrow \text{RGDP demanded}$$

The Interest Rate Effect

The effect of the price level on interest rates can also cause the aggregate demand curve to have a negative slope. Suppose the price level increases. As a result, most goods and services will now have a higher price tag. Consequently, consumers will wish to hold more dollars in order to purchase those items that they want to buy, which will increase the demand for money. If the demand for money increases and the Bank of Canada, the controller of the money supply, does not alter the money supply, then interest rates will rise. In other words, if the demand for money increases relative to the supply, then the demanders of dollars will bid up the price of those dollars—the interest rate. At higher interest rates, the opportunity cost of borrowing rises, and fewer interest-sensitive investments will be profitable, reducing the quantity of investment goods demanded. Businesses contemplating replacing worn-out equipment or planning to expand capacity may cancel or delay their investment decisions unless interest rates decline again. Also, at the higher interest rate, many consumers may give up plans to buy new cars, boats, or houses. That is, the higher interest rate also has a consumption link. The net effect of the higher interest rate, then, is that it will result in fewer investment goods demanded and, consequently, a lower RGDP demanded.

On the other hand, if the price level fell, and people demanded less money as a result, then interest rates would fall. Lower interest rates would trigger greater investment spending, and a larger real GDP demanded would result. We can summarize this process as follows:

$$\uparrow\text{Price level} \Rightarrow \uparrow\text{Money demand (Money supply unchanged)} \Rightarrow \uparrow\text{Interest rate} \Rightarrow$$
$$\downarrow\text{Investment} \Rightarrow \downarrow\text{RGDP demanded}$$

and

$$\downarrow\text{Price level} \Rightarrow \downarrow\text{Money demand (Money supply unchanged)} \Rightarrow \downarrow\text{Interest rate} \Rightarrow$$
$$\uparrow\text{Investment} \Rightarrow \uparrow\text{RGDP demanded}$$

The Open Economy Effect of Changes in the Price Level

Many goods and services are bought and sold in global markets. If the prices of goods and services in the domestic market rise relative to those in global markets due to a higher domestic price level, consumers and businesses will buy more from foreign producers and less from domestic producers. Because real GDP is a measure of domestic output, the reduction in the willingness of consumers to buy from domestic producers leads to a lower real GDP demanded at the higher domestic price level. And if domestic prices of goods and services fall relative to foreign prices, more domestic products will be bought, increasing real GDP demanded. This relationship can be shown as follows:

$$\uparrow\text{Price level} \Rightarrow \downarrow\text{Demand for domestic goods} \Rightarrow \downarrow\text{RGDP demanded}$$

and

$$\downarrow\text{Price level} \Rightarrow \uparrow\text{Demand for domestic goods} \Rightarrow \uparrow\text{RGDP demanded}$$

Section Check

1. An aggregate demand curve shows the inverse relationship between the amounts of real goods and services (RGDP) that are demanded at each possible price level.
2. The aggregate demand curve is downward sloping because of the real wealth effect, the interest rate effect, and the open economy effect.

section

8.4

Shifts in the Aggregate Demand Curve

- What variables shift the aggregate demand curve to the right?
- What variables shift the aggregate demand curve to the left?
- What is the difference between a movement along and a shift in the aggregate demand curve?

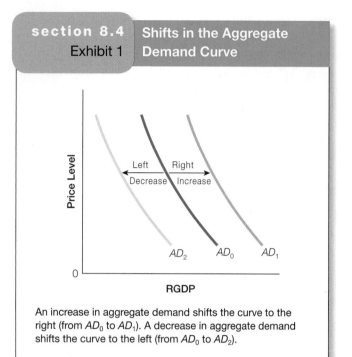

An increase in aggregate demand shifts the curve to the right (from AD_0 to AD_1). A decrease in aggregate demand shifts the curve to the left (from AD_0 to AD_2).

DOES A CHANGE IN THE PRICE LEVEL SHIFT THE AGGREGATE DEMAND CURVE?

As with the supply and demand curves in microeconomics (see Chapter 3), there can be both shifts in and movements along the aggregate demand curve. In the previous section, we discussed three factors—the real wealth effect, the interest rate effect, and the open economy effect—that result in the downward slope of the aggregate demand curve. Each of these factors, then, generates a movement *along* the aggregate demand curve because the general price level changed. In this section, we will discuss some of the many factors that can cause the aggregate demand curve to shift to the right or left.

The whole aggregate demand curve can shift to the right or left, as seen in Exhibit 1. Put simply, if some non–price-level determinant causes total spending to increase, then the aggregate demand curve will shift to the right. If a non–price-level determinant causes the level of total spending to decline, then the aggregate demand curve will shift to the left. Now let's look at some specific factors that could cause the aggregate demand curve to shift.

AGGREGATE DEMAND CURVE SHIFTERS

Anything that changes the amount of total spending in the economy (holding price levels constant) will impact the aggregate demand curve. An increase in any component of GDP (C, I, G, or $X - M$) can cause the aggregate demand curve to shift rightward. Conversely, decreases in C, I, G, or ($X - M$) will shift aggregate demand leftward.

Changing Consumption (C)

A whole host of changes could alter consumption patterns. For example, an increase in consumer confidence, an increase in wealth, an increase in transfer payments, or a tax cut each can increase consumption and shift the aggregate demand curve to the right. An increase in population will also increase the aggregate demand because more consumers will be spending more money on goods and services.

Of course, the aggregate demand curve could shift to the left due to decreases in consumption demand. For example, if consumers sensed that the economy was headed for a recession or if the government imposed a tax increase, this would result in a leftward shift of the aggregate demand curve. Because consuming less is saving more, an increase in saving, *ceteris paribus,* will shift aggregate demand to the left. High levels of accumulated consumer debt may also be a reason that some consumers might put off additional spending.

Changing Investment (I)

Investment is also an important determinant of aggregate demand. Increases in the demand for investment goods occur for a variety of reasons. For example, if business confidence increases or real interest rates fall, business investment will increase and aggregate demand will shift to the right. A reduction in business taxes would also shift the aggregate demand curve to the right because businesses would now retain more of their profits to invest. However, if interest rates or business taxes rise, then we would expect to see a leftward shift in aggregate demand.

ACTIVE LEARNING EXERCISE

CHANGES IN AGGREGATE DEMAND

Q: Any aggregate demand category that has the ability to change total purchases in the economy will shift the aggregate demand curve. That is, changes in consumption purchases, investment purchases, government purchases, or net export purchases shift the aggregate demand curve. For each component of aggregate demand (C, I, G, and $X - M$), list some changes that can increase aggregate demand. Then, list some changes that can decrease aggregate demand.

A: Below we list some aggregate demand curve shifters.

INCREASES IN AGGREGATE DEMAND (RIGHTWARD SHIFT)	DECREASES IN AGGREGATE DEMAND (LEFTWARD SHIFT)
Consumption (C) —lower personal taxes —a rise in consumer confidence —greater stock market wealth —an increase in transfer payments	Consumption (C) —higher personal taxes —a fall in consumer confidence —reduced stock market wealth —a reduction in transfer payments
Investment (I) —lower real interest rates —optimistic business forecasts —lower business taxes	Investment (I) —higher real interest rates —pessimistic business forecasts —higher business taxes
Government Purchases (G) —an increase in government purchases	Government Purchases (G) —a reduction in government purchases
Net Exports ($X - M$) —income increases abroad, which will likely increase foreign sales of domestic goods (exports) —exchange rate depreciation	Net Exports ($X - M$) —income falls abroad, which will lead to a reduction in the foreign sales of domestic goods (exports) —exchange rate appreciation

Changing Government Purchases (G)

Government purchases are also part of total spending and therefore must impact aggregate demand. An increase in government purchases, other things equal, shifts the aggregate demand curve to the right, whereas a reduction shifts aggregate demand to the left.

Changing Net Exports (X − M)

Global markets are also important in a domestic economy. For example, if Canada's major trading partner, the United States, were to slide into a recession, then U.S. demand for Canadian goods and services would decline. This would cause Canadian net exports ($X - M$) to fall, shifting aggregate demand to the left. Alternatively, an economic boom in the U.S. economy might lead to an increase in our exports to the United States, causing net exports ($X - M$) to rise and aggregate demand to increase.

Another factor that has an important effect on net exports is the exchange rate. The exchange rate is the price of one unit of a country's currency in terms of another country's currency. For example, if it takes US$0.75 to buy one Canadian dollar (as was the case on July 26, 2004), then the exchange rate is US$0.75 per Canadian dollar. When the Canadian dollar appreciates in value (to, say, US$1.09 per Canadian dollar—as was the case on November 7, 2007), that makes it more expensive for foreigners to buy Canadian dollars, and therefore more expensive for foreigners to buy Canadian goods and services (which are priced in Canadian dollars). At the same time, it becomes less expensive for

In The **NEWS**

SMALL GAIN EXPECTED FOR GDP

BY ALLAN ROBINSON

The Canadian economy is expected to barely stay above water in the second quarter, while the U.S. appears to go swimmingly along despite facing sharks like the housing crisis and the credit crunch.

The Canadian second-quarter gross domestic product (GDP) is forecast to have increased at an annual rate of 0.6 per cent, compared with a 0.3-per cent decline in the first quarter, according to a survey of economists by Bloomberg. Meanwhile, data released yesterday showed the U.S. grew at an annual rate of 3.3 per cent during the quarter.

"The Canadian economy likely managed to eke out a trace of growth in the second quarter, just avoiding a second consecutive quarter of declining GDP and averting a technical recession (for now)," said Douglas Porter, the deputy chief economist for BMO Nesbitt Burns Inc. "The Canadian economy will do well to grind out even modest growth in the second half of the year, with consumer confidence hobbled, the housing market cooling and U.S. activity likely staying in very low gear."

"I don't get too concerned with the short-term macroeconomic data," said James Cole, senior vice-president and portfolio manager for AIC Investment Services Inc. and manager of AIC Canadian Focused, Canadian Balanced and Dividend Income funds. "Canada remains in very good shape in the world," he said. He also expects energy demand will remain firm.

How will Markets React?

The challenges remain in the manufacturing sector as a result of the strong Canadian dollar in recent years, while the real estate sector is slowing, Mr. Cole said. Nevertheless, the government still has a budget surplus, debt has been reduced and the tax rate lowered. "Our stock market has vastly outperformed others in the world and I expect that will continue to be the case."

But the strength in the Canadian dollar in recent years continues to weigh on industrials. "One element you can zero in on explaining some or a good part of the divergence [in U.S. and Canadian] GDP is the export picture," said Stewart Hall, the currency and fixed-income analyst with HSBC Securities Canada Inc. Exports have been a drag on the Canadian economy with weakness in the auto sector and a decline in natural gas shipments, he said.

Furthermore, the data are not yet reflecting much of the recent drop in commodity prices such as oil and metals.

SOURCE: Adapted from Allan Robinson, "Small gain expected for GDP," *Globe & Mail*, Toronto, Ontario, August 29, 2008, p. B10. Reprinted with permission from *The Globe and Mail*.

CONSIDER THIS:

Real GDP is expected to increase by just 0.6 percent in the second quarter of 2008. Before we look at some of the reasons why, let us recall the aggregate demand shifters: *C, I, G,* or *X − M*. The slowdown in economic growth is being caused by: low consumer confidence, which is causing *C* to decline; a cooling housing market, which is causing *I* to decline; and a strong Canadian dollar, which is causing *X* to decline and *M* to increase. Given the available information, it is not at all surprising that the Canadian economy is expecting small gains in GDP for 2008.

Canadians to buy U.S. dollars, and therefore less expensive for Canadians to buy U.S. goods and services (which are priced in U.S. dollars). As a result, Canadian exports decline and Canadian imports increase. Therefore, an appreciation of the Canadian dollar decreases Canadian net exports and shifts the aggregate demand curve to the left. On the other hand, when the Canadian dollar depreciates in value (to, say, US$0.65 per Canadian dollar—as was the case on February 12, 2003), Canadian net exports increase, and the aggregate demand curve shifts to the right.

Section Check

1. A change in the price level causes a movement along the aggregate demand curve, not a shift in the aggregate demand curve.
2. Aggregate demand is made up of total spending, or *C* + *I* + *G* + (*X* − *M*). Any change in these factors will cause the aggregate demand curve to shift.

Summary

Section 8.1

- Aggregate demand is defined as the sum of the demand for all goods and services in the economy as well as the quantity of real GDP demanded at different price levels.
- The four major components of aggregate demand are consumption (*C*), investment (*I*), government purchases (*G*), and net exports (*X* − *M*).
- Aggregate demand is equal to $C + I + G + (X - M)$.
- Empirical evidence suggests that consumption increases directly with any increase in disposable income.
- The additional consumption spending stemming from an additional dollar of disposable income is called the marginal propensity to consume (MPC).

Section 8.2

- At high real interest rates, firms will only pursue those few investment activities with still higher expected rates of return.
- At lower real interest rates, projects with lower expected rates of return become profitable for firms, and the quantity of investment demanded rises.

- At equilibrium in the saving and investment market, desired investment equals desired national saving at the intersection of the investment demand curve and the saving supply curve.
- National saving is the sum of private saving and public saving.

Section 8.3

- An aggregate demand curve shows the inverse relationship between the price level and real gross domestic product (RGDP) demanded.
- The aggregate demand curve is downward sloping because of the real wealth effect, the interest rate effect, and the open economy effect.
- A change in the price level causes a movement along the aggregate demand curve, not a shift in the aggregate demand curve.

Section 8.4

- Aggregate demand is made up of total spending, or $C + I + G + (X - M)$—any change in these factors will cause the aggregate demand curve to shift.

Key Terms and Concepts

For a complete glossary of chapter key terms, visit the textbook's Web site at http://www.sextonmacro2e.nelson.com.

aggregate demand (*AD*) 197
average propensity to consume
  (*APC*) 198
marginal propensity to consume
  (*MPC*) 198

open economy 199
net exports 199
national savings 201
closed economy 203
private savings 203

public savings 203
dissaving 204
aggregate demand curve 205

Review Questions

1. Suppose an elderly person draws upon past savings and spends more each month than she receives from the Canada Pension Plan. What economic theory is illustrated by the behaviour of this person?

2. If retailers such as Canadian Tire and Zellers find that inventories are rapidly being depleted, would it have been caused by a rightward or leftward change in the aggregate demand curve? What

   are the likely consequences for output and investment?

3. Evaluate the following statement: "A higher price level decreases the purchasing power of the dollar and reduces RGDP."

4. How does a higher price level in the Canadian economy affect purchases of imported goods? Explain.

5. Which of the following both decreases consumption *and* shifts the aggregate demand curve to the left?

   a. an increase in financial wealth

   b. an increase in taxes

   c. an increase in the price level

   d. a decrease in interest rates

6. Predict how each of the following would impact investment expenditures.

   a. inventory levels are depleted

   b. banks scrutinize borrower credit more carefully and interest rates rise

   c. decreasing profit rates over the last few quarters

   d. factories operate at 60 percent capacity, down from 80 percent

7. Identify which expenditure category each of the following will directly impact, and also which direction the Canadian aggregate demand curve will shift as a result.

   a. income increases abroad

   b. a decrease in interest rates

   c. Parliament passes a permanent tax cut

   d. firms become more optimistic about the outlook for the economy

   e. stocks traded on the Toronto Stock Exchange lose 40 percent of their value in one month's time

8. Explain how a recession in the United States may affect aggregate demand in the Canadian economy.

Fill in the Blanks

Section 8.1

1. Aggregate demand (*AD*) refers to the quantity of _____ at different price levels.

2. _____ is by far the largest component of *AD*.

3. At higher real interest rates, households save _____ and consume _____.

4. The additional consumption that results from an additional dollar of disposable income is the _____ propensity to consume.

5. If a person with $10 000 in total disposable income spent $6000 on consumption, her average propensity to consume would be equal to _____.

6. Government purchases tend to be a _____ volatile category of aggregate demand than investment.

7. Models that include international trade effects are called _____ models.

8. Exports minus imports equals _____.

Section 8.2

9. If we put the investment demand for the whole economy and national savings together, we can establish the _____ interest rate in the saving and investment market.

10. As the real interest rate _____, additional projects with lower expected rates of return become profitable for firms, and the quantity of investment demanded _____.

11. If firms expect lower rates of return on their investments, for a given interest rate, the investment demand curve will shift to the _____.

12. Higher business taxes will lead to _____ potential after-tax profits on investment projects and shift the investment demand curve to the _____.

13. At a lower real interest rate, a _____ quantity of saving is supplied.

14. If disposable income fell, there would be _____ saving at any given interest rate.

15. If you expected lower future earnings, you would tend to save _____ now at any given interest rate, shifting the saving supply curve to the _____.

16. The equilibrium _____ interest rate is determined by the intersection of the investment demand curve and the saving supply curve.

17. At a higher-than-equilibrium real interest rate, the quantity of saving supplied would be _____ than the quantity of investment demanded—there would be a _____ of savings at this real interest rate.

Section 8.3

18. The *AD* curve slopes _____, which means that there is an _____ relationship between the price level and real gross domestic product (RGDP) demanded.

19. Three complementary explanations exist for the negative slope of the aggregate demand curve: the _____ effect, the _____ effect, and the _____ effect.

20. As the price level decreases, the real value of people's cash balances _____, so that their planned purchases of goods and services _____.

21. The real wealth effect can be summarized as follows: a higher price level → _____ real wealth → _____ purchasing power → _____ RGDP demanded.

22. At a higher price level, consumers will wish to hold _____ dollars in order to purchase those items that they want to buy, which will _____ the demand for money.

23. At higher interest rates, the opportunity cost of borrowing _____, and _____ interest-sensitive investments will be profitable, which will result in a _____ quantity of RGDP demanded.

24. If the prices of goods and services in the domestic market rise relative to those in global markets due to a higher domestic price level, consumers and businesses will buy _____ from foreign producers and _____ from domestic producers.

25. The open economy effect can be summarized as follows: a decreased price level → _____ the demand for domestic goods → _____ RGDP demanded.

Section 8.4

26. An increase in any component of GDP (*C, I, G,* and *X − M*) can cause the *AD* curve to shift _____.

27. If consumers sensed the economy was headed for a recession or the government imposed a tax increase, this would result in a _____ shift of the *AD* curve.

28. Since consuming less is saving more, an increase in savings, *ceteris paribus,* would shift *AD* to the _____.

29. A reduction in business taxes would shift *AD* to the _____, whereas an increase in real interest rates or business taxes would shift *AD* to the _____.

30. An increase in government purchases, other things being equal, shifts *AD* to the _____.

31. If Canada's major trading partners are experiencing economic slowdowns, then they will demand _____ Canadian goods and services, shifting *AD* to the _____.

32. If the Canadian dollar appreciates, net exports will _____, shifting *AD* to the _____.

True or False

Section 8.1

1. Aggregate demand (AD) = Consumption (C) + Investment (I) + Government purchases (G) + Net exports $(X - M)$.

2. Because consumption is such a stable part of GDP, analyzing its determinants is not very important to an understanding of the forces leading to changes in aggregate demand.

3. At the level of individuals, consumption increases with after-tax, or disposable, income.

4. The fraction of their total disposable income that households spend on consumption is called the marginal propensity to consume.

5. If a person's consumption spending went from $8000 to $14 000 when his total disposable income went from $10 000 to $20 000, his marginal propensity to consume would be 0.7.

6. Good business conditions tend to increase the level of investment by firms.

7. Either an increase in exports or a decrease in imports would increase net exports.

8. *Ceteris paribus,* negative net exports would decrease aggregate demand.

Section 8.2

9. As the real interest rate falls, additional projects with lower expected rates of return become profitable for firms, and the demand for investment curve shifts right.

10. Either changes in technology or business taxes can shift the investment demand curve.

11. Firms with excess inventories of finished goods have an increased incentive to invest in new capital to put those inventories to productive use.

12. If business taxes are lowered, potential after-tax profits on investment projects will increase and shift the investment demand curve to the right.

13. Households, firms, and the government can all supply savings in the economy.

14. At a higher real interest rate, the supply of saving shifts to the right.

15. If disposable (after-tax) income were to rise, more saving would occur at any given interest rate.

16. If the real interest rate is above the equilibrium real interest rate, forces within the economy would tend to restore the equilibrium.

17. If the real interest rate is below the equilibrium real interest rate, the quantity of investment demanded is greater than the quantity of saving supplied at that interest rate, and a shortage of saving occurs.

Section 8.3

18. The AD curve is downward sloping for the same reasons that the demand curve for a particular product is downward sloping.

19. An increase in the price level causes the quantity of RGDP demanded to fall.

20. A lower price level, other things being equal, will lead to increased real wealth and an increase in the quantity of RGDP demanded.

21. At a higher price level, if the money supply does not increase, then interest rates will fall, other things being equal.

22. A lower price level, other things being equal, would decrease money demand and the interest rate, and increase both the level of investment and the quantity of RGDP demanded.

23. If domestic prices of goods and services fall relative to foreign prices, more domestic products will be bought, increasing RGDP demanded.

24. An increased price level will tend to increase the demand for domestic goods and increase RGDP demanded.

25. A change in the price level will not shift aggregate demand.

Section 8.4

26. Decreases in any of C, I, G, or $X - M$ for reasons other than changes in the price level will shift AD leftward.

27. An increase in consumer confidence, an increase in wealth, or a tax cut can each increase consumption and shift AD to the right.

28. An increase in consumer debt, other things being equal, would tend to shift AD to the left.

29. If either business confidence increases or real interest rates rise, business investment will increase and AD will shift to the right.

30. A reduction in government purchases shifts AD to the left.

31. An economic boom in the economies of major trading partners may lead to an increase in Canadian exports to them, causing net exports to rise and AD to increase.

32. A depreciation of the Canadian dollar may lead to a decrease in net exports and a decrease in AD.

Multiple Choice

Section 8.1

1. The largest component of aggregate demand is
    a. government purchases.
    b. net exports.
    c. consumption.
    d. investment.

2. A reduction in personal income taxes, other things being equal, will
    a. leave consumers with less disposable income.
    b. decrease aggregate demand.
    c. leave consumers with more disposable income.
    d. increase aggregate demand.
    e. do both c and d.

3. Empirical evidence suggests that consumption _____ with any _____.
    a. decreases; increase in income
    b. decreases; tax cut
    c. increases; decrease in consumer confidence
    d. increases; increase in income
    e. Both a and b are true.

4. Investment (I) includes
   a. the amount spent on new factories and machinery.
   b. the amount spent on stocks and bonds.
   c. the amount spent on consumer goods that last more than one year.
   d. the amount spent on purchases of art.
   e. all of the above.

5. If private consumption in Canada were 67 percent of GDP, investment were 16 percent, government purchases were 13 percent, exports were 12 percent, and imports were 8 percent, net exports would be equal to _____ percent of GDP.
   a. 4
   b. −4
   c. 20
   d. −20
   e. none of the above

6. If our exports of final goods and services increase more than our imports, other things being equal, aggregate demand will
   a. increase.
   b. be negative.
   c. decrease by the change in net exports.
   d. stay the same.
   e. do none of the above.

7. If Rhonda's taxes rose by $20 000, other things being equal,
   a. her consumption would fall by $15 000 if her MPC were equal to 0.75.
   b. her consumption would fall by $15 000 if her APC were equal to 0.75.
   c. her consumption would rise by $15 000 if her MPC were equal to 0.75.
   d. her consumption would rise by $15 000 if her APC were equal to 0.75.

8. A given change in disposable income would have the greatest effect on consumption with which of the following marginal propensities to consume?
   a. 0.2
   b. 0.4
   c. 0.6
   d. 0.8

9. Which of the following changes in disposable income would lead to the greatest increase in consumption?
   a. a $20 000 increase in disposable income, if MPC equals 0.5
   b. a $12 000 increase in disposable income, if MPC equals 0.75
   c. a $15 000 increase in disposable income, if MPC equals 0.6
   d. a $30 000 increase in disposable income, if MPC equals 0.25

Section 8.2

10. I. The investment demand curve for the economy is downward sloping.
   II. The supply of national saving curve for the economy is upward sloping.
   a. I and II are both true.
   b. I and II are both false.
   c. I is true, and II is false.
   d. I is false, and II is true.

11. Which of the following will *not* shift the investment demand curve?
    a. the introduction of new profitable technology investment opportunities
    b. business inventories that have fallen far below desired levels
    c. a decrease in real interest rates
    d. business expectations of higher future sales and profits
    e. none of the above

12. A combination of the discovery of profitable new technology investment opportunities and inventories that have fallen far below desired levels
    a. would increase the investment demand curve.
    b. would decrease the investment demand curve.
    c. would leave the investment demand curve unchanged.
    d. could either increase or decrease the investment demand curve.

13. A combination of higher business taxes, reduced expected future profitability of businesses, and a reduction in the level of new profitable technology investment opportunities
    a. would increase the investment demand curve.
    b. would decrease the investment demand curve.
    c. would leave the investment demand curve unchanged.
    d. could either increase or decrease the investment demand curve.

14. Which of the following would increase the supply of national saving curve?
    a. an increase in disposable income
    b. a decrease in disposable income
    c. an increase in expected future earnings
    d. Both a and c would increase the supply of national saving curve.
    e. Both b and c would increase the supply of national saving curve.

15. If at a given interest rate the quantity of saving supplied is greater than the quantity of investment demanded,
    a. there is a surplus of saving, and real interest rates will rise.
    b. there is a surplus of saving, and real interest rates will fall.
    c. there is a shortage of saving, and real interest rates will rise.
    d. there is a shortage of saving, and real interest rates will fall.

16. An increase in the investment demand curve would
    a. increase real interest rates.
    b. decrease real interest rates.
    c. increase the dollar amount of investment.
    d. decrease the dollar amount of investment.
    e. do both a and c.

17. A decrease in the supply of national savings curve would
    a. increase real interest rates.
    b. decrease real interest rates.
    c. increase the dollar amount of investment.
    d. do both a and c.
    e. do both b and c.

Section 8.3

18. The aggregate demand curve
   a. is negatively sloped.
   b. demonstrates an inverse relationship between the price level and real gross domestic product demanded.
   c. shows how real gross domestic product demanded changes with the changes in the price level.
   d. All of the above are correct.

19. According to the real wealth effect, if you are living in a period of falling price levels on a fixed income (that is not indexed), the cost of the goods and services you buy _____ and your real income _____.
   a. decreases; decreases
   b. increases; increases
   c. decreases; remains the same
   d. decreases; increases

20. As the price level decreases, real wealth _____, purchasing power _____, and the quantity of RGDP demanded _____.
   a. increases; decreases; increases
   b. increases; increases; increases
   c. decreases; decreases; decreases
   d. decreases; decreases; increases
   e. increases; decreases; decreases

21. As the price level increases, money demand (money supply unchanged) _____, interest rates _____, investments _____, and the quantity of RGDP demanded _____.
   a. increases; decrease; increase; decreases
   b. increases; increase; increase; decreases
   c. decreases; decrease; decrease; increases
   d. decreases; decrease; increase; increases
   e. increases; increase; decrease; decreases

22. What is the open economy effect?
   a. If prices of the goods and services in the domestic market rise relative to those in global markets due to a higher domestic price level, consumers and businesses will buy less from foreign producers and more from domestic producers.
   b. People are allowed to trade with anyone, anywhere, anytime.
   c. It is the ability of firms to enter or leave the marketplace—easy entry and exit with low entry barriers.
   d. If prices of the goods and services in the domestic market rise relative to those in global markets due to a higher domestic price level, consumers and businesses will buy more from foreign producers and less from domestic producers, other things being equal.

23. Which of the following will result as part of the interest rate effect when the price level rises?
   a. Money demand will increase.
   b. Interest rates will increase.
   c. The dollar amount of investment will decrease.
   d. A lower quantity of real GDP will be demanded.
   e. All of the above will result.

24. Which of the following will *not* decrease when the price level falls?
   a. money demand
   b. the real interest rate
   c. the real level of investment
   d. a and b
   e. b and c

25. A decrease in the Canadian price level will
   a. increase Canadian exports.
   b. increase Canadian imports.
   c. increase RGDP demanded in Canada.
   d. both a and c.
   e. both b and c.

Section 8.4

26. An economic bust or severe downturn in the Japanese economy will likely result in a(n)
   a. decrease in Canadian exports and Canadian aggregate demand.
   b. increase in Canadian exports and Canadian aggregate demand.
   c. decrease in Canadian imports and Canadian aggregate demand.
   d. increase in Canadian imports and Canadian aggregate demand.

27. Which of the following will cause consumption, and as a result, aggregate demand, to decrease?
   a. a tax increase
   b. a fall in consumer confidence
   c. reduced stock market wealth
   d. rising levels of consumer debt
   e. all of the above

28. A massive increase in highway construction will affect aggregate demand through which sector? Will this increase or decrease aggregate demand?
   a. investment, increase
   b. government purchases, increase
   c. government purchases, decrease
   d. consumption, decrease

29. An increase in government purchases, combined with a decrease in investment, would have what effect on aggregate demand?
   a. *AD* would increase.
   b. *AD* would decrease.
   c. *AD* would stay the same.
   d. *AD* could either increase or decrease, depending on which change was of greater magnitude.

30. An increase in consumption, combined with an increase in exports, would have what effect on aggregate demand?
   a. *AD* would increase.
   b. *AD* would decrease.
   c. *AD* would stay the same.
   d. *AD* could either increase or decrease, depending on which change was of greater magnitude.

31. What would happen to aggregate demand if the federal government increased military purchases and provincial and local governments decreased their road-building budgets at the same time?
   a. *AD* would increase because only federal government purchases affect *AD*.
   b. *AD* would decrease because only provincial and local government purchases affect *AD*.
   c. *AD* would increase if the change in federal purchases were greater than the change in provincial and local purchases.
   d. *AD* would decrease if the change in federal purchases were greater than the change in provincial and local purchases.

32. If exports and imports both decreased, but exports decreased more than imports,
   a. *AD* would decrease.
   b. *AD* would increase.
   c. *AD* would be unaffected.
   d. *AD* could either increase or decrease.

33. If the Canadian dollar depreciated,
   a. *AD* would decrease.
   b. *AD* would increase.
   c. *AD* would be unaffected.
   d. *AD* could either increase or decrease.

Problems

1. **[Section 8.1]**
   Assume that Melanie had $200 000 of disposable income and spent $180 000 on consumption in 2006, and had $300 000 of disposable income and spent $240 000 on consumption in 2007.
   a. What was Melanie's average propensity to consume in 2006?
   b. What was Melanie's average propensity to consume in 2007?
   c. What is Melanie's marginal propensity to consume?
   d. If Melanie's income went up to $400 000 in 2008, how much would she be likely to spend on consumption that year? What would be her average propensity to consume?
   e. If Melanie's income went down to $100 000 in 2008, how much would she be likely to spend on consumption that year? What would be her average propensity to consume?

2. **[Section 8.2]**
   In the saving and investment market,
   a. what happens to the investment demand curve when the real interest rate declines?
   b. what happens to the investment demand curve when firms' inventories are rising above what the firms desire?
   c. what happens to the investment demand curve when technological advances give rise to popular new products?
   d. what happens to the saving supply curve when the real interest rate increases?
   e. what happens to the saving supply curve when disposable income increases?

3. **[Section 8.2]**

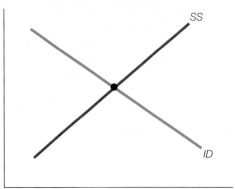

Label the axes for the saving and investment market. Then, explain and illustrate what would happen in the saving and investment market if
a. businesses became more optimistic about future business conditions.
b. individuals became less optimistic about their future incomes.
c. business taxes increased.
d. individuals' disposable incomes increased.

4. **[Section 8.3]**
Fill in the blanks in the following explanations.
a. The real wealth effect is described by the following: An increase in the price level leads to a(n) _____ in real wealth, which leads to a(n) _____ in purchasing power, which leads to a(n) _____ in RGDP demanded.
b. The interest rate effect is described by the following: A decrease in the price level leads to a(n) _____ in money demand, which leads to a(n) _____ in the interest rate, which leads to a(n) _____ in investments, which leads to a(n) _____ in RGDP demanded.
c. The open economy effect is described by the following: An increase in the domestic price level leads to a(n) _____ in the demand for domestic goods, which leads to a(n) _____ in RGDP demanded.

5. **[Sections 8.3 and 8.4]**
Describe what the effect on aggregate demand would be, other things being equal, if
a. exports increase.
b. both imports and exports decrease.
c. consumption decreases.
d. investment increases.
e. investment decreases and government purchases increase.
f. the price level increases.
g. the price level decreases.

Aggregate Supply and Macroeconomic Equilibrium

The Aggregate Supply Curve

- What does the aggregate supply curve represent?
- Why do producers supply more as the price level increases in the short run?
- Why is the long-run aggregate supply curve vertical at the natural rate of output?

WHAT IS THE AGGREGATE SUPPLY CURVE?

The **aggregate supply curve (AS)** is the relationship between the total quantity of final goods and services that suppliers are *willing* and *able* to produce and the overall price level. The aggregate supply curve represents how much real gross domestic product (RGDP) suppliers are willing to produce at different price levels. In fact, there are two aggregate supply curves—a **short-run aggregate supply curve (SRAS)** and a **long-run aggregate supply curve (LRAS).** The short-run relationship refers to a period when output prices can change in response to supply and demand, but input prices have not yet been able to adjust. For example, nominal wages are assumed to adjust slowly in the short run. The long-run relationship refers to a period long enough for the prices of outputs and all inputs to fully adjust to changes in the economy.

WHY IS THE SHORT-RUN AGGREGATE SUPPLY CURVE POSITIVELY SLOPED?

In the short run, the aggregate supply curve is upward sloping, as shown in Exhibit 1. This means that at a higher price level, producers are willing to supply more real output, and at lower price levels, they are willing to supply less real output. Why would producers be willing

aggregate supply curve (AS)
the total quantity of final goods and services suppliers are willing and able to produce at a given price level

short-run aggregate supply curve (SRAS)
the graphical relationship between RGDP and the price level when output prices can change but input prices are unable to adjust

long-run aggregate supply curve (LRAS)
the graphical relationship between RGDP and the price level when output prices and input prices can fully adjust to economic changes

section 9.1

Exhibit 1

**The Short-Run
Aggregate Supply Curve**

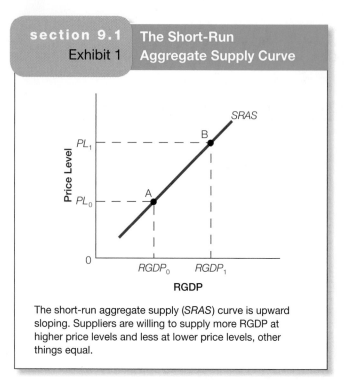

The short-run aggregate supply (*SRAS*) curve is upward sloping. Suppliers are willing to supply more RGDP at higher price levels and less at lower price levels, other things equal.

to supply more output just because the price level increases? There are two possible explanations: the profit effect and the misperception effect.

The Profit Effect

To many firms, input costs—like wages and rents—are relatively constant in the short run. The slow adjustments of input prices are due to contracts that do not adjust quickly to output price level changes. So when the price level rises, output prices rise relative to input prices (costs), raising producers' short-run profit margins. This is the short-run profit effect. The increased profit margins make it in the producers' self-interest to expand production and sales at higher price levels.

If the price level falls, output prices fall and producers' profits tend to fall. Again, this is because many input costs, such as wages and other contracted costs, are relatively constant in the short run. When output price levels fall, producers find it more difficult to cover their input costs and, consequently, reduce their level of output.

The Misperception Effect

The second explanation of the upward-sloping short-run aggregate supply curve is that producers can be fooled by price changes in the short run. For example, say a wheat farmer sees the price of his wheat rising. If he thinks that the relative price of his wheat is rising (i.e., that wheat is becoming more valuable in real terms), he will supply more. In actuality, however, it might be that it was not just wheat prices that were rising; the prices of many other goods and services could also be rising at the same time as a result of an increase in the price level. The relative price of wheat, then, was not actually rising, although it appeared so in the short run. In this case, the producer was fooled into supplying more based on the *short-run misperception* of relative prices. In other words, producers may be fooled into thinking that the relative price of the item they are producing is rising, so they increase production.

WHY IS THE LONG-RUN AGGREGATE SUPPLY CURVE VERTICAL?

Along the short-run aggregate supply curve, we assume that wages and other input prices are constant. This is not the case in the long run, which is a period long enough for the price of all inputs to fully adjust to changes in the economy. When we move along the long-run aggregate supply curve, then we are looking at the relationship between RGDP produced and the price level, once input prices have been able to respond to changes in output prices. Along the long-run aggregate supply (*LRAS*) curve, two sets of prices are changing—the price of outputs and the price of inputs. That is, along the *LRAS* curve, a 10 percent increase in the price of goods and services is matched by a 10 percent increase in the price of inputs. The long-run aggregate supply curve, then, is insensitive to the price level. As you can see in Exhibit 2, the *LRAS* curve is drawn as perfectly vertical, reflecting the fact that the level of RGDP producers are willing to supply is not affected by changes in the price level. Note that the vertical long-run aggregate supply curve will always be positioned at the natural rate of output, where all resources are fully employed

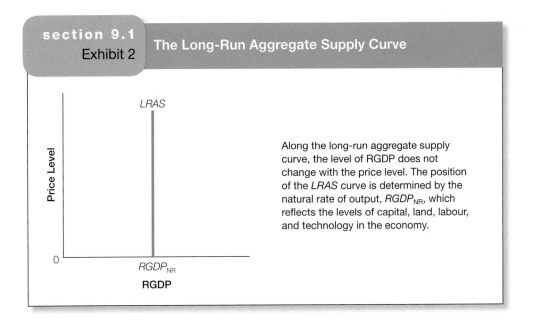

section 9.1
Exhibit 2   **The Long-Run Aggregate Supply Curve**

LRAS

Price Level

Along the long-run aggregate supply curve, the level of RGDP does not change with the price level. The position of the *LRAS* curve is determined by the natural rate of output, $RGDP_{NR}$, which reflects the levels of capital, land, labour, and technology in the economy.

0

$RGDP_{NR}$

RGDP

($RGDP_{NR}$). That is, in the long run, firms will always produce at the maximum level allowed by their capital, labour, and technology, regardless of the price level.

The long-run equilibrium level is where the economy will settle when undisturbed and when all resources are fully employed. Remember that the economy will always be at the intersection of short-run aggregate supply and aggregate demand, but that will not always be at the natural rate of output, $RGDP_{NR}$. Long-run equilibrium will only occur where the short-run aggregate supply and aggregate demand curves intersect along the long-run aggregate supply curve at the natural, or potential, rate of output.

Section Check

1. The short-run aggregate supply curve measures how much RGDP suppliers are willing to produce at different price levels.
2. In the short run, producers supply more as the price level increases because wages and other input prices tend to change more slowly than output prices. For this reason, producers can make a profit by expanding production when the price level rises. Producers also may be fooled into thinking that the relative price of the item they are producing is rising, so they increase production.
3. In the long run, the aggregate supply curve is vertical. In the long run, input prices change proportionally with output prices. The position of the *LRAS* curve is determined by the level of capital, land, labour, and technology at the natural rate of output, $RGDP_{NR}$.

section

Shifts in the Aggregate Supply Curve   **9.2**

■ Which factors of production affect the short-run and the long-run aggregate supply curves?
■ Which factors exclusively shift the short-run aggregate supply curve?

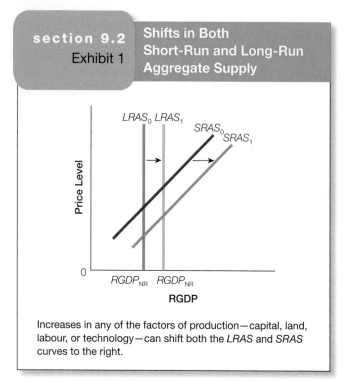

section 9.2
Exhibit 1

Shifts in Both Short-Run and Long-Run Aggregate Supply

Increases in any of the factors of production—capital, land, labour, or technology—can shift both the *LRAS* and *SRAS* curves to the right.

SHIFTING LONG-RUN AND SHORT-RUN AGGREGATE SUPPLY CURVES

We will now examine the determinants that can shift the short-run and the long-run aggregate supply curves to the right or left, as shown in Exhibit 1. Any change in the quantity of any factor of production available—capital, land, labour, or technology—can cause a shift in both the long-run and short-run aggregate supply curves. We will now see how these factors can change the position of both types of aggregate supply curves.

How Capital Affects Aggregate Supply

Changes in the stock of capital will alter the amount of goods and services the economy can produce. Investing in capital improves the quantity and quality of the capital stock, which lowers the cost of production in the short run. This in turn shifts the short-run aggregate supply curve rightward, and allows output to be permanently greater than before, shifting the long-run aggregate supply curve rightward, *ceteris paribus.*

Changes in human capital can also alter the aggregate supply curve. Investments in human capital may include educational or vocational programs or on-the-job training. All of these investments in human capital cause productivity to rise. As a result, the short-run aggregate supply curve shifts to the right because a more skilled workforce lowers the cost of production; in turn, the *LRAS* curve shifts to the right because greater output is achievable on a permanent, or sustainable, basis, *ceteris paribus.*

Technology and Entrepreneurship

Bill Gates of Microsoft, Ted Rogers of Rogers Communications, and Michael Lazaridis of Research in Motion (RIM) are just a few examples of entrepreneurs who, through inventive activity, have developed innovative technology. For example, computers and specialized software have led to many cost savings—ATMs, bar code scanners, biotechnology, and increased productivity across the board. These activities shift both the short-run and long-run aggregate supply curves outward by lowering costs and expanding real output possibilities.

Land (Natural Resources)

Remember that land is an all-encompassing definition that includes all natural resources. An increase in natural resources, such as successful oil exploration in Alberta, would presumably lower the costs of production and expand the economy's sustainable rate of output, shifting both the short-run and long-run aggregate supply curves to the right. Likewise, a decrease in natural resources available would result in a leftward shift of both the short-run and long-run aggregate supply curves.

The Labour Force

The addition of workers to the labour force, *ceteris paribus,* can increase aggregate supply. For example, during the 1960s and 1970s, women and baby boomers entered the labour force in large numbers. More recently, however, immigrants have become a major contributor to Canada's labour force—accounting for over one-fifth of Canada's labour force in 2006. This increase tended to depress wages and increase short-run aggregate supply,

section 9.2
Exhibit 2

Shifts in Short-Run Aggregate Supply but Not Long-Run Aggregate Supply

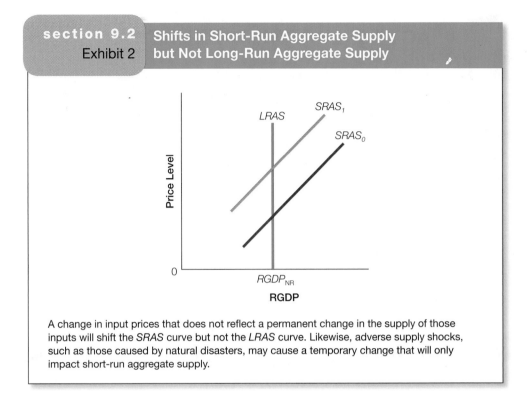

A change in input prices that does not reflect a permanent change in the supply of those inputs will shift the *SRAS* curve but not the *LRAS* curve. Likewise, adverse supply shocks, such as those caused by natural disasters, may cause a temporary change that will only impact short-run aggregate supply.

ceteris paribus. The expanded labour force also increased the economy's potential output, increasing long-run aggregate supply.

Government Regulations

Increases in government regulations can make it more costly for producers. This increase in production costs results in a leftward shift of the short-run aggregate supply curve, and a reduction in society's potential output shifts the long-run aggregate supply curve to the left as well. Likewise, a reduction in government regulations on businesses would lower the costs of production and expand potential real output, causing both the *SRAS* and *LRAS* curves to shift to the right.

WHAT FACTORS SHIFT SHORT-RUN AGGREGATE SUPPLY ONLY?

Some factors shift the short-run aggregate supply curve but do not impact the long-run aggregate supply curve. The most important of these factors are changes in input prices, temporary natural disasters, and other unexpected supply shocks. Exhibit 2 illustrates the impact of these factors on short-run aggregate supply.

Input Prices

The price of factors, or inputs, that go into producing outputs will affect only the short-run aggregate supply curve if they don't reflect permanent changes in the supplies of some factors of production. For example, if wages increase without a corresponding increase in labour productivity, then it will become more costly for suppliers to produce goods and services at every price level, causing the *SRAS* curve to shift to the left. As Exhibit 3 shows, long-run aggregate supply will not shift because with the same supply of labour as before,

ACTIVE LEARNING EXERCISE

SHIFTS IN THE SHORT-RUN AGGREGATE SUPPLY CURVE

Q: Why do wage increases (and other input prices) impact the short-run aggregate supply but *not* the long-run aggregate supply?

A: Remember, in the short run, wages and other input prices are assumed to be constant along the *SRAS* curve. If the firm has to pay more for its workers or any other input, its costs will rise; that is, the *SRAS* curve will shift to the left. This is shown in Exhibit 3 in the shift from $SRAS_0$ to $SRAS_1$. The reason the *LRAS* curve will not shift is that unless these input prices reflect permanent changes in input supply, those changes will only be temporary, and output will not be permanently or sustainedly different as a result. Other things being equal, if an input price is to be permanently higher relative to other goods, its supply must have decreased, but that would mean that potential real output, and hence long-run aggregate supply, would also shift left.

section 9.2
Exhibit 3

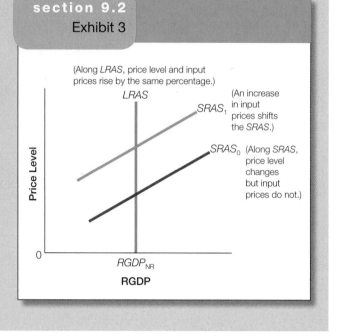

Temporary natural disasters like droughts can destroy crops and leave land parched like in the picture above. This may shift the SRAS curve but not the LRAS curve.

potential output does not change. If the price of steel rises, automobile producers will find it more expensive to do business because their production costs will rise, again resulting in a leftward shift in the short-run aggregate supply curve. The *LRAS* curve will not shift, however, as long as the capacity to make steel has not been reduced.

It is supply and demand in factor markets (like capital, land, and labour) that causes input prices to change. The reason that changes in input prices only affect short-run aggregate supply and not long-run aggregate supply, unless they reflect permanent changes in the supplies of those inputs, lies in our definition of long-run aggregate supply. Recall that the long-run aggregate supply curve is vertical at the natural level of real output, determined by the supplies of the various factors of production. A fall in input prices, which shifts the short-run aggregate supply curve to the right, only shifts long-run aggregate supply to the right if potential output has risen, and that only occurs if the supply of those inputs is increased.

Temporary Supply Shocks

Supply shocks are unexpected temporary events that can either increase or decrease aggregate supply. For example, major widespread flooding, earthquakes, droughts, and other natural disasters can increase the costs of production, causing the short-run aggregate supply curve to shift to the left, *ceteris paribus*. However, once the temporary effects of these disasters have been felt, no appreciable change in the economy's productive capacity has occurred, so the long-run aggregate supply doesn't shift as a result. Other temporary supply shocks, such as disruptions in trade due to war, electric power blackouts, or labour strikes, will have similar effects on short-run aggregate supply.

SECTION CHECK

Section Check

1. Any increase in the quantity of any of the factors of production—capital, land, labour, or technology—available will cause both the long-run and short-run aggregate supply curves to shift to the right. A decrease in any of these factors will shift both of the aggregate supply curves to the left.
2. Changes in input price and temporary supply shocks shift the short-run aggregate supply curve but do not affect the long-run aggregate supply curve.

section 9.3

Macroeconomic Equilibrium

- What is short-run macroeconomic equilibrium?
- What are contractionary and expansionary gaps?
- What is demand-pull inflation?
- What is cost-push inflation?
- How does the economy self-correct?
- What is wage and price inflexibility?

DETERMINING MACROECONOMIC EQUILIBRIUM

The short-run equilibrium level of real output and the price level are shown by the intersection of the aggregate demand curve and the short-run aggregate supply curve. When this equilibrium occurs at the potential output level, or natural rate of output, the economy is operating at full employment on the long-run aggregate supply curve, as seen in Exhibit 1. Only a short-run equilibrium that is at potential output is also a long-run

section 9.3
Exhibit 1 **Long-Run Macroeconomic Equilibrium**

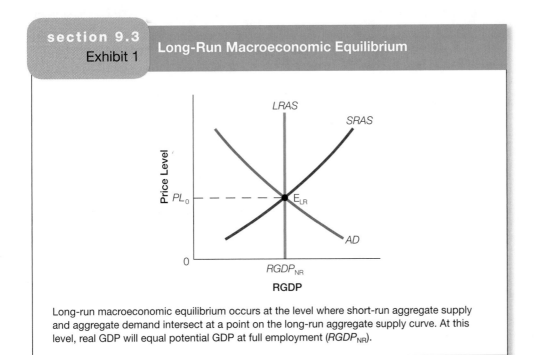

Long-run macroeconomic equilibrium occurs at the level where short-run aggregate supply and aggregate demand intersect at a point on the long-run aggregate supply curve. At this level, real GDP will equal potential GDP at full employment ($RGDP_{NR}$).

equilibrium. Short-run equilibrium can change when the aggregate demand curve or the short-run aggregate supply curve shifts rightward or leftward, but the long-run equilibrium level of RGDP only changes when the *LRAS* curve shifts. Sometimes, these supply or demand changes are anticipated; at other times, however, the shifts occur unexpectedly. Economists call these unexpected shifts **shocks.**

shocks

unexpected aggregate supply or aggregate demand changes

CONTRACTIONARY AND EXPANSIONARY GAPS

As we just discussed, equilibrium will not always occur at full employment. In fact, equilibrium can occur at less than the potential output of the economy, $RGDP_{NR}$ (a **contractionary gap**), temporarily beyond $RGDP_{NR}$ (an **expansionary gap**), or at potential GDP. Exhibit 2 shows these three possibilities. In (a) we have a contractionary gap at the short-run equilibrium, E_{SR}, at $RGDP_0$. When RGDP is less than $RGDP_{NR}$, there is a contractionary gap—aggregate demand is insufficient to fully employ all of society's resources, so unemployment will be above the natural rate. In (c) we have an expansionary gap at the short-run equilibrium, E_{SR}, at $RGDP_2$, where aggregate demand is so high that the economy is temporarily operating beyond full capacity ($RGDP_{NR}$), which will usually lead to inflationary pressure, so unemployment will be below the natural rate. In (b) the economy is just right where AD_1 and *SRAS* intersect at $RGDP_{NR}$—the long-run equilibrium position.

contractionary gap

the output gap that occurs when the actual output is less than the potential output

expansionary gap

the output gap that occurs when the actual output is greater than the potential output

DEMAND-PULL INFLATION

demand-pull inflation

a price level increase due to an increase in aggregate demand

Demand-pull inflation occurs when the price level rises as a result of an increase in aggregate demand. Consider the case in which an increase in consumer optimism results in a corresponding increase in aggregate demand. Exhibit 3 shows that an increase in aggregate demand causes an increase in the price level and an increase in real output. The movement is along *SRAS* from point E_0 to point E_1. This causes an expansionary gap. Recall that there is an increase in output as a result of the increase in the price level in the

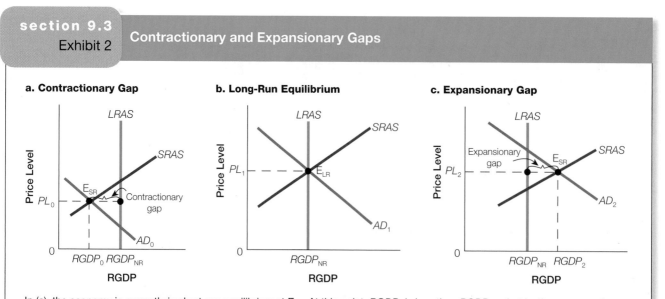

section 9.3
Exhibit 2   **Contractionary and Expansionary Gaps**

a. Contractionary Gap

b. Long-Run Equilibrium

c. Expansionary Gap

In (a), the economy is currently in short-run equilibrium at E_{SR}. At this point, $RGDP_0$ is less than $RGDP_{NR}$; that is, the economy is producing less than its potential output and the economy is in a contractionary gap. In (c), the economy is currently in short-run equilibrium at E_{SR}. At this point $RGDP_2$ is greater than $RGDP_{NR}$. The economy is temporarily producing more than its potential output and we have an expansionary gap. In (b) the economy is producing its potential output at the $RGDP_{NR}$. At this point the economy is in long-run equilibrium and is not experiencing an expansionary or contractionary gap.

short run because firms have an incentive to increase real output when the prices of the goods they are selling are rising faster than the costs of the inputs they use in production.

Note that E_1 in Exhibit 3 is positioned beyond $RGDP_{NR}$—an expansionary gap. It seems peculiar that the economy can operate beyond its potential, but this is possible, temporarily, as firms encourage workers to work overtime, extend the hours of part-time workers, hire recently retired employees, reduce frictional unemployment through more extensive searches for employees, and so on. However, this level of output and employment *cannot* be sustained in the long run.

COST-PUSH INFLATION

The mid-1970s to early 1980s witnessed a phenomenon known as **stagflation,** where lower growth and higher prices occurred together. Some economists believe that this was caused by a leftward shift in the short-run aggregate supply curve, as seen in Exhibit 4. If the aggregate demand curve did not increase considerably but the price level increased significantly, then the inflation was caused by supply-side forces. This is called **cost-push inflation.**

The increase in oil prices was the primary culprit responsible for the leftward shift in the aggregate supply curve. As we discussed in the last section, an increase in input prices can cause the short-run aggregate supply curve to shift to the left, and this spelled big trouble for the Canadian economy—higher price levels, lower output, and higher rates of unemployment. The impact of cost-push inflation is illustrated in Exhibit 4.

In Exhibit 4, we see that the economy is initially at full employment equilibrium at point E_0. Now suppose there is a sudden increase in input prices, such as the increase in the price of oil. This increase would shift the *SRAS* curve to the left—from $SRAS_0$ to $SRAS_1$. As a result of the shift in short-run aggregate supply, the price level rises to PL_1 and real output falls from $RGDP_{NR}$ to $RGDP_1$ (point E_1). Now firms demand fewer workers as a result of the higher input costs that cannot be passed on to the consumers. The result is higher prices, lower real output, and more unemployment—and it leads to a contractionary gap.

stagflation
a situation in which lower growth and higher prices occur together

cost-push inflation
a price level increase due to a negative supply shock or increases in input prices

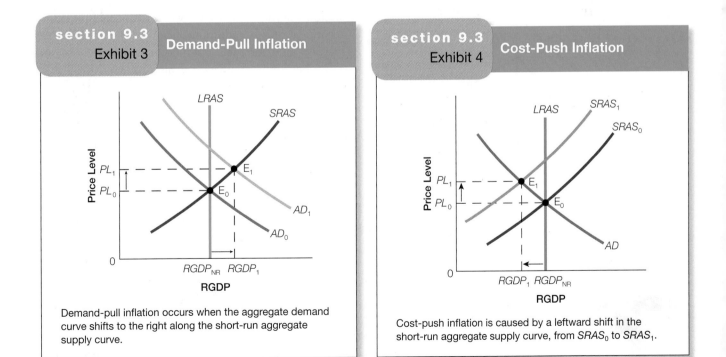

section 9.3
Exhibit 3 — **Demand-Pull Inflation**

Demand-pull inflation occurs when the aggregate demand curve shifts to the right along the short-run aggregate supply curve.

section 9.3
Exhibit 4 — **Cost-Push Inflation**

Cost-push inflation is caused by a leftward shift in the short-run aggregate supply curve, from $SRAS_0$ to $SRAS_1$.

section 9.3
Exhibit 5
**Short-Run Decrease
in Aggregate Demand**

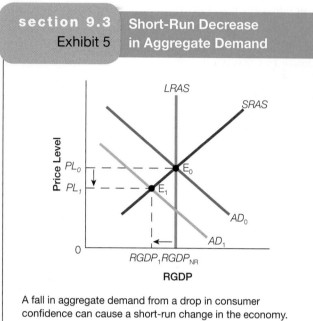

A fall in aggregate demand from a drop in consumer confidence can cause a short-run change in the economy. The decrease in aggregate demand (shown in the movement from point E_0 to E_1) causes lower output and higher unemployment in the short run.

section 9.3
Exhibit 6
**Adjusting to a
Contractionary Gap**

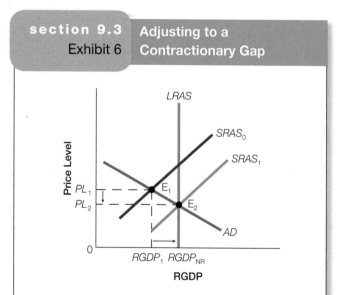

At point E_1, the economy is in a contractionary gap. However, the economy may self-correct as labourers and other input suppliers are now willing to accept lower wages and prices for the use of their resources. This results in a reduction in production costs that shifts the short-run supply curve from $SRAS_0$ to $SRAS_1$. Eventually, the economy returns to a long-run equilibrium at point E_2, at $RGDP_{NR}$, and a lower price level, PL_2. However, if wages and other input prices are sticky, the economy's adjustment mechanism might take many months, or even a few years, to totally self-correct.

ANOTHER CAUSE OF A CONTRACTIONARY GAP

Just as cost-push inflation can cause a contractionary gap, so can a decrease in aggregate demand. For example, consider the case in which consumer confidence plunges and the stock market crashes. As a result, aggregate demand would fall, shown in Exhibit 5 as the shift from AD_0 to AD_1, and the economy would be in a new short-run equilibrium at point E_1. Now, households are buying fewer goods and services at every price level. In response to this drop in demand, output would fall from $RGDP_{NR}$ to $RGDP_1$, and the price level would fall from PL_0 to PL_1. So in the short run, this fall in aggregate demand causes higher unemployment and a reduction in output—and it too can lead to a contractionary gap.

ADJUSTING TO A CONTRACTIONARY GAP

Many recoveries from a contractionary gap occur because of increases in aggregate demand—perhaps consumer and business confidence picks up or the government lowers taxes and/or lowers interest rates to stimulate the economy. That is, there is eventually a rightward shift in the aggregate demand curve that takes the economy back to potential output—$RGDP_{NR}$.

However, it is possible that the economy could *self-correct* through declining wages and prices. In Exhibit 6, at point E_1, the intersection of PL_1 and $RGDP_1$, the economy is in a contractionary gap—the economy is producing less than its potential output. At this lower level of output, firms lay off workers to avoid inventory accumulation. In addition, firms may cut prices to increase sales for their products. Unemployed workers and other input suppliers may also bid down wages and prices. That is, labourers and other input suppliers are now willing to accept lower wages and prices for the use of their resources, and the resulting reduction in production costs shifts the short-run supply curve from $SRAS_0$ to $SRAS_1$. Eventually, the economy returns to a long-run equilibrium at E_2 at $RGDP_{NR}$, and a lower price level, PL_2.

SLOW ADJUSTMENTS TO A CONTRACTIONARY GAP

Many economists believe that wages and prices may be very slow to adjust, especially downward. This downward **wage and price inflexibility** may lead to prolonged periods of a contractionary gap.

For example, in Exhibit 6 we see that the economy is in a recession at E_1 at $RGDP_1$. The economy will eventually self-correct to $RGDP_{NR}$ at E_2, as workers and other input owners

In The **NEWS**

SHORTAGES AND INFLATION ON VERGE OF BECOMING NEW GLOBAL DANGER

The new danger is global inflation—most worryingly in food prices, but also in prices for commodities, raw materials and products that require petroleum energy, which includes almost everything.

Prices for these goods have been skyrocketing in international markets.

It risks a kind of inflation that would trigger panic buying, hoarding and fears of mass political protest.

Actually, this is already happening in Asia, according to the *New York Times*.

The price of rice in global markets has nearly doubled in the last three months, reports the *Times'* Keith Bradsher. Fearing shortages, some major rice producers—including Vietnam, India, Egypt and Cambodia—have sharply limited their rice exports so they can be sure they can feed their own people.

Bradsher summarizes the evidence that food shortages and inflation are fuelling political unrest: "Since January, thousands of troops have been deployed in Pakistan to guard trucks carrying wheat and flour. Protests have erupted in Indonesia over soybean shortages, and China has put price controls on cooking oil, grain, meat, milk and eggs. Food riots have erupted in recent months in Guinea, Mauritania, Mexico, Morocco, Senegal, Uzbekistan and Yemen."

World Bank president Robert Zoellick rang the alarm bell in a speech. He noted that since 2005, the prices of staples have risen 80 per cent. The real price of rice rose to a 19-year record last month, he said, while the real price of wheat hit a 28-year high.

Zoellick warned that this inflation is having political repercussions: "The World Bank Group estimates that 33 countries around the world face potential political and social unrest because of the acute hike in food and energy prices."

SOURCE: From *The Washington Post* 4/3/2008 © 2008 *The Washington Post*. All rights reserved. Used by permission and protected by the Copyright Laws of the United States. The printing, copying, redistribution, or retransmission of the Material without express written permission is prohibited.

CONSIDER THIS:

The emergence of global inflation as the economic danger has its roots in supply-side shocks. Increases in the prices of commodities, raw materials, and products that require petroleum energy (which includes virtually every good and service) have caused dramatic declines in the aggregate supply curve, causing what is known as cost-push inflation.

---

accept lower wages and prices for their inputs, shifting the *SRAS* curve to the right from $SRAS_0$ to $SRAS_1$. However, if wages and other input prices are sticky, the economy's adjustment mechanism might take many months, or even a few years, to totally self-correct.

wage and price inflexibility
the tendency for prices and wages to only adjust slowly downward to changes in the economy

WHAT CAUSES WAGES AND PRICES TO BE STICKY DOWNWARD?

Empirical evidence supports several reasons for the downward stickiness of wages and prices. Firms may not be able to legally cut wages because of long-term labour contracts (particularly with union workers) or a legal minimum wage. Efficiency wages may also limit a firm's ability to lower wage rates. Menu costs may cause price inflexibility as well.

Efficiency Wages

In economics, it is generally assumed that as productivity rises, wages will rise, and that workers can raise their productivity through investments in human capital like education and on-the-job training. However, some economists believe that in some cases, *higher wages will lead to greater productivity.*

In the efficiency wage model, employers pay their employees more than the equilibrium wage as a means to increase efficiency. Proponents of this theory suggest that higher-than-equilibrium wages may attract the most productive workers, lower job turnover and training costs, and improve morale. Because the efficiency wage rate is greater than the equilibrium wage rate, the quantity of labour that would be willingly supplied is greater than the quantity of labour demanded, resulting in greater amounts of unemployment.

However, aside from creating some additional unemployment, it may also cause wages to be inflexible downward. For example, in the event that there is a decrease in aggregate demand, firms that pay efficiency wages may be reluctant to cut wages in the fear that it could lead to lower morale, greater absenteeism, and general productivity losses. In short, if firms are paying efficiency wages, they may be reluctant to lower wages in a recession, leading to downward wage inflexibility.

Menu Costs

As we explained in Chapter 5, there is a cost to changing prices in an inflationary environment. Thus the higher price level in an inflationary environment is often reflected slowly, as restaurants, mail-order houses, and department stores change their prices gradually so that they incur fewer *menu costs* (the costs of changing posted prices) in printing new catalogues, new mailers, new advertisements, and so on. Since businesses are not likely to change these prices instantly, we can say that some prices are sticky, or slow to change. For example, many outputs, like steel, are inputs in the production of other products, like automobiles. As a result, these prices are slow to change.

Suppose that there was an unexpected reduction in the money supply that led to a decrease in aggregate demand. This could lower the price level. Although some firms may adjust to the change quickly, others may move more slowly because of menu costs. The potential result is that their prices may become too high (above equilibrium); sales and output will fall, causing a potential recession.

If some firms are not responding quickly to changes in demand, there must be a reason, and to some economists, menu costs are at least part of that reason.

ADJUSTING TO AN EXPANSIONARY GAP

In Exhibit 7, the economy is currently in an expansionary gap at E_1, where $RGDP_0$ is greater than $RGDP_{NR}$. Because the price level, PL_1, is now higher than workers anticipated, PL_0, workers become disgruntled with wages that have not yet adjusted to it (if prices have risen, but wages have not risen as much, real wages have fallen). Recall that along the *SRAS* curve, wages and other input prices are assumed to be constant. Therefore, workers' and input suppliers' purchasing power falls as output prices rise. Real (adjusted for inflation) wages have fallen. Consequently, workers and other suppliers demand higher prices, to be willing to supply their inputs. As input prices respond to the higher level of output prices, the short-run aggregate supply curve shifts to the left, from $SRAS_0$ to $SRAS_1$. Suppliers will continually seek higher prices for their inputs until they reach the long-run equilibrium, at point E_2 in Exhibit 7. At point E_2, input suppliers' purchasing power is now restored at the long-run equilibrium, at $RGDP_{NR}$, and a new higher price level, PL_2.

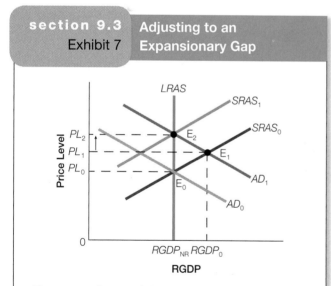

section 9.3
Exhibit 7

Adjusting to an Expansionary Gap

The economy is currently in an expansionary gap at E_1, where $RGDP_0$ is greater than $RGDP_{NR}$. Because the price level is now higher than workers anticipated (that is, it is PL_1 rather than PL_0), workers become disgruntled with wages that have not yet adjusted to the new price level. Consequently, workers and other suppliers demand higher prices to be willing to supply their inputs. As input prices respond to the higher level of output prices, the short-run aggregate supply curve shifts to the left, from $SRAS_0$ to $SRAS_1$. Suppliers will continually seek higher prices for their inputs until they reach the long-run equilibrium, at point E_2. At point E_2, input suppliers' purchasing power is now restored at the natural rate, $RGDP_{NR}$, at a new higher price level, PL_2.

HOW PRECISE IS THE AGGREGATE SUPPLY AND DEMAND MODEL?

In this chapter, we have been shifting the aggregate supply and aggregate demand curves around as if we knew exactly what we were doing. But it is very important to mention that the *AD/AS* model is a crude tool.

In the supply and demand curves of microeconomics covered in Chapters 3 and 4, we saw how this simple tool is very rich in explanatory power. But even that supply and demand analysis does not always provide precise estimates of the shifts or of the exact price and output changes that accompany those shifts. However, although microeconomic supply and demand analysis is not perfect, it does provide a framework to predict the direction that certain important variables will change under different circumstances.

The same is true in the *AD/AS* model, but it is less precise because of the complexities and interrelationships that exist in the macroeconomy. The slopes of the aggregate demand and short-run aggregate supply curves, the magnitudes of the shifts, and the interrelationship of the variables are to some extent a mystery. For example, if a reduction in aggregate demand leads to lower RGDP and, as a result, there are fewer workers that are willing to look for work, it impacts the short-run aggregate supply curve. There are other examples of the interdependence of the aggregate demand and aggregate supply curves that make this analysis not completely satisfactory. Nevertheless, the framework still provides important insights into the workings of the macroeconomy.

Section Check

1. Short-run macroeconomic equilibrium is shown by the intersection of the aggregate demand curve and the short-run aggregate supply curve. A short-run equilibrium is also a long-run equilibrium only if it is at potential output on the long-run aggregate supply curve.

2. If short-run equilibrium occurs at less than the potential output of the economy, $RGDP_{NR}$, there is a contractionary gap. If short-run equilibrium temporarily occurs beyond $RGDP_{NR}$, there is an expansionary gap.

3. Demand-pull inflation occurs when the price level rises as a result of an increase in aggregate demand.

4. Cost-push inflation is caused by a leftward shift in the short-run aggregate supply curve.

5. It is possible that the economy could *self-correct* through declining wages and prices. For example, during a recession, labourers and other input suppliers are willing to accept lower wages and prices for the use of their resources, and the resulting reduction in production costs increases the short-run supply curve. Eventually, the economy returns to the long-run equilibrium, at $RGDP_{NR}$, and a lower price level.

6. Wages and other input prices may be very slow to adjust, especially downward. This downward wage and price inflexibility may lead to prolonged periods of recession.

7. Firms might not be willing to lower nominal wages in the short run for several reasons, leading to downward wage and price inflexibility or sticky prices. Firms may not be able to legally cut wages because of long-term labour contracts (particularly with union workers) or due to a legal minimum wage. In addition, efficiency wage and menu costs may lead to sticky wages and prices.

Summary

Section 9.1

- The short-run aggregate supply curve measures how much RGDP suppliers will be willing to produce at different price levels given fixed input prices.
- In the short run, profitability induces producers to supply more as the price level increases because wages and other input prices tend to be slower to change than output prices.
- Producers also may be fooled into thinking that the relative price of the item they are producing is rising, so they increase production.
- In the long run, the aggregate supply curve is vertical as input prices change proportionally with output prices.
- The position of the *LRAS* curve is determined by the level of capital, land, labour, and technology at the natural rate of output, $RGDP_{NR}$.

Section 9.2

- Any increase in the quantity of any of the factors of production—capital, land, labour, or technology—available will cause both the long-run and short-run aggregate supply curves to shift to the right.
- A decrease in any of these factors will shift both of the aggregate supply curves to the left.
- Changes in input price and temporary supply shocks shift the short-run aggregate supply curve but do not affect the long-run aggregate supply curve.

Section 9.3

- Short-run macroeconomic equilibrium is shown by the intersection of the aggregate demand curve and the short-run aggregate supply curve.

- A short-run equilibrium is also a long-run equilibrium only if it is at potential output on the long-run aggregate supply curve.
- If short-run equilibrium occurs at less than the potential output of the economy, $RGDP_{NR}$, there is a contractionary gap.
- If short-run equilibrium temporarily occurs beyond $RGDP_{NR}$, there is an expansionary gap.
- Demand-pull inflation occurs when the price level rises as a result of an increase in aggregate demand.
- A contractionary gap can be caused by cost-push inflation, which is caused by a leftward shift in the short-run aggregate supply curve, or insufficient aggregate demand.
- Most recoveries from contractions occur because of increases in aggregate demand; however, it is possible that the economy could self-correct through declining wages and other input prices.
- Downward wage and price inflexibility may lead to prolonged periods of recession as firms might not be willing to lower prices in the short run (sticky prices) and firms may not be able to legally cut wages because of long-term labour contracts (particularly with union workers) or due to a legal minimum wage.
- Efficiency wage and menu costs may also lead to sticky wages and prices.

Key Terms and Concepts

For a complete glossary of chapter key terms, visit the textbook's Web site at http://www.sextonmacro2e.nelson.com.

aggregate supply curve (*AS*) 223
short-run aggregate supply
  curve (*SRAS*) 223
long-run aggregate supply curve
  (*LRAS*) 223

shocks 230
contractionary gap 230
expansionary gap 230
demand-pull inflation 230
stagflation 231

cost-push inflation 231
wage and price inflexibility 233

Review Questions

1. You operate a business in which you manufacture furniture. You are able to increase your furniture prices by 5 percent this quarter. You assume that the demand for your furniture has increased and begin increasing furniture production. Only later do you realize that prices in the macroeconomy are rising generally at a rate of 5 percent per quarter. This is an example of what effect? What does it imply about the slope of the short-run aggregate supply curve?

2. What would each of the following do to the short-run aggregate supply curve?
   a. a decrease in wage rates
   b. passage of more stringent environmental and safety regulations affecting businesses
   c. technological progress
   d. an increase in consumer optimism
   e. an electric power blackout in Ontario

3. What would each of the following do to the long-run aggregate supply curve?
   a. advances in medical technologies
   b. increased immigration of skilled workers
   c. an increase in wage rates
   d. An epidemic involving a new strain of the flu kills hundreds of thousands of people.

4. Indicate whether the following events affect short-run aggregate supply or long-run aggregate supply and the direction of impact.
   a. Unusually cold weather in Saskatchewan reduces the wheat crop.
   b. A devastating earthquake in British Columbia destroys hundreds of buildings and kills thousands of people.
   c. Economywide wage increases are made.
   d. Advances in computers and wireless technologies improve the efficiency of production.

5. How does an increase in aggregate demand affect output, unemployment, and the price level in the short run?

6. How does a decrease in short-run aggregate supply affect output, unemployment, and the price level in the short run?

7. Distinguish cost-push from demand-pull inflation. Provide an example of an event or shock to the economy that would cause each.

8. Which of the following leads to stagflation, assuming an economy currently operating at full employment?
   a. an increase in government spending on education
   b. striking workers demand and receive large nominal wage increases
   c. a decrease in federal spending on national defence
   d. a temporary increase in OPEC oil production
   e. a temporary decrease in OPEC oil production

9. Is it ever possible for an economy to operate above the full-employment level in the short term? Explain.

Appendix

THE SIMPLE KEYNESIAN AGGREGATE EXPENDITURE MODEL

The Keynesian aggregate expenditure model is based on the condition that the components of aggregate demand (consumption, investment, government spending, and net exports) must equal total output. Recall from Chapter 7 that Keynes was concerned with explaining and reducing short-term fluctuations in the economy. Keynes believed that total spending was a critical determinant of the overall level of economic activity. When total spending increases, firms increase their output and hire more workers. Even though Keynes ignored an important economic component—aggregate supply—his model still provides a great deal of information about aggregate demand.

Why Do We Assume the Price Level Is Fixed?

In most of this appendix, we will assume that the price level is fixed or constant. If the price level is fixed, then changes in nominal income will be equivalent to changes in real income. That is, when we assume the price level is fixed, we do not have to distinguish real variable changes from nominal variable changes. Keynes believed that prices and wages were rigid or fixed until we reached full employment. But let us begin by looking at the most important aggregate demand determinant—consumption spending.

What Are the Autonomous Factors That Influence Consumption Spending? Even though income is given for the representative household, other economic factors that influence consumption spending are not. When consumption (or any of the other components of spending, such as investment) does not depend on income, we call it *autonomous* (or independent). Let's look at some of these other autonomous factors and see how they would change consumption spending.

Real Wealth. The larger the value of a household's real wealth (the money value of wealth divided by the price level, which indicates the amount of consumption goods that the wealth could buy), the larger the amount of consumption spending, other things being equal. Thus, in Exhibit 1, an increase in real wealth would raise consumption to C_2, at point D, for a given level of current income. Similarly, something that would lower the value of real wealth, such as a decline in property values or a stock market decline would tend to lower the level of consumption to C_1, at point B in Exhibit 1.

Interest Rate. A higher interest rate tends to make the consumption items that we buy on credit more expensive, which reduces expenditures on those items. An increase in the interest rate increases the monthly payments made to buy such things as automobiles, furniture, and major appliances and reduces our ability to spend out of a given income. This shift is shown as a decrease in consumption from point A to point B in Exhibit 1. Moreover, an increase in the interest rate provides a higher future return from reducing current spending, which motivates increasing savings. Thus, a higher interest rate in the current period would likely motivate an increase in savings today, which would permit households to consume more goods and services at some future date.

Household Debt.   Remember when that friend of yours ran up his credit card obligations so high that he stopped buying goods except the basic necessities? Well, our average household might find itself in the same situation if its outstanding debt exceeds some reasonable level relative to its income. So, as debt increases, other things being equal, consumption expenditure would fall from point A to point B in Exhibit 1.

Expectations.   Just as in microeconomics, decisions to spend may be influenced by a person's expectations of future disposable income, employment, or certain world events. Based on monthly surveys conducted that attempt to measure consumer confidence, an increase in consumer confidence generally acts to increase household spending (a movement from point A to point D in Exhibit 1) and a decrease in consumer confidence would act to decrease spending (a movement from A to B in Exhibit 1).

Tastes and Preferences.   Of course, each household is different. Some are young and beginning a working career; some are without children; others have families; still others are older and perhaps retired from the workforce. Some households like to save, putting dollars away for later spending, whereas others spend all their income, or even borrow to spend more than their current disposable income. These saving and spending decisions often vary over a household's life cycle.

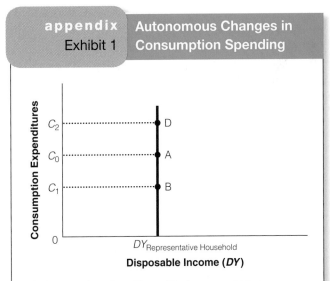

appendix Exhibit 1 — Autonomous Changes in Consumption Spending

An increase in real wealth would raise consumption spending to C_2, at point D. A decrease in real wealth would tend to lower the level of consumption spending to C_1, at point B. A higher interest rate tends to cause a decrease in consumption spending from point A to point B. As household debt increases, other things equal, consumption spending would fall from point A to point B. In general, an increase in consumer confidence would act to increase household spending (a movement from point A to point D) and a decrease in consumer confidence would act to decrease household spending (a movement from point A to point B).

As you can see, many economic factors affect consumption expenditures. The factors already listed represent some of the most important. All of these factors are considered **autonomous determinants of consumption expenditures;** that is, those expenditures that are not dependent on the level of current disposable income.

autonomous determinants of consumption expenditures
expenditures not dependent on the level of current disposable income that can result from factors such as real wealth, the interest rate, household debt, expectations, and tastes and preferences

CONSUMPTION IN THE KEYNESIAN MODEL

In our first model, we looked at the economic variables that affected consumption expenditures when disposable income was fixed. This assumption is clearly unrealistic, but it allows us to develop some of the basic building blocks of the Keynesian expenditure model. Now we'll look at a slightly more complicated model in which consumption also depends on disposable income.

If you think about what determines your own current consumption spending, you know that it depends on many factors previously discussed, such as your age, family size, interest rates, expected future disposable income, wealth, and, most importantly, your current disposable income. Recall from earlier chapters, disposable income is your after-tax income. Your personal consumption spending depends primarily on your current disposable income. In fact, empirical studies confirm that most people's consumption spending is closely tied to their disposable income.

Revisiting Marginal Propensity to Consume and Save. What happens to current consumption spending when a person earns some additional disposable income? Most people will spend some of their extra income and save some of it. The percentage of your

marginal propensity to consume (MPC)
the additional consumption resulting from an additional dollar of disposable income

extra disposable income that you decide to spend on consumption is what economists call your **marginal propensity to consume (MPC).** That is, MPC is equal to the *change* in consumption spending (ΔC) divided by the *change* in disposable income (ΔDY).

$$MPC = \Delta C / \Delta DY$$

For example, suppose you won a lottery prize of $1000. You might decide to spend $750 of your winnings today and save $250. In this example, your marginal propensity to consume is 0.75 (or 75 percent) because out of the extra $1000, you decided to spend 75 percent of it ($0.75 \times \$1000 = \$750$).

The term *marginal propensity to consume* has two parts: (1) *marginal* refers to the fact that you received an extra amount of disposable income—in addition to your income, not your total income; and (2) *propensity to consume* refers to how much you tend to spend on consumer goods and services out of your additional income.

The flip side of the marginal propensity to consume is the **marginal propensity to save (MPS),** which is the proportion of an addition to your income that you would save or not spend on goods and services today. That is, MPS is equal to the *change* in savings (ΔS) divided by the change in disposable income (ΔDY).

marginal propensity to save (MPS)
the additional saving that results from an additional dollar of income

$$MPS = \Delta S / \Delta DY$$

In the earlier lottery example, your marginal propensity to save is 0.25, or 25 percent, because you decided to save 25 percent of your additional disposable income ($0.25 \times \$1000 = \$250$). Because your additional disposable income must be either consumed or saved, the marginal propensity to consume plus the marginal propensity to save must add up to 1, or 100 percent.

Let's illustrate the marginal propensity to consume in Exhibit 2. Suppose you estimated that you had to spend $8000 a year, even if you earned no income for the year, for necessities such as food, clothing, and shelter. And suppose for every $1000 of added disposable income you earn, you spend 75 percent of it and save 25 percent of it. So if your disposable income is $0, you spend $8000 (that means you have to borrow or reduce your existing savings just to survive). If your disposable income is $20 000, you'll spend $8000 plus 75 percent of $20 000 (which equals $15 000), for total spending of $23 000. If your disposable income is $40 000, you'll spend $8000 plus 75 percent of $40 000 (which equals $30 000), for total spending of $38 000.

What's your marginal propensity to consume? In this case, if you spend 75 percent of every additional $1000 you earn, your marginal propensity to consume is 0.75 or 75 percent. And if you save 25 percent of every additional $1000 you earn, your marginal propensity to save is 0.25.

In Exhibit 2, the slope of the line represents the marginal propensity to consume. To better understand this concept, look at what happens when your disposable income rises from $18 000 to $20 000. At a disposable income of $18 000, you spend $8000 plus 75 percent of $18 000 (which is $13 500), for total spending of $21 500. If your

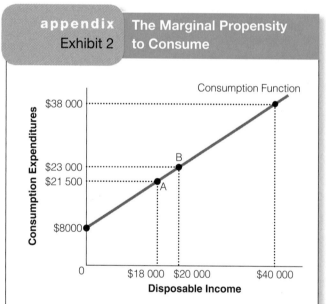

appendix Exhibit 2 **The Marginal Propensity to Consume**

Consumption Function

(y-axis) Consumption Expenditures: $38 000, $23 000, $21 500, $8000

(x-axis) Disposable Income: $18 000, $20 000, $40 000

The slope of the line represents the marginal propensity to consume. At a disposable income of $18 000, you spend $8000 plus 75 percent of $18 000 (which is $13 500), for total spending of $21 500. If your disposable income rises to $20 000, you spend $8000 plus 75 percent of $20 000 (which is $15 000), for total spending of $23 000. So when your disposable income rises by $2000 (from $18 000 to $20 000), your spending goes up by $1500 (from $21 500 to $23 000). Your marginal propensity to consume is $1500 (the increase in spending) divided by $2000 (the increase in disposable income), which equals 0.75, or 75 percent. But notice that this MPC calculation is also the calculation of the slope of the line from point A to point B.

disposable income rises to $20 000, you spend $8000 plus 75 percent of $20 000 (which is $15 000), for total spending of $23 000. So when your disposable income rises by $2000 (from $18 000 to $20 000), your spending goes up by $1500 (from $21 500 to $23 000). Your marginal propensity to consume is $1500 (the increase in spending) divided by $2000 (the increase in disposable income), which equals 0.75, or 75 percent. But notice that this calculation is also the calculation of the slope of the line from point A to point B in the exhibit. Recall that the slope of the line is the rise (the change on the vertical axis) over the run (the change on the horizontal axis). In this case, that's $1500 divided by $2000, which makes 0.75 the marginal propensity to consume. So the marginal propensity to consume is the same as the slope of the line in our graph of consumption and disposable income.

Now, let's take this same logic and apply it to the economy as a whole. If we add up, or aggregate, everyone's consumption and everyone's income, we'll get a line that looks like the one in Exhibit 2, but that applies to the entire economy. This line or functional relationship is called a *consumption function.* Let's suppose consumption spending in the economy is $1 billion plus 75 percent of income.

Now, with consumption equal to $1 billion plus 75 percent of income, consumption is partly autonomous (the $1 billion part, which people would spend no matter what their income, which depends on the current interest rate, real wealth, debt, and expectations), and partly *induced,* which means it depends on income. The induced consumption is the portion that's equal to 75 percent of income.

What is the total amount of expenditure in this economy? Because we've assumed that investment, government purchases, and net exports are zero, aggregate expenditure is just equal to the amount of consumption spending represented by our consumption function.

EQUILIBRIUM IN THE KEYNESIAN MODEL

The next part of the Keynesian aggregate expenditure model is to examine what conditions are needed for the economy to be in equilibrium. This discussion also tells us why the Keynesian expenditure model is sometimes called a Keynesian-cross model. In order to determine equilibrium, we need to show (1) that income equals output in the economy, and (2) that in equilibrium, aggregate expenditure (or consumption in this example) equals output. First, income equals output because people earn income by producing goods and services. For example, workers earn wages because they produce some product that is then sold on the market, and owners of firms earn profits because the products they sell provide more income than the cost of producing them. So any income that is earned by anyone in the economy arises from the production of output in the economy. From now on, we'll use this idea and say that income equals output; we'll use the terms *income* and *output* interchangeably.

The second condition needed for equilibrium (aggregate expenditure in the economy equals output) is the distinctive feature of the Keynesian expenditure model. Just as income must equal output (because income comes from selling goods and services), aggregate expenditure equals output because people can't earn income until the products they produce are sold to someone. Every good or service that is produced in the economy must be purchased by someone or added to inventories. Exhibit 3 plots aggregate expenditure against output. As you can see, it's a 45-degree line (slope = 1). The 45-degree line shows that the number on the horizontal axis, representing the amount of output in the economy, real GDP (Y), is equal to the number on the vertical axis, representing the amount of real aggregate expenditure (AE) in the economy. If output is $5 billion, then in equilibrium, aggregate expenditure must equal $5 billion. All points of macroeconomic equilibrium lie on the 45-degree line.

appendix
Exhibit 3

In Equilibrium, Aggregate Expenditure Equals Output

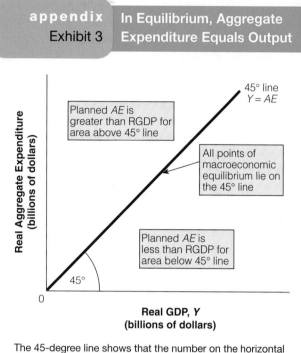

The 45-degree line shows that the number on the horizontal axis, representing the amount of output in the economy, is equal to the number on the vertical axis, representing the amount of aggregate expenditure in the economy. If output is $5 billion, then in equilibrium, aggregate expenditure must equal $5 billion.

DISEQUILIBRIUM IN THE KEYNESIAN MODEL

What would happen if, for some reason, output were lower than its equilibrium level, as would be the case if output were Y_1 in Exhibit 4?

Looking at the vertical dotted line, we see that when output is Y_1, aggregate expenditure (shown by the consumption function) is greater than output (shown by the 45-degree line). This amount is labelled the distance AB on the graph. So, people would be trying to buy more goods and services (*A*) than were being produced (*B*), which would cause producers to increase the amount of production, which would increase output in the economy. This process would continue until output reached its equilibrium level, where the two lines intersect. Another way to think about this disequilibrium is that consumers would be buying more than is currently produced, causing a decrease in inventories on shelves and in warehouses from their desired levels. Clearly, profit-seeking businesspeople would increase production to bring their inventory stocks back up to the desired levels. In doing so, they would move production to the equilibrium level.

Similarly, if output were above its equilibrium level, as would occur if output were Y_2 in Exhibit 4, economic forces would act to reduce output. At this point, as you can see by looking at the graph above point Y_2 on the horizontal axis, aggregate expenditure (D) is less than output (C). People wouldn't want to buy all the output that is being produced, so producers would want to reduce their production. They would keep reducing their output until reaching the equilibrium level. Using the inventory adjustment process, inventories would be bulging from shelves and warehouses and firms would reduce output and production until inventory stocks returned to the desired level. More discussion of this inventory adjustment process can be found later in the chapter when the complete model has been developed.

This basic model—in which we've assumed that consumption spending is the only component of aggregate expenditure (that is, we've ignored investment, government spending, and net exports) and that some consumption spending is autonomous—is quite simple, yet it is the essence of the Keynesian-cross model. From Exhibit 4, you can see where the "cross" part of its name comes from. Equilibrium in this model, and in more complicated versions of the model, always occurs where one line representing aggregate expenditure crosses another line that represents the equilibrium condition where aggregate expenditure equals output (the 45-degree line). The "Keynesian" part of the name reflects the fact that the model is a simple version of John Maynard Keynes' description of the economy from more than 70 years ago.

Now let's put Exhibits 2 and 3 together to find the equilibrium in the economy, shown in Exhibit 4. As you might guess, the point where the two lines cross is the equilibrium point. Why? Because it is only at this point that aggregate expenditure is equal to output. Aggregate expenditure is shown by the flatter line (Aggregate expenditure = Consumption). The equilibrium condition is shown by the 45-degree line ($Y = AE$). The only point for which consumption spending equals aggregate expenditure equals output is the point where those two lines intersect, labelled "Equilibrium." Because these points are on the 45-degree line, equilibrium output equals equilibrium aggregate expenditure.

appendix
Exhibit 4 **Disequilibrium and Equilibrium In the Keynesian Model**

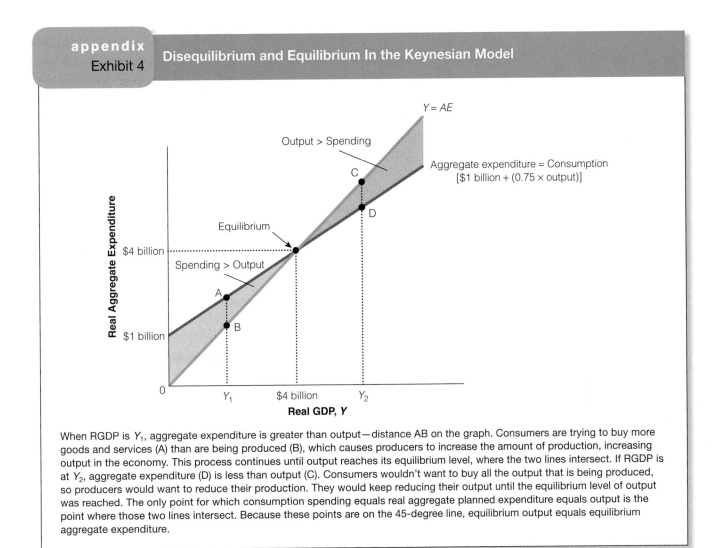

When RGDP is Y_1, aggregate expenditure is greater than output—distance AB on the graph. Consumers are trying to buy more goods and services (A) than are being produced (B), which causes producers to increase the amount of production, increasing output in the economy. This process continues until output reaches its equilibrium level, where the two lines intersect. If RGDP is at Y_2, aggregate expenditure (D) is less than output (C). Consumers wouldn't want to buy all the output that is being produced, so producers would want to reduce their production. They would keep reducing their output until the equilibrium level of output was reached. The only point for which consumption spending equals real aggregate planned expenditure equals output is the point where those two lines intersect. Because these points are on the 45-degree line, equilibrium output equals equilibrium aggregate expenditure.

ADDING INVESTMENT, GOVERNMENT PURCHASES, AND NET EXPORTS

Now we can complicate our model in another important way by adding in the other three major components of expenditure in the economy: investment, government purchases, and net exports. We'll add these components to the model but assume that they are autonomous, that is, they don't depend on the level of income or output in the economy.

Suppose that consumption depends on the level of income or output in the economy, but investment, government purchases, and net exports don't; instead, they depend on other things in the economy, such as interest rates, political considerations, or the condition of foreign economies. Now, aggregate expenditure (AE) consists of consumption (C) plus investment (I) plus government purchases (G) plus net exports (NX):

$$AE \equiv C + I + G + NX$$

This equation is nothing more than a definition (indicated by the $\equiv$ rather than =): Aggregate expenditure equals the sum of its components.

When we add up all the components of aggregate expenditure, we'll get an upward-sloping line, as we did in the previous section because consumption increases as income increases. But because we're now allowing for investment, government purchases, and net

appendix
Exhibit 5 **Adding Investment, Government Purchases, and Net Exports to Aggregate Expenditures**

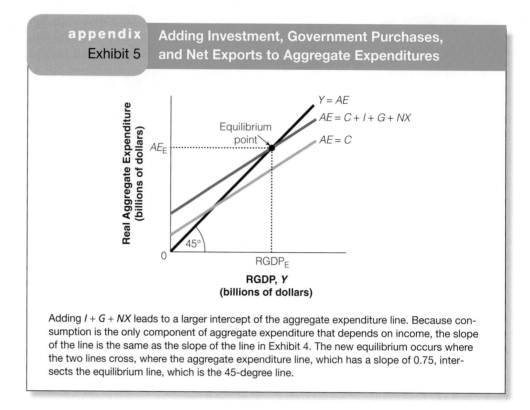

Adding $I + G + NX$ leads to a larger intercept of the aggregate expenditure line. Because consumption is the only component of aggregate expenditure that depends on income, the slope of the line is the same as the slope of the line in Exhibit 4. The new equilibrium occurs where the two lines cross, where the aggregate expenditure line, which has a slope of 0.75, intersects the equilibrium line, which is the 45-degree line.

exports, the autonomous portion of aggregate expenditure is larger. Thus, the intercept of the aggregate expenditure line is higher, as shown in Exhibit 5.

What is the new equilibrium? As before, the equilibrium occurs where the two lines cross, that is, where the aggregate expenditure line intersects the equilibrium line, which is the 45-degree line.

Now that we've added in the other components of spending, especially investment spending, we can begin to discuss some of the more realistic factors related to the business cycle. This discussion of what happens to the economy during business cycles is a major element of Keynesian theory, which was designed to explain what happens in recessions.

If you look at historical economic data, you'll see that investment spending fluctuates much more than overall output in the economy. In recessions, output declines, and a major portion of the decline occurs because investment falls sharply. In expansions, investment is the major contributor to economic growth. The two major explanations for the volatile movement of investment over the business cycle involve planned investment and unplanned investment.

The first explanation for investment's strong business cycle movement is that *planned* investment responds dramatically to perceptions of future changes in economic activity. If business firms think that the economy will be good in the future, they'll build new factories, buy more computers, and hire more workers today, in anticipation of being able to sell more goods in the future. On the other hand, if firms think the economy will be weak in the future, they'll cut back on both investment and hiring. Economists find that planned investment is extremely sensitive to firms' perceptions about the future. And if firms desire to invest more today, it generates ripple effects that make the economy grow even faster.

The second explanation for investment's movement over the business cycle is that businesses encounter *unplanned* changes in investment as well. The idea here is that recessions, to some extent, occur as the economy is making a transition, before it reaches equilibrium. We'll use Exhibit 6 to illustrate this idea. In the exhibit, equilibrium occurs at output of Y_0. Now, consider what would happen if, for some reason, firms produced too many goods, bringing the economy to output level Y_1. At output level Y_1, aggregate expenditure is less than output because the aggregate expenditure line is below the 45-degree line at that point. When people aren't buying all the products that firms are producing, unsold goods begin piling up. In the national income accounts, unsold goods in firms' inventories are counted in a subcategory of investment—inventory investment. The firms didn't plan for this to happen, so the piling up of inventories reflects **unplanned inventory investment.** Of course, once firms realize that inventories are rising because they've produced too much, they cut back on production, reducing output below Y_1. This process continues until firms' inventories are restored to normal levels and output returns to Y_0.

Now let's look at what would happen if firms produced too few goods, as occurs when output is at Y_2. At output level Y_2, aggregate expenditure is greater than output because the aggregate expenditure line is above the 45-degree line at that point. People want to buy more goods than firms are producing, so firms' inventories begin to decline or become depleted. Again, this change in inventories shows up in the national income accounts, this time as a decline in firms' inventories and thus a decline in investment. Again, the firms didn't plan for this situation, so once they realize that inventories are declining because they haven't produced enough, they'll increase production beyond Y_2. Equilibrium is reached when firms' inventories are restored to normal levels and output returns to Y_0. So, our Keynesian aggregate expenditure model helps to explain the process of the business cycle, working through investment.

appendix
Exhibit 6 — Unplanned Inventory Investment

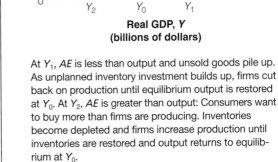

At Y_1, AE is less than output and unsold goods pile up. As unplanned inventory investment builds up, firms cut back on production until equilibrium output is restored at Y_0. At Y_2, AE is greater than output: Consumers want to buy more than firms are producing. Inventories become depleted and firms increase production until inventories are restored and output returns to equilibrium at Y_0.

unplanned inventory investment
collection of inventory that results when people do not buy the products firms are producing

Key Terms and Concepts

For a complete glossary of chapter key terms, visit the textbook's Web site at http://www.sextonmacro2e.nelson.com.

Fill in the Blanks

Section 9.1

1. The _____ curve is the relationship between the total quantity of final goods and services that suppliers are willing and able to produce and the overall price level.

2. There are two aggregate supply curves—a _____ aggregate supply curve and a _____ aggregate supply curve.

3. The short-run relationship refers to a period when _____ prices can change in response to supply and demand, but _____ prices have not yet been able to adjust.

4. In the short run, the aggregate supply curve is _____ sloping.

5. In the short run, at a higher price level, producers are willing to supply _____ real output, and at lower price levels, they are willing to supply _____ real output.

6. The two explanations for why producers would be willing to supply more output when the price level increases are the _____ effect and the _____ effect.

7. When the price level rises in the short run, output prices _____ relative to input prices (costs), _____ producers' short-run profit margins.

8. If the price level falls, output prices _____, producers' profits will _____, and producers will _____ their level of output.

9. If the overall price level is rising, producers can be fooled into thinking that the _____ price of their output is rising, so they will supply _____ in the short run.

10. The long run is a period long enough for the price of _____ to fully adjust to changes in the economy.

11. Along the *LRAS* curve, two sets of prices are changing—the prices of _____ and the prices of _____.

12. The level of RGDP producers are willing to supply in the long run is _____ by changes in the price level.

13. The vertical *LRAS* curve will always be positioned at the _____ of output.

14. The long-run equilibrium level is where the economy will settle when undisturbed and all resources are _____ employed.

15. Long-run equilibrium will only occur where *SRAS* and *AD* intersect along the _____.

Section 9.2

16. The underlying determinant of shifts in short-run aggregate supply is _____.

17. _____ production costs will motivate producers to produce less at any given price level, shifting the short-run aggregate supply curve _____.

18. A permanent increase in the available amount of capital, entrepreneurship, land, or labour can shift the *LRAS* and *SRAS* curves to the _____.

19. A decrease in the stock of capital will _____ real output in the short run and _____ real output in the long run, *ceteris paribus*.

20. Investments in human capital would cause productivity to _____.

21. A(n) _____ in the amount of natural resources available would result in a leftward shift of both *SRAS* and *LRAS*.

22. An increase in the number of workers in the labour force, *ceteris paribus*, tends to _____ wages and _____ short-run aggregate supply.

23. _____ output per worker causes production costs to rise and potential real output to fall, resulting in a _____ shift in both *SRAS* and *LRAS*.

24. A(n) _____ in government regulations on businesses would lower the costs of production and expand potential real output, causing both *SRAS* and *LRAS* to shift to the right.

25. The most important of the factors that shift *SRAS* but do not impact *LRAS* are change in _____ prices and _____.

26. If the price of steel rises, it will shift *SRAS* _____, whereas the *LRAS* will _____ as long as the capacity to make steel has not been reduced.

27. A fall in input prices, which shifts *SRAS* right, shifts *LRAS* right only if _____ has risen, and that only occurs if the _____ of those inputs is increased.

28. _____ supply shocks, such as natural disasters, can increase the costs of production.

Section 9.3

29. Only a short-run equilibrium that is at _____ output is also a long-run equilibrium.

30. The short-run equilibrium level of real output and the price level are determined by the intersection of the _____ curve and the _____ curve.

31. The long-run equilibrium level of RGDP changes only when the _____ curve shifts.

32. Economists call unexpected shifts in supply or demand _____.

33. When short-run equilibrium occurs at less than the potential output of the economy, it results in a _____ gap.

34. _____ inflation occurs when the price level rises as a result of an increase in aggregate demand.

35. Demand-pull inflation causes a(n) _____ in the price level and an _____ in real output in the short run, illustrated by a movement up along the *SRAS* curve.

36. Demand-pull inflation causes a(n) _____ gap.

37. When *AD* increases, real (adjusted for inflation) wages _____ in the short run.

38. In response to an expansionary gap in the short run, wages and other input prices will tend to _____, which is illustrated by a _____ shift in the *SRAS* curve.

39. _____ is the situation in which lower economic growth and higher prices occur together.

40. An increase in input prices can cause the *SRAS* curve to shift to the _____, resulting in _____ price levels, _____ real output, and _____ rates of unemployment in the short run.

41. Starting with the economy initially at full employment equilibrium, a sudden increase in oil prices would result in _____ unemployment and in real output _____ than potential output in the short run.

42. Falling oil prices would result in a _____ shift in the *SRAS* curve.

43. Holding *AD* constant, falling oil prices would lead to _____ prices, _____ output, and _____ rates of unemployment in the short run.

44. An economy can self-correct from a contractionary gap through _____ wages and prices.

45. The long-run result of a fall in aggregate demand is an equilibrium _____ potential output and a _____ price level.

46. Wages and prices may be sticky downward because of _____ labour contracts, a legal _____ wage, employers paying _____ wages, and _____ costs.

47. If the economy is currently in an expansionary gap, with output greater than potential output, the price level is _____ than workers anticipated.

48. The _____ of the *AD* and *AS* curves makes the *AD/AS* analysis not completely satisfactory.

True or False

Section 9.1

1. The aggregate supply curve represents how much RGDP suppliers will be willing to produce at different price levels.

2. Nominal wages are assumed to adjust quickly in the short run.

3. The long-run relationship refers to a period long enough for the prices of outputs and all inputs to fully adjust to changes in the economy.

4. In the short run, the aggregate supply curve is vertical.

5. In the short run, the slow adjustments of input prices are due to the longer-term input contracts that do not adjust quickly to price-level changes.

6. When price level rises in the short run, it will increase producers' profit margins and make it in the producers' self-interest to expand their production.

7. If the price level falls, input prices, producers' profits, and real output will fall in the short run.

8. When the price level falls, producers can be fooled into supplying more based on a short-run misperception of relative prices.

9. Along the short-run aggregate supply curve, we assume that wages and other input prices have time to adjust.

10. Along the long-run aggregate supply curve, we are looking at the relationship between RGDP produced and the price level, once input prices have been able to respond to changes in output prices.

11. Along the *LRAS* curve, a 10 percent increase in the price of goods and services is matched by a 10 percent increase in the price of inputs.

12. Along the *LRAS* curve, the economy is assumed to be at full employment.

13. In the long run, the economy will produce at the maximum sustainable level allowed by its capital, labour, and technological inputs, regardless of the price level.

14. Long-run equilibrium occurs wherever *SRAS* and *AD* intersect.

15. The economy can be in short-run equilibrium without being in long-run equilibrium.

Section 9.2

16. *Ceteris paribus,* lower production costs will motivate producers to produce more at any given price level, shifting *SRAS* rightward.

17. Any permanent change in the quantity of any factor of production available— capital, entrepreneurship, land, or labour—can cause a shift in the long-run aggregate supply curve but not the short-run aggregate supply curve.

18. Less and lower-quality capital will shift both the short-run aggregate supply curve and the long-run aggregate supply curve to the left.

19. Added investments in human capital would shift the short-run aggregate supply curve right but leave the long-run aggregate supply curve unchanged.

20. If entrepreneurs can find ways to lower the costs of production, then the short-run and long-run aggregate supply curves both shift to the right.

21. Successful oil exploration would leave *LRAS* unchanged because it would not change the total amount of oil in the earth.

22. An expanded labour force increases the economy's potential output, increasing *LRAS*.

23. Increases in government regulations that make it more costly for producers shift *SRAS* left but leave *LRAS* unchanged.

24. The prices of factors, or inputs, that go into producing outputs will affect only *SRAS* if they don't reflect permanent changes in the supplies of some factors of production.

25. If wages increase without a corresponding increase in labour productivity, *SRAS* will shift to the left, but *LRAS* will not shift because with the same supply of labour as before, potential output does not change.

26. Changes in input prices only affect *SRAS* if they reflect permanent changes in the supplies of those inputs.

27. Adverse supply shocks can increase the costs of production, shifting *SRAS* to the left; but once the temporary effects of these disasters have been felt, no appreciable change in the economy's productive capacity occurs, so *LRAS* doesn't shift as a result.

Section 9.3

28. In long-run equilibrium, the economy operates at full employment, regardless of the level of the aggregate demand curve.

29. Short-run equilibrium can change only when the short-run aggregate supply curve shifts.

30. A change in aggregate demand will change RGDP in the short-run equilibrium, but not in the long run.

31. When short-run equilibrium occurs beyond the economy's level of potential output, it results in an expansionary gap.

32. Demand-pull inflation causes a contractionary gap.

33. Demand-pull inflation causes the prices of the goods producers sell to rise faster than the costs of the inputs they use in production.

34. The economy can never operate beyond its potential output.

35. Short-run real output beyond potential output (and employment beyond full employment) cannot be sustained in the long run.

36. In response to an expansionary gap in the short run, real wages and other real input prices will tend to rise.

37. When an increase in *AD* causes an expansionary gap in the short run, the only long-run difference from the initial equilibrium is the new, higher price level.

38. A leftward shift in the aggregate supply curve can cause cost-push inflation.

39. The primary culprits responsible for the leftward shift in *SRAS* in the 1970s were oil price decreases.

40. Starting with the economy initially at full employment equilibrium, a sudden increase in oil prices would result in a contractionary gap.

41. Holding *AD* constant, falling oil prices would lead to lower prices, lower output, and lower rates of unemployment.

42. A fall in *AD* would reduce real output and the price level and increase unemployment in the short run—a contractionary gap.

43. In a recession, unemployed workers and other input suppliers will bid down wages and prices, and the resulting reduction in production costs shifts the short-run aggregate supply curve to the right.

44. Downward wage stickiness may lead to prolonged periods of recession in response to decreases in aggregate demand by making the economy's adjustment mechanism slower.

45. If the economy is currently in a contractionary gap, with output less than potential output, the price level is higher than workers anticipated.

46. When aggregate demand increases, workers' and input suppliers' purchasing power falls in the short run, but workers' and input suppliers' purchasing power is restored at a higher price level in the long run.

47. The *AD/AS* model is a very precise tool for analyzing the economy.

Multiple Choice

Section 9.1
1. The short-run aggregate supply curve slopes
   a. downward because firms can sell more, and hence, will produce more when prices are lower.
   b. downward because firms find it costs less to purchase labour and other inputs when prices are lower, and hence, they produce more.
   c. upward because when the price level rises, output prices rise relative to input prices (costs), raising profit margins and increasing production and sales.
   d. upward because firms find that it costs more to purchase labour and other inputs when prices are higher, and hence, they must produce and sell more in order to make a profit.

2. If the price level rises, what will happen to the quantity of RGDP produced along the long-run aggregate supply curve?
   a. It will increase.
   b. It will usually increase, but not always.
   c. Nothing will happen to it.
   d. It will decrease.
   e. It will usually decrease, but not always.

3. If the price level rises, what happens to the level of real GDP supplied?
   a. It will increase in both the short run and the long run.
   b. It will increase in the short run but not in the long run.
   c. It will decrease in both the short run and the long run.
   d. It will decrease in the short run but not in the long run.
   e. It will usually decrease, but not always.

4. What is the typical response of firms to an increase in the price of what they sell, for given input prices?
   a. an increase in output
   b. an increase in hiring factors of production
   c. an increase in the profit level of firms
   d. an increase in employment in the industry
   e. all of the above

5. The short run is
   a. a time period in which the prices of output cannot change, but in which the prices of inputs have time to adjust.
   b. a time period in which output prices can change in response to supply and demand, but in which all input prices have not yet been able to completely adjust.
   c. a time period in which neither the prices of output nor the prices of inputs are able to change.
   d. any time period of less than a year.

6. The profit effect is explained in the text as follows:
   a. When the price level decreases, output prices rise relative to input prices (costs), raising producers' short-run profit margins.
   b. At equilibrium prices, when costs rise, profit margins are able to float with them and be passed along.
   c. The profit effect is only a long-run phenomenon.
   d. When the price level rises, output prices rise relative to input prices (costs), raising producers' short-run profit margins.

7. The text's explanation for the misperception effect for an upward-sloping short-run aggregate supply curve is based on
   a. falling profit margins as the price level rises.
   b. rising costs of production as the price level rises.
   c. fixed-wage labour contracts.
   d. the fact that producers may be fooled into thinking that the relative price of the item they are producing is rising, so they increase production.

8. In the short run, a decrease in the price level
   a. increases output prices relative to input prices.
   b. increases the profit margins of many producers.
   c. decreases RGDP supplied.
   d. decreases unemployment rates.
   e. does none of the above.

Section 9.2

9. Which of the following would shift the long-run aggregate supply curve if it changed?
   a. the level of capital in the economy
   b. the amount of land in the economy
   c. the amount of labour in the economy
   d. the technology in the economy
   e. any of the above

10. The short-run aggregate supply curve will shift to the left, other things being equal, if
    a. energy prices fall.
    b. technology and productivity increase in the nation.
    c. there is a short-term increase in input prices.
    d. the capital stock of the nation increases.

11. An increase in input prices causes
    a. the short-run aggregate supply curve to shift outward, which means the quantity supplied at any price level declines.
    b. the short-run aggregate supply curve to shift inward, which means the quantity supplied at any price level declines.
    c. the short-run aggregate supply curve to shift inward, which means the quantity supplied at any price level increases.
    d. the short-run aggregate supply curve to shift outward, which means the quantity supplied at any price level increases.

12. How will an increase in money wages affect the short-run aggregate supply curve?
    a. It will shift left (a decrease in short-run aggregate supply).
    b. It will shift left (an increase in short-run aggregate supply).
    c. It will shift right (a decrease in short-run aggregate supply).
    d. It will shift right (an increase in short-run aggregate supply).

13. An unusual series of rainstorms washes out the grain crop in the prairie provinces, severely curtailing the availability of corn and wheat, as well as soybeans. What effect would this have on aggregate supply?
    a. It would shift the *SRAS* left, but not the *LRAS*.
    b. It would shift both the *SRAS* and the *LRAS* left.
    c. It would shift the *SRAS* right, but not the *LRAS*.
    d. It would shift both the *SRAS* and the *LRAS* right.

14. Any permanent increase in the quantity of any of the factors of production—capital, land, labour, or technology—available, will cause
    a. *SRAS* to shift to the left and *LRAS* to remain constant.
    b. *SRAS* to shift to the right and *LRAS* to remain constant.
    c. both *SRAS* and *LRAS* to shift to the right.
    d. both *SRAS* and *LRAS* to shift to the left.

15. Which of the following could be expected to shift the short-run aggregate supply curve upward?
    a. a rise in the price of oil
    b. a natural disaster
    c. wage increases without increases in labour productivity
    d. all of the above

16. A temporary positive supply shock will shift _____; a permanent positive supply shock will shift _____.

    a. *SRAS* and *LRAS* right; *SRAS* and *LRAS* right

    b. *SRAS* but not *LRAS* right; *SRAS* and *LRAS* right

    c. *SRAS* and *LRAS* right; *SRAS* but not *LRAS* right

    d. *SRAS* but not *LRAS* right; *SRAS* but not *LRAS* right

17. A year of unusually good weather for agriculture would

    a. increase *SRAS* but not *LRAS.*

    b. increase *SRAS* and *LRAS.*

    c. decrease *SRAS* but not *LRAS.*

    d. decrease *SRAS* and *LRAS.*

18. When there is a temporary sharp increase in the price of oil, which curve(s) will shift left?

    a. *SRAS*

    b. *LRAS*

    c. neither *SRAS* nor *LRAS*

    d. both *SRAS* and *LRAS*

Section 9.3

19. Inflation that occurs due to a decrease in aggregate supply is called

    a. cost-push.

    b. demand-pull.

    c. inflationary push.

    d. none of the above.

20. Assuming a constant level of aggregate demand, the short-run effects of an adverse supply shock include

    a. an increase in the price level and a decrease in real output.

    b. an increase in the price level and an increase in real output.

    c. a decrease in the price level and an increase in real output.

    d. a decrease in the price level and a decrease in real output.

21. Cost-push inflation occurs when

    a. the aggregate demand curve shifts right at a faster rate than short-run aggregate supply.

    b. the short-run aggregate supply curve shifts left while aggregate demand is fixed.

    c. the aggregate demand curve shifts left and aggregate supply is fixed.

    d. the short-run aggregate supply curve shifts right.

22. A recession could result from

    a. a decrease in aggregate demand.

    b. an increase in long-run aggregate supply.

    c. an increase in aggregate demand.

    d. an increase in short-run aggregate supply.

    e. none of the above.

23. When *SRAS* and *AD* intersect at the natural level of real output, it is

    a. a short-run equilibrium and a long-run equilibrium.

    b. a short-run equilibrium but not necessarily a long-run equilibrium.

    c. a long-run equilibrium but not necessarily a short-run equilibrium.

    d. not necessarily either a short-run equilibrium or a long-run equilibrium.

24. Where *SRAS* and *AD* currently intersect at a real output level greater than the natural level of real output,
    a. it is a short-run equilibrium, and real output will tend to fall from its current level as it adjusts to long-run equilibrium.
    b. it is a short-run equilibrium, and real output will tend to rise from its current level as it adjusts to long-run equilibrium.
    c. it is a short-run disequilibrium, and real output will tend to fall from its current level as it adjusts to long-run equilibrium.
    d. it is a short-run disequilibrium, and real output will tend to rise from its current level as it adjusts to long-run equilibrium.

25. Starting from long-run equilibrium, an increase in aggregate demand will cause
    a. an expansionary gap in the short run.
    b. a contractionary gap in the short run.
    c. an expansionary gap in the short run and the long run.
    d. a contractionary gap in the short run and the long run.
    e. neither an expansionary nor a contractionary gap in the short run or the long run.

26. When there is a contractionary gap,
    a. real output exceeds the natural level of output, and unemployment exceeds its natural rate.
    b. real output exceeds the natural level of output, and unemployment is less than its natural rate.
    c. real output is less than the natural level of output, and unemployment exceeds its natural rate.
    d. real output is less than the natural level of output, and unemployment is less than its natural rate.

27. Which of the following could begin an episode of demand-pull inflation?
    a. an increase in consumer optimism
    b. a faster rate of economic growth by a major trading partner country
    c. expectations of higher rates of return in investment
    d. any of the above
    e. none of the above

28. If real output is currently less than the natural level of real output, a decrease in aggregate demand will
    a. make the current expansionary gap larger.
    b. make the current expansionary gap smaller.
    c. make the current contractionary gap larger.
    d. make the current contractionary gap smaller.

29. In the short run, demand-pull inflation
    a. increases both unemployment and the price level.
    b. increases unemployment but decreases the price level.
    c. decreases both employment and the price level.
    d. decreases unemployment and increases the price level.

30. In a stagflation situation,
    a. unemployment increases, and the price level increases.
    b. unemployment increases, and the price level decreases.
    c. unemployment decreases, and the price level increases.
    d. unemployment decreases, and the price level decreases.

31. A sharp fall in oil prices will cause a(n) _____; a sudden increase in the wages demanded by workers will cause a(n) _____.
   a. contractionary gap; expansionary gap
   b. contractionary gap; contractionary gap
   c. expansionary gap; expansionary gap
   d. expansionary gap; contractionary gap

32. Starting from long-run equilibrium, an increase in aggregate demand
   a. causes an expansionary gap.
   b. results in a lower price level.
   c. increases unemployment.
   d. does all of the above.
   e. does b and c, but not a.

33. During the self-correction process after a fall in aggregate demand,
   a. the price level increases and real output increases.
   b. the price level increases and real output decreases.
   c. the price level decreases and real output increases.
   d. the price level decreases and real output decreases.

34. Which of the following can contribute to slowing the adjustment process to a contractionary gap?
   a. efficiency wages
   b. the minimum wage
   c. menu costs
   d. all of the above
   e. b and c, but not a

35. An unexpected increase in aggregate demand will
   a. increase real wages in the short run but not the long run.
   b. increase real wages in the short run and the long run.
   c. decrease real wages in the short run but not the long run.
   d. decrease real wages in the short run and the long run.

Problems

1. [Section 9.2]
   How will each of the following changes alter aggregate supply?

Change	Short-Run Aggregate Supply	Long-Run Aggregate Supply
An increase in aggregate demand	_____	_____
A decrease in aggregate demand	_____	_____
An increase in the stock of capital	_____	_____
A reduction in the size of the labour force	_____	_____
An increase in input prices (that does not reflect permanent changes in their supplies)	_____	_____
A decrease in input prices (that does reflect permanent changes in their supplies)	_____	_____
An increase in usable natural resources	_____	_____
A temporary adverse supply shock	_____	_____
Increases in the cost of government regulations	_____	_____

2. [Section 9.3]

Use the following diagram to answer questions a and b.

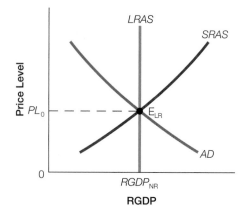

a. On the exhibit provided, illustrate the short-run effects of an increase in aggregate demand. What happens to the price level, real output, employment, and unemployment?

b. On the exhibit provided, illustrate the long-run effects of an increase in aggregate demand. What happens to the price level, real output, employment, and unemployment?

3. [Section 9.3]

Use the following diagram to answer questions a and b.

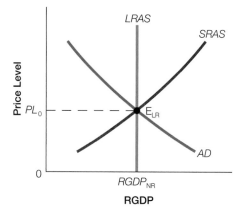

a. On the exhibit provided, illustrate the short-run effects of a decrease in aggregate demand. What happens to the price level, real output, employment, and unemployment?

b. On the exhibit provided, illustrate the long-run effects of a decrease in aggregate demand. What happens to the price level, real output, employment, and unemployment?

4. [Section 9.3]
Use the following diagram to answer questions a and b.

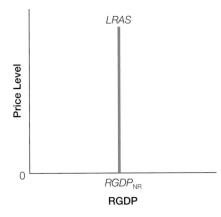

a. Illustrate a contractionary gap on the diagram provided.
b. Given the illustration in a, illustrate and explain the eventual long-run equilibrium in this case.

5. [Section 9.3]
Use the following diagram to answer questions a and b.

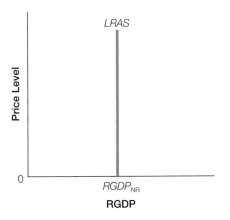

a. Illustrate an expansionary gap on the diagram provided.
b. Given the illustration in a, illustrate and explain the eventual long-run equilibrium in this case.

chapter 10

Fiscal Policy

---

section 10.1 Fiscal Policy

- What is fiscal policy?
- How does expansionary fiscal policy affect the government's budget?
- How does contractionary fiscal policy affect the government's budget?

FISCAL POLICY

fiscal policy
use of government spending and/or taxes to alter equilibrium output and prices

Fiscal policy is the use of government spending and/or taxes to alter RGDP and the price level. Sometimes it is necessary for the government to use fiscal policy to stimulate the economy during a contraction (or recession) or to try to curb an expansion in order to bring inflation under control. In the early 1980s, the U.S. government implemented large tax cuts, which helped the U.S. economy out of a recession. In 2001 and 2003, tax cuts were again implemented to combat an economic slowdown and promote long-term economic growth. In the 1990s, Japan used large government spending programs to help pull itself out of a recessionary slump. Beginning in the early 2000s, the federal government in Canada began cutting income taxes to promote long-term economic growth, a policy objective they have continued in subsequent budgets. When should the government use such policies and how well do they work are just a couple of the questions we will answer in this chapter.

When government spending (for purchases of goods and services and for transfer payments to individuals, like EI benefits) exceeds tax revenues, there is a **budget deficit.** When tax revenues are greater than government spending, a **budget surplus** exists. A balanced budget, where government expenditures equal tax revenues, may seldom occur unless efforts are made to deliberately balance the budget as a matter of public policy.

FISCAL STIMULUS AFFECTS THE BUDGET

When the government wishes to stimulate the economy by increasing aggregate demand, it will increase government spending on goods and services, lower taxes, or use some combination of these approaches. Any of those options will increase the budget deficit (or reduce the budget surplus). Thus, **expansionary fiscal policy** is associated with increased government budget deficits. Likewise, if the government wishes to dampen a boom in the economy by reducing aggregate demand, it will reduce its spending on goods and services, increase taxes, or use some combination of these approaches. Thus, **contractionary fiscal policy** will tend to increase a budget surplus (or reduce a budget deficit).

budget deficit
government spending exceeds tax revenues for a given fiscal year

budget surplus
tax revenues are greater than government expenditures for a given fiscal year

expansionary fiscal policy
use of fiscal policy tools to foster increased output by increasing government spending and/or lowering taxes

contractionary fiscal policy
use of fiscal policy tools to reduce output by decreasing government spending and/or increasing taxes

Section Check

1. Fiscal policy is the use of government spending on goods and services and/or taxes to affect aggregate demand and to alter RGDP and the price level.
2. Expansionary fiscal policies will increase the budget deficit (or reduce a budget surplus) through greater government spending, lower taxes, or both.
3. Contractionary fiscal policies will increase a budget surplus (or reduce a budget deficit) through reduced government spending, higher taxes, or both.

Government: Spending and Taxation

section 10.2

- How does government finance its spending?
- On what does the public sector spend its money?
- What are progressive and regressive taxes?

CATEGORIES OF GOVERNMENT SPENDING

In 2008, the federal government spent $237.0 billion on goods and services and on transfer payments to individuals. The provincial and local governments combined spent $395.7 billion on goods and services and on transfer payments to individuals. Where is all of this money spent? Exhibit 1 illustrates the major categories of government spending as a proportion of total government spending.

Exhibit 1(a) shows that 31 percent of federal government spending in 2008 went to social services, including Employment Insurance and Old Age Security programs.

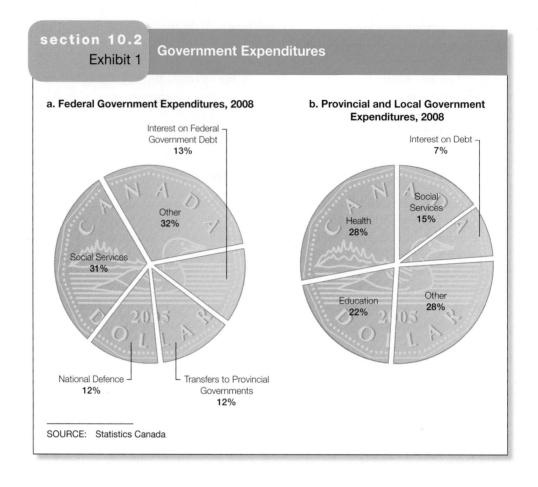

section 10.2
Exhibit 1   Government Expenditures

a. Federal Government Expenditures, 2008

Interest on Federal
Government Debt
13%

Other
32%

Social Services
31%

National Defence
12%

Transfers to Provincial
Governments
12%

**b. Provincial and Local Government
Expenditures, 2008**

Interest on Debt
7%

Social
Services
15%

Health
28%

Education
22%

Other
28%

SOURCE: Statistics Canada

Transfers of money from the federal government to provincial governments (for provincial spending on post-secondary education and health care) amounted to 12 percent of federal government expenditure. Interest payments that the federal government makes on its outstanding debt account for 13 percent of total spending, whereas national defence accounts for 12 percent. The remaining 32 percent of federal government spending includes foreign affairs and international aid, the environment, recreation and culture, resource conservation, and industrial development.

Exhibit 1(b) shows that provincial and local government spending is quite different from federal government spending. Health care and education spending, at 28 percent and 22 percent, respectively, account for virtually one-half of all spending by provincial and local governments. Social services, such as welfare and social assistance programs, account for 15 percent of total spending. Like the federal government, the provincial and local levels of government must also make interest payments on their outstanding debt, accounting for about 7 percent of spending. The remaining 28 percent of provincial and local government expenditure involves items such as housing, the environment, police and fire protection, and transportation and communication services.

GENERATING GOVERNMENT REVENUE

Governments have to pay their bills like any person or institution that spends money. But how do they obtain revenue? Two major avenues are open: taxation and borrowing. When the government runs a budget deficit, spending exceeds tax revenue and therefore part of the spending must be financed by borowing. When the budget is balanced, there is no borrowing requirement, and all spending is financed by tax revenue.

TYPES OF FEDERAL GOVERNMENT REVENUE

Exhibit 2 shows the revenue sources for the federal government and the provincial and local governments. At the federal level (Exhibit 2(a)), the majority of revenue, 67 percent, comes in the form of income taxes on individuals and corporations, called personal income taxes and corporate income taxes, respectively. Consumption taxes, such as the Goods and Services Tax (GST) and federal excise taxes on gasoline, alcohol, and tobacco products, account for 20 percent of federal revenue. Social security contributions, like Employment Insurance premiums paid by both employees and employers, amount to 7 percent of federal government revenue. Other revenue, at 6 percent, comes largely from investment income and sales of goods and services.

A Progressive Tax

One impact of substantial taxes on personal income is that the effective take-home income of Canadians is significantly altered by the tax system. **Progressive taxes,** of which the federal personal income tax is one example, are designed so that those with higher incomes pay a greater proportion of their income in taxes. A progressive tax is one tool that the government can use to redistribute income.

progressive tax
the amount of an individual's tax rises as a proportion of income, as the person's income rises

A Regressive Tax

Some people consider an **excise tax**—a sales tax on individual products such as alcohol, tobacco, and gasoline—to be the most unfair type of tax because it is generally the most regressive. A **regressive tax** takes a greater proportion of the income of lower-income groups than higher-income groups. This type of tax on specific items will impose a far greater burden, as a percentage of income, on the poor and middle class than on the wealthy, because low-income families pay a greater proportion of their income on these taxes than do high-income families.

In addition, excise taxes may lead to economic inefficiencies. By isolating a few products and subjecting them to discriminatory taxation, consumption taxes subject economic choices to political manipulation and lead to inefficiency.

excise tax
a sales tax on individual products such as alcohol, tobacco, and gasoline

regressive tax
the amount of an individual's tax falls as a proportion of income, as the person's income rises

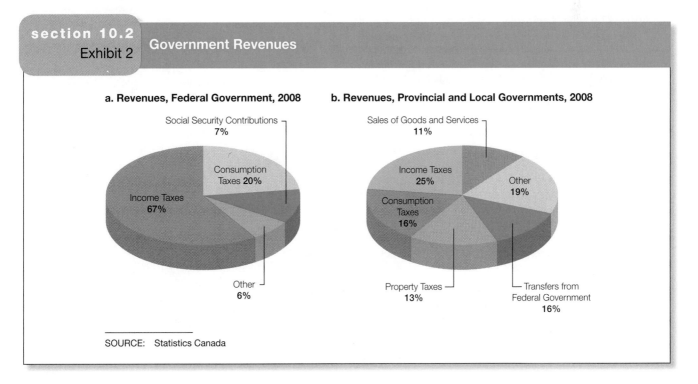

section 10.2 Exhibit 2 — Government Revenues

SOURCE: Statistics Canada

FINANCING PROVINCIAL AND LOCAL GOVERNMENT SPENDING

Exhibit 2(b) shows that income taxes and consumption taxes accounted for 25 percent and 16 percent, respectively, of total provincial and local government revenue, with virtually all that revenue going to provincial governments. Property taxes, however, are the major revenue source for local levels of government, and amount to 13 percent of total provincial and local government revenue. Transfers of money from the federal government are an important source of revenue to lower levels of government, accounting for 16 percent of their revenue. Revenue from the sale of goods and services makes up 11 percent of total revenue. The remaining 19 percent of revenue comes from items such as investment income, health premiums, and other taxes.

In The **NEWS**

THE DISTORTIONARY IMPACT OF THE TAX STRUCTURE IN CANADA

BY WILLIAM WATSON

If you're in the forestry industry in Prince Edward Island, you know what tax rate you pay on the income generated by your next dollar of investment? Minus 58.2 percent. Minus because the value of various tax credits and deductions the federal and provincial governments make available to such investment is more than half again what you can expect to earn by cutting down trees and selling the proceeds.

Outside P.E.I., as well, it's hard to see the trees for the forestry subsidies. The tax rate on a new dollar of income from forestry in Newfoundland and Labrador is minus 42.7 percent. It's also negative in two other Atlantic provinces (minus 21.6 percent in Nova Scotia and minus 27.5 percent in New Brunswick). In Quebec the effective marginal tax rate for forestry is just three percent. The highest forestry tax rate in the country is in Ontario—good old Ontario, our version of Taxachusetts—at 20.8 percent. The average tax rate across all provinces is just 11.0 percent.

Compare this with tax rates on investment in communications, including telecommunications, one of those new 21st-century industries we hear so much about: 49.8 percent in P.E.I, 46.2 percent in Ontario, 45.9 percent in Manitoba, 39.3 percent for the country as a whole.

Another big beneficiary of the current tax structure is manufacturing. It faces a Canada-wide average tax rate of 19.3 percent on new investments, ranging from a low of minus 30.1 percent in P.E.I. to a high of 24.1 percent in Ontario, and comparing with cross-Canada industry-wide averages of 39.3 percent in communications, 38.5 percent in construction, 33.7 percent in retail, and 28.1 percent in transportation.

Millions of good people work in manufacturing. But millions of good people work in all these other industries, too. Why do we favour manufacturing over everything else—everything else except forestry, that is?

Some of these differences in tax rates are accidental. If you tax business capital and some industries use more capital per dollar of profit than others, then their effective tax rates will be higher.

But other differences are the result of deliberate decisions to create differences. Many of our governments, federal and provincial, provide specific tax benefits to forestry and manufacturing companies that are simply not available to companies in other industries.

This is very unlikely to be efficient. Governments have no special insight into which industries or firms will bring the biggest benefits to Canada.

What's needed instead are governments that don't take a position on which types of investments Canadian industry should be making. They should keep tax rates low and tax bases broad by eliminating special exemptions and deductions. The function of the tax system should be to raise revenue for governments, not shape the Canadian economy.

SOURCE: Adapted from William Watson, "It's hard to see the trees for the forestry subsidies," *Ottawa Citizen,* Ottawa, Ontario, September 2, 2008, p. A13. Material reprinted with the express permission of: *The National Post Company,* a CanWest Partnership.

CONSIDER THIS:

The marginal tax rate (the percentage of the next dollar of profit made that must be given to the government) in the forestry industry in Price Edward Island is minus 58.2 percent. In Ontario, the forestry tax rate is 20.8 percent—an astounding difference of nearly 80 percent! Average tax rates in the manufacturing sector are among some of the lowest in Canada at an average of just 19.3 percent, whereas companies in the communications sector pay an average of 39.3 percent. Such variations in tax rates are inefficient. Government should keep tax rates low and eliminate special deductions for certain industries.

SECTION CHECK

Section Check

1. Over 30 percent of federal government spending goes to social services, such as Employment Insurance and Old Age Security programs.
2. A progressive tax takes a greater proportion of the income of higher-income groups than of lower-income groups.
3. A regressive tax takes a greater proportion of the income of lower-income groups than of higher-income groups.

The Multiplier Effect

- What is the multiplier effect?
- How does the marginal propensity to consume affect the multiplier effect?

CHANGES IN RGDP

The RGDP will change anytime the amount of any one of the four forms of purchases—consumption, investment, government purchases, and net exports—changes. If, for any reason, people generally decide to purchase more in any of these categories out of given income, aggregate demand will shift rightward. If they decide to purchase less, there will be a reduction in aggregate demand.

Any one of the major spending components of aggregate demand (C, I, G, or $X - M$) can initiate changes in aggregate demand, and thus a new short-run equilibrium. Changes in total output are often brought about by alterations in investment plans because investment purchases are a relatively volatile category of expenditures. However, if policymakers are unhappy with the present short-run equilibrium GDP, perhaps because they consider unemployment too high, they can deliberately manipulate the level of government purchases in order to obtain a new short-run equilibrium value. Similarly, by changing taxes or transfer payments, they can alter the amount of disposable income of households and thus bring about changes in consumption purchases.

THE MULTIPLIER EFFECT

Usually when an initial increase in purchases of goods or services occurs, the ultimate increase in total purchases will tend to be greater than the initial increase; this is called the **multiplier effect.** But how does this effect work? Suppose the federal government increases its national defence budget by $100 million to buy new search-and-rescue helicopters. When the government purchases the helicopters, not only does it add to the total demand for goods and services directly, it also provides $100 million in added income to the companies that actually construct the helicopters. Those companies will then hire more workers and buy more capital equipment and other inputs in order to produce the new output. The owners of these inputs therefore receive more income because of the increase in government purchases. And what will they do with this additional income? Although behaviour will vary somewhat among individuals, collectively they will probably spend a substantial part of the additional income on additional consumption purchases, pay some additional taxes incurred because of

multiplier effect
a chain reaction of additional income and purchases that results in total purchases that are greater than the initial increase in purchases

the income, and save a bit of it as well. The marginal propensity to consume (*MPC*) is the fraction of additional disposable income that a household consumes rather than saves.

THE MULTIPLIER EFFECT AT WORK

Suppose that out of every dollar in *added* disposable income generated by increased government purchases, individuals collectively spend two-thirds, or 67 cents, on consumption purchases. In other words, the *MPC* is 2/3. The initial $100 million increase in government purchases causes both a $100 million increase in aggregate demand and an income increase of $100 million to suppliers of the inputs used to produce helicopters; the owners of those inputs, in turn, will spend an additional $66.7 million (two-thirds of $100 million) on additional consumption purchases. A chain reaction has been started. The added $66.7 million in consumption purchases by those deriving income from the initial government purchase brings a $66.7 million increase in aggregate demand and in new income to suppliers of the inputs that produced the goods and services. These persons, in turn, will spend some two-thirds of their additional $66.7 million in income, or $44.4 million on consumption purchases. This means $44.4 million more in aggregate demand and income to still another group of people, who will then proceed to spend two-thirds of that amount, or $29.6 million, on consumption purchases.

The chain reaction continues, with each new round of purchases providing income to a new group of people who in turn increase their purchases. As successive changes in consumption purchases occur, the feedback becomes smaller and smaller. The added income generated and the number of resulting consumer purchases get smaller because some of the increase in income goes to savings and tax payments that do not immediately flow into greater investment or government expenditure. As Exhibit 1 indicates, the fifth change in consumption purchases is indeed much smaller than the first change in consumption purchases. What is the total impact of the initial increase in purchases on additional purchases and income? We can find that out using the multiplier formula, calculated as follows:

$$\text{Multiplier} = 1/(1 - MPC)$$

In this case,

$$\text{Multiplier} = 1/(1 - 2/3) = 1/(1/3) = 3$$

An initial increase in purchases of goods or services of $100 million will increase total purchases by $300 million ($100 million × 3), as the initial $100 million in government purchases also generates an additional $200 million in consumption purchases.

section 10.3 Exhibit 1   **The Multiplier Process**

Change in government purchases	$100 million—direct effect on *AD*
First change in consumption purchases	66.7 million (2/3 of 100)
Second change in consumption purchases	44.4 million (2/3 of 66.7)
Third change in consumption purchases	29.6 million (2/3 of 44.4)
Fourth change in consumption purchases	19.8 million (2/3 of 29.6)
Fifth change in consumption purchases	13.2 million (2/3 of 19.8)

The sum of the indirect effect on *AD*, through induced additional consumption purchases, is equal to $200 million

$300 million = Total effect on purchases (*AD*)

CHANGES IN THE *MPC* AFFECT THE MULTIPLIER PROCESS

Note that the larger the marginal propensity to consume, the larger the multiplier effect, because relatively more additional consumption purchases out of any given income increase generates relatively larger secondary and tertiary income effects in successive rounds of the process. For example, if the *MPC* is 3/4, the multiplier is 4:

$$\text{Multiplier} = 1/(1 - 3/4) = 1/(1/4) = 4$$

If the *MPC* is only 1/2, however, the multiplier is 2:

$$\text{Multiplier} = 1/(1 - 1/2) = 1/(1/2) = 2$$

THE MULTIPLIER AND THE AGGREGATE DEMAND CURVE

As we discussed earlier, when the Department of National Defence decides to buy additional helicopters, it affects aggregate demand. It increases the incomes of owners of inputs used to make the helicopters, including profits that go to owners of the firms involved. That is the initial effect. The secondary effect, the greater income that results, will lead to increased consumer purchases. So the initial effect of the government's purchases will tend to have a multiplied effect on the economy. In Exhibit 2, we see that the initial impact of a $100 million additional purchase by the government directly shifts the aggregate demand curve from AD_0 to AD_1. The multiplier effect then causes the aggregate demand to shift out $200 million further, to AD_2. The total effect on aggregate demand of a $100 million increase in government purchases is therefore $300 million, if the marginal propensity to consume equals 2/3.

It is important to note that the multiplier is most effective when it brings idle resources into production. If all resources are already fully employed, the expansion in demand and the multiplier effect will lead to a higher price level, not increases in employment and RGDP.

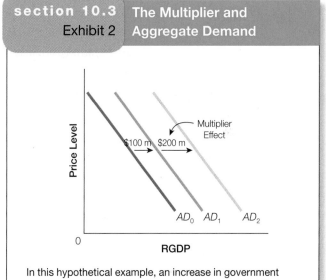

section 10.3 **The Multiplier and**
Exhibit 2 **Aggregate Demand**

In this hypothetical example, an increase in government purchases of $100 million for new helicopters will shift the aggregate demand curve to the right by more than the $100 million initial purchase, other things being equal. It will shift aggregate demand by a total of $300 million, to AD_2.

TAX CUTS AND THE MULTIPLIER

If the government finds that it needs to use fiscal stimulus to move the economy to the natural rate, increased government spending is only one alternative. The government can also stimulate business and consumer spending through tax cuts. Both the United States (2001 and 2003) and Canada (2000 and 2003) have employed tax cuts to stimulate their economies.

How much of an *AD* shift do we get from a change in taxes? As in the case of government spending, it depends on the marginal propensity to consume. However, the tax multiplier is smaller than the government spending multiplier because government spending has a direct impact on aggregate demand, whereas a tax cut has only an indirect impact on aggregate demand. Why? Because consumers will save some of their income from the tax cut. So if the *MPC* is 3/4, then when their disposable income rises by $1000, households will increase their consumption by $750 ($1000 × 3/4) while saving $250 of the added income.

To compare the multiplier effect of a tax cut with an increase in government purchases, suppose there was a $100 million tax cut and that the *MPC* was 2/3. The initial increase in consumption spending from the tax cut would be $2/3 \times 100$ million ($MPC \times$ tax cut) $= \$66.7$ million. Because in this case people would save one-third of their tax-cut income, the effect on aggregate demand of the change in taxes would be smaller than that of a change of equal size in government spending. The cumulative change in spending (the increase in AD) due to the $100 million tax cut is found by plugging the initial effect of the changed consumption spending into our earlier formula: $1/(1 - MPC) \times \$66.7$ million, which is $3 \times \$66.7 = \$200$ million. So the initial tax cut of $100 million leads to a stimulus of $200 million in consumer spending. Although this is less than the $300 million from government spending, it is easy to see why the tax cuts and government spending are both attractive policy prescriptions for a slow economy.

TAXES AND INVESTMENT SPENDING

Taxes can stimulate investment spending. For example, if a cut in corporate-profit taxes leads to expectations of greater after-tax profits, it could fuel additional investment spending. That is, tax cuts designed for consumers and investors can stimulate both the C and I components of aggregate demand. A number of governments have used this strategy to stimulate aggregate spending and shift the aggregate demand curve to the right: the United States (2000 and 2003), Canada (2003), and South Korea (2008).

SPENDING CUTS AND TAX INCREASES

Spending cuts and tax increases are magnified by the multiplier effect, too. Suppose there was a cutback in the public sector. Not only would it decrease government purchases directly, but civil servants would be laid off and unemployed workers would cut back on their consumption spending; this would have a multiplying effect through the economy, leading to an even greater reduction in aggregate demand. Similarly, tax hikes would leave consumers with less disposable income, so they would cut back on their consumption. This would lower aggregate demand and set off the multiplier process, leading to an even larger cumulative effect on aggregate demand.

TIME LAGS, SAVING, TAXES, AND IMPORTS REDUCE THE SIZE OF THE MULTIPLIER

The multiplier process is not instantaneous. If you get an additional $100 in income today, you may spend two-thirds of that on consumption purchases eventually, but you may wait six months or even longer to do it. Such time lags mean that the ultimate increase in purchases resulting from an initial increase in purchases may not be achieved for a year or more. The extent of the multiplier effect visible within a short time period will be less than the total effect indicated by the multiplier formula. In addition, saving, taxes, and money spent on import goods (which are not part of aggregate demand for domestically produced goods and services) will reduce the size of the multiplier because each of them reduces the fraction of a given increase in income that will go to additional purchases of domestically produced consumption goods.

It is also important to note that the multiplier effect is not restricted to changes in government purchases. The multiplier effect can apply to changes that alter spending in any of the components of aggregate demand: consumption, investment, government purchases, or net exports.

SECTION CHECK

Section Check

1. The multiplier effect is a chain reaction of additional income and purchases that results in a final increase in total purchases that is greater than the initial increase in purchases.
2. An increase in the marginal propensity to consume leads to an increase in the multiplier effect.
3. Because of a time lag, the full impact of the multiplier effect on GDP may not be felt until a year or more after the initial purchase.
4. An increase in government purchases will also cause an increase in aggregate income and stimulate additional consumer purchases, which will result in a magnified (or multiplying) effect on aggregate demand.

Fiscal Policy and the *AD/AS* Model

section 10.4

■ How can government stimulus of aggregate demand reduce unemployment?
■ How can government reduction of aggregate demand reduce inflation?

FISCAL POLICY AND THE *AD/AS* MODEL

The primary tools of fiscal policy, government spending and taxes, can be presented in the context of the aggregate supply and demand model. In Exhibit 1, we have used the *AD/AS* model to show how the government can use fiscal policy as an expansionary tool to help control the economy.

BUDGET DEFICITS AND FISCAL POLICY

As we discussed earlier, when the government spends more, and/or taxes less, the size of the government's budget deficit will grow, or the size of the budget surplus will fall. Although budget deficits are often thought to be bad, a case can be made for using budget deficits to stimulate the economy when it is operating at less than full capacity. Such expansionary fiscal policy may have the potential to move an economy out of a contraction (or a recession) and closer to full employment.

Expansionary Fiscal Policy at Less than Full Employment

If the government decides to spend more and/or cut taxes, other things constant, total purchases will rise. That is, increased government spending and tax cuts can increase consumption and investment and government purchases, shifting the aggregate demand curve to the right. The effect of this increase in aggregate demand depends on the position of the macroeconomic equilibrium prior to the government stimulus. For example, in Exhibit 1, the initial

section 10.4
Exhibit 1
Expansionary Fiscal Policy in a Recessionary Gap

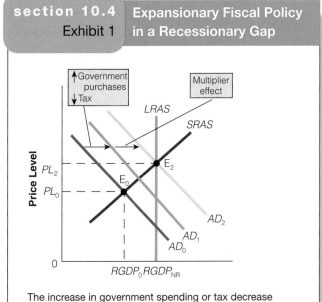

The increase in government spending or tax decrease causes an increase in aggregate demand from AD_0 to AD_1. This triggers the multiplier effect (AD_1 to AD_2) and the result is a new equilibrium at E_2, reflecting a higher price level and a higher RGDP. Because this result is on the *LRAS* curve, it is a long-run, sustainable equilibrium.

equilibrium is at E_0, a recession scenario, with real output below potential RGDP. Starting at this point and moving along the short-run aggregate supply curve, an increase in government spending and/or a tax cut would increase the size of the budget deficit and lead to an increase in aggregate demand, ideally from AD_0 to AD_2. The result of such a change would be an increase in the price level, from PL_0 to PL_2, and an increase in RGDP, from $RGDP_0$ to $RGDP_{NR}$. We must remember, of course, that some of this increase in aggregate demand is caused by the multiplier process (from AD_1 to AD_2), so the magnitude of the change in aggregate demand will be larger than the magnitude of the stimulus package of tax cuts and/or government spending (from AD_0 to AD_1). If the policy change is of the right magnitude and timed appropriately, the expansionary fiscal policy might stimulate the economy, pull it out of the contraction and/or recession, and result in full employment at $RGDP_{NR}$.

BUDGET SURPLUSES AND FISCAL POLICY

When the government spends less and/or taxes more the size of the government's budget deficit will fall or the size of the budget surplus will rise, other things being equal. Sometimes such a change in fiscal policy may help "cool off" the economy when it has overheated and inflation has become a serious problem. Then, contractionary fiscal policy has the potential to offset an overheated, inflationary boom.

Contractionary Fiscal Policy Beyond Full Employment

Suppose that the price level is at PL_0 and that short-run equilibrium is at E_0, as shown in Exhibit 2. Say that the government decides to reduce its spending and increase taxes. A government spending change may directly affect aggregate demand. A tax increase on consumers will reduce households' disposable incomes, thus reducing purchases of consumption goods and services, and higher business taxes will reduce investment purchases. The reductions in consumption, investment, and/or government spending will shift the aggregate demand curve leftward, ideally from AD_0 to AD_2. This lowers the price level from PL_0 to PL_2 and brings RGDP back to the full employment level at $RGDP_{NR}$, resulting in a new short- and long-run equilibrium at E_2.

---

section 10.4
Exhibit 2

Contractionary Fiscal Policy in an Inflationary Gap

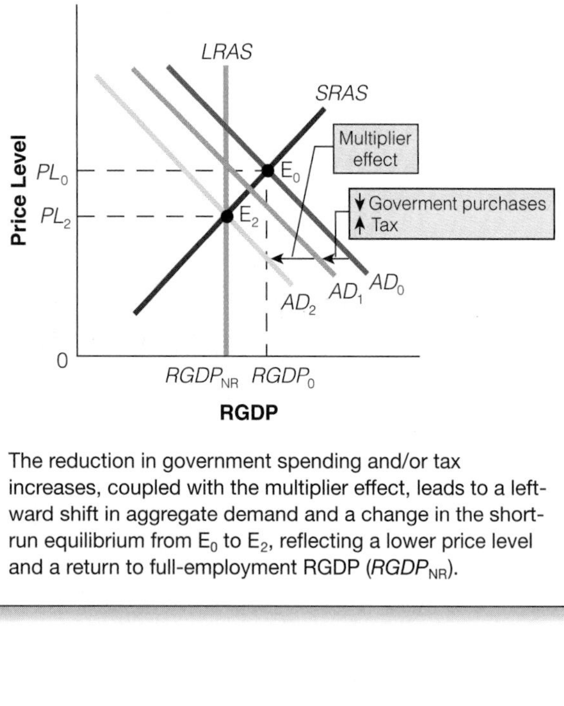

The reduction in government spending and/or tax increases, coupled with the multiplier effect, leads to a leftward shift in aggregate demand and a change in the short-run equilibrium from E_0 to E_2, reflecting a lower price level and a return to full-employment RGDP ($RGDP_{NR}$).

Section Check

1. If the government decided to spend more and/or cut taxes, that would increase total purchases and shift out the aggregate demand curve.
2. If the correct magnitude of expansionary fiscal policy is used in a recession, it could potentially bring the economy to full employment at a higher price level.
3. Contractionary fiscal policy has the potential to offset an overheated inflationary boom.

Automatic Stabilizers

- What are automatic stabilizers?
- Which automatic stabilizers are the most important?

AUTOMATIC STABILIZERS

Some changes in government transfer payments and taxes take place automatically as business cycle conditions change, without deliberations in Parliament. Changes in government transfer payments or tax collections that automatically tend to counter business cycle fluctuations are called **automatic stabilizers.**

automatic stabilizers
changes in government transfer payments or tax collections that automatically help counter business cycle fluctuations

HOW DOES THE TAX SYSTEM STABILIZE THE ECONOMY?

The most important automatic stabilizer is the tax system. For example, with the personal income tax, as incomes rise, tax liabilities also increase automatically. Progressive personal income taxes vary directly in amount with income and, in fact, rise or fall by greater percentage terms than income itself. Big increases and big decreases in GDP are both lessened by automatic changes in income tax receipts. In addition, there is the corporate profit tax. Because incomes, earnings, and profits all fall during a recession, the government collects less in taxes. This reduced tax burden partially offsets the magnitude of the recession.

BRIGITTE BOUVIER, PMO

Beyond this, the employment insurance program is another example of an automatic stabilizer. During recessions, unemployment is usually high and employment insurance benefits increase, providing income that will be consumed by recipients. During boom periods, such benefit payments will fall as the number of unemployed declines. The system of social assistance (welfare) payments tends to be another important automatic stabilizer because the number of low-income persons eligible for some form of social assistance grows during recessions (stimulating aggregate demand) and declines during booms (reducing aggregate demand).

Automatic stabilizers work without legislative action. The stabilizers serve as a shock absorber to the economy. But the key is that they do it quickly.

Section Check

1. Automatic stabilizers are changes in government transfer payments or tax collections that happen automatically and with effects that vary inversely with business cycles.
2. The tax system is the most important automatic stabilizer; it has the greatest ability to smooth out swings in GDP during business cycles. Other automatic stabilizers are employment insurance and social assistance payments.

section
10.6

Possible Obstacles to Effective Fiscal Policy

- How does the crowding-out effect limit the economic impact of increased government purchases or reduced taxes?
- How do time lags in policy implementation affect policy effectiveness?

THE CROWDING-OUT EFFECT

The multiplier effect of an increase in government purchases implies that the increase in aggregate demand will tend to be greater than the initial fiscal stimulus, other things being equal. However, this may not be true, because all other things will not tend to stay equal in this case. For example, when an increase in government purchases stimulates aggregate demand, it also drives the interest rate up. In particular, when the federal government's borrowing competes with private borrowers for available savings, it drives up interest rates. As a result of the higher interest rate, consumers may decide against buying a car, a home, or other interest-sensitive good, and businesses may cancel or scale back plans to expand or buy new capital equipment. In short, the higher interest rate will choke off private investment spending, and as a result, the impact of the increase in government purchases may be smaller than we first assumed. Economists call this the **crowding-out effect.** The crowding-out effect happened in Canada in the late 1980s and early 1990s, when record levels of government borrowing contributed, in part, to interest rates rising above 12 percent.

crowding-out effect
theory that government borrowing drives up the interest rate, lowering consumption by households and investment spending by firms

In Exhibit 1, suppose there was an initial $100 million increase in government purchases. This by itself would shift aggregate demand right by $100 million times the multiplier, from AD_0 to AD_1. However, when the government borrows in the money market to pay for increases in government purchases, the interest rate increases. The higher interest rate crowds out investment spending. This causes the aggregate demand curve to shift left, from AD_1 to AD_2. Because both these processes are taking place at the same time, the net effect is an increase in aggregate demand from AD_0 to AD_2 rather than AD_0 to AD_1.

section 10.6   The Crowding-Out
Exhibit 1   Effect

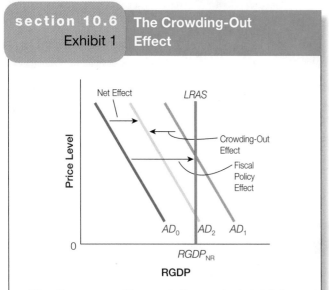

When the government borrows to finance a budget deficit, this leads to a higher interest rate and lower levels of private investment spending. The lower levels of private spending can crowd out the fiscal policy effect, shifting aggregate demand to the left from AD_1 to AD_2; the net effect of the fiscal policy is AD_0 to AD_2, not the larger increase, AD_0 to AD_1.

Critics of the Crowding-Out Effect

Critics of the crowding-out effect argue that the increase in government spending, particularly if the economy is in a severe recession, could actually improve consumer and business expectations and actually encourage private investment spending. It is also possible that the monetary authorities could actually increase the money supply to offset the higher interest rates from the crowding-out effect.

The Crowding-Out Effect in the Open Economy

Another form of crowding out can take place in international markets. For example, when the government increases purchases, it tends to drive up interest rates (assuming the money supply is unchanged). This is the basic crowding-out effect. However, the higher Canadian interest rate will attract funds from abroad. In order to invest in the Canadian economy, foreigners will have to first convert their currencies into Canadian dollars. The increase in the demand for dollars relative to other currencies will cause the dollar to appreciate in value. This will cause net exports $(X - M)$ to fall for two reasons. One, because of the higher relative price of the Canadian dollar, imports become cheaper for those in Canada, and imports will increase. Two, because of the higher relative price of the dollar, Canadian-made goods become more expensive to foreigners, so exports fall. The increase in imports and the decrease in exports causes a reduction in net exports and a fall in aggregate demand. The net effect is that to the extent net exports are crowded out, fiscal policy has a smaller effect on aggregate demand than it would otherwise.

TIME LAGS IN FISCAL POLICY IMPLEMENTATION

It is important to recognize that in a democratic country, fiscal policy is implemented through the political process, and that process takes time. Often, the lag between the time that a fiscal response is desired and the time an appropriate policy is implemented and its effects felt is considerable. Sometimes a fiscal policy designed to deal with a contracting economy may actually take effect during a period of economic expansion, or vice versa, resulting in a stabilization policy that actually destabilizes the economy.

The Recognition Lag

Suppose the economy is beginning a downturn. It may take from three to six months before enough data are gathered to indicate the actual presence of a downturn. This is called the *recognition lag*. Sometimes a future downturn can be forecast through econometric models or by looking at the index of leading indicators, but usually decision makers are hesitant to plan policy on the basis of forecasts that are not always accurate.

The Implementation Lag

At some point, however, policymakers may decide that some policy change is necessary. If, for example, a tax cut is recommended, what form should the cut take and how large should it be? Across-the-board income tax reductions? Reductions in corporate taxes? More generous exemptions and deductions from the income tax (e.g., for child care, education)? In other words, who should get the benefits of lower taxes? Likewise, if the decision is made to increase government expenditures, which programs should be expanded or initiated and by how much? These are questions with profound political consequences, so reaching a decision is not always easy and usually involves much compromise and a great deal of time.

Finally, once the budget is formulated by the staff at the Department of Finance, the finance minister presents the budget to Parliament, which must eventually give approval to the budget. This is all part of what is called the *implementation lag*.

The Impact Lag

Even after legislation is passed, it takes time to bring about the actual fiscal stimulus desired. If the legislation provides for a reduction in income taxes, for example, it might take a few months before the changes actually show up in workers' paycheques. With respect to changes in government purchases, the delay is usually much longer. If the government increases spending for public works projects like sewer systems, new highways, or urban transit systems, it takes time to draw up plans and get permissions, to advertise for bids from contractors, to get contracts, and then to begin work. And there may be further delays because of government regulations. For example, an environmental impact assessment must be completed before most public works projects can begin, a process that often takes many months or even years. This is called the *impact lag*.

Timing Is Critical

The timing of fiscal policy is crucial. Because of the significant lags before the fiscal policy has its impact, the increase in aggregate demand may occur at the wrong time. For example, imagine that we are initially at E_0 in Exhibit 2. The economy is currently suffering from low levels of output and high rates of unemployment. In response, policymakers decide to increase government purchases and implement a tax cut. But from the time when the policymakers recognized the problem to the time when the policies had a chance to work themselves through the economy, business and consumer confidence increased, shifting the aggregate demand curve rightward from AD_0 to AD_1—increasing RGDP and employment. Now when the fiscal policy takes effect, the policies will have the undesired effect of causing inflation, with little permanent effect on output and employment. This is seen in Exhibit 2, as the aggregate demand curve shifts from AD_1 to AD_2. At E_2, input owners will require higher input prices, shifting the *SRAS* leftward from $SRAS_0$ to $SRAS_1$ to the new long-run equilibrium at E_3.

section 10.6
Exhibit 2   Timing Expansionary Fiscal Policy

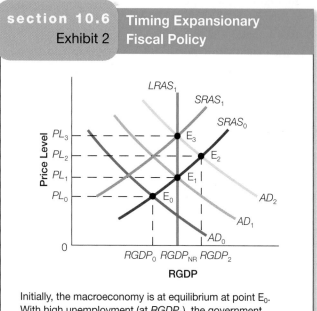

Initially, the macroeconomy is at equilibrium at point E_0. With high unemployment (at $RGDP_0$), the government decides to increase government purchases and cut taxes to stimulate the economy. This shifts aggregate demand from AD_0 to AD_1 over time, perhaps 12 to 16 months. In the meantime, if consumer confidence increases, the aggregate demand curve might shift to AD_2, leading to much higher prices (PL_3) in the long run, rather than at the target level, E_1, at price level PL_1.

Section Check

1. The crowding-out effect states that as the government borrows to finance the budget deficit, it drives up the interest rates and crowds out private investment spending.
2. If crowding out causes a higher Canadian interest rate, it will attract foreign funds. In order to invest in the Canadian economy, foreigners will have to first convert their currencies into Canadian dollars. The increase in the demand for dollars relative to other currencies will cause the dollar to appreciate in value, making imports relatively cheaper in Canada and Canadian exports relatively more expensive in other countries. This will cause net exports ($X - M$) to fall. This is the crowding-out effect in the open economy.
3. The lag time between when a fiscal policy may be needed and when it eventually affects the economy is considerable.

The Federal Government Debt

- How is the budget deficit financed?
- What has happened to the federal budget balance?
- What impact does a budget deficit have on interest rates?
- What impact does a budget surplus have on interest rates?

HOW GOVERNMENT FINANCES THE BUDGET DEFICIT

For many years, the Canadian government ran budget deficits and built up a large federal debt. How did it finance those budget deficits? After all, it has to have some means of paying out the funds necessary to support government expenditures that are in excess of the funds derived from tax payments. One thing the federal government can do is simply print money. However, printing money to finance activities is highly inflationary and also undermines confidence in the government. Typically, the budget deficit is financed by issuing debt. The federal government in effect borrows an amount necessary to cover the deficit by issuing bonds, or IOUs, payable typically at some maturity date. The sum total of the values of all bonds outstanding constitutes the federal government debt.

Exhibit 1 shows the improvement in the federal budget balance since the early 1990s as a result of economic growth, increased tax revenue, and the efforts of the federal government to control the growth of government spending. Indeed, the improvement in federal government finances is quite remarkable. The yearly budget deficit increased steadily from 1989 to 1994, reaching a record $40 billion in both 1993 and 1994. In 1998, however, the government ran its first budget surplus in almost 25 years, and has succeeded in posting annual budget surpluses for 11 consecutive years, to 2008.

section 10.7
Exhibit 1   **Federal Budget Balance, 1989–2008**

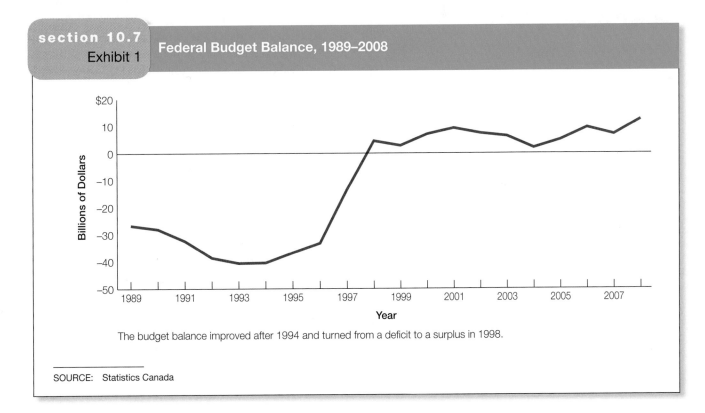

The budget balance improved after 1994 and turned from a deficit to a surplus in 1998.

SOURCE: Statistics Canada

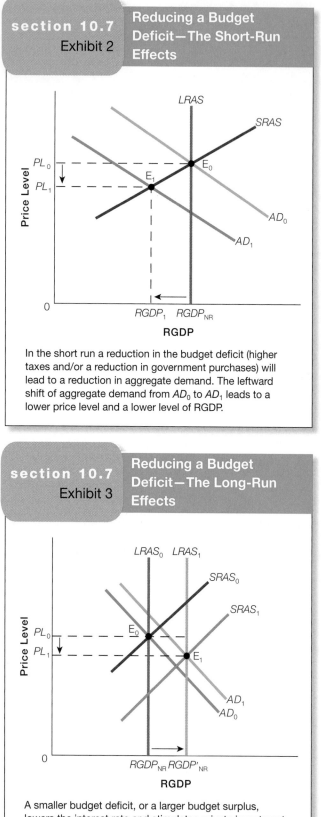

section 10.7

Exhibit 2

Reducing a Budget Deficit—The Short-Run Effects

In the short run a reduction in the budget deficit (higher taxes and/or a reduction in government purchases) will lead to a reduction in aggregate demand. The leftward shift of aggregate demand from AD_0 to AD_1 leads to a lower price level and a lower level of RGDP.

section 10.7

Exhibit 3

Reducing a Budget Deficit—The Long-Run Effects

A smaller budget deficit, or a larger budget surplus, lowers the interest rate and stimulates private investment and capital formation, leading to an increase in RGDP from $RGDP_{NR}$ to $RGDP'_{NR}$. Even with an increase in aggregate demand the price level would be lower than it would have been without the shift in the SRAS and LRAS curves.

WHY RUN A BUDGET DEFICIT?

Budget deficits can be important because they provide the federal government with the flexibility to respond appropriately to changing economic circumstances. For example, the government may run deficits in times of special emergencies like military involvement, earthquakes, fires, or floods. The government may also use a budget deficit to avert an economic downturn.

Historically the largest budget deficits and a growing government debt occur during war years when defence spending escalates and taxes typically do not rise as rapidly as spending. For example, during the Second World War, the federal government debt increased by over 300 percent between 1940 and 1946. The federal government will also typically run budget deficits during recessions as tax revenue falls and government spending increases. However, in the late 1980s deficits and debt soared in a relatively peaceful and prosperous time. The result was huge budget deficits and a growing federal government debt that continued through the early 1990s, as seen in Exhibit 1.

Recall that when the government borrows to finance a budget deficit, it causes the interest rate to rise. The higher interest rate will crowd out private investment by households and firms. But we know that higher private investment and increases in capital formation are critical in a growing economy. So what would happen if the government reduced the budget deficit? In the short run, deficit reduction is the same as running contractionary fiscal policy; either tax increases and/or a reduction in government purchases will shift the aggregate demand curve to the left from AD_0 to AD_1, as seen in Exhibit 2. Unless this is offset by expansionary monetary policy (see Chapter 13), this will lead to a lower price level and lower RGDP. That is, in the short run an aggressive program of deficit reduction can lead to a recession.

In the long run, however, the story is different. Lowering the budget deficit, or running a larger budget surplus, leads to lower interest rates, which increase private investment and stimulate higher growth in capital formation and economic growth. In fact, this is what happened in the late 1990s as the budget deficit was reduced and finally turned into a budget surplus. The reduction in the deficit increased the natural rate of output, shifting the SRAS and LRAS curves rightward in Exhibit 3. The final effect was a higher RGDP and a lower price level than would have otherwise prevailed. Both investment and RGDP grew as the budget deficit shrank. The long-run effects of the deficit reduction are greater economic growth and a lower price level, *ceteris paribus*. The short-run recessionary effects of a budget deficit reduction can be avoided through the appropriate monetary policy, as we will explore in Chapter 13.

What to Do with a Budget Surplus

When Canada has a budget surplus, policymakers have to decide what to do with it. Some favour paying down the government debt, arguing this might drive interest rates down further and stimulate private investment and economic growth. Others think that we should cut taxes since economic theory indicates that taxes can lead to a misallocation of resources. Still others believe the surplus should be used for improvements in education, health care, and research and development that will lead to greater economic growth.

THE BURDEN OF GOVERNMENT DEBT

The burden of the federal government debt is a topic that has long interested economists, particularly whether it falls on present or future generations. Exhibit 4 shows the level of the outstanding federal government debt and the debt expressed as a percentage of GDP from 1930 to 2007. The debt–GDP ratio measures the size of the debt in relation to the size of our national income. The lower the debt–GDP ratio, the smaller the burden of the debt, because less of our national income goes to the federal government in taxes so that the government can service the debt (i.e., make interest payments to the bondholders). Conversely, the higher the debt–GDP ratio, the greater the burden of the debt, because more of our national income goes to the federal government in taxes so that the government can service the debt.

It is interesting to note that between 1930 and 1950, the debt–GDP ratio increased sharply from 39 percent to 63 percent, as the growth in the debt (caused largely by the Great Depression in the 1930s and the Second World War in the 1940s) far exceeded the growth in GDP. Although the debt continued to rise to $72 billion in 1980, the debt–GDP ratio fell to 23 percent as strong economic growth reduced the debt in relation to the size of the economy. Between 1980 and 2000, large budget deficits added almost $500 billion in additional debt, bringing the debt to $562 billion, and the debt–GDP ratio up to a burdensome 52 percent. The debt–GDP ratio peaked, in fact, in 1996 at 69 percent. However, on a much more positive note, the budget surpluses the federal government has posted since 2000 have been used to pay down some of the debt, and combined with good economic growth, the debt–GDP ratio declined significantly to 33 percent in 2007.

Arguments can be made that the generation of taxpayers living at the time that the debt is issued shoulders the true cost of the debt, because the debt permits the government to take command of resources that might be available for other, private uses. In a sense, the resources it takes to purchase government bonds might take away from private activities, such as private investment financed by private debt. There is no denying, however, that the issuance of debt does involve some intergenerational transfer of incomes. Long after federal debt is issued, a new generation of taxpayers is making interest payments to people of the generation that bought the bonds issued to finance that debt. If public debt is created intelligently, however, the burden of the debt should be less than the benefits derived from the resources acquired as a result; this is particularly true when the debt allows for an expansion in real economic activity or for the development of

section 10.7
Exhibit 4

Federal Government Debt, Selected Years

Year	Debt (billions of dollars)	Debt as a Percentage of GDP
1930	$ 2.2	39%
1940	3.3	49
1950	11.6	63
1960	12.0	31
1970	18.1	20
1980	72.6	23
1990	362.9	53
2000	561.7	52
2003	526.5	43
2004	523.7	41
2005	523.3	38
2006	514.1	35
2007	508.1	33

SOURCE: Statistics Canada

vital infrastructure for the future. The opportunity cost of expanded public activity may be very small in terms of private activity that must be forgone to finance the public activity, if unemployed resources are put to work. The real issue of importance is whether the government's activities have benefits that are greater than costs; whether taxes are raised, money is printed, or deficits are run are for the most part financing issues.

Parents can offset some of the intergenerational debt by leaving larger bequests. In addition, if the parents save now to bear the cost of the burden of future taxes, the reduced consumption and increased savings will lower interest rates or, more precisely, offset the higher interest rate caused by the budget deficit. Many parents might not respond that way, but some might.

It is possible that if the budget deficits led people to believe there would be higher future taxes, a budget surplus might lead them to think there would be lower future taxes—and perhaps they would save less and consume more. So do we pay down the debt or cut taxes? They may be equivalent policy prescriptions since each tends to lead to increases in consumption spending.

In The **NEWS**

THE FEDERAL GOVERNMENT AND CANADA'S PUBLIC DEBT

BY ANONYMOUS

Feds Should Not Hide Surplus

Imagine if over the course of 10 years your spouse hid an extra $85,000, money which he silently and solely decided to spend or save according to his own priorities.

A scenario akin to the above has played out over the past decade between Canadians and the federal government. The Certified General Accountants Association of Canada, in a recent report, noted how in 10 of the past 11 years, "surprise" surpluses appeared in the federal books at the end of the fiscal year. Those unplanned surpluses—as distinct from planned surpluses—amounted to $85 billion, according to the CGA, which notes such surprises, even when happy ones, erode the credibility of the budget process.

Surprise surpluses only add to temptation to spend and all parties are guilty of it and the results of such year-end fiscal "happy hours" are clear: According to the CGA report, the federal government could have paid down the federal debt by an additional $30 billion over the past 10 years had "surprise" surpluses not morphed in "surprise" spending at year's end.

In fact, notes the report, "Our estimates reveal that the cumulative level of surprise surpluses could have been at least $50 billion higher than reported had in-year policy measures not been introduced." In other words, successive federal governments have spotted large surpluses coming and also spent extra money mid-year so as to try and shrink the eventual surplus size.

It is not that Ottawa should do away with a commitment to running surpluses, or budget within pennies of such a balanced budget. Because of chronic overspending in the 1970s and 1980s and the resulting deficits and then debt, Canadians still pay interest in 2008 on money borrowed to finance health care delivered in 1982 and civil servant salaries paid in 1990. So a return to deficit spending just to shrink surprise surpluses would be unwelcome. It's that the federal government should be frank about the possible size of the surpluses in advance, say at budget time.

The federal debt stood at $455 billion at the end of March, the end of the last fiscal year and interest charges amounted to $33.2 billion. That's almost $55,000 in federal debt for a family of four and $4,000 annually in federal interest charges for that same family.

The federal government can and should use pleasant year-end revelations in the fiscal balance to pay down the federal debt.

SOURCE: Adapted from Anonymous, "Feds should not hide surplus," *Calgary Herald,* Calgary, Alberta, July 30, 2008, p. A12. Material reprinted with the express permission of: *Calgary Herald Group Inc.,* a CanWest Partnership.

CONSIDER THIS:

With budget surpluses, either planned or unplanned, the federal government has choices to make: cut taxes, increase spending, pay down the debt, or some combination of the three. Paying down the debt frees up money in the future that would otherwise have been used to pay interest on the debt. That money could be used in the future to finance increased spending on Canada's aging population and associated health-care costs.

Section Check

1. The budget deficit is financed by issuing debt.
2. Improvement in the federal budget balance since the mid-1990s resulted from economic growth, increased tax revenues, and the efforts of the federal government to control the growth of government spending.
3. When the government borrows to finance a budget deficit, it causes the interest rate to rise.
4. If the government runs a budget surplus, this lowers the interest rate and stimulates private investment and capital formation.

Summary

Section 10.1

- Fiscal policy is the use of government spending on goods and services and taxes to affect aggregate demand, real GDP, and price levels.
- Expansionary fiscal policies will increase the budget deficit (or reduce a budget surplus) through greater government spending, lower taxes, or both.
- Contractionary fiscal policies will increase a budget surplus (or reduce a budget deficit) through reduced government spending, higher taxes, or both.

Section 10.2

- The federal government spends most of its money on social services.
- Nearly half of all provincial and local government spending is for health care and education.
- Income tax represents the single-largest source of revenue for the federal government.

Section 10.3

- The multiplier effect is a chain reaction of additional income and purchases that results in a final increase in total purchases that is greater than the initial increase in purchases.
- An increase in the marginal propensity to consume leads to an increase in the multiplier effect.
- Because of a time lag, the full impact of the multiplier effect on GDP may not be felt until a year or more after the initial purchase.

Section 10.4

- If the government decided to spend more and/or cut taxes, the aggregate demand curve would shift outward. Made to the correct magnitude, these changes could potentially close a contractionary gap, bringing the economy to full employment.

- Expansionary fiscal policy has the potential to stimulate an economy, pulling it out of a contraction and/or recession.
- If the government decided to spend less and/or increase taxes, the aggregate demand curve would shift inward; made to the correct magnitude, these changes could potentially close an inflationary gap, bringing the economy to full employment.
- Contractionary fiscal policy has the potential to offset an overheated inflationary boom.

Section 10.5

- Automatic stabilizers are changes in government transfer payments or tax collections that happen automatically and that have effects that vary inversely with business cycles.
- The tax system is the most important automatic stabilizer; it has the greatest ability to smooth out swings in real GDP during business cycles.
- Other automatic stabilizers are employment insurance benefits and welfare payments.

Section 10.6

- The crowding-out effect states that as the government borrows to finance the budget deficit, it drives up the interest rates and crowds out private investment spending and consumption.
- The crowding-out effect in the open economy sees government borrowing causing an appreciation of domestic currency and ultimately a decline in net exports.
- The lag time between when a fiscal policy may be needed and when it eventually impacts the economy is considerable.

Section 10.7

- The government finances a budget deficit primarily by issuing debt to private individuals and financial institutions.

- Government borrowing to finance budget deficits causes the interest rate to rise.

- Budget surpluses lower the interest rate and stimulate private investment and capital formation.

Key Terms and Concepts

For a complete glossary of chapter key terms, visit the textbook's Web site at http://www.sextonmacro2e.nelson.com.

fiscal policy 258
budget deficit 259
budget surplus 259
expansionary fiscal policy 259

contractionary fiscal policy 259
progressive tax 261
excise tax 261
regressive tax 261

multiplier effect 263
automatic stabilizers 269
crowding-out effect 270

Review Questions

1. Calculate the spending multiplier when the *MPC* equals
   a. 0.75.
   b. 0.8.
   c. 0.6.

2. Estimate the potential impact on real GDP of each of the following events.
   a. an increase in government spending of $5 billion in order to build new highways
   b. a decrease in federal spending of $1 billion due to peacetime military cutbacks
   c. consumer optimism leading to an $8 billion spending increase
   d. gloomy business forecasts leading to a $12 billion decline in investment spending

3. The economy is experiencing a contractionary gap of $30 billion. If the *MPC* = 0.75, what government spending stimulus would you recommend to move the economy back to full employment? if the *MPC* = 0.66?

4. The economy is experiencing a $25 billion expansionary gap. Absent government intervention, what can you predict will happen to the economy in the long run? (Use aggregate demand–aggregate supply analysis in your answer.) If the government decides to intervene using changes in spending, would you recommend a spending increase or decrease? of what magnitude?

5. Illustrate the impact of a tax cut using aggregate demand–aggregate supply analysis when the economy is operating above full employment. Is this a wise policy? Why or why not?

6. Can government spending that causes crowding out be detrimental to long-run economic growth? Explain.

7. What happens to the following variables during an expansion?
   a. employment insurance benefits
   b. welfare payments
   c. income tax receipts
   d. government budget deficit (surplus)

8. Suppose a proportional tax system that eliminated all deductions replaced the current Canadian income tax system. Would there be any change in the incentive to engage in tax avoidance? What about the incentive to work? (On what might that depend?) Explain.

Fill in the Blanks

Section 10.1

1. _____ is the use of government spending and taxes to alter real GDP and price levels.

2. When government spending (for purchases of goods and services and transfer payments) exceeds tax revenues, there is a budget _____.

3. When the government wishes to stimulate the economy by increasing aggregate demand, it will _____ government spending on goods and services, _____ taxes, or use some combination of these approaches.

4. Expansionary fiscal policy is associated with _____ government budget deficits.

5. If the government wishes to dampen a boom in the economy, it will _____ its spending on goods and services, _____ taxes, or use some combination of these approaches.

Section 10.2

6. Governments obtain revenue through two major avenues: _____ and _____.

7. The single-largest source of spending for the federal government is _____.

8. A progressive tax system is designed so that those with higher incomes pay a _____ proportion of their incomes in taxes.

Section 10.3

9. By changing taxes or transfer payments, the government can alter the amount of _____ income of households and thus bring about changes in _____ purchases.

10. The _____ effect explains why, when an initial increase in purchases of goods or services occurs, the ultimate increase in total purchases will tend to be greater than the initial increase.

11. When the government purchases additional goods and services, not only does it add to the total demand for goods and services directly, but the purchases also add to people's _____.

12. When people's incomes rise because of increased government purchases of goods and services, collectively people will spend a substantial part of the additional income on additional _____ purchases.

13. The additional consumption purchases made as a portion of one's additional income is measured by the _____.

14. With each additional round of the multiplier process, the added income generated and the resulting consumer purchases get _____ because some of each round's increase in income goes to _____ and _____ payments.

15. The _____ is equal to 1 divided by (1 minus the marginal propensity to consume).

16. The larger the marginal propensity to consume, the _____ the multiplier effect.

17. If the marginal propensity to consume were smaller, a given increase in government purchases would have a _____ effect on consumption purchases.

18. The extent of the multiplier effect visible within a short time period will be _____ than the total effect indicated by the multiplier formula.

19. Savings, taxes, and money spent on imported goods will each _____ the size of the multiplier.

Section 10.4

20. Increased budget _____ will stimulate the economy when it is operating at less than full capacity.

21. The result of an expansionary fiscal policy in the short run would be an _____ in the price level and a(n) _____ in RGDP.

22. If the government wanted to use fiscal policy to help "cool off" the economy when it has overheated and inflation has become a serious problem, it would tend to _____ government purchases, _____ taxes, and/or _____ transfer payments.

23. A tax _____ on consumers will reduce households' disposable incomes, reducing purchases of _____ goods and services, whereas higher business taxes will reduce _____ purchases.

24. Contractionary fiscal policy will result in a _____ price level and _____ employment in the short run.

25. The multiplier effect of an increase in government purchases implies that the increase in aggregate demand will tend to be _____ than the initial fiscal stimulus, other things being equal.

Section 10.5

26. Changes in government transfer payments or tax collections that automatically tend to counter business cycle fluctuations are called _____.

27. The most important automatic stabilizer is the _____ system.

28. Big increases and big decreases in GDP are both _____ by automatic changes in income tax receipts.

29. Because incomes, earnings, and profits all fall during a recession, the government collects _____ in taxes. This reduced tax burden partially _____ any contractionary fall in aggregate demand.

Section 10.6

30. When the government borrows money to finance a deficit, it _____ the overall demand for money in the money market, driving interest rates _____.

31. The _____ effect refers to the theory that when the government borrows money to finance a deficit, it drives interest rates up, choking off some private spending on goods and services.

32. The monetary authorities could _____ the money supply to offset the _____ interest rates from the crowding-out effect of expansionary fiscal policy.

33. Expansionary fiscal policy will tend to _____ the demand for dollars relative to other currencies.

34. Expansionary fiscal policy will tend to cause net exports to _____.

35. The larger the crowding-out effect, the _____ the actual effect of a given change in fiscal policy.

36. Because of the _____ in implementing fiscal policy, a fiscal policy designed to deal with a contracting economy may actually take effect during a period of economic expansion.

37. Timed correctly, contractionary fiscal policy could correct an _____; timed incorrectly, it could cause a _____.

Section 10.7
38. A budget surplus _____ to national savings and _____ the interest rate, _____ private investment and capital formation.

39. Typically, a budget deficit is financed by issuing _____.

40. Parents could offset some of the intergenerational burden of the government debt by leaving _____ bequests.

True or False

Section 10.1
1. The government can use fiscal policy to stimulate the economy out of a recession or to try to bring inflation under control.

2. When tax revenues are greater than government spending, a budget surplus exists.

3. A budget surplus is the most common result of government fiscal policy.

4. In recent years, the federal budget has never been in surplus.

5. A cut in taxes would increase the budget surplus.

6. An increase in government purchases of goods and services would stimulate the economy.

7. An increase in taxes would stimulate the economy.

8. Contractionary fiscal policy will tend to reduce a federal budget surplus or increase a federal budget deficit.

Section 10.2
9. Government spending on social programs is the largest component of federal government expenditure.

10. The composition of provincial and local spending is very different from that of federal spending.

11. A large majority of government activity is financed by borrowing.

Section 10.3
12. Real GDP will tend to change anytime the amount of consumption, investment, government purchases, or net exports changes.

13. If policymakers are unhappy about the present short-run equilibrium GDP, they can deliberately manipulate the level of government purchases in order to obtain a new short-run equilibrium value.

14. When an initial increase in government purchases of goods or services occurs, the ultimate increase in total purchases will tend to be greater than the initial increase.

15. If the marginal propensity to consume is two-thirds, a $6 million increase in disposable income to certain households will lead them to increase their consumption spending by $18 million.

16. The multiplier is equal to 1 divided by the marginal propensity to consume.

17. The multiplier would be smaller if the marginal propensity to consume were smaller.

18. If the *MPC* were equal to two-thirds, the multiplier would be equal to 3.

19. The multiplier process is virtually instantaneous.

20. Savings, taxes, and money spent on imported goods will each reduce the size of the multiplier because each of them reduces the fraction of a given increase in income that will go to additional purchases of domestically produced consumption goods.

Section 10.4

21. Expansionary fiscal policy has the potential to move an economy out of a recession.

22. Starting from an initial recession equilibrium, expansionary fiscal policy could potentially increase employment to the full-employment level.

23. Starting from an initial recession equilibrium, a government tax increase would tend to reduce the severity of the recession.

24. An increase in government spending, and/or a tax cut will tend to move the economy up along its short-run aggregate supply curve.

25. Contractionary fiscal policy has the potential to offset an overheated, inflationary boom.

26. Contractionary fiscal policy will tend to increase a current government budget deficit.

Section 10.5

27. One of the advantages of automatic stabilizers is that they take place without the necessity for deliberations in Parliament.

28. Employment insurance benefits and social assistance payments act as automatic stabilizers, stimulating aggregate demand during recessions and reducing aggregate demand during booms.

Section 10.6

29. The crowding-out effect will tend to reduce the magnitude of the effects of increases in government purchases.

30. The crowding-out effect implies that expansionary fiscal policy will tend to reduce private purchases of interest-sensitive goods.

31. The crowding-out effect does not occur with a tax change.

32. Critics of the crowding-out effect argue that an increase in government purchases (or a tax cut), particularly if the economy is in a severe recession, could improve consumer and business expectations and actually encourage private investment spending.

33. Expansionary Canadian fiscal policy will tend to move funds out of Canada.

34. Expansionary fiscal policy will tend to be partly crowded out by a reduction in net exports.

35. Sometimes fiscal policy designed to stabilize the economy can actually destabilize the economy.

36. Time lags in the legislative process are a serious problem in the implementation of fiscal policy.

37. After expansionary fiscal policy legislation is passed, it takes time to bring about the actual fiscal stimulus desired.

Section 10.7

38. The sum total of the values of all bonds outstanding constitutes the federal government debt.

39. Printing money to finance government activities is inflationary.

40. If government debt is created intelligently, the burden of the debt should be less than the benefits derived from the resources acquired as a result.

Multiple Choice

Section 10.1

1. Traditionally, government has used _____ to influence _____.
   a. taxing and spending; the demand side of the economy
   b. spending; the supply side of the economy
   c. supply management; the demand side of the economy
   d. demand management; the supply side of the economy

2. Contractionary fiscal policy consists of
   a. increased government spending, and increased taxes.
   b. decreased government spending, and decreased taxes.
   c. decreased government spending, and increased taxes.
   d. increased government spending, and decreased taxes.

3. Budget deficits are created when
   a. government spending exceeds its tax revenues.
   b. government tax revenues exceed its spending.
   c. government spending equals its tax revenues.
   d. none of the above.

4. If the government wanted to move the economy out of a current recession, which of the following might be an appropriate policy action?
   a. decrease taxes
   b. increase government purchases of goods and services
   c. increase transfer payments
   d. any of the above

Section 10.2

5. Provincial and local governments spending is mainly concentrated on _____ and _____.
   a. national defense; health care
   b. education; health care
   c. social services; environment
   d. foreign aid; outstanding debt

6. A regressive tax takes a(n) _____ proportion of income from lower-income groups than from higher-income groups.
    a. smaller
    b. equal
    c. greater
    d. indeterminate

Section 10.3

7. If the marginal propensity to consume is two-thirds, the multiplier is
    a. 30.
    b. 66.
    c. 1.5.
    d. 3.

8. The multiplier effect is based on the fact that _____ by one person is _____ to another.
    a. income; income
    b. expenditure; expenditure
    c. expenditure; income
    d. income; expenditure

9. The multiplier is
    a. $1/MPC$.
    b. $1/(1 - MPC)$.
    c. $(1 - MPC)/1$.
    d. $1/$change in MPC.

10. The federal government buys $20 million worth of computers. If the MPC is 0.60, what will be the impact on aggregate demand, other things being equal?
    a. Aggregate demand will increase $12 million.
    b. Aggregate demand will increase $13.33 million.
    c. Aggregate demand will increase $20 million.
    d. Aggregate demand will increase $50 million.
    e. Aggregate demand will not change.

11. When taxes are increased, disposable income _____, and hence, consumption _____.
    a. increases; increases
    b. increases; decreases
    c. decreases; increases
    d. decreases; decreases
    e. stays the same; stays the same

12. Starting at full employment, if $MPC = 2/3$, an increase in government purchases of $10 billion would lead AD to _____ and _____ real output in the long run.
    a. increase $30 billion; increase
    b. increase $30 billion; not change
    c. decrease $30 billion; decrease
    d. decrease $30 billion; not change
    e. none of the above

Section 10.4

Using the following graph, answer question 13.

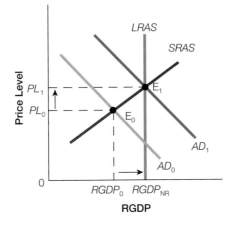

13. In order for the economy pictured above to get back to $RGDP_{NR}$, this economy could use
    a. decreased taxes and increased government spending.
    b. increased taxes and increased government spending.
    c. decreased taxes and decreased government spending.
    d. increased taxes and decreased government spending.

14. If government policymakers were worried about the inflationary potential of the economy, which of the following would not be a correct fiscal policy change?
    a. increase consumption taxes
    b. increase government purchases of goods and services
    c. reduce transfer payments
    d. increase the budget surplus

15. In the short run, expansionary fiscal policy can cause a rise in real GDP
    a. in combination with a rise in the price level.
    b. in combination with no rise in the price level.
    c. in combination with a reduction in the price level.
    d. in combination with a rise or a reduction in the price level, depending on the economy.

16. If the government wanted to offset the effect of a boom in consumer and investor confidence on *AD*, it might
    a. decrease government purchases.
    b. decrease taxes.
    c. decrease transfer payments.
    d. do either a or c.

17. An increase in taxes combined with a decrease in government purchases would
    a. increase *AD*.
    b. decrease *AD*.
    c. leave *AD* unchanged.
    d. have an indeterminate effect on *AD*.

18. A combination of an increase in investment and a decrease in exports would
    a. increase *AD*.
    b. decrease *AD*.
    c. leave *AD* unchanged.
    d. have an indeterminate effect on *AD*.

19. A decrease in government purchases will do which of the following in the long run?
    a. increase unemployment
    b. decrease real output
    c. decrease the price level
    d. all of the above

20. *AD* will shift to the right, other things being equal, when
    a. the government budget deficit increases because government purchases rose.
    b. the government budget deficit increases because taxes fell.
    c. the government budget deficit increases because transfer payments rose.
    d. any of the above circumstances exist.

Section 10.5

21. Automatic stabilizers
    a. reduce the problems that lags cause when using fiscal policy as a stabilization tool.
    b. are changes in fiscal policy that act to stimulate *AD* automatically when the economy goes into a recession.
    c. are changes in fiscal policy that act to restrain *AD* automatically when the economy is growing too fast.
    d. All of the above are correct.

22. During a recession, government transfer payments automatically _____ and tax revenue automatically _____.
    a. fall; falls
    b. increase; falls
    c. increase; increases
    d. fall; increases

Section 10.6

23. One of the real-world complexities of countercyclical fiscal policy is that
    a. fiscal policy is based on forecasts, which are not foolproof.
    b. there is a lag between a change in fiscal policy and its effect.
    c. there is uncertainty about how much of the multiplier effect will take place in a given amount of time.
    d. All of the above are correct.

24. After legislation is passed, the time it takes to bring about the actual fiscal stimulus is called the
    a. recognition lag.
    b. implementation lag.
    c. impact lag.
    d. crowding-out lag.

25. If Canadian budget deficits (which require the borrowing of funds) raise interest rates and attract investment funds from abroad,

    a. the foreign exchange value of the Canadian dollar will appreciate, and Canadian net exports will decrease.

    b. the foreign exchange value of the Canadian dollar will depreciate, and Canadian net exports will decrease.

    c. the foreign exchange value of the Canadian dollar will depreciate, and Canadian net exports will increase.

    d. the foreign exchange value of the Canadian dollar will appreciate, and Canadian net exports $(X - M)$ will increase.

26. When the crowding-out effect of an increase in government purchases is included in the analysis,

    a. AD shifts left.

    b. AD doesn't change.

    c. AD shifts right, but by more than the simple multiplier analysis would imply.

    d. AD shifts right, but by less than the simple multiplier analysis would imply.

Section 10.7

27. How does the government finance budget deficits?

    a. The Bank of Canada creates new money.

    b. It issues debt to financial institutions and private investors.

    c. It is primarily financed by foreign investors.

    d. It does nothing to finance budget deficits.

28. When the government borrows, future generations will

    a. inherit a lower tax liability.

    b. inherit neither higher taxes nor interest payment liability.

    c. inherit higher taxes.

    d. none of the above.

Problems

1. [Section 10.1]

Answer the following questions.

    a. If there is currently a budget surplus, what would an increase in government purchases do to it?

    b. What would that increase in government purchases do to aggregate demand?

    c. When would an increase in government purchases be an appropriate fiscal policy?

2. [Section 10.1]

Answer the following questions.

    a. If there is currently a budget deficit, what would an increase in taxes do to it?

    b. What would that increase in taxes do to aggregate demand?

    c. When would an increase in taxes be an appropriate fiscal policy?

3. [Section 10.3]

What would the multiplier be if the marginal propensity to consume were

    a. 1/3?

    b. 1/2?

    c. 3/4?

4. [Section 10.3]

If there were a $2 billion increase in government spending, other things being equal, what would be the resulting change in aggregate demand, and how much of the change would be a change in consumption, if the *MPC* were

a. 1/3?

b. 1/2?

c. 2/3?

d. 3/4?

e. 4/5?

5. [Section 10.4]

Use the following diagram to answer questions a–f.

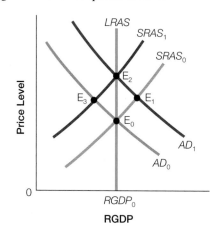

a. At what short-run equilibrium point might expansionary fiscal policy make sense to help stabilize the economy?

b. What would be the result of appropriate fiscal policy in that case?

c. What would be the long-run result if no fiscal policy action were taken in that case?

d. At what short-run equilibrium point might contractionary fiscal policy make sense to help stabilize the economy?

e. What would be the result of appropriate fiscal policy in that case?

f. What would be the long-run result if no fiscal policy action were taken in that case?

chapter

11

Money and the Banking System

What Is Money?

section

11.1

- What is money?
- In what forms is money held?
- What is liquidity?
- What is included in the money supply?
- What backs our money?

Money is anything that is generally accepted in exchange for goods or services. Hundreds of years ago, commodities such as tobacco and furs were sometimes used as money. At some times and in some places, even cigarettes and playing cards have been used as money. But commodities have several disadvantages when used as money, the most important of which is that many commodities deteriorate easily after a few trades. Precious metal coins have been used for money for millennia, partly because of their durability.

money
anything generally accepted in exchange for goods or services

CURRENCY

Currency consists of coins and paper notes that some institution or government has created to be used in the trading of goods and services and the payment of debts. Currency in the form of metal coins is still used as money throughout the world today. But metal currency has a disadvantage: It is bulky. Also, certain types of metals traditionally used in coins, like gold and silver, are not available in sufficient quantities to meet our demands for a monetary instrument. For these reasons, metal coins have been supplemented by paper currency. In Canada, the Bank of Canada issues Bank of Canada notes in various

currency
coins and paper notes created to be used to facilitate the trade of goods and services and the payment of debts

denominations, and this paper currency, along with coins, provides the basis for most transactions of relatively modest size in Canada today.

CURRENCY AS LEGAL TENDER

In Canada and in most other nations of the world, metallic coins and paper currency are the only forms of **legal tender.** In other words, coins and paper money have been officially declared to be money—to be acceptable for the settlement of debts incurred in financial transactions. In effect, the government says, "We declare these instruments to be money, and citizens are expected to accept them as a medium of exchange." Legal tender is **fiat money**—a means of exchange that has been established not by custom and tradition, or because of the value of the metal in a coin, but by government fiat, or declaration.

DEMAND DEPOSITS

Most of the money that we use for day-to-day transactions, however, is not official legal tender. Rather, it is a monetary instrument that has become generally accepted in exchange over the years and has now, by custom and tradition, become money. What is this instrument? It is balances in chequing accounts in chartered banks, more formally called **demand deposits.** Demand deposits are defined as balances in bank accounts that depositors can access on demand by simply writing a cheque or using a debit card.

THE POPULARITY OF DEMAND DEPOSITS

Demand deposits have replaced paper and metallic currency as the major source of money used for larger transactions in Canada and in most other relatively well-developed nations for several reasons, including safety of transactions, lower transaction costs, and transaction records.

Safety of Transactions

Paying for goods and services with a cheque is less risky than paying with paper money. Paper money is readily transferable: If someone takes a $20 bill from you, it is gone, and the thief can use it to buy goods with no difficulty. If, however, someone steals a cheque that you have written to the telephone company to pay a monthly bill, that person probably will have great difficulty using it to buy goods and services, because the individual has to be able to identify himself as a representative of the telephone company. If your chequebook is stolen, a person can use your cheques as money only if he can successfully forge your signature and provide some identification. Hence, transacting business by cheque is much less risky than using legal tender; an element of insurance or safety exists in the use of demand deposits instead of currency.

Lower Transaction Costs

Suppose you decide that you want to buy a compact disc player that costs $81.28 from the current Sears mail-order catalogue. It is much cheaper, easier, and safer for you to send a cheque for $81.28 rather than four $20 bills, a $1 coin, a quarter, and three pennies. Demand deposits are popular precisely because they lower transaction costs compared with the use of metal or paper currency. In very small transactions, the gains in safety and convenience of cheques are outweighed by the time and cost required to write and process them; in these cases, transaction costs are lower with paper and metallic currency. For this reason, it is unlikely that the use of paper or metallic currency will disappear entirely.

---

legal tender
coins and paper notes officially declared to be acceptable for the settlement of financial debts

fiat money
a means of exchange established by government declaration

demand deposits
balances in bank accounts that depositors can access on demand

Transaction Records

Another useful feature of demand deposits is that they provide a record of financial transactions. Each month, the bank sends the depositor a statement recording the deposit and withdrawal of funds. In an age where detailed records are often necessary for tax purposes, this is a useful feature. Of course, it can work both ways. Paper currency transactions are also popular in business activities where participants prefer no records for tax auditors to review.

SAVINGS DEPOSITS

Coins, paper currency, and demand deposits are certainly forms of money, because all are accepted as direct means of payment for goods and services. Money also includes **savings deposits,** which are bank accounts against which the depositor cannot directly write cheques. If these funds cannot be used directly as a means of payment, then why do people hold such accounts? People use these accounts primarily because they generally pay higher interest rates than demand deposits.

LIQUIDITY

Money is an asset that we generally use to buy goods or services. In fact, it is so easy to convert money into goods and services that we say it is the most liquid of assets. When we speak of **liquidity** we are speaking about the ease with which one asset can be converted into another asset or goods and services. For example, to convert a stock or bond into goods and services would prove to be somewhat more difficult—contacting your broker or going on-line, determining at what price to sell your stock, paying the commission, and waiting for the completion of the transaction. Clearly, stocks and bonds are not as liquid an asset as money. But other assets are even less liquid, like converting your painting collection or your hockey card collection into other goods and services.

THE MONEY SUPPLY

There is no unique official measure of the Canadian money supply. The most common definition of the money supply is called **M2,** which consists of currency held outside the chartered banks plus demand and savings deposits at chartered banks. Exhibit 1 shows that in June 2008, the M2 measure of the money supply in Canada was $818.6 billion, comprising $50.0 billion of currency held outside the chartered banks plus $768.6 bil-

What makes this paper money valuable? Paper money is valuable if it is acceptable to people who want to sell goods and services. Sellers must be confident that the money that they accept is also acceptable at the place where they want to buy goods and services. Imagine if money in Alberta was not accepted as money in Ontario or Nova Scotia. It would certainly make it more difficult to carry out transactions.

savings deposits
funds that cannot be used for payment directly

liquidity
the ease with which one asset can be converted into another asset or into goods and services

M2
currency outside chartered banks plus demand and savings deposits at chartered banks

section 11.1 Exhibit 1	Two Definitions of the Money Supply: M2 and M2+

Currency held outside chartered banks	$ 50.0 billion
Demand deposits and savings deposits at chartered banks	768.6 billion
M2	818.6 billion
Deposits at other financial institutions	315.5 billion
M2+	1 134.1 billion

SOURCE: Bank of Canada, June 2008

In The **NEWS**

TINY MICRONESIAN ISLAND USES GIANT STONES AS CURRENCY

BY ART PINE

YAP, Micronesia— On this tiny South Pacific island, life is easy and the currency is hard. Elsewhere, the world's troubled monetary system creaks along; floating exchange rates wreak havoc in currency markets, and devaluations are commonplace. But on Yap the currency is as solid as a rock. In fact, it is rock. Limestone to be precise. For

© ISTOCKPHOTO.COM/TAMMY PELUSO

nearly 2,000 years the Yapese have used large stone wheels to pay for major purchases, such as land, canoes and permission to marry. Yap is a U.S. trust territory, and the [U.S.] dollar is used in grocery stores and gas stations. But reliance on stone money, like the island's ancient caste system and the traditional dress of loincloths and grass skirts, continues.

Buying property with stones is "much easier than buying it with U.S. dollars," says John Chodad, who recently purchased a building lot with a 30-inch stone wheel. "We don't know the value of the U.S. dollar." Others on this 37-square-mile island 530 miles southwest of Guam use both dollars and stones. Venito Gurtmag, a builder, recently accepted a four-foot-wide stone disk and $8,700 for a house he built in an outlying village.

Stone wheels don't make good pocket money, so for small transactions, Yapese use other forms of currency, such as beer. Beer is proffered as payment for all sorts of odd jobs, including construction. The 10,000 people on Yap consume 40,000 to 50,000 cases a year, mostly of Budweiser. In fact, Yapese drink so much that sales taxes on alcoholic beverages account for 25 percent of local tax revenue.

Besides stone wheels and beer, the Yapese sometimes spend "gaw," consisting of necklaces of stone beads strung together around a whale's tooth. They also can buy things with "yar," a currency made from large sea shells. But these are small change.

The people of Yap have been using stone money ever since a Yapese warrior named Anagumang first brought the huge stones over from limestone caverns on neighboring

Palau, some 1,500 to 2,000 years ago. Inspired by the moon, he fashioned the stone into large circles. The rest is history.

Yapese lean the stone wheels against their houses or prop up rows of them in village "banks." Most of the stones are 2½ to 5 feet in diameter, but some are as much as 12 feet across. Each has a hole in the center so it can be slipped onto the trunk of a fallen betel-nut tree and carried. It takes 20 men to lift some wheels.

By custom, the stones are worthless when broken. You never hear people on Yap musing about wanting a piece of the rock.

There are some decided advantages to using massive stones for money. They are immune to black-market trading, for one thing, and they pose formidable obstacles to pickpockets. In addition, there aren't any sterile debates about how to stabilize the Yapese monetary system. With only about 6,600 stone wheels remaining on the island, the money-supply level stays put. "If you have it, you have it," shrugs Andrew Ken, a Yapese monetary thinker.

SOURCE: Art Pine, "Fixed Assets, Or: Why a Loan in Yap Is Hard to Roll Over—Tiny Micronesian Island Uses Giant Stones as Currency; Don't Forget Your Change," *The Wall Street Journal*, March 29, 1984, p. 1. WALL STREET JOURNAL (EASTERN EDITION) by Art Pine. Copyright 1984 by Dow Jones & Company Inc. Reproduced with permission of Dow Jones & Company, Inc. in the format Textbook via Copyright Clearance Center.

CONSIDER THIS:

Although there are advantages to using stones for money, the people of Yap still use U.S. dollars for certain purchases. In particular, they would need to use U.S. dollars to pay for any imported goods.

M2+

M2 plus demand and savings deposits at trust companies, mortgage loan companies, credit unions, caisses populaires, and other financial institutions

lion of demand deposits and savings deposits at the chartered banks. A broader definition of the money supply is called **M2+,** which consists of M2 plus demand and savings deposits at trust companies, mortgage loan companies, credit unions, caisses populaires, and other financial institutions. M2+ totalled $1 134.1 billion in June 2008. Of these two different definitions of the money supply, it is the M2 measurement that is more commonly used as the official money supply.

WHAT BACKS THE MONEY SUPPLY?

Why do people accept currency in exchange for goods? After all, a $20 bill is generally a piece of wrinkled paper with virtually no inherent utility or worth. Do we accept these bills because it states on the front of the bills, "This note is legal tender"? Perhaps, but we accept demand deposits without that statement.

The true backing behind money in Canada is faith that people will take it in exchange for goods and services. People accept with great eagerness these small pieces of coloured paper simply because we believe that they will be exchangeable for goods and services with an intrinsic value. If you were to drop two pieces of paper of equal size on the floor in front of 100 students, one a blank piece of paper and the other a $100 bill, and then leave the room, the group would probably start fighting for the $100 bill while the blank piece of paper would be ignored. Such is our faith in currency's practical value that some will even fight for it. As long as people have confidence in something's convertibility into goods and services, money will exist and no further backing is necessary.

In The **NEWS**

SURGE IN COUNTERFEIT $20 BANK OF CANADA NOTES

BY ERIC BEAUCHESNE

A sharp rise in the production of counterfeit bills may force merchants who already refuse $100 and $50 denominations to start declining $20 notes as well.

The flood of counterfeit bills in circulation early [in 2004]—with a face value of nearly $4-million—hit record levels in 2003, and has surged [in 2004], led by a wave of phony $20 bills, according to new figures from the Bank of Canada.

The bank reports a record 160,313 counterfeit notes surfaced during the first three months of [2004], far more than the previous high of 129,799 in the final quarter of [2003]. That surge in counterfeit bills includes 111,586 fake $20s, up from the previous record 74,617 in the final quarter of [2003].

Counterfeiters have turned to making bills in smaller denominations because $100 and $50 bills are typically either scrutinized or refused at the point of sale.

"The issue is of concern to retailers," said Sharon Maloney of the Retail Council of Canada. "It's very difficult because they want to give customers service, but are at risk of accepting counterfeit currency."

Counterfeiting incidents reported to police jumped 72% [in 2003] to 138,000, making it the sixth most common crime in Canada. And the increase was widespread, tripling in Newfoundland, nearly doubling in Ontario, Quebec and British Columbia, and increasing in all provinces except Prince Edward Island.

"We had over $13-million in counterfeit notes passed successfully in this country [in 2003]," said RCMP Sergeant Moshe Gordon, adding that's a "dramatic increase" from $4.9-million in 2002.

The increase, despite improved security features on the notes, is blamed by the RCMP on better and more affordable computer and image reproduction technology.

"The technology that's available to the bad guys . . . has made counterfeiting a lot easier," he said.

The surge in counterfeit $20 notes more than offset a decline in counterfeit $100 and $50 notes to boost the total face value of counterfeits that surfaced from January through March [2004] to a record $3.99-million. That is up from the previous quarterly high of $3.6-million in the final quarter of 2003, when record numbers of fake $100, $50, $20, $10 and even $5 notes were in circulation.

To help counter the increase in counterfeiting, the central bank is unveiling a new $20 note . . . , which will go into circulation at the end of September [2004], and which will have increased anti-counterfeit security features, similar to those on the new $100 notes.

"The efforts by the Bank of Canada in educating the public and in changing the notes go a long way in addressing this problem," Ms. Maloney said. "But the reality is that we're all challenged by very, very and increasingly sophisticated criminals."

SOURCE: Adapted from Eric Beauchesne, "Techie 'Bad Guys' Churn Out Fake $20s: Flood of Phony Bills Hits Record High," *National Post*, July 29, 2004, p. A4. Material reprinted with the express permission of: "CANWEST NEWS SERVICE", a CanWest Partnership.

CONSIDER THIS:
Although Bank of Canada notes are legal tender, merchants will sometimes refuse to accept them, especially $100 and $50 denominations, because of the risk of accepting counterfeit currency. Better and more affordable computer and image reproduction technology has recently led to a surge in counterfeit $20 notes.

Because governments represent the collective will of the people, they are the institutional force that traditionally defines money in the legal sense. People are willing to accept pieces of paper as money only because of their faith in the government. When people lose faith in the exchangeability of pieces of paper that the government decrees as money, even legal tender loses its status as meaningful money. Something is money only if people will generally accept it. Although governments play a key role in defining money, much of it is actually created by chartered banks. A majority of Canadian money, whether M2 or M2+, is in the form of deposits at privately owned financial institutions.

People who hold money, then, must not only have faith in their government, but also in banks and other financial institutions as well. If you accept a cheque drawn on a bank, you believe that bank or, for that manner, any bank will be willing to convert that cheque into legal tender (currency), enabling you to buy goods or services that you want to have. Thus you have faith in the bank as well. In short, our money is money because of confidence that we have in private financial institutions as well as our government.

Section Check

1. Money is anything that is generally accepted in exchange for goods or services.
2. Coins, paper currency, and demand deposits are all forms of money.
3. The ease with which one asset can be converted into another asset or goods and services is called liquidity.
4. M2 is made up of currency outside chartered banks plus demand and savings deposits at chartered banks. M2+ includes M2 plus demand and savings deposits at trust companies, mortgage loan companies, credit unions, caisses populaires, and other financial institutions.
5. Money is backed by our faith that others will accept it from us in exchange for goods and services.

section
11.2
The Functions of Money

- Is using money better than barter?
- How does money lower the costs of making transactions?
- How does money serve as a store of value?
- Is it less risky to make loans of money or of goods?

medium of exchange
the primary function of money, which is to facilitate transactions and lower transactions costs

barter
direct exchange of goods and services without the use of money

MONEY AS A MEDIUM OF EXCHANGE

We have already indicated that the primary function of money is to serve as a **medium of exchange,** to facilitate transactions, and to lower transactions costs; that is, sellers will accept it as payment in a transaction. However, money is not the only medium of exchange; rather, it is the only medium that is generally accepted for most transactions. How would people trade with one another in the absence of money? They would **barter** for goods and services they desire.

The Barter System Is Inefficient

Under a barter system, individuals pay for goods or services by offering other goods and services in exchange. Suppose you are a farmer who needs some salt. You go to the merchant selling salt and offer her 30 kilograms of wheat for 2 kilograms of salt. The wheat that you use to buy the salt is not money, because the salt merchant may not want wheat and therefore may not accept it as payment. That is one of the major disadvantages of barter: The buyer may not have appropriate items of value to the seller. The salt merchant may reluctantly take the wheat that she does not want, later bartering it away to another customer for something that she does want. In any case, barter is inefficient because several trades may be necessary in order to receive the desired goods.

Moreover, barter is extremely expensive over long distances. What would it cost a customer living in Saskatchewan to send wheat to Toronto in return for an item in the Sears catalogue? It is much cheaper to mail a cheque. Finally, barter is time consuming because of difficulties in evaluating the value of the product that is being offered for barter. For example, the person that is selling the salt may wish to inspect the wheat first to make sure that it is pure and not filled with dirt or other unwanted items. Barter, in short, is expensive and inefficient and generally prevails only where limited trade is carried out over short distances, which generally means in relatively primitive economies. The more complex the economy (e.g., the higher the real per capita GDP), the greater the economic interactions between people, and consequently, the greater the need for one or more universally accepted assets serving as money. Only in a Robinson Crusoe economy, where people live in isolated settlements and are generally self-sufficient, is the use of money unnecessary.

MONEY AS A MEASURE OF VALUE

Besides serving as a medium of exchange, money is also a measure of value. With a barter system, one does not know precisely what 30 kilograms of wheat are worth relative to 2 kilograms of salt. With money, a common "ruler" exists so that the values of diverse goods and services can be very precisely compared. Thus, if wheat costs 50 cents a kilogram and salt costs $1 a kilogram, we can say that a kilogram of salt is valued precisely two times as much as a kilogram of wheat ($1 divided by 50 cents = 2). By providing a universally understood measure of value, money serves to lower the information costs involved in making transactions. Without money, a person might not know what a good price for salt is, because so many different commodities can be bartered for it. With money, there is but one price for salt, and that price is readily available as information to the potential consumer.

MONEY AS A STORE OF VALUE

Money also serves as a store of value. It can provide a means of saving or "storing" things of value in an efficient manner. The farmer in a barter society who wants to save for retirement might accumulate enormous inventories of wheat, which he would then gradually trade away for other goods in his old age. This is a terribly inefficient way to save. Storage buildings would have to be constructed to hold all of the wheat, and the interest payments that the farmer would earn on the wheat would actually be negative, as rats will eat part of it or it will otherwise deteriorate. Most important, physical goods of value would be tied up in unproductive use for many years. With money, the farmer saves pieces of paper that can be used to purchase goods and services in old age. It is both cheaper and safer to store paper rather than wheat.

MONEY AS A MEANS OF DEFERRED PAYMENT

means of deferred payment
the attribute of money that makes it easier to borrow and to repay loans

Finally, money is a **means of deferred payment.** Money makes it much easier to borrow and to repay loans. With barter, lending is cumbersome and subject to an added problem. What if a wheat farmer borrows some wheat and agrees to pay it back in wheat next year, but the value of wheat soars because of a poor crop resulting from drought? The debt will be paid back in wheat that is far more valuable than that borrowed, causing a problem for the borrower. Of course, fluctuations in the value of money can also occur, and indeed, inflation has been a major problem in our recent past and continues to be a problem in many countries. But the value of money fluctuates far less than the value of many individual commodities, so lending in money imposes fewer risks on buyers and sellers than lending in commodities.

Section Check

1. Barter is inefficient compared to money because a person may have to make several trades before receiving something that is truly wanted.
2. By providing a universally understood measure of value, money serves to lower the information costs involved in making transactions.
3. Money is both cheaper and easier to store than other goods.
4. Because the value of money fluctuates less than specific commodities, it imposes fewer risks on borrowers and lenders.

section
11.3   How Banks Create Money

- How is money created?
- What is a desired reserve ratio?
- How do desired reserve ratios affect how much money can be created?

THE FUNCTIONS OF BANKS

Banks offer a large number of financial functions. For example, they often will pay an individual's monthly bills by automatic withdrawals, provide financial planning services, rent safe-deposit boxes, and so on. Most important, though, they accept demand deposits and savings deposits from individuals and firms. They can create money by making loans. In making loans, financial institutions act as intermediaries (the middle persons) between savers, who supply funds, and borrowers, who demand funds.

HOW DO BANKS CREATE MONEY?

As we have already learned, most money, narrowly defined, is in the form of demand deposits, assets that can be directly used to buy goods and services. But how did the balance in, say, a chequing account get there in the first place? Perhaps it was through a loan made by a chartered bank. When a bank lends to a person, it does not typically give the borrower cash (paper and metallic currency). Rather, it gives the person the funds by a cheque or by adding funds to an existing chequing account of the borrower. If you go into a bank and borrow $1000, the bank probably will simply add $1000 to your chequing account at the bank. In doing so, a new demand deposit—money—is created.

HOW DO BANKS MAKE PROFITS?

Banks make loans and create demand deposits in order to make a profit. How do they make their profit? By collecting higher interest payments on the loans they make than the interest they pay their depositors for those funds. If you borrow $1000 from Loans R Us National Bank, the interest payment you make, less the expenses the bank incurs in making the loan, including its costs of acquiring the funds, represents profit to the bank.

FRACTIONAL RESERVE SYSTEM

Because the way to make more profit is to make more loans, banks want to make a large volume of loans. Shareholders, or owners, of banks want the largest profits possible, so what keeps banks from making nearly infinite quantities of loans? A prudent bank would put some limit on its loan (and therefore deposit) volume. For people to accept demand deposits as money, the cheques written must be generally accepted in exchange for goods and services. People will accept cheques only if they know that they are quickly convertible at par (face value) into legal tender. For this reason, banks must have adequate cash reserves on hand to meet the needs of customers who wish to convert their demand deposits into currency.

Our banking system is sometimes called a **fractional reserve system** because banks find it necessary to keep cash reserves on hand equal to some fraction of their demand deposits. If a bank were to create $100 in demand deposits for every $1 in cash reserves that it had, the bank might well find itself in difficulty before too long. Why? Consider a bank with $10 000 000 in demand deposits and $100 000 in cash reserves. Suppose a couple of large companies with big accounts decide to withdraw $120 000 in cash on the same day. The bank would be unable to convert into legal tender all of the funds requested. The word would then spread that the bank's deposits are not convertible into lawful money. This would cause a so-called "run on the bank." The bank would have to quickly convert some of its other assets into currency, or it would be unable to meet its obligations to convert its demand deposits into currency, and it would have to close.

fractional reserve system
a system where banks hold reserves equal to some fraction of their demand deposits

Therefore, few banks would risk maintaining fewer reserves on hand than they thought prudent for their amount of deposits (particularly demand deposits). Although banks must maintain a prudent level of reserves, they do not want to keep any more of their funds as additional reserves than necessary for safety, because cash reserves do not earn any interest for the bank.

A BALANCE SHEET

balance sheet
a financial record that indicates the balance between a bank's assets and its liabilities plus capital

Earlier in this chapter, we learned that money is created when banks make loans. We will now look more closely at the process of bank lending and its impact on the stock of money. In doing so, we will take a closer look at the structure and behaviour of our hypothetical bank, the Loans R Us National Bank. To get a good picture of the size of the bank, what it owns, and what it owes, we look at its **balance sheet,** which is sort of a financial photograph of the bank at a single moment in time. Exhibit 1 presents a balance sheet for the Loans R Us National Bank.

Assets

The assets of a bank are those things of value that the bank owns (e.g., cash reserves, bonds, and its buildings), including contractual obligations of individuals and firms to pay funds to the bank (loans). The largest asset item for most banks is loans. Banks maintain most of their assets in the form of loans because interest payments on loans are the primary means by which they earn revenue. Some assets are kept in the form of non–interest-bearing cash reserves, to meet the cash demands of customers. Banks also keep some assets in the form of bonds (usually Government of Canada bonds) that are quickly convertible into cash if necessary, but also earn interest revenue.

Liabilities

All banks have substantial liabilities, which are financial obligations that the bank has to other people. The predominant liability of virtually all banks is deposits. If you have money in a demand deposit account, you have the right to demand cash for that deposit

section 11.3 — Exhibit 1 Balance Sheet, Loans R Us National Bank

Assets			Liabilities and Capital		
Cash reserves	$	900 000	Demand deposits	$	5 000 000
Loans		7 200 000	Savings deposits		4 000 000
Bonds		1 500 000	Total Liabilities	$	9 000 000
			Capital		1 000 000
Bank building, equipment, fixtures		400 000			
Total Assets		**$10 000 000**	**Total Liabilities and Capital**		**$10 000 000**

at any time. Basically, the bank owes you the amount in your chequing account. Savings deposits similarly constitute a liability of banks.

Capital

For a bank to be healthy and solvent, its assets, or what it owns, must exceed its liabilities, or what it owes others. In other words, if the bank were liquidated and all the assets converted into cash and all the obligations to others (liabilities) paid off, there would still be some cash left to distribute to the owners of the bank, its shareholders. This difference between a bank's assets and its liabilities constitutes the bank's capital. Note that this definition of capital differs from the earlier definition, which described capital as goods used to further production of other goods (machines, structures, tools, etc.). As you can see in Exhibit 1, capital is included on the right side of the balance sheet so that both sides (assets and liabilities plus capital) are equal in amount. Anytime the aggregate amount of bank assets changes, the aggregate amount of liabilities and capital also must change by the same amount, by definition.

THE DESIRED RESERVE RATIO

Suppose for simplicity that the Loans R Us National Bank desires to hold cash reserves equal to 10 percent of its deposits. That percentage is often called the **desired reserve ratio.** But what does a desired reserve ratio of 10 percent mean? This means that the bank *wants to* keep cash on hand equal to one-tenth (10 percent) of its deposits. For example, if the desired reserve ratio was 10 percent, banks would want to hold $100 000 in reserves for every $1 million in deposits. The remaining 90 percent of cash is called **excess reserves.**

> Reserves in the form of vault cash earn no revenue for the bank; no profit is made from holding vault cash. Whenever excess reserves appear, banks will invest the excess reserves in interest-earning assets, sometimes bonds but usually loans.

desired reserve ratio
the percentage of deposits that a bank chooses to hold as cash reserves

excess reserves
cash reserves that are in excess of desired reserves

LOANING EXCESS RESERVES

Let's see what happens when someone deposits $100 000 at the Loans R Us National Bank. We will continue to assume that the desired reserve ratio is 10 percent. That is, the bank wants to hold $10 000 in reserves for this new deposit of $100 000. The remaining 90 percent, or $90 000, becomes excess reserves, and most of this will likely become available for loans for individuals and businesses. Notice that at this point, the money supply (M2) is unchanged. Demand deposits have increased by $100 000 while currency outside the chartered banks has decreased by $100 000 as the currency is now stored in the bank's vault.

However, this is not the end of the story. Let us say that the bank loans all of its new excess reserves of $90 000 to an individual who is remodelling her home. At the time that the loan is made, the money supply will increase by $90 000. Specifically, no one has less money—the original depositor still has $100 000 and the bank now adds $90 000 to the borrower's chequing account (demand deposit). A new demand deposit, or chequing account, of $90 000 has been created. *Since demand deposits are money, the issuers of the new loan have created money.*

Furthermore, borrowers are not likely to keep the money in their chequing accounts for long, since you usually take out a loan to buy something. If that loan is used for remodelling, then the borrower pays the construction company whose owner will likely deposit the money into his account at another bank to add even more funds for additional money expansion. This whole process is summarized in Exhibit 2.

section 11.3
Exhibit 2 **Fractional Reserve Banking System**

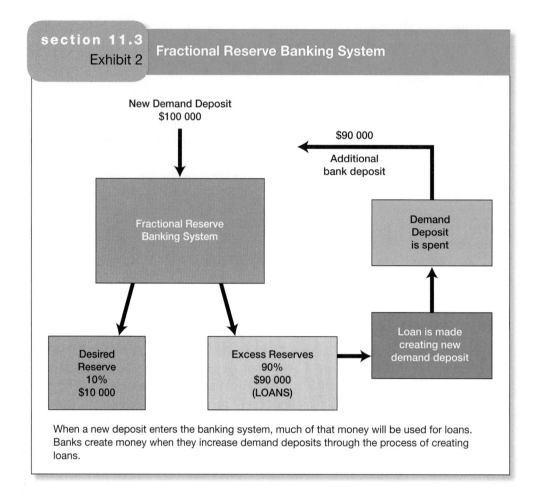

When a new deposit enters the banking system, much of that money will be used for loans. Banks create money when they increase demand deposits through the process of creating loans.

IS MORE MONEY MORE WEALTH?

When banks create more money by putting their excess reserves to work, they make the economy more liquid. There is clearly more money in the economy after the loan, but is the borrower any wealthier? The answer is no. Although borrowers have more money to buy goods and services, they are not any richer because the new liability, the loan, has to be repaid.

In short, banks create money when they increase demand deposits through the process of creating loans. However, the process does not stop here. In the next section, we will see how the process of loans and deposits has a multiplying effect throughout the banking industry.

Section Check

1. Money is created when banks make loans. Borrowers receive newly created demand deposits.
2. Desired reserves are the amount of cash that banks choose to keep on hand.
3. A balance sheet is a financial record that indicates the balance between a bank's assets and its liabilities plus capital.

The Money Multiplier

■ How does the multiple expansion of the money supply process work?
■ What is the money multiplier?

THE MULTIPLE EXPANSION EFFECT

We have just learned that banks can create money (demand deposits) by making loans and that the monetary expansion of an individual bank is limited to its excess reserves. Although this is true, it ignores the further effects of a new loan and the accompanying expansion in the money supply. New loans create new money directly, but they also create excess reserves in other banks, which leads to still further increases in both loans and the money supply. There is a multiple expansion effect, where a given volume of bank reserves creates a multiplied amount of money.

NEW LOANS AND MULTIPLE EXPANSIONS

To see how the process of multiple expansion works, let us extend our earlier example. Say Loans R Us National Bank receives a new cash deposit of $100 000. For convenience, say the bank desires to keep new cash reserves equal to one-tenth (10 percent) of new deposits. With that, Loans R Us chooses to hold $10 000 of the $100 000 deposit for reserves. Thus, Loans R Us now has $90 000 in excess reserves as a consequence of the new cash deposit.

The Loans R Us National Bank, being a profit maximizer, will probably put its newly acquired excess reserves to work in some fashion earning income in the form of interest. Most likely, it will make one or more new loans totalling $90 000.

When the borrowers from Loans R Us National Bank get their loans, the borrowed money will almost certainly be spent on something—such as new machinery, a new house, a new car, or greater store inventories. The new money will lead to new spending.

The $90 000 spent by people borrowing from Loans R Us National Bank likely will end up in bank accounts in still other banks, such as Bank A shown in Exhibit 1. Bank A now has a new deposit of $90 000 with which to make more loans and create still more money. This process continues with Bank B, Bank C, Bank D, and others. Loans R Us National Bank's initial cash deposit, then, has a chain-reaction impact that ultimately involves many banks and a total monetary impact that is far greater than suggested by the size of the original deposit of $100 000; that is, every new loan gives rise to excess reserves, which lead to still further lending and deposit creation. Each round of lending is smaller than the preceding one because some (we are assuming 10 percent) of the new money created will be kept as desired reserves.

THE MONEY MULTIPLIER

The **money multiplier** measures the potential amount of demand deposit money that the banking system generates with each dollar of reserves. The following formula can be used to measure the potential impact on demand deposits:

Potential demand deposit creation = Initial deposit × Money multiplier

money multiplier
measures the potential amount of demand deposit money that the banking system generates with each dollar of reserves

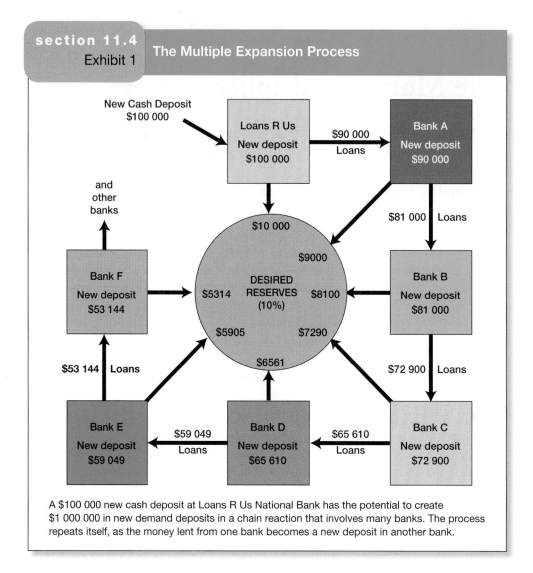

section 11.4
Exhibit 1   The Multiple Expansion Process

A $100 000 new cash deposit at Loans R Us National Bank has the potential to create
$1 000 000 in new demand deposits in a chain reaction that involves many banks. The process
repeats itself, as the money lent from one bank becomes a new deposit in another bank.

To find the size of the money multiplier we simply divide 1 by the desired reserve ratio ($1/R$). The larger the desired reserve ratio, the smaller the money multiplier. Thus, a desired reserve ratio of 25 percent, or one-fourth, means a money multiplier of four. Likewise, a desired reserve ratio of 10 percent, or one-tenth, means a money multiplier of 10.

In the example in Exhibit 1, where Loans R Us National Bank (with a 10 percent desired reserve ratio) receives a new $100 000 cash deposit, initial deposit equals $100 000. Potential demand deposit creation, then, equals $100 000 (initial deposit) multiplied by 10 (the money multiplier), or $1 000 000. Using the money multiplier, we can calculate that the total potential impact of the initial $100 000 deposit is some $1 000 000 in demand deposit money being created. What is the final impact on the money supply (M2)? Demand deposits at the chartered banks are up by $1 000 000, but currency outside the chartered banks is down by $100 000 (as the initial deposit is in the banks' vaults), so the money supply has increased by $900 000.

WHY IS IT ONLY "POTENTIAL" MONEY CREATION?

Note that the expression "potential" money creation was used in describing the impact of creating loans and deposits out of excess reserves. Why "potential"? Because it is possible that some banks will choose not to lend all of their excess reserves. Some banks may simply be extremely conservative and keep some extra newly acquired cash assets in that form. When that happens, the chain reaction effect is reduced by the amount of excess reserves not loaned out.

Moreover, some borrowers may not spend all of their newly acquired bank deposits, or they may wait a considerable period of time before doing so. Others may choose to keep some of their loans as currency in their pockets. Such leakages and time lags in the bank money expansion process usually mean that the actual monetary impact of an initial deposit created out of excess reserves within a short time period is less than indicated by the money multiplier. Still, the multiplier principle does work, and a multiple expansion of deposits will generally occur in a fractional reserve banking system.

HOW IS MONEY DESTROYED?

The process of money creation can be reversed, and in the process, money is destroyed. When a person pays a loan back to a bank, she usually does so by writing a cheque to the bank for the amount due. As a result, demand deposits decline, directly reducing the money supply.

Section Check

1. New loans mean new money (demand deposits), which can increase spending as well as the money supply.
2. The banking system as a whole can potentially create new money equal to several times the amount of new reserves. The exact amount is determined by the money multiplier, which is equal to one divided by the desired reserve ratio.

Summary

Section 11.1
- Money is anything generally accepted as a medium of exchange for goods and services.
- Coins, paper currency, and demand deposits are all forms of money.
- M2 is made up of currency outside chartered banks plus demand and savings deposits at chartered banks.
- M2+ is made up of M2 plus demand and savings deposits at trust companies, mortgage loan companies, credit unions, caisses populaires, and other financial institutions.
- Money is backed by our faith that others will accept it as a medium of exchange.

Section 11.2
- The primary function of money is as a medium of exchange—where sellers accept it as payment in a transaction.
- Barter is inefficient compared to money because a person may have to make several trades before receiving something that is truly wanted.

- The other functions of money include: measure of value, store of value, and means of deferred payment.

Section 11.3
- Money is created when banks make loans.
- Borrowers receive the newly created demand deposits when a loan is created.
- Desired reserves are the amount of cash reserves, equal to a certain proportion of deposits, that banks choose to keep on hand.
- Banks create money by increasing demand deposits through the process of making loans.
- New loans mean new money (demand deposits), which can increase the spending as well as the stock of money.

Section 11.4
- The banking system as a whole can potentially create new money equal to several times the amount of new reserves.
- The exact amount of new money creation is determined by the money multiplier, which is equal to one divided by the desired reserve ratio.

Key Terms and Concepts

For a complete glossary of chapter key terms, visit the textbook's Web site at http://www.sextonmacro2e.nelson.com.

money 289
currency 289
legal tender 290
fiat money 290
demand deposits 290
savings deposits 291

liquidity 291
M2 291
M2+ 292
medium of exchange 294
barter 294
means of deferred payment 296

fractional reserve system 297
balance sheet 298
desired reserve ratio 299
excess reserves 299
money multiplier 301

Review Questions

1. Explain the difficulties that an economics professor might face in purchasing a new car under a barter system.

2. Why do people who live in countries experiencing rapid inflation often prefer to hold another country's currency (for example, U.S. dollars) rather than their own country's currency? Explain.

3. Which one of each of the following pairs of assets is most liquid?

   a. Air Canada stock or a savings deposit

   b. a 30-year bond or a six-month Treasury bill

   c. a term deposit or a demand deposit

   d. a savings account or residential real estate

4. Indicate whether each of the following belong on the asset or liability side of a bank's balance sheet.

   a. loans

   b. holdings of government bonds

   c. demand deposits

   d. vault cash

   e. savings deposits

   f. bank buildings

   g. term deposits

5. Calculate the money multiplier when the desired reserve ratio is

   a. 10 percent.

   b. 2 percent.

   c. 20 percent.

   d. 8 percent.

6. If the desired reserve ratio is 10 percent, calculate the potential change in demand deposits in the banking system under the following circumstances.

   a. You take $5000 from under your mattress and deposit it in your bank.

   b. You withdraw $50 from the bank and leave it in your wallet for emergencies.

   c. You write a cheque for $2500 drawn on your bank (CIBC) to an auto mechanic who deposits the funds in his bank (TD Bank).

7. Calculate the magnitude of the money multiplier if banks were to hold 100 percent of deposits in reserve. Would banks be able to create money in such a case? Explain.

8. Examine the balance sheet for a bank below:

Assets		Liabilities	
Reserves	$ 500 000	Demand Deposits	$2 000 000
Loans	1 600 000	Capital	1 300 000
Buildings	1 200 000		

If the desired reserve ratio is 10 percent, what are the bank's excess reserves? If the bank were to loan out those excess reserves, what is the potential expansion in demand deposits in the banking system?

Fill in the Blanks

Section 11.1

1. The most important disadvantage of using commodities as money is that they _____ easily after a few trades.

2. _____ consists of coins and paper notes that some institution or government has created to be used in the trading of goods and services and the payment of debts.

3. Legal tender is _____ money.

4. Assets in chequing accounts in banks are more formally called _____ deposits.

5. Demand deposits are deposits in banks that can be _____ on demand by simply writing a cheque.

6. Demand deposits are a popular monetary instrument precisely because they lower _____ costs compared with the use of metal or paper currency.

7. M2 consists of currency outside chartered banks, plus _____ and _____ deposits at the chartered banks.

8. _____ deposits are fund accounts against which the depositor cannot directly write cheques.

9. _____ is a broader measure of the money supply than _____.

10. Assets that can be quickly converted into money are considered highly _____ assets.

11. _____ includes M2, plus demand and savings deposits at other financial institutions.

12. Something is money only if people will generally _____ it.

13. Our money is money because of confidence that we have in _____ institutions as well as in our _____.

Section 11.2

14. The primary function of money is to serve as a _____.

15. The more complex the economy, the _____ the need for one or more universally accepted assets serving as money.

16. Money is both a _____ of value and a _____ of value.

17. With money, a common _____ exists so that the values of diverse goods and services can be very precisely compared.

18. The value of money fluctuates far _____ than the value of many individual commodities.

Section 11.3

19. In making loans, financial institutions act as intermediaries between _____, who supply funds, and _____, who demand funds.

20. If you go into a bank and borrow $1000, the bank probably will simply _____ to your chequing account at the bank.

21. Banks make their profit by collecting _____ interest payments on the loans they make than they pay their depositors for those funds.

22. Our banking system is sometimes called a _____ system because banks find it necessary to keep cash on hand equal to some fraction of their demand deposits.

23. Money is created when banks _____.

24. The largest asset item for most banks is _____.

25. Demand deposits and savings deposits constitute _____ of banks.

26. Anytime the aggregate amount of bank _____ changes, the aggregate amount of liabilities and capital also must change by the same amount, by definition.

27. Desired reserves equal _____ times _____.

28. Whenever excess reserves appear, banks will convert the _____ reserves into other _____ assets.

Section 11.4

29. The monetary expansion of an individual bank is limited to its _____ reserves.

30. Potential money creation from a cash deposit equals that initial deposit times _____.

31. The actual monetary impact of an initial deposit created out of excess reserves within a short time period is _____ indicated by the money multiplier.

32. When a person pays a loan back to a bank, demand deposits _____, and the money supply _____.

True or False

Section 11.1

1. Money is anything that is generally accepted in exchange for goods or services.

2. In Canada, the Bank of Canada issues paper currency.

3. Cheques provide the basis for most transactions of relatively small size in Canada today.

4. Metallic coins and paper currency are the only forms of legal tender.

5. Most of the money that we use for day-to-day transactions is official legal tender.

6. There is an element of insurance or safety in the use of demand deposits instead of currency.

7. Credit cards are included in some measures of the money supply.

8. Economists are not completely in agreement on what constitutes money for all purposes.

9. People use savings accounts primarily because they generally pay higher interest rates than demand deposits.

10. Liquidity refers to the ease with which one asset can be converted into another asset or goods and services.

11. People prefer to keep the bulk of their liquid assets as currency or in demand deposits rather than in the form of savings accounts of various kinds.

12. As long as people have confidence in something's convertibility into goods and services, no further backing is necessary for it to serve as money.

13. When people lose faith in the exchangeability of pieces of paper that the government decrees as money, even legal tender loses its status as meaningful money.

Section 11.2

14. An economy that relies on barter is as efficient as one that uses money to facilitate transactions.

15. As a measure of value, money serves to lower information costs involved in making transactions.

16. Money makes borrowing and repaying loans much easier.

Section 11.3

17. Financial institutions can create money by making loans.

18. If you go into a bank and borrow $1000, the bank probably will simply add $1000 to your chequing account at the bank, but it will not create new money in the process.

19. Although banks choose to hold some proportion of deposits as reserves, they do not want to keep any more of their funds as additional reserves than necessary for safety because cash assets do not earn any interest.

20. The predominant liability of virtually all banks is deposits.

21. The difference between a bank's assets and its liabilities constitutes the bank's capital, or net worth.

22. Actual reserves equal desired reserves minus excess reserves.

23. If a bank lends out its excess reserves of $90 000, at the time the loan is made, the money supply will increase by $90 000.

24. When banks create more money, they also directly create wealth.

Section 11.4

25. New loans create new money directly, but they also create excess reserves in other banks, which leads to still further increases in both loans and the stock of money.

26. Assume that Loans R Us National Bank receives a new cash deposit of $100 000. With a 10 percent desired reserve ratio, this creates $10 000 of desired reserves and $90 000 of excess reserves.

27. The money multiplier is 1 divided by the desired reserve ratio.

28. The higher the desired reserve ratio, the larger the money multiplier.

29. If some banks choose not to lend all of their excess reserves, the total amount of money created by an initial cash deposit will be smaller.

30. When a person pays a loan back to a bank, demand deposits decline, directly reducing the money supply.

Multiple Choice

Section 11.1

1. The money supply that includes currency outside chartered banks plus demand and savings deposits at the chartered banks is called
   a. M1.
   b. M2.
   c. M2+.
   d. M3.

2. Money is
   a. whatever is generally accepted in exchange for goods and services.
   b. an object to be consumed.
   c. a highly illiquid asset.
   d. widely used in a barter economy.

3. An increase in demand deposits combined with an equal decrease in currency in circulation would
   a. have no direct effect on M2 or M2+.
   b. increase both M2 and M2+.
   c. increase M2 and decrease M2+.
   d. decrease M2 and increase M2+.

4. Liquidity is defined as
   a. the cash value of fiat money.
   b. the value of fiat money when used to buy a good or a service.
   c. the speed at which money is spent.
   d. the ease with which money can be divided to make payments.
   e. the ease with which an asset can be converted into cash.

Section 11.2

5. Money's principal role is to serve as
   a. a standard for credit transactions.
   b. a medium of exchange.
   c. a standard for making bank loans.
   d. a standard for the Bank of Canada.

6. Barter is inefficient compared to using money for trading because
   a. it is more expensive over long distances.
   b. potential buyers may not have appropriate items of value to sellers with which to barter.
   c. it is more time consuming, as it is more difficult to evaluate the products that are being offered for barter than to evaluate money.
   d. all of the above.
   e. none of the above.

7. Currency is a poor store of value when
   a. the unemployment rate is high.
   b. banks are failing at an abnormally high rate.
   c. the rate of inflation is very high.
   d. gold can be purchased at bargain prices.
   e. all of the above are correct.

8. Money makes it easier to borrow and repay loans. This function of money is referred to as
   a. a store of value.
   b. a means of deferred payment.
   c. a unit of account.
   d. a standard of value.
   e. none of the above.

9. Without money to serve as a medium of exchange,
   a. gains from trade would be severely limited.
   b. our standard of living probably would be reduced.
   c. the transactions costs of exchange would increase.
   d. all of the above are true.

Section 11.3

10. Under fractional reserve banking, when a bank lends to a customer,
    a. bank credit decreases.
    b. reserves drain away from the system.
    c. the bank is protected from a run.
    d. borrowers receive a newly created demand deposit; that is, money is created.
    e. bank profitability is decreased.

11. Desired reserves of a bank are a certain percentage of their
    a. loans.
    b. cash on hand.
    c. total assets.
    d. deposits.

12. Which of the following will lead to an increase in the money supply?
    a. You pay back a $10 000 loan that you owe to your bank.
    b. Your bank gives you a $10 000 loan by adding $10 000 to your chequing account.
    c. You pay $10 000 in cash for a new motorcycle.
    d. You bury $10 000 in cash in your backyard.

13. If a banking transaction created new excess reserves in the banking system, the result would tend to be
    a. an increase in the amount of loans made by banks and an increase in the supply of money.
    b. an increase in the amount of loans made by banks and a decrease in the supply of money.
    c. a decrease in the amount of loans made by banks and an increase in the supply of money.
    d. a decrease in the amount of loans made by banks and a decrease in the supply of money.

14. If many people were to suddenly deposit into their chequing accounts large sums of cash previously kept in their wallets, this would eventually result in
    a. a reduction in the money supply.
    b. a decrease in M2 but an increase in M2+.
    c. an increase in interest rates.
    d. an increase in reserves of banks and therefore an increase in the money supply.
    e. both a and c.

Section 11.4

15. A reserve ratio of 20 percent means a money multiplier of
   a. 1.25.
   b. 2.
   c. 5.
   d. 20.

16. If the desired reserve ratio were increased, then
   a. the money supply would tend to decrease, but the outstanding loans of banks would tend to increase.
   b. both the money supply and the outstanding loans of banks would tend to decrease.
   c. the money supply would tend to increase, but the outstanding loans of banks would tend to decrease.
   d. both the money supply and the outstanding loans of banks would tend to increase.

Problems

1. **[Section 11.1]**
   What would each of the following changes do to M2 and M2+?

Change	M2	M2+
An increase in currency in circulation	_____	_____
A decrease in demand deposits	_____	_____
An increase in savings deposits	_____	_____
A transfer of demand deposit balances from credit unions to chartered banks	_____	_____

2. **[Sections 11.3 and 11.4]**
   Assume there was a new $100 000 deposit into a demand deposit at a bank.
   a. What would be the resulting excess reserves created by that deposit if banks faced a desired reserve ratio of

   10 percent? _____

   20 percent? _____

   25 percent? _____

   50 percent? _____

   b. How many additional dollars could that bank lend out as a result of that deposit if banks faced a desired reserve ratio of

   10 percent? _____

   20 percent? _____

   25 percent? _____

   50 percent? _____

   c. How many additional dollars of demand deposit money could the banking system as a whole create in response to such a new deposit if banks faced a desired reserve ratio of

   10 percent? _____

   20 percent? _____

   25 percent? _____

   50 percent? _____

3. **[Sections 11.3 and 11.4]**

   Answer questions a and b.

   a. If a bank had reserves of $30 000 and demand deposits of $200 000 (and no other deposits), how much could it lend out if had a desired reserve ratio of

   10 percent? _____

   15 percent? _____

   20 percent? _____

   b. If the bank then received a new $40 000 deposit in a customer's demand deposit account, how much could it now lend out (including the amount in a) if it had a desired reserve ratio of

   10 percent? _____

   15 percent? _____

   20 percent? _____

4. **[Section 11.4]**

   What would the money multiplier be if the desired reserve ratio were

   5 percent? _____

   10 percent? _____

   20 percent? _____

   25 percent? _____

   50 percent? _____

The Bank of Canada

section

12.1

The Bank of Canada

- What is the Bank of Canada?
- What are the functions of the Bank of Canada?

THE BANK OF CANADA

In most countries of the world, the job of controlling the supply of money belongs to the central bank. The Bank of Canada is Canada's central bank. It was established in 1935, largely as a result of the economic problems of the Great Depression and the need for better control of the money supply. Chartered banks' goal, remember, is to maximize profits for their shareholders. However, the banks' behaviour can have adverse effects on the nation's money supply. For example, during a period of economic recession, banks may have increasing concerns about the ability of new borrowers to repay their loans, or they may find that their customers are withdrawing more cash due to fears that the banks may fail. As a result, the banks may choose to hold more excess reserves for safety and liquidity, rather than loaning those excess reserves out. Thus, during a period of economic recession there is a tendency for the money supply to decrease, which further destabilizes the economy. A central bank, however, can use certain tools to adjust the money supply in order to help stabilize the economy.

The Bank of Canada is owned by the federal government. It is controlled by a board of directors, which is appointed by the government. The governor of the Bank of Canada, who is the chief executive, is appointed for a seven-year term. The current governor, Mark Carney, was appointed in 2008. Although the government has final responsibility for the Bank of Canada's actions, the governor has considerable independence in the day-to-day operations of the Bank of Canada. If there was a very significant disagreement between the governor and the government, the government could issue a written directive to the governor, forcing him or her to either comply with the directive or resign.

The objectives of the Bank of Canada are outlined in the Bank of Canada Act, which says:

> Whereas it is desirable to establish a central bank in Canada to regulate credit and currency in the best interests of the economic life of the nation, to control and protect the external value of the national monetary unit and to mitigate by its influence fluctuations in the general level of production, trade, prices and employment, so far as may be possible within the scope of monetary action, and generally to promote the economic and financial welfare of Canada.

The Bank of Canada has recently adopted an explicit inflation-control strategy for its objective. Inflation control is how the Bank of Canada contributes to improved economic performance. Low inflation allows the economy to function more efficiently, resulting in better economic growth over time and reduced short-run cyclical fluctuations in output and employment. In 1991, the Bank of Canada and the federal government jointly announced inflation targets. The current inflation target aims to keep the annual inflation rate within a target range of 1 to 3 percent.

THE FUNCTIONS OF THE BANK OF CANADA

The Bank of Canada has five main functions. The first function is to issue currency for circulation in Canada. The Bank of Canada has monopoly power over issuing legal tender in the form of Bank of Canada notes. The Bank of Canada is responsible for note design, for overseeing the printing and distribution of banknotes, and for replacing worn-out currency.

The second function is to act as a banker to the federal government. The federal government has a demand deposit account at the Bank of Canada and at the chartered banks as well. The Bank of Canada manages the government's bank accounts in these different financial institutions. In addition, the Bank of Canada acts as a fiscal agent to the federal government in managing the government's foreign currency reserves and its bonds.

The third function of the Bank of Canada is to act as a bank to the chartered banks. In Chapter 11, we explained that the chartered banks hold their reserves as currency in their vaults. However, they also hold a small amount of their reserves as a demand deposit at the Bank of Canada. These deposits at the Bank of Canada allow the chartered banks to make payments to each other. For example, let's say you pay your monthly rent by writing a cheque for $800 on your chequing account at the TD Bank. Your landlord deposits the cheque in her chequing account at the Royal Bank. The Royal Bank will credit your landlord's chequing account for $800. But the Royal Bank will want payment of $800 from the TD Bank. Therefore, as the cheque clears, $800 will be deducted from the TD Bank's reserve account at the Bank of Canada and transferred to the Royal Bank's reserve account at the Bank of Canada. Of course, once the cheque clears, the TD Bank will deduct $800 from your chequing account.

The fourth function is to serve as a "lender of last resort." When a bank finds itself in financial distress because it is short of reserves and cannot meet the withdrawal demands of its customers, the Bank of Canada may act as a lender of last resort and lend reserves to the bank in order to help maintain stability in the financial system.

The Bank of Canada's fifth and most important function is controlling the supply of money. The policy decisions that the Bank of Canada makes in controlling the money supply, consistent with its inflation control objective, form the basis of the Bank of Canada's monetary policy.

In The NEWS

INDEPENDENCE AND THE CENTRAL BANK

"There have been three great inventions since the beginning of time: fire, the wheel and central banking," quipped Will Rogers, an American humorist. Yet central banking as we know it today is an invention of the 20th century.

Central banks' original task was not to conduct monetary policy or support the banking system, but to finance government spending. The world's oldest central bank, the Bank of Sweden, was established in 1668 largely as a vehicle to finance military spending. The Bank of England was created in 1694 to fund a war with France. Even as recently as the late 1940s, a Labour chancellor of the exchequer, Stafford Cripps, took great pleasure in describing the Bank of England as "his bank." Today most central banks are banned from financing government deficits.

The United States managed without a central bank until early [in the 20th] century. Private banks used to issue their own notes and coins, and banking crises were fairly frequent. But following a series of particularly severe crises, the Federal Reserve was set up in 1913, mainly to supervise banks and act as a lender of last resort. Today the Fed is one of the few major central banks that is still responsible for bank supervision; most countries have handed this job to a separate agency.

At first, governments in most countries kept a tight grip on the monetary reins, telling central banks when to change interest rates. But when inflation soared, governments saw the advantage of granting central banks independence in matters of monetary policy. Short-sighted politicians might try to engineer a boom before an election, hoping that inflation would not rise until after the votes had been counted, but an independent central bank insulated from political pressures would give higher priority to price stability. If, as a result of independence, policy is more credible, workers and firms are likely to adjust their wages and prices more quickly in response to a tightening of policy, and so, the argument runs, inflation can be reduced with a smaller loss of output and jobs . . .

Several studies in the early 1990s confirmed that countries with independent central banks did indeed tend to have lower inflation rates (see Exhibit 1). And better still, low inflation did not appear to come at the cost of slower growth. . . . No central bank is completely independent. Before the ECB was set up, the German Bundesbank was the most in-dependent central bank in the world, yet the German government chose to ignore its advice on the appropriate exchange rate for unification, and thereby stoked inflationary pressures. Some central banks, such as the Bank of England, have full independence in the setting of monetary policy, but their inflation target is set by the government.

Independent central banks are more likely to achieve low inflation than finance ministers because they have a longer time horizon. But independence is no panacea: central banks can still make mistakes. Note that Germany's Reichsbank was statutorily independent when the country suffered hyperinflation in 1923.

---

section 12.1
Exhibit 1

Central Bank Independence and Inflation, 1960–1992

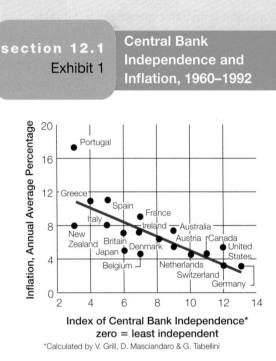

Index of Central Bank Independence*
zero = least independent
*Calculated by V. Grill, D. Masciandaro & G. Tabellini

There is often a stong negative correlation between a country's average annual inflation rate and the degree of independence of its central bank.

SOURCE: "Monetary Metamorphosis," *The Economist,* September 25, 1999. From "A Survey of the World Economy: The Navigators," pp. 1–42, appearing on p. 4. ECONOMIST by The Economist. Copyright 1999 by Economist Newspaper Group. Reproduced with permission of Economist Newspaper Group in the format Textbook via Copyright Clearance Center.

CONSIDER THIS:

The Bank of Canada is managed by a board of directors, appointed by the federal government. Ultimately, the Bank of Canada is controlled by the Canadian government. However, in practice, the Bank of Canada is largely independent of the federal government. The governor of the Bank of Canada is appointed for a seven-year term, which, to a great extent, allows him or her considerable independence in day-to-day operations.

SECTION CHECK

Section Check

1. Of the five main functions of a central bank, the most important is its role in regulating the money supply.
2. The Bank of Canada is owned by the federal government, which has final responsibility for the Bank of Canada's policies. However, the governor of the Bank of Canada has considerable independence in formulating the Bank of Canada's monetary policy.

section

12.2

The Equation of Exchange

- What is the equation of exchange?
- What is the velocity of money?
- How is the equation of exchange useful?

As we discussed in the previous section, the most important function of the Bank of Canada is its ability to regulate the money supply. In order to fully understand the significant role that the Bank of Canada plays in the economy, we will first examine the role of money in the national economy.

THE EQUATION OF EXCHANGE

The role that money plays in determining equilibrium GDP, the level of prices, and real output of goods and services has attracted the attention of economists for generations. There is a useful relationship that helps our understanding of the role of money in the national economy, called the **equation of exchange.** The equation of exchange can be presented as follows:

$$M \times V = P \times Q$$

where M is the money supply, however defined (usually M2 or M2+), V is the velocity of money, P is the average level of prices of final goods and services, and Q is the physical quantity of final goods and services produced in a given period (usually one year).

The velocity of money, V, represents the average number of times that a dollar is used in purchasing final goods or services in a one-year period. Thus, if individuals are hoarding their money, velocity will be low; if individuals are writing lots of cheques on their chequing accounts and spending currency as fast as they receive it, velocity will tend to be high.

The expression $P \times Q$ represents the dollar value of all final goods and services sold in a country in a given year. Does that sound familiar? It should, because that is the definition of nominal gross domestic product (GDP). Thus, for our purposes, we may consider the average level of prices (P) times the physical quantity of final goods and services in a given time period (Q) to be equal to nominal GDP. We could say then, that

$$M \times V = \text{Nominal GDP}$$
$$\text{or,}$$
$$V = \text{Nominal GDP}/M$$

equation of exchange
the money supply (M) *times velocity* (V) *of circulation equals the price level* (P) *times quantity of goods and services produced in a given period* (Q)

That, in fact, is the definition of velocity: The total output of goods in a year divided by the amount of money is the same thing as the average number of times a dollar is used in final goods transactions in a year.

For simplicity, let us use some hypothetical numbers to derive the velocity of money:

$$V = \text{Nominal GDP}/M2 = \$1600 \text{ billion}/\$800 \text{ billion} = 2$$

The average dollar of money, then, turns over two times in the course of a year.

USING THE EQUATION OF EXCHANGE

The equation of exchange is a useful tool when we try to assess the impact on the aggregate economy of a change in the supply of money (M). If M increases, then one of the following must happen:

1. V must decline by the same magnitude, so that $M \times V$ remains constant, leaving $P \times Q$ unchanged.

2. P must rise.

3. Q must rise.

4. P and Q must each rise some, so that the product of P and Q remains equal to $M \times V$.

In other words, if the money supply increases and the velocity of money does not change by an offsetting amount, there will be either higher prices (inflation), greater output of final goods and services, or a combination of both. If one considers a macroeconomic policy to be successful if output is increased but unsuccessful if the only effect of the policy is inflation, then an increase in M is an effective policy if Q increases but an ineffective policy if P increases.

Likewise, dampening the rate of increase in M or even causing it to decline will cause nominal GDP to fall, unless the change in M is counteracted by a rising velocity of money. Intentionally decreasing M can also either be good or bad, depending on whether the declining money GDP is reflected mainly in falling prices (P) or in falling output (Q).

Therefore, expanding the money supply, unless counteracted by increased hoarding of currency (leading to a decline in V) will have the same type of impact on aggregate demand as an expansionary fiscal policy—increasing government spending, or reducing taxes. Likewise, policies designed to reduce the money supply will have a contractionary impact (unless offset by a rising velocity of money) on aggregate demand, similar to the impact obtained from increasing taxes or decreasing government spending.

In sum, what these relationships illustrate is that monetary policy can be used to obtain the same objectives as fiscal policy. Some economists, often called monetarists, believe that monetary policy is the most powerful determinant of macroeconomic results.

HOW VOLATILE IS THE VELOCITY OF MONEY?

Economists once considered the velocity of money a given. We now know that it is not constant, but moves in a fairly predictable pattern over a long period of time. Thus, the connection between money supply and GDP is still fairly predictable. However, velocity is less stable when measured over short periods of time. For example, an increase in velocity can occur with anticipated inflation. When individuals expect inflation, they will spend their money more quickly. They don't want to be caught holding money that is going to be worth less in the future. Also, an increase in interest rates will cause people to hold less money. That is, people want to hold less money when the opportunity cost of holding money increases. This, in turn, means that the velocity of money increases.

THE RELATIONSHIP BETWEEN THE INFLATION RATE AND THE GROWTH IN THE MONEY SUPPLY

The inflation rate tends to rise more in periods of rapid monetary expansion than in periods of slower growth in the money supply. The relationship between the growth in the money supply and higher inflation is particularly strong with hyperinflation—inflation that is greater than 50 percent. The most famous case of hyperinflation was in Germany in the 1920s—inflation was roughly 300 percent *per month* for over a year. The German government incurred large amounts of debt during the First World War and could not raise enough money to pay its expenses, so it printed huge amounts of money.

In The **NEWS**

IT'S NOT JUST INFLATION—IT'S HYPERINFLATION!

BY CHRIS BOUTET

As if the appearance of newly-minted $50,000,000 bank notes worth all of about US$1.20, or the equivalent of three loaves of bread, wasn't enough of an indication that Zimbabwe is experiencing extreme economic turmoil, that country's Central Statistical Office revealed today that the inflation rate—already by far the highest in the world—has soared to an astronomical 164,900% year-on-year in February.

According to the CSO, that annual percentage change marks a 64,320.1% gain on the January rate of 100,590.2% for a February month-to-month inflation rate of 125.9%, gaining 5.1 percentage points on the January rate of 120.8%. If those strike you as alarmingly big numbers, rest assured that they are (compare, for example, Canada's measly year-on-year inflation rate of 1.8% for February). The inflation gripping Zimbabwe is so out-of-control, in fact, that economists have a special word for it: hyperinflation.

So what is hyperinflation? According to a 2007 paper prepared for the International Monetary Fund on Zimbabwe's economic crisis, hyperinflation is a largely modern phenomenon associated with the printing of money to finance large fiscal deficits due to wars, revolutions, the end of empires and the establishment of new states. In 1956, economist Phillip Cagan defined hyperinflation as beginning the month that inflation first exceeds 50% per month and ends when the inflation rate drops below 50% for at least one year.

Zimbabwe fell into a state of hyperinflation in 2000, when the Mugabe government began seizing commercial farms, forcing foreign investors to flee the country and causing manufacturing to grind to a halt and prices to shoot up. Inflation passed 600% in January, 2006, but really began to take off after the government revealed it had printed at least $21-trillion in Zimbabwe currency to pay the IMF US$221-million in arrears that endangered the country's

Zimbabwe's new $50 million note, issued by the Reserve Bank on April 4, 2008.

membership in the organization. Zimbabwe's annual inflation passed 1,000% in April, 2006. Explains Reuters, Zimbabwe was then in its eighth year of recession at this time and had the dubious distinction of having the world's fastest shrinking economy outside a war zone, not to mention the highest inflation rate on the globe. Things, as we know, have only gotten worse from there.

SOURCE: Posted: April 16, 2008, 5:02 PM by Chris Boutet. http://network.nationalpost.com/np/blogs/posted/archive/2008/04/16/primer-it-s-not-just-inflation-it-s-hyperinflation.aspx. Material reprinted with the express permission of: "CANWEST NEWS SERVICE", a CanWest Partnership.

CONSIDER THIS:

Imagine being fortunate enough to have a good-paying job, but unable to buy even the most basic necessities of life. Imagine going to your local store and seeing the prices of items increase on an hourly basis. Although these images seem foreign to us in Canada, this is the reality in Zimbabwe, due to hyperinflation.

The inflation was so bad that store owners would change their prices in the middle of the day, firms had to pay workers several times a week, and many resorted to barter. Recently, Zimbabwe [see In The News], Brazil, Argentina, and Russia have all experienced hyperinflation. The cause of hyperinflation is simply excessive money growth—printing too much money.

Section Check

1. The equation of exchange is $M \times V = P \times Q$, where M is the money supply, V is the velocity of money, P is the average level of prices of final goods and services, and Q is the physical quantity of final goods and services produced in an economy in a given year.
2. The velocity of money (V) represents the average number of times that a dollar is used in purchasing final goods or services in a one-year period.
3. The equation of exchange is a useful tool when analyzing the effects of a change in the money supply on the aggregate economy.

section 12.3

Tools of the Bank of Canada

- What are the major tools of the Bank of Canada?
- What is the purpose of the Bank of Canada's tools?

HOW DOES THE BANK OF CANADA MANIPULATE THE SUPPLY OF MONEY?

As noted previously, the most important function of the Bank of Canada is to regulate the supply of money. The Bank of Canada decides whether to expand the money supply and, it is hoped, the real level of economic activity, or to contract the money supply, hoping to cool inflationary pressures. How does the Bank of Canada control the money supply, particularly when it is the privately owned chartered banks that actually create and destroy money by making loans, as we discussed earlier?

The Bank of Canada has two major methods that it can use to control the supply of money: It can engage in open market operations, or it can change the bank rate. Open market operations are the most important tool used by the Bank of Canada to influence the money supply.

OPEN MARKET OPERATIONS

open market operations
purchase and sale of government securities by the Bank of Canada

Open market operations involve the purchase and sale of Government of Canada securities (bonds and Treasury bills) by the Bank of Canada. When the Bank of Canada purchases Government of Canada bonds from the public, say, an investment dealer, the Bank of Canada pays for the bonds with a cheque drawn on itself. The investment dealer receiving the payment will likely deposit the cheque in its chequing account at its chartered bank, thereby increasing the money supply in the form of demand deposits. More important, the chartered bank will collect payment of this cheque from the Bank of

ACTIVE LEARNING EXERCISE

OPEN MARKET OPERATIONS

Q: How does the money supply increase as the result of open market operations?

A: In order for people to want to put more money in banks and less in government bonds, the Bank of Canada must offer bondholders an attractive price.

If the Bank of Canada's price is high enough, it will tempt some investors to sell their government bonds. When those individuals place the proceeds from the sale in the bank, new deposits are created, increasing reserves in the banking system. The excess reserves can then be loaned by the banks, creating more new deposits and increasing the excess reserves in still other banks.

Canada. The Bank of Canada will credit the chartered bank's reserve account at the Bank of Canada. Therefore, the chartered bank, in return for crediting the chequing account of the investment dealer with a new deposit, gets a credit in its reserve account at the Bank of Canada.

For example, suppose the Loans R Us National Bank has no excess reserves and that one of its customers, an investment dealer, sells a bond for $10 000 to the Bank of Canada. The customer deposits the cheque from the Bank of Canada for $10 000 in its account, and the Bank of Canada credits the Loans R Us National Bank with $10 000 in reserves. Suppose the desired reserve ratio is 10 percent. The Loans R Us National Bank, then, only needs new reserves of $1000 ($10 000 × 0.10) to support the $10 000 demand deposit, meaning that it has acquired $9000 in new excess reserves ($10 000 new actual reserves minus $1000 in new desired reserves). Loans R Us National Bank can, and probably will, lend out its excess reserves of $9000, creating $9000 in new deposits in the process. The recipients of the loans, in turn, will likely spend the money, leading to still more new deposits and excess reserves in other banks, as discussed in Chapter 11.

In other words, the Bank of Canada's purchase of the bond directly creates $10 000 in money in the form of demand deposits, and indirectly permits up to $90 000 in additional money to be created through the multiple expansion in bank deposits. (The money multiplier is 1/0.10, or 10. 10 × $9000 = $90 000.) Thus, if the desired reserve ratio is 10 percent, a potential total of up to $100 000 in new money is created by the purchase of one $10 000 bond by the Bank of Canada.

The process works in reverse when the Bank of Canada sells a bond. The investment dealer purchasing the bond will pay the Bank of Canada by cheque, lowering demand deposits in the banking system. Reserves of the bank where the investment dealer has a bank account will likewise fall. If the bank had zero excess reserves at the beginning of the process, it will now be short of reserves. The bank will likely reduce its volume of loans, which will lead to a further reduction of demand deposits. A multiple contraction of deposits, and money, will begin.

Open Market Activities and the Equation of Exchange

Generally, in a growing economy where the real value of goods and services is increasing over time, an increase in the supply of money is needed even to maintain stable prices. If the velocity of money (V) in the equation of exchange is fairly constant and real GDP (denoted by Q in the equation of exchange) is rising between 3 and 4 percent a year, then a 3 or 4 percent increase in M is consistent with stable prices. We would expect, then, that over long time expanses, the Bank of Canada's open market operations would more often lead to monetary expansion than monetary contraction. In other words, the Bank of Canada would more often purchase bonds than sell them. Moreover, in periods of rising prices, if *V* is fairly constant, the growth of *M* likely will exceed the 3 to 4 percent annual growth that appears to be consistent with long-term price stability.

THE BANK RATE

bank rate
interest rate that the Bank of Canada charges chartered banks for the loans it extends to them

We have seen that chartered banks hold a very small proportion of their deposits as reserves, choosing instead to lend out the vast majority of their deposits as interest-earning loans. The main reason that banks are able to operate with such a low ratio of reserves is that they are able to borrow reserves from the Bank of Canada when they find that their reserves have dropped below their desired level. The interest rate that the Bank of Canada charges on these borrowed reserves is called the **bank rate**.

If the Bank of Canada raises the bank rate, it makes it more costly for banks to borrow funds from it to increase their reserves. The higher the interest rate banks have to pay on the borrowed funds, the lower the potential profit from any new loans made from borrowed reserves, so fewer new loans will be made and less money created. Thus, if the Bank of Canada wants to contract the money supply, it will raise the bank rate. Conversely, if the Bank of Canada wants to expand the money supply, it will lower the bank rate, making it cheaper for banks to borrow funds from it. The lower the interest rate banks have to pay on the borrowed reserves, the higher the potential profit from any new loans made from the reserves, so more new loans will be made and more money created.

overnight interest rate
interest rate that chartered banks charge each other for one-day loans

The Bank of Canada sets the bank rate in relation to another important interest rate in the economy called the **overnight interest rate**. The overnight interest rate is the interest rate that chartered banks charge each other for one-day loans. The Bank of Canada sets a range for the overnight interest rate by using the bank rate as the upper limit of the range.

For example, say the Bank of Canada sets the bank rate at 3.25 percent. That means that chartered banks can borrow funds from the Bank of Canada at an interest rate of 3.25 percent. At the same time, however, the Bank of Canada pays chartered banks interest on their reserve deposits at the Bank of Canada. That interest rate, called the bankers' deposit rate, is set at the bank rate minus one-half of a percentage point. In this case, the banker's deposit rate would be 2.75 percent. We can now see that if one chartered bank needed to borrow reserves overnight (because its actual reserves were less than its desired reserves), it would first try to borrow those reserves from a second bank that was then in a position of having some excess reserves. What overnight interest rate might those two banks find it beneficial to agree to?

The overnight interest rate will fall somewhere between 2.75 percent and 3.25 percent. The first bank will not borrow reserves from the second bank for more than 3.25 percent, since it can borrow reserves from the Bank of Canada at that interest rate. Likewise, the second bank will not lend reserves to the first bank for less than 2.75 percent, since it can earn that rate of interest by holding its excess reserves at the Bank of Canada. Thus, an overnight interest rate of, say, 3.0 percent would benefit the chartered bank trying to borrow reserves overnight as well as the chartered bank trying to lend excess reserves overnight.

HOW THE BANK OF CANADA REDUCES THE MONEY SUPPLY

The Bank of Canada can do two things to reduce the money supply or reduce the rate of growth in the money supply: (1) sell bonds or (2) raise the bank rate. Of course, the Bank of Canada could also opt to use some combination of these two tools in its approach.

These moves would tend to decrease aggregate demand, reducing nominal GDP, hopefully through a decrease in *P* rather than *Q*. These actions would be the monetary policy equivalent of a fiscal policy of raising taxes, lowering transfer payments, and/or lowering government spending.

HOW THE BANK OF CANADA INCREASES THE MONEY SUPPLY

If the Bank of Canada is concerned about underutilization of resources (e.g., unemployment), it would engage in precisely the opposite policies: (1) buy bonds or (2) lower the bank rate. The Bank of Canada could also use a combination of these two approaches.

These moves would tend to increase aggregate demand, increasing nominal GDP, hopefully through an increase in Q (in the context of the equation of exchange) rather than P. Equivalent expansionary fiscal policy actions would be to reduce taxes, and/or increase government spending.

Section Check

1. The two major tools of the Bank of Canada are open market operations and changing the bank rate.
2. If the Bank of Canada wants to stimulate the economy (increase aggregate demand), it will increase the money supply by buying government bonds and/or lowering the bank rate.
3. If the Bank of Canada wants to restrain the economy (decrease aggregate demand), it will lower the money supply by selling bonds and/or raising the bank rate.

Summary

Section 12.1

- The Bank of Canada has five main functions: issuing currency for circulation in Canada; acting as the banker to the federal government; acting as the bank to the chartered banks; serving as a "lender of last resort"; and regulating the money supply.
- Of the five main functions of a central bank, the most important is its role in regulating the money supply.
- The Bank of Canada is owned by the federal government, which has final responsibility for the Bank of Canada's policies.
- The governor of the Bank of Canada has considerable independence in formulating bank policy.

Section 12.2

- The equation of exchange is $M \times V = P \times Q$, where M is the money supply, V is the velocity of money, P is the average level of prices of final goods and services, and Q is the physical quantity of final goods and services produced in an economy in a given year.

- The velocity of money (V) represents the average number of times that a dollar is used in purchasing final goods and services in a one-year period.
- The equation of exchange is a useful tool when analyzing the effects of a change in the supply of money on the aggregate economy, provided that the velocity is constant or at least predictable.

Section 12.3

- The two major tools of the Bank of Canada are open market operations and changing the bank rate.
- If the Bank of Canada wants to stimulate the economy, it will increase the money supply by buying government bonds and/or lowering the bank rate.
- If the Bank of Canada wants to restrain the economy, it will lower the money supply by selling government bonds and/or raising the bank rate.

Key Terms and Concepts

For a complete glossary of chapter key terms, visit the textbook's Web site at http://www.sextonmacro2e.nelson.com.

equation of exchange 315   bank rate 320   overnight interest rate 320

open market operations 318

Review Questions

1. Which of the following are functions of the Bank of Canada?

    a. provide loans to developing economies

    b. supervise banks

    c. back the Canadian dollar with gold

    d. issue currency

    e. regulate the money supply

    f. loan reserves to banks

    g. act as the bank for the Canadian government

    h. set interest rates on mortgages

2. Suppose that velocity and the money supply remain constant. If real GDP grows at an annual rate of 5 percent, what can you predict will happen to the price level using the equation of exchange? if real GDP falls by 2 percent?

3. If the Bank of Canada purchases $10 million worth of government bonds in the open market when the desired reserve ratio is 5 percent, what is the potential change in the money supply? if the desired reserve ratio is 25 percent?

4. If the Bank of Canada sells a $10 000 bond to an investor, what is the potential change in the money supply if the desired reserve ratio is 10 percent?

5. The following table shows the balance sheet for the Loans R Us National Bank. If the desired reserve ratio decreases from 10 percent to 5 percent, what happens to the "reserves" and "excess reserves" on the bank's balance sheet? What is the potential change in the money supply?

Loans R Us National Bank			
Assets		**Liabilities**	
Reserves	$100 000	Demand Deposits	$1 000 000
Excess Reserves	$0	Equity Capital	$50 000
Loans	$700 000		
Securities	$250 000		

6. Answer Question 5 again for the situation where the bank increases the desired reserve ratio from 10 percent to 12.5 percent. Where can the bank acquire the additional funds necessary to cover the desired reserves?

Fill in the Blanks

Section 12.1

1. In most countries, the job of manipulating the supply of money belongs to the _____.

2. The Bank of Canada is owned by _____.

3. The governor of the Bank of Canada is appointed for a _____ term.

4. The Bank of Canada has an _____ control strategy.

5. The most important function of the Bank of Canada is its ability to regulate the _____.

Section 12.2

6. The equation of exchange can be presented as: _____ = _____.

7. _____ represents the average number of times that a dollar is used in purchasing final goods or services in a one-year period.

8. If M increases and V remains constant, then P must _____, Q must _____, or P and Q must each _____.

9. Expanding the money supply, other things being equal, will have the same type of impact on aggregate demand as _____ government spending, or _____ taxes.

10. Some economists, often called _____, believe that monetary policy is the most powerful determinant of macroeconomic results.

11. Velocity is _____ stable when measured over shorter periods of time.

12. An increase in the interest rates will cause people to hold _____ money, which, in turn, means that the velocity of money _____.

13. Higher rates of anticipated inflation would tend to _____ velocity.

14. The inflation rate tends to rise _____ in periods of rapid monetary expansion.

Section 12.3

15. The Bank of Canada has two major methods that it can use to control the supply of money: It can engage in _____ operations, or change its _____ rate.

16. _____ are the most important device used by the Bank of Canada to influence the money supply.

17. Open market operations involve the purchase or sale of _____ by _____.

18. When the Bank of Canada buys government bonds in an open market operation, it _____ the money supply.

19. The most a bank can lend out at a given time is equal to its _____.

20. If the desired reserve ratio is 10 percent, a total of up to _____ in new money is potentially created by the purchase of $100 000 of government bonds by the Bank of Canada.

21. When the Bank of Canada sells a bond, the reserves of the bank where the bond buyer keeps his bank account will _____.

22. If the Bank of Canada _____ government bonds, it will create excess reserves in the banking system.

23. An increase in the bank rate would result in a _____ in the money supply.

24. The Bank of Canada would _____ the bank rate to stimulate the economy.

25. Banks that are short of reserves can borrow reserves directly from the Bank of Canada at an interest rate called the _____ rate.

26. If the Bank of Canada raises the bank rate, it makes it _____ costly for banks to borrow funds from it, which will result in _____ new loans being made and _____ money created.

27. If the Bank of Canada wants to expand the money supply, it will _____ the bank rate.

28. When banks have short-term needs for cash, they are more likely to take a very short-term (often overnight) loan from _____ than to borrow from the Bank of Canada.

29. The Bank of Canada can do two things if it wants to reduce the money supply. It can _____ government bonds, or _____ the bank rate.

30. An increase in the money supply would tend to _____ nominal GDP.

True or False

Section 12.1

1. A central bank has only one function—controlling the supply of money in a country.

2. The central bank typically serves as a bank for the federal government.

3. The central bank implements monetary and fiscal policy for the government.

4. The Bank of Canada is owned by the federal government.

5. The board of directors of the Bank of Canada is appointed by the federal government.

6. The Bank of Canada has no independence from the federal government.

7. The governor of the Bank of Canada is appointed for a seven-year term.

8. The Bank of Canada has an inflation control strategy.

Section 12.2

9. The money supply times velocity equals the price level times real GDP.

10. If individuals are writing lots of cheques on their chequing accounts and spending currency as fast as they receive it, velocity will tend to be low.

11. Velocity equals nominal GDP divided by the money supply.

12. The magnitude of velocity does not depend on the definition of money that is used.

13. If the money stock increases and the velocity of money does not change, there will be higher prices (inflation), greater real output of goods and services, or a combination of both.

14. Expanding the money supply, unless counteracted by increased hoarding of currency (leading to a decline in V), will have the same type of impact on aggregate demand as an expansionary fiscal policy.

15. Reducing the money supply, other things being equal, will have a contractionary impact on aggregate demand.

16. The velocity of money is a constant.

17. If velocity changes, but it moves in a fairly predictable pattern, the connection between money supply and GDP is still fairly predictable.

18. The cause of hyperinflation is excessive money growth.

Section 12.3

19. The Bank of Canada controls the supply of money, even though privately owned chartered banks actually create and destroy money by making and reducing loans.

20. Open market purchases or sales of securities by the Bank of Canada have an ultimate impact on the money supply that is several times the amount of the purchase or sale.

21. If the Bank of Canada buys bonds in an open market operation, and the seller deposits the payment in her bank account, the money supply will increase, and there will be an increase in the bank's reserves.

22. With a 10 percent desired reserve ratio, a $10 000 cash deposit in a bank would result in an increase in the bank's excess reserves by $1000.

23. With a 10 percent desired reserve ratio, a $1000 bond purchase by the Bank of Canada directly creates $1000 in money in the form of bank deposits, and indirectly permits up to $9000 in additional money to be created through the multiple expansion in bank deposits.

24. The Bank of Canada selling government bonds will tend to cause a multiple expansion of bank deposits.

25. Generally, in a growing economy where the real value of goods and services is increasing over time, an increase in the supply of money is needed to maintain stable prices.

26. Changes in the bank rate have no impact on the money supply.

27. If the Bank of Canada raises the bank rate, the money supply will tend to increase.

28. The overnight interest rate is the interest rate chartered banks charge on loans to each other.

29. The overnight interest rate will always be less than or equal to the bank rate.

30. If the Bank of Canada wanted to increase the money supply, it would buy bonds or lower the bank rate.

Multiple Choice

Section 12.1

1. The most important function of the Bank of Canada is
   a. raising or lowering taxes.
   b. regulating the supply of money.
   c. increasing or reducing government spending.
   d. none of the above.

2. Which of the following is *not* a function of the Bank of Canada?
   a. being a lender of last resort
   b. issuing currency
   c. serving as a bank for the federal government
   d. setting currency exchange rates

3. The Bank of Canada is largely independent. A major advantage of this is that
   a. monetary policy is subject to regular ratification by parliamentary votes.
   b. monetary policy is not subject to control by politicians.
   c. monetary policy cannot be changed once it has been completed.
   d. monetary policy will always be coordinated with fiscal policy.
   e. monetary policy will always offset fiscal policy.

Section 12.2

4. The *P* in the equation of exchange represents the
   a. profit earned in the economy.
   b. average level of prices of final goods and services in the economy.
   c. marginal level of prices.
   d. marginal propensity to spend.

5. The equation of exchange can be written as
   a. $M \times P = V \times Q$.
   b. $M \times V = P \times Q$.
   c. $M \times Q = P \times V$.
   d. $Q \times M = P \times V$.

6. If an economist divides the level of nominal GDP by the number of dollars in the money supply, she has computed
   a. the velocity of money.
   b. the price level.
   c. the level of real GDP.
   d. the economic growth rate.

7. If nominal GDP is $1200 billion, and M2 is $150 billion, then velocity is
   a. 0.5.
   b. 2.
   c. 4.
   d. 8.
   e. 400.

8. According to the equation of exchange, a change in the money supply of 6.5 percent would, holding velocity constant, lead to
   a. a 6.5 percent change in real GDP.
   b. a 6.5 percent change in nominal GDP.
   c. a 6.5 percent change in velocity.
   d. a 6.5 percent change in aggregate supply.

9. If people expect increasing inflation, what would be the expected reaction of velocity in the equation of exchange?
    a. Velocity would be expected to remain the same.
    b. Velocity would be expected to decrease.
    c. Velocity would be expected to increase.
    d. None of the above

10. If M increases and V increases,
    a. nominal GDP increases.
    b. nominal GDP decreases.
    c. nominal GDP stays the same.
    d. there is an indeterminate effect on nominal GDP.

11. If the velocity of money (V) and real output (Q) were increasing at approximately the same rate, then
    a. it would be impossible for monetary authorities to control inflation.
    b. monetary acceleration would not lead to inflation.
    c. inflation would be closely related to the long-run rate of monetary expansion.
    d. both a and b would be true.

Section 12.3

12. In order to increase the rate of growth of the money supply, the Bank of Canada can
    a. raise the bank rate.
    b. lower the bank rate.
    c. buy government securities on the open market.
    d. sell government securities on the open market.
    e. do both b and c.

13. The monetary policies generated by the Bank of Canada
    a. must be consistent with fiscal policies that are made in Parliament.
    b. are sometimes inconsistent with fiscal policies.
    c. must be ratified by Parliament.
    d. must be approved by the minister of finance.

14. If the Bank of Canada buys a bond from an investment dealer, what is the effect on the money supply?
    a. There will be no effect at all.
    b. The money supply will shrink.
    c. The money supply will grow by smaller amounts than if the Bank of Canada bought from a bank.
    d. The money supply will grow by larger amounts than if the Bank of Canada bought from a bank.
    e. The effect will be the same as if the Bank of Canada had bought the bond from a bank.

15. When the Bank of Canada purchases government securities from a chartered bank, the bank
    a. automatically becomes poorer.
    b. loses equity.
    c. receives reserves that can be used to make additional loans.
    d. loses its ability to make loans.

16. If the Bank of Canada wishes to expand the money supply, it
    a. buys stocks.
    b. sells stocks.
    c. buys government bonds.
    d. sells government bonds.

17. If the Bank of Canada sells a government bond to a member of the public,
    a. the banking system has more reserves, and the money supply tends to grow.
    b. the banking system has fewer reserves, and the money supply tends to grow.
    c. the banking system has more reserves, and the money supply tends to fall.
    d. the banking system has fewer reserves, and the money supply tends to fall.

18. An open market purchase of government bonds by the Bank of Canada would tend to cause
    a. the money supply to fall and bond prices to go up.
    b. the money supply to rise and bond prices to go up.
    c. the money supply to rise and bond prices to go down.
    d. the money supply to fall and bond prices to go down.

19. If the Bank of Canada lowers the bank rate, what will be the effect on the money supply?
    a. The money supply will tend to increase.
    b. The money supply will tend to decrease.
    c. There will be no change—there has been no deposit to begin an expansion or contraction process.
    d. Not enough data are given to answer.

20. When the Bank of Canada sells a Canadian government bond,
    a. the volume of loans issued by the banking system increases, and investment will tend to increase.
    b. the volume of loans issued by the banking system increases, and investment will tend to decrease.
    c. the volume of loans issued by the banking system decreases, and investment will tend to increase.
    d. the volume of loans issued by the banking system decreases, and investment will tend to decrease.

21. Lowering the bank rate, other things being equal, would tend to
    a. increase the dollar volume of loans made by the banking system.
    b. increase the money supply.
    c. increase aggregate demand.
    d. all of the above.
    e. do a and b, but not c.

22. A combination of an open market purchase by the Bank of Canada and a decrease in the bank rate would
    a. increase the money supply.
    b. decrease the money supply.
    c. leave the money supply unchanged.
    d. have an indeterminate effect on the money supply.

Problems

1. **[Section 12.2]**

   Answer questions a–e.
   a. What is the equation of exchange?
   b. In the equation of exchange, if V doubled, what would happen to nominal GDP as a result?
   c. In the equation of exchange, if V doubled and Q remained unchanged, what would happen to the price level as a result?
   d. In the equation of exchange, if M doubled and V remained unchanged, what would happen to nominal GDP as a result?
   e. In the equation of exchange, if M doubled and V fell by half, what would happen to nominal GDP as a result?

2. **[Section 12.3]**

   In which direction would the money supply change if
   a. the Bank of Canada raised the bank rate?
   b. the Bank of Canada conducted an open market sale of government bonds?
   c. the Bank of Canada lowered the bank rate?
   d. the Bank of Canada conducted an open market sale of government bonds and raised the bank rate?
   e. the Bank of Canada conducted an open market purchase of government bonds and raised the bank rate?

Monetary Policy

Money, Interest Rates, and Aggregate Demand

- What causes the demand for money to change?
- How do changes in income change the money market equilibrium?
- How does the Bank of Canada buying and selling bonds affect RGDP in the short run?
- What is the relationship between bond prices and the interest rate?
- Why does the Bank of Canada target the interest rate rather than the money supply?
- How are the real and nominal interest rates connected in the short run?

THE MONEY MARKET

The Bank of Canada's policies with respect to the money supply have a direct impact on short-run real interest rates, and accordingly, on the components of aggregate demand. The **money market** is the market where money demand and money supply determine the equilibrium *nominal* interest rate. When the Bank of Canada acts to change the money supply, it alters the money market equilibrium.

Money has several functions, but why would people hold money instead of other financial assets? That is, what is responsible for the demand for money? Transaction purposes, precautionary reasons, and asset purposes are at least three determinants of the demand for money.

money market
market in which money demand and money supply determine the equilibrium interest rate

Transaction Purposes

First, the primary reason that money is demanded is for transaction purposes—to facilitate exchange. The higher one's income, the more transactions a person will make (because consumption is income related), the greater will be GDP, and the greater the demand for money for transaction purposes, other things being equal.

Precautionary Reasons

Second, people like to have money on hand for precautionary reasons. If unexpected expenses require an unusual outlay of cash, people like to be prepared. The extent to which people demand cash for precautionary reasons depends partly on an individual's income and partly on the opportunity cost of holding money, which is determined by market rates of interest. The higher market interest rates, the higher the opportunity cost of holding money, and people will hold less of their financial wealth as money.

Asset Purposes

Third, money has a trait (liquidity) that makes it a desirable asset. Other things equal, people prefer more-liquid assets to less-liquid assets. That is, they would like to easily convert some of their assets into goods and services. For this reason, most people wish to have some of their portfolio in money form. At higher interest rates on other assets, the amount of money desired for this purpose will be smaller because the opportunity cost of holding money will have risen.

THE DEMAND FOR MONEY AND THE NOMINAL INTEREST RATE

The quantity of money demanded varies inversely with the nominal interest rate. When interest rates are higher, the opportunity cost—in terms of the interest income on alternative assets—of holding monetary assets is higher, and people will want to hold less money. At the same time, the demand for money, particularly for transaction purposes, is highly dependent on income levels, because the transaction volume varies directly with income. And lastly, the demand for money depends on the price level. If the price level increases, buyers will need more money to purchase goods and services. Or if the price level falls, buyers will need less money to purchase goods and services.

The demand curve for money is presented in Exhibit 1. At lower interest rates, the quantity of money demanded is greater, a movement from A to B in Exhibit 1. An increase in income will lead to an increase in the demand for money, depicted by a rightward shift in the money demand curve, a movement from A to C in Exhibit 1.

WHY IS THE SUPPLY OF MONEY RELATIVELY INELASTIC?

The supply of money is largely governed by the monetary policies of the central bank. Whether interest rates are 4 percent or 14 percent, banks seeking to maximize profits will increase lending as long as they have reserves above their desired level. Even a 4 percent return on loans provides more

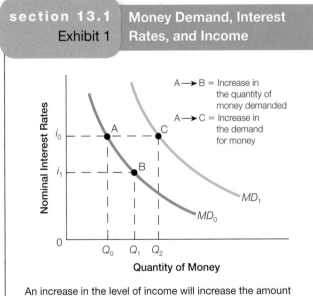

section 13.1
Exhibit 1
Money Demand, Interest Rates, and Income

A → B = Increase in the quantity of money demanded

A → C = Increase in the demand for money

(Graph: vertical axis "Nominal Interest Rates" with i_0 and i_1; horizontal axis "Quantity of Money" with Q_0, Q_1, Q_2; curves MD_0 and MD_1; points A, B, C)

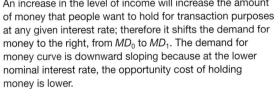

An increase in the level of income will increase the amount of money that people want to hold for transaction purposes at any given interest rate; therefore it shifts the demand for money to the right, from MD_0 to MD_1. The demand for money curve is downward sloping because at the lower nominal interest rate, the opportunity cost of holding money is lower.

section 13.1
Exhibit 2

section 13.1
Exhibit 2   **Changes in the Money Market Equilibrium**

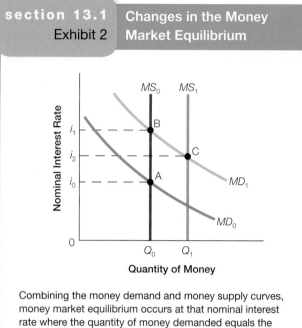

Combining the money demand and money supply curves, money market equilibrium occurs at that nominal interest rate where the quantity of money demanded equals the quantity of money supplied, initially at point A and interest rate i_0. An increase in income will shift the money demand curve to the right, from MD_0 to MD_1, raising the interest rate from i_0 to i_1 and resulting in a new equilibrium at point B. If the economy is presently at point B, an increase in the money supply resulting from expansionary monetary policies (e.g., the Bank of Canada buying bonds or lowering the bank rate) will shift the money supply curve to the right (from MS_0 to MS_1), lowering the nominal interest rate from (from i_1 to i_2) and shifting the equilibrium to point C.

profit than maintaining those excess reserves in non–interest-bearing cash. Given this fact, the money supply is effectively almost perfectly inelastic with respect to interest rates over their plausible range. Therefore, we draw the money supply curve as vertical, other things equal, in Exhibit 2, with changes in Bank of Canada policies acting to shift the money supply curve.

CHANGES IN MONEY DEMAND AND MONEY SUPPLY AND THE NOMINAL INTEREST RATE

Equilibrium in the money market is found by combining the money demand and money supply curves in Exhibit 2. Money market equilibrium occurs at that *nominal* interest rate, where the quantity of money demanded equals the quantity of money supplied. Initially, the money market is in equilibrium, at point A in Exhibit 2.

For example, rising national income increases the demand for money, shifting the money demand curve to the right from MD_0 to MD_1, and leading to a new higher equilibrium interest rate. If the economy is now at point B, an increase in the money supply (e.g., the Bank of Canada buys bonds) will shift the money supply curve to the right from MS_0 to MS_1, lowering the nominal rate of interest from i_1 to i_2, and shifting the equilibrium to point C.

THE BANK OF CANADA BUYS BONDS

Suppose the economy is headed for a recession and the Bank of Canada wants to pursue an expansionary monetary policy to increase aggregate demand. It will buy bonds on the open market. The Bank of Canada increases the demand for bonds, shifting the demand curve for bonds to the right, and the price of bonds rises in the bond market as seen in Exhibit 3(a). When the Bank of Canada buys bonds, bond sellers will likely deposit their cheque from the Bank of Canada in their bank and the money supply increases. The immediate impact of expansionary monetary policy is to decrease the interest rates, as seen in Exhibit 3(b). The lower interest rate, or the fall in the cost of borrowing money, then leads to an increase in aggregate demand for goods and services at the current price level. The lower interest rate will increase home sales, car sales, business investments, and so on. That is, when the Bank of Canada buys bonds, there is an increase in the demand for bonds and the price of bonds rises. The increase in the money supply will lead to lower interest rates and an increase in aggregate demand, as seen in Exhibit 3(c).

THE BANK OF CANADA SELLS BONDS

Now suppose the Bank of Canada wants to contain an overheated economy—that is, pursue a contractionary monetary policy to reduce aggregate demand. It will sell bonds on the open market. The Bank of Canada increases the supply of bonds and the price of bonds falls in the bond market. This is seen in Exhibit 4(a). As we just learned, when the Bank of Canada sells bonds to the private sector, the bond purchaser takes the money out of his chequing account to pay for the bond and that bank's reserves are reduced by the

section 13.1
Exhibit 3
The Bank of Canada Buys Bonds, Increases the Money Supply

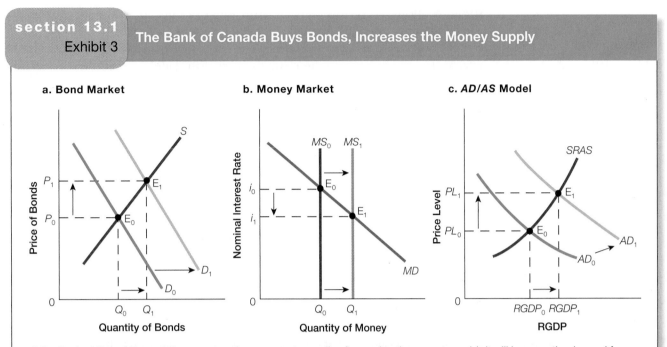

a. Bond Market

b. Money Market

c. *AD/AS* Model

If the Bank of Canada is pursuing an expansionary monetary policy (increasing the money supply), it will increase the demand for bonds, shifting the demand curve for bonds to the right, and the price of bonds rises in the bond market, as seen in Exhibit 3(a). When the Bank of Canada buys bonds, bond sellers will likely deposit their cheque from the Bank of Canada in their bank and the money supply increases. This will lower the interest rates, as seen in Exhibit 3(b). At lower interest rates, households and businesses will invest more and buy more goods and services, shifting the aggregate demand curve to the right, as seen in Exhibit 3(c).

section 13.1
Exhibit 4
The Bank of Canada Sells Bonds, Decreases the Money Supply

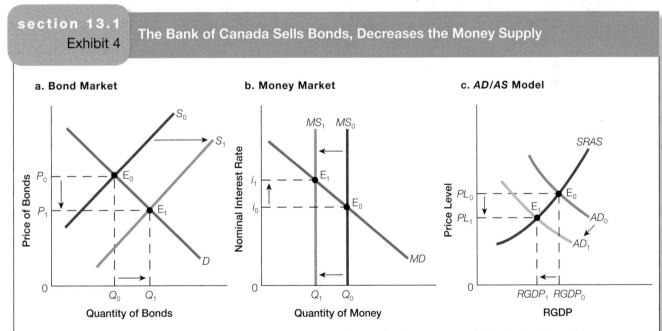

a. Bond Market

b. Money Market

c. *AD/AS* Model

If the Bank of Canada is pursuing a contractionary monetary policy (decreasing the money supply) the Bank of Canada increases the supply of bonds and the price of bonds falls in the bond market. This is seen in Exhibit 4(a). When the Bank of Canada sells bonds to the private sector, the bond purchasers take the money out of their chequing accounts to pay for the bonds and those banks' reserves are reduced by the size of the cheque. This reduction in reserves leads to a reduction in the money supply or a leftward shift, as seen in the money market in Exhibit 4(b). The reduction of the money supply leads to an increase in the interest rate in the money market. The higher interest rate, or the rise in the cost of borrowing money, then leads to a reduction in aggregate demand for goods and services, as seen in Exhibit 4(c).

size of the cheque. This reduction in reserves leads to a reduction in the money supply or a leftward shift, as seen in the money market in Exhibit 4(b). The reduction of the money supply leads to an increase in the interest rate in the money market. The higher interest rate, or the rise in the cost of borrowing money, then leads to a reduction in aggregate demand for goods and services, as seen in Exhibit 4(c). That is, the higher interest rate will lead to a decrease in home sales, car sales, business investments, and so on. In sum, when the Bank of Canada sells bonds, there is an increase in the supply of bonds, and bond prices fall. When bonds are bought at the new lower price, there is a reduction in the money supply, which leads to a higher interest rate and a reduction in aggregate demand, at least in the short run.

BOND PRICES AND INTEREST RATES

Notice the relationship between the interest rate and bond prices. When the Bank of Canada sells bonds—increases the supply of bonds—bond prices fall. However, when the Bank of Canada sells bonds, the money supply is reduced because bond buyers write cheques against their banks; the reduction in the supply of money leads to higher interest rates. That is, there is an inverse relationship between the interest rate and the price of bonds. When the price of bonds falls, the interest rate rises.

This relationship also holds when the Bank of Canada buys bonds on the open market. When the Bank of Canada buys bonds, this leads to an increase in demand for bonds and bond prices rise. However, when the Bank of Canada buys bonds, bond sellers put their cheques in their banks; this increases the money supply and lowers the interest rate. When the price of bonds rises, the interest rate falls.

section 13.1
Exhibit 5

Bank of Canada Targeting: Money Supply versus the Interest Rate

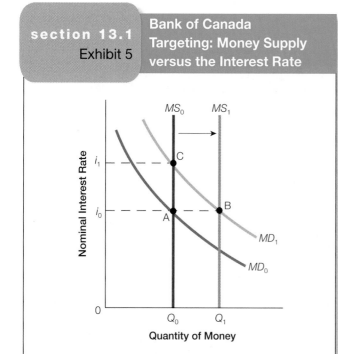

When the demand curve for money shifts out, the Bank of Canada must either settle for a higher interest rate, a greater money supply, or both. The Bank of Canada cannot completely control the growth in the money supply and the interest rate. If it attempts to keep the interest rate steady, it must increase the growth in the money supply. And if it tries to keep the growth of the money supply in check, the interest rate will rise.

DOES THE BANK OF CANADA TARGET THE MONEY SUPPLY OR THE INTEREST RATE?

Some economists believe the Bank of Canada should try to control the money supply. Other economists believe the Bank of Canada should try to control the interest rate. Unfortunately, the Bank of Canada cannot do both—it must pick one or the other.

The economy is initially at point A in Exhibit 5, where the interest rate is i_0 and the quantity of money is at Q_0. Now suppose the demand for money were to increase because of an increase in national income, or an increase in the price level, or overall, people desire to hold more money. As a result, the demand curve for money would shift to the right from MD_0 to MD_1. If the Bank of Canada decides it does not want the money supply to increase, it can pursue a no-monetary-growth policy; this will lead to an increase in the interest rate to i_1 at point C in Exhibit 5. The Bank of Canada could also try to keep the interest rate stable at i_0, but it can only do so by increasing the growth in the money supply through expansionary monetary policy. Since the Bank of Canada cannot simultaneously pursue a no-monetary-growth policy and expansionary monetary policy, it must choose—a higher interest rate or a greater money supply or some combination. The Bank of Canada cannot completely control both the growth in the money supply and the interest rate. If it attempts to keep the interest rate steady in the face of increased money demand, it must increase the growth in the money supply. And if it tries to keep the growth of the money supply in check in the face of increased money demand, the interest rates will rise.

The Problem

The problem with targeting the money supply is that the demand for money fluctuates considerably in the short run. Focusing on the growth in the money supply when the demand for money is changing unpredictably will lead to large fluctuations in the interest rate. These erratic changes in the interest rate could seriously disrupt the investment climate.

Keeping interest rates in check would also create problems. For example, when the economy grows, the demand for money also grows, so the Bank of Canada would have to increase the money supply to keep interest rates from rising. And if the economy were in a recession, the Bank of Canada would have to contract the money supply to keep the interest rate from falling. This would lead to the wrong policy prescription—expanding the money supply during a boom would eventually lead to inflation and contracting the money supply during a recession would make the recession even worse.

WHICH INTEREST RATE DOES THE BANK OF CANADA TARGET?

The Bank of Canada targets the overnight interest rate. Remember, the overnight interest rate is the interest rate that chartered banks charge each other for one-day loans. A bank that may be short of reserves might borrow from another bank that has excess reserves. The Bank of Canada has been targeting the overnight interest rate since about 1996. Announcements regarding the overnight interest rate—whether it will be increased, decreased, or made to stay the same—are made by the Bank of Canada on eight prespecified dates during the year.

Monetary policy actions can be conveyed through either the money supply or the interest rate. That is, if the Bank of Canada wants to pursue a contractionary monetary policy, this can be thought of as a reduction in the money supply or a higher interest rate. And, if the Bank of Canada wants to pursue an expansionary monetary policy, this can be thought of as an increase in the money supply or a lower interest rate. So why is the interest rate used? First, as we mentioned earlier, changes in the demand for money can significantly affect money supply targets. Second, many economists believe that the primary effects of monetary policy are felt through the interest rate. Finally, people are more familiar with changes in interest rates than changes in the money supply.

DOES THE BANK OF CANADA INFLUENCE THE REAL INTEREST RATE IN THE SHORT RUN?

In Chapter 8, we saw how the equilibrium real interest rate was found at the intersection of the investment demand curve and the saving supply curve in the saving and investment market. In this chapter, we have seen how the equilibrium nominal interest rate is found at the intersection of the demand for money and the supply of money in the money market. Both are important and the saving and investment market and money markets are interconnected.

Most economists believe that in the short run the Bank of Canada can control the nominal interest rate and the real interest rate. Recall that the *real interest rate is equal to the nominal interest rate minus the expected inflation rate.* So a change in the nominal interest rate tends to change the real interest rate by the same amount because the expected inflation rate is slow to change in the short run. That is, if the expected inflation rate does not change, there is a direct relationship between the nominal and real interest rates; a 1 percent reduction in the nominal interest rate will generally lead to a 1 percent reduction in the real interest rate in the short run. However, in the long run, over several years after the inflation rate has adjusted, the equilibrium real interest rate is found by the intersection of the saving supply curve and investment demand curve.

Section Check

1. The money market is the market where money demand and money supply determine the equilibrium interest rate.
2. Money demand has three possible motives: transaction purposes, precautionary reasons, and asset purposes.
3. The quantity of money demanded varies inversely with interest rates (a movement along the money demand curve) and directly with income (a shift of the money demand curve). Monetary policies that increase the supply of money will lower interest rates in the short run, other things being equal.
4. Rising incomes increase the demand for money. This will lead to a new higher equilibrium interest rate, other things being equal.
5. The supply of money is effectively almost perfectly inelastic with respect to interest rates over their plausible range, as controlled by Bank of Canada policies.
6. Money market equilibrium occurs at the intersection of the money demand and money supply curves. At the equilibrium nominal interest rate, the quantity of money demanded equals the quantity of money supplied.
7. When the Bank of Canada sells bonds to the private sector, bond purchasers take the money out of their chequing accounts to pay for the bonds and those banks' reserves are reduced by the size of the cheque. This reduction in bank reserves leads to a reduction in the money supply, which in turn leads to a higher interest rate and a reduction in aggregate demand, at least in the short run.
8. When the Bank of Canada buys bonds, bond sellers will likely deposit their cheque from the Bank of Canada in their bank and the money supply increases. The increase in the money supply will lead to lower interest rates and an increase in aggregate demand.
9. There is an inverse relationship between the interest rate and the price of bonds. When the price of bonds rises (falls) the interest rate falls (rises).
10. A change in the nominal interest rate tends to change the real interest rate by the same amount in the short run.
11. The Bank of Canada signals its intended monetary policy through the overnight interest rate target it sets.

section 13.2

Expansionary and Contractionary Monetary Policy

■ What is expansionary monetary policy?
■ What is contractionary monetary policy?

EXPANSIONARY MONETARY POLICY IN A RECESSIONARY GAP

Suppose the initial equilibrium is E_0, the point at which AD_0 intersects the short-run aggregate supply curve in Exhibit 1(c). At this point, output is equal to $RGDP_0$ and the

section 13.2
Exhibit 1
Expansionary Monetary Policy in a Recessionary Gap

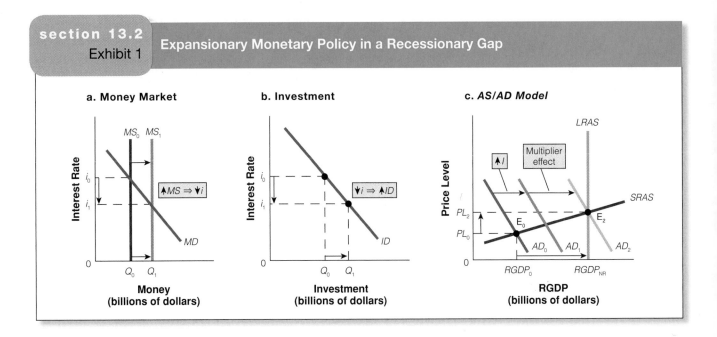

a. Money Market   b. Investment   c. AS/AD Model

price level is PL_0. If the Bank of Canada engages in expansionary monetary policy to combat a recessionary gap, the increase in the money supply will lower the interest rate, as seen in Exhibit 1(a). The lower interest rate leads to an increase in investment demanded, as seen in Exhibit 1(b). For example, business executives invest in new plant and equipment whereas individuals increase their investment in housing at the lower interest rate. In short, lower interest rates lead to greater investment spending. Since investment spending is one of the components of aggregate demand ($C + I + G + [X - M]$), when interest rates fall, total expenditures rise. That is, as investment expenditures increase, the aggregate demand curve shifts from AD_0 to AD_1, as seen in Exhibit 1(c). The increase in aggregate expenditures then triggers the multiplier effect, which shifts aggregate demand even further, from AD_1 to AD_2. The result is greater RGDP and a higher price level, at E_2. In this case, the Bank of Canada has eliminated the recession and RGDP is equal to the potential level of output at $RGDP_{NR}$.

During 2001, the Bank of Canada aggressively lowered the bank rate to stimulate aggregate demand when faced with a slowing economy. Between January 2001 and January 2002, the Bank of Canada cut the bank rate by 3.5 percentage points, from 5.75 percent to 2.25 percent, clearly demonstrating that it was concerned that the economy was dangerously close to falling into a recession.

CONTRACTIONARY MONETARY POLICY IN AN INFLATIONARY GAP

The Bank of Canada may engage in contractionary monetary policy if the economy faces an inflationary gap. Suppose the economy is at initial short-run equilibrium, E_0, in Exhibit 2(c). In order to combat inflation, suppose the Bank of Canada engages in an open market sale of bonds. This would lead to a decrease in the money supply, shifting the MS_0 leftward to MS_1, causing the interest rate to rise from i_0 to i_1, as seen in Exhibit 2(a). The higher interest rate leads to a decrease in the quantity of investment demanded, from Q_0 to Q_1, as seen in Exhibit 2(b). Investment expenditures fall as firms find it more costly to invest in plant and equipment and households find it more costly to finance new homes. Since the decrease in investment spending causes a reduction in

Contractionary Monetary Policy in an Inflationary Gap

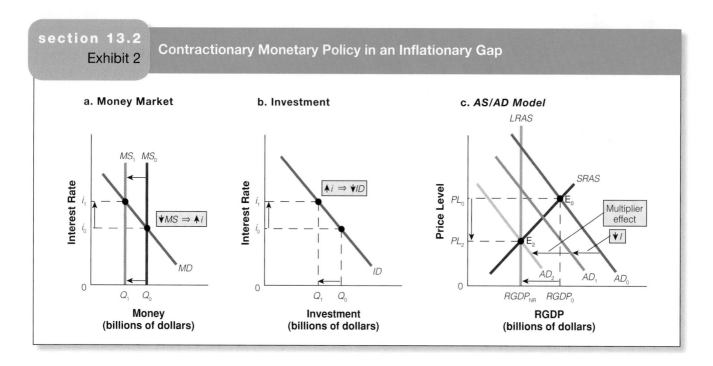

aggregate expenditures, the aggregate demand curve shifts leftward from AD_0 to AD_1 in Exhibit 2(c). The decrease in aggregate expenditures triggers the multiplier effect that reduces aggregate demand even further, shifting the aggregate demand curve from AD_1 to AD_2. The result is a lower RGDP and a lower price level, at E_2. The economy is now at $RGDP_{NR}$ where RGDP equals the potential level of output.

ACTIVE LEARNING EXERCISE

MONEY AND THE *AD/AS* MODEL

Q: During the Great Depression in Canada, the price level fell, real GDP fell, and unemployment reached almost 20 percent. Investment fell and the money supply fell. Can you show the effect of these changes from a vibrant 1929 economy to a battered 1933 economy using the *AD/AS* model?

A: The 1929 economy was at PL_{1929} and $RGDP_{1929}$ in Exhibit 3. The lack of consumer confidence coupled with the reduction in the money supply and falling investment sent the aggregate demand curve reeling. As a result, the aggregate demand curve fell from AD_{1929} to AD_{1933}, real GDP fell to $RGDP_{1933}$, and the price level fell to PL_{1933}—deflation.

section 13.2
Exhibit 3

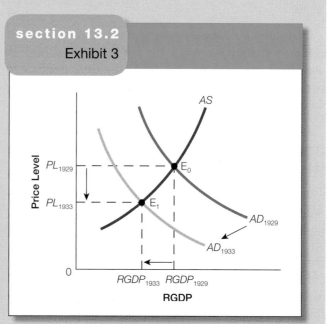

MONETARY POLICY IN THE OPEN ECONOMY

For simplicity we have assumed that the global economy does not impact Canadian monetary policy. This is incorrect. Suppose the Bank of Canada decides to pursue an expansionary policy by buying bonds on the open market. As we have seen, if the Bank of Canada buys bonds on the open market, the immediate effect is that the money supply will increase and the interest rate in Canada will fall. As some Canadian investors now seek to invest funds in foreign markets, they will exchange Canadian dollars for foreign currency, leading to a depreciation of the dollar (a decrease in the value of the dollar). The depreciation of the dollar makes Canadian goods and services more attractive to foreign buyers, and foreign goods and services relatively less attractive to Canadian buyers. That is, there is an increase in net exports—fewer imports and greater exports—and an increase in RGDP in the short run.

Similarly, if the Bank of Canada reduces the money supply and causes Canadian interest rates to rise, foreign investors will convert their currencies to Canadian dollars to take advantage of the relatively higher interest rates in Canada. This will lead to an appreciation of the dollar (an increase in the value of the dollar). The appreciation of the dollar will make Canadian goods and services relatively more expensive to foreign buyers, and foreign goods and services relatively cheaper to Canadian buyers. This leads to a decrease in net exports and a reduction in RGDP in the short run.

In The **NEWS**

BANK OF CANADA FACES BIG DECISION ON INTEREST RATES

BY ERIC BEAUCHESNE

OTTAWA—The Bank of Canada faces a critical interest rate decision as concerns grow over the country's ability to avoid a major hit from the global economic slowdown.

The central bank is widely expected to keep rates stable as it continues to weigh the risks of economic weakness against the threat of higher inflation from rising oil and world food prices.

Many analysts expect its next interest-rate move, when it comes, will be to start raising rates again. Inflation, now at 2.2 per cent, has risen above the central bank's two per cent target and is expected to rise above the upper limit of its one to three per cent target range.

While Canada's housing market has so far avoided the meltdown that has occurred in the U.S., and that has now spilled over into European and Asian housing markets, it will not escape unscathed.

"Canada has thus far avoided a housing adjustment," Export Development Canada noted. "But Canada's turn may come soon. Although imbalances in the marketplace appear to be small, starts are currently well ahead of requirements, and are unlikely to continue indefinitely at today's pace."

That view was echoed in the construction industry analysis.

"There are many signs that the pendulum may be starting to swing back toward lower volumes of new housing starts . . . through 2009," it says, citing more spending caution due to high gasoline prices and a riskier job market, higher levels of unsold inventories facing builders, the slowdown in the migration of workers to Western Canada and falling home sales.

"Even with respect to one of the few positives for housing starts, low interest and mortgage rates, the outlook may be clouding over," it observed. "It is unlikely that interest rates will be dropping further this year, given the increasing concerns that central bankers around the world are having about inflationary pressures."

"Therefore, expect a period of adjustment ahead," it warns.

SOURCE: Adapted from Eric Beauchesne, "Bank of Canada Faces Big Decision on Interest Rates," *Star–Phoenix*, Saskatoon, Saskatchewan, July 15, 2008, p. C7. Material reprinted with the express permission of: "CANWEST NEWS SERVICE", a CanWest Partnership.

CONSIDER THIS:

The Bank of Canada is expected to keep rates steady as it evaluates the results from a number of recent economic reports. The importance of the housing market to the Canadian business cycle is front and center as experts attempt to determine whether the mortgage crisis in the United States will spill over into Canada. A decline in the housing sector could shift the aggregate demand curve leftward and put downward pressure on inflation.

Thus, you can see that in an open economy, like Canada's, monetary policy operates on aggregate demand through two channels: the interest rate and the exchange rate. An expansionary monetary policy causes interest rates to fall and the exchange rate to depreciate, both of which, in turn, cause aggregate demand to increase. Similarly, a contractionary monetary policy causes interest rates to rise and the exchange rate to appreciate, both of which, in turn, cause aggregate demand to decrease.

Section Check

1. An expansionary monetary policy can combat a recessionary gap, causing an increase in real GDP and the price level.
2. A contractionary monetary policy can close an inflationary gap, causing a decline in real GDP and the price level.

section 13.3 Problems in Implementing Monetary and Fiscal Policy

- What problems exist in implementing monetary policy?
- What problems exist in coordinating monetary and fiscal policies?

PROBLEMS IN CONDUCTING MONETARY POLICY

The lag problem inherent in adopting fiscal policy changes is much less acute for monetary policy, largely because the decisions are not slowed by the same budgetary process. The Bank of Canada, because of its independence, can act very quickly in undertaking open market operations. However, the length and variability of the impact lag before its effects on output and employment are felt are still significant, and the time before the full price level effects are felt is even longer and more variable. The major effects of a change in monetary policy on growth in the overall production of goods and services and on inflation are usually spread over six to eight quarters (18 months to two years).

HOW DO CHARTERED BANKS IMPLEMENT THE BANK OF CANADA'S MONETARY POLICIES?

One limitation of monetary policy is that it ultimately must be carried out through the banking system. The central bank can change the environment in which banks act, but the banks themselves must take the steps necessary to increase or decrease the money supply. Usually, when the Bank of Canada is trying to constrain monetary expansion, there is no difficulty in getting chartered banks to make appropriate responses. If the Bank of Canada sells bonds and/or raises the bank rate, banks will call in loans that are due for collection, and in the process of collecting loans, they lower the money supply.

When the Bank of Canada wants to induce monetary expansion, however, it can provide banks with excess reserves (by buying government bonds), but it cannot force the banks to make loans, thereby creating new money. Ordinarily, of course, banks want to convert their excess reserves to interest-earning income by making loans. But in a deep recession or depression, banks might be hesitant to make enough loans to put all those reserves to work, fearing that they will not be repaid. Their pessimism might lead them to perceive that the risks of making loans to many normally creditworthy borrowers outweigh any potential interest earnings (particularly at the low real interest rates that are characteristic of depressed times).

FISCAL AND MONETARY COORDINATION PROBLEMS

Another possible problem that arises out of existing institutional policymaking arrangements is the coordination of fiscal and monetary policy. The Canadian government makes fiscal policy decisions, whereas monetary policy decision making is in the hands of the Bank of Canada. A macroeconomic problem arises if the federal government's fiscal decision makers differ with the Bank of Canada's monetary decision makers on policy objectives or targets. For example, the Bank of Canada may be more concerned about keeping inflation low, whereas fiscal policymakers may be more concerned about keeping unemployment low.

Some people believe that monetary policy should be more directly controlled by the federal government so that all macroeconomic policy will be determined more directly by the political process. Others, however, argue that it is dangerous to turn over control of the nation's money supply to politicians, rather than allowing decisions to be made by an independent central bank, which is more focused on price stability and more insulated from political pressures.

THE SHAPE OF THE AGGREGATE SUPPLY CURVE AND POLICY IMPLICATIONS

Many economists argue that the short-run aggregate supply curve is relatively flat at very low levels of real GDP, when the economy has substantial excess capacity, and very steep when the economy is near maximum capacity, as shown in Exhibits 1 and 2.

Why is the *SRAS* curve in Exhibit 1 flat over the range where there is considerable excess capacity? Firms are operating well below their potential output at $RGDP_{NR}$, so the marginal cost of producing more rises little as output expands. Firms can also hire more labour without increasing the wage rate. With many idle resources, producers are willing to sell additional output at current prices because there are few shortages to push prices upward. In addition, many unemployed workers are willing to work at the going wage rate, which diminishes the power of workers to increase wages. In short, when the economy is operating at levels significantly lower than full-employment output, input prices are sticky (relatively inflexible). Empirical evidence for the period 1983–1987, when the Canadian economy was experiencing significant unemployment, appears to confirm that the short-run aggregate supply curve was very flat when the economy was operating with significant excess capacity.

Near the top of the *SRAS* curve, however, the economy is operating close to maximum capacity (and beyond the

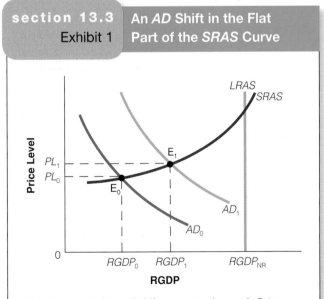

section 13.3 Exhibit 1 An *AD* Shift in the Flat Part of the *SRAS* Curve

If an aggregate demand shift occurs on the nearly flat portion of the *SRAS* curve, it causes a large change in RGDP and a small change in the price level.

An *AD* Shift in the Steep Part of the *SRAS* Curve

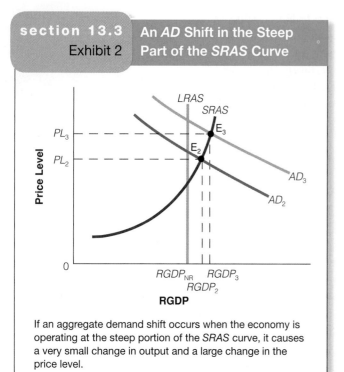

If an aggregate demand shift occurs when the economy is operating at the steep portion of the *SRAS* curve, it causes a very small change in output and a large change in the price level.

output level that could be sustained over time). That is, at this level of output, it will be very difficult or impossible for firms to expand output any further—firms may already be running double shifts and paying overtime. At this point, an increase in aggregate demand will be met almost exclusively with a higher price level in the short run.

In short, if the government is using fiscal and/or monetary policy to stimulate aggregate demand, it must carefully assess where it is operating on the *SRAS* curve. As we have seen in Exhibit 1, if the economy is operating on the flat portion of the *SRAS* curve, far from full capacity, an increase in the money supply, a tax cut, or an increase in government spending will result in an increase in output but little change in the price level—a movement from E_0 to E_1 in Exhibit 1. In this case, the expansionary policy works well: higher RGDP and employment with little change in the price level. However, if the shift in aggregate demand occurs when the economy is operating near maximum capacity, the result will be a substantial increase in the price level, with very little change in the output level—a movement from E_2 to E_3 in Exhibit 2. That is, if the economy is operating on the steep portion of the *SRAS* curve, expansionary policy does not work well.

Furthermore, what if the expansionary policy involves an increase in government spending, with no change in the money supply? If the economy is operating in the steep portion of the *SRAS* curve, the increase in *AD* largely causes the price level to rise. The increase in the price level leads to an increase in the demand for money and higher interest rates, which act to crowd out consumer and business investment. This also undermines the effectiveness of the government policy.

It is also easy to see in Exhibits 1 and 2 that contractionary monetary or fiscal policy (a tax increase, a decrease in government spending, and/or a decrease in the money supply) to combat inflation is more effective in the steep region of the *SRAS* curve than in the flat region. In the steep region, contractionary monetary and/or fiscal policy results in a large fall in the price level and a small change in real GDP; in the flat region of the *SRAS* curve, the contractionary policy would result in a large decrease in output and a small change in the price level.

OVERALL PROBLEMS WITH MONETARY AND FISCAL POLICY

Much of macroeconomic policy in this country is driven by the idea that the federal government can counteract economic fluctuations: stimulating the economy (with increased government purchases, tax cuts, transfer payment increases, and easy money) when it is weak, and restraining it when it is overheating. But policymakers must adopt the right policies in the right amounts at the right time for such "stabilization" to do more good than harm. And for this, government policymakers need far more accurate and timely information than experts can give them.

First, economists must know not only which way the economy is heading, but also how rapidly. And the unvarnished truth is that in our incredibly complicated world, no one knows exactly what the economy will do, no matter how sophisticated the econometric models used. It has often been said, and not completely in jest, that the purpose of economic forecasting is to make astrology look respectable.

But let's assume that economists can outperform astrologers at forecasting. Indeed, let's be completely unrealistic and assume that economists can provide completely accurate economic forecasts of what will happen if macroeconomic policies are unchanged. Even then, they could not be certain of how best to promote stable economic growth.

If economists knew, for example, that the economy was going to dip into another recession in six months, they would then need to know exactly how much each possible policy would spur activity in order to keep the economy stable. But such precision is unattainable, given the complex forecasting problems faced. Furthermore, despite assurances to the contrary, economists aren't always sure what effect a policy will have on the economy. Will an increase in government purchases quicken economic growth? It is widely assumed so. But how much? And increasing government purchases increases the budget deficit, which could send a frightening signal to the bond markets. The result can be to drive up interest rates and choke off economic activity. So even when policymakers know which direction to nudge the economy, they can't be sure which policy levers to pull, or how hard to pull them, to fine-tune the economy to stable economic growth.

But let's further assume that policymakers know when the economy will need a boost, and also which policy will provide the right boost. A third crucial consideration is how long it will take a policy before it has its effect on the economy. The trouble is that, even when increased government purchases or expansionary monetary policy does give the economy a boost, no one knows precisely how long it will take to do so. The boost may come very quickly, or many months (or even years) in the future, when it may add inflationary pressures to an economy that is already overheating, rather than helping the economy recover from a recession.

In this way, macroeconomic policymaking is like driving down a twisting road in a car with an unpredictable lag and degree of response in the steering mechanism. If you turn the wheel to the right, the car will eventually veer to the right, but you don't know exactly when or how much. In short, there are severe practical difficulties in trying to fine-tune the economy. Even the best forecasting models and methods are far from perfect. Economists are not exactly sure where the economy is or where or how fast it is going, making it very difficult to prescribe an effective policy. Even if we do know where the economy is headed, we cannot be sure how large a policy's effect will be or when it will take effect.

Some economists believe that fine-tuning the economy is like driving a car with an unpredictable steering lag on a winding road.

Unexpected Global and Technological Events

The Bank of Canada must take into account the influences of many different factors that can either offset or reinforce monetary policy. This isn't easy because sometimes these developments occur unexpectedly, and because the size and timing of their effects are difficult to estimate.

For example, during the 1997–1998 currency crisis in East Asia, economic activity in several countries in that region either slowed or declined. This led to a reduction in the aggregate demand for Canadian goods and services. In addition, the foreign exchange value of most of their currencies depreciated, and this made Asian-produced goods less expensive for us to buy and Canadian-produced goods more expensive in Asian countries. Both of these factors would reduce aggregate demand in Canada and lower output and employment. So the Bank of Canada must consider these global events in formulating its monetary policy.

During the late 1990s, the Canadian economy experienced a productivity increase through high-tech and other developments. This "new" economy increased productivity growth, allowing for greater economic growth without creating inflationary pressures. The Bank of Canada was then faced with estimating how fast productivity was increasing and whether those increases were temporary or permanent. Not an easy task.

By 2007, the Canadian economy was facing a new set of global challenges—the Canadian dollar was trading around par with its American counterpart (a reality that had last occurred during the mid-1970s), the U.S. economy was experiencing an economic slowdown, and oil prices had risen to near-record levels. An added complication for the Bank of Canada was the fact that, unlike the 1970s, the high oil prices had not produced strong inflationary expectations for consumers. To successfully navigate this set of challenges, the Bank of Canada would have to carefully consider a wide range of policy options.

Section Check

1. Monetary policy faces somewhat different implementation problems than fiscal policy. Both face difficult forecasting and lag problems. But the Bank of Canada can take action much more quickly. However, its effectiveness depends largely on the reaction of the private banking system to its policy changes.
2. In Canada, monetary and fiscal policy are carried out by different decision makers, thus requiring cooperation and coordination for effective policy implementation.

section 13.4 The Phillips Curve

- What is the Phillips curve?
- How does the Phillips curve relate to the aggregate supply and demand model?

UNEMPLOYMENT AND INFLATION IN THE SHORT RUN

We usually think of inflation as an evil—higher prices mean lower real incomes for people on fixed incomes, whereas those with the power to raise the prices charged for goods or services they provide may actually benefit. Nevertheless, some economists believe that in the short run, inflation could actually help eliminate unemployment. For example, if output prices rise but money wages do not go up as quickly or as much, real wages fall. At the lower real wage, unemployment is less because the lower wage makes it profitable to hire more, now cheaper, employees than before. The result is real wages that are closer to the full-employment equilibrium wage that clears the labour market. Hence, with increased inflation, one might expect lower unemployment in the short run. In the long run, there is no tradeoff between unemployment and inflation. In the long run, output is determined by the LRAS curve, and unemployment is at its natural rate.

THE PHILLIPS CURVE

In fact, an inverse short-run relationship between the rate of unemployment and the changing level of prices has been observed in many periods and places in history. Credit for identifying this relationship generally goes to British economist A. H. Phillips, who in the late 1950s published a paper setting forth what has since been called the *Phillips curve*. Phillips and many others since have suggested that at higher rates of inflation, the rate of unemployment is lower, whereas during periods of relatively stable or falling prices, unemployment is substantial. In summary, the cost of lower unemployment appears to be greater inflation, and the cost of greater price stability appears to be higher unemployment, at least in the short run.

Exhibit 1 shows the actual inflation-unemployment relationship for Canada for the 1960s. The points in this graph represent the combination of the inflation rate and the rate of unemployment for the period 1960–1969. The curved line—the Phillips curve—is the smooth line that best fits the data points.

THE SLOPE OF THE PHILLIPS CURVE

In examining Exhibit 1, it is evident that the slope of the Phillips curve is not the same throughout its length. The curve is steeper at higher rates of inflation and lower levels of unemployment. This relationship suggests that once the economy has relatively low unemployment rates, further reductions in the unemployment rate can occur only if the economy can accept larger increases in the inflation rate. Once the unemployment rate is low, it takes larger and larger doses of inflation to eliminate a given quantity of unemployment. Presumably, at lower unemployment rates, an increased part of the economy is already operating at or near full capacity. Further fiscal or monetary stimulus primarily triggers inflationary pressures in sectors already at capacity, while eliminating decreasing amounts of unemployment in those sectors where some excess capacity and unemployment still exist.

THE PHILLIPS CURVE AND AGGREGATE SUPPLY AND DEMAND

In Exhibit 2, we see the relationship between aggregate supply and demand analysis and the Phillips curve. Suppose the economy moved from a 2 percent annual inflation rate to a

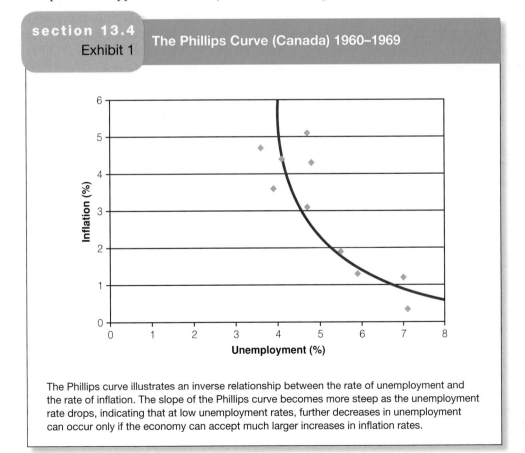

section 13.4
Exhibit 1   **The Phillips Curve (Canada) 1960–1969**

The Phillips curve illustrates an inverse relationship between the rate of unemployment and the rate of inflation. The slope of the Phillips curve becomes more steep as the unemployment rate drops, indicating that at low unemployment rates, further decreases in unemployment can occur only if the economy can accept much larger increases in inflation rates.

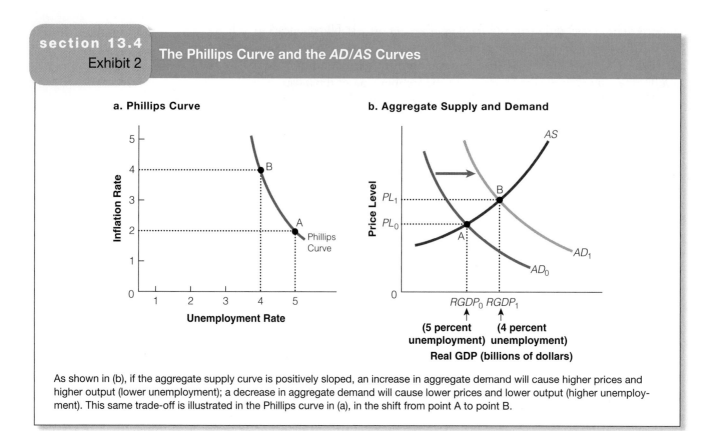

section 13.4
Exhibit 2 The Phillips Curve and the *AD/AS* Curves

As shown in (b), if the aggregate supply curve is positively sloped, an increase in aggregate demand will cause higher prices and higher output (lower unemployment); a decrease in aggregate demand will cause lower prices and lower output (higher unemployment). This same trade-off is illustrated in the Phillips curve in (a), in the shift from point A to point B.

4 percent inflation rate, and the unemployment rate simultaneously fell from 5 percent to 4 percent. In the Phillips curve, we see this change as a move up the curve from point A to point B in Exhibit 2(a). We can see a similar relationship in the *AD/AS* model in Exhibit 2(b). Imagine that an increase in aggregate demand occurs. Consequently, the price level increases from PL_0 to PL_1 (the inflation rate rises) and output increases from $RGDP_0$ to $RGDP_1$ (the unemployment rate falls). To increase output, firms employ more workers, so employment increases and unemployment falls—the movement from point A to point B in Exhibit 2(b).

Section Check

1. The inverse relationship between the rate of unemployment and the rate of inflation is called the Phillips curve.
2. The Phillips curve relationship can also be seen indirectly from the *AD/AS* model.

Summary

Section 13.1
- The equilibrium nominal interest rate in the money market is determined by the intersection of money demand and money supply curves.

- Money demand has three possible motives: transaction purposes, precautionary reasons, and asset purposes.
- The quantity of money demanded varies inversely with the interest rate and directly with income.

- The supply of money, controlled by Bank of Canada policies, is effectively almost perfectly inelastic with respect to interest rates.
- When the Bank of Canada sells bonds to the private sector, this leads to a reduction in the money supply, which in turn leads to a higher interest rate and a reduction in aggregate demand, at least in the short run.
- When the Bank of Canada buys bonds, the money supply increases, interest rates are lowered, and aggregate demand increases.

Section 13.2

- Expansionary monetary policy can be used to address a recessionary gap, causing an increase in real GDP and the price level.
- Contractionary monetary policy can be used to address an inflationary gap, causing a decrease in real GDP and the price level.

Section 13.3

- Monetary policy faces somewhat different implementation problems than fiscal policy.
- Although both face difficult forecasting and lag problems, the Bank of Canada can implement monetary policy much more quickly.
- The effectiveness of monetary policy depends largely on the reaction of the private banking system.
- In Canada, monetary and fiscal policy are carried out by different decision makers, thus requiring cooperation and coordination for effective policy implementation.

Section 13.4

- The inverse relationship between the unemployment rate and the rate of inflation in the short run is called the Phillips curve.
- The Phillips curve relationship can also be seen indirectly from the *AD/AS* model.

Key Terms and Concepts

For a complete glossary of chapter key terms, visit the textbook's Web site at http://www.sextonmacro2e.nelson.com.

money market 330

Review Questions

1. What is the motive for holding money in each of the following cases (precautionary, transaction, or asset)?

    a. Concerned about the fluctuations of the stock market, you sell stock and keep cash in your brokerage account.

    b. You keep ten $20 bills in your earthquake-preparedness kit.

    c. You go to Toronto with a large sum of money in order to complete your holiday shopping.

    d. You keep $20 in your glove compartment just in case you run out of gas.

2. Money is said to be "neutral" in the long run. Using the aggregate demand–aggregate supply framework, explain why an increase in the money supply when an economy is operating at full employment affects only the price level in the long run.

3. What use of the monetary policy tools do you think would have been appropriate to help bring the Canadian economy out of the Great Depression? Explain.

4. Predict the impact of a decrease in the money supply on the following variables in the short run and in the long run.

    a. the inflation rate

    b. the unemployment rate

    c. real output

    d. real wages

Fill in the Blanks

Section 13.1

1. People have three basic motives for holding money instead of other assets: for _____ purposes, _____ purposes, and _____ purposes.

2. The quantity of money demanded varies _____ with the rate of interest.

3. If the price level falls, buyers will need _____ money to purchase their goods and services.

4. We draw the money supply curve as _____, other things being equal, with changes in _____ policies acting to shift the money supply curve.

5. Money market equilibrium occurs at that _____ interest rate where the quantity of money demanded equals the quantity of money supplied.

6. Rising national income will shift the demand for money to the _____, leading to a new _____ equilibrium nominal interest rate.

7. An increase in the money supply will lead to _____ interest rates and an _____ in aggregate demand.

8. When the Bank of Canada sells bonds, it _____ the price of bonds, _____ interest rates, and _____ aggregate demand in the short run.

9. If the demand for money increases, but the Bank of Canada doesn't allow the money supply to increase, interest rates will _____, and aggregate demand will _____.

10. When the economy grows, the Bank of Canada would have to _____ the money supply to keep interest rates from rising.

11. The _____ is the interest rate the Bank of Canada targets.

12. A contractionary policy can be thought of as a(n) _____ in the money supply or a(n) _____ in the interest rate.

13. The _____ interest rate is determined by investment demand and saving supply; the _____ interest rate is determined by the demand and supply of money.

14. The real interest rate is equal to _____ minus _____.

Section 13.2

15. Countercyclical monetary policy would _____ the supply of money to combat a potential inflationary boom.

16. The Bank of Canada selling bonds will lead to a(n) _____ in the money supply, a(n) _____ in interest rates, a(n) _____ of the dollar, a(n) _____ in net exports, and a(n) _____ in RGDP in the short run.

Section 13.3

17. The lag problem inherent in adopting fiscal policy changes is much _____ acute for monetary policy.

18. The major effects of a change in policy on growth in the overall production of goods and services and on inflation tend to involve lags of _____ quarters.

19. In the process of calling in loans to obtain necessary banking reserves, banks _____ the supply of money.

20. Ordinarily, banks want to convert excess reserves into interest-earning _____, but in a deep recession or depression, banks might be hesitant to make enough loans to put all those reserves to work.

21. The Bank of Canada finds it easier to _____ the money supply than _____ the money supply.

22. Decision making with respect to fiscal policy is made by _____, whereas monetary policy decision making is in the hands of _____.

23. Some people believe that monetary policy should be more directly controlled by the federal government, so that all macroeconomic policy will be determined _____ directly by the political process.

24. Policymakers must adopt the _____ policies in the _____ amounts at the _____ time for such "stabilization" to do more good than harm.

25. When increased government purchases or expansionary monetary policy does give the economy a boost, _____ knows precisely how long it will take to do so.

Section 13.4

26. The Phillips curve describes a short run trade-off between _____ and _____.

27. If output prices rise but money wages do not go up as quickly, real wages will _____, tending to _____ unemployment.

28. The Phillips curve suggests that at lower rates of inflation, the rate of unemployment will be _____.

29. The Phillips curve is _____ at higher rates of inflation and lower rates of unemployment.

30. An increase in aggregate demand would cause the economy to move _____ along the Phillips curve, causing the inflation rate to _____ and the rate of unemployment to _____.

31. When moving up along the Phillips curve, employment rates tend to _____.

True or False

Section 13.1

1. When interest rates are lower, the opportunity cost of holding monetary assets is higher.

2. The demand for money, particularly for transaction purposes, is highly dependent on income levels because the transaction volume varies directly with income.

3. At lower interest rates, the quantity of money demanded, but not the demand for money, is greater.

4. An increase in the money supply raises the equilibrium nominal interest rate.

5. The Bank of Canada buying bonds on the open market is an example of an expansionary monetary policy.

6. When the price of bonds rises, the interest rate rises.

7. The Bank of Canada cannot control both the money supply and the interest rate at the same time.

8. If the demand for money increases, and the Bank of Canada wants to keep the interest rate stable, it will have to increase the money supply.

9. Focusing on the growth in the money supply when the demand for money is changing unpredictably will lead to large fluctuations in the interest rate.

10. An expansionary policy can be thought of as an increase in the money supply or an increase in the interest rate.

11. A change in the nominal interest rate tends to change the real interest rate by the same amount in the short run because the expected inflation rate is slow to change in the short run.

12. In the long run, the real interest rate is determined by the intersection of the saving supply curve and investment demand curve.

Section 13.2

13. The Bank of Canada buying bonds on the open market will lead to an appreciation of the Canadian dollar, an increase in net exports, and an increase in RGDP in the short run.

14. Expansionary monetary policy can be implemented to combat an inflationary gap.

15. Contractionary monetary policy will see the money supply decrease, interest rates increase, and the aggregate demand curve shift leftward.

Section 13.3

16. The Bank of Canada is unable to act quickly in emergencies.

17. The length and variability of the impact lag before the effects of monetary policy on output and employment are felt are longer and are more variable than for fiscal policy.

18. The Bank of Canada can change the environment in which banks act, but the banks themselves must take the steps necessary to increase or decrease the supply of money.

19. If the Bank of Canada sells bonds and/or raises the bank rate, banks will call in loans that are due for collection, and in the process of contracting loans, they lower the supply of money.

20. When the Bank of Canada is trying to constrain monetary expansion, it often has difficulty in getting banks to make appropriate responses.

21. When the Bank of Canada wants to induce monetary expansion, it can provide banks with excess reserves, but it cannot force the banks to make loans, thereby creating new money.

22. Banks maintaining excess reserves hinder attempts by the Bank of Canada to induce monetary expansion.

23. Even if economists could provide completely accurate economic forecasts of what will happen if macroeconomic policies are unchanged, they could not be certain of how best to promote stable economic growth.

24. Given the difficulties of timing stabilization policy, an expansionary monetary policy intended to reduce the severity of a recession may instead add inflationary pressures to an economy that is already overheating.

25. If the "new" economy increases productivity, the Bank of Canada, in trying to allow for greater economic growth without creating inflationary pressures, must estimate how much faster productivity is increasing and whether those increases are temporary or permanent.

Section 13.4

26. The inverse relationship between the rate of unemployment and the rate of inflation is called the Phillips curve.

27. If output prices rise faster than money wages, real wages will fall, as will the unemployment rate.

28. According to the short-run Phillips curve, the cost of lower unemployment appears to be greater inflation, and the cost of lower inflation appears to be higher unemployment.

29. Along any particular Phillips curve, the slope and therefore the trade-off between unemployment and inflation is constant.

Multiple Choice

Section 13.1

1. When the money supply increases, other things being equal,
   a. nominal interest rates fall, and investment spending rises.
   b. nominal interest rates fall, and investment spending falls.
   c. nominal interest rates rise, and investment spending falls.
   d. nominal interest rates rise, and investment spending rises.

2. The money demand curve shows
   a. the various amounts of money that individuals will hold at different price levels.
   b. the various amounts of money that individuals will spend at different levels of GDP.
   c. the various amounts of money that individuals will hold at different interest rates.
   d. the quantity of bonds that the Bank of Canada will buy at different price levels.

3. What will happen to the demand for money if real GDP rises?
   a. It will decrease.
   b. It will be unchanged.
   c. It will increase.
   d. It depends on what happens to interest rates.

4. When money demand increases, the Bank of Canada can choose between
   a. increasing interest rates or increasing the supply of money.
   b. increasing interest rates or decreasing the supply of money.
   c. decreasing interest rates or increasing the supply of money.
   d. decreasing interest rates or decreasing the supply of money.

5. The quantity of money that households and businesses will demand
   a. increases if income rises but decreases if interest rates rise.
   b. increases if income rises and increases if interest rates rise.
   c. decreases if income rises but increases if interest rates rise.
   d. decreases if income rises and decreases if interest rates rise.
   e. None of the above is true.

Section 13.2

6. Contractionary monetary policy will tend to have what effect?
   a. increase the money supply and lower interest rates
   b. increase the money supply and increase interest rates
   c. decrease the money supply and lower interest rates
   d. decrease the money supply and increase interest rates

7. The combination of an increase in the bank rate and an open market sale of government securities by the Bank of Canada will tend to result in
   a. a higher loan volume issued by the chartered banking system.
   b. higher bond prices.
   c. a lower price level.
   d. a decrease in unemployment rates.

8. The flatter the *SRAS* curve,
   a. the harder it is for fiscal policy to change real GDP in the short run.
   b. the easier it is for fiscal policy to change real GDP in the short run.
   c. the harder it is for monetary policy to change real GDP in the short run.
   d. the easier it is for monetary policy to change real GDP in the short run.
   e. both b and d are true.

9. If a reduction in the money supply were desired to slow inflation, the Bank of Canada might
   a. decrease the bank rate.
   b. buy government bonds on the open market.
   c. raise the bank rate.
   d. do either b or c.

10. The Bank of Canada increasing the money supply will cause an increase in aggregate demand because
   a. real interest rates will fall, stimulating business investment and consumer purchases.
   b. the dollar will depreciate on the foreign exchange market, leading to an increase in net exports.
   c. lower interest rates will tend to increase asset prices, which increases wealth and thereby stimulates current consumption.
   d. of all the above reasons.

11. Which one of the following would be the most appropriate stabilization policy if the economy is operating beyond its long-run potential capacity?
   a. an increase in the bank rate
   b. an increase in government purchases, holding taxes constant
   c. a purchase of bonds by the Bank of Canada
   d. a reduction in taxes, holding government purchases constant

12. In the long run, a sustained increase in growth of the money supply relative to the growth rate of potential real output will most likely
   a. cause the nominal interest rate to fall.
   b. cause the real interest rate to fall.
   c. reduce the natural rate of unemployment.
   d. increase real output growth.
   e. do none of the above.

13. Which of the following would tend to reduce the price level?
   a. a chartered bank using excess reserves to extend a loan to a customer
   b. a chartered bank purchasing government securities from an individual as an investment
   c. an increase in the bank rate
   d. a purchase of government securities by the Bank of Canada

Section 13.3

14. Compared to fiscal policy, which of the following is an advantage of using monetary policy to attain macroeconomic goals?
   a. It takes a long time for fiscal policy to have an effect on the economy, but the effects of monetary policy are immediate.
   b. The effects of monetary policy are certain and predictable, whereas the effects of fiscal policy are not.
   c. The implementation of monetary policy is not slowed down by the same budgetary process as fiscal policy.
   d. The economists that help conduct monetary policy are smarter than those who help with fiscal policy.

15. An important limitation of monetary policy is that
   a. it is conducted by people in Parliament who are under pressure to get re-elected.
   b. when the Bank of Canada tries to buy bonds, it is often unable to find a seller.
   c. when the Bank of Canada tries to sell bonds, it is often unable to find a buyer.
   d. it must be conducted through the chartered banking system, and the Bank of Canada cannot always make banks do what it wants them to do.

Section 13.4

16. If output prices rise faster than money wages, the likely result will be that
   a. real wages will fall, as will the unemployment rate.
   b. real wages will fall, and the unemployment rate will rise.
   c. real wages will rise, as will the unemployment rate.
   d. real wages will rise, and the unemployment rate will fall.

17. According to the Phillips curve, society faces a trade-off between
   a. government deficits and unemployment.
   b. inflation and unemployment.
   c. the actual unemployment rate and the natural rate of unemployment.
   d. inflation and real output.

18. If the Phillips curve is steeper at higher rates of inflation, it suggests that
   a. once the economy has relatively low unemployment rates, further reductions in the unemployment rate can occur only by accepting larger increases in the inflation rate.
   b. once the economy has relatively low unemployment rates, further reductions in the unemployment rate can occur only by reducing the rate of inflation.
   c. only reducing the rate of inflation can reduce the high unemployment rate.
   d. when the economy is experiencing low inflation rates, the unemployment rate can be reduced only by accepting lower rates of inflation.

Problems

1. [Section 13.1]

Using the following diagram, answer questions a and b.

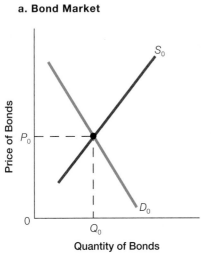 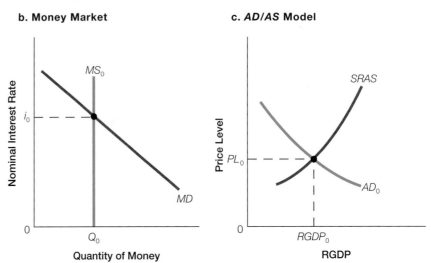

a. Bond Market

Price of Bonds

S_0

P_0

D_0

0 Q_0

Quantity of Bonds

b. Money Market

Nominal Interest Rate

MS_0

i_0

MD

0 Q_0

Quantity of Money

c. *AD/AS* Model

Price Level

$SRAS$

PL_0

AD_0

0 $RGDP_0$

RGDP

a. Show the effects in each of the indicated markets of an open market purchase of government bonds by the Bank of Canada.

b. Show the effects in each of the indicated markets of an open market sale of government bonds by the Bank of Canada.

2. [Section 13.2]

Using the following diagram, answer questions a–c.

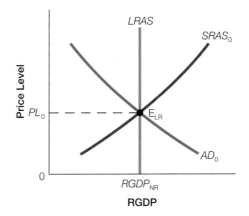

Price Level

$LRAS$

$SRAS_0$

PL_0 E_{LR}

AD_0

0

$RGDP_{NR}$

RGDP

a. On the diagram, illustrate the short-run effects of an increase in aggregate demand caused by expanding the money supply.

b. On the diagram, illustrate the long-run effects of an increase in aggregate demand caused by expanding the money supply.

14

International Trade

Canada's Merchandise Trade

- Who trades with Canada?
- What does Canada import and export?

CANADA'S TRADING PARTNERS

In its early history, Canadian international trade was largely directed towards Europe and to Great Britain in particular. Now Canada trades with a vast number of countries. Exhibit 1 shows the country's most important trading partners. The single-most important Canadian trading partner is the United States, accounting for an enormous 77 percent of our exports of goods and 65 percent of our imports of goods. Trade with countries of the European Union (EU) and Japan is also particularly important.

CANADA'S EXPORTS AND IMPORTS

Throughout its history, Canada has been a large exporter of natural resource–based products to the rest of the world. Today, as Exhibit 2 shows, Canada's exports of natural resource–based products, including agricultural and fishing products, energy products, forestry products, and industrial goods and materials, total nearly $260 billion, or about 56 percent of our exports of goods. However, Canada's exports of automotive products, and machinery and equipment total $170 billion, or about 37 percent of our exports of goods.

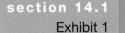

section 14.1
Exhibit 1   Major Canadian Trading Partners

Top Trading Partners— Exports of Goods in 2007		
Rank	**Country**	**Percent of Total**
1	United States	77%
2	European Union	8
3	Japan	2
4	Other countries	13

SOURCE: Statistics Canada.

Top Trading Partners— Imports of Goods in 2007		
Rank	**Country**	**Percent of Total**
1	United States	65%
2	European Union	10
3	Japan	3
4	Other countries	22

SOURCE: Statistics Canada.

section 14.1
Exhibit 2   Canada's Exports and Imports by Category of Good, 2007

	Exports (billions of dollars)	Percent of Total	Imports (billions of dollars)	Percent of Total	Trade Balance (billions of dollars)
Agricultural and fishing products	$34.4	7.4%	$25.5	6.1%	$ 8.9
Energy products	91.7	19.8	36.6	8.8	55.1
Forestry products	29.3	6.3	3.0	0.7	26.3
Industrial goods and materials	104.4	22.6	85.1	20.5	19.3
Machinery and equipment	93.4	20.2	116.6	28.1	−23.2
Automotive products	77.3	16.7	80.0	19.3	−2.7
Consumer goods	18.7	4.0	54.8	13.2	−36.1
Other transactions and adjustments	13.9	3.0	13.4	3.3	−0.5
Total	463.1	100.0	415.0	100.0	48.1

SOURCE: Statistics Canada.

On the import side, Canada's imports are much more concentrated on finished goods. Imports of machinery and equipment, automotive products, and consumer goods total $116 billion, $80 billion, and $54 billion, respectively, and account for 60 percent of our imports of goods.

When we compare the trade balance (exports of goods minus imports of goods) for the major categories of goods, we can see that the largest trade surpluses exist for energy products ($55.1 billion), forestry products ($26.3 billion), and industrial goods and materials ($19.3 billion). By far, the largest trade deficit is in the consumer goods category ($36.1 billion).

Section Check

1. Our single-most important trading partner, the United States, accounts for 77 percent of our exports and 65 percent of our imports. Trade with Japan and the countries of the European Union is also particularly important to Canada.
2. Exports of natural resource-based products make up over one-half of our exports of goods. Our imports are concentrated in finished goods, like machinery and equipment, automotive products, and consumer goods.

International Trade Agreements

section 14.2

- What has happened to the volume of international trade over time?
- What international trade agreements is Canada involved in?

IMPACT OF INTERNATIONAL TRADE FOR CANADA

In a typical year, about 15 percent of the world's output is traded in international markets. Of course, the importance of the international sector varies enormously from country to country. Some nations are almost closed economies (no interaction with other economies), with foreign trade equalling only a very small portion (perhaps 5 percent) of total output. The impact of international trade on the Canadian economy is illustrated in Exhibit 1, which shows the current dollar value of Canadian exports and imports of goods and services as a percentage of GDP. As Exhibit 1 shows, the value of both exports and imports has grown from around 20 percent in the 1960s to about 35 percent of GDP for exports and 33 percent of GDP for imports in 2007. In the United States, by contrast, exports were only 12 percent of GDP, whereas imports were 17 percent of GDP, in 2007.

INTERNATIONAL TRADE AGREEMENTS

International trade agreements have been a positive force in expanding global trade, and thereby contributing to economic growth and prosperity in countries covered by such agreements. Government trade policies have contributed to the remarkable rise in international trade for Canada. Listed below are the major trade agreements to which Canada is a participant.

THE GENERAL AGREEMENT ON TARIFFS AND TRADE (GATT)

Canada and 22 other nations in 1947 signed the General Agreement on Tariffs and Trade (GATT). The objective of GATT was to reduce barriers to international trade, such as tariffs (taxes on imported goods) and quotas (government-imposed restrictions on the quantity of imports allowed). GATT was based on a few key principles. First, each member nation was to apply any tariffs equally to all countries—that is, in a nondiscriminatory

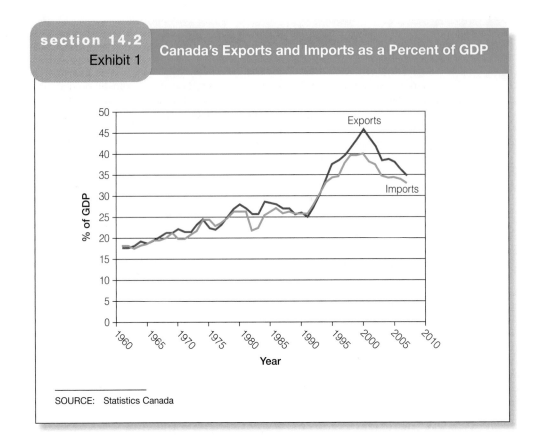

section 14.2
Exhibit 1   Canada's Exports and Imports as a Percent of GDP

SOURCE: Statistics Canada

manner. Second, reductions in tariffs were to be the result of multilateral negotiations. And third, quotas were to be eliminated and replaced by tariffs. (We will examine the economic impact of tariffs and quotas later in this chapter.)

Eight rounds of multilateral negotiations have taken place under GATT, with the last round of negotiations, called the Uruguay Round, having taken effect in 1995. That agreement eliminated or reduced trade barriers on a wide range of goods and services. It also gave the world's poorer countries greater access to markets in developed (richer) nations for textiles and garments. On the agricultural side, export subsidies were to be reduced, and import quotas on agricultural products were to be replaced by tariffs. Canadian egg and dairy farmers have had their trade protection from quotas replaced by high tariffs. Although this has protected Canadian farmers in the short run, as these tariffs are reduced over time, we would expect a higher level of Canadian imports of these products.

THE WORLD TRADE ORGANIZATION (WTO)

In 1995, GATT was replaced by the World Trade Organization (WTO), another multilateral trade organization. The WTO has over 140 nations as members, who negotiate on areas such as liberalizing trade in services, protecting intellectual property rights, and giving fair treatment to foreign investment. Member countries have their international trade disputes resolved by a WTO arbitration board. When the board makes its ruling, the losing country must comply with the ruling. If it does not comply, the winning country can impose trade sanctions on the losing country.

THE EUROPEAN UNION (EU)

In addition to multilateral trade agreements, there are also a large number of regional trade agreements in effect around the world. The largest such trading bloc is the European Union (EU), consisting of 25 European nations, including France, Germany, Italy, and the United Kingdom. An important aspect of the EU is that it allows for the free movement of labour and capital between member nations. As well, nearly all products are traded freely among member nations, and there is a common system of tariffs for goods from outside the EU.

NORTH AMERICAN FREE TRADE

Canada's first major bilateral trade agreement was the Canada–U.S. Free Trade Agreement (FTA), which came into effect in 1989. It called for the reduction or elimination of tariffs and other barriers to trade, free trade in energy products, freer trade in services, and a reduction in subsidies. As well, it set up a dispute-settlement mechanism to resolve trade disputes between the two countries. This free trade agreement, in particular, has had a significant impact on the volume of exports and imports for Canada. Since 1989, Canadian exports and imports have increased sharply, as shown in Exhibit 1, with virtually all this rise the result of increased trade with the United States.

In 1994, the Canada–U.S. Free Trade Agreement was replaced by the North American Free Trade Agreement (NAFTA), creating a trading bloc for Canada, the United States, and Mexico. NAFTA's objectives are to eliminate trade barriers between the three countries over a 15-year period, promote fair competition, increase investment opportunities, protect intellectual property rights, and resolve trade disputes.

Since 1994, as expected, Canada's exports and imports with the United States and Mexico have increased substantially. There have been concerns, however, about the impact of free trade with Mexico on Canadian industries and workers. Mexico's lower labour and environmental standards, as well as fears that Canadian businesses would relocate to Mexico to take advantage of the lower wages there, were often discussed. Economists, however, have tried to emphasize the benefits to Canada of freer trade that result from increased specialization and exchange (a topic we look at in the next section). There certainly have been labour market adjustments in Canada since NAFTA, as some Canadian industries have contracted, resulting in reduced employment in those sectors. At the same time, however, the United States and Mexico represent a combined market of almost 400 million people, providing many Canadian businesses with the opportunity to expand their sales and create additional jobs in Canada. In addition to NAFTA, Canada has also entered into bilateral agreements with several other economies including: Israel (Canada–Israel Free Trade Agreement—1997), Chile (Canada–Chile Free Trade Agreement—1997), Costa Rica (Canada–Costa Rica Free Trade Agreement—2002), and the European Union (Canada–European Free Trade Agreement—2008).

Section Check

1. The volume of international trade has increased substantially in Canada over the last 50 years. During that time, exports and imports have grown from about 20 percent of GDP to about 35 percent.
2. A major reason why Canada has experienced a rise in international trade is the numerous trade agreements in which Canada is an active participant.

Comparative Advantage and Gains from Trade

■ Does voluntary trade lead to an improvement in economic welfare?
■ What is the principle of comparative advantage?
■ What benefits are derived from specialization?

ECONOMIC GROWTH AND TRADE

Using simple logic, we conclude that the very existence of trade suggests that trade is economically beneficial. This is true if one assumes that people are utility maximizers and are rational and intelligent, and engage in trade on a voluntary basis. Because almost all trade is voluntary, it would seem that trade occurs because the participants feel that they are better off because of the trade. Both participants of an exchange of goods and services anticipate an improvement in their economic welfare. Sometimes, of course, anticipations are not realized (because the world is uncertain), but the motive behind trade remains an expectation of some enhancement in utility or satisfaction by both parties.

Granted, "trade must be good because people do it" is a rather simplistic explanation. The classical economist David Ricardo is usually given most of the credit for developing the economic theory that more precisely explains how trade can be mutually beneficial to both parties, raising output and income levels in the entire trading area.

THE PRINCIPLE OF COMPARATIVE ADVANTAGE

Ricardo's theory of international trade centres on the concept of comparative advantage. A person, a region, or a country can gain by specializing in the production of the good in which they have a comparative advantage. That is, if they can produce a good or service at a lower opportunity cost than others, we say that they have a **comparative advantage** in the production of that good or service. In other words, a country or a region should specialize in producing and selling those items that it can produce at a lower opportunity cost than other regions or countries.

comparative advantage *occurs when a person or a country can produce a good or service at a lower opportunity cost than others*

Comparative advantage analysis does not mean that nations or areas that export goods will necessarily be able to produce those goods or services more cheaply than other nations in an absolute sense. What is important is *comparative* advantage, not *absolute* advantage. For example, Canada may be able to produce more clothing per worker than India, but that does not mean Canada should necessarily sell clothing to India. Indeed, Canada has an absolute advantage or productive superiority over India in nearly every good, given the higher levels of output per person in Canada. Yet India's inferiority in producing some goods is much less than for others. In goods where India's productivity is only slightly less than that of Canada, such as perhaps in clothing, it probably has a comparative advantage over Canada. How? For a highly productive nation to produce goods in which it is only marginally more productive than other nations, the nation must take resources from the production of other goods in which its productive abilities are markedly superior. As a result, the opportunity costs in India of making clothing may be less than in Canada. With that, both can gain from trade, despite potential absolute advantages for every good in Canada.

COMPARATIVE ADVANTAGE AND THE PRODUCTION POSSIBILITIES CURVE

To help illustrate the concepts involved, the principle of comparative advantage can be applied to trading areas. In fact, trade has evolved in large part because different geographic areas have different resources and therefore different production possibilities. In Exhibit 1, we show the production possibilities curves for two trading areas. A "trading area" may be a locality, a region, or (as in this example) a nation. We see that if Canada devotes all its resources to producing food, it can produce 40 kilograms of food per day; if it devotes all its resources to producing cloth, it can produce 100 metres of cloth per day. We also see that when India uses all its resources to produce food, it can only produce 30 kilograms per day, and when it uses all its resources to produce cloth, it can produce 30 metres per day.

Canada and India have various potential combinations of food and cloth that they can produce. For each region, the cost of producing more food is the output of cloth that must be forgone, and vise versa. We see in Exhibit 1 that Canada can produce more food (40 kilograms per day) and more cloth (100 metres per day) than India can (30 kilograms and 30 metres per day, respectively), perhaps reflecting superior resources (more or better labour, more land, and so on). This means that Canada has an absolute advantage in both products.

Suppose that, before specialization, Canada chooses to produce 75 metres of cloth and 10 kilograms of food per day. Similarly, suppose India decides to produce 12 metres of cloth and 18 kilograms of food per day. Collectively, then, the two areas are producing 87 metres of cloth (75 + 12) and 28 kilograms of food (10 + 18) per day before specialization.

Looking at Exhibit 2, now suppose the two nations specialize. Canada decides to specialize in cloth and devotes all its resources to making that product. As a result, cloth output in Canada rises to 100 metres per day, some of which is sold to India. India, in turn, devotes all its resources to food, producing 30 kilograms of food per day and selling some of it to Canada. Together, the two nations are producing more of both cloth and food than before—100 metres instead of 87 metres of cloth and 30 kilograms instead of 28 kilograms of food per day. Both areas could, as a result, have more of both products than before they began specializing and trading.

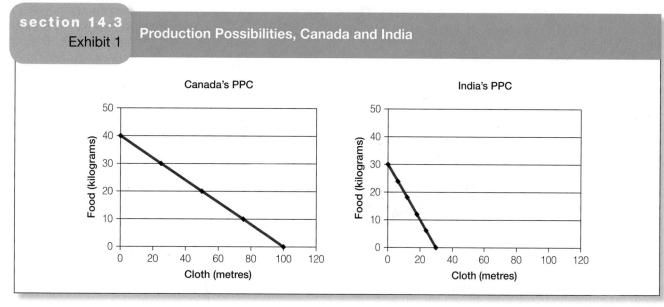

section 14.3
Exhibit 1 **Production Possibilities, Canada and India**

ACTIVE LEARNING EXERCISE

section 14.3
Exhibit 2
Specialization and Trade

Region	Food	Cloth
Canada	(kilograms per day)	(metres per day)
	0	100
	10	75
	20	50
	30	25
	40	0
India	0	30
	6	24
	12	18
	18	12
	24	6
	30	0
Before Specialization		
Canada	10	75
India	18	12
Total	28	87
After Specialization		
Canada	0	100
India	30	0
Total	30	100

How can this happen? In Canada, the opportunity cost of producing food is very high—25 metres of cloth must be forgone to get 10 more kilograms of food. The cost of 1 kilogram of food is 2.5 metres of cloth (25 divided by 10). In India, by contrast, the opportunity cost of producing 6 more kilograms of food is six metres of cloth that must be forgone; so the cost of 1 kilogram of food is 1 metre of cloth. In Canada, a kilogram of food costs 2.5 metres of cloth, whereas in India the same amount of food costs only 1 metre of cloth. Food is more costly in Canada in terms of cloth forgone than in India, so India has a comparative advantage in food even though Canada has an absolute advantage in food.

With respect to cloth production, an increase in output by 25 metres, say, from 25 to 50 metres, costs 10 kilograms of food forgone in Canada. The cost of one more metre of cloth is 0.4 kilograms of food (10 divided by 25). In India, the cost of 1 metre of cloth is 1 kilogram of food. Cloth is more costly (in terms of opportunity cost) in India and cheaper in Canada, so Canada has a comparative advantage in the production of cloth.

Thus, by specializing in products in which it has a comparative advantage, an area has the potential of consuming more goods and services, assuming it trades the additional output for other desirable goods and services that others can produce at a lower opportunity cost. In the scenario presented here, the people in Canada would

ACTIVE LEARNING EXERCISE

COMPARATIVE ADVANTAGE AND ABSOLUTE ADVANTAGE

Q: Renée, a successful artist, can complete one painting in each 40-hour workweek. Each painting sells for $3000. As a result of her enormous success, however, Renée is swamped in paperwork. To solve the problem, Renée hires Drake to handle all of the bookkeeping and typing associated with buying supplies, answering inquiries from prospective buyers and dealers, writing art galleries, and so forth. Renée pays Drake $400 per week for his work. After a couple of weeks in this arrangement, Renée realizes that she can handle Drake's chores more quickly than Drake does. In fact, she estimates that she is twice as fast as Drake, completing in 20 hours what it takes Drake 40 hours to complete. Should Renée fire Drake?

A: Clearly Renée has an absolute advantage over Drake in both painting and paperwork because she can do twice as much paperwork in 40 hours as

Drake can, and Drake can't paint well at all. Still, it would be foolish for Renée to do both jobs. If Renée did her own paperwork, it would take her 20 hours per week, leaving her only 20 hours to paint. Because each watercolour takes 40 hours to paint, Renée's output would fall from one painting per week to one painting every two weeks.

When Drake works for her, Renée's net income is $2600 per week ($3000 per painting minus $400 in Drake's wages); when Drake does not work for her, it is only $1500 per week (one painting every two weeks). Although Renée is both a better painter and better at Drake's chores than Drake, it pays for her to specialize in painting, in which she has a comparative advantage, and allow Drake to do the paperwork. The opportunity cost to Renée of paperwork is high. For Drake, who lacks skills as a painter, the opportunity costs of doing the paperwork are much less.

In The **NEWS**

THE MIRACLE OF TRADE

It is mere common sense that if one country is very good at making hats, and another is very good at making shoes, then total output can be increased by arranging for the first country to concentrate on making hats and the second on making shoes. Then, through trade in both goods, more of each can be consumed in both places.

That is a tale of absolute advantage. . . . Each country is better than the other at making a certain good, and so profits from specialization and trade. Comparative advantage is different: a country will have it despite being bad at the activity concerned. Indeed, it can have a comparative advantage in making a certain good even if it is worse at making that good than any other country.

This is not economic theory, but a straightforward matter of definition: a country has a comparative advantage where its margin of superiority is greater, or its margin of inferiority smaller.

[W]hen people say of Africa, or Britain, or wherever, that it has no comparative advantage in anything, they are simply confusing absolute advantage (for which their claim may or may not be true) with comparative advantage (for which it is certainly false).

Why does this confusion over terms matter? Because the case for free trade is often thought to depend on the existence of absolute advantage and is therefore thought to collapse whenever absolute advantage is absent. But economics shows that gains from trade follow, in fact, from comparative advantage. Since comparative advantage is never absent, this gives the theory far broader scope than more popular critics suppose.

In particular, it shows that even countries which are desperately bad at making everything can expect to gain from international competition. If countries specialize according to their comparative advantage, they can prosper through trade regardless of how inefficient, in absolute terms, they may be in their chosen specialty.

SOURCE: "The Miracle of Trade," *The Economist*, January 27, 1996, pp. 61, 62. ECONOMIST by The Economist. Copyright 1996 by Economist Newspaper Group. Reproduced with permission of Economist Newspaper Group in the format Textbook via Copyright Clearance Center.

CONSIDER THIS:

The gains from trade are based on comparative advantage, not absolute advantage. Canada, a rich country based on absolute advantage, can gain from trade, as can Mexico, a poor country, gain from trade.

specialize in cloth, and the people in India would specialize in food. If Canada exports 20 metres of cloth and imports 11 kilograms of food, it can consume 80 metres of cloth and 11 kilograms of food after trade. Likewise, if India exports 11 kilograms of food and imports 20 metres of cloth, it can consume 20 metres of cloth and 19 kilograms of food after trade. We can see from this example that specialization increases both the division of labour and the interdependence among nations.

Section Check

1. Voluntary trade occurs because the participants feel that they are better off because of the trade.
2. A nation, a geographic area, or even a person can gain from trade if the good or service is produced relatively cheaper than anyone else can produce it. That is, an area should specialize in producing and selling those items that it can produce at a lower opportunity cost than others.
3. Through trade and specialization in products in which it has a comparative advantage, a country can enjoy a greater array of goods and services at a lower cost.

section 14.4

Supply and Demand in International Trade

■ What is consumer surplus?

■ What is producer surplus?

■ Who benefits and who loses when a country becomes an exporter?

■ Who benefits and who loses when a country becomes an importer?

consumer surplus
the difference between what the consumer is willing and able to pay and what the consumer actually pays for a quantity of a good or service

producer surplus
the difference between the lowest price at which a supplier is willing and able to supply a good or service and the actual price received for a given quantity of a good or service

THE IMPORTANCE OF TRADE: PRODUCER AND CONSUMER SURPLUS

The difference between the most a consumer would be willing to pay for a quantity of a good and what a consumer actually has to pay is called **consumer surplus.** The difference between the lowest price a supplier is willing to supply a quantity of a good or service for and the price a supplier actually receives for selling it is called **producer surplus.** With the tools of consumer and producer surplus, we can better analyze the impact of trade. Who gains? Who loses? What happens to net welfare?

The demand curve represents maximum prices that consumers are willing and able to pay for different quantities of a good or service; the supply curve represents minimum prices suppliers require to be willing to supply different quantities of that good or service. In Exhibit 1, for example, for the first unit of output, the consumer is willing to pay up to $7 and the producer would demand at least $1 for producing that unit. However, the equilibrium price is $4, as indicated by the intersection of the supply and demand curves. It is clear that the two would gain from getting together and trading that unit because the consumer would receive $3 of consumer surplus ($7 − $4) and the producer would receive $3 of producer surplus ($4 − $1). Both would also benefit from trading the second and third unit of output—in fact, from every unit up to the equilibrium output. Once the equilibrium output is reached at the equilibrium price, all of the mutually beneficial opportunities from trade between suppliers and demanders will have taken place; the sum of consumer surplus and producer surplus is maximized.

It is important to recognize that the total gains to the economy from trade are the sum of consumer and producer surplus. That is, consumers benefit from additional amounts of consumer surplus and producers benefit from additional amounts of producer surplus.

section 14.4 Exhibit 1	Consumer and Producer Surplus

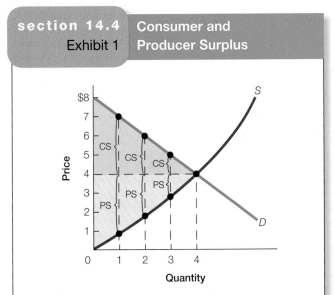

Consumer surplus is the difference between the price a consumer has to pay ($4) and the price the consumer is willing to pay. For unit 1, consumer surplus is $3 ($7 − $4). Producer surplus is the difference between the price a seller receives for selling a good or service ($4) and the price at which he is willing to supply that good or service. For unit 1, producer surplus is $3 ($4 − $1).

FREE TRADE AND EXPORTS—DOMESTIC PRODUCERS GAIN MORE THAN DOMESTIC CONSUMERS LOSE

Using the concepts of consumer and producer surplus, we can graphically show the net benefits of free trade. Imagine an economy with no trade, where the equilibrium price, P_{BT},

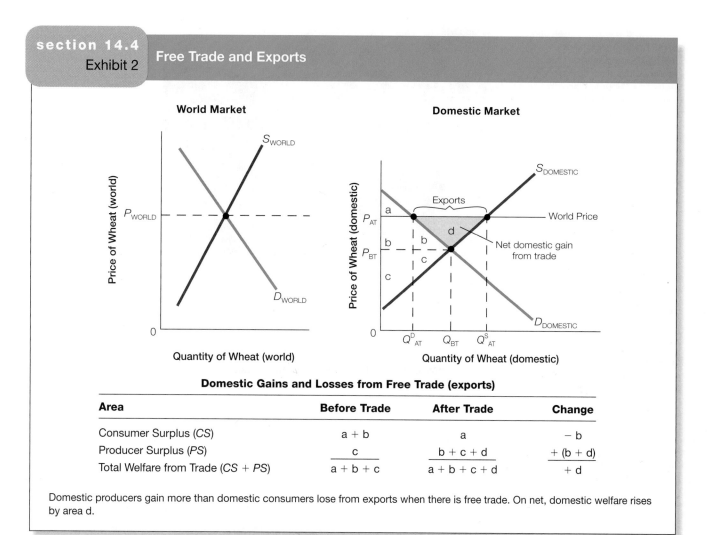

World Market

Domestic Market

Domestic Gains and Losses from Free Trade (exports)

Area	Before Trade	After Trade	Change
Consumer Surplus (*CS*)	a + b	a	− b
Producer Surplus (*PS*)	c	b + c + d	+ (b + d)
Total Welfare from Trade (*CS* + *PS*)	a + b + c	a + b + c + d	+ d

Domestic producers gain more than domestic consumers lose from exports when there is free trade. On net, domestic welfare rises by area d.

and the equilibrium quantity, Q_{BT}, of wheat are determined exclusively in the domestic economy, as seen in Exhibit 2. Say that this imaginary economy decides to engage in free trade. You can see that the world price (established in the world market for wheat), P_{WORLD}, is higher than the domestic price before trade, P_{BT}. In other words, the domestic economy has a comparative advantage in wheat because it can produce wheat at a lower relative price than the rest of the world. So this wheat-producing country sells some wheat to the domestic market and some wheat to the world market, all at the going world price.

The price after trade (P_{AT}) is higher than the price before trade (P_{BT}). Because the world market is huge, the demand from the rest of the world at the world price (P_{WORLD}) is assumed to be perfectly elastic. That is, domestic wheat farmers can sell all the wheat they want at the world price. If you were a wheat farmer in Saskatchewan, would you rather sell all of your bushels of wheat at the higher world price or the lower domestic price? As a wheat farmer, you would surely prefer the higher world price. But this is not good news for domestic cereal and bread eaters, who now have to pay more for products made with wheat, because P_{AT} is greater than P_{BT}.

Graphically, we can see how free trade and exports affect both domestic consumers and domestic producers. At the higher world price, P_{AT}, domestic producers supply Q_{AT}^{S}, whereas domestic consumers demand Q_{AT}^{D}. The difference between these two quantities is the amount of wheat exported to the world market. At the higher world price, P_{AT}, domestic wheat producers are receiving larger amounts of producer surplus. Before trade, they received a surplus equal to area c; after trade, they received surplus b + c + d, for a

In 1993, the North American Free Trade Agreement (NAFTA) was passed. This lowered the trade barriers between Mexico, Canada, and the United States. Proponents of freer trade, especially economists, viewed the agreement as a way to gain greater wealth through specialization and trade for all three countries—one of our ten powerful ideas. Opponents thought the agreement would take away Canadian and U.S. jobs and lower living standards.

© PHOTOPIA

net gain of area b + d. However, part of the domestic producers' gain comes at domestic consumers' expense. Specifically, consumers had a consumer surplus equal to area a + b before the trade (at P_{BT}), but they now only have area a (at P_{AT})—a loss of area b.

Area b reflects a redistribution of income because producers are gaining exactly what consumers are losing. Is that good or bad? We can't say objectively whether consumers or producers are more deserving. However, the net benefits from allowing free trade and exports are clearly visible in area d. Without free trade, no one gets area d. That is, on net, members of the domestic society gain when domestic wheat producers are able to sell their wheat at the higher world price. Although domestic wheat consumers lose from the free trade, those negative effects are more than offset by the positive gains captured by producers. Area d is the net increase in domestic welfare (the welfare gain) from free trade and exports.

FREE TRADE AND IMPORTS—DOMESTIC CONSUMERS GAIN MORE THAN DOMESTIC PRODUCERS LOSE

Now suppose that our economy does not produce shirts as well as other countries of the world. In other words, other countries have a comparative advantage in producing shirts. This means that the domestic price for shirts is above the world price. This scenario is illustrated in Exhibit 3. At the new, lower world price, the domestic producer will supply quantity Q_{AT}^S. However, at the lower world price, the domestic producers will not produce the entire amount demanded by domestic consumers, Q_{AT}^D. At the world price, reflecting the world supply and demand for shirts, the difference between what is domestically supplied and what is domestically demanded is supplied by imports.

At the world price (established in the world market for shirts), we assume the world supply curve to the domestic market is perfectly elastic—that the producers of the world can supply all that domestic consumers are willing to buy at the going price. At the world price, Q_{AT}^S is supplied by domestic producers and the difference between Q_{AT}^D and Q_{AT}^S is imported from other countries.

Who wins and who loses from free trade and imports? Domestic consumers benefit from paying a lower price for shirts. In Exhibit 3, before trade, consumers only received area a in consumer surplus. After trade, the price fell and quantity purchased increased, causing the area of consumer surplus to increase from area a to area a + b + d, a gain of b + d. Domestic producers lose because they are now selling their shirts at the lower world price, P_{AT}. The producer surplus before trade was b + c. After trade, the producer surplus falls to area c, reducing producer surplus by area b. Area b, then, represents a redistribution from producers to consumers, but area d is the net increase in domestic welfare (the welfare gain) from free trade and imports.

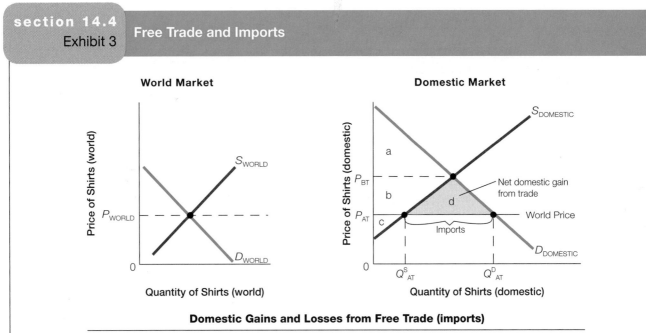

section 14.4
Exhibit 3 — Free Trade and Imports

World Market

Price of Shirts (world) — S_{WORLD}

P_{WORLD}

D_{WORLD}

0 — Quantity of Shirts (world)

Domestic Market

Price of Shirts (domestic) — $S_{DOMESTIC}$

a

P_{BT}

b

d — Net domestic gain from trade

P_{AT} — c — World Price

Imports

$D_{DOMESTIC}$

0 — Q^S_{AT} — Q^D_{AT} — Quantity of Shirts (domestic)

Domestic Gains and Losses from Free Trade (imports)

Area	Before Trade	After Trade	Change
Consumer Surplus (CS)	a	a + b + d	+ (b + d)
Producer Surplus (PS)	b + c	c	− b
Total Welfare from Trade (CS + PS)	a + b + c	a + b + c + d	+ d

Domestic consumers gain more than domestic producers lose from imports when there is free trade. On net, domestic welfare rises by area d.

In The **NEWS**

GLOBALIZATION IS NOT KILLING CANADIAN WELL-PAID JOBS

BY ERIC BEAUCHESNE

Fears that globalization has led to the loss of well-paying Canadian jobs to low-wage countries have been overblown, two new reports suggest.

While that may change, in part because the stronger dollar is making Canada a more expensive place to do business, Statistics Canada said there's little evidence so far that highly skilled service sector jobs are being outsourced.

"Recent media reports in the United States and in Canada have raised the possibility that new forms of outsourcing, involving service sector positions with high skill requirements, may be driving jobs offshore and contribute to the elimination of well-paid jobs in Canada," the federal agency said [in January 2005].

"Although this study does not directly examine the link between outsourcing and job loss, it finds little evidence that

well-paid jobs have been disappearing in Canada in recent years or since the early 1980s."

The federal agency's suspicion that Canada is not losing good jobs to outsourcing was reinforced by a separate private sector report. . . .

That report, based on a survey of over 1,300 CEOs around the world by PricewaterhouseCoopers, found that Canadian corporate bosses were less likely than their global counterparts to outsource jobs to low-wage countries or to see that as a cost-saving move or one that would give them a competitive edge.

Currently 23 percent of Canadian CEOs said they have outsourced jobs, compared with 28 percent of CEOs globally.

Further, only 30 percent of Canadian CEOs, compared with 46 percent of American CEOs, believe that outsourcing reduces costs, it said. And only 23 percent of Canadians believe outsourcing would give them a competitive advantage, compared with 32 percent of American bosses.

(continued)

IN THE NEWS *(continued)*

"A lot of it boils down to the cost differential," said PwC's Robert Scott.

"It's generally been cheaper to do business in Canada than the U.S. . . . and the price differential between Canada and some of the low-cost centres was not as high," he said.

However, he said there's evidence that outsourcing by Canadian companies may be on the increase, in part because the stronger Canadian dollar has boosted relative employment costs.

But the proportion of Canadian CEOs who were looking at outsourcing as a future business strategy at the time of the survey [in 2004] was still a small minority of only 14 percent, Scott noted.

Statistics Canada's suspicion that Canada isn't outsourcing good jobs is because the proportion of Canadian workers with good paying jobs—those earning $30 an hour or more in inflation-adjusted dollars—has increased almost steadily over the past two decades, and especially since 1997.

In 2004, 11.4 percent of workers earned $30 or more an hour, up from 9.4 percent in 1997 and 8.5 percent in 1981.

Also, the proportion holding the poorest paying jobs—less than $10 an hour—has eased slightly over the past two decades to 15.7 percent.

While the real wages of Canadian workers have changed little over the last two decades, despite their growing experience and educational attainment, the relative importance of well-paid jobs in the Canadian labour market did not decline.

But the quality of jobs for younger workers has deteriorated.

"For instance, newly hired men aged 25 to 64 saw their median wages drop 13 percent between 1981 and 2004," it said.

SOURCE: Adapted from Eric Beauchesne, "Globalization Has Not Yet Cost Canada Well-Paid Jobs," *Edmonton Journal*, January 27, 2005, p. G1. Reprinted with permission by Canwest News Service.

CONSIDER THIS:
There is little evidence that well-paid jobs have been disappearing in Canada in recent years due to NAFTA or globalization. The proportion of Canadian workers earning $30 or more an hour (in constant dollars) has increased from 8.5 percent in the 1980s to 11.4 percent in 2004.

Section Check

1. The difference between what a consumer is willing and able to pay and what a consumer actually has to pay is called consumer surplus.
2. The difference between what a supplier is willing and able to receive and the price a supplier actually receives for selling a good or service is called producer surplus.
3. With free trade and exports, domestic producers gain more than domestic consumers lose.
4. With free trade and imports, domestic consumers gain more than domestic producers lose.

---

section

14.5   Tariffs, Import Quotas, and Subsidies

- What is a tariff?
- What are the effects of a tariff?
- What are the effects of an import quota?
- What is the economic impact of subsidies?

TARIFFS

A **tariff** is a tax on imported goods. Tariffs are usually relatively small revenue producers that retard the expansion of trade. They bring about higher prices and revenues to domestic producers, and lower sales and revenues to foreign producers. Moreover, tariffs lead to higher prices for domestic consumers. In fact, the gains to producers are more than offset by the loss to consumers. Let us see how this works graphically.

tariff
a tax on imports

THE DOMESTIC ECONOMIC IMPACT OF TARIFFS

The domestic economic impact of tariffs is presented in Exhibit 1, which illustrates the supply and demand curves for domestic consumers and producers of shoes. In a typical international supply and demand illustration, the intersection of the world supply and demand curves would determine the domestic market price. However, with import tariffs, the domestic price of shoes is greater than the world price, as in Exhibit 1. We consider the world supply curve (S_{WORLD}) to domestic consumers to be perfectly elastic; that is, we can buy all we want at the world price (P_{WORLD}). At the world price, domestic producers are only willing to provide quantity Q_S, but domestic consumers are willing to buy quantity Q_D—more than domestic producers are willing to supply. Imports make up the difference.

section 14.5
Exhibit 1   **Free Trade and Tariffs**

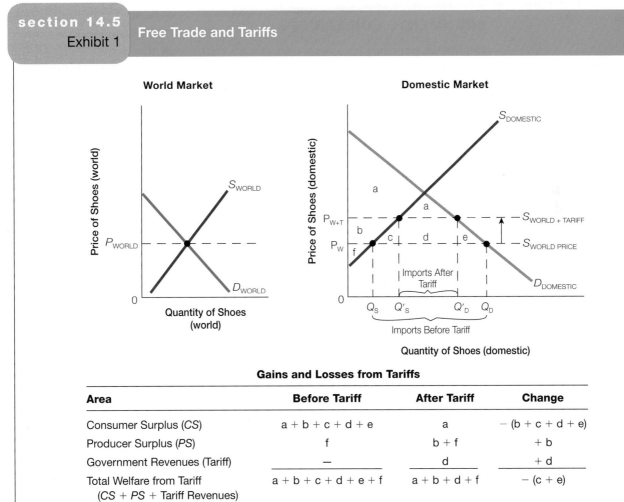

Gains and Losses from Tariffs

Area	Before Tariff	After Tariff	Change
Consumer Surplus (*CS*)	a + b + c + d + e	a	− (b + c + d + e)
Producer Surplus (*PS*)	f	b + f	+ b
Government Revenues (Tariff)	—	d	+ d
Total Welfare from Tariff (*CS* + *PS* + Tariff Revenues)	a + b + c + d + e + f	a + b + d + f	− (c + e)

In the case of a tariff, we see that consumers lose more than producers and government gain. On net, the deadweight loss associated with the new tariff is represented by area c + e.

As you can see in Exhibit 1, the imposition of the tariff shifts up the perfectly elastic supply curve from foreigners to domestic consumers from S_{WORLD} to $S_{WORLD + TARIFF}$, but it does not alter the domestic supply or demand curve. At the resulting higher domestic price (P_{W+T}), domestic suppliers are willing to supply more, Q'_S, but domestic consumers are willing to buy less, Q'_D, reducing the quantity of imported shoes. Overall, then, tariffs lead to: (1) a smaller total quantity sold; (2) a higher price for shoes for domestic consumers; (3) greater sales of shoes at higher prices for domestic producers; and (4) lower sales of foreign shoes.

Although domestic producers do gain more sales and higher earnings, consumers lose much more. The increase in price from the tariff results in a loss in consumer surplus, as shown in Exhibit 1. After the tariff, shoe prices rise to P_{W+T}, and, consequently, consumer surplus falls by area b + c + d + e, representing the welfare loss to consumers from the tariff. Area b in Exhibit 1 shows the gain to domestic producers as a result of the tariff. That is, at the higher price, domestic producers are willing to supply more shoes, representing a welfare gain to producers resulting from the tariff. As a result of the tariff revenues, government gains area d. This is the import tariff—the revenue government collects on imports. However, we see from Exhibit 1 that consumers lose more than producers and government gain from the tariff. That is, on net, the deadweight loss associated with the tariff is represented by area c + e.

ARGUMENTS FOR TARIFFS

Despite the preceding arguments against trade restrictions, they continue to be levied. Some rationale for their existence is necessary. Three common arguments for the use of trade restrictions deserve our critical examination.

Temporary Trade Restrictions Help Infant Industries Grow

A country might argue that a protective tariff will allow a new industry to more quickly reach a scale of operation at which economies of scale and production efficiencies can be realized. That is, temporarily shielding the young industry from competition from foreign firms will allow the infant industry a chance to grow. With the early protection, these firms will eventually be able to compete effectively in the global market. It is presumed that without this protection, the industry could never get on its feet. At first hearing, the argument sounds valid, but there are many problems with it. How do you identify "infant industries" that genuinely have potential economies of scale and will quickly become efficient with protection? We do not know the long-run average total cost curves of industries, a necessary piece of information. Moreover, if firms and governments are truly convinced of the advantages of allowing an industry to reach a large scale, would it not be wise to make massive loans to the industry, allowing it to instantly begin large-scale production rather than slowly and at the expense of consumers? In other words, the goal of allowing the industry to reach its efficient size can be reached without protection. Finally, the history of infant industry tariffs suggests that the tariffs often linger long after the industry is mature and no longer in need of protection.

Tariffs Can Reduce Domestic Unemployment

Exhibit 1 showed how tariffs increase output by domestic producers, thus leading to increased employment and reduced unemployment in industries where tariffs were imposed. Yet the overall employment effects of a tariff imposition are not likely to be positive; the argument is incorrect. Why? First, the imposition of a tariff by Canada on, say, foreign steel is going to be noticed in the countries adversely affected by the tariff. If a new tariff on steel lowers Japanese steel sales to Canada, the Japanese likely will retaliate by imposing tariffs on Canadian exports to Japan, say, on beef exports. The retaliatory tariff will lower Canadian sales of beef and thus employment in the Canadian beef industry. As a result, the gain in employment in the steel industry will be offset by a loss of employment elsewhere.

Even if the other countries did not retaliate, Canadian employment would likely suffer outside the industry gaining the tariff protection. The way that other countries pay for Canadian goods is by getting Canadian dollars from sales to Canada—imports to us. If new tariffs lead to restrictions on imports, fewer Canadian dollars will be flowing overseas in payment for imports, which means that foreigners will have fewer Canadian dollars available to buy our exports. Other things being equal, this will tend to reduce our exports, thus creating unemployment in the export industries.

Tariffs Are Necessary for National Security Reasons

Sometimes it is argued that tariffs are a means of preventing a nation from becoming too dependent on foreign suppliers of goods vital to national security. That is, by making foreign goods more expensive, we can protect domestic suppliers. For example, if oil is vital to running planes and tanks, a cutoff of foreign supplies of oil during wartime could cripple a nation's defences.

In The NEWS

CANADIAN FIRMS SURVIVE THE DROP IN TARIFFS UNDER THE CANADA-U.S. FREE TRADE AGREEMENT

BY ERIC BEAUCHESNE

The reduction in tariffs between Canada and the United States under free trade boosted the odds of survival for more than two-thirds of Canadian manufacturing firms, according to a . . . Statistics Canada study released [in 2004].

And those most likely to survive the drop in tariffs were firms that had relatively low levels of debt and were relatively more productive, concluded the study, which bolsters claims that, on balance, free trade has been good for Canadian businesses.

"Somewhat surprisingly, firm size does not affect the sensitivity of firms to changes in tariffs," stated the study, titled Changing Trade Barriers and Canadian Firms: Survival and Exit After the Canada–U.S. Free Trade Agreement.

"On one hand, tariff reductions effectively increase competition by exposing firms to foreign competitors in the domestic market," it noted. "This decline in protection threatens to reduce the market share of domestic firms less efficient than their foreign rivals."

"However, declining tariffs also provide domestic firms with access to foreign markets without the cost disadvantages imposed by high tariffs," it said. "Access to this larger market may be advantageous for domestic firms able to compete with foreign producers."

The report noted there was a dramatic drop in tariffs under free trade.

For example, in 1988, and just prior to the free trade deal, 21% of Canadian manufacturing industries were protected by tariffs of 10% or more, but by 1995, there were no industries in this position.

On balance, the combined Canadian and American tariff reductions were associated with an improved probability of survival for 69% of Canadian firms.

It appears higher productivity and low debt levels shelter firms from the impact of falling tariff protection, it concluded. "However, this general conclusion was not true for all firms," it noted.

The chances of survival increased significantly in industries where the reduction in U.S. tariffs was much greater than the drop in Canadian tariffs, and that was the case even for Canadian firms with lower levels of productivity and higher debt loads, it said.

SOURCE: Adapted from Eric Beauchesne, "Free Trade Benefits Canada, StatsCan Finds," *National Post*, April 29, 2004, p. FP8. Reprinted with permission by Canwest News Service.

CONSIDER THIS:

In 1988, prior to the Canada–U.S. Free Trade Agreement, 21 percent of Canadian manufacturing industries were protected by tariffs of 10 percent or more. By 1995, no Canadian industries had that level of tariff protection. The Canadian firms that were most likely to survive the drop in tariffs were firms that had relatively low levels of debt and were relatively more productive.

The national security argument is usually not valid. If a nation's own resources are depletable, tariff-imposed reliance on domestic supplies will hasten depletion of domestic reserves, making the country even *more* dependent on imports in the future. If we impose a high tariff on foreign oil to protect domestic producers, we will increase domestic output of oil in the short run, but in the process, we will deplete the stockpile of available reserves. Thus, the defence argument is often of questionable validity. From a defence standpoint, it makes more sense to use foreign oil in peacetime and perhaps stockpile "insurance" supplies so that larger domestic supplies would be available during wars.

IMPORT QUOTAS

import quota

a legal limit on the imported quantity of a good that is produced abroad and can be sold in domestic markets

Like tariffs, **import quotas** directly restrict imports, leading to reductions in trade and thus preventing nations from fully realizing their comparative advantage. The case for quotas is probably even weaker than the case for tariffs. Suppose that the Japanese have been sending 50 000 cars annually to Canada but now are told that, because of quota restrictions, they can only send 30 000 cars. If the Japanese manufacturers are allowed to determine how the quantity reduction is to occur, they will likely collude, leading to higher prices. Suppose that each producer is simply told to reduce sales by 40 percent. They will substantially raise the price of the cars to Canadians above what the 50 000 original buyers would have paid for them.

THE GOVERNMENT DOES NOT COLLECT REVENUES FROM IMPORT QUOTAS

Unlike what occurs with a tariff, the Canadian government does not collect any revenue as a result of the import quota. Despite the higher prices, the loss in consumer surplus, and the loss in government revenue, quotas come about because people often view them as being less "protectionist" than tariffs—the traditional, most maligned form of protection.

Besides the rather blunt means of curtailing imports by using tariffs and quotas, nations have devised still other, more subtle means to restrict international trade. For example, nations sometimes impose product standards, ostensibly to protect consumers against inferior merchandise. Effectively, however, sometimes those standards are simply a means to restrict foreign competition. For example, France might keep certain kinds of wine out of the country on the grounds that they were made with allegedly inferior grapes or had an inappropriate alcoholic content. Likewise, Canada might prohibit automobile imports that do not meet certain standards in terms of pollutants, safety, and fuel efficiency. Even if these standards are not intended to restrict foreign competition, the regulations may nonetheless have that impact, restricting consumer choice.

THE DOMESTIC ECONOMIC IMPACT OF AN IMPORT QUOTA

The domestic economic impact of an import quota on autos is presented in Exhibit 2. The introduction of an import quota increases the price from the world price, P_W (established in the world market for autos) to P_{W+Q}. The quota causes the price to rise above the world price. The domestic quantity demanded falls and the domestic quantity supplied rises. Consequently, the number of imports is much smaller than it would be without the import quota. Compared to free trade, domestic producers are better off but domestic consumers are worse off. Specifically, the import quota results in a gain in producer surplus of area b and a loss in consumer surplus of area b + c + d + e. However, unlike the tariff case, where the govern-

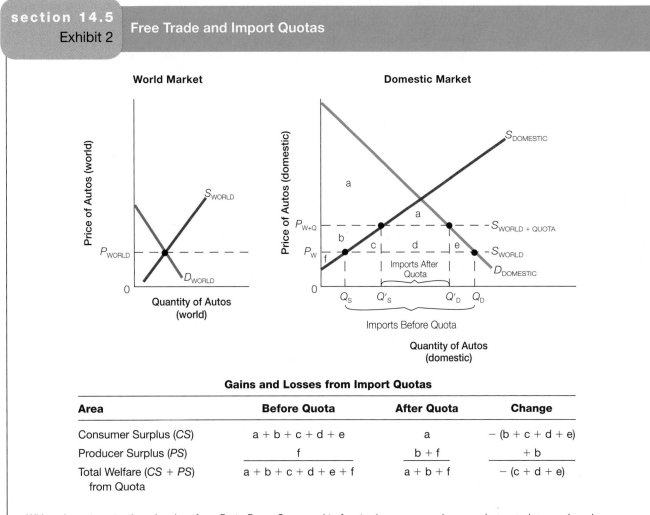

section 14.5
Exhibit 2   **Free Trade and Import Quotas**

World Market

Domestic Market

Gains and Losses from Import Quotas

Area	Before Quota	After Quota	Change
Consumer Surplus (*CS*)	a + b + c + d + e	a	− (b + c + d + e)
Producer Surplus (*PS*)	f	b + f	+ b
Total Welfare (*CS* + *PS*) from Quota	a + b + c + d + e + f	a + b + f	− (c + d + e)

With an import quota, the price rises from P_W to P_{W+Q}. Compared to free trade, consumers lose area b + c + d + e and producers gain area b. The deadweight loss from the quota is area c + d + e. Under quotas, consumers lose and producers gain. The difference in deadweight loss between quotas and tariffs is area d that the government is not able to pick up with import quotas.

ment gains area d in revenues, the government does not gain any revenues with a quota. Consequently, the deadweight loss is even greater with quotas than with tariffs. That is, on net, the deadweight loss associated with the quota is represented by area c + d + e. Recall that the deadweight loss was only c + e for tariffs.

If tariffs and import quotas hurt importing countries, why do they exist? The reason they exist is that producers can make large profits or "rents" from tariffs and import quotas. Economists call these efforts to gain profits from government protection **rent seeking.** Because this is money, time, and effort that could have been spent producing something else rather than spent on lobbying efforts, the deadweight loss from tariffs and quotas that we just illustrated will likely understate the true deadweight loss to society.

rent seeking
producer efforts to gain profits from government protections such as tariffs and import quotas

THE ECONOMIC IMPACT OF SUBSIDIES

Working in the opposite direction, governments sometimes try to encourage exports by subsidizing producers. With a subsidy, revenue is given to producers for each exported unit of output. This stimulates exports. Although not a barrier to trade like tariffs and quotas, objections can be raised that subsidies distort trade patterns and lead to inefficiencies. How does this happen? With subsidies, producers will export goods not because their costs are lower than that of a foreign competitor, but because their costs have been artificially reduced by government action, transferring income from taxpayers to the exporter. The subsidy does not reduce the actual labour, raw material, and capital costs of production—society has the same opportunity costs as before. A nation's taxpayers end up subsidizing the output of producers who, relative to producers in other countries, are inefficient. The nation, then, exports products in which it does not have a comparative advantage. Gains from trade in terms of world output are reduced by such subsidies. Thus, subsidies, usually defended as a means of increasing exports and improving a nation's international financial position, are usually of dubious worth to the world economy and even to the economy doing the subsidizing.

Section Check

1. A tariff is a tax on imported goods.
2. Tariffs bring about higher prices and revenues to domestic producers, and lower sales and revenues to foreign producers. Tariffs lead to higher prices and reduce consumer surplus for domestic consumers. Tariffs result in a net loss in welfare because the loss in consumer surplus is greater than the gain to producers and the government.
3. Arguments for the use of tariffs include: tariffs help infant industries grow; tariffs can reduce domestic unemployment; and tariffs are necessary for national security reasons.
4. Like tariffs, import quotas restrict imports, lowering consumer surplus and preventing countries from fully realizing their comparative advantage. There is a net loss in welfare from quotas, but it is proportionately larger than for a tariff because there are no government revenues.
5. Sometimes government tries to encourage production of a certain good by subsidizing its production with taxpayer dollars. Because subsidies stimulate exports, they are not a barrier to trade like tariffs and import quotas. However, they do distort trade patterns and cause overall inefficiencies.

Summary

Section 14.1
- The single-most important Canadian trading partner is the United States—it accounts for nearly 80 percent of Canadian exports and 65 percent of Canadian imports.
- Trade with Japan and countries of the European Union is also particularly important to Canada.

Section 14.2
- The volume of international trade has increased substantially in Canada over the last several decades.
- Exports and imports have grown from about 20 percent to about 35 percent of GDP.
- A major reason why international trade has experienced such dramatic growth is the various free trade agreements that Canada is involved in, most notably the North American Free Trade Agreement (NAFTA).

Section 14.3
- As economic growth occurs, regions and countries tend to specialize in what they produce best, resulting in more total output from the available scarce resources.
- A nation, a geographic area, or even a person can gain from trade if a good or service is produced relatively cheaper (a lower opportunity cost) than other areas or people can produce it.
- Through trade and specialization in products in which it has a comparative advantage, a country can consume a greater array of goods and services at a lower cost.

Section 14.4
- The difference between what a consumer is willing and able to pay and what a consumer actually has to pay is called consumer surplus.

■ The difference between what a supplier is willing and able to supply and the price a supplier receives for selling a good or service is called producer surplus.

■ With free trade and exports, domestic producers gain more than domestic consumers lose.

■ With free trade and imports, domestic consumers gain more than domestic producers lose.

Section 14.5

■ A tariff is a tax imposed on goods that brings about higher prices and revenues to domestic producers and lower sales and revenues to foreign producers.

■ Tariffs lead to higher prices and reduced consumer surplus for domestic consumers.

■ Arguments for the use of tariffs include: tariffs help infant industries grow; tariffs can reduce domestic unemployment; and tariffs are necessary for national security reasons.

■ Import quotas restrict imports, lower consumer surplus, and prevent countries from fully realizing their comparative advantage.

■ Sometimes government tries to encourage production of a certain good by subsidizing its production with taxpayer dollars.

■ Because subsidies stimulate exports, they are not a barrier to trade; however, they do distort trade patterns and cause overall inefficiencies.

Key Terms and Concepts

For a complete glossary of chapter key terms, visit the textbook's Web site at http://www.sextonmacro2e.nelson.com.

comparative advantage 360
consumer surplus 364

producer surplus 364
tariff 369

import quota 372
rent seeking 373

Review Questions

1. The following represents the production possibilities in two countries.

Country A		Country B	
Good X	**Good Y**	**Good X**	**Good Y**
0	32	0	24
4	24	4	18
8	16	8	12
12	8	12	6
16	0	16	0

Which country has a comparative advantage at producing Good X? How can you tell? Which country has a comparative advantage at producing Good Y?

2. Suppose Canada can produce cars at an opportunity cost of 2 computers for each car it produces. Suppose Mexico can produce cars at an opportunity cost of 8 computers for each car it produces. Indicate how both countries can gain from free trade.

3. Evaluate the following statement: "Small developing economies must first become self-sufficient before benefiting from international trade."

4. Evaluate the following statement: "Canada has an absolute advantage in growing wheat. Therefore, it must have a comparative advantage in growing wheat."

5. Explain why imposing a tariff causes a net welfare loss to the domestic economy.

6. If imposing tariffs and quotas harms consumers, why don't consumers vigorously oppose the implementation of these protectionist policies?

7. NAFTA (North American Free Trade Agreement) is an agreement between Canada, the United States, and Mexico to reduce trade barriers and promote the free flow of goods and services across borders. Some Canadian labour groups were opposed to NAFTA. Can you explain why? Can you predict how NAFTA might alter the goods and services produced in the participating countries?

Fill in the Blanks

Section 14.1

1. Nations import and export _____, such as tourism, as well as _____ (goods).

2. When exports of goods exceed imports of goods, there is a merchandise trade _____.

3. In the global economy, one country's exports are another country's _____.

Section 14.2

4. In a typical year, about _____ percent of the world's output is traded in international markets.

5. The objective of GATT was to _____ barriers to international trade, such as _____ and _____.

6. Canada's first bilateral trade agreement was the _____ Free Trade Agreement (FTA), which came into effect in 1989.

Section 14.3

7. _____ trade implies that both participants of an exchange of goods and services anticipate an improvement in their economic welfare.

8. The theory that explains how trade can be beneficial to both parties centres on the concept of _____.

9. A person, a region, or a country has a comparative advantage over another person, region, or country in producing a particular good or service if it produces a good or service at a lower _____ than others do.

10. What is important for mutually beneficial specialization and trade is _____ advantage, not _____ advantage.

Section 14.4

11. The difference between the most a consumer would be willing to pay for a quantity of a good and what a consumer actually has to pay is called _____ surplus.

12. We can better analyze the impact of trade with the tools of _____ and _____ surplus.

13. Once the equilibrium output is reached at the equilibrium price, the sum of _____ and _____ is maximized.

14. When the domestic economy has a comparative advantage in a good because it can produce it at a lower relative price than the rest of the world can, international trade _____ the domestic market price to the world price, benefiting domestic _____ but harming domestic _____.

15. When the domestic economy has a comparative advantage in a good, allowing international trade redistributes income from domestic _____ to domestic _____, but _____ surplus increases more than _____ surplus decreases.

16. When a country does not produce a good relatively as well as other countries do, international trade will _____ the domestic price to the world price, with the difference between what is domestically supplied and what is domestically demanded supplied by _____.

17. When a country does not produce a good relatively as well as other countries do, international trade redistributes income from domestic _____ to domestic _____ and causes a net _____ in domestic welfare.

Section 14.5

18. A _____ is a tax on imported goods.

19. Tariffs bring about _____ prices and revenues to domestic producers, _____ sales and revenues to foreign producers, and _____ prices to domestic consumers.

20. With import tariffs, the domestic price of goods is _____ than the world price.

21. If import tariffs are imposed, at the new price, the domestic quantity demanded is _____, and the quantity supplied domestically is _____, _____ the quantity of imported goods.

22. Import tariffs benefit domestic _____ and _____, but harm domestic _____.

23. One argument for tariffs is that tariff protection is necessary _____ to allow a new industry to more quickly reach a scale of operation at which economies of scale and production efficiencies can be realized.

24. Tariffs lead to _____ output and employment and reduced unemployment in domestic industries where tariffs are imposed.

25. If new tariffs lead to restrictions on imports, _____ dollars will be flowing overseas in payment for imports, which means that foreigners will have _____ dollars available to buy Canadian exports.

26. If a nation's own resources are depletable, tariff-imposed reliance on domestic supplies will _____ depletion of domestic reserves.

27. An import _____ gives producers from another country a maximum number of units of the good in question that can be imported within any given time span.

28. The case for import quotas is _____ than the case for import tariffs.

29. Tariffs and import quotas are rather suspect and exist because of producers' lobbying efforts to gain profits from government protection, called _____.

30. Governments sometimes try to encourage exports by _____ producers.

31. With subsidies, a nation's taxpayers end up subsidizing the output of producers who, relative to producers in other countries, are _____.

32. Gains from trade in terms of world output are _____ by export subsidies.

True or False

Section 14.1

1. When Canada runs a trade surplus in goods, it must run a trade deficit in services.

2. In the global economy, imports equal exports because one country's exports are another country's imports.

3. Japan is Canada's largest trading partner in terms of imports.

4. On the import side, Canada's imports are much more concentrated on finished goods.

Section 14.2

5. Although the importance of the international sector varies enormously from place to place, the volume of international trade has increased substantially.

6. Exports and imports account for a larger percentage of GDP in the United States than in Canada.

7. The North American Free Trade Agreement (NAFTA) created a trading bloc between Canada, the United States, and Mexico.

Section 14.3

8. In voluntary trade, both participants of an exchange anticipate an improvement in their economic welfare.

9. An area should specialize in producing and selling those items in which it has an absolute advantage.

10. Differences in opportunity costs provide an incentive to gain from specialization and trade.

11. By specialization according to comparative advantage and trade, two parties can each achieve consumption possibilities that would be impossible for them without trade.

Section 14.4

12. The difference between the least price for which a supplier is willing to supply a quantity of a good or service and the price a supplier actually receives for selling it is called consumer surplus.

13. Trading at the market equilibrium price generates both consumer surplus and producer surplus.

14. Once the equilibrium output is reached at the equilibrium price, all of the mutually beneficial opportunities from trade between suppliers and demanders will have taken place.

15. The total gain to the economy from trade is the sum of consumer and producer surplus.

16. When the domestic economy has a comparative advantage in a good, allowing international trade benefits domestic consumers but harms domestic producers.

17. When the domestic economy has a comparative advantage in a good, exporting that good increases domestic welfare because, although domestic consumers lose from the free trade, those negative effects are more than offset by the positive gains captured by producers.

18. When a country does not produce a good relatively as well as other countries do, international trade benefits domestic consumers but harms domestic producers.

19. When a country does not produce a good relatively as well as other countries do, allowing international trade will increase consumer surplus by less than producer surplus decreases.

Section 14.5

20. Tariffs are usually relatively large revenue producers for governments.

21. Tariffs lead to gains to domestic producers that are more than offset by the losses to domestic consumers.

22. The history of infant industry tariffs suggests that the tariffs often linger long after the industry is mature and no longer in "need" of protection.

23. The overall domestic employment effects of a tariff imposition are likely to be positive and large.

24. If the imposition of a tariff leads to retaliatory tariffs by other countries, domestic employment outside the industry gaining the tariff protection would likely suffer.

25. Exporters in a country would generally be supportive of their country imposing import tariffs.

26. From a national defence standpoint, it makes more sense to use foreign supplies in peacetime, and perhaps stockpile "insurance" supplies so that large domestic supplies would be available during wars, than to impose import tariffs.

27. Like tariffs, quotas directly restrict imports, but the Canadian government does not collect any revenue as a result of the import quota, unlike with tariffs.

28. Nations have sometimes used product standards ostensibly designed to protect consumers against inferior, unsafe, dangerous, or polluting merchandise as a means to restrict foreign competition.

29. Because resources being spent on lobbying efforts could have produced something instead, the measured deadweight loss from tariffs and quotas will likely understate the true deadweight loss to society.

30. Unlike import tariffs and quotas, export subsidies tend to increase efficiency.

31. With subsidies, producers export goods not because their costs are lower than those of a foreign competitor, but because their costs have been artificially reduced by government action transferring income from taxpayers to the exporter.

32. Export subsidies lead nations to export products in which they do not have a comparative advantage.

Multiple Choice

Section 14.1

1. Why would a new limit on trade in goods with Canada by the United States be more important to the Canadian economy than the same type of policy in Italy?
   a. Americans speak English, so Canadian citizens are more interested in what they do.
   b. The United States ranks behind only the United Kingdom as our second-most important trade partner.
   c. The United States is Canada's largest trading partner.
   d. The United States imports most of the hockey players who play for the National Hockey League.

2. In terms of Canada's trade balance, the largest trade surpluses exist in _____.
   a. the consumer goods category
   b. the automotive category
   c. the energy category
   d. all of the above

Section 14.2

3. Which of the following is correct?
   a. Canadian international trade represents about 5 percent of Canadian GDP.
   b. Less than 5 percent of world output is sold in a country different from the one in which it is produced.
   c. Canada is best characterized as a closed economy.
   d. The volume of international trade has grown rapidly.

4. Which of the following were stated objectives of NAFTA?
   a. eliminate trade barriers
   b. promote fair competition and increase investment opportunities
   c. protect intellectual property
   d. resolve trade disputes
   e. all of the above

Section 14.3

5. Assume that the opportunity cost of producing a pair of pants in Canada is 2 kilograms of apples, whereas in China, it is 5 kilograms of apples. As a result,
   a. Canada has a comparative advantage over China in the production of pants.
   b. China has a comparative advantage over Canada in the production of apples.
   c. there can be mutual gains from trade to the two countries if Canada exports apples to China in exchange for pants.
   d. there can be mutual gains from trade to the two countries if Canada exports pants to China in exchange for apples.
   e. all of the above except c are true.

6. In Samoa the opportunity cost of producing 1 coconut is 4 pineapples, whereas in Guam the opportunity cost of producing 1 coconut is 5 pineapples. In this situation,
   a. if trade occurs, both countries will be able to consume beyond their original production possibilities frontiers.
   b. Guam will be better off if it exports coconuts and imports pineapples.
   c. both Samoa and Guam will be better off if Samoa produces both coconuts and pineapples.
   d. mutually beneficial trade cannot occur.

7. Mutually beneficial trade will occur whenever the terms of trade between the goods involved are set at a level where
   a. each country can export a good at a price above the opportunity cost of producing the good in the domestic market.
   b. each country can import a good at a price above the opportunity cost of producing the good in the domestic market.
   c. the terms of trade are exactly equal to the opportunity cost of producing the good in each country.
   d. each country will specialize in the production of those goods in which it has an absolute advantage.
   e. either b or d is true.

Questions 8–10 refer to the following data: Alpha can produce either 18 oranges or 9 apples in an hour, whereas Omega can produce either 16 oranges or 4 apples in an hour.

8. The opportunity costs of producing 1 apple for Alpha and Omega, respectively, are
   a. 0.25 oranges and 0.5 oranges.
   b. 9 oranges and 4 oranges.
   c. 2 oranges and 4 oranges.
   d. 4 oranges and 2 oranges.
   e. 0.5 orange and 0.25 oranges.

9. Which of the following statements is true?
   a. Alpha should export to Omega, but Omega should not export to Alpha.
   b. Since Alpha has an absolute advantage in both goods, no mutual gains from trade are possible.
   c. If Alpha specializes in growing apples and Omega specializes in growing oranges, they could both gain by specialization and trade.
   d. If Alpha specializes in growing oranges and Omega specializes in growing apples, they could both gain by specialization and trade.
   e. Since Alpha has a comparative advantage in producing both goods, no mutual gains from trade are possible.

10. Which of the following terms of trade between apples and oranges would allow both Alpha and Omega to gain by specialization and exchange?
    a. 1 apple for 3 oranges
    b. 3 apples for 3 oranges
    c. 2 apples for 3 oranges
    d. 1 orange for 0.2 apples
    e. 1 orange for 0.8 apples

11. If Canada could produce 0.5 tonnes of potatoes or 1 tonne of wheat per worker per year, whereas Ireland could produce 3 tonnes of potatoes or 2 tonnes of wheat per worker per year, the country with the comparative advantage in producing wheat is _____, and the country with the absolute advantage in producing potatoes is _____.
    a. Canada; Canada
    b. Canada; Ireland
    c. Ireland; Canada
    d. Ireland; Ireland

12. According to international trade theory, a country should
    a. import goods in which it has an absolute advantage.
    b. export goods in which it has an absolute advantage.
    c. import goods in which it has a comparative disadvantage.
    d. import goods in which it has an absolute disadvantage.

Section 14.4
13. If nations begin to specialize in production for the purpose of trade:
    a. consumer surplus will increase, but not total output.
    b. total world output will increase, and consumer surplus will increase as well.
    c. total world output will increase, but consumer surplus will not increase.
    d. neither total output nor consumer surplus will change.

14. Compared to the no-trade situation, when a country imports a good:

    a. domestic consumers gain, domestic producers lose, and the gains outweigh the losses.

    b. domestic consumers lose, domestic producers gain, and the gains outweigh the losses.

    c. domestic consumers gain, domestic producers lose, and the losses outweigh the gains.

    d. domestic consumers gain and domestic producers lose an equal amount.

Section 14.5

15. After Canada introduces a tariff in the market for widgets, the price of widgets in Canada will

    a. decrease.

    b. increase.

    c. remain the same.

    d. change in an indeterminate manner.

16. The infant industry argument for protectionism suggests that an industry must be protected in the early stages of its development so that

    a. firms will be protected from subsidized foreign competition.

    b. domestic producers can attain the economies of scale to allow them to compete in world markets.

    c. there will be adequate supplies of crucial resources in case they are needed for national defence.

    d. None of the above reflect the infant industry argument.

17. Protectionist legislation is often passed because

    a. employers in the affected industry lobby more effectively than the workers in that industry.

    b. both employers and workers in the affected industry lobby for protectionist policies.

    c. trade restrictions often benefit domestic consumers in the long run, though they must pay more in the short run.

    d. none of the above.

18. Introducing a tariff on vitamin E would

    a. reduce imports of vitamin E.

    b. increase Canadian production of vitamin E.

    c. decrease Canadian consumption of vitamin E.

    d. do all of the above.

    e. do none of the above.

19. A new Canadian import quota on imported steel would be likely to

    a. raise the cost of production to steel-using Canadian firms.

    b. generate tax revenue to the government.

    c. decrease Canadian production of steel.

    d. increase the production of steel-using Canadian firms.

    e. do all of the above.

20. An import quota does which of the following?

    a. decreases the price of the imported goods to consumers

    b. increases the price of the imported goods to consumers

    c. redistributes income away from domestic producers toward domestic consumers

    d. a and c

    e. b and c

21. A crucial difference between the impact of import quotas compared to that of tariffs is that
   a. import quotas generate revenue to the domestic government, but tariffs do not.
   b. import quotas generate no revenue to the domestic government, but tariffs do.
   c. tariffs increase the prices paid by domestic consumers, but quotas do not.
   d. a and c.
   e. b and c.

Problems

1. **[Section 14.4]**
   Using the following graph, illustrate the domestic effects of opening up the domestic market to international trade on the domestic price, the domestic quantity purchased, the domestic quantity produced, imports or exports, consumer surplus, producer surplus, and the total welfare gain from trade.

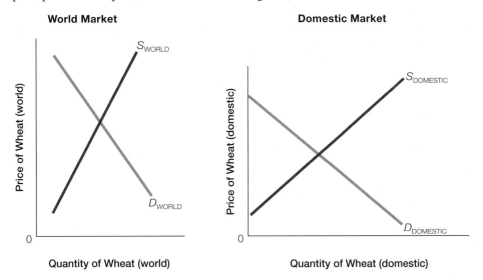

2. **[Section 14.5]**
   Use the following graph to illustrate the domestic effects of imposing a tariff on imports on the domestic price, the domestic quantity purchased, the domestic quantity produced, the level of imports, consumer surplus, producer surplus, the tariff revenue generated, and the total welfare effect from the tariff.

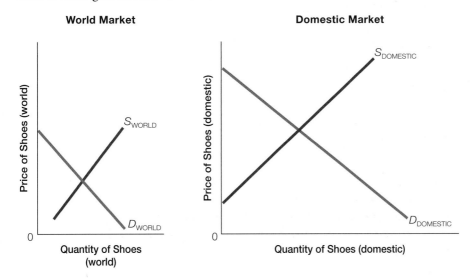

International Finance

15.1 THE BALANCE OF PAYMENTS

What are the three main components of the balance of payments?

15.2 EXCHANGE RATES

How do exchange rates affect the demand for foreign goods?

15.3 EQUILIBRIUM CHANGES IN THE FOREIGN EXCHANGE MARKET

What factors cause the supply of and demand for a currency to shift?

15.4 FLEXIBLE EXCHANGE RATES

How does a system of flexible exchange rates work?

---

section
15.1

The Balance of Payments

- What is the balance of payments?
- What are the three main components of the balance of payments?

BALANCE OF PAYMENTS

balance of payments
the record of international transactions in which a nation has engaged over a year

The record of all of the international financial transactions of a nation over a year is called the **balance of payments.** The balance of payments is a statement that records all the exchanges requiring an outflow of funds to foreign nations or an inflow of funds from other nations. Just as an examination of gross domestic product accounts gives us some idea of the economic health and vitality of a nation, the balance of payments provides information about a nation's world trade position. The balance of payments is divided into three main sections: the current account, the capital account, and an "error term" called the statistical discrepancy. These are highlighted in Exhibit 1. Let us look at each of these components beginning with the current account, which is largely made up of imports and exports of goods and services.

THE CURRENT ACCOUNT
Export Goods and the Current Account

current account
a record of a country's imports and exports of goods and services, net investment income, and net transfers

A **current account** is a record of a country's imports and exports of goods and services, net investment income, and net transfers. Anytime a foreign buyer purchases a good from a Canadian producer, the foreign buyer must pay the Canadian producer for the good.

Canadian Balance of Payments, 2007 (billions of dollars)

Type of Transaction

Current Account			Capital Account		
1. Exports of goods	$ 463		10. Net flow of Canadian assets	$ −170	
2. Imports of goods	−415		11. Net flow of Canadian liabilities	148	
3. Merchandise trade balance (lines 1 + 2)		48	12. Financial account balance (lines 10 + 11)		−22
4. Exports of services	67		13. Statistical discrepancy		8
5. Imports of services	−86		14. Net balance (lines 9 + 12 + 13)		$0
6. Services trade balance (lines 4 + 5)		−19			
7. Net investment income		−14			
8. Net transfers		−1			
9. Current account balance (lines 3 + 6 + 7 + 8)		14			

SOURCE: Adapted from the *Statistics Canada* web site, "Canada's balance of international payments (Current account)", http://www40.statcan.ca/l01/cst01/econ01a.htm and "Canada's balance of international payments (Capital and financial account)", http://www40.statcan.ca/l01/cst01/econ01b.htm, 2008.

Usually, the foreigner must pay for the good in Canadian dollars because the seller wants to pay his workers and for other inputs with dollars. This requires the foreign buyer to exchange units of his currency at a foreign exchange dealer for Canadian dollars. Because Canada obtains foreign currency, exports of Canadian goods abroad are considered a credit or plus (+) item in the Canadian balance of payments.

Import Goods and the Current Account

When a Canadian consumer buys an imported good, however, the reverse is true: The Canadian importer must pay the foreign producer, usually in that nation's currency. Typically, the Canadian buyer will go to a foreign exchange dealer and exchange Canadian dollars for units of that foreign currency. Imports are thus a debit (−) item in the balance of payments, because Canada loses foreign currency in order to buy imports.

Services and the Current Account

Although imports and exports of goods are the largest components of the balance of payments, they are not the only ones. Nations import and export services as well. A particularly important service is tourism. When Canadian tourists go abroad, they are buying foreign-produced services. Those services include the use of hotels, sightseeing tours, restaurants, and so forth. In the current account, these services are included in imports. On the other hand, foreign tourism in Canada provides us with foreign currencies, so they are included in exports.

© ROYALTY-FREE/CORBIS

When a foreign tourist visits the CN Tower in Toronto, how does that affect the current account? Tourism provides Canada with foreign currency, which is included in exports.

Net Transfers and Net Investment Income

Other items that affect the current account are net transfers, which are largely private and government grants and gifts to and from other countries. When the Canadian government gives foreign aid to another country, this creates a debit in the Canadian balance of payments. Private gifts, such as Canadian individuals receiving money from relatives or friends in foreign countries, show up in the current account as a credit item.

There is also net investment income in the current account—Canadian investors hold foreign assets and foreign investors hold Canadian assets. When Canadian investors hold foreign assets, they earn investment income in the form of interest and dividends, which is a credit item. When foreign investors hold Canadian assets, they earn investment income in the form of interest and dividends, which is a debit item. In Exhibit 1, investment income paid to foreigners on their Canadian assets exceeded the investment income received by Canadians on their foreign assets by $14 billion.

Current Account Balance

The balance on the current account is the net amount of credits or debits after adding up all transactions of goods (merchandise imports and exports), services, investment income, and transfer payments. If the sum of credits exceeds the sum of debits, the nation is said to run a surplus on the current account. If debits exceed credits, however, the nation is running a deficit on the current account.

The current account balance for 2007 is presented in Exhibit 1. Note that exports and imports of goods are by far the largest credits and debits. Note also that Canadian exports of goods were $48 billion more than Canadian imports of goods. Canada, therefore, experienced a $48 billion surplus in the merchandise trade balance. However, some of the $48 billion merchandise trade surplus was offset by a $19 billion deficit in the services trade balance. When the $14 billion net investment income payment and the $1 billion net transfers payment are also included, the overall current account surplus was $14 billion.

THE CAPITAL ACCOUNT

What happens to the current account surplus? We lend it to the rest of the world. The current account surplus is reflected by movements of financial, or capital, assets. These transactions are recorded in the capital account, so a current account surplus is reflected by a capital account deficit.

What Does the Capital Account Record?

Capital account transactions include items such as international bank loans, purchases of corporate stocks and bonds, government bond purchases, and direct investments in foreign subsidiary companies. In Exhibit 1, we see that Canadians purchased an additional $170 billion of foreign assets in 2007, which was a debit because Canada loses foreign currency. On the other hand, foreigners purchased an additional $148 billion of Canadian assets in 2007, which was a credit because it provided Canadians with foreign currency. On balance, then, there was a deficit in the capital account from capital movements of $22 billion, offsetting the $14 billion surplus in the current account.

It is important to highlight one particular capital account transaction: purchases and sales of foreign currencies by the Bank of Canada in the foreign exchange market. The Bank of Canada can intervene in the foreign exchange market to counter disruptive short-term movements in the external value of the Canadian dollar. For example, to moderate a decline in the value of the Canadian dollar, the Bank of Canada can sell foreign currency (usually U.S. dollars) and buy Canadian dollars on the foreign exchange market, thereby putting upward pressure on the Canadian dollar. Similarly, if the Canadian dollar is appreciating too rapidly, the Bank of Canada can buy foreign currency (usually U.S. dollars) and sell Canadian dollars on the foreign exchange market, thereby putting downward pressure on the Canadian dollar. These purchases and sales of foreign currencies by the Bank of Canada affect the level of Canada's official international reserves (the Government of Canada's holdings of foreign currencies) and these transactions are recorded in the capital account of the balance of payments.

The Statistical Discrepancy

In the final analysis, it is true that the overall balance of payments account must balance so that credits and debits are equal. Why is this so? Because every unit of foreign currency used (debit) must have a source (credit). We can see that the current account surplus ($14 billion credit) does not exactly equal the capital account deficit ($22 billion debit). That is because there are considerable international flows of goods and capital which government authorities are unable to measure and record (for example, smuggling of goods, or undeclared financial investments). These "errors" are entered

In The **NEWS**

CURRENT ACCOUNT BALANCE MAY BE BACK IN A DEFICIT

BY ERIC BEAUCHESNE

Canada has lost its status as the world's No. 1 supplier of goods to the U.S. and is also in danger of suffering its first deficit in a decade in its dealings with the rest of the world.

"Even with the firestorm over unsafe products and toy recalls recently, China surpassed Canada as the No. 1 supplier to the U.S. market in 2007," BMO Capital Markets economist Douglas Porter noted in an analysis of the year-end trade reports from both sides of the border titled—North American Trade: End of an Era.

The U.S. Commerce Department reported that the U.S. imported $321.5 billion U.S. worth of merchandise from China in 2007, up 11.7 percent from 2006, and $313.1 billion U.S. from Canada, up 3.5 percent.

Meanwhile, Canada's merchandise trade surplus—eroded by the strong dollar, weakening U.S. economy and increased offshore competition—plunged more than expected to a nine-year low in December, increasing the risk that Canada will—or even already has—slipped back into an overall deficit in its dealings with the rest of the world.

"Goodbye twin surpluses," said Mr. Porter.

He was referring to Canada's boast that it's the only major industrial country to be running both a national government budget surplus as well as a surplus in its trade in goods and services investments with the rest of the world.

The sharp shrinkage in the merchandise trade surplus suggests that it will no longer be large enough to offset Canada's chronic deficit in services trade.

The news that Canada's merchandise trade surplus fell to $2.4 billion in December from $3.8 billion in November as exports dropped 3.1 percent while imports edged up 0.7 percent, was "disappointing," said National Bank of Canada economist Stefane Marion.

Statistics Canada reported yesterday that the trade surplus last year slipped to $49.7 billion from $51.3 billion in 2006. Both exports and imports hit record highs in 2007, but the growth in imports was greater.

Exports—led by a surge in oil shipments along with other resources, which offset weakness in autos and forestry products—rose 2.1 percent to a record $465.4 billion, while imports increased 2.8 percent to $415.7 billion, also a record.

While in Canadian dollars, exports to the U.S. fell, shipments to other countries rose dramatically, Statistics Canada noted. As a result, the U.S. share of Canadian exports fell to 76.4 percent from 79.2 percent.

SOURCE: Adapted from Eric Beauchesne, "Canada No Longer Top Exporter to the U.S.," *Ottawa Citizen*, Ottawa, Ontario, February 15, 2008, p. C1.

CONSIDER THIS:

Canada's current account balance is determined by the sum of the merchandise trade balance, services trade balance, net investment income, and net transfers (see Exhibit 1). Of all these accounts, the only one that has been in surplus in recent years has been the merchandise trade account. Should the merchandise trade surplus continue to decline, Canada may find itself back in a position of an overall current account deficit with the rest of the world.

into the balance of payments as the statistical discrepancy. In Exhibit 1, the statistical discrepancy was $8 billion (credit). By including the statistical discrepancy with the current account balance and the capital account balance, the overall balance of payments does balance.

Balance of Payments: A Useful Analogy

In concept, the international balance of payments is similar to the personal financial transactions of individuals. Each individual has his or her own "balance of payments," reflecting that person's trading with other economic units: other individuals, corporations, or governments. People earn income or credits by "exporting" their labour service to other economic units, or by receiving investment income (a return on capital services). Against that, they "import" goods from other economic units; we call these imports "consumption." This debit item is sometimes augmented by payments made to outsiders (e.g., banks) on loans, and so forth. Fund transfers, such as gifts to children or charities, are other debit items (or credit items for recipients of the assistance).

As individuals, if our spending on our consumption ("imports") exceeds our income from our "exports" of our labour and capital services, we have a "deficit" that must be financed by borrowing or selling assets. On the other hand, if we "export" more than we "import," we can make new investments and/or increase our "reserves" (savings and investment holdings). Like nations, individuals who run a deficit in daily transactions must make up for it through accommodating transactions (e.g., borrowing or reducing one's savings or investment holdings) to bring about an ultimate balance of credits and debits to their personal account. Likewise, individuals who run a surplus in daily transactions must make new investments and/or increase their savings and investment holdings to bring about a balance of credits and debits.

In summary, the international balance of payments works like this: A country that runs a current account surplus lends that surplus to the rest of the world, creating a capital account deficit; a country that runs a current account deficit finances that deficit by borrowing from the rest of the world, thus creating a capital account surplus.

Section Check

SECTION CHECK

1. The balance of payments is the record of all the international financial transactions of a nation for any given year.
2. The balance of payments is made up of the current account, the capital account, as well as an "error term" called the statistical discrepancy.
3. The merchandise trade balance refers strictly to the imports and exports of (merchandise) goods with other nations. If our imports of foreign goods are less than our exports, we are said to have a merchandise trade surplus.

section

15.2

Exchange Rates

- What are exchange rates?
- How are exchange rates determined?
- How do exchange rates affect the demand for foreign goods?

THE NEED FOR FOREIGN CURRENCIES

When Canadian consumers buy goods from people in other countries, the sellers of those goods want to be paid in their own domestic currencies. The Canadian consumers, then, must first exchange Canadian dollars for the seller's currency in order to pay for those goods. Canadian importers must, therefore, constantly buy U.S. dollars, yen, euros, pesos, and other currencies in order to finance their purchases. Similarly, people in other countries buying Canadian goods must sell their currencies to obtain Canadian dollars in order to pay for those goods.

THE EXCHANGE RATE

The price of one unit of one country's currency in terms of another country's currency is called the **exchange rate.** If a Canadian importer has agreed to pay euros (the new currency of the European Union) to buy a cuckoo clock made in the Black Forest in Germany, she would then have to exchange Canadian dollars for euros. If it takes $2 to buy 1 euro, then the exchange rate is $2 per euro. From the German perspective, the exchange rate is 0.50 euros per Canadian dollar.

Exhibit 1 shows the exchange rate for the Canadian dollar against the currencies of some of our major trading partners. The exchange rates listed were the average exchange rates for the year 2007. It took 0.9304 U.S. dollars to buy one Canadian dollar (that is the exchange rate of the Canadian dollar in terms of the U.S. dollar). Conversely, it took 1.0748 Canadian dollars to buy one U.S. dollar (that is the exchange rate of the U.S. dollar in terms of the Canadian dollar). Note carefully that 1.0748 equals 1 divided by

exchange rate
the price of one unit of a country's currency in terms of another country's currency

---

section 15.2
Exhibit 1 — **Exchange Rates for the Canadian Dollar in 2007**

Country	Currency	Units of Foreign Currency per Canadian Dollar	Canadian Dollars per Unit of Foreign Currency
Australia	Dollar	1.1133	0.8982
China	Renminbi	7.0822	0.1412
European Monetary Union	Euro	0.6840	1.4619
Hong Kong	Dollar	7.2622	0.1377
India	Rupee	38.3142	0.0261
Japan	Yen	109.8901	0.0091
Mexico	Peso	10.1729	0.0983
New Zealand	Dollar	1.2671	0.7892
Norway	Krone	5.4585	0.1832
Russia	Rouble	23.8095	0.0420
South Korea	Won	833.3333	0.0012
Sweden	Krona	6.2933	0.1589
Switzerland	Franc	1.1178	0.8946
United Kingdom	Pound	0.4664	2.1487
United States	Dollar	0.9304	1.0748

SOURCE: Bank of Canada.

© C-SQUARED STUDIOS PHOTO DISC/GETTY ONE IMAGES

ACTIVE LEARNING EXERCISE

EXCHANGE RATES

Q: Why is a strong Canadian dollar a mixed blessing?

A: A strong Canadian dollar will lower the price of imports and make trips to foreign countries less expensive. Lower prices on foreign goods also help keep inflation in check. A strong dollar will also make investments in foreign financial markets (foreign stocks and bonds)

relatively cheaper. However, it makes Canadian exports more expensive. Consequently, foreigners will buy fewer Canadian goods and services. The net effect is a fall in exports and a rise in imports—net exports fall. Note that some Canadians are helped (vacationers going to foreign countries and those preferring foreign goods), whereas others are harmed (producers of Canadian exports, operators of hotels dependent on foreign visitors in Canada). A stronger dollar also makes it more expensive for foreign investors to invest in Canada.

0.9304. Similarly, it took 109.8901 Japanese yen to buy one Canadian dollar, and it took 0.0091 Canadian dollars (1 divided by 109.8901) to buy one Japanese yen.

CHANGES IN EXCHANGE RATES AFFECT THE DOMESTIC DEMAND FOR FOREIGN GOODS

Prices of goods in their currencies combine with exchange rates to determine the domestic price of foreign goods. Suppose the cuckoo clock sells for 100 euros in Germany. What is the price to Canadian consumers? Let us assume that tariffs and other transactions costs are zero. If the exchange rate is $2 = 1 euro, then the equivalent Canadian dollar price of the cuckoo clock is 100 euros times $2 per euro, or $200. If the exchange rate were to change to $3 = 1 euro, fewer clocks would be demanded in Canada. This is because the effective Canadian dollar price of the clocks would rise to $300 (100 euros times $3 per euro). The new higher relative value of a euro compared to the dollar (or equivalently, the lower relative value of a dollar compared to the euro) would lead to a reduction in Canadian demand for German-made clocks.

With the introduction of the euro it will be easy to compare prices for the same goods in different European countries using this currency. For example, if you use mail order or shop on the Internet, it will be easier to spot the bargains between countries.

derived demand
the demand for an input derived from consumers' demand for the good or service produced with that input

THE DEMAND FOR A FOREIGN CURRENCY

The demand for foreign currencies is a **derived demand.** This is because the demand for a foreign currency derives directly from the demand for foreign goods and services or for foreign assets. The more foreign goods are demanded, the more of that foreign currency will be needed to pay for those goods. Such an increased demand for the currency will push up the exchange rate of that currency relative to other currencies.

THE SUPPLY OF A FOREIGN CURRENCY

Similarly, the supply of foreign currency is provided by foreigners who want to buy the exports of another nation. For example, the more that foreigners demand Canadian products, the more of their currencies they will supply in exchange for Canadian dollars, which they use to buy our products.

DETERMINING EXCHANGE RATES

We know that the demand for foreign currencies is derived in part from the demand for foreign goods, but how does that affect the exchange rate? Just as in the product market, the answer lies with the forces of supply and demand. In this case, it is the supply of and demand for a foreign currency that determine the equilibrium price (exchange rate) of that currency.

THE DEMAND CURVE FOR A FOREIGN CURRENCY

As Exhibit 2 shows, the demand curve for a foreign currency—the euro, for example—is downward sloping, just as a demand curve is in product markets. In this case, however, the demand curve has a negative slope because as the price of the euro falls relative to the Canadian dollar (that is, the euro depreciates in value), European products become relatively cheaper to Canadian consumers, who therefore buy more European goods. To do so, the quantity of euros demanded by Canadian consumers will increase to buy more European goods as the price of the euro falls. This is why the demand for foreign currencies is considered to be a derived demand.

THE SUPPLY CURVE FOR FOREIGN CURRENCY

The supply curve for a foreign currency is upward sloping, just as a supply curve is in product markets. In this case, as the price of the euro increases relative to the Canadian dollar (that is, the euro appreciates in value), Canadian products will become relatively cheaper to European buyers and they will increase the quantity of dollars they demand. Europeans will, therefore, increase the quantity of euros supplied to the foreign exchange market by buying more Canadian products. Hence, the supply curve is upward sloping.

EQUILIBRIUM IN THE FOREIGN EXCHANGE MARKET

Equilibrium is reached where the demand and supply curves for a given currency intersect. In Exhibit 2, the equilibrium price of a euro is $1.20. As in the product market, if the Canadian dollar price of euros is higher than the equilibrium price, an excess quantity of

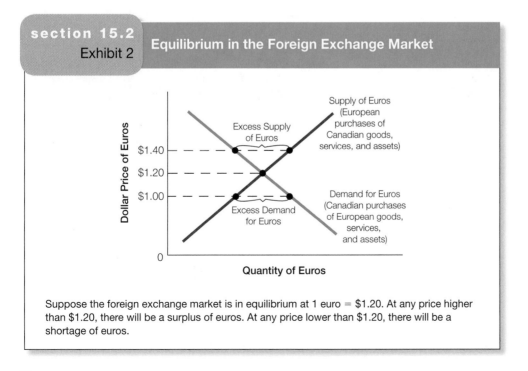

section 15.2
Exhibit 2   **Equilibrium in the Foreign Exchange Market**

Suppose the foreign exchange market is in equilibrium at 1 euro = $1.20. At any price higher than $1.20, there will be a surplus of euros. At any price lower than $1.20, there will be a shortage of euros.

In The **NEWS**

WHAT'S A LOONIE REALLY WORTH?

BY WILLIAM WATSON

"So what's the right value for the loonie?" asked the CBC lady who came calling [in November 2004] after our dollar made one of its big jumps.

Good question, but it's not clear it has an answer. What's the right value of a bag of potatoes? Depends if you're buying or selling. If you're buying, you like the price low. If you're selling, you want it high.

Who buys loonies? Anyone who wants to visit here or buy Canadian goods, services or assets. People who work in tourism or exports obviously aren't happy about a steroidal loonie. There are estimates that an 80 cents-plus loonie will cost us 500,000 manufacturing jobs.

On the other hand, if you're selling loonies these days, you're ecstatic. Who does that? Anyone who buys foreign currencies, but especially U.S. dollars. That includes Canadians heading south, investing in the United States (when their pension rules allow them) and buying U.S. goods—which of course means just about all of us. Canadians who buy in the United States but don't sell there are unambiguously better off with a strong loonie. Unfortunately, we seldom count in stories about the rising dollar, which always focus on its dire implications for exporters. Some of my best friends are exporters, but consumers are people, too. How we feel about the loonie should matter, too.

If potato prices fall, potato growers have three choices: live with lower profits, become more productive or try something else. Exporters who can't hack a higher loonie face the same three choices. If the loonie's rise is permanent, we may end up with a smaller export sector but the people and capital currently employed there will ultimately find uses in non-export sectors.

In fact, economists' position on the price of potatoes isn't quite agnostic. Tax potatoes, thus artificially raising their price, and people don't consume enough potatoes. Subsidize them, thus artificially lowering their price, and that's bad, too, since people end up eating too many. The potato price economists favour—the "right" price, as the CBC lady would say—is whatever price an unfettered potato market produces.

Is the foreign exchange market as "efficient" as the potato market? Unfortunately, there's always a lurking suspicion that the currency values such markets produce don't really "mean" anything, that people are buying (or selling) loonies just because they think their price is going up (or down). "Purchasing-power parity" calculations have suggested for the last 15 years that the Canadian dollar should be trading at US80 cents to US85 cents. What that means is that if you take a representative bundle of Canadian goods—say, ear muffs, doughnuts, beer and hockey sticks—sell them for Canadian dollars, use the proceeds to buy U.S. dollars and then buy U.S. goods, 80 cents to 85 cents is the exchange rate that would get you the same bundle of goods. You'd think that with open borders, prices would tend in that direction. But for a decade and a half they didn't. They're there now, but is anyone confident they'll stay?

Does that mean we should regulate the exchange rate—maybe fix its value for good—so that we don't let a seemingly capricious market move exchange rates in ways that have nothing to do with economic "fundamentals," thereby whiplashing the "real" bits of our economy?

Suppose we do that. How do we choose which value to fix it at? If we let a committee of economists pick it, that's one thing. But I bet we'd do it more democratically, which means we'll end up choosing the value most pleasing to voters in swing ridings. Central Canada being our electoral Ohio, the suburban rings around Toronto and Montreal will call the shots. As usual.

Maybe we're best off forgetting about the "right" value of the loonie and living with what an admittedly imperfect market gives us.

SOURCE: Adapted from William Watson, "What's a Loonie Really Worth?" *National Post*, November 18, 2004, p. A20. Reprinted with permission from the author.

CONSIDER THIS:
When the Canadian dollar appreciates in value against the U.S. dollar, it hurts Canadian exporters of goods and services (like tourism services). On the other hand, a stronger exchange rate for the Canadian dollar lowers the Canadian dollar price of imports from the United States, making Canadian consumers better off.

---

euros will be supplied at that price, or a surplus of euros. Competition among euro sellers will push the price of euros down toward equilibrium. Likewise, if the dollar price of euros is lower than the equilibrium price, an excess quantity of euros will be demanded at that price, or a shortage of euros. Competition among euro buyers will push the price of euros up toward equilibrium.

SECTION CHECK

Section Check

1. The price of a unit of one foreign currency in terms of another currency is called the exchange rate.
2. The exchange rate for a currency is determined by the supply of and demand for that currency in the foreign exchange market.
3. If the dollar appreciates in value relative to foreign currencies, foreign goods become cheaper to Canadian consumers, increasing Canadian demand for foreign goods.

section

15.3

Equilibrium Changes in the Foreign Exchange Market

- What factors cause the demand curve for a currency to shift?
- What factors cause the supply curve for a currency to shift?

DETERMINANTS IN THE FOREIGN EXCHANGE MARKET

The equilibrium exchange rate of a currency changes many times daily. Sometimes, these changes can be quite significant. Any force that shifts either the demand for or supply of a currency will shift the equilibrium in the foreign exchange market, leading to a new exchange rate. These factors include changes in consumer tastes for goods, changes in income, changes in tariffs, changes in relative interest rates, changes in relative inflation rates, and speculation.

INCREASED TASTES FOR FOREIGN GOODS

Because the demand for foreign currencies is derived from the demand for foreign goods, any change in the demand for foreign goods will shift the demand schedule for foreign currency in the same direction. For example, if a cuckoo clock revolution sweeps through Canada, German producers would have reason to celebrate, knowing that many Canadian buyers will turn to Germany for their cuckoo clocks. The Germans, however, will only accept payment in the form of euros, and so Canadian consumers and retailers must convert their dollars into euros before they can purchase their clocks. The increased taste for European goods in Canada would, therefore, lead to an increased demand for euros. As shown in Exhibit 1, this increased demand for euros shifts the demand curve to the right, resulting in a new, higher equilibrium dollar price of euros.

CANADIAN INCOME INCREASES OR REDUCTIONS IN CANADIAN TARIFFS

Any change in the average income of Canadian consumers will also change the equilibrium exchange rate, *ceteris paribus*. If, on the whole, incomes increased in Canada, Canadians would buy more goods, including imported goods, so more European goods would be bought. This increased demand for European goods would lead to an

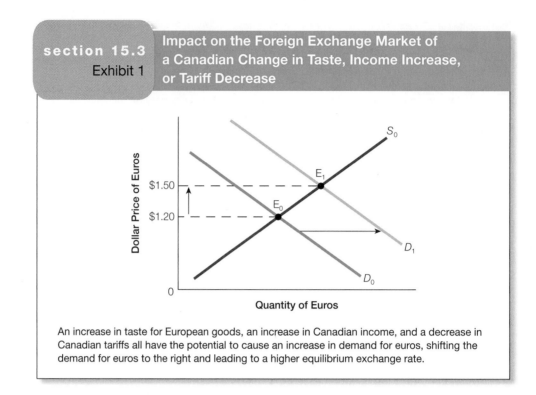

section 15.3
Exhibit 1

Impact on the Foreign Exchange Market of a Canadian Change in Taste, Income Increase, or Tariff Decrease

An increase in taste for European goods, an increase in Canadian income, and a decrease in Canadian tariffs all have the potential to cause an increase in demand for euros, shifting the demand for euros to the right and leading to a higher equilibrium exchange rate.

What impact will an increase in travel to Paris by Canadian consumers have on the Canadian dollar price of euros? In order for a consumer to buy souvenirs at the Eiffel Tower, she will need to exchange dollars for euros. This would increase the demand for euros and result in a new higher dollar price of euros.

© COURTESY OF ROBERT SEXTON

increased demand for euros, resulting in a higher exchange rate for the euro. A decrease in Canadian tariffs on European goods would tend to have the same effect as an increase in incomes by making European goods more affordable. As Exhibit 1 shows, this would again lead to an increased demand for European goods and a higher equilibrium exchange rate for the euro.

CHANGES IN EUROPEAN INCOME, TARIFFS, OR TASTES

If European incomes rose, European tariffs on Canadian goods fell, or European tastes for Canadian goods increased, the supply of euros in the foreign exchange market would increase. Any of these changes would cause Europeans to demand more Canadian goods, and therefore more Canadian dollars in order to purchase those goods. To obtain those added dollars, Europeans must exchange more of their euros, increasing the supply of euros on the foreign exchange market. As Exhibit 2 demonstrates, the effect of this would be a rightward shift in the euro supply curve, leading to a new equilibrium at a lower exchange rate for the euro.

HOW DO CHANGES IN RELATIVE INTEREST RATES AFFECT EXCHANGE RATES?

If interest rates in Canada were to increase relative to, say, European interest rates, other things equal, the rate of return on Canadian bonds would increase relative to that on European bonds. European investors would thus increase their demand for Canadian bonds, and therefore offer euros for sale to buy dollars to buy Canadian bonds, shifting the supply curve for euros to the right, from S_0 to S_1 in Exhibit 3.

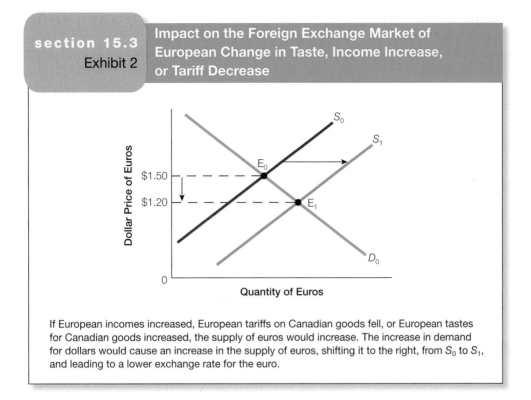

section 15.3
Exhibit 2

Impact on the Foreign Exchange Market of European Change in Taste, Income Increase, or Tariff Decrease

If European incomes increased, European tariffs on Canadian goods fell, or European tastes for Canadian goods increased, the supply of euros would increase. The increase in demand for dollars would cause an increase in the supply of euros, shifting it to the right, from S_0 to S_1, and leading to a lower exchange rate for the euro.

In this scenario, Canadian investors would also shift their investments away from Europe by decreasing their demand for euros, from D_0 to D_1 in Exhibit 3. A subsequent lower equilibrium exchange rate ($1.50) would result for the euro due to an increase in the Canadian interest rate. That is, the euro would depreciate. In short, the higher Canadian interest rate attracted more investment to Canada and led to a relative appreciation of the dollar and a relative depreciation of the euro.

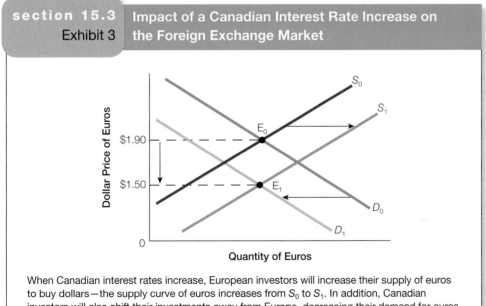

section 15.3
Exhibit 3

Impact of a Canadian Interest Rate Increase on the Foreign Exchange Market

When Canadian interest rates increase, European investors will increase their supply of euros to buy dollars—the supply curve of euros increases from S_0 to S_1. In addition, Canadian investors will also shift their investments away from Europe, decreasing their demand for euros and shifting the demand curve from D_0 to D_1. This will lead to a depreciation of the euro and an appreciation of the dollar.

You may remember this analysis from our discussion of monetary policy in the open economy in Chapter 13. When the Bank of Canada runs a contractionary monetary policy and causes Canadian interest rates to rise, the Canadian dollar appreciates, which leads to a decrease in net exports and a reduction in real GDP in the short run.

CHANGES IN THE RELATIVE INFLATION RATE

If Europe experienced an inflation rate greater than that experienced in Canada, other things being equal, what would happen to the exchange rate? In this case, European products would become relatively more expensive to Canadian consumers. Canadians would decrease the quantity of European goods demanded and, therefore, decrease their demand for euros. The result would be a leftward shift of the demand curve for euros.

On the other side of the Atlantic, Canadian goods would become relatively cheaper to Europeans, leading Europeans to increase the quantity of Canadian goods demanded, and therefore, to demand more Canadian dollars. This increased demand for dollars translates into an increased supply of euros, shifting the supply curve for euros rightward. Exhibit 4 shows the shifts of the supply and demand curves and the new lower equilibrium exchange rate for the euro resulting from the higher European inflation rate.

EXPECTATIONS AND SPECULATION

Every trading day, billions of Canadian dollars trade hands in the foreign exchange markets. Suppose currency traders believed Canada was going to experience more rapid inflation in the future than Japan. If currency speculators believe that the value of the dollar will soon be falling because of the anticipated rise in the Canadian inflation rate, those traders that are holding dollars will convert them to yen. This leads to an increase

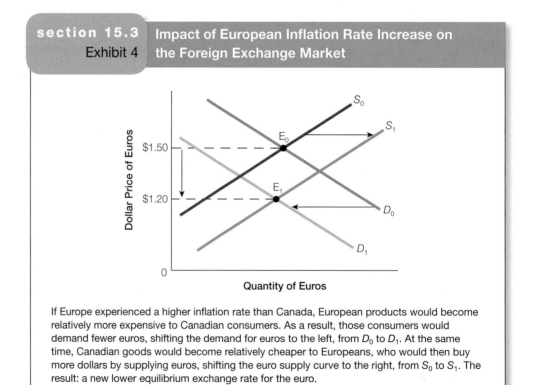

section 15.3
Exhibit 4
Impact of European Inflation Rate Increase on the Foreign Exchange Market

If Europe experienced a higher inflation rate than Canada, European products would become relatively more expensive to Canadian consumers. As a result, those consumers would demand fewer euros, shifting the demand for euros to the left, from D_0 to D_1. At the same time, Canadian goods would become relatively cheaper to Europeans, who would then buy more dollars by supplying euros, shifting the euro supply curve to the right, from S_0 to S_1. The result: a new lower equilibrium exchange rate for the euro.

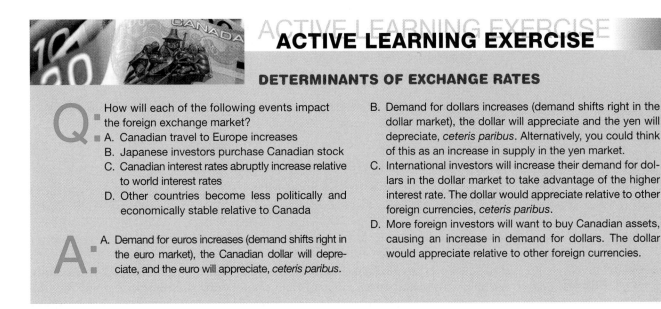

ACTIVE LEARNING EXERCISE

ACTIVE LEARNING EXERCISE

DETERMINANTS OF EXCHANGE RATES

Q: How will each of the following events impact the foreign exchange market?

A. Canadian travel to Europe increases

B. Japanese investors purchase Canadian stock

C. Canadian interest rates abruptly increase relative to world interest rates

D. Other countries become less politically and economically stable relative to Canada

A: A. Demand for euros increases (demand shifts right in the euro market), the Canadian dollar will depreciate, and the euro will appreciate, *ceteris paribus*.

B. Demand for dollars increases (demand shifts right in the dollar market), the dollar will appreciate and the yen will depreciate, *ceteris paribus*. Alternatively, you could think of this as an increase in supply in the yen market.

C. International investors will increase their demand for dollars in the dollar market to take advantage of the higher interest rate. The dollar would appreciate relative to other foreign currencies, *ceteris paribus*.

D. More foreign investors will want to buy Canadian assets, causing an increase in demand for dollars. The dollar would appreciate relative to other foreign currencies.

in the demand for yen—the yen appreciates and the dollar depreciates relative to the yen, *ceteris paribus*. In short, if speculators believe that the price of a country's currency is going to rise, they will buy more of that currency, pushing up the price and causing the country's currency to appreciate.

Section Check

1. Any force that shifts either the demand or supply curves for a foreign currency will shift the equilibrium in the foreign exchange market and lead to a new exchange rate.
2. Any changes in tastes, tariffs, income levels, relative interest rates, relative inflation rates, or speculation will cause the demand for and supply of a currency to shift.

section

section

Flexible Exchange Rates

15.4

■ How are exchange rates determined today?

■ How are exchange rate changes different under a flexible-rate system than in a fixed-rate system?

■ What major problems exist in a fixed-rate system?

■ What are the major arguments against flexible rates?

THE FLEXIBLE EXCHANGE RATE SYSTEM

Since 1973, the world has essentially operated on a system of flexible exchange rates. Flexible exchange rates mean that currency prices are allowed to fluctuate with changes in supply and demand, without governments stepping in to prevent those changes. Before that, governments operated under what was called the *Bretton Woods fixed exchange rate system,* in which they would maintain a stable exchange rate by buying or selling currencies or reserves to bring demand and supply for their currencies together at the fixed exchange rate. The present system evolved out of the Bretton Woods fixed-rate system and occurred by accident, not design. Governments were unable to agree on an alternative fixed-rate approach when the Bretton Woods system collapsed, so nations simply let market forces determine currency values.

ARE EXCHANGE RATES MANAGED AT ALL?

To be sure, governments sensitive to sharp changes in the exchange value of their currencies do still intervene from time to time to prop up their currency's exchange rate if it is considered to be too low or falling too rapidly, or to depress its exchange rate if it is considered to be too high or rising too rapidly. However, present-day fluctuations in exchange rates are not determined solely by market forces. Economists sometimes say that the current exchange rate system is a **dirty float system,** meaning that fluctuations in currency values are partly determined by market forces and partly influenced by government intervention. Over the years, however, such governmental support attempts have been insufficient to dramatically alter exchange rates for long, and currency exchange rates have changed dramatically.

dirty float system
a description of the exchange rate system that means that fluctuations in currency values are partly determined by government intervention

WHEN EXCHANGE RATES CHANGE

When exchange rates change, they affect not only the currency market but the product markets as well. For example, if Canadian consumers were to receive fewer and fewer British pounds and Japanese yen per Canadian dollar, the effect would be an increasing price for foreign imports, *ceteris paribus.* It would now take a greater number of dollars to buy a given number of yen or pounds, which Canadian consumers use to purchase those foreign products. It would, however, lower the cost of Canadian exports to foreigners. If, however, the dollar increased in value relative to other currencies, then the relative price of foreign goods would decrease, *ceteris paribus.* But foreigners would find that Canadian goods were more expensive in terms of their own currency prices, and, as a result, would import fewer Canadian products.

The exchange rate is the rate at which one country's currency can be traded for another country's currency. Under a flexible-rate system, the government allows the forces of supply and demand to determine the exchange rate. Changes in exchange rates occur daily or even hourly.

THE ADVANTAGES OF FLEXIBLE RATES

As mentioned earlier, the present system of flexible exchange rates was not planned. Indeed, most central bankers thought that a system where rates were not fixed would lead to chaos. What in fact has happened? Since the advent of flexible exchange rates, world trade has not only continued but expanded. Over a one-year period, the world economy adjusted to the shock of a four-fold increase in the price of its most important internationally traded commodity, oil. Although the OPEC oil cartel's price increase certainly had adverse economic effects, it did so without paralyzing the economy of any one nation.

The most important advantage of the flexible-rate system is that the recurrent crises that led to speculative rampages and major currency revaluations under the fixed Bretton Woods system have significantly diminished. Under the fixed-rate system, price changes in currencies came infrequently, but when they came, they were of a large magnitude: 20 percent or 30 percent changes overnight were fairly common. Today, price changes occur daily or even hourly, but each change is much smaller in magnitude, with major changes in exchange rates typically occurring only over periods of months or years.

FIXED EXCHANGE RATES CAN RESULT IN CURRENCY SHORTAGES

Perhaps the most significant problem with the fixed-rate system is that it can result in currency shortages, just as domestic price and wage controls lead to shortages. Suppose we had a fixed-rate system with the price of one euro set at $1, as shown in Exhibit 1. In this example, the original quantity of euros demanded and supplied is indicated by curves D_0 and S, so $1 is the equilibrium price. That is, at a price of $1, the quantity of euros demanded (by Canadian importers of European products and others wanting euros) equals the quantity supplied (by European importers of Canadian products and others).

Suppose that some event happens to increase Canadian demand for Dutch goods. For this example, let us assume that Royal Dutch Shell discovers new oil reserves in the North Sea and thus has a new product to export. As Canadian consumers begin to demand Royal Dutch Shell oil, the demand for euros increases. That is, at any given dollar price of euros, Canadian consumers want more euros, shifting the demand curve to the right, to D_1. Under a fixed exchange rate system, the dollar price of euros must remain at $1, where the quantity of euros demanded, Q_1, now exceeds the quantity supplied, Q_0. The result is a shortage of euros—a shortage that must be corrected in some way. As a solution to the shortage, Canada may borrow euros from the Netherlands, or perhaps ship the Netherlands some of its reserves of gold. The ability to continually make up the shortage (deficit) in this manner, however, is limited, particularly if the deficit persists for a substantial time.

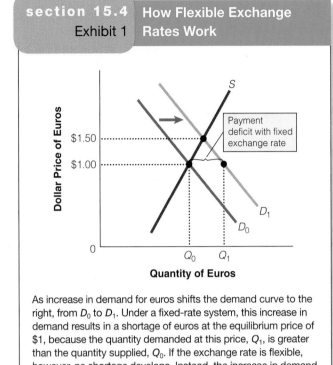

section 15.4 Exhibit 1 How Flexible Exchange Rates Work

As increase in demand for euros shifts the demand curve to the right, from D_0 to D_1. Under a fixed-rate system, this increase in demand results in a shortage of euros at the equilibrium price of $1, because the quantity demanded at this price, Q_1, is greater than the quantity supplied, Q_0. If the exchange rate is flexible, however, no shortage develops. Instead, the increase in demand forces the exchange rate higher, to $1.50. At this higher exchange rate, the quantity of euros demanded doesn't increase as much, and the quantity of euros supplied increases as a result of the now relatively lower cost of imports from Canada.

FLEXIBLE RATES SOLVE THE CURRENCY SHORTAGE PROBLEM

Under flexible exchange rates, a change in the supply or demand for euros does not pose a problem. Because rates are allowed to change, the rising Canadian demand for European goods (and thus for euros) would lead to a new equilibrium price for euros, say, at $1.50. At this higher price, European goods are more costly to Canadian buyers. Some of the increase in demand for European imports, then, is offset by a decrease in quantity demanded resulting from higher import prices. Similarly, the change in the exchange rate will make Canadian goods cheaper to Europeans, thus increasing Canadian exports and, with that, the quantity of euros supplied. For example, a $40 software program that cost Europeans 40 euros when the exchange rate was $1 per euro costs less than 27 euros when the exchange rate increases to $1.50 per euro ($40 divided by $1.50).

FLEXIBLE RATES AFFECT MACROECONOMIC POLICIES

With flexible exchange rates, the imbalance between debits and credits arising from shifts in currency demand and/or supply is accommodated by changes in currency prices, rather than through the special financial borrowings or reserve movements necessary with fixed rates. In a pure flexible exchange rate system, deficits and surpluses in the balance of payments tend to disappear automatically. The market mechanism itself is able to address world trade imbalances, dispensing with the need for bureaucrats attempting to achieve some administratively determined price. Moreover, the need to use restrictive monetary and/or fiscal policy to end such an imbalance while maintaining a fixed exchange rate is alleviated. Nations are thus able to feel less constraint in carrying out internal macroeconomic policies under flexible exchange rates. For these reasons, many economists welcomed the collapse of the Bretton Woods system and the failure to arrive at a new system of fixed or quasi-fixed exchange rates.

THE DISADVANTAGES OF FLEXIBLE RATES

Despite the fact that world trade has grown and dealing with balance-of-payments problems has become less difficult, flexible exchange rates have not been universally endorsed by everyone. Several disadvantages of this system have been cited.

Flexible Rates and World Trade

Traditionally, the major objection to flexible rates was that they introduce considerable uncertainty into international trade. For example, if you order some perfume from France with a commitment to pay 1000 euros in three months, you are not certain what the dollar price of euros, and therefore of the perfume, will be three months from now because the exchange rate is constantly fluctuating. Because people prefer certainty to uncertainty and are generally risk averse, this uncertainty raises the costs of international transactions. As a result, flexible exchange rates can reduce the volume of trade, thus reducing the potential gains from international specialization.

Proponents of flexible rates have three answers to this argument. First, the empirical evidence shows that international trade has, in fact, grown in volume faster since the introduction of flexible rates. The exchange rate risk of trade has not had any major adverse effect. Second, it is possible to, in effect, buy insurance against the proposed adverse effect of currency fluctuations. Rather than buying currencies for immediate use in what is called the "spot" market for foreign currencies, one can contract today to buy foreign currencies in the future at a set exchange rate in the "forward" or "future" market. By using this market, a perfume importer can buy euros now for delivery to her in three months; in doing so, she can be certain of the dollar price she is paying for the perfume. Since floating exchange rates began, booming futures markets in foreign currencies have opened in Toronto, Chicago, New York, and other foreign financial centers. The third argument is that the alleged certainty of currency prices under the old Bretton Woods system was fictitious because the possibility existed that nations might, at their whim, drastically revalue their currencies to deal with their own fundamental balance-of-payments problems. Proponents of flexible rates, then, argue that they are therefore no less disruptive to trade than fixed rates.

Flexible Rates and Inflation

A second, more valid criticism of flexible exchange rates is that they can contribute to inflationary pressures. Under fixed rates, domestic monetary and fiscal authorities have an incentive to constrain their domestic prices because lower domestic prices increase the attractiveness of exported goods. This discipline is not present to the same extent with flexible rates. The consequence of a sharp monetary or fiscal expansion under flexible rates would be a decline in the value of one's currency relative to those of other countries.

Advocates of flexible rates would argue that inflation need not occur under flexible rates. Flexible rates do not cause inflation; rather, it is caused by the expansionary macroeconomic policies of governments and central banks. Actually, flexible rates give government decision makers greater freedom of action than fixed rates; whether they act responsibly is determined not by exchange rates but by domestic policies.

Section Check

1. Today, rates are free to fluctuate based on market transactions, but governments occasionally intervene to increase or depress the price of their currencies.
2. Changes in exchange rates occur more often under a flexible-rate system, but the changes are much smaller than the drastic, overnight revaluations of currencies that occurred under the fixed-rate system.
3. Under a fixed-rate system, the supply and demand for currencies shift, but currency prices are not allowed to shift to the new equilibrium, leading to surpluses and shortages of currencies.
4. The main arguments presented against flexible exchange rates are that international trade levels will be diminished due to uncertainty of future currency prices and that the flexible rates would lead to inflation. Proponents of flexible exchange rates have strong counter-arguments to those views.

Summary

Section 15.1

■ The balance of payments is the record of all the international financial transactions of a nation for a given year.

■ The balance of payments is made up of the current account, the capital account, as well as an "error term" called the statistical discrepancy.

■ The merchandise trade balance refers strictly to the imports and exports of (merchandise) goods with other nations.

■ If imports of foreign goods are greater than exports, there is a merchandise trade deficit. If exports are greater than imports, there is a merchandise trade surplus.

Section 15.2

■ The exchange rate is the price in one country's currency of one unit of another country's currency.

■ The exchange rate for a currency is determined by supply and demand in the foreign exchange market.

■ If the Canadian dollar appreciates in value relative to foreign currencies, foreign goods become cheaper to Canadian consumers, increasing Canadian demand for foreign goods.

Section 15.3

■ Any force that shifts either the demand or supply curves for foreign currency will shift the equilibrium in the foreign exchange market and lead to a new exchange rate.

■ Any changes in tastes, tariffs, income levels, relative interest rates, relative inflation rates, or speculation will cause the demand for and supply of a currency to shift.

Section 15.4

■ Flexible-rate systems allow exchange rates to fluctuate freely based on market transactions, but governments occasionally intervene to increase or depress the price of their currencies.

■ Changes in exchange rates are more frequent under a flexible-rate system, but the changes are much smaller as compared to the fixed-rate system.

■ The main arguments against flexible exchange rates are that international trade will diminish due to uncertainty of future currency prices, and that the flexible rates would lead to inflation.

Key Terms and Concepts

For a complete glossary of chapter key terms, visit the textbook's Web site at http://www.sextonmacro2e.nelson.com.

balance of payments 384
current account 384

exchange rate 389
derived demand 390

dirty float system 398

Review Questions

1. Indicate whether each of the following represents a credit or debit on the Canadian current account.

   a. a Canadian imports a BMW from Germany

   b. a Japanese company purchases software from a Canadian company

   c. Canada gives $100 million in financial aid to Afghanistan

   d. a Canadian company sells lumber to Great Britain

2. Indicate whether each of the following represents a credit or debit on the Canadian capital account.

   a. a French bank purchases $100 000 worth of Canadian government bonds

   b. Nortel purchases an American telecommunications company

   c. a Canadian resident buys a stock on the Japanese stock market

   d. a Japanese company purchases a shopping mall in Vancouver

3. How are each of the following events likely to affect the Canadian merchandise trade balance?

   a. the European price level increases relative to the Canadian price level

   b. the Canadian dollar appreciates in value relative to the currencies of its trading partners

   c. the Canadian government offers subsidies to firms that export goods

   d. the Canadian government imposes tariffs on imported goods

   e. the United States experiences a severe recession

4. How are each of the following events likely to affect the value of the Canadian dollar relative to the euro?

   a. interest rates in the European Union increase relative to Canada

   b. the European Union price level rises relative to the Canadian price level

   c. the Bank of Canada intervenes by buying Canadian dollars on the foreign exchange market

   d. the price level in Canada rises relative to the price level in Europe

5. What happens to the supply curve for Canadian dollars in the foreign exchange market under the following conditions?

   a. Canadians wish to buy more Japanese consumer electronics

   b. a Canadian mutual fund wants to buy stock in Microsoft

Fill in the Blanks

Section 15.1

1. A current account is a record of a country's current _____ and _____ of goods and services.

2. Because Canada obtains foreign currency, all exports of Canadian goods abroad are considered a _____ or _____ item in the Canadian balance of payments.

3. Nations import and export _____, such as tourism, as well as _____ (goods).

4. When exports of goods exceed imports of goods, there is a merchandise trade _____.

Section 15.2

5. Foreigners buying Canadian goods must _____ their currencies to obtain _____ in order to pay for Canadian goods.

6. The price of a unit of one foreign currency in terms of another currency is called the _____.

7. A change in the euro–dollar exchange rate from $1 per euro to $2 per euro would _____ the Canadian dollar price of German goods, _____ the number of German goods that would be demanded in Canada.

8. The demand for foreign currencies is a derived demand because it derives directly from the demand for foreign _____ or for foreign _____.

9. The more foreigners demand Canadian products, the _____ of their currencies they will supply in exchange for Canadian dollars.

10. The supply of and demand for a foreign currency determine the equilibrium _____ of that currency.

11. The quantity of euros demanded by Canadian consumers will increase to buy more European goods as the price of the euro _____.

12. As the price, or value, of the euro increases relative to the Canadian dollar, Canadian products become relatively _____ expensive to European buyers, which will _____ the quantity of dollars they will demand.

13. The supply curve of a foreign currency is _____ sloping.

14. If the dollar price of euros is higher than the equilibrium price, there will be an excess quantity of euros _____ at that price, and competition among euro _____ will push the price of euros _____ toward equilibrium.

Section 15.3

15. An increased demand for euros will result in a _____ equilibrium exchange rate for euros, whereas a decreased demand for euros will result in a _____ equilibrium exchange rate for euros.

16. Changes in a currency's exchange rate can be caused by changes in _____ for goods, changes in _____, changes in relative _____ rates, changes in relative _____ rates, and _____.

17. An increase in tastes for European goods in Canada would _____ the demand for euros, _____ the equilibrium exchange rate of euros.

18. A decrease in incomes in Canada would _____ the amount of European imports purchased by Canadians, which would _____ the demand for euros, resulting in a _____ exchange rate for euros.

19. If European incomes _____, European tariffs on Canadian goods _____, or European tastes for Canadian goods _____, Europeans would demand more Canadian goods, leading them to increase their supply of euros to obtain the added dollars necessary to make those purchases.

20. If interest rates in Canada were to increase relative to European interest rates, other things being equal, the rate of return on Canadian investments would _____ relative to that on European investments, _____ Europeans' demand for Canadian investments.

21. If Europe experienced a higher inflation rate than Canada, European products would become relatively _____ expensive to Canadian consumers, _____ the quantity of European goods demanded by Canadians, and therefore _____ the demand for euros.

Section 15.4

22. A _____ refers to an exchange rate system where fluctuations in the currency value is partly determined by government intervention.

23. Under a fixed-rate system, changes in the supply and demand for currencies leads to _____ and _____ of currencies.

24. The two major objections to flexible exchange rates are: reduced _____ due to increased uncertainty regarding future currency prices; and increased _____.

True or False

Section 15.1

1. Canadian imports are considered a credit item in the balance of payments because Canada obtains foreign currency.

2. Our imports provide the Canadian dollars with which foreigners can buy our exports.

3. Canada's imports and exports of services are the largest component of the balance of payments.

4. When Canada runs a trade surplus in goods and services with the rest of the world, the rest of the world must be running a trade deficit in goods and services with Canada.

Section 15.2

5. Canadian consumers must first exchange Canadian dollars for a foreign seller's currency in order to pay for imported goods.

6. The exchange rate can be expressed either as the number of units of currency A per unit of currency B or its reciprocal, the number of units of currency B per unit of currency A.

7. The more foreign goods that are demanded, the more of that foreign currency will be needed to pay for those goods, which will tend to push down the exchange rate of that currency relative to other currencies.

8. The supply of foreign currency is provided by foreigners who want to buy the exports of another nation.

9. As the price of the euro falls relative to the Canadian dollar, European products become relatively cheaper to Canadian consumers, who therefore buy more European goods.

10. As the value of the euro increases relative to the Canadian dollar, Canadian products become relatively cheaper to European buyers. Europeans will, therefore, increase the quantity of euros supplied.

11. If the dollar price of euros is lower than the equilibrium price, there will be a surplus of euros, and competition among euro sellers will push the price of euros down toward equilibrium.

Section 15.3

12. Any force that shifts either the demand for or supply of a currency will shift the equilibrium in the foreign exchange market, leading to a new exchange rate.

13. Any change in the demand for foreign goods will shift the demand curve for foreign currency in the opposite direction.

14. A decrease in tastes for European goods in Canada would decrease the demand for euros, decreasing the equilibrium exchange rate of euros.

15. An increase in incomes in Canada would increase the amount of European imports purchased by Canadians, which would increase the demand for euros, resulting in a higher exchange rate for euros.

16. If European incomes rose, European tariffs on Canadian goods decreased, or European tastes for Canadian goods increased, the exchange rate for euros would tend to be higher.

17. A decrease in Canadian tariffs on European goods would tend to have the same effect on the exchange rate for euros as an increase in Canadian incomes.

18. If interest rates in Canada were to increase relative to European interest rates, the result would be a new lower exchange rate for euros, other things being equal.

19. If Europe experienced a higher inflation rate than Canada, both the supply of euros would tend to increase and the demand for euros would tend to decrease, leading to a new lower exchange rate for euros.

20. If currency speculators believe that Canada is going to experience more rapid inflation than Japan in the future, they believe that the value of the Canadian dollar will soon be falling, which will increase the demand for yen, so the yen will appreciate relative to the Canadian dollar.

Section 15.4

21. Under a flexible-rate system, price changes in currencies are infrequent, but when they do come, they are large in magnitude.

22. Under a flexible-rate system, an increase in the demand for foreign currency forces the exchange rate higher, thereby avoiding a shortage of foreign currency.

23. Flexible exchange rates have been universally endorsed as the optimal system for valuing currency.

Multiple Choice

Section 15.1

1. Which of the following would be recorded as a credit in the Canadian balance of payments accounts?
   a. the purchase of a German business by a Canadian investor
   b. the import of Honda trucks by a Canadian automobile distributor
   c. European travel expenditures of a Canadian university student
   d. the purchase of a Canadian government bond by a French investment company

2. What is the difference between the merchandise trade balance and the balance of payments?
   a. Only the value of goods imported and exported is included in the merchandise trade balance, whereas the balance of payments includes the value of all payments to and from foreigners.
   b. The value of goods imported and exported is included in the merchandise trade balance, whereas the balance of payments includes only capital account transactions.
   c. The value of all goods, services, and transfers is included in the merchandise trade balance, whereas the balance of payments includes both current account and capital account transactions.
   d. Merchandise trade balance and balance of payments both describe the same international exchange transactions.

3. If consumers in Europe and Asia develop strong preferences for Canadian goods, Canada's current account will
   a. not be affected since purchases of Canadian goods by foreigners are recorded in the capital account.
   b. not be affected since purchases of Canadian goods based on mere preferences are recorded under statistical discrepancy.
   c. move toward surplus since purchases of Canadian goods are recorded as credits on our current account.
   d. move toward deficit since purchases of Canadian goods by foreigners are counted as debits in our current account.

4. Which of the following would supply Canadian dollars to the foreign exchange market?
   a. the sale of a Canadian automobile to a Mexican consumer
   b. the spending by British tourists in Canada
   c. the purchase of German wine by a Canadian consumer
   d. the sale of a Canadian corporation to a Japanese investor

5. Which of the following will enter as a credit in the Canadian balance of payments capital account?
   a. the purchase of a Japanese automobile by a Canadian consumer
   b. the sale of Canadian lumber to Japan
   c. the sale of a Canadian manufacturing company to a Japanese industrialist
   d. the purchase of a Japanese electronics plant by a Canadian firm

6. If the value of a nation's merchandise exports exceeds merchandise imports, then the nation is running a
   a. balance of payments deficit.
   b. balance of payments surplus.
   c. merchandise trade deficit.
   d. merchandise trade surplus.

7. When goods or services cross international borders,
    a. money must generally move in the opposite direction.
    b. payment must be made in another good, using barter.
    c. a future shipment must be made to offset the current sale/purchase.
    d. countries must ship gold to make payment.

8. The balance of payments records information about
    a. purchases of Canadian financial assets by foreigners.
    b. purchases of foreign financial assets by Canadians.
    c. the levels of imports and exports of goods and services for a country.
    d. all of the above.

9. Suppose Canada imposed a high tariff on a major imported item. This would tend to
    a. cause the dollar to appreciate in value.
    b. cause the dollar to depreciate in value.
    c. decrease the Canadian merchandise trade surplus.
    d. increase Canadian exports of goods.

10. A deficit in a country's current account will be matched by
    a. a deficit in the capital account.
    b. a surplus in the capital account.
    c. a surplus in the merchandise trade balance.
    d. a deficit in the merchandise trade balance.

11. If high-yield investment opportunities attract capital from abroad and lead to a capital account surplus, then the
    a. nation's currency must appreciate.
    b. nation's currency must depreciate.
    c. nation must run a current account deficit.
    d. nation must run a current account surplus.
    e. a and c.

Section 15.2

12. If the Canadian dollar *depreciates,* it can be said that
    a. foreign countries no longer respect Canada.
    b. other currencies appreciate.
    c. it rises in value.
    d. it takes fewer dollars to buy units of other currencies.
    e. all of the above are correct.

13. Assume it costs US$0.667 to buy one Canadian dollar. How many Canadian dollars would it take to buy one U.S. dollar?
    a. $1.50
    b. $1.33
    c. $1.00
    d. $0.67

14. If the exchange rate between the Canadian dollar and the euro changes from $2 = 1 euro to $3 = 1 euro, then
    a. European goods will become less expensive for Canadians, and imports of European goods to Canada will rise.
    b. European goods will become less expensive for Canadians, and imports of European goods to Canada will fall.
    c. European goods will become more expensive for Canadians, and imports of European goods to Canada will rise.
    d. European goods will become more expensive for Canadians, and imports of European goods to Canada will fall.

15. If the price in Canadian dollars of Mexican pesos changes from $0.10 per peso to $0.14 per peso, the peso has
    a. appreciated.
    b. depreciated.
    c. devalued.
    d. stayed at the same exchange rate.

16. Which of the following is most likely to cause the depreciation of the Canadian dollar?
    a. a German professor on vacation in Quebec
    b. a Canadian professor on extended vacation in Paris
    c. a Canadian farmer who relies on exports
    d. a foreign student studying in Canada

17. If the dollar appreciates relative to other currencies, which of the following is true?
    a. It takes more of the other currency to buy a dollar.
    b. It takes less of the other currency to buy a dollar.
    c. There is no change in the currency needed to buy a dollar.
    d. There is not enough information to make a determination.

18. Suppose that the Canadian dollar rises from 100 to 125 Japanese yen. As a result,
    a. exports to Japan will likely increase.
    b. Japanese tourists will more likely visit Canada.
    c. Canadian businesses will be less likely to use Japanese shipping lines to transport their products.
    d. Canadian consumers will more likely buy Japanese-made automobiles.

19. A depreciation in the Canadian dollar would
    a. discourage foreigners from making investments in Canada.
    b. discourage foreign consumers from buying Canadian goods.
    c. reduce the number of dollars it would take to buy a Swiss franc.
    d. encourage foreigners to buy more Canadian goods.

20. If the exchange rate between euros and dollars were 2 euros per dollar, when a Canadian purchased a good valued at 80 euros, its cost in dollars would be
    a. $160.
    b. $80.
    c. $40.
    d. none of the above.

21. Suppose that the exchange rate between Mexican pesos and Canadian dollars is 8 pesos per dollar. If the exchange rate goes to 10 pesos per dollar, it would tend to
    a. increase Canadian exports to Mexico.
    b. decrease Canadian exports to Mexico.
    c. increase Mexican exports to Canada.
    d. decrease Mexican exports to Canada.
    e. do both b and c.

22. If the Canadian dollar is cheaper in terms of a foreign currency than the equilibrium exchange rate, a _____ exists at the current exchange rate that will put _____ pressure on the exchange rate of the dollar.
    a. surplus of dollars; downward
    b. surplus of dollars; upward
    c. shortage of dollars; downward
    d. shortage of dollars; upward

23. In foreign exchange markets, the supply of dollars is determined
    a. by the level of Canadian imports and the demand for foreign assets by Canadian citizens.
    b. solely by the level of Canadian merchandise exports.
    c. solely by the level of Canadian merchandise imports.
    d. solely by the levels of Canadian merchandise exports and merchandise imports.
    e. by the level of Canadian exports and the demand for Canadian assets by foreigners.

Section 15.3

24. In foreign exchange markets, the effect of an increase in the demand for dollars on the value of the dollar is the same as that of
    a. an increase in the supply of foreign currencies.
    b. a decrease in the supply of foreign currencies.
    c. a decrease in the demand for dollars.
    d. none of the above.

25. If the demand by foreigners for Canadian government bonds increased, other things being equal, it would tend to:
    a. increase the exchange rate of the dollar and increase Canadian merchandise exports.
    b. increase the exchange rate of the dollar and decrease Canadian merchandise exports.
    c. decrease the exchange rate of the dollar and increase Canadian merchandise exports.
    d. decrease the exchange rate of the dollar and decrease Canadian merchandise exports.

26. If the rate of inflation in Canada falls relative to the rate of inflation in foreign nations, Canadian net exports will tend to _____, causing the exchange rate of the Canadian dollar to _____.
    a. rise; rise
    b. rise; fall
    c. fall; rise
    d. fall; fall

27. If real incomes in foreign nations were growing more rapidly than Canadian real incomes, one would expect that as a result,
    a. the exchange rate of the dollar would decline relative to other currencies.
    b. the exchange rate of the dollar would increase relative to other currencies.
    c. there would likely be no effect on the exchange rate of the dollar relative to other currencies.
    d. there would be an indeterminate effect on the exchange rate of the dollar relative to other currencies.

28. If interest rates in Canada fell relative to interest rates in other countries, other things being equal,
    a. the exchange rate of the dollar would decline relative to other currencies.
    b. the exchange rate of the dollar would increase relative to other currencies.
    c. there would likely be no effect on the exchange rate of the dollar relative to other currencies.
    d. there would be an indeterminate effect on the exchange rate of the dollar relative to other currencies.

29. Sweden's currency would tend to appreciate if
    a. the demand for Sweden's exports increases.
    b. the demand for imports by Swedes increases.
    c. interest rates in Sweden decrease relative to those of the rest of the world.
    d. Sweden's inflation rate rises relative to inflation in the rest of the world.

30. A country would tend to experience currency depreciation relative to that of other countries if
    a. the profitability of investments in other countries increases relative to the profitability in that country.
    b. traders in the foreign currency markets expect the value of the currency to fall in the near future.
    c. the foreign demand for its exports decreases.
    d. any of the above occurs.
    e. any of the above except c occurs.

31. If the Canadian dollar depreciates relative to the Japanese yen, we would expect
    a. that the Japanese trade surplus with Canada would increase.
    b. that Japanese imports from Canada would decrease.
    c. that Japanese exports to Canada would decrease.
    d. that a and b would occur.

32. As the number of British pounds that exchange for a Canadian dollar falls on foreign currency markets,
    a. the British will have an incentive to import fewer Canadian goods.
    b. the British will find it easier to export goods to Canada.
    c. the British will find Canadian goods to be more expensive in their stores.
    d. all of the above will be true.
    e. none of the above will be true.

33. If interest rates in Canada rose and interest rates in the United States fell, we would expect people to
    a. increase their demand for U.S. dollars.
    b. borrow more from Canadian sources.
    c. buy relatively more Canadian assets.
    d. buy relatively more U.S. assets.
    e. do both b and c.

34. If the Bank of Canada were to sell Canadian dollars on the foreign exchange market, a likely result would be
    a. a rightward shift in the dollar supply curve.
    b. at least a temporary decline in the exchange rate of the Canadian dollar.
    c. at least a temporary increase in the exchange rate of the Canadian dollar.
    d. a and b.
    e. a and c.

Section 15.4

35. In a dirty float system, who is seen as intervening in the market to partly determine currency values?
    a. foreign investors
    b. domestic consumers
    c. the government
    d. currency speculators

36. Under which system of currency valuation will changes in the demand and supply of foreign currency not result in surpluses and shortages of foreign currency?
   a. fixed-rate system
   b. flexible-rate system
   c. constant-rate system
   d. all of the above

37. Which of the following is a criticism against flexible exchange rate systems?
   a. they reduce uncertainty and therefore limit the growth of international trade
   b. they allow for greater opportunity for illegal 'laundering' of currency for organized crime
   c. they contribute to inflationary pressures
   d. all of the above

Problems

1. [Section 15.2]
Assume that a product sells for $100 in Canada.
   a. If the exchange rate between British pounds and Canadian dollars is $2 per pound, what would the price of the product be in the United Kingdom?
   b. If the exchange rate between Mexican pesos and Canadian dollars is 8 pesos per dollar, what would the price of the product be in Mexico?
   c. Which direction would the price of the $100 Canadian product change in a foreign country if Canadians' tastes for foreign products increased?
   d. Which direction would the price of the $100 Canadian product change in a foreign country if incomes in the foreign country fell?
   e. Which direction would the price of the $100 Canadian product change in a foreign country if interest rates in Canada fell relative to interest rates in other countries?

2. [Section 15.3]
How would each of the following affect the supply of euros, the demand for euros, and the dollar price of euros?

Change	Supply of Euros	Demand for Euros	Dollar Price of Euros
Reduced Canadian tastes for European goods			
Increased incomes in Canada			
Increased Canadian interest rates			
Decreased inflation in Europe			
Reduced Canadian tariffs on imports			
Increased European tastes for Canadian goods			

CHAPTER 1

Fill in the Blanks

1. limited; unlimited **2.** scarcity **3.** inputs **4.** scarcity; value **5.** trade-offs **6.** macroeconomics; microeconomics **7.** theories; explain; predict **8.** hypothesis **9.** *ceteris paribus* **10.** correlation **11.** fallacy of composition **12.** positive **13.** wants; resources **14.** labour; land; capital; entrepreneurship **15.** knowledge and skill; education and on-the-job training **16.** production techniques; products; profits **17.** competition **18.** wants and desires **19.** choices; wants and desires **20.** opportunity cost **21.** how much **22.** marginal; marginal; adding to; subtracting from **23.** expected marginal benefits; expected marginal costs **24.** rise; fall; fall; rise **25.** positive **26.** specialize; lower **27.** comparative advantage **28.** skill; wasted; best **29.** language; relative availability of products; relative value; less; more **30.** voluntary; price **31.** market failure

True or False

1. T **2.** F **3.** F **4.** T **5.** F **6.** F **7.** T **8.** F **9.** T **10.** T **11.** F **12.** T **13.** T **14.** T **15.** T **16.** F **17.** T **18.** T **19.** T **20.** F **21.** T **22.** F **23.** F **24.** T **25.** T **26.** F **27.** T **28.** T **29.** T **30.** T **31.** T **32.** T

Multiple Choice

1. b **2.** d **3.** d **4.** d **5.** b **6.** d **7.** d **8.** c **9.** c **10.** c **11.** d **12.** c **13.** d **14.** d **15.** d **16.** e **17.** e **18.** d **19.** b **20.** d **21.** b **22.** d **23.** b **24.** b **25.** c **26.** b **27.** b **28.** a **29.** b **30.** e **31.** b **32.** b **33.** c **34.** c

Problems

1. **a.** microeconomics
   b. macroeconomics
   c. microeconomics
   d. macroeconomics
   e. microeconomics
2. **a.** both normative and positive statements
   b. normative statements
   c. positive statements
   d. both normative and positive statements
   e. positive statements
3. **a.** $50; $25
   b. 3; 5; Mark would go as long as his marginal benefit was greater than the admission price.
   c. Yes; 6; Mark would buy the pass because his total benefits exceed his total cost. Once he has the pass, the marginal cost of attending one more day becomes zero, so he will go as long as his marginal benefits exceed zero.
4. **a.** $57; $88
   b. 43; 44; He would produce as long as the price (marginal benefit) exceeded the marginal cost.

CHAPTER 2

Fill in the Blanks

1. what; how; for whom **2.** decentralized **3.** mixed **4.** least **5.** labour intensive; capital intensive **6.** product **7.** inputs; firms; factor; input **8.** circular flow; product; factor; firms **9.** production possibilities **10.** resources; technology **11.** inefficiently; potential **12.** unemployed; better **13.** efficiency; most **14.** concave; increasing **15.** opportunity cost; increases **16.** fewer; more **17.** technology; labour productivity; natural resource finds **18.** scarcity; trade-offs **19.** scarcity; choice; opportunity costs; efficiency; economic growth

True or False

1. T **2.** T **3.** T **4.** F **5.** T **6.** T **7.** F **8.** T **9.** F **10.** T **11.** F **12.** F **13.** T **14.** T **15.** T **16.** F **17.** F **18.** F

Multiple Choice

1. a **2.** c **3.** d **4.** c **5.** a **6.** d **7.** e **8.** e **9.** e **10.** c **11.** d **12.** c **13.** c **14.** e **15.** b **16.** b **17.** c **18.** d **19.** a **20.** c **21.** c **22.** e **23.** b

Problems

1.

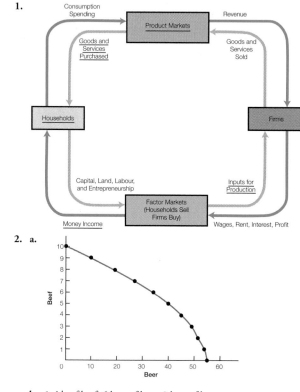

2. **a.**

b. 1 side of beef; 6 kegs of beer; 9 kegs of beer
c. 35 kegs of beer
d. No; that combination is inside the production possibilities curve, which means more of one good could be produced without giving up any production of the other good.
e. No; that combination is beyond the production possibilities curve and therefore unattainable.

3. **a.** Yes; the bowed-outward shape of the production possibilities curve indicates increasing opportunity costs.
b. Zero; because point I is inside the production possibilities curve, moving from point I to point D means that the output of food can increase with no decrease in the output of shelter.
c. 10 units of food
d. All of the points on the production possibilities curve are efficient because at any of those points more of one good could be produced only by sacrificing some output of the other good. However, the curve does not tell us which of those points is best from the perspective of society.
e. N; additional resources or new technology (shifting the PPC outward).
f. I; economy must ensure that all resources are being utilized to their fullest extent, no wasted resources.

CHAPTER 3

Fill in the Blanks

1. market; exchanging **2.** trade **3.** buyers; sellers **4.** competitive **5.** quantity demanded **6.** substitution **7.** individual demand schedule **8.** market demand curve **9.** money (or absolute or nominal); relative **10.** a good's price; moving along **11.** prices of related goods; income; number; tastes; expectations **12.** rightward; leftward **13.** substitutes **14.** increase; decrease **15.** increase

16. quantity supplied; quantity supplied **17.** profits; production; higher
18. positive **19.** willing; able **20.** input; expectations; number; technology;
regulation; taxes and subsidies; weather **21.** lower; right **22.** increases
23. decreases

True or False
1. T **2.** F **3.** T **4.** T **5.** F **6.** T **7.** T **8.** T **9.** T **10.** F **11.** F **12.** T **13.** F **14.** T
15. F **16.** T **17.** F **18.** T **19.** F **20.** F

Multiple Choice
1. e **2.** d **3.** d **4.** b **5.** d **6.** d **7.** b **8.** b **9.** c **10.** b **11.** d **12.** c **13.** d **14.** c

Problems

1. a.

P	Q_D
$5	4
4	8
3	12
2	16
1	20

b.

P	Q_D
$5	6
4	12
3	18
2	24
1	30

c.

P	Q_D
$5	5
4	10
3	15
2	20
1	25

2.

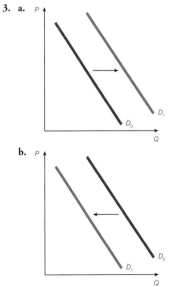

3. a.

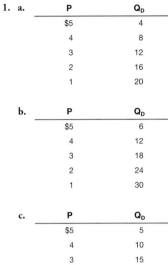

b.

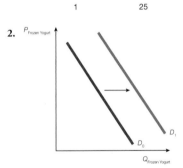

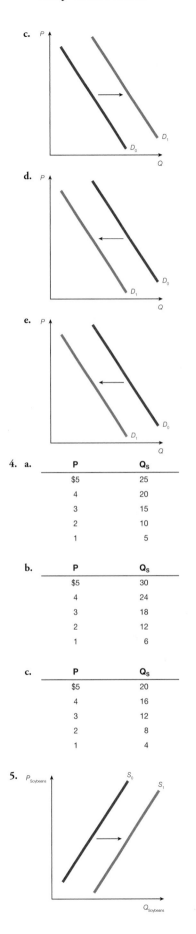

4. a.

P	Q_S
$5	25
4	20
3	15
2	10
1	5

b.

P	Q_S
$5	30
4	24
3	18
2	12
1	6

c.

P	Q_S
$5	20
4	16
3	12
2	8
1	4

5.

6. a.

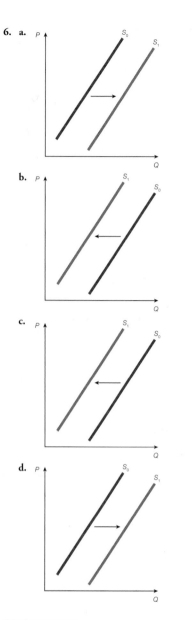

b.

c.

d.

CHAPTER 4

Fill in the Blanks

1. equilibrium; equilibrium **2.** surplus **3.** shortage **4.** surplus; more; cut back; more **5.** greater; greater **6.** higher; lower **7.** decrease **8.** increase; be indeterminate **9.** ceiling; floor **10.** shortages **11.** decline **12.** additional **13.** unintended consequences

True or False

1. F **2.** T **3.** F **4.** T **5.** T **6.** F **7.** T **8.** T **9.** F **10.** F

Multiple Choice

1. c **2.** d **3.** a **4.** d **5.** c **6.** b **7.** a **8.** c **9.** b **10.** a **11.** a **12.** c **13.** e **14.** e **15.** a **16.** c

Problems

1. a.

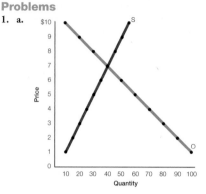

b. $7; 40 units traded

c. Surplus; at $9, above the equilibrium price, there will be a surplus of 30 units of Z (the quantity supplied at $9 [50] minus the quantity demanded at $9 [20]).

d. Shortage; at $3, below the equilibrium price, there will be a shortage of 60 units of Z (the quantity demanded at $3 [80] minus the quantity supplied at $3 [20]).

e. $8, with 45 units traded (at the new supply and demand intersection)

f. $6, with 50 units traded (at the new supply and demand intersection)

2. a. To get to point A would require a decrease in supply; to get to point B would require a decrease in supply and an increase in demand; to get to point C would require an increase in demand; to get to point D would require a decrease in supply and a decrease in demand; point E is the current equilibrium; to get to point F would require an increase in supply and an increase in demand; to get to point G would require a decrease in demand; to get to point H would require an increase in supply and a decrease in demand; to get to point I would require an increase in supply.

b. B; because it indicates a decrease in supply and an increase in demand.

c. Indeterminate; because one of the changes decreases supply and the other increases supply, we don't know what the net effect is on supply. If the effects were of the same magnitude, the result would be E; if the increase in supply were greater than the decrease in supply, the answer would be I; if the decrease in supply were greater than the increase in supply, the answer would be A.

d. C; A; A

e. G; I; G

3.

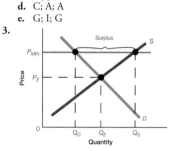

a. If the price floor is raised, the quantity supplied increases, the quantity demanded decreases, and the surplus increases; if the price floor is lowered, the quantity supplied decreases, the quantity demanded increases, and the surplus decreases.

b. The quantity supplied does not change, the quantity demanded increases, and the surplus decreases.

c. The quantity supplied increases, the quantity demanded does not change, and the surplus increases.

4.

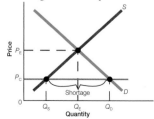

a. If the price ceiling is raised, the quantity supplied increases, the quantity demanded decreases, and the shortage is reduced; if the price ceiling is lowered, the quantity supplied decreases, the quantity demanded increases, and the shortage is increased.

b. The quantity supplied does not change, the quantity demanded increases, and the shortage is increased.

c. The quantity supplied increases, the quantity demanded does not change, and the shortage is decreased.

CHAPTER 5

Fill in the Blanks
1. high; stable; high **2.** real GDP **3.** output **4.** unemployed; the labour force **5.** employed; unemployed **6.** discouraged; labour force **7.** only partly **8.** losers; leavers; re-entrants new **9.** job losers **10.** inflation **11.** mismatches **12.** high; low **13.** labour force participation **14.** short; normal **15.** greater **16.** lower **17.** structural **18.** cyclical **19.** aggregate demand **20.** structural **21.** frictional; structural **22.** natural **23.** frictional; structural **24.** technological, demographic; institutional **25.** potential **26.** greater **27.** temporarily **28.** co-ordinating **29.** high **30.** consumer price index **31.** erodes **32.** uncertainty **33.** raise **34.** relative **35.** menu **36.** shoe-leather **37.** nominal; inflation **38.** lower; higher **39.** leftward **40.** accurately **41.** cost-of-living **42.** short-term; long-term **43.** expansion; peak; contraction; trough **44.** rising; falling; high **45.** peak; trough **46.** forecasts **47.** leading indicators **48.** depth; duration

True or False
1. T **2.** T **3.** F **4.** T **5.** F **6.** T **7.** T **8.** T **9.** F **10.** T **11.** T **12.** F **13.** T **14.** F **15.** T **16.** T **17.** T **18.** T **19.** T **20.** F **21.** T **22.** T **23.** F **24.** T **25.** F **26.** T **27.** F **28.** T **29.** T **30.** T **31.** T **32.** T **33.** F **34.** F **35.** T **36.** T **37.** F **38.** T **39.** T **40.** T **41.** F **42.** T **43.** F **44.** T

Multiple Choice
1. d **2.** c **3.** c **4.** c **5.** e **6.** a **7.** b **8.** b **9.** b **10.** c **11.** a **12.** b **13.** e **14.** b **15.** a **16.** c **17.** b **18.** e **19.** c **20.** a **21.** b **22.** c **23.** d **24.** c **25.** e **26.** a **27.** c **28.** c **29.** d **30.** c **31.** b **32.** d **33.** b **34.** d **35.** c **36.** e **37.** a **38.** e **39.** a

Problems
1. a. Its labour force participation rate is 80 percent (160 million ÷ 200 million) and its unemployment rate is 12.5 percent (20 million ÷ 160 million).

b. Its labour force participation rate would be 90 percent (180 million ÷ 200 million) and its unemployment rate would be 16.7 percent (30 million ÷ 180 million).

c. Its labour force participation rate would be 75 percent (150 million ÷ 200 million) and its unemployment rate would be 6.7 percent (10 million ÷ 150 million).

d. Its labour force participation rate would be 75 percent (150 million ÷ 200 million) and its unemployment rate would be 6.7 percent (10 million ÷ 150 million).

2. a.

job losers	**increase**
job leavers	**decrease**
re-entrants	**decrease**
new entrants	**decrease**

b. Good job prospects would tend to increase the number of job leavers by making them confident they could find better jobs; good job prospects would also attract re-entrants (for example, homemakers or retirees) and new entrants (for example, students who would leave school if offered a good enough job).

3. a.

retirees on fixed incomes	**hurt**
workers	**hurt (unless wages kept up with inflation)**
debtors	**help**
creditors	**hurt**
shoe-leather costs	**increase**
menu costs	**increase**

b. Workers, debtors, and creditors would be unaffected. If retirees stayed on their fixed incomes, they would be hurt. Shoe-leather costs would be unaffected but menu costs would rise.

4. a. 4 percent; 7 percent

b. Nothing, it would remain at 5 percent; 3 percent.

CHAPTER 6

Fill in the Blanks
1. national income **2.** GDP **3.** final; intermediate **4.** expenditure; income **5.** expenditure **6.** consumption; investment; government purchases; net exports **7.** nondurable; durable; services **8.** households **9.** vehicles **10.** more **11.** capital; produce other goods **12.** fixed; inventory **13.** increase **14.** transfer **15.** excluded **16.** income **17.** income **18.** wages; rent; interest; profits **19.** productive; factor **20.** depreciation **21.** disposable **22.** index **23.** consumer price index **24.** final **25.** households **26.** current; base **27.** nominal GDP; GDP deflator **28.** real; total population **29.** reliable **30.** in the home **31.** omitted

True or False
1. T **2.** F **3.** T **4.** T **5.** T **6.** F **7.** F **8.** T **9.** F **10.** T **11.** F **12.** T **13.** T **14.** F **15.** F **16.** T **17.** T **18.** T **19.** T **20.** F **21.** T **22.** F **23.** T **24.** T **25.** F **26.** F **27.** T **28.** T **29.** T **30.** F **31.** F **32.** T **33.** F **34.** F **35.** T

Multiple Choice
1. a **2.** c **3.** d **4.** c **5.** c **6.** c **7.** b **8.** b **9.** c **10.** d **11.** b **12.** a **13.** d **14.** e **15.** c **16.** c **17.** e **18.** e **19.** e **20.** d **21.** c **22.** c **23.** c **24.** d **25.** c **26.** d **27.** b **28.** c **29.** e **30.** a **31.** e **32.** d **33.** c **34.** e **35.** e **36.** b

Problems
1. a. GDP is the value of all final goods and services produced within a country during a given period of time (almost always one year).

b. To count intermediate goods as well as final goods and services would result in double counting the value of some goods and services.

c. GDP is an attempt to measure domestic output; therefore, it must exclude goods and services produced in other countries (even if those goods and services are produced by Canadians in other countries).

d. The value of used goods was included in GDP when those goods were newly produced, so sales of used goods are not counted as part of GDP (although any sales commissions on such sales would be counted as newly produced services).

e. Because such sales simply rearrange existing ownership claims, they are not counted because they are not payments for newly produced goods or services (although any sales commissions on such sales would be counted as newly produced services).

2. Consumption: $5400
Consumption of durable goods: $1200
Consumption of nondurable goods: $1800
Consumption of services: $2400
Investment: $1400
Fixed investment: $800
Inventory investment: $600
Government expenditures on goods and services: $1600
Government transfer payments: $500
Exports: $500
Imports: $650
Net exports: −$150
GDP: $8250

3.

Year	GDP Deflator	Nominal GDP (in billions)	Real GDP (in billions)
2004	90.9	$700	$770
2005	100	$800	$800
2006	125	$1000	$800
2007	140	$1400	$1000
2008	150	$1800	$1200

4. a. 110 **b.** 180 **c.** 200

CHAPTER 7

Fill in the Blanks
1. short-term **2.** crucial **3.** real GDP per capita **4.** quantity; quality **5.** increases **6.** greater **7.** growth **8.** developed; less-developed **9.** labour; land; capital; technological **10.** rises; longer **11.** human **12.** capital **13.** innovation **14.** labour; land (natural resources); capital **15.** higher; greater **16.** quality; type **17.** new; improvements; innovations; doing **18.** property rights **19.** free trade **20.** fall; grows **21.** reducing; raising **22.** higher **23.** fall **24.** negative; subsistence **25.** developing

True or False
1. T **2.** T **3.** F **4.** T **5.** T **6.** T **7.** F **8.** T **9.** T **10.** F **11.** T **12.** T **13.** F **14.** F **15.** T **16.** T **17.** T **18.** T **19.** T **20.** T **21.** T **22.** F **23.** T **24.** F **25.** F **26.** T

Multiple Choice
1. d **2.** c **3.** d **4.** c **5.** d **6.** b **7.** d **8.** b **9.** e **10.** e **11.** e **12.** a **13.** a **14.** a **15.** d **16.** b **17.** d **18.** e **19.** d **20.** c **21.** b **22.** e **23.** a **24.** c **25.** c **26.** a

Problems

1. a.

0.5 percent:	140	years
1 percent:	70	years
1.4 percent:	50	years
2 percent:	35	years
2.8 percent:	25	years
3.5 percent:	20	years
7 percent:	10	years

b.

1.4 percent?	$200 billion
2.8 percent?	$400 billion
7 percent?	$3200 billion

2.

	Real GDP Growth	Real GDP Growth per Capita
An increase in population	increase	indeterminate
An increase in labour force participation	increase	increase
An increase in population and labour force participation	increase	increase
An increase in current consumption	decrease	decrease
An increase in technology	increase	increase
An increase in illiteracy	decrease	decrease
An increase in tax rates	decrease	decrease
An increase in productivity	increase	increase
An increase in tariffs on imported goods	decrease	decrease
An earlier retirement age in the country	decrease	decrease
An increase in technology and a decrease in labour force participation	indeterminate	indeterminate
An earlier retirement age and an increase in the capital stock	indeterminate	indeterminate

CHAPTER 8

Fill in the Blanks

1. real GDP demanded **2.** consumption **3.** more; less **4.** marginal **5.** 0.6 **6.** less **7.** open economy **8.** net exports **9.** real **10.** falls; rises **11.** left **12.** lower; left **13.** lower **14.** less **15.** more; right **16.** real **17.** greater; surplus **18.** downward; inverse **19.** real wealth; interest rate; open economy **20.** rises; increase **21.** reduced; reduced; reduced **22.** more; increase **23.** rises; fewer; lower **24.** more; less **25.** increases; increases **26.** rightward **27.** leftward **28.** left **29.** right; left **30.** right **31.** fewer; left **32.** decrease; left

True or False

1. T **2.** F **3.** T **4.** F **5.** F **6.** T **7.** T **8.** T **9.** F **10.** T **11.** F **12.** T **13.** T **14.** F **15.** T **16.** T **17.** T **18.** F **19.** T **20.** T **21.** F **22.** T **23.** T **24.** F **25.** T **26.** T **27.** T **28.** T **29.** F **30.** T **31.** T **32.** F

Multiple Choice

1. c **2.** e **3.** d **4.** a **5.** a **6.** a **7.** a **8.** d **9.** a **10.** a **11.** c **12.** a **13.** b **14.** a **15.** b **16.** e **17.** a **18.** d **19.** d **20.** b **21.** e **22.** d **23.** e **24.** c **25.** d **26.** a **27.** e **28.** b **29.** d **30.** a **31.** c **32.** a **33.** b

Problems

1. a. 0.90
b. 0.80
c. 0.60
d. $300 000; 0.75
e. $120 000; 1.2

2. a. The quantity of investment demanded increases but the investment demand curve does not shift.
b. The investment demand curve shifts to the left.
c. The investment demand curve shifts to the right.
d. The quantity of saving supplied increases but the saving supply curve does not shift.
e. The saving supply curve shifts to the right.

3.

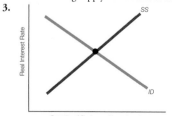

a. The investment demand (*ID*) curve would shift to the right, increasing both interest rates and the dollar amount of investment demanded.

b. The saving supply (*SS*) curve would shift to the right, decreasing interest rates and increasing the dollar amount of investment demanded.
c. The investment demand (*ID*) curve would shift to the left, decreasing both interest rates and the dollar amount of investment demanded.
d. The saving supply (*SS*) curve would shift to the right, decreasing interest rates and increasing the dollar amount of investment demanded.

4. a. decrease; decrease; decrease
b. decrease; decrease; increase; increase
c. decrease; decrease

5. a. increase
b. indeterminate
c. decrease
d. increase
e. indeterminate
f. no change (change in quantity of RGDP demanded)
g. no change (change in quantity of RGDP demanded)

CHAPTER 9

Fill in the Blanks

1. aggregate supply **2.** short-run; long-run **3.** output; input **4.** upward **5.** more; less **6.** profit; misperception **7.** rise; raising **8.** fall; fall; reduce **9.** relative; more **10.** all inputs **11.** outputs; inputs **12.** not affected **13.** natural rate **14.** fully **15.** long-run aggregate supply curve **16.** production costs **17.** higher; leftward **18.** right **19.** reduce; reduce **20.** rise **21.** decrease **22.** depress; increase **23.** lower; leftward **24.** reduction **25.** input; natural disasters **26.** left; not shift **27.** potential output; supply **28.** adverse **29.** potential **30.** aggregate demand; short-run aggregate supply **31.** *LRAS* **32.** shocks **33.** contractionary **34.** demand-pull **35.** increase; increase **36.** expansionary **37.** fall **38.** rise; leftward **39.** stagflation **40.** left; higher; lower; higher **41.** higher; less **42.** rightward **43.** lower; greater; lower **44.** declining **45.** at; lower **46.** long-term; minimum; efficiency; menu **47.** higher **48.** interdependence

True or False

1. T **2.** F **3.** T **4.** F **5.** T **6.** T **7.** F **8.** F **9.** F **10.** T **11.** T **12.** T **13.** T **14.** F **15.** T **16.** T **17.** F **18.** T **19.** F **20.** T **21.** F **22.** T **23.** F **24.** T **25.** T **26.** F **27.** T **28.** T **29.** F **30.** T **31.** T **32.** T **33.** T **34.** F **35.** T **36.** T **37.** T **38.** T **39.** F **40.** T **41.** F **42.** T **43.** T **44.** T **45.** F **46.** T **47.** F

Multiple Choice

1. c **2.** c **3.** b **4.** e **5.** b **6.** d **7.** d **8.** c **9.** e **10.** c **11.** b **12.** a **13.** a **14.** c **15.** d **16.** b **17.** a **18.** a **19.** a **20.** a **21.** b **22.** a **23.** a **24.** a **25.** a **26.** c **27.** d **28.** c **29.** d **30.** a **31.** d **32.** a **33.** c **34.** d **35.** c

Problems

1.

Change	Short-Run Aggregate Supply	Long-Run Aggregate Supply
An increase in aggregate demand	no change	no change
A decrease in aggregate demand	no change	no change
An increase in the stock of capital	increase (shift right)	increase (shift right)
A reduction in the size of the labour force	decrease (shift left)	decrease (shift left)
An increase in input prices (that does not reflect permanent changes in their supplies)	decrease (shift left)	no change
A decrease in input prices (that does reflect permanent changes in their supplies)	increase (shift right)	increase (shift right)
An increase in usable natural resources	increase (shift right)	increase (shift right)
A temporary adverse supply shock	decrease (shift left)	no change
Increases in the cost of government regulations	decrease (shift left)	decrease (shift left)

2. a.

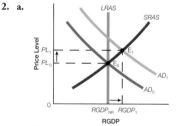

The price level increases, real output increases, employment increases, and unemployment decreases.

b.

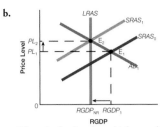

The price level ends up higher, real output ends up back where it began at potential output, employment ends up back where it began at full employment, and unemployment ends up back where it began at the natural rate of unemployment.

3. a.

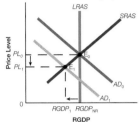

The price level falls, real output falls, employment falls, and unemployment rises.

b.

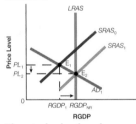

The price level ends up lower, real output ends up back where it began at potential output, employment ends up back where it began at full employment, and unemployment ends up back where it began at the natural rate of unemployment.

4. a.

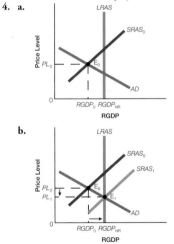

b.

In the long run, the price level will end up lower than before, but real output and unemployment will return to their long-run equilibrium levels.

5. a.

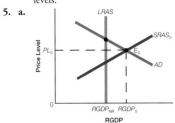

b.

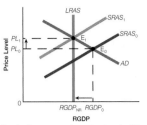

In the long run, the price level will end up higher than before, but real output and unemployment will return to their long-run equilibrium levels.

CHAPTER 10

Fill in the Blanks

1. fiscal policy **2.** deficit **3.** increase; lower **4.** increased **5.** reduce; increase **6.** taxation; borrowing **7.** social services **8.** greater **9.** disposable; consumption **10.** multiplier **11.** incomes **12.** consumption **13.** marginal propensity to consume **14.** smaller; savings; tax **15.** multiplier **16.** larger **17.** smaller **18.** less **19.** reduce **20.** deficits **21.** increase; increase **22.** reduce; increase; decrease **23.** increase; consumption; investment **24.** lower; lower **25.** greater **26.** automatic stabilizers **27.** tax **28.** lessened **29.** less; offsets **30.** increases; up **31.** crowding-out **32.** increases; higher **33.** increase **34.** fall **35.** smaller **36.** time lags **37.** inflationary boom; recession **38.** adds; lowers; increasing **39.** debt **40.** larger

True or False

1. T **2.** T **3.** F **4.** F **5.** F **6.** T **7.** F **8.** F **9.** T **10.** T **11.** F **12.** T **13.** T **14.** T **15.** F **16.** F **17.** T **18.** T **19.** F **20.** T **21.** T **22.** T **23.** F **24.** T **25.** T **26.** F **27.** T **28.** T **29.** T **30.** T **31.** F **32.** T **33.** F **34.** T **35.** T **36.** T **37.** T **38.** T **39.** T **40.** T

Multiple Choice

1. a **2.** c **3.** a **4.** d **5.** b **6.** c **7.** d **8.** c **9.** b **10.** d **11.** d **12.** b **13.** a **14.** b **15.** a **16.** d **17.** b **18.** d **19.** c **20.** d **21.** d **22.** b **23.** d **24.** c **25.** a **26.** d **27.** b **28.** c

Problems

1. a. An increase in government spending would decrease a budget surplus.
   b. An increase in government spending would increase aggregate demand.
   c. When the threat of a recession is developing.
2. a. An increase in taxes would decrease a budget deficit.
   b. An increase in taxes would decrease aggregate demand.
   c. When the threat of an unsustainable, inflationary boom is likely.
3. a. 1.5 **b.** 2 **c.** 4
4.

		Change in Aggregate Demand	Change in Consumption
a.	1/3	$3 billion	$1 billion
b.	1/2	$4 billion	$2 billion
c.	2/3	$6 billion	$4 billion
d.	3/4	$8 billion	$6 billion
e.	4/5	$10 billion	$8 billion

5.

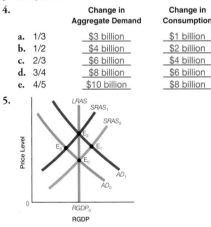

   a. At point E_3.
   b. The economy would end up at a long-run equilibrium at point E_2.
   c. The economy would end up at a long-run equilibrium at point E_0.
   d. At point E_1.
   e. The economy would end up in long-run equilibrium at E_0.
   f. The economy would end up in long-run equilibrium at E_2.

CHAPTER 11

Fill in the Blanks
1. deteriorate 2. currency 3. fiat 4. demand 5. withdrawn 6. transaction
7. demand; savings 8. savings 9. M2+; M2 10. liquid 11. M2+ 12. accept
13. financial; government 14. medium of exchange 15. greater 16. measure;
store 17. ruler 18. less 19. saver; borrowers 20. add $1000 21. higher
22. fractional reserve 23. make loans 24. loans 25. liabilities 26. assets
27. deposits; desired reserve ratio 28. non–interest-earning; interest-earning
29. excess 30. money multiplier 31. less than 32. decline; declines

True or False
1. T 2. T 3. F 4. T 5. F 6. T 7. F 8. T 9. T 10. T 11. F 12. T 13. T 14. F
15. T 16. T 17. T 18. F 19. T 20. T 21. T 22. F 23. T 24. F 25. T 26. T
27. T 28. F 29. T 30. T

Multiple Choice
1. b 2. a 3. a 4. e 5. b 6. d 7. c 8. b 9. d 10. d 11. d 12. b 13. a 14. d 15. c 16. b

Problems

1.
Change	M2	M2+
An increase in currency in circulation	increase	increase
A decrease in demand deposits	increase	increase
An increase in savings deposits	increase	increase
A transfer of demand deposit balances from credit unions to chartered banks	increase	no change

2.
a.	10 percent	$90 000
	20 percent	$80 000
	25 percent	$75 000
	50 percent	$50 000
b.	10 percent	$90 000
	20 percent	$80 000
	25 percent	$75 000
	50 percent	$50 000
c.	10 percent	$1 000 000
	20 percent	$500 000
	25 percent	$400 000
	50 percent	$200 000

3.
a.	10 percent	$10 000
	15 percent	zero (it has zero excess reserves)
	15 percent	zero (it has insufficient reserves)
b.	10 percent	$46 000
	15 percent	$34 000
	20 percent	$22 000

4.
5 percent	20
10 percent	10
20 percent	5
25 percent	4
50 percent	2

CHAPTER 12

Fill in the Blanks
1. central bank 2. the federal government 3. seven-year 4. inflation 5. money
supply 6. $M \times V$; $P \times Q$ 7. velocity 8. rise; rise; rise 9. increasing; reducing
10. monetarists 11. less 12. less; increases 13. increase 14. more
15. open market; bank 16. open market operations 17. government securities;
the Bank of Canada 18. increases 19. excess reserves 20. $1 000 000
21. fall 22. buys 23. decrease 24. lower 25. bank 26. more; fewer; less
27. lower 28. other banks 29. sell; raise 30. raise

True or False
1. F 2. T 3. F 4. T 5. T 6. F 7. T 8. T 9. T 10. F 11. T 12. F 13. T 14. T
15. T 16. F 17. T 18. T 19. T 20. T 21. T 22. F 23. T 24. F 25. T 26. F
27. F 28. T 29. T 30. T

Multiple Choice
1. b 2. d 3. b 4. b 5. b 6. a 7. d 8. b 9. c 10. a 11. c 12. e 13. b 14. e 15. c
16. c 17. d 18. b 19. a 20. d 21. d 22. a

Problems
1. a. MV = PQ
   b. Nominal GDP would double.
   c. The price level would double.
   d. Nominal GDP would double.
   e. Nominal GDP would remain unchanged.
2. a. decrease b. decrease c. increase d. decrease e. indeterminate

CHAPTER 13

Fill in the Blanks
1. transactions; precautionary; asset 2. inversely 3. less 4. vertical; Bank of
Canada 5. nominal 6. right; higher 7. lower; increase 8. lowers; raises; reduces
9. rise; fall 10. increase 11. overnight interest rate 12. decrease; increase 13. real;
nominal 14. the nominal interest rate; the expected inflation rate 15. reduce
16. decrease; increase; appreciation; decrease; decrease 17. less 18. six to eight
19. reduce 20. loans 21. decrease/increase 22. the federal government; the Bank
of Canada 23. more 24. right; right; right 25. no one 26. inflation; unemployment 27. fall; reduce 28. higher 29. steeper 30. up; rise; fall 31. rise

True or False
1. F 2. T 3. T 4. F 5. T 6. T 7. T 8. T 9. T 10. T 11. T 12. T 13. F 14. F
15. T 16. T 17. T 18. T 19. T 20. F 21. T 22. T 23. T 24. T 25. T 26. T
27. T 28. T 29. F

Multiple Choice
1. a 2. c 3. c 4. a 5. a 6. d 7. c 8. e 9. c 10. d 11. a 12. e 13. c 14. c 15. d
16. a 17. b 18. a

Problems

1. a.

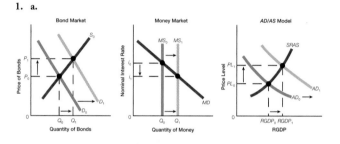

b.

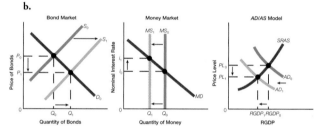

2. a.

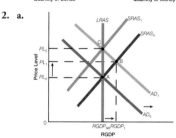

The short-run result is indicated by the movement from point A to
point B in the diagram above.

b.

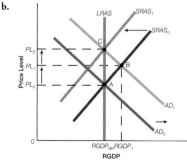

The long-run result is indicated by the movement from point B to
point C in the diagram above.

CHAPTER 14

Fill in the Blanks

1. services; merchandise **2.** surplus **3.** imports **4.** 15 **5.** reduce; tariffs; quotas **6.** Canada—U.S. **7.** voluntary **8.** comparative advantage **9.** opportunity cost **10.** comparative; absolute **11.** consumer **12.** consumer; producer **13.** consumer surplus; producer surplus **14.** raises; producers; consumers **15.** consumers; producers; producer; consumer **16.** lower; imports **17.** producers; consumers; increase **18.** tariff **19.** higher; lower; higher **20.** greater **21.** lower; greater; reducing **22.** producers; the government; consumers **23.** temporarily **24.** increased **25.** fewer; fewer **26.** hasten **27.** quota **28.** weaker **29.** rent seeking **30.** subsidizing **31.** inefficient **32.** reduced

True or False

1. F **2.** T **3.** F **4.** T **5.** T **6.** F **7.** T **8.** T **9.** F **10.** T **11.** T **12.** T **13.** T **14.** T **15.** T **16.** F **17.** T **18.** T **19.** F **20.** F **21.** T **22.** T **23.** F **24.** T **25.** F **26.** T **27.** T **28.** T **29.** T **30.** T **31.** T **32.** T

Multiple Choice

1. c **2.** c **3.** d **4.** e **5.** e **6.** a **7.** a **8.** c **9.** c **10.** a **11.** b **12.** c **13.** b **14.** a **15.** b **16.** b **17.** b **18.** d **19.** a **20.** b **21.** b

Problems

1.

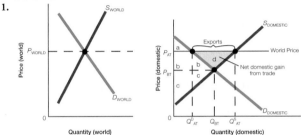

Domestic Gains and Losses from Free Trade (exports)

Area	Before Trade	After Trade	Change
Consumer Surplus (*CS*)	a + b	a	− b
Producer Surplus (*PS*)	c	b + c + d	+ (b + d)
Total Welfare from Trade (*CS* + *PS*)	a + b + c	a + b + c + d	+ d

2.

Gains and Losses from Tariffs

Area	Before Tariff	After Tariff	Change
Consumer Surplus (*CS*)	a + b + c + d + e	a	− (b + c + d + e)
Producer Surplus (*PS*)	f	b + f	+ b
Government Revenues (Tariff)	0	d	+ d
Total Welfare from Tariff (*CS* + *PS* + Tariff Revenues)	a + b + c + d + e + f	a + b + d + f	− (c + e)

CHAPTER 15

Fill in the Blanks

1. imports; exports **2.** credit; plus **3.** services; merchandise **4.** surplus **5.** sell; Canadian dollars **6.** exchange rate **7.** increase; reducing **8.** goods and services; assets **9.** more **10.** exchange rate **11.** falls **12.** less; increase **13.** upward **14.** supplied; sellers; down **15.** higher; lower **16.** tastes; income; interest; inflation; speculation **17.** increase; increasing **18.** decrease; decrease; lower **19.** rose; decreased; increased **20.** increase; increasing **21.** more; decreasing; decreasing **22.** dirty float system **23.** shortages; surpluses **24.** international trade; inflation

True or False

1. F **2.** T **3.** F **4.** T **5.** T **6.** T **7.** F **8.** T **9.** T **10.** T **11.** F **12.** T **13.** F **14.** T **15.** T **16.** F **17.** T **18.** T **19.** T **20.** T **21.** F **22.** T **23.** F

Multiple Choice

1. d **2.** a **3.** c **4.** c **5.** c **6.** d **7.** a **8.** d **9.** a **10.** b **11.** e **12.** b **13.** a **14.** d **15.** a **16.** b **17.** a **18.** d **19.** d **20.** c **21.** e **22.** d **23.** a **24.** a **25.** b **26.** a **27.** b **28.** a **29.** a **30.** d **31.** c **32.** e **33.** c **34.** d **35.** c **36.** b **37.** c

Problems

1. **a.** 50 pounds
b. 800 pesos
c. The Canadian dollar would depreciate, making the Canadian product cheaper in the other country.
d. The Canadian dollar would depreciate, making the Canadian product cheaper in the other country.
e. The Canadian dollar would depreciate, making the Canadian product cheaper in the other country.

2.

Change	Supply of Euros	Demand for Euros	Dollar Price of Euros
Reduced Canadian tastes for European goods	no change	decreases	decreases
Increased incomes in Canada	no change	increases	increases
Increased Canadian interest rates	increases	decreases	decreases
Decreased inflation in Europe	decreases	increases	increases
Reduced Canadian tariffs on imports	no change	increases	increases
Increased European tastes for Canadian goods	increases	no change	decreases

aggregate the total amount—such as the aggregate level of output

aggregate demand (*AD*) the total demand for all the final goods and services in the economy

aggregate demand curve graph that shows the inverse relationship between the price level and RGDP demanded

aggregate supply curve (*AS*) the total quantity of final goods and services suppliers are willing and able to supply at a given price level

automatic stabilizers changes in government transfer payments or tax collections that automatically help counter business cycle fluctuations

autonomous determinants of consumption expenditures expenditures not dependent on the level of current disposable income that can result from factors such as real wealth, the interest rate, household debt, expectations, and tastes and preferences

average propensity to consume (*APC*) the fraction of total disposable income that households spend on consumption

balance of payments the record of international transactions in which a nation has engaged over a year

balance sheet a financial record that indicates the balance between a bank's assets and its liabilities plus capital

bank rate interest rate that the Bank of Canada charges chartered banks for the loans it extends to them

bar graph represents data using vertical bars rising from the horizontal axis

barter direct exchange of goods and services without the use of money

boom periods of prolonged economic expansion

budget deficit government spending exceeds tax revenues for a given fiscal year

budget surplus tax revenues are greater than government expenditures for a given fiscal year

business cycles short-term fluctuations in the economy relative to the long-term trend in output

capital the equipment and structures used to produce goods and services

capital intensive production that uses a large amount of capital

causation when one event brings on another event

ceteris paribus holding all other things constant

change in demand the prices of related goods, income, number of buyers, tastes, and expectations can change the demand for a good. That is, a change in one of these factors shifts the entire demand curve

change in quantity demanded a change in a good's price leads to a change in quantity demanded, a move along a given demand curve

circular flow model of income and output an illustration of the continuous flow of goods, services, inputs, and payments between firms and households

closed economy an economy with no international trade—net exports are zero and imports are zero

command economies economies where the government uses central planning to coordinate most economic activities

comparative advantage occurs when a person or a country can produce a good or service at a lower opportunity cost than others

competitive market a market where the many buyers and sellers have very little market power—each buyer's and seller's effect on market price is negligible

complement an increase (a decrease) in the price of one good shifts the demand curve for another good to the left (right)

consumer price index (CPI) a measure of the prices of a basket of consumable goods and services that serves to gauge inflation

consumer sovereignty consumers vote with their dollars in a market economy; this explains what is produced

consumer surplus the difference between what the consumer is willing and able to pay and what the consumer actually pays for a quantity of a good or service

consumption purchases of consumer goods and services by households

contraction when the economy's output is falling—measured from the peak to the trough

contractionary fiscal policy use of fiscal policy tools to reduce output by decreasing government spending and/or increasing taxes

contractionary gap the output gap that occurs when the actual output is less than the potential output

correlation two events that usually occur together

cost-push inflation a price level increase due to a negative supply shock or increases in input prices

crowding-out effect theory that government borrowing drives up the interest rate, lowering consumption by households and investment spending by firms

currency coins and paper notes created to be used to facilitate the trade of goods and services and the payment of debts

current account a record of a country's imports and exports of goods and services, net investment income, and net transfers

cyclical unemployment unemployment due to short-term cyclical fluctuations in the economy

deflation a decrease in the overall price level, resulting in an increase of the purchasing power of money

demand deposits balances in bank accounts that depositors can access on demand

demand-pull inflation a price level increase due to an increase in aggregate demand

depressions severe recessions, or contraction in output

derived demand the demand for an input derived from consumers' demand for the good or service produced with that input

desired reserve ratio the percentage of deposits that a bank chooses to hold as cash reserves

dirty float system a description of the exchange rate system that means that fluctuations in currency values are partly determined by government intervention

discouraged worker an individual who has left the labour force because he or she could not find a job

disposable income the personal income available after taxes

dissaving consuming more than total available income

double counting adding the value of a good or service twice by mistakenly counting intermediate goods and services in GDP

durable goods longer-lived consumer goods, such as automobiles

economic growth an upward trend in the real per capita output of goods and services

the economic problem scarcity forces us to choose, and choices are costly because we must give up other opportunities that we value

economics the study of the allocation of our limited resources to satisfy our unlimited wants

efficiency getting the most from society's scarce resources

empirical analysis the use of data to test a hypothesis

entrepreneurship the process of combining labour, land, and capital together to produce goods and services

equation of exchange the money supply (M) times velocity (V) of circulation equals the price level (P) times quantity of goods and services produced in a given period (Q)

equilibrium price the price at the intersection of the market supply and demand curves; at this price the quantity demanded equals the quantity supplied

equilibrium quantity the quantity at the intersection of the market supply and demand curves; at the equilibrium quantity, the quantity demanded equals the quantity supplied

excess reserves cash reserves that are in excess of desired reserves

exchange rate the price of one unit of a country's currency in terms of another country's currency

excise tax a sales tax on individual products such as alcohol, tobacco, and gasoline

expansion when output (real GDP) is rising significantly—the period between the trough of a recession and the next peak

expansionary fiscal policy use of fiscal policy tools to foster increased output by increasing government spending and/or lowering taxes

expansionary gap the output gap that occurs when the actual output is greater than the potential output

expenditure approach calculation of GDP by adding the expenditures of market participants on final goods and services over a given period

factor (or input) markets the market where households sell the use of their inputs (capital, land, labour, and entrepreneurship) to firms

factor payments wages (salaries), rent, interest payments, and profits paid to the owners of productive resources

fallacy of composition the incorrect view that what is true for the individual is always true for the group

fiat money a means of exchange established by government declaration

fiscal policy use of government spending, and/or taxes, to alter equilibrium output and prices

fixed investments all new spending on capital goods by producers

fractional reserve system a system where banks hold reserves equal to some fraction of their demand deposits

frictional unemployment unemployment from normal turnovers in the economy, such as when individuals change from one job to another

GDP deflator a price index that helps to measure the average price level of all final goods and services produced in the economy

goods items we value or desire

goods and services flow the continuous flow of inputs and outputs in an economy

gross domestic product (GDP) the measure of economic performance based on the value of all final goods and services produced in a given period

human capital the productive knowledge and skill people receive from education and on-the-job training

hypothesis a testable proposition

implicit costs the opportunity costs of production that do not require a monetary payment

import quota a legal limit on the imported quantity of a good that is produced abroad and can be sold in domestic markets

income approach calculation of GDP based on the summation of incomes received by the owners of resources used in the production of goods and services

income effect at higher prices, buyers feel poorer, causing a lowering of quantity demanded

income flow the continuous flow of income and expenditure in an economy

increasing opportunity cost the opportunity cost of producing additional units of a good rises as society produces more of that good

individual demand curve a graphical representation that shows the inverse relationship between price and quantity demanded

individual demand schedule a schedule that shows the relationship between price and quantity demanded

individual supply curve a graphical representation that shows the positive relationship between the price and the quantity supplied

inferior good if income increases, the demand for a good decreases; if income decreases, the demand for a good increases

inflation a rise in the overall price level, which decreases the purchasing power of money

innovation applications of new knowledge that create new products or improve existing products

inventory investment purchases that add to the stocks of goods kept by the firm to meet consumer demand

investment the creation of capital goods to augment future production

job leaver a person who quits his or her job

job loser an individual who has been laid off or fired

labour the physical and human effort used in the production of goods and services

labour force persons 15 years of age and older who are employed or are unemployed and seeking work

labour force participation rate the percentage of the population (aged 15 and over) in the labour force

labour intensive production that uses a large amount of labour

land the natural resources used in the production of goods and services

law of demand the quantity of a good or service demanded varies inversely (negatively) with its price, *ceteris paribus*

law of supply the higher (lower) the price of the good, the greater (smaller) the quantity supplied

leading economic indicators factors that typically change before changes in economic activity

legal tender coins and paper notes officially declared to be acceptable for the settlement of financial debts

liquidity the ease with which one asset can be converted into another asset or into goods and services

long-run aggregate supply curve *(LRAS)* the graphical relationship between RGDP and the price level when output prices and input prices can fully adjust to economic changes

M2 currency outside chartered banks plus demand and savings deposits at chartered banks

M2+ M2 plus demand and savings deposits at trust companies, mortgage loan companies, credit unions, caisses populaires, and other financial institutions

macroeconomics the study of the whole economy including the topics of inflation, unemployment, and economic growth

marginal propensity to consume *(MPC)* the additional consumption resulting from an additional dollar of disposable income

marginal thinking focusing on the additional, or marginal, choices; marginal choices involve the effects of adding or subtracting from the current situation, the small (or large) incremental changes to a plan of action

market the process of buyers and sellers exchanging goods and services

market demand curve the horizontal summation of individual demand curves

market economy an economy that allocates goods and services through the private decisions of consumers, input suppliers, and firms

market failure when the economy fails to allocate resources efficiently on its own

market supply curve a graphical representation of the amount of goods and services that suppliers are willing and able to supply at various prices

means of deferred payment the attribute of money that makes it easier to borrow and to repay loans

medium of exchange the primary function of money, which is to facilitate transactions and lower transactions costs

menu costs the cost imposed on a firm from changing listed prices

microeconomics the study of household and firm behaviour and how they interact in the marketplace

mixed economy an economy where government and the private sector determine the allocation of resources

money anything generally accepted in exchange for goods or services

money market market in which money demand and money supply determine the equilibrium interest rate

money multiplier measures the potential amount of demand deposit money that the banking system generates with each dollar of reserves

money price the price that one pays in dollars and cents, sometimes called an absolute or nominal price

multiplier effect a chain reaction of additional income and purchases that results in total purchases that are greater than the initial increase in purchases

national income accounting a uniform means of measuring economic performance

national savings the sum of public and private saving

natural rate of unemployment the "average" unemployment rate, equal to the sum of frictional and structural unemployment

negative incentives incentives that either increase costs or reduce benefits resulting in a decrease in the activity or behaviour

negative relationship when two variables change in opposite directions

net domestic income at factor cost a measure of income earned by the owners of factors of production

net exports the difference between the value of exports and the value of imports

new entrant an individual who has not held a job before and is now seeking employment

nominal interest rate the reported interest rate that is not adjusted for inflation

nondurable goods tangible items that are consumed in a short period of time, such as food

normal good if income increases, the demand for a good increases; if income decreases, the demand for a good decreases

normative analysis a subjective, nontestable statement—how the economy should be

open economy a type of model that includes international trade effects

open market operations purchase and sale of government securities by the Bank of Canada

opportunity cost the value of the best forgone alternative that was not chosen

overnight interest rate interest rate that chartered banks charge each other for one-day loans

peak the point in time when the expansion comes to an end, when output is at the highest point in the cycle

personal income the amount of income received by households before taxes

pie chart a circle subdivided into proportionate slices that represent various quantities that add up to 100 percent

positive analysis an objective testable statement—how the economy is

positive incentives incentives that either reduce costs or increase benefits resulting in an increase in the activity or behaviour

positive relationship when two variables change in the same direction

potential output the amount of real output the economy would produce if its labour and other resources were fully employed—that is, at the natural rate of unemployment

price ceiling a legally established maximum price

price controls government mandated minimum or maximum prices

price floor a legally established minimum price

price index a measurement that attempts to provide a measure of the trend in prices paid for a certain bundle of goods and services over a given period

price level the average level of prices in the economy

private savings the amount of income households have left over after consumption and net taxes

producer goods capital goods that increase future production capabilities

producer surplus the difference between the lowest price at which a supplier is willing and able to supply a good or service and the actual price received for a given quantity of a good or service

production possibilities curve the potential total output combinations of any two goods for an economy

productivity the amount of goods and services a worker can produce per hour

product markets the market where households are buyers and firms are sellers of goods and services

progressive tax the amount of an individual's tax rises as a proportion of income, as the person's income rises

public savings the amount of income the government has left over after paying for its spending

re-entrant an individual who worked before and is now re-entering the labor force

real gross domestic product (RGDP) the total value of all final goods and services produced in a given time period such as a year or a quarter, adjusted for inflation

real gross domestic product per capita real output of goods and services per person

real interest rate the nominal interest rate minus the inflation rate; also called the inflation-adjusted interest rate

recession a period of significant decline in output and employment

regressive tax the amount of an individual's tax falls as a proportion of income, as the person's income rises

relative price the price of one good relative to other goods

rent seeking producer efforts to gain profits from government protections such as tariffs and import quotas

research and development (R&D) activities undertaken to create new products and processes that will lead to technological progress

resources inputs used to produce goods and services

rule of rational choice individuals will pursue an activity if the expected marginal benefits are greater than the expected marginal costs

savings deposits funds that cannot be used for payment directly

scarcity exists when human wants (material and nonmaterial) exceed available resources

service an intangible act that people want, like treatment from a doctor or a dentist

services intangible items of value provided to consumers, such as haircuts

shocks unexpected aggregate supply or aggregate demand changes

shoe-leather cost the cost incurred when individuals reduce their money holdings because of inflation

shortage a situation where quantity demanded exceeds quantity supplied

short-run aggregate supply curve *(SRAS)* the graphical relationship between RGDP and the price level when output prices can change but input prices are unable to adjust

slope the ratio of rise (change in the Y-variable) over the run (change in the X-variable)

specializing concentrating in the production of one, or a few, goods

stagflation a situation in which lower growth and higher prices occur together

structural unemployment unemployment persisting due to lack of skills necessary for available jobs

substitute an increase (a decrease) in the price of one good causes the demand curve for another good to shift to the right (left)

substitution effect at higher prices, buyers increasingly substitute other goods for the good that now has a higher relative price

surplus a situation where quantity supplied exceeds quantity demanded

tariff a tax on imports

theory statement or proposition used to explain and predict behaviour in the real world

theory of rational expectations belief that workers and consumers incorporate the likely consequences of government policy changes into their expectations by quickly adjusting wages and prices

time-series graph a type of line chart that plots data trends over time

trough the point in time when output stops declining; it is the moment when business activity is at its lowest point in the cycle

underemployment a situation in which workers have skills higher than necessary for a job

unemployment rate the percentage of the people in the labour force who are unemployed

unintended consequences the secondary effects of an action that may occur after the initial effects

variable something that is measured by a number, such as your height

wage and price inflexibility the tendency for prices and wages to only adjust slowly downward to changes in the economy

***X*-axis** the horizontal axis on a graph

***Y*-axis** the vertical axis on a graph

Index